American Public Opinion

American Public Opinion

EIGHTH EDITION

Robert S. Erikson
Columbia University

Kent L. Tedin
University of Houston

Longman

Boston Columbus Indianapolis New York San Francisco Upper Saddle River
Amsterdam Cape Town Dubai London Madrid Milan Munich Paris Montreal Toronto
Delhi Mexico City São Paulo Sydney Hong Kong Seoul Singapore Taipei Tokyo

Editor-in-Chief: Eric Stano
Editorial Assistant: Elizabeth Alimena
Senior Marketing Manager: Lindsey Prudhomme
Production Manager: Wanda Rockwell
**Project Coordination, Text Design, and Electronic
  Page Makeup:** Integra Software Services, Ltd.
Creative Director: Jayne Conte
Cover Designer: Mary Steiner
Cover Illustration/Photo: Fotolia
Cover Printer and Binder: Courier Companies, Inc.

1 2 3 4 5 6 7 8 9 10—CRS—13 12 11 10

Library of Congress Cataloging-in-Publication Data

Erikson, Robert S.
  American public opinion / Robert S. Erikson, Kent L. Tedin.—8th ed.
    p. cm.
  Includes bibliographical references and index.
  ISBN-13: 978-0-205-74543-2 (alk. paper)
  ISBN-10: 0-205-74543-1 (alk. paper)
    1. Public opinion—United States.   I. Tedin, Kent L.   II. Title.
HN90.P8E74 2011
303.3'80973—dc22   2010009424

Longman
is an imprint of

www.pearsonhighered.com

ISBN-10:   0-205-74543-1
ISBN-13: 978-0-205-74543-2

Dedicated to the memory of Maggie Banks Tedin (1947–2008),
companion and wife of Kent Tedin for 32 years,
and friend of Bob Erikson and his family.

Contents

List of Figures
and Tables

Figures

Tables

Credits for Figures and Tables

Figures

Figure 2.1: Compiled by Robert S. Erikson and Christopher Wlezien.

Figure 3.1: American National Election Studies, 2008 election data.

Figure 3.2: American National Election Studies, 2008 election data.

Figure 3.3: American National Election Studies, 2008 election data.

Figure 3.4: American National Election Studies, 2008 election data.

Figure 4.1: American National Election Studies, 1970–2008.

Figure 4.2: American National Opinion Research Center, Gallup, and General Social Survey.

Figure 4.3: The U.S. Role in the World Poll, 1996: University of Maryland; Gallup; National Opinion Research Center; General Social Survey; Transatlantic Trends Survey.

Figure 4.4: Roper, General Social Survey, and Gallup.

Figure 4.5: Richard G. Niemi, John Mueller, and Tom W. Smith, *Trends in Public Opinion* (New York: Greenwood, 1989); General Social Survey (1989–2006); Harold W. Stanley and Richard G. Niemi, *Vital Statistics of American Politics, 2007–2008* (Washington, DC: Congressional Quarterly, 2009); FBI Uniform Crime Reports.

Figure 4.6: Gallup, GSS.

Figure 4.7: CBS/NYT Polls averaged yearly.

Figure 4.8: James A. Stimson.

Figure 4.9: Compiled from Gallup Polls.

Figure 4.10: Gallup Poll.

Figure 4.11: Gallup Poll.

Figure 5.1: CIRP Freshman Study, Higher Education Research Institute, University of California, Los Angeles.

Figure 5.2: "America's Views and Mood 1998," *Public Perspective* (December/January 1999), p. 65.

Figure 5.3: University of Michigan Political Socialization Study Data. Recalls of vote decisions are from 1973, 1982, and 1997 survey waves.

Figure 6.1: Surveys by *Los Angeles Times, Newsweek,* Pew Center.

Figure 6.2: American National Election Studies (1958–2008).

Figure 7.1: American National Election Studies, 2008.

Figure 7.2: American National Election Studies, 2008 election data.

Figure 7.3: National Election Studies data.

Figure 7.4: Gallup Poll, 1952–1976; National Election Studies, 1980–1992; Voter News Service, 1996–2000; NEP, 2004–2008.

Figure 7.5: National Election Studies.

Figure 7.6: National Election Studies.

Figure 8.1: Harold W. Stanley and Richard G. Niemi, *Vital Statistics on American Politics 2007–2008* (Washington: CQ Press, 2008), augmented by data from *Editor and Publisher* and *Pew* Web sites.

Figure 8.2: ANES election studies.

Figure 9.1: Compiled by authors.

Figure 9.2: American National Election Studies election data.

Figure 9.3: American National Election Studies election data.

Figure 9.4: Compiled by authors.

Figure 9.5: National Election Studies data.

Figure 9.6: Compiled by authors.

Figure 9.7: National Election Studies data.

Figure 10.1: NEP Exit Polls.

Figure 10.2: http://voteview.com.

Figure 10.3: http://voteview.com.

Figure 10.4: http://voteview.com.

Figure 10.5: http://voteview.com.

Figure 11.1: Updated from Erikson, MacKuen, and Stimson (2002, Figure 9.1).

Figure 11.2: Robert S. Erikson, Gerald C. Wright, and John P. McIver, *Statehouse Democracy* (New York: Cambridge University Press, 1994).

Tables

Table 2.2: fivethirtyeight.com.

Table 3.1: ANES (American National Election Studies); D&K (Delli Carpini and Keeter 1996); Luntz (Luntz Research); IRC (IRC Survey Research Group); WP (*Washington Post*); Pew (Pew Center for People and the Press); CBS/NYT (CBS News/*New York Times*); GSS (General Social Survey); Ipsos (Ipsos Public Affairs); TNS (TNS Intersearch); G&C (Gibson and Caldeira 2009).

Table 3.2: National Election Studies, 2008.

Table 3.3: National Election Studies, 1989 pilot study data.

Table 3.4: National Election Studies, 1989 pilot study.

Table 3.5: National Election Studies, 2004 election data.

Table 3.6: Adapted from National Election Studies, 1994.

Table 3.7: National Election Studies, 2008.

Table 3.8: National Election Studies, 2008 election data.

Table 3.9: Paul R. Hagner and John C. Pierce, "Correlative Characteristics of Levels of Conceptualization in the American Public, 1956–1976," *Journal of Politics* 44 (August 1982), pp. 779–809, 1980–1988; compiled by Paul Hagner and Kathleen Knight 2000; Lewis-Beck et al. 2008, 279.

Table 3.10: National Election Studies, 2008 data.

Table 3.11: National Election Studies data.

Table 3.12: National Election Studies, 2008 data.

Table 4.1: General Social Survey, 2008; General Social Survey, (2006).

Table 4.2: Gallup Poll, (2009); ANES (2008); GSS (2006); GSS (2004); Pew (2009).

Table 5.1: M. Kent Jennings and Richard G. Niemi, *The Political Character of Adolescence* (Princeton, NJ: Princeton University Press, 1974), p. 78. Reprinted by permission of Princeton University Press.

Table 5.2: M. Kent Jennings and Richard G. Niemi, *The Political Character of Adolescence* (Princeton, NJ: Princeton University Press, 1974), p. 41. Reprinted by permission of Princeton University Press.

Table 5.3: Adapted from Amy Liu, Sylvia Ruiz, Linda DeAngelo, and John Pryor. 2009. "Findings from the 2008 Administration of the College Senior Survey (CSS); National Aggregates." Report from the Higher Education Research Institute, UCLA, Table 42.

Table 5.4: For 1984 students and faculty, Ernest Boyer and Mary Jean Whitelaw, *The Condition of the Professoriate: Attitudes and Trends, 1989* (New York: Harper, 1989); for 1999 faculty, Denise E. Magner, "Faculty Attitudes and Characteristics: Results of a 1998–1999 Survey," *Chronicle of Higher Education* (Sept. 3, 1999), pp. A20–A21; the 1999 college seniors data are courtesy of Dr. Jerry Jacobs, Department of Sociology, University of Pennsylvania.

Table 5.5: 2006 Biannual Youth Survey on Politics and Public Service, Institute for Politics, John F. Kennedy School of Government, Harvard University; 1998–2008 pooled General Social Survey (18–23 year olds, whites only).

Table 5.6: CBS News/*New York Times* polls.

Table 6.1: John L. Sullivan, James Piereson, and George E. Marcus, *Political Tolerance and American Democracy* (Chicago: University of Chicago Press, 1982), p. 203; ★The Freedom Forum (June 12–July 5, 2002).

Table 6.2: John Sullivan, James Piereson, and George Marcus, *Political Tolerance and American Democracy* (Chicago: University of Chicago Press, 1982); General Social Survey (GSS), 1985; CBS: Robert Chandler, *Public Opinion* (New York: Bowker, 1972); Herbert McClosky, 1958; Herbert McCloskey "Consensus and Ideology in American Politics," *American Political Science Review* 58 (June 1964); CLS: Herbert McClosky and Alida Brill, *Dimensions of Political Tolerance* (New York: Russell Sage Foundation, 1983); Louis Harris and Alan F. Westin, *The Dimensions of Privacy* (Stevens Point, WI: Sentry Insurance, 1979); James L. Gibson, *Freedom and Tolerance in the United States* (NORC: unpublished codebook, 1987); *Washington Pos/CBS News 1970, 2006*; Pew Research Center (PEW) 2009; The Freedom Forum, 1997; First Amendment Center (FAC), 2005; *Fox News* (2002).

Table 6.3: 1954 data are from Samuel Stouffer, *Communism, Conformity, and Civil Liberties* (New York: Wiley, 1954); 1972 and 2006 data are from the General Social Survey.

Table 6.4: James Gibson, *Freedom and Tolerance in the United States* (National Opinion Research Center: unpublished codebook, 1987).

Table 7.1: ANES, 2000; GSS, 2008; GSS 2006; ANES, 2008.

Table 7.2: ANES, 2008; GSS, 2008.

Table 7.3: American National Election Studies, 2008 election data.

Table 7.4: Princeton Survey Research Associates; Gallup; General Social Survey; ANES.

Table 7.5: American National Election Studies; Gallup.

Table 7.6: American National Election Studies; GSS; *Washington Post* poll.

Table 7.7: National Election Studies; General Social Survey; ABC News; Pew combined surveys (n = 74,446).

Table 7.8: Adapted from Corwin Smidt, Lyman Kellsteadt, and James Guth "The Role of Religion in American Politics" In Corwin Smidt (ed), *Oxford Handbook of Religion and American Politics* (Oxford: Oxford Press, 2009).

Table 7.9: 2008 National Election Study.

Table 7.10: 1956 data adapted from Howard Schuman, Charlotte Steeh, and Lawrence Bobo, *Racial Attitudes in America* (Cambridge, MA: Harvard University Press, 1985), p. 78; the 1985 data are from the General Social Survey.

Table 7.11: American National Election Studies; CNN/ORC; General Social Survey.

Table 8.1: Pew Research Center, "Public's News Habits Little Changed by September 11" (June 9, 2002); "News Audiences Increasingly Politicized" (June 8, 2004); "Key News Audiences Now Blend Online and Traditional Sources" (August 17, 2008).

Table 8.2: David H. Weaver and G. Cleveland Wilhoit, *The American Journalist in the 1990s* (Mahwah, NJ: Erlbaum, 1996), pp. 15–18; William Schneider and I. A. Lewis, "Views on the News," *Public Opinion* 8 (Aug.–Sept. 1985), p. 7.

Table 8.3: Adapted from Farnsworth and Lichter, 2007; Media Monitor, 2009.

Table 8.4: American National Election Studies, 2008 election data.

Table 8.5: American National Election Studies, 2008 election data.

Table 8.6: American National Election Studies, 2008 election data.

Table 9.1: American National Election Studies, 2008 election data.

Table 9.2: American National Election Studies, 2008 election data.

Table 9.3: American National Election Studies, 2008 election data.

Table 9.4: American National Election Studies, 2008 election data.

Table 9.5: American National Election Studies, 2008 election data.

Table 9.6: American National Election Studies, 2008 election data.

Table 9.7: American National Election Studies, 2008 election data.

Table 9.8: Compiled by authors.

Table 10.1: Stanley and Niem, 2009.

Table 10.2: Kathleen A. Frankovic and Laurily K. Epstein, "Congress and Its Constituency: The New Machine Politics," paper delivered at American Political Science Association Meeting, Washington DC, Sept. 1979.

Table 10.3: Compiled by authors.

Table 10.4: Harold W. Stanley and Richard G. Niemi, *Vital Statistics of American Politics, 2005–2006* (Washington, DC: Congressional Quarterly Press, 2006), p. 75.

Table 10.5: American National Election Studies, 2008 election data.

Table 11.1: Alan D. Monroe, "Consistency Between Public Preferences and National Policy Decisions," *American Politics Quarterly* 7 (Jan. 1979), p. 9. Copyright © 1979 by Sage Publications. Reprinted by permission of Sage Publications, Inc.

Preface

In this eighth edition of *American Public Opinion*, we present an accounting of the role of public opinion in the democratic politics of the United States. As with the previous editions, this edition discusses the contemporary literature on public opinion, supplementing it with our own illustrations and analyses of contemporary public opinion data. It provides an in-depth analysis of public opinion, beginning with its origins in political socialization, the impact of the media, the extent and breadth of democratic values, and the role of public opinion in the electoral process. *American Public Opinion* is unique in that it goes beyond a simple presentation of data and discussion of the formation of opinion, to include a critical analysis of the role of public opinion in American democracy. As in previous editions, the eighth edition examines the relationship between public opinion and policy.

New to This Edition

Because public opinion and electoral politics are always changing, each edition of this book requires extensive revision. In this eighth edition, we strive to keep the discussion as current as possible, and professors and students will notice the following:

- The most recent data on contemporary issues such as abortion, gay rights, gun control, race relations, and health care policy
- Data on the 2008 presidential election from the American National Election Studies
- The most recent literature is updated and incorporated throughout the text
- Extensive changes in Chapter 8, "The News Media and Political Opinions," reflect the rapid transformation of American news media
- New election data has been introduced in Chapter 9

Despite the extensive rewrite of material, readers familiar with the seventh edition (including the updated version) will notice few changes in format. The chapter titles are identical to those from the seventh edition. The within-chapter headings have changed little.

Acknowledgments

As this book has evolved through multiple editions over thirty years, so too has the list of authors. The first edition (1973) was authored by Robert S. Erikson and Norman L. Luttbeg. With the second edition, Kent L. Tedin joined the team as a third author. That triumvirate held through three editions. By the time of the fifth edition, Luttbeg left the team to pursue other scholarly pursuits. This is the third edition solely authored by Erikson and Tedin. But Luttbeg's contribution to the book remains, most notably in the five linkage models which he originated.

The preparation of this volume relies heavily on the survey data of the American National Election Studies, conducted by the University of Michigan, supported by grants from the National Science Foundation, and made available by the Interuniversity Consortium for Political and Social Research. We also relied extensively on the General Social Survey (also funded by the National Science Foundation) and the data available online from the Roper Center Data Archive at the University of Connecticut. These organizations bear no responsibility for the analysis or interpretations presented here. We are greatly indebted to them for making their data available to us, and to other scholars on whose research we depend. We benefit from the assistance provided by our editor, Eric Stano, and to colleagues, students, and staff at Columbia University and the University of Houston. Our special gratitude goes to Kathleen Knight of Columbia University for her advice at many stages of this project. We would like to thank those who most recently reviewed this text: Ted G. Jelen, University of Nevada–Las Vegas; Geoff Peterson, University of Wisconsin–Eau Claire; Greg Shaw, Illinois Wesleyan University; and Allen R. Wilcox, University of Nevada–Reno.

Special thanks go to Aaron Diamond, Yair Ghitza, and Kelly Rader, for their invaluable research assistance.

Robert S. Erikson
Kent L. Tedin

1 Public Opinion in Democratic Societies

Few Americans in the twenty-first century can remember a time when public opinion polls—like television, shopping malls, and eight-lane freeways—were not part of the popular landscape. Polls tell us which television shows are the most popular, how frequently people attend church, what person Americans most admire, plus a myriad of opinions on current political topics. We shall see, however, that the study of public opinion is much broader than simply gauging popular reaction to recent events. It is, for example, also concerned with how people learn about government, their trust in existing political institutions, their support for the political rules of the game, the interrelationships among their opinions, and their beliefs about the effectiveness of political participation. The list could go on. But more than anything else, the study of public opinion is justified by the simple notion that democratic institutions should result in government decisions that reflect the views of everyday people. In the words of Robert Dahl, the most eminent political theorist of the post–World War II war era, "I assume that a key characteristic of a democracy is the continued responsiveness of the government to the preferences of its citizens, considered as political equals" (Dahl 1971, 1). It is this presumption, and its implications, that guides the systematic analysis of mass opinion.

1-1 Public Opinion and Government

Rousseau, in 1744, was among the first to use the term *public opinion* (*l'opinion publique*), meaning the customs and manners of all members of society (as opposed to some elite). By 1780, French writers were using the term interchangeably with *common will*, *public spirit*, and *public conscience* to refer to the political aspects of mass opinion (Price 1992, 8). *Public opinion* soon came into common usage among those writing about government.

1

However, long before scientific methods were developed to measure attitudes or the term *public opinion* gained currency, political theorists speculated about the "group mind" or the "general will" and how it might influence the political order. Writers beginning with Plato and Aristotle, through Locke and Hobbes as well as Rousseau, did not see public opinion as an aggregation of individual opinions, as is common today. Rather, they saw the whole as greater than the sum of its parts, much in the way a mob with a united purpose behaves in a fashion that would be foreign to any individual member. To these predemocratic theorists, public opinion was a mass entity, which if brought to bear on public affairs had potential for enormous influence. It was like a force of nature, constrained perhaps by certain regularities, but a unified whole that changed continually, like the currents in the ocean (Palmer 1936; Spitz 1984).

It was not until the rise of popular sovereignty that thinking about public opinion began to consider individual or group characteristics. By the eighteenth century, no Western political regime could afford to ignore the views of the masses. This change was brought about by the construction of electoral institutions and parliamentary bodies for regular consultation with the public and the gradual extension of the franchise to the lower classes. Henceforth, governments would find it necessary to take account of public opinion and its distribution throughout the polity. This accounting was not simply a question of government responsiveness to mass policy desires. Government also had to take account of popular support for the ongoing political order. A strong argument can be made that only when the political status quo was threatened did political elites, in an act of self-preservation, grudgingly extend the franchise to portions of the mass public (Ginsberg 1982). But with the granting of the franchise, there soon developed an ethical imperative that governments are morally obligated to heed public opinion in formulating policies.

In the early years of the American republic, to speak of "public opinion" was mostly to speak about the thin layer of the educated, affluent public in a position to communicate their views to government. While the nation's founders agreed on the principle of popular government, they greatly distrusted the wisdom and judgment of the masses on matters political. To Alexander Hamilton,

> The voice of the people has been said to be the voice of God; and however generally this maxim has been quoted and believed, it is not true in fact. The people are turbulent and changing; they seldom judge or determine right. (Farrand 1961, 299–300)

While not all took such an uncharitable position, it was generally thought that public opinion was easily swayed and subject to fits of passion. Thus institutions were developed, such as the Electoral College and the indirect election of senators, to distance political leaders from the opinions of everyday citizens.

Nevertheless, by the mid-nineteenth century, many who followed the American political scene voiced concern about an excess of influence on political decision making by public opinion. One reason was the integration of the working class into the electorate via the universal franchise. By the 1850s, it became impossible to argue that the public's opinion could be ignored. Writing in 1848, Alexis de Tocqueville, perhaps the most astute observer of nineteenth-century America, thought "there was no country in which . . . there is less independence of mind and true freedom of discussion than in America" (Tocqueville 1966, 254). He felt the numerical majority intimidated the minority so that only a narrow range of opinion could be expressed. In the end, he feared that the views of the majority could result in either social or governmental tyranny (Spitz 1984, 70). History was, of course, to prove him wrong. But those writing later agreed with his assessment of the importance of public opinion. In 1888, the perceptive British journalist and author James Bryce would claim that "in no country is public opinion so powerful as in the United States" (Bryce 1900). He also noted, "the obvious weakness of government by opinion is the difficulty of ascertaining it."

Of those writing before the development of the modern opinion poll, perhaps the most influential critic of public opinion was Walter Lippmann (1922, 1925). Like many of the Founders, Lippmann believed mass opinion was subject to passions that could be induced by elite propaganda. He was convinced that the manipulation of public opinion by those opposed to the League of Nations was responsible for the tragedy of America's failure to join after World War I. Famously, Lippmann perceptively observed that the images of politics received by the public are not direct pictures of events, immediate experiences of action, or provable economic and social theories. Rather, they are "pictures in people's heads" generated by political interests to benefit their cause. In a prescient analysis of major findings by modern survey research, Lippmann challenged traditional democratic theory and its notion of an informed and rational public basing opinions on a considered judgment of the facts. He argued that the average person had little time for affairs of state and would rather read the comics than consider the pros and cons of weighty political issues. It should not be expected, therefore, that the mass public be competent in matters of state. Lippmann's prescription for democracy was for the public to choose leaders but for public policy to be developed and implemented by scientifically oriented experts.

The debate over the role of public opinion in democracy was given a new focus by the appearance of scientific polling in 1936. Among the most outspoken proponents of polls as a guide to government decision making was George Gallup, a pioneer of the new technology (Gallup and Rae 1940). Gallup was a prairie populist with a Ph.D. in psychology, who believed in the collective wisdom of everyday citizens. He distrusted intellectuals and experts, and he thought that elite rule and democratic government were incompatible. The challenge for democracy, as he saw it, was, "Shall the common people be free to express their basic needs and purposes, or shall they be dominated by a small ruling clique?" In other words, how does one make those holding high public office responsive to the needs and wishes of the public?

Poll results, Gallup argued, could be considered a "mandate from the people," a concrete expression of the policies the public desires the government to enact. No longer would elected officials have to rely on the ambiguities of elections, claims by self-serving interest groups, newspaper stories, communications from constituents, or other nonrepresentative channels of public sentiment. Rather, they could turn to the latest opinion poll. In the past, claims that elected officials should heed popular preferences directly when formulating policy could always be countered with arguments like those of sixteenth-century political theorist Michel de Montaigne (1967), who wrote that "public opinion is a powerful, bold, and unmeasurable party."

Gallup saw the modern opinion poll as the high-tech equivalent of the New England town meeting—an opportunity for all citizens (or at least a representative sample) to voice their opinions. The scientific poll gave crispness, clarity, and reliability to mass opinion. Gallup and his supporters argued that through polls, the will of the people could accurately be determined. No longer could failure to take seriously popular preferences when enacting public policy be justified by claims that public opinion is unknowable. With the aid of the modern opinion poll, it was the moral responsibility of elected officials to convert the public will into public policy.

Not all were enthusiastic about the new polling technology and George Gallup's prescriptions for it. Sociologist Herbert Blumer and political scientist Lindsay Rogers soon launched frontal assaults on the opinion poll and its implications. Blumer (1948) asserted the "one person, one vote" definition of public opinion inherent in polls was precisely what public opinion was not. Public opinion could not be reduced to a nose count of citizens. Rather, it was the interactions and communications among functional groups that percolated through society and came to the attention of government. These interactions and communications were not aggregations of individual opinions but "an organic whole of interacting, interrelated parts." To Blumer, not all opinions counted equally. They merited the label *public opinion* only to the extent opinions surfaced in a public forum and were taken seriously by those in government with power and influence. This view, of course, clashed directly with the populist inclinations of Gallup and other early pollsters.[1]

Lindsay Rogers, on the other hand, was convinced that the public was not intellectually or emotionally fit to play the role Gallup's opinion-poll democracy required of it (Fried 2006). In any case, polls were not technically able to ascertain the public's message. Rogers (1949) reformulated the position of the English philosopher Edmund Burke that it is the duty of elected representatives to follow their conscience and best judgment and not be slaves to moments of popular passion.[2] Only in this fashion, argued Rogers, could the true public interest be served. Rogers was also one of the first to raise serious methodological questions about polls—that is, to challenge pollsters on their own turf. He addressed questions of measurement, opinion aggregation, intensity, and framing effects that occupy a great deal of attention among contemporary students of public opinion. In essence, he claimed that polls of public opinion did not really measure "public opinion." Notably, polls do not allow for the deliberation of issues, and a sophisticated understanding of issues requires deliberation. Deliberation, in turn, requires group discussion and analysis. Rogers argued that "Dr. Gallup does not make the public more articulate. He only estimates how in replying to certain questions it would say 'yes,' 'no,' or 'don't know.' Instead of feeling the pulse of democracy, Dr. Gallup listens to its baby talk" (Rogers 1949, 17).

Rogers' perspective on public opinion has intellectual roots in the writings of Founding Father James Madison. According to Colleen Sheehan (2004, 406), Madison rejected the notion of public opinion as simply an aggregation of public sentiments. Rather, he saw it as a process of community conversation and deliberation, with citizens influencing each other through public and private discourse, ultimately influencing political decisions through an "enlightened public voice" (Sheehan 2004, 406).

The critiques of Blumer and Rogers helped spawn the development of an important methodological innovation in public opinion—the deliberative poll (Delli Carpini, Cook, and Jacobs 2004). Gastil (2000, 22) defines public deliberation as the careful examination of a political problem, identification of solutions to that problem, and debate over the merits of proposed solutions. Lindeman (2002, 119) sees deliberation as "a cognitive process in which individuals form, alter, or reinforce their opinions as they weigh evidence and arguments from various points of view." Luskin, Fishkin, and Jowell (2002, 456) assert that "Now several decades' experience the wiser, we know that opinion polls . . . have not been the great boon to democracy that Gallup envisioned." The problem, in their view, is responses to conventional opinion questions is mostly ill-considered and barren of information (see also Bartels 2008). A somewhat different critique is offered by Scott Althaus (2003, 278), who argues that fair representation is undermined by the uneven distribution of political knowledge. In particular, the poorly informed is less likely to have opinions than the better informed.

The general idea behind deliberation is that individuals will revise, modify, or change their opinions in light of new information and the force of argument made by fellow discussants. A by-product of deliberation is that the policy preferences are more "informed, enlightened, and authentic" (Page 1996, 1).

The deliberative poll, pioneered by James Fishkin (1997), combines the strength of the representative sample survey with the internal validity of the experimental design, which allows for comparison of deliberate polls with traditional polling methods. In national deliberative polls, a representative sample of 600 or so participants is selected by a telephone survey and transported to a single site. They are broken into small groups, given detailed information on key issues facing the nation, and engage in two-to-four days of deliberation. As we shall see shortly, everyday citizens found in their normal environment bear little resemblance to the democratic ideal often caricatured by the New England town meeting. The purpose of the deliberative poll is to create the conditions whereby a representative sample of Americans can express informed and thoughtful opinions—a situation unlike the 1936 polling innovation of George Gallup (at least according to critics like Lindsay Rogers).

There have now been a number of studies involving the deliberative poll (Luskin, Fishkin, and Jowell 2002; Barabas 2004; Sturgis, Roberts, and Allum 2005; Jackman and Sniderman 2006; Goidel, Freeman Procoio, and Zewe 2008). The research is decided a mixed bag, with many conflicting results. Compared to traditional polling, participants in deliberative polls are (sometimes) better informed, have stronger interrelationships among their opinions (constraints), tend to change their opinions based on the policy issues discussed, and are more politically efficacious (more likely to participate in the political process). However, deliberation only rarely changes opinions. Those participating in deliberative polls, while they gain information, usually do not change their opinions (Visser, Hobrook, and Krosnick 2008).

Critics of deliberative polls claim that the dynamics of small groups shows that even when opinion moves, it generally moves in the direction of the group majority. Also, better-educated, higher status deliberators tend to be disproportionately vocal and persuasive in group discussions (Mendelberg 2002). In addition, Hibbing and Theiss-Morse (2002) show many citizens recoil from the discord and disagreement that naturally accompanies open political deliberation. Many citizens don't like to argue about politics, and when placed in that situation develop feelings of frustration and powerlessness, rather than the more positive consequences attributed to deliberation by its advocates.

A different argument flowing from the critique of Lindsay Rogers holds that public opinion changes in a capricious fashion—that is, over short periods of time, policy preferences shift rapidly, frequently, and arbitrarily. This belief was used by the author of Federalist Paper No. 63 to argue for an indirectly elected Senate, which would serve as "an anchor against popular fluctuations" and protect the people against their own "temporary errors and delusions." This argument has been advanced most notably in the realm of foreign affairs— where public interest and information tend to be lower than for domestic matters. In 1950, political scientist Gabriel Almond (1950, 53) argued that on matters of foreign policy, the public reacts with "formless and plastic moods which undergo frequent alteration in response to changes in events."[3] This view of public opinion was used to buttress arguments about limiting the role of mass opinion in policy decisions and is still a touchstone of the "realist" school of foreign policy (Russett and Graham 1989).

Recently, however, scholars have "rehabilitated" the public on matters of foreign policy. According to the revisionist approach, citizens make decisions about foreign affairs based on the principle of "low information rationality" (Brewer, Gross, Aday, and Willnat 2004). While not possessing extensive knowledge of world events, they are nevertheless able to use informational shortcuts to form stable and reasonable reactions to international events (Page and Shapiro 1992; Holsti 2004). Among these shortcuts are the images they hold of foreign countries as allies or threats to American security, or isolationist versus internationalist perspectives on America's proper role in the world (Drezner 2008). We shall elaborate on these points in chapter 4.

The liberal democracy school of thought (Dahl 1989) holds that an essential element of democracy is the creation of institutions and practices that allow for meaningful public input into the governing process. Democratic government works best when elected officeholders and appointed officials respond to the popular will. Citizens are more likely to comply with government decisions when they are backed by the moral force of popular approval. In addition, advocates of liberal democracy argue that decisions based on popular will are most likely to be the correct decisions. This idea traces its heritage to Aristotle's view that the pooled judgments of the many are likely to contain more wisdom than the judgments of the few.[4] The liberal democratic model does not hold that public policy must be driven only by the engine of public opinion. Rather, public opinion must count for something of consequence in government decision making.

The arguments we have just outlined are still occasionally elaborated upon today. However, most current research on public opinion does not address normative issues about the proper role of opinion in the governmental process. Rather, empirical questions dominate the field—that is, questions about "what really is" as opposed to "what ought to be." But empirical questions often have important normative implications. Clearly of consequence are, "How much does the public know about public affairs, and how is that knowledge organized?" "How is public opinion articulated?" "Whose voices are heard?" "Are some segments of society (presumably the more affluent) better able to communicate their opinions to political decision makers than those with fewer economic resources?" The answers to these questions are important for theories of how the just polity should be structured.

1-2 Public Opinion Defined

Public opinion is notoriously difficult to define. There are scores, if not hundreds, of variations on a definition (see Childs 1965 for a sampling). V.O. Key, Jr., famously defined public opinion as "those opinions held by private persons which governments finds it prudent to heed" (Key 1961b, 14). But what if government does not find it prudent to heed a particular opinion held by the public? Is it then not a "public opinion?"

We take a somewhat different approach. A standard definition of *public* is a group that has something in common. Some argue that there is no such thing as a single public; rather, there are many publics (MacDougall 1966). Thus, one can refer to the tennis-playing public, the snowmobiling public, or the television-watching public. Others, however, take a broader view. For political scientists, what members of the "public" in *public opinion* have in common is a connection to government. At a minimum, all citizens eighteen and older have the right to vote. That binds them together with a common interest, even if they choose not to exercise the right. And, of course, everyone is affected in some way by government. That creates a common interest as well. Students of government also regularly speak of several specialized publics. They talk of the "attentive public," those persons who generally pay close attention to politics, and "issue publics," those persons who focus on specific issues while paying less attention to others. It is perhaps helpful to think of these as "subpublics" of the overall public (i.e., the adult population).

We may first describe an opinion as a verbal expression of an attitude.[5] There are, of course, other ways in which attitudes can be expressed, such as marches, demonstrations, or riots. But we reserve the term *opinion* as the manifestation of attitudes in words or writing.[6] Attitudes are latent; they cannot be directly observed. Social psychologists typically define an attitude as an enduring predisposition to respond. Normally, attitudes do not change weekly or monthly. Although change is clearly possible, attitudes are mostly stable over extended periods. Opinions are imperfect indicators of the underlying, unobserved attitude. Because opinions are imperfect measures, we sometimes find they are inconsistent or display contradictions. We deal with this problem at length in chapter 3.

Second, opinions are disagreements about matters of preference, which cannot be resolved using the rules of science. Thus, when it comes to music, I may prefer opera. You may prefer hard rock. But there is no systematic way of demonstrating the virtue or goodness of one over the other. The same is true for opinions about welfare policy, foreign aid, or same-sex marriage. Disagreements about questions of fact are not opinions, but beliefs.[7] There was once disagreement about whether the earth circled the sun. Some believed the reverse—that the sun revolved around the earth. That disagreement has been resolved by scientific methods. There is still disagreement over whether massive doses of vitamin C will prevent colds and other illness. Some believe this notion is nothing more than a hoax; others take large doses of the vitamin daily. But one's position on this issue is a belief, not an opinion, because in principle the question may someday be resolved with finality. Disagreements over classical versus rock music will not be resolved.

No one has yet advanced a definition of *public opinion* that satisfies a substantial number of students in the field. We prefer to keep our definition short and simple. We define *public opinion* as the preferences of the adult population on matters of relevance to government. The first implication is that not all opinions are public opinion. Thus, one's preference for computer operating systems—Windows, Linux, Mac OS X—is excluded from our definition because it has nothing to do with government. The second implication is that while in the broadest sense we are talking about all adults, that does not exclude the possibility of referencing subgroups, such as the attentive public. A third point is that by the term *preferences* we mean more than simply the affective component of an opinion. *Affect* refers to feelings—like or dislike, approve or disapprove. However, we must also be concerned with the cognitive component of an opinion. *Cognition* refers to the process of knowing, to the intellectual sophistication one brings to the ordering of political opinions. Obviously, the amount of political information one has affects the ability to link one political concept with another and is important for our understanding of public opinion. Finally, while we have defined *opinions* as verbal manifestations of attitudes, events such as riots, demonstrations, and marches are also indicators of public opinion for certain attentive publics.

In the recent era, the meaning of *public opinion* sometimes seems to have evolved into whatever opinion polls show public opinion to be. In the opinion of CBS News Poll director Kathleen Frankovic, "Polls are not only part of the news today, they are news. They not only sample public opinion, they define it"

(Frankovic 1998, 150). In many ways, the findings of public opinion polls (or survey research in general) should inspire trust. Counterintuitive though it may seem, mathematical statistics and decades of experience reveal that one *can* generalize from a random sample of one or two thousand individuals to the nation as a whole. And one rarely has reason to believe that survey respondents systematically lie to pollsters.

We must be careful, however, not to reify. Public opinion and the results of public opinion polls are not the same thing. A public opinion poll is an indirect measure of "public opinion," much like an IQ test is an indirect measure of "intelligence." As shown in later chapters, the results of opinion polls must be interpreted with great care. Findings can vary considerably with different question wordings or different shadings of how issues are presented to respondents. Also, survey respondents sometimes tend to give socially desirable responses. For this reason, surveys often underreport attitudes and behaviors such as nonvoting, racist feelings, and tolerance for pornography because of a tendency for respondents to give a favorable accounting of themselves.

1-3 The Evolution of the Public Opinion Poll

Before the appearance of the modern public opinion poll in 1936, popular sentiment was assessed by newspapers and magazines through a variety of informal and haphazard soundings called *straw polls*.[8] The *Harrisburg Pennsylvanian* is credited with conducting the first of these polls in the summer of 1824. It showed presidential candidate Andrew Jackson, with 63 percent of the vote, an easy winner over John Quincy Adams and Henry Clay.[9]

But it was not until 1896 that straw polling became a serious business. In that year, the *Chicago Record* conducted an elaborate and expensive straw poll to tap voter preferences in the bitterly fought presidential contest between William McKinley and William Jennings Bryan. It sent out postcard ballots to every eighth voter in twelve Midwestern states, as well as ballots to every registered voter in Chicago.[10] The owner of the *Chicago Record* had clear Republican sympathies, and the Democratic Party feared the poll was nothing more than a Republican trick. The party urged Democrats not to return the ballots. Nevertheless, with the aid of a team of eminent mathematicians, the *Record* predicted in October that McKinley would win Chicago with 57.95 percent of the vote. Amazingly, he received 57.91 percent on Election Day. Outside of Chicago, however, the *Record*'s predictive record was a failure (Jensen 1968).

With the dawn of the twentieth century, straw polls were becoming a regular feature in many magazines and newspapers. Like today, the poll results were "newsworthy." Approximately eighty-four straw polls were conducted during the 1928 presidential election, of which six were national. The straw polls occupied thousands of column inches in the print media. If anything, they were featured even more prominently than is currently the case.[11] The polls were of major importance to their sponsors as a promotional gimmick. They created interest in the publication. Also, those publishers using mail–out ballots usually included a special subscription offer along with the ballot. By all indications, the scheme worked remarkably well to boost circulation (Robinson 1932).

Like current opinion polls, the straw polls did not limit themselves simply to electoral contests. They polled on the issues as well, most notably the burning issue of the 1920s: Prohibition. The wet–dry controversy was as emotion laden as any issue to surface in American politics. If popular sentiment on the issue were to be measured by a cutout ballot from a newspaper, one side would sometimes attempt to secure a monopoly on that issue and send in all the ballots. Or one side would urge its people not to participate in a straw poll when the sponsor's sentiments on the issue were known. Thus a poll in Delaware sponsored by Pierre du Pont, a well-known wet, was boycotted by drys. It wound up showing 97 percent of its respondents in favor of repeal. Mr. du Pont wisely decided against publishing the poll results as an indicator of public opinion. Rather, he submitted the returned ballots as a petition to the Delaware legislature urging the repeal of Prohibition (Robinson 1932).

The straw polls were a public relations disaster waiting to happen. By the 1930s, considerable advances had been made by market researchers in the field of applied sampling. However, the magazines and newspapers sponsoring the straw polls were oblivious. Their major concern with straw polls was how they contributed to profitability, not the technical quality of the poll itself. Methodologically, straw polls stayed in the rear guard, learning nothing from the advances in sampling methods, using the same outdated methods year after year.

Straw polls were, in fact, known to be notoriously unreliable. In 1932, Claude Robinson published an analysis of the state-by-state error margins of the major straw polls of the day.[12] The average error of the polls conducted by the Hearst newspapers was 12 percent in 1924. The poll by *The Pathfinder*, a weekly magazine, was off by an average of 14 percent in 1928. The *Farm-Journal* poll of thirty-six states in 1928 had an average error of 17 percent. Even the best known and most professionally operated of the straw polls—the *Literary Digest* poll—was off the mark by an average of 12 percent in both 1924 and 1928.

It was the 1936 election and the notorious misprediction of its outcome by the *Literary Digest* that brought an end to the era of straw polls. The *Literary Digest* was the largest circulation general magazine of its time, with over 2 million subscribers. Much of this success could be traced directly to its straw poll, a regular feature since 1916. While the *Digest* poll experienced more than its share of mispredictions, it had managed each time to get the winner of the presidential election right. And it was not modest. The *Digest* claimed "uncanny accuracy" for its poll, congratulating itself frequently on its amazing record. But in the 1936 presidential election, the *Digest* poll wildly mispredicted the outcome, giving Alf Landon 57 percent of the vote and Franklin Roosevelt 43 percent. Roosevelt won with 62.5 percent of the vote. The *Digest* was off the mark by almost 20 percentage points. Its credibility shattered, the *Literary Digest* went bankrupt a year later.[13]

In that same year, three young pollsters with backgrounds in market research, using "scientific" methods of sampling, did correctly predict the win by Roosevelt. The three were Archibald Crossley, Elmo Roper, and George Gallup, each of whom went on to found his own poll. The best known of these was, of course, George Gallup, founder of the Gallup Poll.

Gallup was a talented self-promoter. In the 1936 election season he taunted the *Literary Digest*, offering clients a money-back guarantee that his poll would be closer to the actual vote on Election Day than the *Digest's*.[14] He urged newspapers and magazines to run the two polls side by side (J. Converse 1987, 116–20).

Gallup used in-person interviews as opposed to mail questionnaires, and he employed "quotas" to ensure that his samples looked demographically like the overall population. His poll forecast Roosevelt with 55.7 percent of the vote— 6.8 percent off the mark. But he got the winner right, and he used that fact, along with the *Digest's* disaster, to quickly become the nation's preeminent pollster.

But all was not right with the Gallup Poll. While Gallup continued to forecast the correct winner in the 1940 and 1944 presidential contests, his surveys consistently overestimated the Republican vote (Moore 1992, 66–68). Then, in 1948, the Gallup Poll incorrectly forecast that Republican Thomas Dewey would defeat Democrat Harry Truman by a margin of 49.5 to 44.5 percent. It is important to note that the Crossley Poll and the Roper Poll also predicted a win by Dewey. Roper had the margin at 52.2 percent Dewey and 37.1 percent Truman. Something was clearly wrong with the sampling methodology used by all three of these polls. That something was quota sampling. In a comprehensive study of the failure of the polls in 1948, the Social Science Research Council recommended the abandonment of quota samples and their replacement with probability samples (Bradburn and Sudman 1988). Probability sampling is the method used in "scientific" public opinion polls (see chapter 2).

Gallup, Crossley, and Roper were commercial pollsters. They did polls for clients and by necessity were concerned with costs and profitability. They had little incentive for pure research or for the lengthy surveys necessary to answer complex academic questions.[15] Those topics would be addressed by the major academic survey organizations, most notably the National Opinion Research Center (NORC) at the University of Chicago and the Survey Research Center (SRC)[16] at the University of Michigan. NORC was founded in 1941, and its associates produced several classics in the field of public opinion, including *The American Soldier* (Stouffer 1949) and *Communism, Conformity, and Civil Liberties* (Stouffer 1955). The SRC, founded in 1946, has focused on studies of the American electorate. Perhaps the most influential book to date on public opinion and voting, *The American Voter* (Campbell et al. 1960), was published by a group associated with the SRC.

Both the NORC and the SRC devote considerable resources to technical issues involving sampling and question wording. The NORC pioneered the split-ballot technique, in which different forms of a question are asked of random halves of a sample to investigate the effects of question wording. Researchers associated with the SRC have also devoted extensive time and energy to problems of question wording (Schuman and Presser 1996). But most important are the periodic surveys conducted by each of these institutions.

Every other year since 1948, the SRC and the Center for Political Studies have conducted the American National Election Studies (ANES).[17] These are large, in-person national surveys of issues relevant to elections. In presidential years, respondents are interviewed in the autumn before the election, and then reinterviewed after the election is over. The total interview time is often three to five hours, and hundreds of questions are asked. The ANES surveys voters in midterm election years as well, with shorter interviews usually conducted only after the election.

Since 1971, NORC has sponsored the General Social Survey (GSS), conducted on an annual or biennial basis. The GSS has a general set of questions, often repeated from one survey to the next, and a topical module that addresses a specific substantive concern at considerable length. Both the ANES and GSS are publicly available, formatted and ready for analysis with common computer statistical packages. Much of the data presented in this book comes from these two sources.

While both the ANES and GSS interview people in their homes; this is an expensive undertaking. By the early 1970s, techniques were being developed to scientifically sample telephone numbers using a random-digit-dialing methodology. This greatly reduced the cost of surveys and encouraged the media to conduct their own public opinion polls, much as they did in the days of the straw polls. In 1976, CBS News and the *New York Times* went into partnership to conduct their own polls. They were soon followed by the NBC/*Wall Street Journal*, the ABC/*Washington Post* polls, and CNN.[18] The principal advantage to the media of in-house polls is that they can decide on the topics and timing of the surveys rather than being confined to the topics and timing of independent pollsters like Gallup. In-house polls also free the media from reliance on leaks from political campaigns about how candidates are faring with the voters. They can find out for themselves on an impartial, firsthand basis. The most significant nonprofit, nonpartisan organization that polls on a regular basis is the Pew Research Center. Unlike media polls that usually address topical issues with an abbreviated number of questions, Pew conducts episodic polls that treat specific topics (such as political trust) in considerable depth.

A relatively new innovation is the Election Day exit poll, developed by CBS News in the late 1960s. It did not, however, gain prominence until the 1980 election, when it was first used to forecast the outcome of a presidential election. With an exit poll, one chooses a representative sample of precincts in a state and interviews voters as they leave the polling place. The networks usually know by 3:00 P.M. who has won the election, although they do not reveal this information for any one state until the polls have closed in that state. Beyond forecasting, exit polls have proved extremely valuable for understanding why people voted for specific candidates. Prior to 1990, each network conducted its own exit polls.

In 1990, the major networks, along with CNN and the Associated Press, formed a consortium, Voter News Service (VNS), to conduct common exit polls and share the information. This worked well until the 2000 presidential election, when VNS prematurely forecast a Gore victory in Florida. Then, in 2002, VNS exit polls were not reported on election night due to concerns over unreliability. As a consequence, VNS was dissolved and replaced by a new consortium called the National Election Pool (NEP).

The most recent innovation in polling is measuring public opinion using the Internet. Respondents are recruited by a variety of methods. Most often they are recruited directly over the Internet and are offered an incentive to participate in online polls. The resulting sample is then adjusted for self-selection and weighted based on Census data. Of course, those lacking an Internet connection cannot be included in the sample (24 percent as of January 2010).[19] Another method is to recruit respondents by telephone, give those lacking Internet access the necessary equipment, and providing everyone with an incentive to participate in the vendor's surveys.

One further innovation in polling worth mentioning is the development of a code of standards for those in the field of public opinion. Unlike physicians, lawyers, and morticians, pollsters are not subject to government regulation. On occasion there have been calls by some in Congress for regulation. The first of these came in 1948, with many Democrats charging that the polls were biased in favor of Republicans. Another came in response to using exit polls to call the winner of the presidential election in 1980 before the voting booths had closed on the West Coast. It was argued that many Democrats failed to vote once they learned that President Carter had been defeated. However, virtually all attempts by the government to regulate opinion polls have run afoul of the First Amendment's guarantee of the right of free speech.

In 1986, the American Association for Public Opinion Research (AAPOR) adopted a code of ethics and practices for the profession.[20] Among the major features of this code are full disclosure, confidentiality, and responsibility to those being interviewed. Pollsters must make available full information about who sponsored the survey and give details of relevant methodology, such as how the sample was selected. They must hold as confidential the responses to questions by specific individuals. They must avoid any practice that would harm or mislead a respondent. While the AAPOR has a standards committee, its only power of sanction is the glare of adverse publicity.

1-4   The Modern Public Opinion Poll and Its Political Consequences

Prior to 1940, politicians judged public sentiment mainly from newspapers (Herbst 1993; Kernell 1993). For example, William McKinley kept tabs on "public opinion" by compiling a scrapbook, called "Current Comment," of newspaper articles from every section of the country (Hilderbrand 1981). Contemporary political leaders clearly have much better information on the content of public opinion than they did prior to the advent of scientific polling. John Geer (1996) argues that politicians well informed about public opinion use a qualitatively different leadership style than those without reliable opinion information. In particular, he argues certain skills historically associated with leadership are found less frequently in today's political leaders. They include the ability to craft good arguments and a willingness to remain committed to a stand.

According to Geer, before polling, politicians were uncertain if the electorate was on their side, and a premium was placed on the ability to convince both citizens and other politicians of the merits of an argument. Today this skill is less essential because more certainty exists about the electorate's preferences. For example, staff disputes on issues are often resolved by reference to public opinion rather than nuanced argument. Modern politicians are also less likely to remain committed to issue positions if the polls show them to be electoral losers. William Jennings Bryan ran for president in 1896 on the "free silver" platform. Despite being soundly defeated, he showcased the same issue in his 1900 presidential bid. Bryan remained convinced that public opinion was on his side (Anderson 1981). Geer argues that in the absence of reliable opinion data as a reality check, politicians' estimate of public opinion is driven by their personal views and reinforced by those around them, who often think as they do. On the other hand, Ronald Reagan in the 1960s and early 1970s was a strong proponent of a voluntary social security program. Because polls showed a large proportion of the public disagreed, it is probably no accident that he dropped the issue when he ran for the presidency. Finally, the modern opinion poll has likely forever changed the standard by which political leadership is judged. Every decision is now evaluated in reference to public opinion. How, for example, would history treat Lincoln's Emancipation Proclamation if a Gallup Poll in June 1862 showed 72 percent of Northerners wanted to abolish slavery (Geer 1996)?

Change is not neutral. Innovations benefit some at the expense of others. The modern public opinion poll is no exception. Benjamin Ginsberg (1986) makes the counterintuitive argument that replacement by the modern opinion poll of traditional methods of expressing public opinion has served to "domesticate" public opinion. In other words, public opinion is a less potent force in American politics now than it was prior to scientific polling. Public opinion polls may serve to reassure people that their opinions are being heeded, when in fact they may be ignored by powerful elites who set public policy mainly with regard to their own interests.

"Traditional methods of expressing public opinion" refers to letters to newspapers and public officials, personal contact, elections, advocacy group activity, marches, demonstrations, and riots—to list the more obvious. Such methods are still available, but when these indicators of public opinion differ from those reported in polls, it is universally assumed that polls are more representative. If one conceives of public opinion as an aggregation of equally weighted preferences, that assumption is almost certainly correct. However, polling by simply totaling individual opinions has, according to Ginsberg, changed some important aspects of "public opinion" as expressed by methods commonly employed before the advent of the scientific survey.

For example, public opinion was once largely a group phenomenon. At election time, elected officials would consult closely with the leaders of advocacy groups, such as farmers and organized labor, to be informed of membership opinion. Opinion polls have undermined the ability of group leaders to speak for their membership, as the members can now be polled directly. Any difference archive contains almost half a million items, which can be accessed through the Internet. Many colleges have an IPOLL subscription. By simply entering one or more keywords, such as "gun control," users can obtain question wording, item frequencies, and basic documentation for questions housed at the archive. The survey data are also sometimes available and can be directly downloaded. The Institute for Research in Social Science at the University of North Carolina houses the surveys conducted by Lou Harris and Associates, plus more than 350 statewide-level polls. An excellent multipurpose site for public opinion data and other social data is Data on the Net, maintained by the University of California at San Diego. It serves as a gateway to almost one hundred data archives throughout the world. Finally, World Associates for Public Opinion Research is a source for public opinion data across a range of subjects. This site tends to focus on market research, but it also archives political surveys. In addition, there are often short feature stories about polling and research methods.

For academic students of public opinion, including undergraduate and graduate students, the most valuable data archive is the Inter-University Consortium for Political and Social Research (ICPSR) at the University of Michigan. Many colleges and universities are members of the Consortium, while membership in other data archives is less frequent. The Consortium publishes annually a complete catalog of its holdings and distributes a newsletter informing members of new acquisitions. This information as well as the frequencies for some of its data sets can be accessed at its Web site. The Consortium also disseminates the American National Election Studies, the General Social Survey, and the World Values Survey. These are three of the most important nonproprietary academic surveys available for secondary analysis, and we rely on them extensively in this book. Each of these studies comes with a completely documented codebook. Both the codebooks and the data sets are routinely received by universities that are Consortium members. In addition, a number of journals regularly publish opinion data. Each issue of the *Public Opinion Quarterly* has a section called "The Polls" in which survey data on a specific topic is reviewed.

Current Polling Data

The Internet is now an important resource for monitoring polls. The following sites make available the latest public opinion polling data on a wide range of topics—from public reaction to an event recently in the news to the latest reading on presidential popularity or the current poll data on a high-profile election.

> www.psr.keele.ac.uk/data.htm A lengthy list of data archives and polling organizations from around the world.
>
> www.fivethirtyeight.com First-rate analysis of polling data by Nate Silver, who expertly combines statistical analysis and popular politics.
>
> www.Pollster.com Thorough site for commentary on polling, run by Mark Blumenthal and Charles Franklin. The editors received an excellence award in 2007 from the American Association for Public Opinion Research.

www.pollingreport.com A service of The Polling Report, a nonpartisan clearinghouse for public opinion data; provides reports on current opinion on politics, the economy, and popular culture.

www.nationaljournal.com/ The *National Journal*; provides up-to-date polling information on electoral contests.

www.hsph.harvard.edu/horp/ Provides public opinion information on health issues and public policy issues.

www.gallup.com The site for the Gallup Poll.

www.americanprogress.org This site contains the column "Public Opinion Watch" by Ruy Teixeira. Teixeira presents insightful commentary and analysis on current polls and polling issues.

www.pipa.org This site reports original polling and discussion on international issues, conducted by the Program on International Policy Attitudes at the University of Maryland.

www.publicagenda.org A site that presents opinion data and commentary on domestic policy issues.

www.people-press.org The site for the Pew Research Center for the People and the Press; an independent research group that conducts surveys in some depth about current issues, regularly conducts polls on public attentiveness to news stories, and charts trends in fundamental social and political values.

www.democracycorps.com Conducts regular polls on current political matters.

www.harrisinteractive.com/harris_poll Home of the Harris Poll, mostly Internet surveys.

www.PublicOpinionPros.com. An official web site of the American Associate for Public Opinion Research that provides informed commentary by polling experts on both substance and method.

www.zogby.com The site for Zogby International, the political polling agency for Reuters; mostly focuses on electoral choice.

Polling Data Archives Earlier in this chapter, we discussed a number of data libraries. The Web sites for these archives are listed below.

www.icpsr.umich.edu The site for the University Consortium for Social and Political Research, home to the National Election Studies (ANES). It archives the General Social Survey (GSS), the World Values Survey, and others.

www.norc.uchicago.edu The site for the National Opinion Research Center, home to the General Social Survey and other NORC studies.

www.ipoll.com The site for the Roper Center Archive, which houses the Gallup Poll, media polls, and others.

www.irss.unc.edu/odum/jsp/home.jsp The Odum Institute archive, associated with the University of North Carolina, home to the Harris Poll and the National Association of State Polls, which houses more than 350 state-level studies.

http://libraries.ucsd.edu/ssds Data on the Net, maintained by the
University of California at San Diego; also provides links to other social
data bases.

gort.ucsd.edu/calpol The archive for the Field Poll, devoted to political
and social issues in California.

Data Archives for Non-American Surveys Survey research now occurs regularly
all over the world. The best of the archives and their Web sites are listed below.

www.gesis.org/en/data_service/issp/index.htm The archive for the
International Social Survey.

http://ec.europa.eu/public_opinion/index_en.htm. This site is for archives
for the Eurobarometer and the Central and Eastern Eurobarometer.

www.mori.com A British-based opinion research firm and archive.
MORI holds mostly British opinion data but also conducts and archives
occasional cross-national studies.

Polling Organizations A number of professional polling organizations offer
useful and interesting information on survey research.

www.aapor.org The site for the American Association for Public Opinion
Research, the oldest and most prestigious of the polling organizations;
includes a complete index to articles published in the *Public Opinion
Quarterly*.

www.worldopinion.com The site for the World Association for Public
Opinion Research; often contains useful articles about opinion
research.

www.casro.org The site for the Council of American Survey Research
Organizations, the primary organization for those doing commercial
survey research.

www.ncpp.org The site for the National Council of Public Polls;
contains information on national standards and how to conduct and
interpret polls.

1-6 Linkage Models Between Public Opinion and Public Policies

In a democracy, public opinion is supposed to influence the decisions by the
elected leaders. But how effective, in practice, is the public at controlling what
its government does? This book attempts to answer this important question. The
mechanisms of popular control are more complicated than one might think.
(For a sampling of contemporary perspectives, see Fearon 1999; Ferejohn 1999;
Manin, Przeworski, and Stokes 1999; Erikson, MacKuen, and Stimson 2002;
Hutchings 2003; Mansbridge 2003; Stimson 2004) Here, we sketch five models,
drawn from Luttbeg (1968), by which public opinion can get reflected by public
policy.

The Rational-Activist Model

This model is the basis for the widely accepted concept of the ideal citizen's role in a democracy. Voting on the basis of issues is at the heart of the rational-activist model. By the standards of this model, individual citizens are expected to be informed politically, involved, rational, and, above all, active. On the basis of an informed and carefully reasoned set of personal preferences and an accurate perception of the various candidates' positions, voters are expected to cast a ballot for those candidates who best reflect their issue preferences. In this way, the victorious candidates in elections will be the ones who best represent constituency policy views.

This model places a burden on citizens, who are expected to hold informed and enlightened views about the policy positions of candidates and vote accordingly. As we have noted, politics does not play a salient role in the lives of most Americans. Many people rarely or never vote. Those who do are often inattentive to policy issues, particularly in low-salience elections.

Certainly, issue voting allows for some influence of public opinion on government policy. But in our search for methods by which political leaders can be held accountable, we must look beyond the rational-activist model.

The Political Parties Model

The political parties model greatly reduces the political demands placed on the citizen. The model depends on the desire of political parties to win elections as a mechanism for achieving popular control. According to the model, a party states its positions on the issues of the day in its platform. Because of their interest in winning elections, parties can be counted on to take stands that appeal to large segments of the electorate. Voters then select among platforms, giving support to the candidate of the party whose platform most conforms to their personal preference. Instead of facing multiple decisions for the numerous offices up for election, voters need only make a single decision among the available choice of parties.

A number of questions are raised by a consideration of this model. For example, to what extent do parties take distinct positions, and to what extent do voters recognize them? Does a party's electoral fortunes reflect the degree of public support for its policies, or is a party's vote largely independent of the policies it advocates?

The Interest Groups Model

In the preceding models, we emphasized the central importance of communication between elected officials and their constituents. For representatives to respond to public demands, they need to know what these demands are. For the public to achieve accountability from representatives, they need to know what the representatives have done and what alternatives were available. Interest groups can perform this function. They can serve as a link between people and their representatives.

Numerous organized groups in society claim to speak for various segments of the electorate—the Sierra Club, the National Organization for Women, and the National Rifle Association, to mention just three. At one extreme, these groups could be so inclusive of individuals in society and could so accurately represent their members' opinions that representatives could achieve accountability merely by recording the choice of each group, weighing them by the number of voters they represent, and voting with the largest group. This would be in accord with what might be called the interest groups model of popular control.

Under ideal circumstances, interest groups might succeed in communicating public opinion to officials between elections and with greater clarity than can be communicated through election outcomes. Interest groups, like political parties, could simplify the choices for the individual voter, making it possible for an electorate that is largely disinterested in politics to nevertheless achieve accountability.

Several questions arise out of the interest groups model. Does group opinion, the somehow combined opinions of all those persons in all the relevant interest groups, coincide with public opinion? Or, do the opinions carried to government by interest groups reflect only the opinions of the wealthy or the business sector of society? Who among everyday citizens belongs to interest groups? Are some segments of society overrepresented and others mostly uninvolved in any type of group activity?

The Delegate Model

When voters are doing their job (via the rational–activist model), elections are decided by policy issues. To win elections under such circumstances, politicians must cater to the views of their prospective voters, and to stay elected, elected officials must anticipate voter preferences in advance of the next election. When politicians take voter preferences seriously in this way, acting as the voters' agent, we say they are behaving as the voters' delegates. This is the delegate model at work.[21] By this model, representation of public opinion can be enhanced simply because elected leaders believe they will be voted out of office if they do not attend to voter opinion—whether or not the voters would actually do so.

Several questions are raised by the delegate model: Can elected officials accurately learn public opinion, or do they receive a distorted view? To what extent do elected officials actually heed public opinion as they perceive it? What do elected leaders view as the consequences of ignoring public opinion? Finally, how often do elected officials see their role as representing constituency preferences as opposed to their (possibly conflicting) personal views of the constituency's best interests?

The Sharing Model

Because as a society we do not designate leaders early in life and hold them as a class apart from then on, it is unlikely that the personal opinions held by elected officials on the issues of the day differ diametrically from those held by the rest of the electorate. This possibility is the final model of political linkage: the sharing model. This model simply states that because many attitudes are broadly held throughout the public, elected leaders cannot help but satisfy public opinion to some degree, even if the public is totally apathetic. Unilateral disarmament, total government takeover of the economy, a termination of public education, a complete disregard for the preservation of the environment—all are examples of actions so contrary to broadly held American attitudes that they would be rejected by any set of government leaders. Even on issues that provoke substantial disagreement, the distribution of opinion among political leaders may be similar to that among the public. If so, even when leaders act according to personal preference and are ignored by disinterested citizens, their actions would often correspond to citizen preferences. For this model, we need to consider how broadly opinions on national issues are shared and how similar the views of elected officials are to those of the public at large.

1-7   Plan of This Book

We have by necessity ordered facts into chapters that strike us as convenient. Chapter 2 discusses the science of assessing public opinion. Chapter 3 is concerned with the psychology of opinion-holding and focuses on the role of political ideology and party identification. Chapter 4 chronicles trends in public opinion over time. Chapter 5 discusses the formation of political attitudes. Chapter 6 evaluates data on broad public acceptance of certain attitudes that may be necessary for a stable democratic government, and Chapter 7 delves into the group basis of public opinion. Chapter 8 analyzes the effect of the media on those attitudes. Chapter 9 is an analysis of public opinion and elections, and Chapter 10 views the reverse aspect of political linkage—how elected officials respond to the views of their constituents. In the final chapter, we assess the linkage models and draw conclusions about public opinion in the United States based on the data presented throughout the book.

Notes

1. The term *pollster* was coined by political scientist Lindsay Rogers in his book *The Pollsters: Public Opinion, Politics, and Democratic Leadership* (1949) to evoke in the minds of readers the word *huckster* (Hitchens 1992, 46).
2. Or, as Winston Churchill put it, "Nothing is more dangerous than to live in the temperamental atmosphere of a Gallup Poll, always feeling one's pulse and taking one's temperature . . . There is only one duty, only one safe course, and that is to try to be right and not to fear to do or waver in what you believe to be right" (quoted in Bogart 1972, 47).
3. For a recent review of the volatility of public opinion on foreign policy, see Drezner (2008).
4. The eighteenth-century French mathematician Marquis de Condorcet, using jury decisions as an example, was able to demonstrate mathematically a greater probability that the majority would come to the right decision than the probability the minority would come to the right decision. For a popular rendition of this idea, see Surowiecki (2004).

5. It also includes the functional equivalent of verbal expressions, such as filling out a written questionnaire.

6. One ambiguity inherent in this conceptualization is that some people may never express orally or in writing some of their opinions. We could possibly conceptualize such opinions as internal, but that has the unhappy consequence of muddying the distinction between attitudes and opinions. Our simple solution for unexpressed opinions is to assert that, if expressed, they would have the same characteristics and qualities of expressed opinion.

7. It should be noted that our distinction between opinions and beliefs is not common to all fields. In a court of law, for example, an expert witness is frequently asked to give an "expert opinion" on a matter of fact. In everyday conversation, it is quite frequent that someone asserts, "It is my opinion that . . ." followed by some assertion of factual truth.

8. The name apparently comes from a practice in rural areas of throwing straw into the air to see which way the wind is blowing. Presumably, a "straw poll" is a method for determining the direction of the political winds. Pioneer pollster Claude Robinson (1932, 6) defined a straw poll as "an unofficial canvass of an electorate to determine the division of popular sentiment on public issues or on candidates for public office." Today, the term generally refers to any assessment of public opinion based on nonscientific sampling methods.

9. The sample consisted of 532 respondents from Wilmington, Delaware, selected "without discrimination of parties" (Gallup and Rae 1940, 35).

10. Straw polls used three methods to gather data. One was the ballot-in-the-paper method, in which the reader filled out the ballot, cut it out of the paper, and mailed it to the sponsoring organization. The second was the personal canvass, in which solicitors took ballots to crowded locations such as theaters, hotels, and trolleys and got willing citizens to complete them. Sometimes ballots were simply left in a crowded area in the morning, and those completed were retrieved in the evening. The third method was to send ballots by mail to a specified list of people and ask that they send them back by return mail.

11. The *Chicago Record* featured daily straw-poll updates on its front page from September 1896 through Election Day. It was typical for newspapers and magazines to publish regular updates of their straw-poll findings.

12. The sample sizes for the straw polls were so large that they typically made projections on a state-by-state basis.

13. Straw polls were not the only method used to handicap the "horse race" of presidential campaigns in the prepoll era. One source for many years was a Wall Street betting market on the election outcome. Market prices on the candidates chances of winning were followed much the same that poll numbers are followed today. Early in the twentieth century, these markets predicted presidential vote outcomes with roughly the accuracy of that polls do in the modern era. However, most elections during this period were one-sided. In the one close race (1916), the election markets predicted the wrong winner. See Rohde and Strumpf (2004).

14. Gallup marketed to newspapers a column, "America Speaks," from 1935 to 1971 which was based on his polls.

15. Although early on, Gallup did do split-ballot question-wording experiments. These were not, however, publicly released.

16. Now a division of the Institute for Social Research.

17. Over the years, these University of Michigan–based surveys have undergone a number of name changes. In the early years, they were dubbed the SRC surveys,

after the Survey Research Center. Then they became the CPS surveys, named after the Center for Political Studies, a division of the Institute for Social Research. Currently they are referred to as the American National Election Studies.

18. However, only the CBS News/*New York Times* has its own in-house polling operation. ABC, NBC, and CNN contract with outside commercial polling houses for their opinion surveys.

19. Survey by Pew Internet and American Life Project and Princeton Survey Research Associates International, November 19–December 20.

20. A copy of the code of ethics can be obtained from the AAPOR Web site at www.aapor.org.

21. In editions 1–6, we labeled this model the role-playing model, following Luttbeg's original formulation. For the politician, an alternative to the delegate role is the role of the trustee who, rather than following constituency preferences, acts according to the politician's conception of the constituents' best interests. See Wahlke et al. (1962) for various formulations of legislator roles.

2 Polling: The Scientific Assessment of Public Opinion

THE USE OF SCIENTIFIC POLLING TO GAUGE and analyze public opinion and elections has now been part of the political landscape for over sixty years. And it continues to grow. This growth is evident in the media's obsession with campaigns as horse races, where journalists' interest lies more in forecasting the outcome than the substance of the campaign. During the presidential election season, the news media is now saturated with polling reports. In recent presidential campaigns, one finds national polls being reported at a rate of greater than one per day, with even more state polls reported on a daily basis (Wlezien and Erikson 2002; Cohen 2007). Perhaps as many as two-thirds of the election stories that are reported on the network news in recent years are supported by polling data (Hess 2000; Fiorina et al. 2009, 18).

2-1 The Value of Polls

Of course, polling is not confined to election polls and the prediction of the next election outcome. As discussed in chapter 1, academic polls advance our knowledge of public opinion. Commercial pollsters (e.g., Gallup) satisfy the public's (and private clients') curiosity regarding trends in public opinion. Although not as highly publicized as the pollsters' election forecasts, polls routinely ascertain public preferences on a variety of policy issues and monitor the public pulse regarding such indicators as party identification, ideological identification, and the approval rating of the current president. This is the stuff of public opinion analysis and the subject of subsequent chapters.

Politicians and the Polls

Politicians have a particularly strong interest in the polls, as their professional careers may depend on reading public opinion accurately. Like the rest of us, politicians have access to commercial opinion polls such as the Gallup Poll. But the politicians often seek further intelligence regarding public opinion by commissioning their own polls. The first president to poll the public was Franklin Roosevelt, who did so in the late 1930s. While his next two successors, Truman and Eisenhower, had little use for private polling, presidential polling picked up in earnest with John Kennedy. Since then, virtually every major presidential decision has been made with the benefit of private polls. Presidents seek updates of public attitudes toward current policies, public reactions to future policy options, and especially information on their own standing with the voters (Jacobs and Shapiro 2000).

Politicians below the presidential level also do their own polling, as do the major political parties. Senate and House members spend about 3 percent of their sizable campaign war chests on polling their states or districts (Fritz and Morris 1992). Although the general purpose of this polling is to monitor their electoral standing against current or future opponents, private constituency polls can also register signals regarding shifts in constituency concerns.

A candidate's poor showing in preelection polls makes fund-raising difficult and dampens volunteer enthusiasm. As observed by Mike Murphy and Mark Mellman (2007), two leading political consultants (one a Republican and the other a Democrat), "Early national polling is used to declare winners and losers. Those declarations affect the flow of money and [media] coverage." Good poll numbers result in more media attention (Traugott and Lavrakas 2008). A strong showing in the polls can legitimize a candidate, ensuring that he or she is taken seriously, and being taken seriously is necessary to raise money.

Polls create expectations about who is the likely election winner. In presidential primaries with a number of more or less unknown candidates, expectations about who will win in the preelection polls help to frame the postelection spin. Sometimes losers manufacture "wins" by beating expectations even when they fail to win the most votes. A classic example occurred in the New Hampshire Democratic primary of 1992, when Bill Clinton came in second (to Paul Tsongas) and hailed himself as the "comeback kid." In the 2004 election, this pattern was repeated when John Edwards received a bonanza of favorable press coverage when he beat expectations in the Wisconsin primary, even though he lost to John Kerry by 6 percent of the vote (Ruttenberg 2005). Thomas Patterson (2002, 2005) makes a compelling argument that the standing in the polls of a presidential candidate determines the way the candidate's personal qualities are described by the media. When poll numbers are good, news stories are positive; when poll numbers are bad, stories turn negative (see also Farnsworth and Lichter 2007). For example, in an analysis of *Newsweek's* reporting of the 1988 presidential campaign, Patterson demonstrates that when polls showed Michael Dukakis doing well in the 1988 presidential race, he was described as "relentless in his attack" and "a credible candidate." As he later dropped in the polls, *Newsweek* described him as "reluctant to attack" and "trying to present himself as a credible candidate." Interestingly, the change in descriptors coincided quite closely with the point he fell behind George Bush in the polls (Patterson 1989, 104–6). Finally, standing in the polls can determine whether or not a candidate is invited to participate in the presidential debates. For example, while Ross Perot's poll numbers justified his appearance in the 1992 debates, his poll support was deemed insufficient for his inclusion in the 1996 presidential debates.

Presidential popularity, now gauged virtually daily, is the public opinion indicator watched with perhaps the most interest by members of Congress, others in the political community, and the media. Arguably, one important aspect of presidential power, including influence over Congress, is the chief executive's personal standing with the public (Canes-Wrone and deMarchi 2002; Bond, Fleisher, and Wood 2003; Canes-Wrone and Shotts 2004). While it is debatable how much a president can leverage popular approval into public support for his favored projects, there is little doubt that members of Congress and Washington insiders believe that a popular president holds the power to persuade public opinion. It was the high job approval enjoyed by President Clinton (about 70 percent) that in the opinion of many (including Clinton) saved his presidency after he was impeached by the House of Representatives.[1] President George W. Bush's surge in popularity following 9/11 smoothed the passage of items from his conservative agenda through Congress.

The Public Looks at the Polls

More and more people say they are paying attention to the polls. In 1944, only 19 percent of the public said that they regularly or occasionally followed poll results; by 1985 it was 41 percent, and in 2000, the figure had risen to 65 percent. In 2008, 89 percent said they had read or heard about the latest polls in the presidential election contest.[2] Yet few citizens have even a rudimentary understanding of how a public opinion poll works. In September 2005, the Gallup organization asked a national sample whether interviews with 1,500 or 2,000 people (typical sample sizes for national polls) "can accurately reflect the views of the nation's population" or whether "it's not possible with so few people." Only 30 percent said a sample of that size could yield accurate results; 68 percent said it was not possible, and the remaining 2 percent had no opinion. While the public may not understand the technicalities of polling, a sizable majority nevertheless believes polls are important guides for public officials (Traugott and Kang 2000a). In 2001, 66 percent said that "polls are useful for elected officials in Washington to understand how the public feels about important issues."[3]

The 2008 political campaign saw polling methodology draw far more than the usual public attention, thanks to the World Wide Web. In 2008, bloggers of both the political left and right complained about alleged biases in favor of one candidate or another. At the same time, access to the Web allowed interested members of the public to learn more about the ins and outs of polling methodology than ever before.[4]

Polling certainly deserves a critical look. Many surveys are badly conceived, poorly executed, and incorrectly interpreted. Nevertheless, much popular criticism of public opinion polls seems ill-informed. Few outside the professional survey community have an appreciation for why candidates who lead in the final preelection poll do not always win, why two surveys taken at the same time report different results, or even why Truman beat Dewey when the Gallup Poll predicted otherwise.

2-2   Sampling

Public opinion polls are based on samples. When the Gallup Poll reports that 50 percent of adult Americans approve of the way the president is handling his job, it is obvious that the Gallup organization has not gone out and interviewed 225 million American adults. Instead, it has taken a sample. The reasons for sampling are fairly straightforward. First, to interview everyone would be prohibitively expensive. The Census for the year 2010 is estimated to cost $11.8 billion. Second, to interview the entire population would take a very long time. Months might pass between the first and last interviews. Public opinion might, in that period, undergo real change.

Sampling provides a practical alternative to interviewing the whole population—be it national, state, or local. Furthermore, when done correctly, sampling can provide accurate estimates of the political opinions of a larger population. The theory of sampling is a branch of the mathematics of probability, and the error involved in going from the sample to the population can be known with precision. However, many surveys of public opinion do not meet the demanding requirements of sampling theory. The attendant result, of course, is a loss in accuracy.

Sampling Theory

The *population* is that unit about which we want information. In most political surveys, the population is one of the following: (1) those eighteen and older, (2) registered voters, or (3) those who will (or do) vote in the next election. These are three quite different groups. It is important that the population be clearly specified. When one sees a poll addressing abortion, presidential popularity, or voter intent in an upcoming election, those reporting the poll should provide a clear description of the population about which they speak. The *sample* is that part of the population selected for analysis. Usually, the sample is considerably smaller than the population. National political surveys conducted by reputable firms employ samples of 1,000 to 1,500 respondents, although smaller samples are sometimes used in state and local contests. But as samples get smaller, the probability of error increases. Sample size should always be reported along with the results of a survey. If that information is missing, the alleged findings should be treated with a great deal of caution.

When samples accurately mirror the population, they are said to be *representative*. The term _randomness_ refers to the only method by which a representative sample can be scientifically drawn. In a simple random sample, each unit of the population has exactly the same chance of being drawn as any other unit. If the population is American attorneys, each attorney is required to have exactly the same probability of being selected in order for the sample to be random. Attorneys in big cities could not have a greater likelihood of getting into the sample than those from rural areas. This situation obviously requires a detailed knowledge of the population. In the case of attorneys, one could get a list from the American Bar Association and then sample from that list. But suppose the population was unemployed adults. To specify the population in a fashion to be able to draw a random sample would be difficult. As a consequence, obtaining a representative sample of the unemployed is not easy.

A *probability sample* is a variant of the principle of random sampling. Instead of each unit having exactly the same probability of being drawn, some units are more likely to be drawn than would others—but this is a known probability. For example, if one were sampling voter precincts in a state, it is of consequence that some precincts contain more people than do others. To make the sample of people in those precincts representative, the larger precincts must have a greater likelihood of being selected than smaller ones.

We use simple random sampling (SRS) to illustrate how the principle of probability works in selecting a representative sample. Let us assume our population is a large barrel containing 1 million marbles, some of which are red and some green. We do not know the percentage of each. Instead of counting them all (a long and tedious job), we will draw a random sample. The question is, How? We could just dip in our hand and take some out, but that would mean that those within our reach would be picked and those close to the bottom would have no chance of being selected. Or we could spin the barrel and take one out after every spin. That would probably work reasonably well, but it still would not be "scientific." Even with a spin, those marbles at the bottom might never get close enough to the surface to get picked. If we are insisting on a pure random sample, we would have to employ a table of random numbers and give each marble a numeral between 1 and one million. Random number tables are computer-generated digits that are completely unrelated to one another (i.e., random). They can be found in the appendix of virtually any statistics book. Let us assume we sample 600 marbles. Our first random number might be 33,382. We would then find the marble with that number and note if it is red or green. Our next random number might be 712,343. We would again note its color. The process would continue until we drew 600 marbles and recorded the color of each.

Having completed that task, let us say our sample shows 65 percent red marbles. Given the sampling method, we now know some things about the population. Sampling theory (the central limit theorem) tells us that the most likely percentage of red marbles is 65 percent. Of course, it is very unlikely that the real percentage of red marbles is precisely 65 percent. It might be 65.5 or 64.3, for example. The sample will not get the population value exactly correct for the same reason that flipping a coin 100 times will not likely yield exactly 50 heads and 50 tails—although it should be close if the coin is honestly flipped.

At this point, we need to introduce the concepts of *confidence level* and *sampling error*. A sample rarely hits the true population value right on the nose. The confidence level tells us the probability that the population value will fall within a specified range. The sampling error specifies that range. A commonly used confidence level is 95 percent (it is sometimes higher, but almost never lower). For a sample of 600, the sampling error is 4 percent. What all this means is that if we took 100 samples from our population, and each of these samples consisted of 600 marbles randomly drawn, then 95 out of 100 times we would be plus or minus 4 percent of the true population value. Our sample came up 65 percent red. While this figure may not be exactly correct, we at least know that 95 out of 100 times (our 95 percent confidence level) we are going to be within four points—one way or the other—of the true proportion of red marbles in the barrel. This much can be proved mathematically.

Let us turn to a political example. The Gallup Poll reported that President Barack Obama's approval rating after his first 100 days in office was 69 percent (*Washington Post/ABC News Poll*, April 26, 2009). Since the sample size in this survey was 1,072, we know that if the poll were repeated 100 times, 95 of the 100 repetitions (the 95 percent confidence level) would produce results that are plus or minus 3 percent (the sampling error) of what we would find if we interviewed all American adults.[5] Thus, Obama's popularity on or about April 29, 2009, could have been as high as 72 percent or as low as 66 percent. The best estimate (according to the central limit theorem) is 69 percent. Sampling error decreases as we move away from a 50/50 split, and it increases as the population has more heterogeneous political attitudes. But by far the most important factor is the size of the sample.

The importance of sample size for sampling accuracy can be easily demonstrated by flipping a coin. We know that, in theory, if a coin is flipped honestly a large number of times it should come up about equal proportions of heads and tails. Suppose we flipped a coin ten times. Given a large number of repetitions of ten flips we might frequently get seven heads, eight tails, and so on. But if instead of flipping the coin ten times we flipped it one hundred times, then our large number of repetitions would only occasionally yield 70 heads or 80 tails, and if we flipped it 1,000 times, our repetitions could tend to cluster around 500 heads and 500 tails, with 700 heads or 800 tails being rare events indeed. The larger the size of the sample (i.e., the number of times the coin is flipped), the closer we will come to the theoretical expectation of one-half heads and one-half tails.

Unlike the size of the sample, the size of the population is of little consequence for the accuracy of the survey.[6] That is, it does not make much difference if we are surveying the city of Houston or the entire United States. With a sample size of 600, the sampling error would be identical for both the city and the nation—all other things being equal. Table 2.1 presents the sampling errors associated with specific sample sizes.

Using a large barrel of marbles and a table of random numbers, we drew a "perfect" sample—that is, the sampling method fit perfectly with the

TABLE 2.1	Sampling Error and Sample Size Employing Simple Random Sampling*

Sample Size	Sampling Error (plus or minus)*
2,430	2.0
1,536	2.5
1,067	3.0
784	3.5
600	4.0
474	4.5
384	5.0
267	6.0
196	7.0
150	8.0
119	9.0
96	10.0
42	15.0

*This computation is based on the assumptions of a simple random sampling (SRS) with a dichotomous opinion that splits 50/50 and a 95 percent confidence level.

mathematics of sampling theory. When we sample humans, we cannot draw a perfect sample. Although a marble cannot refuse to tell us if it is red or green, a person may refuse to be interviewed. Sampling theory does not allow for refusals. Consequently, surveys of public opinion only approximate the underlying theory of sampling.

One way to compensate for the workings of chance in probability surveys and for survey nonresponse is through poststratification weighting. We know from the Census the distribution of key demographic factors among the American population. If the sample does not match the Census, it can be weighted to bring it into line. For example, we know 12 percent of the American population is African American. If a sample of 1,000 contained just 8 percent African Americans, it can be weighted to bring the total up to 12 percent. If this were the only weighting consideration, we would multiply African Americans by 1.50 and everyone else by .957. This would raise the percent of African Americans in the sample to 12 percent but still keep the sample size at 1,000. The demographics normally used for weighting include age, gender, education, race/ethnicity, and homeownership, although the choice of weight factors varies among survey professionals. Weighting is an effective, but still imperfect, solution for adjusting samples that depart from known demographics. Those who refuse to be interviewed may be different from those who consent, and weighting cannot correct for this difference.[7]

Bad Sampling: Two Historical Examples

Historically, there are many instances in which sampling theory was either ignored or those conducting the polls were ignorant. If the poll simply concerns political opinions (favor/oppose abortion, approve/disapprove of tax reform, favor/oppose the registration of handguns, etc.), there is no reality test. The survey may have been done badly and be considerably off the mark, but how would one know?[8] On the other hand, pre–Election Day surveys have a reality test: Election Day. In these surveys, sampling mistakes have, in several dramatic cases, cast opinion pollsters in a highly unfavorable light.

To see how not to sample, it is worth reviewing two classic polling mistakes from the past. One, discussed in chapter 1, was the *Literary Digest* fiasco of 1936. The other was when the seemingly scientific polls all failed in the presidential election of 1948.

The **Literary Digest,** *1948.* The previous chapter discussed the prescientific straw polls that were used to gauge candidate fortunes prior to 1936. The best known of the commercial publications conducting straw polls was the *Literary Digest*. The *Digest* accurately forecast the winner (if not the exact percentage points) of each presidential election between 1920 and 1932. In 1936, as in previous years, it sent out some 10 million postcard ballots "drawn from every telephone book in the United States, from the rosters of clubs and associations, from city directories, lists of registered voters, [and] classified mail order and occupational data" (*Literary Digest*, August 1936, 3). About 2.2 million returned their postal ballots. The result was 1,293,699 (57 percent) for Republican Alf Landon and 972,867 (43 percent) for President Franklin Roosevelt. On Election Day, Roosevelt not only won but also won by a landslide, receiving 62.5 percent of the vote and carrying every state except Maine and Vermont. The *Literary Digest* was not only wrong; it was also wrong by 19.5 percent. On November 14, 1936, the *Literary Digest* published the following commentary:

> What Went Wrong with the Polls?
>
> None of Straw Votes Got Exactly the Right Answer—Why?
>
> In 1920, 1924, 1928 and 1932, the *Literary Digest* Polls were right. Not only right in the sense they showed the winner; they forecast the actual popular vote and with such a small percentage of error (less than 1 percent in 1932) that newspapers and individuals everywhere heaped such phrases as "uncannily accurate" and "amazingly right" upon us. . . . Well this year we used precisely the same method that had scored four bull's eyes in four previous tries. And we were far from correct. Why? We ask that question in all sincerity, because *we want to know.*

Why *did* the poll fare so badly? One reason that can be discounted is sample size. The *Digest* claims to have polled 10 million people (and received 2.2 million responses). Thus, a large sample is no guarantee for accuracy. Rather, their sampling procedure had four fundamental defects. First, the sample was drawn in a biased fashion. The *Digest* clearly did not use random selection or anything approaching it. Even though questionnaires were sent out to 10 million people, a large part of the sample was drawn from telephone directories and lists of automobile owners—during the Depression, a decidedly upper-middle-class group, predominantly Republican in its political sentiments. In other words, the *Digest* did not correctly specify the population. A second factor contributing to the *Digest's* mistake was time. The questionnaires were sent out in early September, making impossible the detection of any late trend favoring one candidate or the other. Third, 1936 was the year that marked the emergence of the New Deal Coalition. The *Digest* had picked the winner correctly since 1920 using the same methods as in 1936, but in 1936 voting became polarized along class lines. The working class and the poor voted overwhelmingly Democratic, while the more affluent classes voted predominantly Republican. Since the *Literary Digest's* sample was heavily biased in the direction of the more affluent, it is not surprising that their sample tended to favor Landon.

Finally, there was the problem of self-selection. The *Digest* sent out its questionnaires by mail. Of the 10 million they mailed, only a little over 2 million were returned—about 22 percent. Those people who self-select to respond to mail surveys are often quite different in their political outlook from those who do not respond. They tend to be better educated, to have higher incomes, and to feel more strongly about the topics dealt with in the questionnaire (Dillman 1978). So even if the sample of 10 million had been drawn in an unbiased fashion, the poll probably still would have been in error due to the self-selection factor (Squire 1988). A fundamental principle of survey sampling is that one cannot allow the respondents to select themselves into the sample.

Despite the failure of the *Literary Digest*, several public opinion analysts did pick Franklin Roosevelt as the winner. Among them was George Gallup, who built his reputation on a correct forecast in 1936. In terms of percentage, Gallup did not get particularly close. He missed by almost 7 percent. But he got the winner right, and that is what most people remember.

"Dewey Defeats Truman," 1948. Following Gallup's success at predicting the 1936 election, "scientific" polling surged in popularity and became perceived within the political class as almost infallible. Gallup and other pollsters predicted the winners of the presidential elections of 1940 and 1944. Then, in 1948 the pollsters all predicted that the Republican presidential candidate, Tom Dewey, would defeat Truman. The pollsters were so confident of Dewey's victory that they did not even poll during the last few weeks of the campaign, seeing it as a waste of time. Virtually all politically knowledgeable observers saw the outcome as certain. Famously, Dewey began to name his cabinet.

The 1948 presidential election jarred the pollsters from their complacency. President Truman defeated Dewey in an upset. Gallup's prediction of Truman's vote was off by 5 percentage points. While this error was actually smaller than that in 1936, the crucial fact was that Gallup got the winner wrong.[9]

Why were Gallup and the other pollsters wrong in 1948? The technique used by Gallup in 1936 and up until the Dewey–Truman disaster is called *quota sampling.* This technique employs the Census to determine the percentage of certain relevant groups in the population. For example, what percentage is male, Catholic, white, and college educated? Within these groups, interviewers are then assigned quotas. They must interview a certain percentage of women, a certain percentage with less than high school education, a certain percentage of blacks, and so on. But there are few, if any, constraints as to which individuals in these groups are to be interviewed. Once the interviews are completed, the sample is weighted so it will be representative of the population on those variables. If 15 percent of the population is male, high school educated, and making over $25,000 a year, the sample is weighted to reflect those proportions.

The principal problem with quota sampling is a variation on the problem of self-selection. The interviewer has too much opportunity to determine who is selected for the sample. An interviewer who must, for instance, get a specified number of females and a specified number of blacks may avoid certain areas of town or may get the entire quota from a single block. There is a natural tendency to avoid shabby residences, long flights of stairs, and homes where there are dogs. Experience with quota samples demonstrates that they systematically tend to underrepresent the poor, the less educated, and racial minorities.

Research on Gallup's misprediction in 1948 reveals he had too many middle- and high-income voters. A second factor contributing to Gallup's mistake was that he quit polling two weeks before the election (Bradburn and Sudman 1988, 29). When significant movement takes place, it often occurs just before the election. For example, in 1980 Jimmy Carter and Ronald Reagan were virtually tied the weekend before the vote. A strong move toward Reagan over the weekend allowed him to pile up a substantial victory. To capture these changes, Gallup and other survey organizations now poll right up to the day of the election.

One irony in Gallup's misprediction is that two years before the *Literary Digest* fiasco, a Polish statistician named Jerzy Neyman (1934) published a landmark article demonstrating the superiority of random sampling to quota samples in survey work. So powerful was his mathematical demonstration that quota samples became an object of ridicule in scientific circles. During World War II, virtually all the voluminous government survey work was based on some variant of random sampling. The problems with quota samples had been known for some time. However, for reasons of cost, Gallup did not think he could abandon the quota method. After the 1948 election, he changed his mind (Frankel and Frankel 1987).

Sampling Methods for In-Person Surveys

From the 1930s into the 1980s, the predominant survey methodology was to interview respondents in-person, in their own homes. Earlier we described simple random sampling to illustrate the principles involved in drawing a scientific sample. However, in-person surveys rarely employ SRS. There is no master list of all Americans who could be sampled. Even if there were, the persons selected would be widely scattered throughout the country, making in-person interviews prohibitively expensive. For example, an interviewer might have to travel to Kerrville, Texas, just to talk to one respondent. Rather, polls where respondents are personally interviewed use *multistage cluster samples.*

The first step in drawing a multistage cluster sample of the American electorate is to divide the country into four geographic regions. Within each region, a set of counties and standard metropolitan statistical areas (SMSAs) is randomly selected. To ensure a representative selection of the national population, each county or SMSA is given a chance to be selected proportional to its population (probability sampling). National surveys typically include about 80 primary sampling units (PSUs). Once selected, the PSUs are often used several years before they are replaced. The reason is economic: Compact geographic areas save time and money. Interviewers are expensive to train, but once trained they can be used over and over.

About twenty respondents are chosen within each PSU. First, four or five city blocks (or their rural equivalents) are randomly selected. Then, four or five households are sampled within each block. It is at the household level that the continued use of probability methods becomes most difficult. Ideally, the interviewer obtains a list of all persons living in the household and samples from the list. And indeed, some academic polls (such as the General Social Survey (GSS) and the American National Election Studies (ANES)) attempt to meet this ideal. Many survey organizations, however, abandon probability methods at the block level and rely on some type of systematic method for respondent selection. The problem is that specific individuals are hard to locate. Interviewers are given a randomly drawn starting point and then instructed to stop at every nth household. The interviewer first asks to speak to the youngest man of voting age; if no man is at home the interviewer asks to speak to the youngest woman. If both refuse, or if no one is home, the interviewer goes to the next adjacent dwelling. Each interviewer has a male/female quota and an age quota, but this is not a quota sample because the interviewer cannot choose who gets into the sample.

Multistage cluster samples work well and are an efficient compromise, given the expense involved in a simple random sample approach. The drawback is that cluster samples have a greater sampling error than SRS, as would be expected because the respondents are clustered into 75 to 100 small geographic areas. A simple random sample of 1,000 has a 3 percent sampling error. Gallup reports that its in-person national samples (multistage cluster samples) of 1,500 have a 4 percent sampling error.

Telephone Surveys

Today, most surveys are conducted by telephone (or over the Internet, see below) rather than in person. The principal advantages are the speed with which telephone (and Internet) surveys can be completed and their low costs. They also free one from having to use clusters, as the physical location of a respondent is irrelevant in phone and Internet surveys. However, there are disadvantages as well.

Nationwide, as many as a third of all phone numbers may be unlisted. Those most likely to have unlisted numbers are younger, lower income, renters, and nonwhite households with children. A solution to this problem is random-digit dialing (RDD). A ten-digit phone number is composed of an area code (the first three numbers), an exchange (the next three), a cluster (the next two), and the two final digits. Since the geographic assignment of area codes, exchanges, and clusters is publicly available, one can define and sample a population. In large cities (e.g., Houston, Texas), there are approximately 10,000 of these eight-digit codes. The following is an example:

713-496-78 __ __

The first eight digits are randomly sampled from the population of 10,000. Then the last two digits are chosen from a table of random numbers or by a computer program that generates random digits. These methods bring persons with unlisted numbers into the sample.[10] On the negative side, many calls are made to nonworking numbers. But the sample of households is representative. Once the household is selected, it is then necessary to sample residents within it. Sophisticated methods to ensure random selection have been developed by statisticians, but they require an enumeration of all household members by age and sex—information many respondents are unwilling to provide over the phone. One simple alternative is the last birthday method. Interviewers ask to speak to the person in the household who had the last—that is, the most recent—birthday. This technique gives a good approximation of random sampling within the household (Lavrakas 1993).

Refusals and Nonresponse. A significant problem with telephone surveys, although it applies to in-person surveys as well, is refusal. The telephone, however, particularly lends itself to abuse, as persons selling aluminum siding, upholstery, or can't-miss real-estate deals sometimes attempt to gain a respondent's confidence by posing as a pollster. The sales pitch comes later. A study by the Roper Organization showed that 27 percent of a national sample had experienced these sales tactics (Turner and Martin 1984, 73). People, especially those in large cities, are becoming wary of callers claiming to be taking polls. However, by 2005 both the state and federal government had instituted "do not call" lists, which bar telemarketers from calling phone numbers registered on the lists. The national list contains more than 1 million phone numbers. The effect of these lists on survey response rates has yet to be determined.

Nonresponse involves more than refusals. It includes any reason why the designated respondent is not interviewed, such as ring–no answer or contacting an answering machine. The response rate is computed as a percentage. In simple terms, it is the number of people successfully interviewed divided by the total number of people called.[11] In the 1960s and earlier, it was common to find response rates in the 80 percent range (Moore 2008, 121).

Most pollsters believe that survey nonresponse has become a serious problem and seems to be getting worse (Groves and Couper 1998; Harris-Kojetin and Tucker 1999; Berinsky 2009). Even high-quality surveys have shown a decline in response rates, such as for the University of Michigan's Survey of Consumer Attitudes, a national telephone poll that has been conducted every month since 1977. Between 1979 and 2003, the response rate for this survey has dropped from 72 to 48 percent. Even maintaining a 48 percent response rate has come at the cost of more time in the field, more interviewer training, more calls to ring–no answer numbers, and sophisticated attempts to convert refusals into successful interviews by calling respondents a second time.[12] The principal cause of the drop has been an increase in refusals, but there was also a significant increase in noncontacts beginning around the mid-1990s (Curtin, Presser, and Singer 2005). For surveys where resources are not abundant and time windows are short (as is often the case in media surveys), response rates are significantly lower than for the Survey of Consumer Attitudes (Steeh et al. 2001). Holbrook, Krosnick, and Pfent (2008) analyzing over a hundred surveys conducted by major field services between 1996 and 2005, found that the response rate declined by a rate of two tens of a percent each month. The average response rate over this period was 30 percent. Nonresponse is of consequence only if those sampled but not interviewed differ on questions of interest from those sampled *and* interviewed.

In an analysis of the ANES and GSS, Brehm (1993) found nonresponse led to an overrepresentation of the elderly, blacks, women, the poor, and the less educated. For simple frequencies, this bias in response can be corrected by weighting the sample. For example, we know from the most recent Census that African Americans are 12 percent of the U.S. adult population.[13] If our sample contained only 9 percent blacks, we could easily use weights to raise the percentage. But weights are not an entirely satisfactory solution, as those reluctant to participate may not share the same opinions as the more willing. Studies by the Pew Research Center (Keeter et al. 2000; Pew Research Center 2004a) showed few opinion differences between those readily willing to be interviewed versus those who were reluctant (who initially refused but were recalled one or more times and convinced to participate). The two groups did, however, differ significantly on race-related questions. The reluctant respondents held views less sympathetic to the political and economic aspirations of African Americans than did the willing respondents.[14]

Groves (2006) conducted an analysis of past research on nonresponse and found little evidence of any direct link between response rates and biased survey results. For there to be bias, respondents must differ from nonrespondents. Groves found occasional bias but, crucially, that its degree was not predictable from the response rate. Rather, it was predicted by other factors that were unique to each survey, such as the correlation between the survey subject matter and the willingness of people to participate. Groves concluded that "blind pursuit of high response rates in probability sample is probably unwise" (668).

Cell Phones. Telephone surveys only interview people with telephones. Until recently, almost all households had land line telephones. This is not so today. Many potential survey respondents rely solely on cell phones, and the number is growing. According to the National Health Interview Survey (a government-funded in-person survey), more than one out-of-five households (20.2 percent) had only wireless telephones in 2008 (Blumberg and Luke 2009). Those adults most likely to rely on cell phones only are between eighteen and twenty-four years old, renters, those attending school, and adults living with unrelated roommates.

While pollsters are concerned about this problem, it is believed that at current levels of cell phone usage, as long as respondents are weighted by age, the exclusion of cell-phone-only households from sampling frames does not bias survey results (Blumberg, Luke, and Cynamon 2006; Piekarski 2005; Keeter 2006). Recently, commercial sampling firms have developed dual frame samples that incorporate both land line numbers and cell phone numbers. However, this strategy is expensive. Sometimes cell phone respondents are offered a monetary incentive to participate in the survey. Also, the Telephone Consumer Protection Act of 1991 prohibits the use of auto dialers when calling cell phones. The numbers have to be dialed manually, which further adds to the expense. Still, in January 2008 Gallup announced its national polls would be based on dual frame samples (Moore 2008, 133), a practice increasingly used by many polling organizations.

Given the likely increase in wireless-only households there has been spirited debate about the future of telephone surveys. Some see it as the end of conventional RDD survey methods. Others argue, perhaps counterintuitively, that as cell-phones-only households become more common the difference between landline-only and wireless-only-households will essentially disappear, and cease to be related to most political opinions (Blumberg, Luke, and Cynamon 2006). As of this writing, there is still debate over the best current way to handle the cell-phone-only problem.[15]

Polling Frontiers: Robotic and Internet Polls

Given the rising cost of high-quality telephone surveys, some have turned to still new methods of polling that reach more respondents for less money. One innovation is robotic polling, whereby respondents punch buttons on their telephone in response to the instructions of automated voices (robots). Another innovation, which eschews the telephone altogether, is to conduct automated interviews via the Internet.

Robotic Polls. Robotic polls are most prevalent at the state or local level, where they are typically conducted for media clients who wish to acquire fast and cheap information about where the public is leaning in the next election. In robotic polls (or as their sponsors prefer to call them, "interactive voice response" polls), the survey research firm samples telephone numbers by random-digit dialing with an auto dialer. The person who answers the telephone hears the recorded voice of a professional announcer describing the poll and receives instructions for answering questions via punching numbers on the telephone. The key difference from regular polling—but a big difference— is that there is no human being at the controls on the pollster's side of the communication.

The allure of automatic polls is the ability to obtain many interviews at low cost. There are no interviewers to train or hire. A robotic poll can readily conduct over a thousand surveys within three days or even sooner upon demand. At least one robotic poll firm—Survey USA—claims a record of considerable accuracy of only about 2.33 percentage points as the average error for general election surveys. Still, considerable controversy follows robotic polls. Their most obvious challenge is that they offer no control over the person in the household (a child? a visitor?), who actually answers the telephone and punches a set of replies. And it is not in everybody's nature to respond to automated surveys. Response rates are often less than five percent. And, as previously noted, federal law forbids the use of auto dialers for cell phone numbers. Many political observers who follow the polls closely are reluctant to treat robotic polls seriously, preferring to focus solely on those conducted by humans.

Internet Polls. Like robotic polling, Internet polling has become a tempting alternative to the standard interview by a human interviewer. Of course, one cannot simply send out a survey on the Internet and expect to get meaningful results. Even assuming a population is clearly defined, this approach suffers from the same self-selection bias as the *Literary Digest* poll. First, there is coverage error. As of January 2010, 23 percent of the public said they do not use the Internet.[16] These people have a zero probability of being included in the sample. Most recruiting for Internet surveys is done over the Internet. One approach involves recruiting Internet participants via popup ads and then using sophisticated weighting schemes so the sample reflects the demographics of the population (Groves et al. 2009). A second approach is to recruit a large representative panel— say 100,000 people—by random-digit dialing and pay people an incentive to participate in a fixed number of Internet surveys. The sample for each individual survey is then drawn from this large panel. The sample is weighted for self selection and for reflect demographics as reported in the Census. Still, as noted, not everyone has access to the Internet. Those who do are younger, white, better educated, and more affluent than the general population. Weights are something less than a perfect solution to this problem. Even when weighting for observable variables relevant to participation in Internet surveys, willing participants might still hold somewhat different opinions from the general population (Moore 2008, 137–38). On the other hand, response rates for professional Internet surveys are quite high—often up to 90 percent. A third approach also involves sampling from a large, representative panel. Respondents without Internet access are offered free WebTV in exchange for participating in opinion surveys. Those with Internet access are offered other incentives for participation. Proponents claim this method meets the standard of probability sampling, and is representative of the adult population.

Polling via the Internet allows for a certain degree of sophistication, as complex questions can be combined with visuals. The principal drawback is that once people agree to participate, they sometimes change their behavior (e.g., pay more attention to politics), so they may not be entirely comparable to a similar group not recruited (Dillman 2008; Harwood and Crossen 2000).

Also, as respondents participate in many surveys, this experience may affect responses. And though Internet polls try to maintain their samples' representativeness, problems of sample selection remain. While Internet polling has many advocates, the accuracy of Internet polling remains an open question.

2-3   Question Wording

It should surprise no one that in survey research, as in everyday life, the answers received are often dependent on the questions asked. This reality has both an upside and a downside for opinion polling. The upside is that people are sensitive to the way survey questions are phrased. That means they are paying reasonably close attention to what they are being asked, and their answers can be taken seriously. If changes in question wording had no impact, the opinion poll would likely be too blunt an instrument to be of much use. The downside is that because the distribution of public opinion can be a function of question wording, incorrect or inappropriate inferences about its true nature are easily possible. Not all variations in question phrasing affect the distribution of responses, but in some cases they clearly do. In this section, we review some of the aspects of question wording that can affect the distribution of public opinion.

Multiple Stimuli

Many questions have more than one stimulus to which respondents may react. Sometimes these are just bad questions. Take, for instance, the following question from a 2007 *Newsweek* Poll: "Do you think the scientific theory of evolution is well-supported by evidence and widely accepted in the scientific community?"[17] How do the substantial number of people who believe the theory of evolution *is not* well-supported by the evidence, but *is* widely accepted by the scientific community respondent to this question?

In other instances, such questions are not faulty but are often a necessary requirement for measuring opinions on complex topics. Examples of commonly used single-stimulus questions are: "Generally speaking, do you consider yourself a Democrat, an Independent, a Republican, or what?" or "Do you approve or disapprove of the way the president is handling his job?" But suppose we were interested in public support for the First Amendment right of free speech. We could ask people to agree or disagree with the statement, "I believe in free speech for all, no matter what their views might be." In 1978, 89 percent of opinion-holders agreed (Sullivan, Piereson, and Marcus 1982). But that tells us little other than in the abstract there is near consensus on a fundamental principle of the American creed. However, real controversies over free speech do not occur in the abstract but in concrete circumstances. Thus we might ask, "Suppose an admitted Communist wanted to make a speech in your community. Should he be allowed to speak or not?" In 2008, only 66 percent of the public said the person should be allowed to speak. If the admitted Communist was teaching in a college, 37 percent said he should be fired. It is quite clear that in specific circumstances, people are responding to both the free speech stimulus and Communist stimulus. As we shall see, the level of support for free speech is a matter of considerable controversy (see chapter 6).

Many less obvious instances of multiple stimuli can affect the distribution of public opinion. One way is to preface the question with the name of an authoritative or admired person or institution. Consider the responses of white Americans to different phrasings of a question about the controversial policy of minority set-asides (Sniderman and Piazza 1993, 113).

Form A		Form B	
Sometimes you hear it said there should be a law to ensure that a certain number of federal contracts go to minority contractors. Do you favor or oppose such a law?		The Congress of the United States—both the House of Representatives and the Senate—has passed a law to ensure that a certain number of federal contracts go to minority contractors. Do you favor or oppose such a law?	
Favor law	43%	Favor law	57%
Oppose law	57%	Oppose law	43%
	100%		100%

Invoking the symbol of the law in this question transforms the policy of set-asides from one backed by a minority of white respondents to one backed by a clear majority—a change that may not be trivial in the politics of affirmative action. The use of authoritative symbols also provides a cue for the uncertain, decreases the don't-knows, and raises the percentage of those favorable and unfavorable among those who know little or nothing about the issue in question (Smith and Squire 1990; Bishop 2004, 33–36).

Question Order Effects

By *order effects*, we mean the effect the previous content of the interview might have on a specific question. For example, respondents usually desire to be consistent in their answers. When asked back in 1980 if "the United States should let Communist newspaper reporters from other countries come here and send back to their papers the news as they see it," 55 percent said yes. But when the question was preceded by one that asks whether "a Communist country like Russia should allow American newspaper reporters to come in and send back the news as they see it," then 75 percent favored letting Communist reporters into the United States (Schuman and Presser 1996, 27; Schuman 2008). Since most answered yes to allowing American reporters into (Communist) Russia, it was obviously inconsistent to bar Communist reporters from the United States. With respect to the abortion issue, general support for abortion will increase if a specific item with a high level of support is asked first. Thus, if respondents are asked if abortion should be permitted "if there is a strong chance of serious defect in the baby" (84 percent say yes), general support for abortion is 13 percent greater than if the specific abortion item is not asked first (Schuman and Presser 1996, 37).

Other examples of order effects include the questionnaire placement of presidential popularity or presidential vote items. Incumbent presidents do worse on both if the question comes late in a survey as opposed to early. The reason is that content of the interview reminds respondents of troublesome aspects of the incumbent's presidency (Sigelman 1981). Pocketbook voting (i.e., voting on the basis of changes in one's personal finances) can be induced by asking questions about finances immediately before ascertaining vote choice (Sears and Lau 1983). Finally, pollsters sometimes provide information on somewhat obscure topics before asking opinions about the topic. Suffice it to say that the content of the information provided in the stem of the question can easily affect the answer given (Bishop 2005).

Balanced Arguments

If a question mentions only one side of a controversy, that side will often get a disproportionate number of responses. An example is, "Do you favor the death penalty?" Because only one option ("favor") is given, we might expect that option would be more frequently chosen than if the question is balanced, as in "Do you favor or oppose the death penalty?" The same is true for questions that use an agree/disagree format (called *Likert scales*). The common practice is to inform the respondent of both the agree and disagree options in the stem of the question.

At best, however, agree/disagree questions present only one side of the issue. Respondents must construct the other side of the issue themselves. In the example below, providing balanced alternatives on a question about unemployment yields quite different results compared to an agree/disagree alternative (Cantril 1991, 126).

Form A		Form B	
Do you agree or disagree with this statement: "Any able-bodied person can find a job and make ends meet."		Some people feel that any able-bodied person can find a job and make ends meet. Others feel there are times when it is hard to get along and some able-bodied people may not be able to find work. Whom do you agree with most?	
Agree	65%	Can make ends meet	43%
No opinion	10	No opinion	18
Disagree	25	Sometimes to get along	39
	100%		100%

The Middle Position

The public seldom splits into polar camps on any issue, and even when a middle position is not offered, many will volunteer an intermediate alternative. When the question wording explicitly includes a middle position, many respondents seize this middle response as the safe alternative. In one study, Schuman and Presser (1996, 166) found that when respondents are asked on political issues if they "are on the liberal side or the conservative side," 16 percent volunteer that they are "middle of the road." But if the "middle of the road" option is offered, it is taken by 54 percent. While there is little doubt about the consequence of offering a middle position (or an "unsure" or "undecided" option for issue questions), there is no consensus about the desirability of doing so. Some argue that most respondents do have a preference, albeit in some cases a weak one. Offering the middle alternative as an in-between sort of response encourages respondents not to express their opinion (Gilljam and Granberg 1993; Schuman 2008).

When questions are framed to offer a middle or compromise position, public opinion can appear in a different light than when they are presented with only a pair of two stark alternatives. For instance, Gallup asked two questions about the death penalty in May 2003, less than three weeks apart. When the public was asked if it favored the death penalty, 70 percent said yes. But when Gallup presented an option of life in prison without the possibility of parole, support for the death penalty dropped to 53 percent. Similar patterns are found, for instance, on the issue of school prayer. When asked about the matter, the vast majority of respondents voice favor for official prayers in public schools, despite their unconstitutionality. But when respondents are given the added option of moments of silence (which could be used for private prayer), much of the support for official prayer moves to this new alternative.

Response Acquiescence

Often when people are asked whether they agree or disagree with an abstract statement, or one about which they know little, they tend to agree rather than disagree. This tendency is called *response acquiescence*. It arises mostly because the public is ill-informed and may not have genuine opinions on many issues (see chapter 3). We can illustrate this with a 1986 study of attitudes about pornography. Respondents were asked whether they agreed or disagreed that "people should have the right to purchase a sexually explicit book, magazine, or movie, if that's what they want to do." Evidently, people saw this statement as a referendum on individual rights, since an overwhelming 80 percent agreed with the statement. However, in the same poll respondents were also asked whether they agreed or disagreed with the opposite statement that "community authorities should be able to prohibit the selling of magazines or movies they consider to be pornographic." Sixty-five percent agreed with this opposite view as well.[18] Overall, a large number of respondents agreed that the public had a right to purchase pornographic materials *and* also agreed that the community has the

right to stop people from purchasing the same material. The most likely explanation of this contradiction is response acquiescence. These examples indicate
the danger of using single Likert-type items to measure the level of public
opinion. The best strategy for dealing with response acquiescence is to use two
or more items where half are worded positively and half negatively—that is, to
support free speech the respondent must agree with one statement and disagree
with another.

Filter Questions

Most people believe that good citizens should have opinions on current political topics. Thus, when interviewed by polling organizations, they tend to offer
opinions on subjects about which they know little or nothing. In an otherwise
conventional survey of the Cincinnati area, Bishop and his colleagues (1980)
included a question asking respondents whether the nonexistent "Public Affairs
Act" should be kept or repealed. Eighteen percent thought it should be kept;
16 percent favored its repeal. Given these findings on a fictitious issue, it should
not be surprising that on real but somewhat obscure issues many will offer
opinions on matters about which they have no true attitude.

One way to reduce this problem is by using filter questions. Respondents
are read a question and response alternatives and then asked, "Where would
you place yourself on this scale, or haven't you thought much about this?"
Using the 2004 NES question that asks people to indicate on a 1–7 scale if they
feel more or less money should be spent on defense, 13 percent of the sample
indicated they had not thought enough about the issue to have an opinion. But
that does not mean that all the remaining 87 percent have a true attitude.
Another 23 percent took the middle position on the scale. It seems likely some
taking this position have either no attitude or one that is poorly developed.

One danger in using screening questions is that some people with real
attitudes, but who are hesitant to express them, may be filtered out of surveys
(Berinsky 1999). An alternative is to use branching questions, where those who
say they are undecided or unsure are encouraged in follow-up probes to make a
choice (Smith 1984; Krosnick and Kerent 1993). But, of course, this strategy
runs the risk of eliciting opinions where no true underlying attitude exists.

Open-Ended Questions

Most survey questions are "closed-ended," asking the respondent to choose
from a fixed menu of options. Sometimes, however, survey researchers ask
"open-ended" questions, without the prompt of a fixed set of alternatives.
With open-ended questions, classifying the responses is a multistep process
with the interviewer recording the answer, and then coders classifying the
answers according to predetermined categories. With the closed-ended
version, almost all respondents choose one of the options that offered. The
open-ended version generates a wide range of responses, often with a high
percentage offering no opinion.

One frequently used open-ended question asks: "What is the most important problem facing the country today?" Schuman and Presser (1996) compared this open-ended format to an identical closed-ended format, where the latter respondents were given a choice among seven possible options. For alternatives such as "inflation" the open and closed formats yielded the same results. But twice as many people mentioned "crime and violence" in the closed-ended format (35 percent) as in the open-ended format (16 percent). The authors claim that listing "crime and violence" in the closed-ended format legitimized the option, if only because the words "facing the country today" used in the stem of the question imply national problems. Many think of crime as a local problem. In this instance, the extent to which crime and violence was seen by the public as the most important problem facing the country is very much dependent on how the question was asked.

Naturally, any option that is offered in a closed-ended question is likely to be chosen more frequently than from the comparable open-ended question. One illuminating example is how the format affects the responses following 9/11 regarding who was responsible for the attacks. Few Americans *volunteered* that Saddam was behind the 9/11 attacks when asked the open-ended version. But when explicitly presented with this possibility as an item from the menu of choices in a closed-ended format, a surprisingly large percentage—often more than 50 percent—saw Saddam as being personally involved (Althaus and Largio 2004). For some, being specifically given the option that Saddam may have been involved made it easier to conclude that he in fact was involved.

Social Desirability

Respondents want to make a good impression on those who interview them. Even though the interviewer is a total stranger, survey respondents often feel pressured to give answers that conform to widely held social norms. This phenomenon, often called social desirability (or impression management), results in reported answers that are more socially acceptable than the respondent's true attitude or belief. For example, people overreport voting. The 2008 election provides one example. Although only 62 percent of eligible citizens cast votes, over 80 percent claimed to have voted in NBC News/*Wall Street Journal* polls after the election. Good citizens vote, and to avoid a negative impression some nonvoters "recall" having voted.

Other examples abound of possible survey contamination from social desirability. Respondents often approach questions about religion as if the survey were a referendum on their faith and overreport the extent to which they attend church (Bishop 2005). During the 2008 Democratic presidential primary campaign, pollsters worried about respondents overreporting a voting preference for Obama on the grounds that it would appear socially undesirable to vote against a plausible black candidate. This concern was shown to be unfounded (Hopkins 2009). And survey respondents may overreport their enthusiasm for platitudes such as free speech, a concern we address in chapter 6.

The Question Wording Experiment

For scientific research, the gold standard is the experimental design. Average citizens most frequently encounter this method when the media reports on trials involving the effectiveness of a new drug. Half of the sample randomly gets the drug; the other half randomly gets a placebo (sugar pill). If the half that gets the drug differs significantly on key indicators from the half that gets the placebo, the drug is deemed effective—at least in the case of this one trial. While question wording experiments have been around for a long time (J. Converse 1987), it is only with the advent of computer-assisted survey interviewing (CATI) that the potential of this method has been fully realized. In a simple survey experiment, half of the sample might randomly get a question on affirmative action for "blacks" and the other half would get exactly the same question, but "women" would be substituted for blacks (Sniderman and Piazza 1993). This would allow the investigator insight into whether opposition to affirmative action was based on principle or on racial resentment. CATI interviewing allows for much more complex experiments, where respondents are assigned multiple different versions of a question (Berinsky and Mendelberg 2005; Feldman and Huddy 2005). The survey experiment is a strong design because (1) the experiment is invisible to the respondent, (2) there is the capacity to make strong causal inferences owing to the experimental design, and (3) there is the ability to generalize from a sample to a population (Tedin and Weiher 2004).

Summary: The Pitfalls of Question Wording

Variations in question wording can clearly influence the distribution of public opinion. That fact should be recognized and considered when using opinion data. Some questions are obviously biased (see next section). Read the questions carefully. What are the stimuli? Are authorities being invoked? Are inferences being made about the level of opinion from single Likert items? Are "no opinion" screens used on obscure issues? Are balanced questions truly presenting both options in a fair manner? Is the format open-ended or closed-ended? Are there reasons to think answers are influenced by impression management? All of these possibilities are cause for concern. Some types of inferences are more reliable than others. Multiple questions on the same issue can give insight into the range of opinion. But the most reliable strategy is to compare responses to the same question. Thus, subgroup differences on the same question are usually quite meaningful, as are differences when groups are randomly assigned different questions. Also effective is comparing change over time in response to the same question. Because the stimulus is identical, variation is likely due to a change in the public's view.

2-4 Polls and Predicting Elections

How accurate are public opinion polls? The one good test occurs on Election Day. Only when comparing the polls to actual election outcomes can the accuracy of the polls be tested objectively. Predicting elections presents the pollsters with the usual challenges to polling accuracy, plus more. Like all other public opinion polls, election polls must deal with the problem of frequent refusals. What if, for instance, supporters of one candidate or party were more likely to agree to be interviewed? And election polls are not immune from even the problem of question wording. There are many ways to ask respondents whom they will vote for, and these sometimes have consequences (McDermott and Frankovic 2003). When trying to predict elections, pollsters face one further challenge that does not arise when simply trying to predict general opinion. That challenge is that pollsters must take into account who votes and who does not. And voters are always prone to overestimate their likelihood of voting.

We will see below that preelection polls have a strong record of accuracy. Yet even polls that are correctly executed do not always predict the actual Election Day winner. Different polls administered during the same time interval sometimes show conflicting numbers. Occasionally poll numbers swing wildly over a short period. These characteristics do not necessarily mean the polls are defective, but they do require explanation.

The media tends to attribute more accuracy to preelection polls than even the best designed polls can possibly deliver. First, an obvious point. Preelection polls refer to sentiment at the time they are conducted, not on Election Day. The horse-race analogy commonly used to discuss elections is, in this case, appropriate. The horse that is ahead going into the stretch is not always the horse (or the candidate) that wins. But even given the overall trend, there are still "house effects"—variations in survey results due to idiosyncratic ways in which survey organizations conduct their polling. For example, there is surprisingly great variation in the way the candidate-choice question is asked in presidential elections.[19] Survey "houses" vary further in such matters as their frequency of callbacks to elicit responses from refusers, how they poststratify and weight their respondents, how they allocate "undecideds," and how they measure and adjust for the respondent's likelihood of voting. Thus, polls from different firms can be at some variance with one another during the campaign for a variety of reasons.

Most importantly, we should remember that polls will inevitably vary because of ordinary sampling error. Commentators during election campaigns have a tendency to overinterpret shifts in the polls as meaningful when they actually represent house effects or sampling error. One study of the preelection polls during the fall of 1996 showed that the evident movement of the polls, a subject of much interpretation by the popular media, was no greater than would be expected from chance alone, given routine sampling error (Erikson and Wlezien 1999). Preferences undoubtedly did shift back and forth during the 2000 Bush–Gore campaign. But in the Bush–Kerry campaign of 2004, the polls were so stable within a narrow range where, arguably, virtually all the "changes" from one poll to the next could have been due to nothing more than sampling error. Even in 2008, when the presidential campaign was conducted during an economic storm, the horse race changed surprisingly little.

Allocating Undecideds

Typically, surveys show 15 percent or more of the electorate to be undecided at any point during a presidential campaign (the figure is much higher for lower-level races), winding down to 5 to 8 percent a few days before the balloting. Survey houses differ in the way they handle these undecideds. While common sense might dictate a simple reporting of candidate preferences plus undecideds, most media polls do not follow that strategy. If voters claim to be unsure, they are pressed in a follow-up question to indicate which candidate they "lean to." Voters who maintain they are really undecided must be quite firm in their conviction in the face of pressure to make a choice. The inevitable result of this strategy is a sizable swing in candidate preferences, mostly accounted for by those forced to make a choice when their initial reaction was undecided (Crespi 1988; Moore 1992).

Late movement by undecided voters can determine the election, yet go undetected if polling ceases before Election Day. The flow of the undecideds was one reason Truman beat Dewey (the final Gallup Poll showed that 19 percent of the electorate was undecided). It is also the reason that Richard Nixon barely squeaked out a win of less than 1 percent over Hubert Humphrey in 1968, when the polls had shown Nixon with a fifteen-point lead in the final weeks of the campaign. And it is the reason Ronald Reagan soundly defeated Jimmy Carter in 1980, when polls showed the contest to be very close, and why Ross Perot performed better in 1992 than almost all preelection polls indicated.

If undecideds in preelection polls do not split evenly on Election Day, how, then, is one to allocate them before the election? There is no one correct answer for all circumstances. Sometimes the undecideds are reported as just that—"undecided." However, the poll will then underestimate the percentage of the vote going to a candidate who has momentum. Sometimes undecided respondents are asked to rate candidates on a 0–10 scale. The undecideds are then allocated to the candidate they like best. If there is a tie on that question, party identification is used to assign the undecideds to a candidate.[20] Other polls exclude the undecideds altogether and base their preelection forecasts only on those voters willing to make a choice.

Deciphering Who Votes

Undoubtedly, the most fundamental problem with pre–Election Day polls as predictors is an inability to define the population properly. Recall that a random sample must be drawn from a finite population. However, it is impossible to precisely define the Election Day population. Only about one-half of adult Americans vote in presidential elections. No one has yet determined a method that predicts with great accuracy who will vote. Yet it is those Election Day voters who constitute the population, not adult Americans or even registered voters. In a preelection survey in 1996, the Pew Research Center asked a national sample of those over eighteen if they were "absolutely certain," "fairly certain," or "not certain" to vote in the upcoming election for president.[21] Here are the results:

Absolutely certain	69%
Fairly certain	18
Not certain/unsure	13
	100%

Actual turnout in 1996 was about 49 percent.

Since respondents' self-reports greatly inflate their likelihood of voting, survey researchers try to screen voters by objectively assessing their likelihood of voting. If all respondents who claimed they would vote were allowed through the screen, the projected election results would be distorted in favor of the party whose supporters are least likely to vote. Historically, the poor and the less educated are the least likely to vote, and these people tend to support Democratic candidates. Election results are also affected by the level of excitement of each party's supporters, which can vary from election to election. Pollsters seem to do a good job of screening in the days leading up to election, when voter interest in the election is fairly easy to ascertain. But screening becomes a challenge to pollsters in the early days of the campaign. The danger is that shifts in the polls of likely voters are often due not to people changing their mind but rather to change in the composition of who counts as a likely voter. Democrats' and Republicans' relative excitement varies in the short term so that first one party and then the next will be overrepresented among likely voters in a way that has little bearing on the vote later on Election Day, when their level of excitement matters (Erikson, Panagopoulos, and Wlezien 2004).

To screen their preelection samples for nonvoting, pollsters first ask respondents whether they are registered and then ignore the choices of the unregistered. Registered respondents are asked a set of questions designed to measure their likelihood of voting. Pollsters use one of two methods at this stage. By the cutoff method, they divide registered respondents into those more and less likely to vote (above or below the cutoff value of voting likelihood) and then count the preferences only of the most likely. (For instance, if they anticipate a 60 percent turnout, they count the preferences of the 60 percent most likely to vote.) By the probable electorate method, the pollster weights registered respondents by their likelihood of voting. For instance, the preferences of a voter estimated at 30 percent likely to vote would be weighted only 0.30 as much as a certain voter. Which method is better is a matter of debate (Erikson 1993; Ferree 1993; Hugick and Molyneux 1993; Daves 2000). The important point is that the type of screen and its application can have an important consequence for a poll result.

How Accurate Are the Polls?

Given the daunting challenges that pollsters face, one might expect that polls do a poor job of predicting elections. But that would be wrong. Polls conducted early in campaigns often give a misleading view of what will transpire on Election Day. But that is because events change beyond the pollsters' control. Similarly, primary elections are difficult to poll accurately even in the final week of the campaign, as preferences leading up to primary elections are historically volatile. (Voters focus late, and they choose within their party rather than between parties.) But general election polls conducted late in the campaign, such as in the final week, show an excellent record of accuracy. This is reassuring not just because we might sometimes want to know outcomes in advance. It assures us that opinion polls should also be reasonably accurate as snapshots of public opinion at the moment, even when we lack the feedback of an election to verify.

Figure 2.1 nicely summarizes the accuracy of presidential polls over fifteen elections, from 1952 to 2008. This graph shows the actual vote (measured as the Democratic percent of the two-party vote) as a function of the Democratic share of the two-party vote in the polls during the final week of the campaign. (The Republican vote in the polls or on Election Day is 100 percent minus the Democratic percent.) The vote in the polls is measured by pooling all polls available where the middate of the polling period is within one week of Election Day.

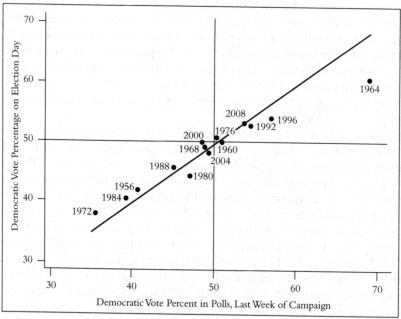

Figure 2.1   Democratic vote for president (as share of two-party vote) by Democratic strength (as percent of two-party vote) in all polls (combined) in the final week of the campaign, 1952–2008. Compiled by Robert S. Erikson and Christopher Wlezien.

In Figure 2.1, the polls would be perfectly accurate if the fifteen annual observations all fell on the diagonal line. They do not of course, since polls are not perfect. Rather, the late polls tend to be accurate within about 1.5 percentage points. This is less than one would expect by chance from sampling error alone, but we must keep in mind that the polls cannot register the late movement in the very final days of the campaign. Historically, the late polls show no bias in favor of one party's candidates or the others. And, contrary to some claims, they do not inflate support for incumbents. One can see from Figure 2.1 that polls tend to exaggerate the sizes of large leads in landslide elections (e.g., 1964, 1972).[22] But when elections are close, presidential polls tend to be quite accurate.

Presidential polls were remarkably accurate in 2000, 2004, and 2008. In 2000, the late polls revealed Gore's late advancement which lead to a virtual tie in the popular vote. (Gore, of course, won the popular vote while Bush won the contested and decisive electoral vote.) In 2004, the polls correctly predicted another close election with most tilting toward Bush, the winner (Traugott 2005). In 2008, the late polls correctly predicted Obama's win and reported the vote margin with impressive accuracy.

Table 2.2 details the record of the final polls of the 2008 race. Here, the vote is measured as the relative strengths of candidates Obama and McCain, allowing for undecideds (in the polls) and votes for minor-party candidates (in the polls and the election), so that the sum of Obama and McCain support does not add quite up to 100 percent. The margin is measured as Obama's lead over McCain.

TABLE 2.2 | Accuracy of Final Polls in the 2008 Presidential Election

Poll	Obama	McCain	Obama Margin
ABC/*Washington Post*	53	44	+9
Battleground	49	44	+5
CBS/*New York Times*	51	42	+9
Diageo/Hotline	50	45	+7
Fox	50	43	+7
GQR	51	44	+7
IBD/Tipp	48	43	+5
Ipsos	53	46	+7
Marist	52	43	+9
NBC/*Wall Street Journal*	51	43	+8
Rasmussen	52	46	+6
Research 2000	52	45	+7
Zogby	54	43	+9
Average (Poll of Polls)	*51.3*	*44.0*	*+7.3*
Actual Vote	**52.9**	**45.7**	**+7.2**

Source: http://www.fivethirtyeight.com

The national polls did vary, but in a range that is more than acceptable in terms of sampling error.

National polls are only the tip of the polling iceberg. For every national poll predicting a presidential election there is at least one poll predicting the presidential vote in some particular state. And pollsters actively survey state electorates for important races such as for governor and U.S. senator. Election polls are found for important local races as well. How well do they do?

Although state polls are not always conducted to the standards of the best national polls, their track record is quite good. In the final week of the 2008 campaign, 236 state polls were conducted for president, U.S. Senate, and governor. Of these, 98.2 percent got the state winner correctly, a record consistent with the state polls' performance in recent elections.[23] Where state polls were in consensus about the likely winner, there were no mistakes. In the rare instances where the state polls were all close, showing no clear leader in the presidential race (Indiana, Missouri, North Carolina), the actual vote margin was within a few tenths of a percentage point. The one Senate race where polling showed no clear leader (Minnesota) was so close it eventually was decided by the courts.

Given the handicaps that pollsters face and the fact that they do not always converge toward a common solution to their common problems, it is remarkable that the polls perform as well as they do. The pollsters' best defense is that, despite possible criticisms of specific procedures, their polls do predict with considerable accuracy. What keeps the pollsters on their toes is the knowledge that if they were systematically off the mark they would be out of business.

Election Day Exit Polls

Now over a quarter century old, the *exit poll* is an important if sometimes controversial innovation in opinion polling. Representative precincts are selected, and voters are interviewed immediately after leaving the voting booth. Questions go beyond vote choice to include demographic and attitudinal information. Exit polls are commissioned by the news media to help them to project the winner soon after the polls close on Election Day and report on the demographic and issue correlates of the vote choice. While the National Election Pool (NEP) provides data to television networks and other news outlets, each news sources hires its own experts to analyze the data and ultimately call the election night winners.

When networks and other news organizations call elections, exit poll results actually play only a partial role compared to such techniques as getting early returns from sample precincts and comparing reported election results with past voting patterns from the same geographic area. The major purpose of exit polls is to provide background data on which types of voters prefer which candidates. As raw data from exit polls stream in throughout Election Day, they are unreliable as indicators of the vote margins in the states and the nation.

The fact that raw exit poll data is not useful for predicting close elections became clear to all in 2004. "Raw" early exit poll numbers clearly favored Kerry, and as this information inevitably leaked out on Election Day, early perceptions were that Kerry—not Bush—had won. It was not until 1:33 A.M. the following day that an NEP exit poll release showed Bush with a lead (Morin 2004; Traugott, Highton, and Brady 2005).

The NEP and its partners moved quickly to seal the leaks for subsequent elections. No results are provided by NEP to its clients until 4:00 P.M. The source of leaks had not been the NEP, but its network clients (Traugott, Highton, and Brady 2005). If clients do not have the data, their employees cannot leak the early results. These fixes were successful in 2006 and 2008.

There are several reasons why raw exit results are unreliable. The large number of polling places to monitor requires many interviewers to be hired on a temporary basis. They are often inexperienced and poorly trained. With mostly young interviewers seeking interviews outside polling places, older voters are more likely to refuse cooperation. Early voting provides a further hurdle. As of 2008, about a 30 percent of all voters cast their vote in presidential elections before the first Tuesday in November. These early voters tend to be more partisan, ideological, and politically interested than Election Day voters. Election night analysts must estimate this early vote and factor that along with the exit poll data and other considerations when making their Election Day projections (Biemer et al. 2003; Frankovic 2003; Stein and Vonnahme 2008).[24]

Although by themselves, the data from exit polls comprise at best only a rough indicator for predicting elections, they are useful for postelection analysis of the vote. After the election results are known, exit poll data can be properly weighted to adjust for such factors as precinct voting and certain demographic patterns to the refusals. Processed in this way, long after the election, exit polls become among the best sources for investigating the variables that affect the vote in different elections. For analytical purposes, exit polls have two advantages to offset their disadvantages. The respondents include only voters, and their responses reflect their thinking on Election Day.

2-5 Conclusion

For more than sixty years, public opinion polls have been part of the political landscape, and there is every sign that their influence is growing. While the scientific pollsters have an admirable track record, it must be recognized that polls are imperfect predictors. Even the best preelection poll is based on a probability model that on rare occasions can go wrong due to an unlucky dose of sampling error. Preelection polls can also go wrong when the behavior they are sampling changes underneath their feet. The electorate's choice is often volatile in the days before an election, and the pollsters race to catch up by means of polling until the last minute. Polls can go wrong because people are increasingly likely to refuse requests to be interviewed. And polls can go wrong when they miscalculate which eligible voters will actually show up to vote. Under the circumstances, contemporary polls do a surprisingly good job at predicting elections. One reason may be that pollsters know they must do a good job because they lose credibility and their jobs if they do not.

In this book, our central interest is in polls regarding public opinion, not election outcomes. A challenge is that unlike with election polls, we do not know for sure how close opinion polls are to the correct result. Unless the target opinion is the outcome of an initiative or referendum election, opinion polls lack direct validation. And opinion polls are sensitive to matters of question framing and question wording. The key to understanding polls is a realization that the numbers do not speak for themselves; they require interpretation. Among the keys to that interpretation are how the sample was selected, how the questions were phrased, an appreciation for the context in which the survey was conducted, and a comparison to other surveys taken at the same time or an analysis of trends over time.

Notes

1. Following the Senate's failure to convict Clinton on impeachment charges, he is reported to have said, "Thank God for public opinion." (Edwards 2003, 4).
2. Pew Research Center and Opinion Research Corporation, October 24–27, 2008.
3. Survey by Princeton University Research Associates, January 3–March 26, 2001.
4. The best sources for informed commentary on contemporary polls practices is www.pollster.com.
5. Strictly speaking, in terms of statistical theory, if the poll were repeated an infinite number of times, in 95 percent of the trials the result would be between 54 and 60 percentage points. We are assuming simple random sampling, which is a useful simplification of Gallup's sampling procedure.
6. The exception is when the population itself is quite small (say, less than 10,000). With a small population, a correction can be made to properly lower the sampling error. Table 2.1 shows that a sample of 384 drawn from a very large population has a sampling error of 5 percent. However, if our barrel contained only 1,000 marbles and we randomly drew 384, then, instead of a sampling error of 5 percent, the true sampling error would be 0.785×5.0 percent, or 3.9 percent. The sampling error correction for small populations is the square root of $N-n/N-1$ where N is the population size and n is the sample size (Wallis and Roberts 1956, 369).
7. Some pollsters extend poststratification to weight by party identification. The idea is that the public is reasonably stable in partisanship, so that when one interviews, say, more Republicans than normal, then Republicans should be weighted down to adjust for the distorted sample. This procedure, designed to add precision to the sample estimates, is controversial. The danger is that, unlike with demographics, partisanship can change in the short run. An unexpected surge of Republican respondents might indicate sampling error, but it could also mean more people decide to call themselves Republicans.
8. One's suspicions are aroused, however, if polls on the same topic at about the same time with similarly worded questions show quite different results.
9. In 1948, Gallup had Dewey at 49.5 percent and Truman at 44.5 percent (with 6 percent going to minor-party candidates). The vote, in fact, was Truman 49.5 percent and Dewey 45.1 percent, with others getting 5.4 percent. The Roper Poll in 1948 was further off the mark than Gallup. Roper had Dewey at 52.2 percent and Truman at 37.1 percent (with 10.7 percent going to minor-party candidates).

10. This description is somewhat of an oversimplification of modern RDD methods. For a detailed explanation, see Lepkowski et al. (2008).

11. Actual formulas, however, are a good deal more complex. Not every unanswered call is included in the denominator, depending on the survey. A detailed discussion of methods for computing response rates can be found at the Web site for the American Association for Public Opinion Research, http://www.aapor.org.

12. While the overall response rate for the Survey of Consumer Attitudes between 1977 and 1999 was 70 percent, it dropped to 66 percent in the period between 1995 and 1999.

13. In actual practice, national surveys are weighted by the Current Population Survey (CPS), which is conducted by the Census Bureau. The CPS is a very large national poll of 50,000 households done every month. It has a high response rate (90 percent or more) because people feel an obligation to cooperate with the Census, and such cooperation is also required by federal law.

14. For this experiment, the Pew Research Center conducted two surveys of 1,000 adults, one rigorous and the other less rigorous. The rigorous survey spanned an eight-week period. In addition, respondents were sent advance letters announcing the survey and offered a small monetary gift for participating; those refusing were recontacted to persuade them to participate. The response rate was 79 percent. The less rigorous survey was conducted over five days and had a response rate of 65 percent. The response rate of 65 percent for the less rigorous survey is still, however, a good deal higher than many critics contend is currently the case for atypical media surveys. Almost all major polling organizations refuse to disclose their response rates, so the exact response rates are difficult to know.

15. For a thorough review of issues in survey research and cell phones, see the special issue of *Public Opinion Quarterly* (Winter 2007).

16. Pew Social Trends Poll, conducted January 14–January 20, 2010.

17. *Newsweek* Poll conducted by Princeton Survey Research Associates, March 28–29, 2007.

18. A 1986 *Time*/Yankelovich Survey, cited in "Opinion Roundup," *Public Opinion* (September/October 1986): 32.

19. For a list of the way the major polling firms ask this question, see Crespi (1988, ch. 5).

20. This practice of pushing undecideds to make a choice is defended by Frank Newport, editor-in-chief of the Gallup Poll, in the following words: "[I]f pollsters allow voters the explicit option to call themselves 'unsure' about their vote, the number of reported undecideds would jump. All major polling organizations, however, eschew this structure because it would make polling less valuable and less interesting. Most voters, when asked in which direction they lean, have a preference and are willing to express it. It would not be very instructive . . . to allow large numbers of voters to claim they are undecided through the election season. We would miss the dynamics of change, we would be unable to tell how well the candidates were doing in response to events, and publicly released polls would be out of synchronization with private, campaign polls" (Letter to the editor, *New York Times*, November 6, 1992, sec. A).

21. The Pew Research Center for the People and the Public. News Release, August 2, 1996.

22. Note that Figure 2.1 effectively assigns the undecideds as either staying home or voting Democratic or Republican in proportion to the choices among those who make a choice in the final poll. Allocating the undecideds as voting, say, 50–50, would lead to slightly lower predictions in landslide elections.

23. Based on reports by the National Council on Public Opinion Polls. http://www.ncpp.org/?q=node/114

24. While the analysts at television networks and other news organizations use exit polls as one tool for predicting state-level races, winners for president and important statewide offices, they have learned to predict cautiously. The most notorious misprediction was the early call that Gore had won Florida in 2000 (and by implication an Electoral College majority.) Faulty exit polls played a part in this misprediction. Since the 2000 fiasco, network analysts have made no serious errors in prematurely calling state winners. It may be said that network analysts know more about forecasting elections than they used to, including knowing more about the limits of what they know.

3 Microlevel Opinion: The Psychology of Opinion-Holding

In THEORY, democracy works best when the people actively attend to public affairs—ideally, when they direct policymakers toward the problems most deserving of attention and actively monitor their deliberations. In this best of all worlds, people might disagree with one another, but their opinions are soundly reasoned and logically consistent. Their preferences transcend conflict among self-interested parties to reflect a concern for the general welfare.

In actuality, public opinion falls considerably short of this ideal. As early survey researchers explored the nature of public opinion, they found several reasons for pessimism. For instance, respondents often express preferences so thoughtless as to be arguably too shallow for consideration as meaningful opinions. The opinions that people do hold sometimes seem like unconnected preferences in no logical relationship to one another. Where predictability exists, opinions often flow from disturbing prejudices rather than thoughtful consideration. Often it appears that political leaders find it all too easy to manipulate political symbols so as to fool a politically gullible mass public.

Although recent discussions of the capabilities of mass opinion vary in theoretical perspectives, they find some significant reason for optimism (compare Popkin 1991; Page and Shapiro 1992; Zaller 1992; Fishkin 1995; Delli Carpini and Keeter 1996; Kuklinski et al. 2001; Stimson 2005; Dalton 2008; Lewis-Beck et al. 2008). Many ordinary people stay politically informed and can be considered politically sophisticated. Actually, it may seem remarkable that people hold political opinions at all. Why, we might ask, do people bother to develop and maintain political opinions when the time spent on politics might be better devoted to dealing with matters that affect their private lives? As most of our political involvement is as passive spectators watching helplessly on the sidelines, why do we not only pay attention but also invest time and effort developing opinions? Indeed, a strong argument can be made that if the main purpose of following politics is to affect policy outcomes, staying informed and thinking about politics is, from a cost-benefit perspective, an irrational investment (Downs 1958).

Because many people are sufficiently political to have ignored such advice, political opinions must be of some benefit to the people who hold them. It has long been recognized that holding political opinions serves several positive psychological functions (Smith, Bruner, and White 1956). Opinions can serve a social function—for instance, when people learn to agree with the prevailing views within their preferred social groups. Opinions can serve a direct psychological function—when political opinions follow as an extension of personality. A frequently cited example is the person who seeks an ordered and disciplined personal environment being more susceptible to authoritarian political ideologies (Altemeyer 1997). Opinions can also promote economic self-interest—when people develop political opinions consistent with their economic standing. Sometimes people develop elaborate ideologies to rationalize their economic status, as when rich people adopt a conservative economic ideology to justify the wealth they have accumulated.

As one would expect, opinions often reflect economic self-interest—for example, when the rich adopt more conservative economic positions than the poor (see chapter 7). But the pull of self-interest is far from universal. People often derive opinions from values that have little if anything to do with obvious self-interest (Sears and Funk 1990). One example is when prosperous citizens concern themselves with the economic plight of others. Another, very different, example is when people express racial animosity in circumstances that lack an obvious economic motive (Kinder and Winter 2001; de Figueiredo and Elkins 2003). Even obvious economic interests are sometimes overridden by alternative calculations. In a study of school districts affected differently by court-ordered financial equalization, property-rich districts had to pay more school taxes and property-poor districts had to pay less. While attitudes toward this decision generally reflected how one's district was affected, many liberals who had to pay more taxes favored the equalization and many conservatives who had to pay less opposed the measure—contrary to their economic self-interest (Tedin 1994b).

While sometimes it seems that people arbitrarily generate opinions, those opinions usually have reasons behind them. Consider opinions about the issue of whether the government should spend more on welfare for the disadvantaged. People who favor less spending argue the principles of limited government and self-reliance, or they voice concern about people falling into a welfare "trap." People who favor more spending cite egalitarian arguments and express sympathy for the immediate needs of the poor (Feldman and Zaller 1992).[1] Abstract values such as authoritarianism, egalitarianism, and liberal/conservative ideology are important to politics because they cause people to have opinions when they have no direct stake in a particular issue (Bawn 1999; Stenner 2005). For example, many Americans living in small, homogeneous Midwestern farming communities have opinions about bilingual education. These opinions have political consequences, even though the lives of the opinion-holders are almost certainly not touched by the issue.

This chapter examines public opinion at the microlevel of the individual citizen, usually when observed as a survey respondent. We first examine the extent of political knowledge and the depth of opinion-holding. We then explore the core values and beliefs that sometimes hold opinions together. For politically sophisticated respondents, it is possible to summarize core political values in terms of position on the liberal–conservative ideological spectrum. Finally, we explore a source of political orientation adhered to by sophisticates and nonsophisticates alike—that is, the respondent's party identification or relative allegiance to the Democratic or Republican Party.

3-1 Political Attention and Opinion-Holding

When public opinion is reported on some issue, underlying the division of opinion is considerable diversity in terms of attention and caring about the matter at hand. At one extreme we find highly attentive citizens who follow public affairs closely and hold informed (if diverse) opinions regarding even complicated questions of public policy. These citizens vote regularly, and their votes are based on issue preferences that have been well thought out. Moreover, they make their views known to elected leaders, even during the time intervals between political campaigns.

At the other extreme, we find citizens who can be best described as "apolitical." Virtually disengaged from politics, they ordinarily pay no attention to the political happenings reported in newspapers and on television, and they do not vote. Their interests in politics is perked up only by unusual events, such as the threat of war or a political sex scandal. But by being passive, they collectively forfeit their influence on policy outcomes.

Most people fall between these two extremes, and their attention to the world of government and politics varies considerably. Cognitive ability or general intelligence is certainly an important factor for understanding politics and holding political opinions (Delli Carpini and Keeter 1996; Althaus 2003; Joslyn 2003). But we should not assume that when people are politically inattentive, they lack the mental capacity to follow public affairs, or that politics is too complicated for ordinary folks to figure out. Whether one follows politics closely is largely a matter of personal taste, similar to the choice of whether to follow certain sports, like football and baseball. And just as sporting events are more fascinating and comprehensible to regular followers, so too is following politics easier for those who have invested time and effort learning about the political world. For those who choose not to invest in an understanding of politics, following political events and holding informed opinions is a considerably more difficult task (Zaller 1992).

Just as it is misleading to describe public opinion by focusing on the typical citizen, it can be misleading to assume that a citizen's attention level regarding one aspect of politics extends to all others. People vary not only in their taste for public affairs but also in the aspects of public affairs that engage their interest most. For instance, some people focus on national politics but ignore their local political environment, while others do the reverse. Some people are issue serialists who become members of the attentive public only when issues dear to their interests enter the public agenda. On some issues, they hold strong opinions and make their views known; on others, they react with indifference. We must also recognize that interest in public affairs is seasonal, peaking during election campaigns as people become more informed when preparing to vote.

Levels of Political Knowledge

Since the 1930s, more than 2,000 factual pop quiz political knowledge questions have been asked of the American public. Table 3.1 presents a sampling of factual questions across a variety of issue domains from a number of polling sources. The table suggests a surprising level of public ignorance.

Although the items presented in Table 3.1 are taken from a range of years, there has been little change over time in the level of political knowledge. Americans appear no better informed about political matters today than they were twenty years ago (Pew 2007) or fifty years ago (Delli Carpini and Keeter 1996). For example, 50 percent could recall the name of their congressional representative in 1942 compared to 42 percent in 1998. Given the rise in levels of education and the greater availability of political media, many find this lack of improvement puzzling. Perhaps there are countertrends that cancel out improvements in education and technology, or there may be inherent limits to how much political information the public can absorb.

The most disconcerting aspect of the public's ignorance during normal times may be people's inability to recall the names of leading political officeholders. Some examples are included in Table 3.1. Over two-thirds of the public can name their state's governor, but few can immediately recall the name of key Washington leaders. When the Republicans gained control of the House of Representatives in 1995, Speaker Newt Gingrich became a rival to the president for the center of the political stage—but he became no household name. At the height of his political power in 1995, only 54 percent could identify him as House speaker. In 2004, just 10 percent could identify the job held by his low-key successor, House Speaker Dennis Hastert. Following the Democrats retaking Congress in 2007, 57 percent (in 2008) could identify the job of Hastert's Democratic successor, Nancy Pelosi. But in 2007, just 15 percent could identify the job held by Harry Reid, the Senate majority leader.

The Distribution of Political Information. How even is the distribution of political information among the public? In order to find out, the Pew Research Center (2007) administered a 23-item multiple choice political knowledge scale to a representative sample of the public. On average, the public answered 12 of the 23 items correctly—a little more than half. On most college campuses, this would not be a passing grade, but then the public is mostly not taking course work on politics. Respondents were categorized into high, medium, and low in political knowledge; 31 percent fell into the high-information group. The best predictor of a high-information score was education. Also men scored higher than women,

TABLE 3.1 | **Level of Information Among the Adult U.S. Population**

Percentage		Year	Source
96	Know United States is a member of the United Nations	1985	D&K
96	Know president's term is four years	1989	D&K
88	Can identify Richard Cheney's job as Vice President	2004	ANES
86	Know Democrats have a House majority	2009	Pew
88	Know Cuba is communist	1988	D&K
77	Know George W. Bush has a plan to change Social Security	2005	CBS
74	Know governor of home state	1989	D&K
72	Know states cannot prohibit abortion	1989	D&K
69	Know Pakistan and Afghanistan share a common boarder	2009	Pew
66	Know Supreme Court justices service a life term	2005	G&C
63	Know party of congressional representative	1995	IRC
58	Know *Roe v. Wade* is about abortion rights	1989	D&K
57	Know how congressional representative voted on Gulf War	1991	D&K
57	Know Supreme Court as the "last say" on the Constitution	2005	G&C
58	Can identify Nancy Pelosi's job as Speaker of the House	2008	ANES
56	Know the Democrats control the House of Representatives	2008	ANES
47	Know congressman's vote on Clinton impeachment	1999	WP
44	Know Auschwitz/Dachau/Treblinka were Nazi concentration camps	2005	TNS
42	Know name of congressional representative	2000	ANES
36	Can name the President (Putin) of Russia	2007	Pew
36	Know how many senators are needed to convict president	1999	Gallup
35	Can name at least one Supreme Court justice	2003	Find Law
34	Can name the secretary of state (Baker)	1990	GSS
33	Can name the secretary of state (Albright)	2000	Gallup
32	Can locate Vietnam on a map	1988	D&K
31	Know what affirmative action is	1985	D&K
29	Can name secretary of defense (Rumsfeld)	2002	Pew
27	Know that more is spent on Medicare than foreign aid	1995	IRC
21	Know House and Senate raised the minimum wage	2007	Pew
19	Know political office held by William Rehnquist (Chief Justice)	2004	IPSOS
15	Can identify office held by Harry Reid (Majority Leader)	2007	Pew
12	Know who presided over Clinton impeachment trial	1999	Pew

Sources: ANES (American National Election Studies); D&K (Delli Carpini and Keeter 1996); Luntz (Luntz Research); IRC (IRC Survey Research Group); WP (*Washington Post*); Pew (Pew Center for People and the Press); CBS/NYT (CBS News/*New York Times*); GSS (General Social Survey); Ipsos (Ipsos Public Affairs); TNS (TNS Intersearch); G&C (Gibson and Caldeira 2009).

and whites scored higher than other racial and ethnic groups. One of the most dramatic difference was due to age. Those between 18 and 29 were least likely to fall into the high-information category (15 percent), compared to 43 percent for those over 65. The best informed were those between 50 and 64, at 47 percent. On the other hand, there was no difference between Democrats and Republicans.

Political Misinformation. Just as alarming as evidence of public ignorance of political facts is the willingness of some to claim beliefs that are decidedly not true. Two examples are the sizeable proportions of the electorate who claimed (well into the late 2000s) that the United States found weapons of mass destruction (WMD) in Iraq or that Sadam Hussein had something to do with the 9/11 attacks even though both claims are clearly false. Similarly, contrary to all evidence, a stubborn minority (11 percent in one Pew poll) insisted during the 2008 campaign that Obama is a Moslem. Some polls in 2009 show strong minority support for the idea that Obama was not born in the United States and would thus under the constitutional be ineligible for the presidency. (Both claims are absurd.)[2]

Why do people persist in asserting belief in things that any knowledgeable person would know to be false? In part, such beliefs are maintained because they are convenient to one's world view at no evident cost. One's preferred belief can be comforting; if it is proved false there is no penalty. In part, false beliefs are maintained for the simple reason that certain segments of the political elite encourage them. Jerit and Barabas (2006) document one example, involving Social Security. According to their analysis, when politicians exaggerated Social Security's financial woes to claim (falsely) that it was going bankrupt, people— including those nominally more informed—became overly pessimistic about potential cuts to the program.

Context and Political information

In March 1999, armed forces of the North Atlantic Treaty Organization (NATO) conducted an intensive bombing raid on Serbia in an attempt to halt "ethnic cleansing" by Serbs in the predominantly Albanian province of Kosovo. Prior to the bombing, it is safe to say, most Americans had never heard of Kosovo. However, within a few days of the bombing, a Pew Research Center poll (March 29, 1999) found that 43 percent of Americans were able to identify Kosovo as a province of Yugoslavia located in central Europe. This was a remarkable amount of learning for a nation often scolded for its lack of geographical knowledge.

But of course this event was understandable. People begin to pay attention to political events that are in the news. Indeed political events can attract near universal attention, but only if they contain the necessary elements of drama— a terrorist attack, a hostage drama, or a sex scandal.

Public knowledge improves in the face of threat, which is a powerful motivator for people to learn about politics (Marcus, Neuman, and MacKuen 2000). Closely following 9/11, public knowledge of issues related to terrorism stood at levels quite unexpected during normal times. In November of 2001, 84 percent of the public knew the Northern Alliance was our ally in Afghanistan, 85 percent knew that Pakistan had a common border with Afghanistan, and 67 percent knew Colin Powell was secretary of state (Prior 2002). However, as the threat receded, political knowledge retreated to levels found during normal times. Less than a year after 9/11, fewer than half of American adults could name Colin Powell as secretary of state, and fewer than a third could name Donald Rumsfeld as secretary of defense.

Measuring Political Knowledge

In assessing the political knowledge of the public, we must contend with numerous methodological considerations. The context of the interview and the way the knowledge question is asked can affect the assessment of information levels. One problem is that the survey format is not conducive to searching long-term memory for answers, as an expectation develops during the interview process that answers should be provided in a matter of seconds. When respondents are given extra time, they are significantly more likely to provide correct answers (Prior and Lupia 2008).

In addition, assessment of the public's level of political knowledge is sensitive to question format. We can distinguish between open-ended questions which require fairly demanding *recall* ("What is the name of the vice-president?") versus less demanding recall ("What is the job of Joe Biden?"). Still different are closed-ended multiple-choice questions that measure *recognition*. This format presents the respondent with a list of possibilities and asks them to identify which on the list holds the office (e.g., "Which of the following people is the vice-president of the United States?").

This latter type of closed-ended question has its adherents. If asked in an open-ended format, "What is the name of your congressional representative?" about 40 percent of respondents can give the correct answer. Using a closed-ended format where a list of possibilities is offered, close to 90 percent can often correctly identify their congressional representative (Tedin and Murray 1979; McDermott and Frankovic 2003; Pew 2007).

Gibson and Caldeira (2009, 439) make a similar argument about the judicial branch. When using appropriately crafted closed-ended questions, they find "respondents demonstrate relatively high knowledge about the Supreme Court." For instance, when asked, "What job or political office the late William Rehnquist held?" only 12 percent identified the former Chief Justice by his title. But when asked to choose among Rehnquist and two plausible ringers from a list of three names, 71 percent answered correctly.

Knowledge and Opinions

One concern about the public's low attention to politics is that policy preferences of the informed public may differ substantially from the uninformed majority. There are two ways of looking at this problem. On one hand, those who believe that informed opinion should carry greater weight can argue that poll results are contaminated by the counting of passive, uninformed opinions.

On the other hand, those who believe that people should have equal influence can argue that disproportionate weight should not be given to the perhaps one-sided views of the assertive minority who make their views known (Berinsky 2004). The differences between informed and uninformed opinion that are known to exist are generally attributed to the greater education and income of those who are more knowledgeable. Generally we would expect the largest differences between the views of the informed and uninformed to be on issues where opinions are in flux. The more knowledgeable will be quicker to learn the new conventional wisdom and adjust their opinions accordingly. One good example comes from the ANES's 1992 survey. Back in 1992, being informed was highly correlated with favoring increased aid to Russia. Evidently, the more knowledgeable were the first to learn that the Cold War had ended and Russia was now more friend than foe.

We present here examples from the 2008 American National Election Studies (ANES) survey. For this task, we introduce a summary index of political information. We score respondents on the basis of their knowledge of candidate policy differences, which studies show to be a good measure of relevant political information (Luskin 1987; Zaller 1992). Details of this index are presented in the Appendix. When we use this index, we compare voters at two information extremes. High-information respondents are the 30 percent (36 percent of voters) who correctly saw McCain to the right of Obama on four issues. Low-information respondents are the bottom 30 percent (24 percent of voters) who could correctly identify candidate differences on no more than one of the four issues. *This information scale is a key predictor of political opinions throughout the book, not just this chapter, and it is important for the reader to spend time reviewing its construction and meaning.*

Table 3.2 shows differences in opinion-holding by knowledge level in the 2008 ANES survey. High-information respondents tend to be more liberal on abortion rights and more opposed to an Iraq withdrawal timetable. Also, the more informed are more likely to label themselves as "liberals." But we see a different story on some social-welfare spending issues, such as a guaranteed job and standard of living and increased government services. On these issues, it is the least informed who are the most liberal.

Converting Information into Opinions

Information is the basis for (most) opinions about politics. But what is the process by which information becomes converted into opinions? One interpretation holds that citizens translate information into opinions using the rules of *instrumental rationality*—that is, for the issue at hand, citizens form opinions based on the personal costs and benefits that accrue to them. For example, farmers favor free trade because it opens more markets for their products. In short, by this view, people form opinions based on personal self-interest.

As we have mentioned, while it obviously plays a role in shaping political opinions, self-interest is far from dominant. One can readily find people whose

TABLE 3.2	Opinion by Level of Political Information, 2008		
Opinion	High Information (%)	Low Information (%)	Difference (%)
Legalize abortions	66	50	+16
Reduce defense spending	43	40	+3
Set Iraq withdrawal timetable	40	74	−34
Oppose death penalty	33	30	+3
Legalize gay marriage	36	39	−1
Favor gun control	40	52	−12
Support equal role for women	96	92	+4
More government aid to blacks	30	25	+5
Support national health insurance	57	54	+3
Favor guaranteed standard of living	29	47	−18
Increase domestic spending	50	76	−26
Liberal (of ideological identifiers)	42	35	+14
Democratic (of party identifiers)	47	66	−19

Source: National Election Studies, 2008. Cell numbers represent percentages among opinion-holders. For measure of high- and low-income respondents, see the Appendix.

political opinions defy their economic circumstances, such as rich people who are advocates for the poor, or chronically ill individuals who oppose national health care. As we discuss in this and subsequent chapters, people's opinions on specific issues are shaped by their broader political predispositions such as their party identification and core political values (e.g., Feldman 1988; Alvarez and Brehm 2002; Goren 2004), which may differ greatly among individuals. For some, these political predispositions take on the status of an ideological world-view. Political predispositions tend to be stable, even over a lifetime. While these predispositions might be influenced by personal circumstance and certainly are subject to change, they have their origin in early political learning or political socialization.

Political psychologists stress the mechanisms by which political opinions are shaped by the way information is processed, in which there are two ways: online and memory-based processing. Suppose one is asked his or her opinion about a political issue. With *online* processing, individuals are able to immediately recall their position, which can be updated as new information arrives. Updated opinions are then stored in long-term memory and recalled when needed (Lodge, Steenbergen, and Brau 1995). *Memory-based* processors lack this immediate recall but instead consult their memory for relevant considerations that favor one side of the issue or the other. Online processing is particularly applicable to political campaigns, where information is relatively abundant and attitudes are accessed with some frequency. When survey respondents are asked their opinions about policies or politicians, the more politically sophisticated are most prone to online processing, as they readily access their updated information and attitudes without needing to think the matter through. The memory-based approach helps us understand opinions where information is less plentiful, and it may be more appropriate for attitudes not accessed as regularly.

Depth of Opinion-Holding

Chapter 2 presented examples of how seemingly minor variations in the framing and wording of survey questions can provoke major variations in survey results. Such phenomena could only occur if people were often ambivalent about their political convictions. On a given political issue, some survey respondents can recall from memory long-term convictions that they have held on the particular subject. Many, however, can offer no more than the top-of-the-head casual opinions of the kind sometimes known as *doorstep opinions*. One consequence is a disturbing degree of response instability when people are interviewed more than once, in what is called a *panel survey*. Many panelists who offer opinions in successive interviews change their position from one side to the other—which is seemingly inconsistent with the traditional notion of an attitude as an enduring predisposition. The implications are important for understanding public opinion.

Table 3.3 shows examples of response turnover from a special (pilot) ANES survey in 1989. The issues varied from the hotly debated (abortion, death penalty, and so on) to the technical and obscure (funding the Stealth bomber, building a new Alaska pipeline, and so on). Respondent views were measured in the summer and again in the fall of 1989. Respondents received no filter to encourage nonresponses, and over 90 percent offered opinions to each question.[3]

The table shows from 13 to 22 percent switching sides between interviews just a few months apart. As discussed later, analysts agree that almost all of such switching represents not true opinion change but rather some sort of response error. As one would expect, more response error appears for obscure issues such as Alaska pipelines and Stealth bombers, about which people typically do not think much, than for salient moral issues like abortion and the death penalty.

The setup of Table 3.3 enhances the observed stability because multiple respondent choices are collapsed into two alternatives. Responses appear less stable when a middle ground is included. Table 3.4 presents the abortion example again, this time with three alternatives.

Whereas in Table 3.3 the choices for restrictions on abortion were combined as one, for Table 3.4 we separate out the extreme "right-to-life" position that abortions should never be permitted or permitted only under exceptional circumstances from the more moderate or middle position that abortions "should be permitted . . . but only after the need has been clearly

TABLE 3.3 | **Turnover of Opinion Response on Selected Issues, 1989 ANES Pilot Study**

Death Penalty

		Summer 1989	
		Oppose	Favor
Fall 1989	Oppose	19%	5%
	Favor	5%	73%

Stealth Bomber

		Summer 1989	
		Oppose	Favor
Fall 1989	Oppose	41%	8%
	Favor	9%	42%

Abortion

		Summer 1989	
		Legal	Restricted
Fall 1989	Legal	34%	5%
	Restricted	6%	53%

More Welfare Spending

		Summer 1989	
		Favor	Opposed
Fall 1989	Favor	35%	11%
	Opposed	11%	43%

Affirmative Action

		Summer 1989	
		Favor	Oppose
Fall 1989	Favor	13%	8%
	Oppose	5%	74%

New Alaska Oil Pipeline

		Summer 1989	
		Oppose	Favor
Fall 1989	Oppose	36%	10%
	Favor	12%	42%

More Gun Control

		Summer 1989	
		Favor	Oppose
Fall 1989	Favor	59%	7%
	Oppose	13%	21%

More Cooperation with Russia

		Summer 1989	
		Favor	Oppose
Fall 1989	Favor	38%	10%
	Oppose	13%	39%

More Spending to Fight AIDS

		Summer 1989	
		Favor	Oppose
Fall 1989	Favor	48%	8%
	Oppose	15%	29%

More Aid to Nicaraguan Contras

		Summer 1989	
		Oppose	Favor
Fall 1989	Oppose	49%	11%
	Favor	10%	30%

Source: National Election Studies, 1989 pilot study data. In some instances, framing of question varied with respondent and with wave.

established." The turnover table now shows 25 percent changing their position from one survey to the next, with many respondents finding the middle position attractive. Notably, however, virtually no respondent switched from pro-choice to pro-life or vice versa.[4]

If the amount of turnover of responses to the abortion question seems high, consider that abortion positions are probably the most stable of political attitude responses, rivaled perhaps only by party identification

TABLE 3.4	Opinion Consistency on Abortion, 1989		
	Summer 1989		
	Never permitted, or only if rape, incest, or woman's life in danger	Other than if rape, incest, or woman's life in danger, after need established	Always permitted as a matter of personal choice
Fall 1989			
Never permitted, or only if rape, incest, or woman's life in danger	31%	6%	1%
Other than if rape, incest, or woman's life in danger, after need established	6%	12%	4%
Always permitted as a matter of personal choice	2%	5%	34%

Source: National Election Studies, 1989 pilot study.

(Converse and Markus 1979; Wetstein 1993; Green, Palmquist, and Schickler 2002). Less morally charged issues show considerably less response stability. Typical is the turnover of responses to the ANES's "spending and services" question between the preelection and postelection surveys in 2004, shown in Table 3.5.

Only a minority of the respondents (37 percent) had a sufficiently firm attitude to take the same side consistently (pro/pro or con/con) in both interviews. A few (6 percent) changed sides completely from one interview to the next, and others (21 percent) took no position in either interview. The remainder (36 percent) took sides in one interview but not in the other.

The most studied patterns of response instability are from several four-year, three-wave panels as part of the ANES (Converse 1964; Converse and Markus 1979). In a 1950s panel, the same respondents were interviewed at two-year intervals—in 1956, 1958, and 1960. The ANES 1970s panel interviewed the same respondents in 1972, 1974, and 1976. In the 1990s, ANES conducted a small panel with the same respondents interviewed in 1992, 1994, and again in 1996. Another multiyear ANES panel study followed a set of respondents from the 2000 election to the end of the 2004 campaign.

One important fact learned from the ANES panel studies is that the time interval between panel waves has little bearing on the observed amount of response stability. For instance, the degrees of response turnover to questions on abortion and guaranteed living standards asked four years apart in the ANES 1970s, 1990s, and 2000s panels are only slightly larger than the amount of response turnover shown in Tables 3.3 and 3.4 for the same issues when the same question was asked only a few months apart.

TABLE 3.5 | **Opinion Consistency on Whether Government Should Provide Fewer or More Services, 2004**

	Preelection Response, 2004		
	Government should provide many fewer services	In between, no opinion	Government should provide many more services
Postelection Response, 2004			
Government should provide many fewer services	14%	6%	4%
In between, no opinion	5%	21%	16%
Government should provide many more services	2%	9%	23%

Source: National Election Studies, 2004 election data.

This evidence suggests that most response change does not represent true change in underlying attitudes. If people were really changing their minds frequently, long time intervals would produce greater decay of initial positions. While scholars agree that response instability generally does not indicate true attitude conversion, they disagree in what the unstable responses mean. One position, developed by Philip E. Converse, holds that people who change positions usually have no position but instead respond randomly. This "nonattitude" explanation has been challenged by other scholars, who prefer a "measurement error" explanation. While the details of the opposing interpretations are too complicated to receive full treatment here, we can present brief sketches of the competing points of view.

The "Nonattitudes" Explanation

After analyzing turnover patterns from the 1950s panel, Converse (1964) proposed that virtually all respondents who change their position over time hold no true convictions but instead express random responses or "nonattitudes." The strong evidence for infrequent true change is that response instability varies little with the time between surveys. Surveys four months and four years apart yield about the same amount of response turnover. If people were actually changing their minds, observed opinions would be more stable over the briefer time interval.

If the nonattitude thesis is correct, most observed response change is random error, as if changers are simply flipping coins. Just as coins can be flipped heads one time and tails the next, they can also be flipped consistently heads or tails both times. Thus, a further implication of the nonattitudes thesis is that many consistent responses are random responses that appear stable only by chance. On one notorious issue from the 1950s panel, the abstract "power and housing" question (whether "the government should leave things like electric power and housing for private businessmen to handle"), Converse reached a startling conclusion (1964, 293). He estimated that less than 20 percent of the adult public held meaningful attitudes on this issue even though about two-thirds ventured a viewpoint on the matter when asked in a survey.

Many have found the implications of the nonattitudes explanation quite disturbing. In a democracy, public officials presumably respond to the policy preferences of the public, enacting these preferences into law. But if large segments of the public do not really have coherent preferences or preferences at all, why should elected officials heed their views? Indeed, if survey responses are largely nonattitudes, why should anyone take public opinion polls seriously? Fortunately, there are ways to avoid such a pessimistic assessment.

The "Measurement Error" Explanation

An obvious implication of the nonattitudes explanation is that the seemingly random element to survey responses is the fault of the respondents themselves, as if their lack of political sophistication is to blame. That is, the assumption is that when people give unstable responses to opinion questions the reason is a lack of the political sophistication necessary to form crystallized opinions. But if instead, response instability is largely unrelated to political sophistication, then we can hardly place blame on the public for its lack of sophistication.

In fact, contrary to this prediction of nonattitude theory, response instability varies little if at all with measures of political sophistication or political knowledge (Achen 1975; Erikson 1979; Feldman 1989). The disturbing level of instability found for surveys of the general public is also found for subsamples representing the sophisticated and informed. If even politically sophisticated individuals respond with a seeming random component, what is to blame? It probably is not a lack of capability on the part of those being interviewed.

For this reason, a measurement error explanation has been proposed to account for response error (Achen 1975; Erikson 1979; Ansolabehere, Rodden, and Synder 2008). This explanation does not challenge the evidence that most response instability represents error rather than true change. However, by the measurement error explanation, the "blame" for the response instability is placed not so much on the capabilities of the respondents as on the survey questions themselves. Even the best survey questions produce some instability from respondents who hold weak or ambivalent attitudes about policy issues. Some inherent limitations in the survey enterprise make measuring attitudes an imprecise task. These include ambiguities in question wording, single item indicators, the problem of investigator-defined responses to closed-ended questions that may not be congruent with the way respondents think about issues, and the problem of respondents having to give immediate answers to perhaps 100 or more questions with virtually no opportunity for reflection or considered judgment. Thus, it is the inherent limitations of the survey method that mostly explain response instability, not the inherent limitations of the respondent.

An Explanation Based on Response Probability

John Zaller and Stanley Feldman offer a "theory of the survey response" that provides a more general explanation for response instability and incorporates the findings of both the nonattitudes and measurement approaches (Zaller 1992; Zaller and Feldman 1992; see also Alvarez and Brehm 2002). From this perspective, respondents do not hold fixed, stable attitudes on many issues, but they *do* have propensities to respond one way or another. The answer they give, however, depends on the considerations that come to mind when a question is asked. A consideration is simply anything that affects how someone decides on a political issue, one way or another. For example, when one is asked for an opinion on universal health insurance, considerations may include higher taxes, sick people unable to get medical care, and big government. The actual survey response depends on the considerations that are accessible when the question is asked. Assuming the considerations listed were of equal importance, the respondent would oppose universal health insurance as two considerations point in that direction versus one that points to support.

But the considerations that come to mind at one point in time may not be the same as at another. Usually, for our hypothetical respondent, the considerations that come to mind induce opposition to universal health care. But perhaps she recently saw a TV news story about a hardworking man paid poverty-level wages who could not afford medical treatment for his bedridden wife. When asked the universal health care question, that consideration may be at the top of the head and induce support for universal health care. But the news story will eventually be forgotten, and considerations that induce opposition will again predominate. Thus, for many issues, responses are probabilistic. There is a propensity to come down on one side of an issue, but the probability is something greater than zero and less than 1.0.

Even though the opinions expressed on an issue may vary, the underlying attitudes that give rise to them may be quite stable. Suppose our hypothetical individual has a 70 percent probability of choosing the conservative response on national health insurance, and further assume that this places her at the eightieth percentile of conservatism on the issue (the respondent is more conservative than 80 percent of citizens). Within a period of two to four years, our respondent should still be near the same eightieth percentile. Stimuli in the environment might cause minor variations in probabilistic responses—for example, a liberal national mood swing might lower everybody's probability of a conservative response. But our hypothetical respondent would still be more conservative than 80 percent of citizens.

We have a paradox. Peoples' *latent* attitudes tend to be stable over time, as described earlier. Yet any particular survey response is problematical. Given this dilemma, how can we improve the measurement of political opinion?

One solution is to ask multiple questions of respondents on similar issues and record their average response. When using multiple items to measure a concept, response stability increases significantly (Ansolabehere, Rodden, and Synder 2008).

If people's attitudes are as unstable as just described at the microlevel, should we expect opinion trends at the macrolevel? We show in the next chapter that net public opinion on an issue is often very stable over time. However, we observe interesting exceptions where public opinion moves in a unidirectional fashion in response to one-sided environmental stimuli (Page and Shapiro 1992; Zaller 1992).

3-2 | Liberal–Conservative Ideology and the Organization of Opinions

When a person expresses viewpoints on a number of political subjects, we might expect that these opinions are connected to each other in some pattern. One expectation is that opinions are connected by logical consistency with core political values. For instance, a person who believes strongly in individual responsibility would be inclined to respond negatively toward government help for the inner cities or toward the government guaranteeing a job and a good standard of living. A person with strong egalitarian values would be expected to respond in an opposite fashion. To take another example, a person committed to traditional social values probably would oppose abortion rights and oppose people who are gay serving in the military. A person with a strong belief in individual choice would take the opposite view.

We could try to account for opinions in terms of how people weight political values such as individual responsibility, equality, tradition, and individual freedom. When we describe a person's core political values in this way, we begin to describe his or her political ideology. In the broadest sense, a person's ideology is any set of beliefs about the proper order of society and how it can be achieved. People with strong ideologies use their personal ideology as a guide for understanding the political world.

As a convenient shorthand, observers often prefer to reduce ideology to the single dimension of the left–right ideological continuum, classifying political values simply according to their relative liberalism versus conservatism. This classification permeates discussions of American politics by the media and political partisans. The left–right ideological distinction between liberals and conservatives contains considerable useful political content when describing the opinions of political elites or politically active people. For instance, delegates to national political conventions clearly understand ideological labels and tend to polarize as consistent liberals or conservatives (Herrera 1992; Jennings 1992). Because the ideological liberal–conservative continuum holds less meaning to those near the bottom of the sophistication ladder, the importance of liberal–conservative ideology within the mass public is a matter of uncertainty and controversy.[5]

A standard poll question asks respondents their ideological identification, usually with the three choices of liberal, moderate, or conservative. As discussed in chapter 2, one-fourth or more decline to classify themselves ideologically given the choice of "no opinion." Of those who choose, almost half choose the "moderate" or "middle-of-the-road" alternative when it is offered.

Ideally, ideological classification is a convenient way to measure individuals' core political values and to summarize their political views on a variety of issues. In practice, the result is mixed. The most politically sophisticated segment of the public approximates the ideal. For them, ideological identification goes a long way toward describing their political convictions. But when less sophisticated people respond to the ideological identification question with a response of liberal, moderate, or conservative, we can be less sure of what the response means. At worst, the response represents some idiosyncratic meaning known only to the respondent, or perhaps a doorstep opinion made up on the spot.

Liberal and Conservative Terminology

What do the terms *liberal* and *conservative* actually mean? At the philosophical level, political thinkers with reputations as liberals and conservatives differ in several ways. Conservatives view society as a control for humanity's worst impulses; liberals view the human condition as relative to the quality of society. Conservatives consider people inherently unequal and due unequal rewards; liberals are egalitarian. Conservatives venerate tradition, order, and authority; liberals believe planned change brings the possibility of improvement.[6]

Of course, people who are liberal or conservative in their practical politics need not strictly adhere to the philosophy associated with their ideological label. Nevertheless, we can see the implications of these philosophic distinctions at work in the common applications of the ideological labels to political points of view. Conservatives are more afraid than liberals of "big government," except on matters of law and order and national security. In foreign policy preferences, conservatives are more aggressive; liberals are more cooperative or yielding. Conservatives are more likely to see harmful consequences of government help for the disadvantaged, while liberals see the benefits. Conservatives tend to be moralistic; liberals are more permissive.

These kinds of relative distinctions are familiar to people who follow politics closely. But the language of ideology holds less meaning for the public as a whole. One test is whether the individual can both identify the Republican as the more conservative party and offer a plausible definition of the term *conservative*. Throughout the years, roughly half the public passes this test of understanding of ideological labels (Converse 1964; Luttbeg and Gant 1985; Lewis-Beck et al. 2008).

What do people think of when they hear the terms *liberal* and *conservative*? Table 3.6 summarizes the responses from a 1994 ANES study of how people describe liberals and conservatives. Respondents were asked, "What sorts of things do you have in mind when you say that someone's political views are liberal?" and similarly, "What sorts of things do you have in mind when you say that someone's political views are conservative?" They were allowed up to three responses to each question, six overall. Seventy-eight percent of the sample gave at least one response.

TABLE 3.6 | Perceived Meaning of Ideological Labels, 1994

Question: *What sorts of things do you have in mind when you say someone's political views are liberal?*

What sorts of things do you have in mind when you say someone's political views are conservative?

Type of Mention	Example	Percentage Mentioning
Change	L's accept change/new ideas/innovative.	23
	C's resist change/protect status quo/rigid.	
Fiscal	L's for socialism/welfare state/give-away programs.	24
	C's for free enterprise/capitalism/oppose social programs.	
Personality	L's are open-minded/not concerned with consequences.	14
	C's are moralists/concerned with consequences.	
Morality	L's not interested in setting moral standards/not religious.	13
	C's have definite moral standards/religious.	
Spend/save	L's free spenders/favor government spending.	24
	C's thrifty/economize on government spending.	
Civil liberties	L's support upholding of Bill of Rights/human rights.	5
	C's want to limit Bill of Rights/human rights.	
Class	L's for little people/working people/unions.	12
	C's for big business/the rich.	
Abortion	L's are pro-choice.	15
	C's are pro-life.	
Gay rights	L's favor gay rights.	9
	C's oppose gay rights.	
Defense	L's weak on defense/national security.	4
	C's strong on defense/national security.	
People	L's identify label with prominent national figures.	5
	C's identify label with prominent national figures.	

$N = 595$.

Source: Adapted from National Election Studies, 1994. The questions allow for multiple responses.

As in other years, economic distinctions were used most often to explain the difference between liberals and conservatives. Liberals spend; conservatives save. Liberals are seen as favoring the welfare state and giving away programs; conservatives are seen as favoring free enterprise and opposing big spending social programs. Liberals were also seen as being more change oriented and innovative, while conservatives were viewed as more status quo–oriented and rigid. All these are reasonably broad distinctions. But the public also sees differences between liberals and conservatives on narrower issues. Conservatives are seen as moralistic and religious, while liberals are seen as having more flexible moral standards and not as religious. The contemporary issues of abortion and gay rights show up in the expected fashion. However, with the end of the Cold War, fewer respondents mention defense and national security issues than in the past. In addition, a number of responses deal with peripheral matters such as liberal and conservative positions on narrow policy issues (see also Lewis-Beck et al. 2008, ch. 9).

When survey respondents are asked to classify themselves on the liberal–conservative spectrum, their answers tend to correspond to their policy positions. Examples of the relationships and positions on specific issues are shown in Table 3.7. Self-declared liberals take issue positions considerably more liberal than do self-declared conservatives.

This tendency is even clearer when issue positions are summed over several issues. Table 3.8 compares people's liberalism–conservatism as measured by their composite stands over the ten issues shown in Table 3.7 with their self-declared ideology. People who are very liberal on the ten issues identify themselves as liberals and people who are very conservative on the ten issues overwhelmingly identify themselves as conservatives. It may also be noted that people with conservative views on issues are more eager to identify themselves ideologically than are people with liberal positions.

TABLE 3.7	Ideological Preferences and Opinions on Selected Policy Issues, 2008*
Belief	**Support Among Self-Declared Liberals**	**Support Among Self-Declared Conservatives**
The government should provide "more services even if it means an increase in spending"	87%	31%
The government should guarantee "that every person has a job and good standard of living"	65	18
Favor "government insurance plan which would cover all medical and hospital expenses for everyone"	87	31
The government "should make every effort to improve the social and economic position of blacks"	60	13
Permit abortion "always" or "if needed"	84	46
The government "should make it more difficult to buy a gun"	59	33
Impose timetable for withdrawal from Iraq	80	35
Legalize gay marriage	63	17
Oppose "death penalty for persons convicted of murder"	47	21
The United States "should spend less on defense"	69	23

*Reported figures are percentage of opinion-holders only.

Source: National Election Studies, 2008.

TABLE 3.8 | **Correspondence of Ideological Self-Ratings and Summary of Positions on Ten Issues, 2008**

Ideological Self-Rating	Summary Position on Ten Issues*				
	Very Liberal	Liberal	Center	Conservative	Very Conservative
Liberal	56%	26%	22%	6%	4%
Moderate	12	32	30	24	16
Conservative	11	18	27	44	71
Don't know	21	25	20	26	9
	100%	100%	100%	100%	100%
(Percentage of total sample)	(16)	(19)	(23)	(20)	(21)

*See the Appendix for construction of ten-item summary scores. The full distribution of scores is shown in Figure 3.1. The categories here are as follows: Very liberal −10 to −5, Liberal −4 to −2, Center −1 to +1, Conservative +2 to +4, and Very Conservative +5 to +10.

Source: National Election Studies, 2008 election data.

Use of Ideological Language

Although ideological terms are within the vocabularies of a large share of the American public, few actually employ them to defend their choices of party or candidates. For each American National Election Study, respondents are asked what they like and dislike about each major party and presidential candidate. Starting with the *The American Voter* (Campbell et al. 1960, 216–49), responses have been recorded according to their "levels of conceptualization."

Table 3.9 enumerates the electorate by these levels based on ANES surveys for presidential year from 1956 to 2000 (data are not available for 1992 and 1996). The researchers were interested not only in the individuals' image of the parties and candidates but also in the conceptual sophistication of the responses. To what extent is the public motivated in evaluating parties and candidates by a reasonably rigorous use of the ideological concepts of liberal and conservative, and what types of thinking motivates others in their vote choice?

Respondents who spontaneously and knowledgeably evaluated the parties and candidates in terms of their placement on the liberal–conservative spectrum were labeled as "ideologues" (meaning political sophisticates, and not as the term is sometimes used in popular discourse, an ideological-driven fanatic). Ideologues evaluate candidates and parties in broad abstract terms consistent with our understanding of liberalism and conservatism.

As can be seen in Table 3.9, only a small portion of the electorate is classed as ideologues, 20 percent in 2000. A typical ideologue in the 2000 election responded as follows when asked, "Is there anything you like about Al Gore?" (Lewis-Beck et al. 2008, 262).

TABLE 3.9	Levels of Political Conceptualization, 1956–2000									
	1956	1960	1964	1968	1972	1976	1980	1984	1988	2000
Ideologues	12%	19%	27%	26%	22%	21%	21%	19%	18%	20%
Group benefits	42	31	27	24	27	26	31	26	36	28
Nature of the times	24	26	20	29	34	30	30	35	25	28
No issue content	22	23	26	21	17	24	19	19	21	24
	100%	99%	100%	100%	100%	101%	101%	99%	99%	100%
Number of cases	1,749	1,701	1,431	1,319	1,372	2,870	1,612	2,257	2,040	1,807

Source: 1956–1976: Paul R. Hagner and John C. Pierce, "Correlative Characteristics of Levels of Conceptualization in the American Public, 1956–1976," Journal of Politics 44 (August 1982), pp. 779–809, 1980–1988; compiled by Paul Hagner and Kathleen Knight (2000); Lewis-Beck et al. (2008): 279.

Yes, I definitely like his stand on Social Security. He'll keep it and improve it. (Anything else?) His strong protection of the environment and stand against drilling oil in Alaska. (Anything else). He is trying to work on the health program, which will be slow going. (Anything else) I love his pro-choice stand and his program for schools.

An added 28 percent of the 2000 sample expressed their likes and dislikes about the candidates (Bush and Gore) and parties in terms of "group benefits." They tend to think in terms of identifiable interests like labor unions or environmental groups rather than along an abstract liberal–conservative continuum. How do the parties and candidates reward or punish favored citizen groups? Seniors, for example, frequently expressed their political likes and dislikes in group benefits terms—for example, mentions of government health insurance were common when asked about Al Gore. One citizen responded, "His health care, so that senior citizens will not have any out-of-pocket expenses; that is the direction we need to heed" (Lewis-Beck et al. 2008, 269). Many group-benefit responses were class-related, evoking the notion that Republicans favor big business while the Democrats favor the "little person."

Moving down the conceptual ladder, another 28 percent of the 2000 respondents referred to the "nature of the times" when evaluating candidates and parties. Nature-of-the-times voters were guided by perceptions of past performance, such as which candidate or party brought economic prosperity or which party kept their promises (or vice versa). A typical nature-of-the-times respondent, when asked what he disliked about the Democrats, said, "They promise too much giveaway at taxpayer expense." The same respondent when asked, "Is there anything you like about the Republican Party?" offered, "They are willing to help you so you can work out your needs. People should not remain on welfare all their lives."

The lowest level of conceptualization, with 24 percent, is "no issue content." About a third of this group in 2000 expressed no likes or dislikes at all about the parties or candidates. Their comments tended to focus on the candidates' personal characteristics. This group evidenced no cognitive organization to their thinking, and often simply fell back on party identification. Typical was the following exchange:

(Anything you like about the Democratic Party)	"No."
(Anything you dislike the Democratic Party)	"The scandal that went on in the Oval Office. It was mockery."
(Anything you like about the Republican Party)	"They do a good job in general, like the Reagan years, which is why we are doing good now. Beyond that, nothing specific."
(Anything you dislike about the Republican Party?)	"No." (Lewis-Beck et al. 2008, 278)

As we might expect, a variety of factors are related to the level of conceptualization, but none of these move the percentage of ideologues above one-third. There are slightly more ideologues among voters than nonvoters, but only by 4 percent. Education is also a strong determinant, with just 3 percent with less than a high school degree being ideologues compared to 31 percent with a college degree (Lewis-Beck et al. 281–88).

The distribution of how people conceptualize partisan politics may be interpreted to mean that Americans are not very ideological, and in one sense this is correct. The authors of *The American Voter* accounted for the scarcity of ideologues in terms of the public's "cognitive limitations," particularly a lack of intellectual ability to think in terms of ideological abstractions (Campbell et al. 1960, 253). Now many political scientists see *The American Voter* judgment as overly harsh. Although the authors did not realize it at the time, the 1956 presidential election was probably the least ideological of all modern campaigns, conducted essentially as a referendum on President Eisenhower's first term. Because the 1956 campaign was not conducted at an ideological level, respondents in that year were not apt to explain their likes and dislikes about parties and candidates in terms of ideological nuances. They chose the easier criteria of group representation and the nature of the times.

Subsequent elections, starting with 1964, focused more sharply on issue differences among the candidates and parties, with the percentage of ideologues increasing noticeably over the percentage reported in 1956. We now know that ideological thinking is, within limits, both a function of citizen capacities and the clarity with which candidates and parties draw issue distinctions. In many ways the 2000 electorate (the last year for which we have data) looks quite typical compared to past elections. The number of ideologues, as classified by ANES surveys, were neither as scarce as in 1956 nor as relatively abundant as in 1964.

There are four lessons to be learned from our analysis of the levels of conceptualization. First, at best one-fifth of the electorate pay meaningful attention to ideological themes. As we have seen, a greater proportion of the electorate can utilize the ideological language than are classifiable as ideologues. One explanation is that many individuals can use ideological labels without pursuing much ideology. For instance, many at the "group-interest" level identify with liberals or conservatives as a group with which they share a common interest, much as some may feel about teachers or labor unions (Tedin 1987).

Second, ideologues have distinctive background attributes. They are among the best educated, most knowledgeable and most politically active segments of the electorate. Third, ideologues are among the most likely to vote (typically 90 percent of ideologues cast their ballot in presidential elections), and tend to be the most partisan segments of the electorate. They are likely to vote consistently for the same party from one election to the next. Fourth, the paucity of ideologues raise serious questions about the extent to which elections can reasonably be interpreted as mandates for policy change, since only about a fifth of the electorate is engaging in sophisticated ideological thinking about parties and candidates (Lewis-Beck et al. 2008, 289).

Ideology as Liberal–Conservative Consistency

Suppose we array the American public on a scale from most liberal to most conservative. What would this distribution look like? Would most people be at the liberal or conservative pole? Or would they cluster in the middle? Figure 3.1 displays the distribution of the American public's liberal–conservative

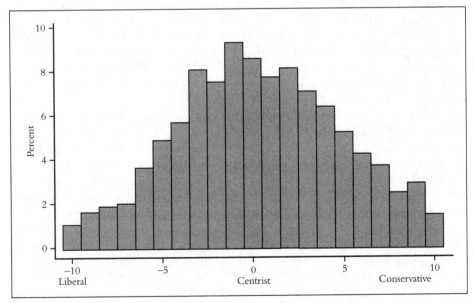

Figure 3.1   Distribution of composite opinion scores, 2008. *Source:* National Election Studies, 2008 election data.

"scores" as measured by their cumulative responses to ten opinion questions in the 2008 ANES survey. A person with all liberal opinions would score at −10, whereas a person who expresses conservative outlooks on all ten issues would score at +10. (For details of the index construction, see the Appendix.) Most respondents were near the midpoint of the scale (0), indicating that their liberal and conservative viewpoints balanced each other out.

Because over a series of issues most people give some liberal and some conservative positions, there is a temptation to label the public as political moderates. But these voters in the center cannot be grouped as sharing the same moderate ideology because they differ greatly in their pattern of responses on individual issues. For instance, one voter with balanced liberal and conservative views may be liberal on social welfare issues and civil rights but conservative on foreign policy and law and order, while another with equally balanced views professes exactly the opposite opinions. Still a third person may have an overall score that is neither very conservative nor very liberal for the reason that he or she expresses few opinions at all.

If ideology influences people's opinions, opinions on two separate issues should be predictable from one another because both are "constrained" by the opinion-holder's ideological perspective. If a conservative ideology binds some to oppose spending programs for example, their conservatism should compel them to support the death penalty or perhaps to oppose abortion rights. Table 3.10 shows examples of the search for ideological constraint.

For a pair of issues, an individual is more likely to offer consistently liberal or conservative positions if the issues are logically related or share content. The top row of Table 3.10 presents two examples. In Table 3.10(a), people's opinions regarding government involvement in health care are predictable from their general views on domestic government spending. In Table 3.10(b), the opinions of 2008 respondents regarding spending more or less for defense were correlated with their beliefs regarding setting a timetable for withdrawal from Iraq. In Table 3.10(c), people's opinions on abortion appear consistent with their views on legalizing gay marriage.

When issues are not closely related in content, liberal–conservative consistency tends to fade. Panels (d) through (f) of Table 3.10 show three examples. One cannot predict an individual's position on abortion from his or her position on national health insurance (d). One has a hard time predicting a person's position on guaranteed jobs from their stand on gay marriage (e). In these instances, while each issue has a liberal and a conservative side as these ideological terms are used, there is no compelling argument why a person could not simultaneously hold a liberal belief on one issue and a conservative belief on the other. But consider also the relationship between "more" domestic spending and "less" military spending, shown in Table 3.10(f). Arguably, people should gravitate toward one side of the trade-off of either more domestic spending and less military spending (liberal) or less domestic spending and more military spending (conservative). Table 3.10(f) shows only a

TABLE 3.10 | Correlations Between Opinions on Selected Issues, 2008

		(a) Increase Domestic Spending				(b) Impose Iraq Withdrawal Deadline	
		Pro	Con			Pro	Con
National Health Insurance	Pro	50%	11%	Cut Military Spending	Pro	31%	10%
	Con	15	24		Con	29	30
	Gamma = .76				Gamma = .53		

		(c) Legalize Abortions				(d) Legalize Abortions	
		Pro	Con			Pro	Con
Legalize Gay Marriage	Pro	29%	9%	National Health Insurance	Pro	37%	21%
	Con	28	34		Con	20	22
	Gamma = .58				Gamma = .31		

		(e) Legalize Gay Marriage				(f) More Domestic Spending	
		Pro	Con			Pro	Con
Guarantee Living Standard	Pro	17%	21%	Cut Military Spending	Pro	28%	11%
	Con	18	43		Con	3,439	2,423
	Gamma = .29				Gamma = .22		

Source: National Election Studies, 2008 data. See the Appendix for the full text of opinion questions.

modest correlation. Favoring spending in one domain does not predict less appetite for spending in the other.[7]

The low levels of ideological constraint within the general public reflect real variations in ideological sophistication. Liberal–conservative opinion consistency is quite high among those most knowledgeable about politics, such as people identified as "ideologues" (Stimson 1975; Knight 1985). We can illustrate this point by comparing the respondents classified as least knowledgeable and most knowledgeable in the 2008 ANES survey. Among the select "high-information" group, opinions on different issues are highly correlated, while for the "low-information" group there is essentially no correlation at all. Our illustration is for the relationship between opinion on a national health insurance program and opinion on abortion.

		Low Information Legal Abortions		High Information Legal Abortions	
		Pro	Con	Pro	Con
National Health	Pro	29%	26%	44%	12%
Insurance	Con	20%	25%	20%	23%
		Gamma = .15		Gamma = .61	

We see that with the accumulation of a high level of political information, people tend toward consistently liberal or consistently conservative positions, while we see no relationship at all for those with low levels of information. A broader illustration compares the high-information, medium-information, and low-information groups in terms of their distributions on the composite ten-item liberal–conservative scale. Figure 3.2 shows the results. The informed show some gravitation toward the liberal and conservative poles, as their opinions are distributed with close to an even density across the ideological spectrum. Meanwhile, the uninformed are highly clustered in the center of the spectrum.

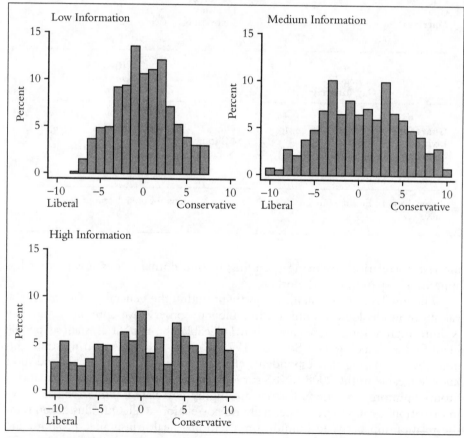

Figure 3.2   Composite opinion by information level. *Source*: National Election Studies, 2008 election data.

Despite the fact that the most knowledgeable are the most responsive to liberal versus conservative distinctions, we should not insist that use of the liberal–conservative dimension is a requirement for political thinking. Liberal–conservative consistency is not the only possible ordering principle for political opinions. On foreign policy, for example, core values regarding the morality of warfare and ethnocentrism appear to be important (Hurwitz and Peffley 1987). More generally, people can make their opinions consistent with their own personal ideologies and need not apply the notion of liberal versus conservative ways of thinking. Consider abortion attitudes, which until recently did not correlate much with conventional liberal–conservative orderings as measured by other policy opinions. According to Kristen Luker, attitudes concerning abortion result from "beliefs and attitudes about motherhood; about sexuality; about men and women; about the role of children; and more broadly, about such global things as morality and the role of rational planning in human affairs" (Luker 1984, 31).

Ideological Thinking: A Summary

The public is mixed in its understanding and usage of ideological language and thinking. Most citizens do not engage in the ideological thinking of the sort found among political elites. But ordinary citizens often use ideological labels in at least a limited way as part of their political vocabulary. Many, however, do not do even this. For perhaps as much as half the electorate, the liberal versus conservative component of political discourse is nothing more than a confusion of background noise. The fact that there is little ideological consistency to people's issue positions demonstrates that few people use their ideological position as a cuing device to arrange their responses to the political world. The kind of attitudinal constraint that motivates people toward consistently liberal, conservative, or moderate political viewpoints is reserved for a relatively small, politically active segment of the public.

In our effort to understand public opinion, we should not ignore this politically sophisticated segment of the American public, which does follow government and politics in terms of the liberal–conservative continuum. Thinking about politics in liberal versus conservative terms is sophisticated not because it is preferable to hold ideologically extreme convictions or to view the political world through a distorted lens. Rather, to have the liberal–conservative spectrum as a political frame of reference is necessary to understand the language of politics as it is practiced by political elites. Many ordinary Americans do follow this ideological discussion.

3-3 Party Identification and the Organization of Political Opinions

So far, we have ignored partisanship as a way of organizing political opinions. More than on the basis of ideology, Americans' political opinions are structured by party identification. Whereas ideological identification may be of particular relevance for a select segment of the public, people at all levels of sophistication appear to hold meaningful party identifications. Whereas ideological identification and questions about core values are intended to summarize a person's political predispositions, party identification represents a person's net evaluation of the Republican and Democratic parties. It is relatively easy to prefer one party over the other while holding little political information or giving even modest thought to most political issues.

For most people, party identification is a central aspect of political identity. Compared to ordinary political opinions, people's party identifications are quite stable over time, both before and after adjustment for measurement error (Green, Palmquist, and Schickler 2002). For instance, when interviewed during two successive presidential campaigns four years apart, most respondents persist with their original basic identification as a Democrat, Independent, or Republican. Only a small percentage of respondents switch party identification from Democratic to Republican or vice versa. Those who switch generally move in and out of the Independent category rather than "convert" from one side to the other.

As discussed in chapter 5, the source of one's party identification is often the political values that were transmitted in the family during childhood. At the other end of the causal chain, party identification is the best predictor of how people vote. Following the sequence through, we find that people tend to vote for the party with which their parents identified.

Survey researchers normally ascertain party identification by asking respondents whether they consider themselves Democrats, Independents, or Republicans. Partisans may then be asked whether they consider themselves "strong" or "not so strong" (often translated as "weak") Republicans or Democrats. Classifying on strength plus partisan direction makes four categories of partisans. Meanwhile, Independents are sometimes asked whether they "lean" toward one of the parties. The Independents can be classified as Republican leaners, Democratic leaners, and pure Independents. Pure Independents typically make up no more than about 10 percent of a national sample, suggesting that few citizens are purely neutral when it comes to partisanship. Altogether, there are seven potential categories of party identification, on a scale from "strong Democrat" to "strong Republican." Usually, however, the three-category classification is sufficient. Except where otherwise indicated, this book employs the simple three-category division of party identification as Republicans (strong plus weak), Democrats (strong plus weak), and Independents (pure plus partisan leaners).

Party identification can be a handy cue by which to orient the remainder of one's political beliefs. An alert Republican, for example, learns that a good Republican is supposed to subscribe to conservative positions on certain issues and responds accordingly. At the same time, we might expect that the rare event of a partisan conversion results when a person becomes aware that his or her ideological views are out of alignment with his or her partisan heritage. These causal processes could not occur, however, unless people were aware of the Democratic versus Republican differences on the issues of the day.

Perceptions of Party Differences

As we show in chapter 10, Democratic and Republican leaders are ideologically different, with the Republicans generally conservative and Democrats generally liberal. In other words, at the leadership level the usual party stereotypes are true. Here we can ask: To what extent does the public perceive these party differences?

The American National Election Studies have regularly asked their respondents to place the major parties' positions on selected issues of the day (although not in their most recent survey from 2008). Respondents are asked to rate the Democrats to the left of the Republicans (correct), the Republicans to the left of the Democrats, rate them tied at the identical position, or declare no interest in the issue. Table 3.11 presents the perceptions of the parties' relative positions in recent ANES surveys. Typically, about half rate the Democrats as the more liberal (left) party. Few guess incorrectly and identify the Republican Party with the liberal position.

Over the years, the public has increasingly seen party differences on the issues. As recently as the early 1960s, the public saw party differences only in terms of social welfare issues. The public image of the parties as distinct on social welfare issues goes back to the New Deal era of the 1930s, when the parties began to develop opposite philosophies toward the role of the federal government in the economy. Until about 1964, party differences on issues outside the social welfare sphere were not sharply focused at the leadership level, such as congressional and presidential politics. It is no surprise, therefore, that before the 1960s people generally did not see either party as liberal or conservative on civil rights or foreign policy issues.

Nowadays, Americans generally perceive the Democrats as the more liberal party not only on social welfare issues but also on civil rights, foreign policy, plus social issues like gay rights. Arguably, this happened largely because the parties became more polarized at the elite level (Poole and Rosenthal 1997; Hacker

TABLE 3.11	Public Perceptions of Party Differences on Issues, 1988–2004		
Perceptions of Which Party Is More in Favor of . . .	**Democrats**	**Republicans**	**No Difference, Don't Know, No Interest**
More domestic spending (2004)	63%	15%	22%
Reducing defense spending (2004)	68	11	21
Guaranteed living standard (2004)	63	10	27
Aid to blacks (2004)	56	8	36
Equal role for women (2004)	42	9	49
National health insurance (1988)	43	8	50
Abortion rights (1996)	57	9	34
Regulating the environment (1996)	48	9	44

Source: National Election Studies data.

and Pierson 2005). Public perceptions simply followed the behavior and the rhetoric of party leaders. The biggest change occurred with the ideological Goldwater election of 1964 (Carmines and Stimson 1989). Senator Goldwater, the 1964 Republican candidate, campaigned as a forthright conservative. By opposing the Civil Rights Act of 1964, he altered the Republican image on civil rights. By his tough posturing about the Soviet Union, he made the Republicans appear to be the most belligerent on foreign policy. His Democratic opponent, President Lyndon Johnson, was able to exploit Goldwater's image as an extreme conservative. Goldwater lost the election in a landslide, but he and his supporters moved the Republican Party sharply to the right in a manner that has lasted into the twenty-first century.

Events after 1964 added to the growing perceptions of party differences, as growing polarization of Democratic and Republican elites fueled a further division between Republican and Democratic identifiers in the mass public (Hetherington 2001). By the 1980s, public perceptions of the parties began to seriously diverge on "social issues" such as abortion, "toughness" on crime, and gay rights, with Republicans seen as moralistic and Democrats as permissive. Today, on virtually all national issues that divide Americans, the two major parties are seen as taking quite different sides. While there was once a time when critics complained that the parties did not offer meaningful policy choices, the more typical complaint today is that the chasm has become too wide. As discussed in chapter 10, a sharpening of divisions between congressional Democrats and Republicans maintains the liberal–conservative party polarization that began in 1964.

Party Identification and Policy Preferences

Increasingly over the years, Americans have become polarized along partisan and ideological lines, clustering as liberal Democrats or conservative Republicans. Table 3.12 displays some examples of partisan divergence on specific issues from the 2008 ANES study. Figure 3.3 displays the difference between Democrats and Republicans in terms of scores on the composite ten-item index of liberalism–conservatism. In terms of their net ideological direction, most Democrats are left of center and most Republicans are right of center, but there are many exceptions. In fact, the reader might be surprised by the proportions of the public who appear as conservative Democrats and liberal Republicans. Clearly, ideology and partisanship are not the same thing.

The correlation between partisanship and ideological direction sharpens if we isolate informed citizens. Figure 3.4 repeats the ideological comparison of Democrats and Republicans, this time separately, for voters with a perfect or "high" information score and for all others, now cast as the "low" information group. Among low-information voters, there exists almost no correlation between partisanship and ideology; in this set, Democrats are only barely to the left of Republicans on average, with considerable overlap. But among high-information voters, virtually all Democrats are to the left of center, and virtually

TABLE 3.12 | **Party Identification and Policy Opinions, 2008**

Issue	Strong Dem.	Weak Dem.	Ind.	Weak Rep.	Strong Rep.	Gamma
		Percent Liberal Among				
More domestic spending	90	81	67	35	27	.66
Job guarantee	78	50	37	12	14	.39
Less defense spending	53	55	39	25	11	.38
Government aid to blacks	66	40	26	11	9	.63
National health insurance	79	75	69	34	14	.59
Set Iraq withdrawal deadline	87	70	62	41	20	.60
Legalize gay marriage	45	46	44	25	9	.24
Oppose death penalty	46	37	29	16	14	.38
Favor gun control	62	52	46	38	29	.29
Favor abortion rights	72	58	61	61	34	.25
Mean	*68*	*56*	*48*	*30*	*19*	*.45*
Liberal identifiers*	77	77	42	9	2	.82

* Percent liberal among liberal and conservative identifiers.

Source: National Election Studies, 2008 data.

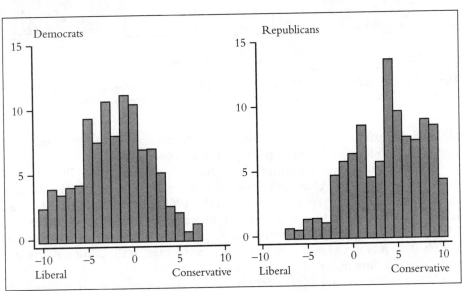

Figure 3.3 Composite opinion by party identification. *Source*: National Election Studies, 2008 election data.

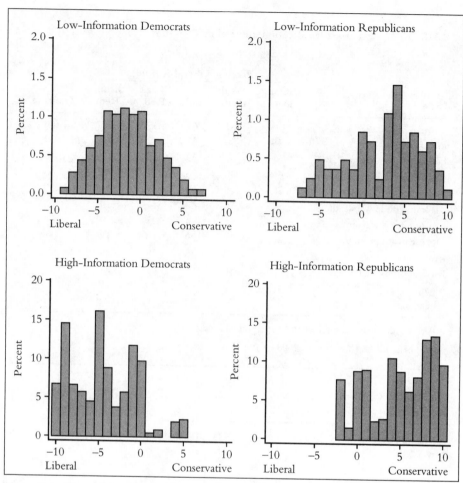

Figure 3.4   Democratic and Republican composite opinion, by information level. Low information scores include all without perfect "high" scores. *Source:* National Election Studies, 2008 election data.

all Republicans to the right. In other words, find an informed voter and partisanship follows ideology, or perhaps it is the other way around.

While Democratic identifiers have been somewhat more liberal than Republicans on social welfare issues since the 1930s, Democrats and Republicans did not differ on other types of issues until the 1960s, starting with the ideological 1964 election. Before that time, Democrats in the electorate were not identifiably more liberal on civil rights, foreign policy, or social issues. Of course, they had no reason to be, as people saw the two parties as differing only on the social welfare dimension.

What causes the consistency between political opinions and party identification? Do people learn their political opinions from their party identifications, or do political opinions shape party identifications? Undoubtedly both causal processes are at work, but their relative contributions can be only roughly estimated.

Because party identification can be such a strong and stable attitude, partisanship often drives policy opinions more than the reverse (Campbell et al. 1960; Goren 2005; Levendusky 2009); parties realign their positions on an issue, and their supporters follow. A classic example occurred among partisans after Republican President Nixon initiated the thaw in U.S. relations with the People's Republic of China in the early 1970s. Republicans abandoned their hostility to "Red China" faster than Democrats did.[8] Similarly, when President Reagan initiated a new friendship with the Soviet Union, Republicans were quicker to think the Cold War was over.[9] When in early 1991 many congressional Democrats balked at supporting President Bush's intervention in the Persian Gulf, the Democratic rank and file became more dovish and the Republican rank and file became more hawkish (Zaller 1992, 104–05). Finally, just the reverse occurred in the spring of 1999 when congressional Republicans balked at supporting President Clinton's policy of halting ethnic cleansing in Kosovo by bombing Serbia.[10]

Partisanship can influence not only attitudes and opinions but also beliefs about the state of the world. Following the Iraq invasion of 2003, it was soon evident that no weapons of mass destruction were found, contrary to the claim that had become the Bush administration's chief justification for the war. Well into 2004, most Republicans in surveys (but few Democrats) continued to insist not only that WMD had been discovered but also that Saddam Hussein had been allied with the terrorist group Al Qaida (Kull, Ramsey, and Lewis 2003–2004; Bloch-Elkon and Shapiro 2005). Similarly, when asked in surveys, Republican identifiers claimed U.S. casualty rates in Iraq that were lower than Democratic identifiers' estimates (Berinsky 2004).

While partisanship influences people's perceptions of the world and shapes their opinions, sometimes it is party identification that changes when initial partisanship and issue positions get out of alignment (Markus and Converse 1979; Page and Jones 1979; Franklin and Jackson 1983; Jacoby 1988; Abramowitz and Saunders 1998; Putz 2002; Carsey and Layman 2006). The gradual conversion of conservative white southerners from the Democratic to the Republican Party is a case in point. Some people who become ideologically disaffected by their home party become Independents. Those who go all the way and shift from one party to the other often display the ideological zeal of true converts.

Party Identification: Psychological Identification or Running Tally?

Political scientists still do not fully understand party identification. *The American Voter* (Campbell et al. 1960) presented one influential interpretation—that one's party identification is essentially a psychological attachment or "affective orientation" to one's favorite party. By this view, party identification can approach blind loyalty, as when people find reason to support their party's position and vote for its candidates long after they have rational reasons for doing so.

Some scholars, however, emphasize the more rational aspects of party identification. By this view, people learn a party identification based on what Morris Fiorina (Fiorina 1977; Fiorina, Abrams, and Pope 2003) calls a "running tally" of their partisan decisions. For example, voters who find repeated reason to vote Republican begin to call themselves Republican—not so much out of psychological attachment as by way of learning a convenient shorthand rule for deciding how to vote. If reasons develop for such voters to vote Democratic instead, they do not blindly continue down the Republican path in the face of contrary evidence. Instead, they vote Democratic or even change partisanship in response to the new running tally.

Both interpretations of partisanship carry some validity. For example, many partisans persist in voting loyally for their party even when it no longer represents their views on issues. But many partisans casually change allegiance when circumstances seem to warrant it. Perhaps our question should be whether by forming a standing decision to vote Democratic or Republican, people enhance or detract from their ability to vote rationally. We address this question in later chapters.

Notes

1. Analysts must be sensitive to the accuracy of the reasons people give for their opinions. For instance, people can recall their position on some matters, but not the original reasons for it, and then rationalize their choice with new reasons that may not have had any bearing on their choice. A lengthy literature exists on how people store and retrieve political information when making or remembering political judgments. For examples, see Lodge and Stroh (1993) and Wyer and Ottati (1993).

2. Another arguable example of people persisting in incorrect beliefs, not directly in the realm of politics, is the division of opinion between scientists, the presumed experts, and the mass public on issues like Darwin's theory of evolution and that human behavior contributes to global warming. Scientists are in near consensus that evolution and human responsibility are correct, yet the public is considerably skeptical. See Pew 2009b (Pew Survey Reports: "Public Praises Science; Scientists Fault Public, Media." July 9, 2009; http://people-press.org/report/528/).

3. Although the responses shown in Table 3.3 are part of a framing experiment, this is not a source of serious distortion. In some instances, different framing in the two waves enhances response turnover. Yet this contamination appears slight. For issues in which some respondents were given variable framings and others the same framing, the effect of this difference in stimulus appears to have been but a few percentage points. Where some respondents repeatedly received an elaborate framing of the underlying arguments for the two points of view while a control group got none, responses were no more stable when respondents received framing.

4. The abortion question was actually asked three times in the 1989 ANES pilot study. The pilot respondents were first asked their views on abortion in late 1988 as part of the regular ANES 1988 election survey. Over three waves, only 26 percent took a consistent pro-life position and only 27 percent took a consistent pro-choice position. An even smaller 5 percent were consistently in the middle, but 42 percent took a middle position in at least one wave.

5. As a practical matter, the single dimension of liberal–conservative ideology is a better measure of underlying political values than specific values measured individually. Zaller (1992, 26) states the case nicely: "There is . . . a tendency for

people to be fairly consistently 'left,' 'right,' or 'centrist' on such dispara-
dimensions as economic individualism, opinions toward Communists, tolera-
nonconformists, racial issues, sexual freedom, and religious authority. The
correlations among these different value dimensions are never so strong as to
suggest that there is one and only one basic value dimension, but they are always
at least moderately strong, and among highly aware persons, the correlations are
sometimes quite strong. And, of course, there are also moderately strong
correlations between people's self-descriptions as liberal or conservative and their
scores on the various value measures."

6. For discussions of the origins of liberal–conservative terminology, see Kerlinger
   (1984) and Rotunda (1986).
7. Correlations between opinions have increased since the early readings in the
   1950s. The greatest jump occurred at the time of the ideological 1964 election
   (Nie and Anderson 1974; Nie, Verba, and Petrocik 1976). Some scholars believe
   this increase is largely illusory, the result of better questions asked by survey
   researchers (Sullivan, Piereson, and Marcus 1978; Bishop 2004).
8. For instance, between 1966 and 1971, the percentage of Democratic
   opinion-holders who told Gallup they favored U.N. admission for China rose
   from one-third to nearly half. Meanwhile, Republican support rose
   from 1 in 4 to a clear plurality in favor of admission.
9. For instance, in 1984 (pre-Gorbachev) and 1988, "strong Democrats"
   (with opinions) increased their support for cooperation with Russia by four
   percentage points. "Strong Republicans" (with opinions) increased their support
   by 24 points (1984 and 1988 ANES data).
10. Pew Research Center poll, June 9–13, 1999.

4 Macrolevel Opinion: The Flow of Political Sentiment

PUBLIC OPINION SPECIALISTS BEGIN their investigations of survey data by analyzing the *frequencies*, or the percentagized divisions, of opinion for the sample. The frequency distributions reflect the content of public opinion at the moment of the poll. When a particular survey question has been repeatedly asked in the past, the latest frequencies also provide information about opinion trends.

Frequency distributions must be interpreted with caution because, as we saw in chapter 2, responses are often influenced by question wording. When the polls show a certain percentage favoring a particular response to a question, we need some anchor, a reference point, by which to measure the significance of the finding. One way is to compare the frequencies for one question with those for slightly different but related questions. This comparison allows us to see what distinctions the mass public makes in the kinds of policies it is willing to support. A particularly useful anchor is to compare answers to the same question over time. If the public displays a different level of support for some policy today than one year ago or five years ago, then we may have located a potentially important change in public opinion.

Unfortunately, the data that would allow for the accurate assessment of trends in public opinion are often not as available as one might expect. Commercial pollsters naturally ask questions of current interest to their media clients. As popular interest fades, those questions are often not repeated. Academic polling units are more concerned with the continuity and comparability of questions over time, but even they are not immune to the wax and wane of topical issues. Thus, questions dealing with civil liberties were frequently asked in the McCarthy era of the early 1950s, when many people thought their basic personal liberties were threatened, but not asked again until the early 1970s. Before the 1960s, questions about race relations were seldom asked; the aspirations of the black minority were given little thought by white politicians, press, and public. Even when the polls monitor opinions on the same issue over time, they often vary question wording, making it difficult to separate real change from question-wording effects.

In the following sections we present an overview of macrolevel public opinion, or what polls tell us about the content of public opinion both today and in the past. We begin by examining opinion on specific policy issues that have been polled over the years, searching for liberal or conservative trends. Second, we consider the possibility of general ideological movement. Poll trends are often described in ideological terms, as if the public's frame of reference is shifting on the liberal–conservative continuum. Third, we examine changes in the distribution of party identification over the years. And finally, we consider one important partisan question well known for its volatility: the president's approval rating.

4-1   The Micro Foundations of Macro Opinion

The previous chapter showed that the survey response tends to be erratic. When survey respondents are asked their opinion on more than one occasion and change their answers, the chances are that the shift represents error (or at best a shift in short-term influences) rather than true opinion change. When it comes to basic political predispositions, true opinion change is incremental if it occurs at all. We might ask, therefore, whether it is meaningful to assess survey responses in the aggregate. Would we expect to find real (statistically significant) changes in opinion, given that responses may contain more randomness than real change? The fact is that observable changes in the aggregate responses at the macrolevel are far more orderly than the individual responses at the microlevel of which they are comprised. This is the "miracle of aggregation." Survey error that is so mischievous at the microlevel, when one analyzes individual responses, tends to cancel out at the macrolevel. Although people rarely change their true opinions, when they do the shifts tend to be uniform. When macrolevel change occurs, a shift by only a small portion of the public can have important political consequences.

For a useful illustration, we turn not to a survey question about politics but instead about economics. In the 1996 ANES panel, respondents were asked whether their personal family economic circumstances had improved, stayed the same, or gotten worse over the previous year. The same respondents had been interviewed two years earlier in 1994. In both 1994 and 1996, the ANES asked respondents about their family income. Although the interviews were two years apart, we might expect considerable correspondence between respondents' recall of family income change and the *actual* change in their reported income between 1994 and 1996. We get:

		Change in Reported Income, 1996 minus 1994		
		Worse	**Same**	**Improved**
Recall of Previous Year's Change in	Worse	28%	20%	21% (118)
Family Income, 1996	Same	36	37	30 (174)
	Improved	36	43	49 (228)
		100%	100%	100%
	N	(134)	(139)	(247)

We can see a relationship of sorts. Respondents whose income improved were slightly more likely to recall a growth in income. But the tendency is weak. We could interpret the table to mean that people are no more than dimly aware of their own economic circumstances. But a better explanation is survey noise. For instance, people have different reference points for "improved" and "worse" in terms of family income, making it seem as if people often respond randomly. But apart from illustrating survey error, the table provides meaningful information about aggregate opinion change. We see that the proportion who claimed their circumstances were improving was roughly twice that of those who claimed a decline. On average, people saw improvement during a time when family income was indeed growing, and growing at a faster rate than inflation. The macrolevel signal peeking through the noise was indeed accurate.

As an aggregate measure, the mean report of family income growth is a useful measure of net economic satisfaction. It has its political uses, as changes in family income help to account for changes in party identification as the electorate gradually shifts its net partisanship in response to how well the presidential party maintains prosperity (Erikson, MacKuen, and Stimson 2002). Other economic survey questions tap respondents' perception of the national economy, both past and future. At any one time, survey respondents will disagree about whether the national economy has improved or worsened over the past year. But their mean perception tends to be accurate. And in the aggregate, survey respondents can predict short-term changes in the national economy, even if most individual responses are vague guesses. In fact, the mean responses regarding whether the economy will improve or worsen form one of the key components of the economists' index of leading economic indicators.

With these economic examples, we can readily understand that the aggregate information contains a signal about the aggregate economy plus random noise. The noise of uninformed respondents, being random, cancels out in the aggregate and the signal remains.[1] In politics, the shifts of attentive citizens provide the signals that overcome the error in individual survey responses. (See Converse 1990 for an excellent exposition.) When public opinion changes beyond the realm of what we would expect by sampling error, the change is real even if most individuals may not be undergoing conversions.

4-2 Trends in Policy Opinions

For convenience, most policy questions can be divided into four general domains: (1) social welfare, (2) civil rights, (3) foreign policy, and (4) cultural issues. Social welfare controversies pertain to the distribution of wealth and government efforts to help the disadvantaged; civil rights refer to the quest for equality under the law; foreign policy, obviously, refers to views about the U.S. role abroad; and cultural issues usually involve differences over lifestyles or "moral values" such as abortion, prayer in the public schools, and capital punishment.

Social Welfare Issues

From the New Deal to the present, the American public has been receptive to government programs to accomplish economic welfare objectives. In fact, on social welfare legislation, mass opinion has often been well ahead of congressional action. For example, the earliest polls revealed an overwhelming majority (89 percent) in favor of "old age pensions" prior to the adoption of the Social Security Act in 1936 (Cantril 1951, 521). A majority also supported the right of workers to organize and bargain collectively before the 1941 Wagner Act transformed these principles into law (Page and Shapiro 1992, 136). Majority approval has continually been found prior to each increase in the federal minimum wage (Erskine 1962b, 26; Gallup Poll Index 1985, 17).

It has long been noted that the American public is ideologically conservative but operationally liberal (Free and Cantril 1967; Cantril and Cantril 1999). Polls persistently show self-identified conservatives outnumbering self-identified liberals. When it comes to specific social welfare programs, however, most people generally are supportive of liberal spending. For example, when the ANES asked in 2008 if the government should "provide fewer services, even in areas such as health and education, in order to reduce spending" or instead "provide more services and spending," 41 percent chose more services and spending, 24 percent chose fewer services and less spending, with the remainder taking the middle position or offering no opinion.[2]

Table 4.1 shows levels of support for federal spending on a variety of federal programs. Program by program, few Americans want reductions in social spending. The most frequent preference, in fact, is not to reduce spending or even to keep spending the same but rather to *increase spending* across a wide variety of social programs such as health, education, and retirement. While it is easy to say "spend more" without appreciating the tax consequences, in the 2006–2008 GSS, respondents were told that if they say "spend more," "it might require a tax increase to pay for it." Still, we see majorities saying "spend more" for health care, the environment, education, and retirement. Few people want to spend less on these programs. The most notable exception is a lack of enthusiasm for increased spending on foreign aid (just 12 percent)—a program which few people feel benefits them directly. Also, more spending on the culture and arts

TABLE 4.1 | **Opinion about Spending Too Little, About Right, or Too Much on Selected Federal Programs**

	Spend Too Little	About Right	Spend Too Much
Health care[a]	76%	19%	05%
The environment[a]	68	24	08
Police and law enforcement[a]	53	38	09
Social Security[b]	63	30	06
Education[a]	71	23	03
Military and defense[a]	24	32	44
Retirement benefits[b]	64	28	08
Unemployment benefits[b]	35	49	15
Culture and Arts[a]	23	48	29
Welfare programs[a]	26	37	37
Poor people[a]	70	22	08
Foreign aid[a]	12	28	60
Space exploration[a]	13	49	38

Sources: [a]General Social Survey (2008); [b]General Social Survey (2006).

generates little enthusiasm. Despite occasional rhetoric to the contrary, the domestic services provided by government to its citizens are popular.

Of course, there are limits to the public's enthusiasm for social welfare programs. Most notably, Americans clearly make the classic distinction between the "deserving poor" (those who have fallen on hard times through no fault of their own) and the "shiftless poor," who would rather receive a government handout than hold a job. Thus, in the mid-1980s one poll showed that 88 percent of people with opinions agreed that the government ought to help those "who are unable to support themselves," while at the same time 91 percent agreed that "too many people on welfare could be working" and 94 percent said "too many people on welfare get money to which they are not entitled" (Page and Shapiro 1992, 125).

This distinction can be seen most graphically by large changes in poll numbers when slight changes are made in the way questions are phrased. For example, in a question-wording experiment (shown in Table 4.1), the 2008 GSS asked in random order if too little, about right, or too much is spent on the poor; 70 percent said "too little." But when asked the same question about "people on welfare," just 26 percent said "too little" was being spent.

More than a mere illustration of question-wording effects, this experiment reflects a belief among Americans that the government should help those who cannot help themselves—the deserving poor. But Americans see people on welfare as able but unwilling to work, and thus meriting little sympathy. There is a widespread belief among the American public that people who receive financial assistance ought to work for their money, even if the work they do is of little use. Even spending more on "unemployment benefits" generates only modest support among the public.

But this may not be all to the story about Americans' hostility toward people on welfare. Race, regrettably, is an important part of the explanation. Many whites harbor the belief that blacks are lazy; they tend to exaggerate the extent to which blacks populate the welfare rolls. The effect of this belief on support for welfare can be seen in the fact that those whites who believe (mistakenly) that most welfare recipients are black are also those who are most opposed to welfare (Gilens 1999; Kuklinski et al. 2001).

Health Care. As we noted earlier, the public has frequently been out in front of elected officials on many innovations in social welfare policy. This has certainly been the case with regard to health care. Since the 1930s, opinion polls have consistently shown the public favors some form of government-subsidized health insurance. In 1937, a Gallup Poll showed that over 70 percent favored the notion that "the federal government should provide free medical and dental care for those who cannot pay." During the 1950s and 1960s, 60 to 65 percent supported the principle of the government paying the medical bills of the elderly, which was enacted into law in 1965 with Medicare (Erskine 1975).

In principle, a majority of people favor health care for all. In 1997, when the issue was mostly on the back burner, 83 percent endorsed "some form of universal health care coverage so that everyone has health insurance" (Harris Poll). How to get there, however, is a source of often heated disagreement. What is the role of the private sector? What is the role of government?

Since 1972, ANES has asked its national samples an identical question on the politics of health care, where the liberal choice is "government health insurance plan which would cover all medical and hospital expenses," and the conservative alternative is that medical expenses would be "paid to individuals through private insurance."[3] In most years, the preferences for the two differing approaches are about equal as shown in Figure 4.1. A key exception occurred in 1992, when health care reform was a prominent theme in Clinton's successful presidential campaign. Preference for a government plan rose to 45 percent, and preference for a private plan dropped to 24 percent. As Congress was poised to act on the Clinton plan, the health care industry mounted a major counterattack; two years later, in 1994, the government plan was preferred by only a 3-point margin; by 1996, a slight plurality preferred the private plan. Subsequently, growing pluralities favored the public plan. In 2008, support for a government health program rose to all-time high of 46 percent, with 33 percent preferring a private health plan.

The failure of the Clinton health care initiative demonstrates the difficulty of achieving fundamental change on a complex issue. It is easy to point out certain negative aspects of a proposal, even if taken in whole the proposal had considerable merit. There seems little doubt that the reversal in public opinion at the time of Clinton's proposed Health Security Act was a major factor leading to its defeat (Koch 1998; Jacobs and Shapiro 2000).

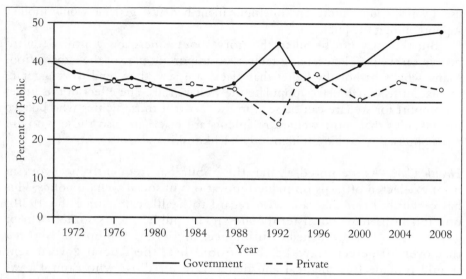

Figure 4.1   Private versus government health insurance. *Source:* National Election Studies, 1970–2008.

In its 2008 survey, support for a government health care program was greater than at any other time in ANES' time series, although still less than a majority. Throughout the 2009–2010 health care debate, there was widespread support for requiring insurers to cover people with preexisting conditions, paying for it by increasing taxes on the rich, and employer-mandated participation in health care insurance. But the circumstances for passage of health care reform were not easy. Powerful interest groups opposed significant change from the status quo and there was a strong public relations campaign against Obama's plan, striking at people's understandable fear of change. Even if concerned about medical costs under the status quo, insured Americans generally were satisfied with the quality of their health care.[4] Americans had questions about three issues: Would reform really improve health care? Would their own health care get better or worse? Would costs significantly increase? When it comes to the government role, opinion was again mixed. In one review of multiple polls, a substantial majority wanted increased regulation of the health system, but 58 percent did not want the government to run the health system (Blendon and Benson 2009). In the end, major health care reform was signed into law by President Obama on March 24, 2010. One week later, the Gallup Poll reported that 47 percent said passing the healthcare bill was "a good thing," 50 percent said it was "a bad thing" and 3 percent had no opinion.

Taxes. Compared to European countries, taxes in the United States take a smaller share of Gross National Product and are less progressive (Alesina and Glaeser 2004). Nevertheless, polls on taxes often portray extreme antitax sentiment by the public. In 2001, 62 percent said the income taxes they "currently pay" were too high (Associated Press). In 2003, 66 percent told the Harris Poll that high taxes had pushed their family to the breaking point. In 2009, 56 percent said they would "not" be willing to pay more taxes to reduce the deficit (CBS News).

The seemingly inconsistent poll data on spending and taxes appear to demonstrate that the public irrationally expects to have its cake and eat it too. Citizens want a plethora of public services (as shown in Table 4.1), but they do not want to pay for them. Of course, survey questions about taxing and spending usually are asked in a vacuum as if spending required no new revenue or as if taxes provided no benefits. When the views of the public are assessed with realistic questions designed to measure the trade-offs between different types of services and the taxes to pay for them, the public appears quite rational. When pressed to make choices with budget constraints, respondents tend to recognize that they cannot have it both ways—more government spending and lower taxes (see also Page and Shapiro 1992; Hansen 1998).

Antitax sentiment has fluctuated over time, partially in response to shifts in the actual tax bite. Since 1947, Gallup has regularly asked its respondents whether federal income taxes are "too high." Antitax sentiment has been at its highest (about 70 percent) following wartime increases from the Korean and the Vietnam War, as well as in the late 1970s as part of an overall antigovernment right turn. At other times, only about half complain about the income tax being too high. One such period of lesser concern about taxes was during the George W. Bush administration, when taxes were cut and stayed cut even though the Iraq War was being fought. By the time of Obama's presidency in 2009, only 46 percent claimed their federal income taxes were "too high" (Gallup).

The most relevant question might not be attitudes toward taxes, but rather the fairness of the tax burden. In general, people see the middle class paying too much while the rich do not pay their fair share (Campbell 2010).[5] Still people do not give the redistributive aspects of tax policy much thought, as shown below.

Public opinion on tax policy took on special relevance during the debate in 2001 over the massive tax cuts benefiting the wealthy that President George W. Bush ultimately pushed through Congress. According to estimates by Citizens for Tax Justice, over the ten-year life of the legislation, the top 1 percent of households would receive an average tax break of $32,247 per household per year, while the bottom 60 percent would get an average annual tax break of only $325.

Bush's tax cuts could probably not have passed without considerable consent among the public. Indeed, the public was polled twenty-five times during the debate over the 2001 Bush tax cut, and on average 56 percent supported it and 33 percent opposed it (Hacker and Pierson 2005). The obvious question is, why did the public seem to support a tax cut that served to promote economic inequality?

One answer is question wording. Hacker and Pierson (2005) contend that the apparent support for the Bush tax cuts was an illusion since respondents were simply asked whether or not they favored a tax cut. There was no mention of costs or trade-offs. Since a majority typically respond that taxes are too high, it is not surprising that when presented with a simple "yes–no" on lower taxes, people tend to say "yes." The authors present examples of instances where tax questions also include trade-offs and find support for tax cuts is noticeably lower.

Another answer is that a favorable opinion about the Bush tax cuts stemmed from an unenlightened sense of self-interest. According to Bartels (2005, 2008), most people disapprove of growing economic inequality but fail to connect this phenomenon to the tax issue, mostly out of simple ignorance. Proponents of the tax cut played on citizen perceptions that their own personal taxes are "too high" and took advantage of the generally low levels of citizen information. The least informed citizens were the ones most likely to favor the tax cuts. Meanwhile, well-informed partisans gravitated to the position of their party. The best informed Republicans were 14 percentage points more likely to favor the tax cuts than the lesser informed. The best informed Democrats were 19 percentage points more likely to oppose the tax cuts than the lesser informed (Lupia et al. 2007).

In any event, the seeming public support for Bush's tax cut that helped it become law seems to have been short lived. In 2009, when asked whether Bush's tax cuts for those making over $250,000 a year should expire, a national survey responded 49 to 42 percent in favor (Democracy Corps).

Civil Rights

Discerning the true attitudes held by white Americans on civil rights issues has proved a difficult and controversial task. Taking easy issues first, polls clearly show at a minimum that Americans have rejected the prevalent white suprema- cist ideology that pervaded mass attitudes as recently as a few decades ago. Poll data from the 1930s and 1940s suggest that perhaps a majority of white Americans once believed blacks to be intellectually inferior and undeserving of equal status with whites. In 1939, a Roper poll found 76 percent of white respondents agreeing that "Negroes" had generally "lower" intelligence than white people (Page and Shapiro 1992). As late as 1944, just 44 percent believed that "Negroes are as intelligent as white people" (Erskine 1962a). By 1994, according to a Harris survey, only 12 percent of whites agreed with the stereo- type that blacks have less native intelligence than other races.

In the analysis of public opinion on racial issues, it is common to distin- guish between questions concerning the goals or ideals of the civil rights movement and government action to actually implement those goals into public policy. The public is more supportive of the abstract goals of the civil rights movement than their implementation. For example, when asked in 1995 if black and white children should go to the same or separate schools, 96 percent of whites preferred the ideal of both races "going to the same schools" (Schuman et al. 1997). But when asked if the government in Washington "should see to it" that black and white children attend the same schools or if this is "not the government's business," just 47 percent of whites supported implementation of the ideal by federal government action (ANES 2000). The same lack of support for implementation was present in 2007 when 63 percent of whites approved of a Supreme Court decision to limit the use of student race in school assignments as a means of integrating schools.[6]

We see a somewhat similar pattern in the trends over time. Whites have become much more liberal on questions concerning the ideals of the civil rights movement, but less so on the implementation of these ideals. In terms of ideals, endorsement of fair employment practices for blacks rose from 42 percent in 1944 to 96 percent by 1972 (Smith and Sheatsley 1984, 14–15. In 1944, 45 percent said, "Negroes should have as good a chance as whites to get a job"; by 1972, a near consensus of 97 percent shared that belief (Page and Shapiro 1992, 69). In 1958, only 38 percent of white respondents indicated they would vote for a well-qualified black presidential candidate; by 2007, 93 percent would do so (see Figure 4.2).

Figure 4.2 presents trends in white support for integrated schools, both in terms of principle and implementation. First, consider the question of whether white and black children should attend the same or separate schools. In 1942, just 30 percent (of whites) said "same school" and 66 percent said "separate schools." Figure 4.2 picks up the series in 1956, when the percent saying "same school" had grown to 49 percent. By 1996 (the last year the question was asked), 96 percent of the white public said they favored black and white children attending the same school. From 1942 to 1996, there was a 65 percentage point increase in white support for integrated schools, perhaps the largest change in public opinion for which we have data.

Figure 4.2 shows a different trend, however, on the question of whether the "government in Washington should see to it" that black and white children go to the same schools. When framed in terms of possible federal action, there is less support for the integration positions, with white Americans more in favor of government action in the 1960s than in the 1970s and later. While opposition to

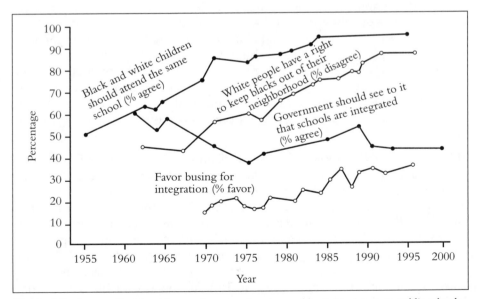

Figure 4.2 Support for school integration, open housing, and busing to integrate public schools.
Source: National Opinion Research Center, Gallup, and General Social Survey.

racial discrimination is almost universal, attitudes about government intervention are anything but consensual.

Still, not all implementation trends are conservative. Figure 4.2 shows that whites became increasingly acceptant of busing children to achieve racial balance in schools and (especially) increasingly opposed to a supposed right to keep blacks from their neighborhoods. By 1996, the number disagreeing that white people "had a right" to keep blacks out of their neighborhood had grown to 87 percent.

Affirmative Action. The most contentious civil rights issue of contemporary politics is "affirmative action" to help blacks (plus other racial minorities and women) advance in the education system and the workplace. While surveys show considerable white opposition to affirmative action programs, the extent of this opposition depends heavily on how the question is framed. If the survey question emphasizes helping the advancement of the disadvantaged, one can obtain majority support for affirmative action in principle. For instance, a 2007 Pew survey randomly asked half its sample, "In order to overcome past discrimination, do you favor or oppose affirmative action programs designed to help blacks, women, and other minorities to get better jobs and education?" Fifty-two percent of whites supported affirmative action, while 37 percent opposed. But when the question emphasizes "preferences" for minorities, support for affirmative action plunges. The other half of the Pew sample was asked, "In order to overcome past discrimination, do you favor or oppose affirmative action programs which give special preferences to qualified blacks in hiring and education?" Support among whites drops to 39 percent, while a plurality of 47 percent now say they oppose affirmative action.

Public reaction to existing affirmative action policies can be interpreted as mixed. When asked about the pace of affirmative action, 36 percent in a 2003 *Los Angeles Times* poll (all races) said affirmative action programs had "gone too far," while 18 percent said they "had not gone far enough." Thirty-six percent saw these programs as "just about adequate now." A CBS poll in 2006 (all races) shows essentially the same results. When asked if affirmative action programs should be ended now, phased out, or continued for the foreseeable future, 12 percent said "end now," 33 percent said "phase out," and 36 percent said "continue."[7]

Whites and Racial Attitudes Today. Some claim that in the twenty-first century, *implicit* racial messages are more likely to elicit negative stereotypes about African Americans than are *explicit* racial messages (Mendelberg 2001, 2008). The distinction can be best illustrated with an example. A random half of a sample got the question: "Some people want to increase spending for new prisons to lock up violent inner city criminals. Others would rather spend this money for antipoverty programs to prevent crime. What about you?" In the other half of the sample the word "inner city" is deleted (Hurwitz and Peffley 2005). The mention of "inner city" yields more support for building prisons. Differences as illustrated by this example suggest that significant racial resentment still exists, but it takes on an increasingly sophisticated guise, sometimes through the use of code words like "inner city." Mendelberg claims that implicit racial messages actually work better than explicit racial messages to ignite racial animosity, although other research suggests the matter is still not settled (Huber and Lapinski 2006, 2008; Hutchings and Jardina 2009).

How does one explain the tepid support among whites for specific remedies to solve the problem of racial discrimination in the face of their overwhelming support for the ideals of racial integration? Two explanations are commonly debated: race per se and the politics of race. The first of these, the "new racism" argument (Sears and Kinder 1971; Kinder and Sanders 1996), holds there has been little change in whites' attitudes about African-Americans, which remain mostly hostile. When asked about policy questions with racial implications, whites are more likely to respond to the racial symbol (e.g., "black") rather than the policy content of the question. However, over the years that public expression of racist sentiment has become increasingly unfashionable. Outright racial discrimination also became illegal. Consequently, people learned it was socially unacceptable to express overtly racist opinions. Instead, racial hostility is expressed indirectly by a glorification of traditional values such as "the work ethic" and *economic* "individualism" (Gomez and Wilson 2006) in which blacks and some other minorities are seen as deficient (Sears et al. 1997; Tarman and Sears 2005). Federico (2006) finds that educated whites are most likely (or best able) to mask their racial attitudes in nontransparent ways. Thus, some of the apparent liberal trend in racial attitudes is not real change but rather reflects the need to express increasingly sophisticated "socially desirable" opinions. Opposition to implementation, usually on grounds other than race, is simply disingenuous.[8]

A rival explanation is simple, straightforward politics. Sniderman and Piazza (1993, 107) argue that "the central problem of racial politics is *not* the problem of prejudice" (italics original). The agenda of the civil rights movement has changed from one of equal opportunity to equal outcomes. No fair-minded person could find consistency between the American Creed and denial of voting rights; segregated universities, workplaces, and lunch counters; and confinement to the back of the bus. But in the eyes of many, the new civil rights agenda of affirmative action very much clashes with the principle of equal treatment for all. Its implementation also requires an activist, expansionist government. Antistatism, manifested as hostility to federal power, is a longstanding tradition in American politics. The political explanation holds that inconsistencies with the American Creed, and concerns about the power and trustworthiness of the federal government, prevent many whites (particularly conservative whites) from translating an abstract commitment to racial equality into support for specific federal policies (Sniderman and Carmines 1997; Sniderman, Crosby, and Howell 2000).[9]

Recent research has shown support for both schools of thought (Feldman and Huddy 2005). The authors looked at support for a college scholarship program where both the race and economic status of the recipient was experimentally manipulated. With the economic class of the hypothetical recipients held constant while their race varied, white respondents were more eager to offer scholarships when told they would go to white students than to African

Americans. Feldman and Huddy also applied a measure of "racial resentment," defined as a belief that blacks are not deserving of special treatment. It was the racially resentful respondents who mainly differentiated by race, more willing to offer scholarships to white children than to black children. This is consistent with the "new racism" thesis. However, complicating matters, this gap was smaller among self-identified "conservatives" than "liberals." Racially resentful conservatives generally opposed scholarships regardless of the recipient's race. This finding, say Feldman and Huddy, is consistent with the "normal politics" explanation. Conservatives who score high on the measure of racial resentment may actually be activating their conservative principles. Further analysis showed that among conservatives, racial resentment "is closely tied to opposition to race-conscious programs regardless of recipient race and is only weakly tied to measures of overt prejudice" (Feldman and Huddy 2005, 168).

To summarize, white racism has been declining, but we should keep in mind that survey respondents have become hesitant to share overtly racist views. Government policies to induce further equality among the races are often opposed. In part, this is due to hidden racial animosity as described earlier. In part, it can be attributed to principled conservatism.

Foreign Policy

Scholars often depict public opinion on questions of foreign policy as being particularly shallow and without meaningful content. Typical is the observation by Light and Lake (1985, 94) that "public opinion polls show that people do not follow foreign affairs closely and often do not know enough about the specifics of a particular issue to form opinions." As applied to most citizens on most foreign policy issues, one cannot easily object to this statement. However, an important foreign policy matter can easily grab public attention and profoundly affect the popularity of the president or the outcome of the next election.

Foreign policy opinions are subject to more abrupt changes than are domestic policy opinions. If *abrupt change* is defined as ten or more percentage points over a single year, abrupt changes are twice as likely on foreign policy as on domestic issues (Page and Shapiro 1989). The explanation is straightforward: There are more dramatic events on the international scene than on the domestic scene. Few domestic occurrences have the impact of the Cuban missile crisis, the Iran hostage crisis, 9/11 and subsequent U.S. involvement in Afghanistan, and the two wars involving Iraq.

Internationalism Versus Isolationism. One indicator of foreign policy sentiment is one's preference for an internationalist versus an isolationist posture in foreign policy. For many people, this dimension serves as a core value that structures other foreign policy opinions. An internationalist, for example, is more likely to favor foreign aid, trade pacts, humanitarian aid, military intervention, and defense spending (Brewer et al. 2004).

Prior to World War II, American opinion was strongly isolationist. In 1937, 70 percent of opinion-holders said U.S. entry into World War I had been a mistake (Free and Cantril 1967, 62). That same year, 94 percent of opinion-holders said the United States should "do everything possible to keep out of foreign wars." But once the United States was involved in World War II, internationalist sentiment increased sharply. By June 1943, 83 percent said the United States would have to play a larger part in world affairs than before the war (Page and Shapiro 1992, 176).

Figure 4.3 tracks post–World War II internationalist versus isolationist sentiment as monitored by the question of whether the United States should "take an active part" or "stay out" of world affairs. Support for internationalism has risen steadily over the years, with one true spike following 9/11. But there have also been two periods of gradual decline, corresponding to the prolonged Vietnam and Iraq Wars, as opposition mounted. With the election of Barack Obama, support for an active U.S. role in global affairs appears to have increased.[10]

Just as Figure 4.3 shows most Americans have favored an internationalist position in foreign affairs, most Americans have historically also favored U.S. participation in the United Nations—despite a minority of vocal critics. In 1997, only 9 percent of the population said we "should give up" our membership in the UN (versus 88 percent who said we should not), and 70 percent had a "mostly favorable" view of the United Nations (21 percent said "mostly unfavorable"). With the advent of the war in Iraq and friction between the United States and the United Nations, by 2005 the "mostly unfavorable" view of the United Nations had risen to 35 percent, returning by 2009 to normal,

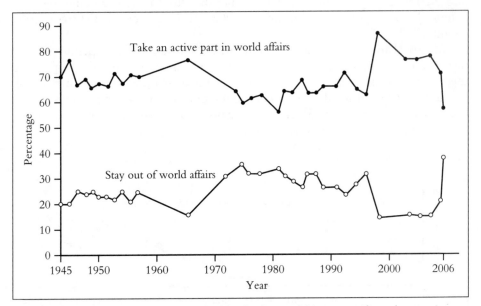

Figure 4.3 "Do you think it would be best for the future of this country if we take an active part in world affairs, or if we stayed out of world affairs?" *Sources:* The U.S. Role in the World Poll, 1996: University of Maryland; Gallup; National Opinion Research Center; General Social Survey; Transatlantic Trends Survey.

with 61 percent having a favorable opinion of the United Nations and just 23 percent an unfavorable opinion (Pew 2009).[11]

Defense Spending. One source of frequently shifting opinion is public perception of the adequacy of defense spending. Figure 4.4 shows a roller coaster of changing beliefs regarding whether the United States is spending "too little on the military, armaments, and defense."

Beginning in 1978, large segments of the public began to believe that U.S. defenses were underfunded. This conservative trend resulted in part from the Soviet Union's invasion of Afghanistan in 1979, which President Carter denounced as "the worst threat to world peace since World War II." Both the Democratic and Republican Party leadership became convinced that the United States was spending too little on defense. Without a credible alternative elite counterargument, public opinion quickly fell into line. Belief that we are spending "too little" on defense reached an all-time high of 56 percent in February of 1980 (GSS).

Following the renewed military buildup under both Carter and Reagan, the citizenry became reassured that America's defenses were again strong. As the 1980s progressed, support for increased defense spending retreated to the level of the early 1970s. With the collapse of the Soviet Union in the early 1990s, support for increases in defense spending fell to record lows. With the advent of war in the Persian Gulf and then the Iraq War, belief that the United States is spending too little on defense began a slow but steady rise. As the war in Iraq bogged down and costs mounted, the belief that "too little" was being spent on defense began a predictable decline, standing at 24 percent in February 2009 (Gallup).

Statistical analysis of trends in public attitudes toward defense spending shows that it follows a rational course. It is not just that spending attitudes respond to the severity of the perceived threat (or the threat people are told to believe). In addition, support for defense spending responds to the waxing and waning of the actual defense buildup. When spending goes up, demand for further spending goes down, and vice versa (Wlezien 1995a).

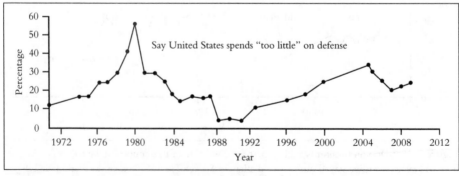

Figure 4.4   Percentage who say the United States is spending "too little" on the military, armaments, and defense. *Source:* Roper, General Social Survey, and Gallup.

Foreign Interventions and War. As we observed in chapter 3, when the United States gets militarily involved in foreign conflicts in remote corners of the world—for example, Nicaragua, Kosovo, or Afghanistan—the public rises from its slumber and begins to pay attention. When the United States gets involved in actual war—from World War II to Iraq—the initial public response has been widespread support. But as wars become prolonged, with an uncertain verdict— Korea, Vietnam, and Iraq—initial support decays.

An important question is, what are the conditions under which the public will support a war effort or cease to do so? One obvious source of eroding support is the steady mounting of casualties (Mueller 1973, 1996, 2005; Gartner and Segura 1998). But casualties can be tolerated when the war is perceived to be just or making progress toward victory (Feaver and Gelpi 2004; Gelpi, Feaver, and Reifler 2004–2005). The United States suffered far more casualties in World War II than in succeeding wars; yet, public opinion polls showed widespread support for continuing toward unconditional victory rather than attempting a negotiated settlement (Berinsky 2009).

Adam Berinsky (2009) argues that the crucial ingredient for obtaining support for a war effort from the public is the support of political elites from whom the public gets its signals. When politicians of all stripes support the war effort, the public generally goes along as well. When elite support divides, as when the parties split over the Iraq War, public support declines—mainly among supporters of the dissenting party. Of course, the degree of elite consensus can influence the degree of consensus among the public. But it can also be that when political leaders and the general public are changing their opinion in the same direction, the leaders and the public are responding to the same flow of events, without one set of individuals necessarily influencing the other.

Cultural Issues

In the first half of the twentieth century, the only types of policy issues that drew strong national attention, including those from pollsters, were social welfare matters involving spending and taxing and foreign affairs. Starting in the 1950s, civil rights pushed toward center stage. Soon after, a new set of concerns called *cultural issues* arrived and never left. In their broadest context, these issues involve conflicts between forces of social change and forces committed to maintaining "traditional moral values." Examples of cultural issues include prayer in public schools, decriminalization of marijuana use, gun control, government restrictions on pornography, and tolerance for gay lifestyles, among others.

On cultural issues, the public is generally thought to be rather conservative. Many but not all the divisions shown in Table 4.2 support this perception. One obvious limitation on the public's social conservatism is a willingness to support sex education in public schools. Despite fierce opposition from some social conservatives, 88 percent of the public believe the schools are a proper forum for teaching the biology of human reproduction.

Even on school prayer, the public's conservatism should not be exaggerated, though when offered only the choice between prayer and no prayer, a substantial

TABLE 4.2	Opinion Distributions on Social Issues (Percentage of Opinion-Holders)		
		Liberal	**Conservative**
Marijuana	Do you think marijuana should be made legal or not?[a]	33 (yes)	67 (no)
Gay rights	Should there be laws to protect homosexuals against job discrimination?[b]	71 (yes)	29 (no)
Pornography	Should there be laws against the distribution of pornography to adults?[c]	61 (no)	39 (yes)
Sex education	Do you favor sex education in the public schools?[c]	88 (yes)	12 (no)
Prayer in schools	Should prayer be permitted in public schools?[d]	29 (no)	69 (yes)
Gun ownership	Right to own guns more important than controlling gun ownership[e]	52 (no)	48 (yes)

Sources: [a]Gallup Poll (2009); [b]ANES (2008); [c]GSS (2006); [d]GSS (2004); [e]Pew (2009).

majority choose prayer (see Table 4.2). But consider responses to a 2005 Gallup survey in which respondents were offered a choice between a spoken prayer or a moment of silence in the public schools. Sixty-nine percent said they preferred a moment of silence.

When it comes to the evolution controversy, a literal interpretation of the Bible holds sway with the public over the views of establishment science. A sizable plurality favors the creationist theory over evolution to account for the origin of human life. Gallup first asked in 1982 which statement came closest to the views of how life began on earth: (1) evolution only, (2) evolution guided by God, or (3) creation by God in the last 10,000 years. In fifteen survey repetitions through 2008, "creation by God in the last 10,000 years" had either a plurality or an outright majority. Evolution becomes a political issue when school boards decide what is to be taught in public schools. When asked by CBS in 2008, 56 percent of Americas favored teaching "creation science" in the public schools along with evolution. In a 2005 Pew poll, 38 percent insisted on teaching creationism *instead* of evolution (Plutzer and Berkman 2008).

Because the cultural issues presented in Table 4.2 have been on the public agenda for no more than a few decades, it is sometimes difficult to establish trend lines of any length. Nevertheless, some trend data are available. In the case of the legalization of marijuana, support has grown steadily but slowly. When the GSS started polling on legalization in 1973, opinion was 81 to 19 percent against legalization. By 2006, the division narrowed to only 2 to 1 against—66 to 34 percent. For pornography laws, the trend has been stable at least since 1973, with those favoring laws against its distribution to anyone ranging between 37 and 42 percent. The same stability occurs for sex education and prayer in the public schools. Opinion in these two areas has been more or less constant for the last thirty years (Niemi, Mueller, and Smith 1989; ANES 2004; GSS 2006).

Not all cultural issues show declining conservatism among the American public. When asked what is more important, protecting the right of Americans to own guns or to control gun ownership, the percentage saying "right to own guns" was at its highest point (51 percent) in May 2009. The low point of 32 percent (1999) followed shortly after the shootings of twelve students at Columbine High School by two of their classmates.[12]

Support for gay rights has increased substantially in recent years (Brewer and Wilcox 2005; Fiorina 2006; Haider-Markel and Joslyn 2008). In 1973, 70 percent of the public said that "sexual relations between adults of the same sex" is always wrong. In 2004, 58 percent said that homosexual relations are "always wrong" (GSS). The public shows greatest support for gays and lesbians when the issue is framed in terms of equal employment rights. In 1977, 56 percent of the public said homosexuals should have "equal rights in terms of job opportunities." By 2008 that figure had risen to 89 percent (Gallup). On the other hand, support for same sex-marriage is mixed, but on a recent upswing. In 1996, 27 percent favored allowing gays and lesbians to marry legally. By May of 2009, 45 percent favored legal marriage between gay and lesbian couples (CNN/ORC). If given a choice of a middle ground, most opt for allowing gays to form "civil unions," but short of marriage.

Law and Order. As can be seen in Figure 4.5, opinions about law and order issues roughly follow changes in the rate of violent crime. In the case of the view that

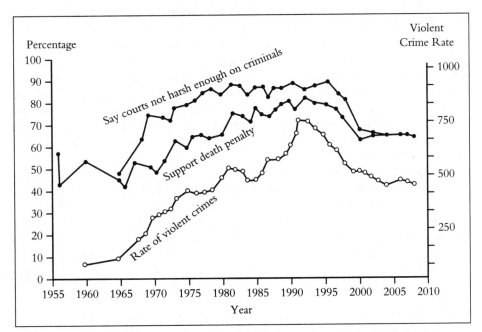

Figure 4.5   Law-and-order opinion and the rate of violent crime. *Sources:* Richard G. Niemi, John Mueller, and Tom W. Smith, *Trends in Public Opinion* (New York: Greenwood, 1989); General Social Survey (1989–2006); Harold W. Stanley and Richard G. Niemi, *Vital Statistics of American Politics, 2007–2008* (Washington, DC: Congressional Quarterly, 2009); FBI Uniform Crime Reports.

courts do not deal harshly enough with criminals, opinion shows a decided conservative trend starting in the mid-1960s through 1995. Then it begins to move in a liberal direction. The data show support for the view that courts do not deal harshly enough with criminals. In 2006, this position was endorsed by 65 percent of the public, up 20 percentage points from 1965, but down from its all-time high of 80 percent in 1998. Interestingly, the public's apparent taste for greater punitiveness has not caught up with the actual trend toward longer criminal sentences. Conceivably some respondents confront the survey question about harshness toward criminals in a factual vacuum and respond simply as if it were a referendum on the goodness or badness of crime.

Public opinion about the death penalty is particularly important. Compared to other issues, citizens have firmer opinions on the death penalty. The public is also aware of the positions on this issue taken by presidential candidates and tell pollsters that it is important for their vote decision[13] (but see Chapter 9 on issue voting). Further, public opinion on the death penalty figures prominently into many Supreme Court decisions on the issue. In both *Furman v. Georgia,* a decision in 1972 banning the death penalty, and *Gregg v. Georgia*, reinstating it in 1976, the court in defining cruel and usual punishment said, using the same words in both cases, that the death penalty "is not fastened to the absolute but many acquire meaning as public opinion becomes enlightened by a humane justice" (Baumgartner, De Boef, and Boydstun 2008).

There is some debate over whether punitive opinion changes in reaction to changes in the crime rate (as would appear from Figure 4.5), media coverage of crime, or both. In a statistical analysis of opinion about the death penalty, Baumgartner, De Boef, and Boydstun (2008) find that homicide rates and media coverage have about equal effects in moving opinion about the death penalty. They also find that there is a significant time lag between changes in crime rates and changes in public opinion. We see that lag illustrated in Figure 4.5, where the rate of violent crime begins to drop sharply in 1990 but public opinion moves much more slowly in a liberal direction. Baumgartner et al. estimate it takes about five years for opinion to catch up with what we would predict statistically based on changes in the violent crime rate.

Support for the death penalty for convicted murderers is influenced significantly by the way the question is asked. The most frequently asked version states, "Are you in favor of the death penalty for persons convicted of murder." The latest reading (October 2009) shows 65 percent in favor (Gallup). If respondents are also offered (in additional to the death penalty) an option of "life imprisonment with no possibility of parole," support for the death penalty drops to 53 percent (CNN 2009). Since forty-eight of the fifty states offer this latter sentencing alterative, it would seem the more appropriate question to ask.

Equality for Women Opinion polls show a growing support across the years for equality for women. From Gallup and GSS, we have data spanning fifty years on the question of whether or not the public would vote for a qualified woman for president—the ultimate nontraditional role. Figure 4.6 shows growth in support, from a minority view in the 1930s to near unanimity in the 1990s, only to

Figure 4.6   Would vote for a qualified woman or a qualified black for president. *Source:* Gallup, GSS.

drop off somewhat in the twenty-first century. However, the question may be contaminated by social desirability. When using a nonobtrusive measurement method (the list experiment), support for a woman president decreases by about 20 percent (Streb, Burrell, Frederick, and Genovese 2008).

Over the decades, the public shifted from general opposition to the idea of a woman president to a general accepting the idea in principle.[14] Other opinion indicators on the role of women show a similar pattern. Since 1972, the ANES has been asking respondents if women should have "an equal role with men in running business, industry, and government" or whether a "woman's place is in the home." In 1972, a mere 59 percent (of opinion-holders) chose the "equal role" option. By 1980, 75 percent did. By 2008, the division among opinion-holders was ninety-three to seven in favor of women having an active role rather than saying women should stay home.[15]

Abortion The most salient of the social issues from the 1970s on into the twenty-first century has been abortion. In 2005, 1.21 million abortions took place in the United States, down from the high point in 1996 when there were 1.36 abortions.[16] Americans tend to oppose abortion on moral grounds while supporting the right to abortion as a matter of public policy. In 2009, for example, 56 percent of respondents said they "personally believe that abortion is wrong" (Gallup) while in October of 2008, 53 percent said abortion should be legal in most cases (Pew). Even for the hot button issue of abortion, many Americans have ambivalent feelings (Craig, Kane, and Martinez 2002).

The public debate on abortion tends to stress the extremes, with the "pro-life" advocates demanding an end to all abortions and the "pro-choice" advocates demanding abortion on request. But most Americans favor neither polar position. In a 2009 Gallup survey, 22 percent said that "abortion should be legal in any circumstances" and 23 percent said that "abortion should be illegal under all circumstances." The majority, 53 percent, said abortion should be legal, but only under certain circumstances (3 percent had no opinion).

We can discover the circumstances under which the public feels abortion should be allowed. Since 1972, the General Social Survey has been asking respondents if "you think it should be possible for a pregnant woman to obtain a legal abortion . . ." and then specifying six different circumstances. We can group these circumstances into "traumatic" and "elective," with traumatic being external circumstances beyond the woman's control including danger to her health, damage to the fetus, and rape or incest. Elective reasons include personal and economic considerations—for example, if a married woman wants no more children, the family cannot afford more children, or if an unmarried pregnant woman does not wish to marry the father. Opinion on these items has been remarkably stable since the *Roe v. Wade* decision in 1973 (Fiorina 2006; GSS). Public support for abortion rights in traumatic and elective circumstances in the 2008 General Social Survey was

Traumatic Abortion		Elective Abortion	
Defective fetus	70%	Married, does not want children	43%
Health danger	85	Cannot afford children	41
Rape/Incest	72	Does not want to marry	39

Most Americans favor some restrictions on abortion rights. According to a 2003 Gallup survey, 88 percent of the public favored a law requiring physicians to inform patients about alternatives to abortion before performing the procedure, and in the same survey 72 percent favored a law requiring "the husband of a married woman be notified" if a woman wants an abortion. In 2005, a Pew Research Poll showed that 73 percent favored a law requiring parental notification before a pregnant teenager under eighteen could get an abortion; also in 2005, a Quinnipiac poll found that 70 percent favored a 24-hour waiting period before an abortion took place.

Despite majorities favoring some restrictions, Americans oppose a total ban on abortion rights, as only a minority of the public favors reversing *Roe v. Wade* (which in most states would effectively outlaw all abortions). When the public was asked in 2009 if the *Roe* decision should be overturned, 68 percent said "no" compared with 30 percent who wanted the ruling overturned (CNN/ORC). At the same time, those who want a total ban seem to hold the most intense opinions. Of the 18 percent in the 2008 ANES survey who said their views on abortion were "extremely important" in terms of casting their vote, 34 percent favored banning all abortions. For everyone else, only 11 percent favored a total ban.

It seems clear that the public wants abortion kept legal, but with some restrictions. Measured by Gallup's standard abortion question, asked every year since 1975, pro-choice support peaked in 1994, when 33 percent said "abortion should be legal under any circumstances." By 2008, only 28 percent said so. The slight decline since then is probably in part due to the highly charged debate over pro-life issues such as "partial birth abortions." Also, there is some evidence that younger people in recent years are less supportive of abortion rights than previous generations (Wilcox and Carr 2010).[17] When the choice is framed as "pro-life" versus "pro-choice," the division is close to an even split.

4-3 General Ideological Movement

The preceding sections have shown trends on specific survey items. For a particular issue, opinion might become more conservative over time, or more liberal—or, as is often the case, it may just stay the same from one survey reading to the next. If there is a general ideological trend from the data we have examined, it would seem to be lost in the details. A challenging question is whether the public regularly undergoes changes in its "ideological mood." Conceivably, one could detect broad currents of opinion that sometimes flow in the liberal direction and sometimes in the conservative direction. We do know that any general ideological movement cannot be large. From one year to the next, net opinion on any issue rarely changes more than a few percentage points. And large movements generally are responses to events unique to the issue, such as when defense spending preferences once fluctuated in response to the momentary intensity of the Cold War.

One way to locate trends in liberalism or conservatism on the part of the public is simply to record changes in the degree to which people call themselves liberals or conservatives. However, as shown in the previous chapter, self-ranking as liberal or conservative is sometimes questionable for the reason that many people lack adequate understanding of these terms. At a minimum, though, changes in how people describe themselves ideologically should reveal shifts in how fashionable are the terms *liberal* and *conservative*.

In polls taken between the late 1930s and the mid-1960s, respondents remained about evenly divided between self-declared liberals and self-declared conservatives. But then a conservative shift began so that by 1970, conservatives clearly outnumbered liberals, typically by a ratio of about 3 to 2. This change is puzzling, as the public's stands on issues did not obviously become more conservative at the same time. Why did the liberal label go into disfavor so suddenly in the late 1960s?

To some extent, the sudden shift toward "conservatism" reflected an increased public concern about issues on which people saw themselves as conservative (e.g., law-and-order issues) and less public concern about issues on which people saw themselves as liberal (e.g., New Deal social welfare issues). Also, in the changing 1960s, opponents of civil rights legislation frequently justified their position in terms of conservative ideology rather than opposition to the equal-opportunity goals of the civil rights movement. Finally, the mid-1960s were a time when much liberal legislation (such as Medicare, federal aid to education, and major civil rights protection) was enacted. As policy became more liberal, people's ideological frame of reference changed. To be a liberal was to seek even more liberal policies rather than simply to support the new status quo.

In any case, the growth of conservative self-identification in the late 1960s was a one-time event. Over the past forty-plus years, people have preferred the "conservative" label to the "liberal" label by a ratio that sometimes approaches 2 to 1, with a plurality choosing the moderate category over both extremes. Figure 4.7 shows the distribution of the electorate's ideological self-identification from 1976 to 2008. The figure is notable for the absence of any trend. In terms of ideological identification, the electorate shows essentially the same distribution for administrations as varied as Carter, Reagan, Clinton, and George W. Bush.[18]

A second way to monitor changes in liberalism/conservatism is to carefully estimate movement in responses to multiple survey items containing left–right policy content. James Stimson (1999) has performed such an investigation, averaging trends in opinion across a range of subject matter. Stimson's updated findings, shown in Figure 4.8, reveal an oscillating movement of what he calls the electorate's ideological "mood." His mood index shows an increase in liberalism in the 1950s and early 1960s, followed by a decline in the late 1960s and 1970s, followed again by a liberal surge in the 1980s, leveling off in the 1990s. The new century saw Stimson's measure of mood swing more conservative following 9/11, only to swing toward liberalism toward the end of the decade. The scale shown represents movement on the scale of the percentage of liberal (among opinion-holders). Thus, the maximum difference in "mood" is a seventeen-point range from the liberal "high" of the early 1960s to a conservative "low" around 1979.[19]

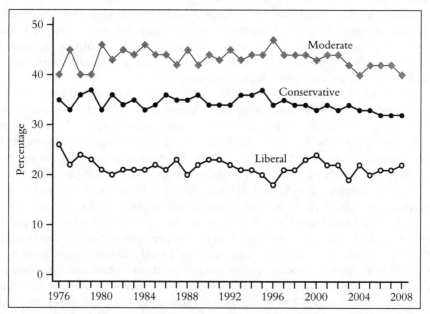

Figure 4.7   Ideological identification of the U.S. Public, 1976–2008 *Question:* "How would you describe your views on most political matters? Generally, do you think of yourself as liberal, moderate, or conservative?" *Source:* CBS/NYT Polls averaged yearly.

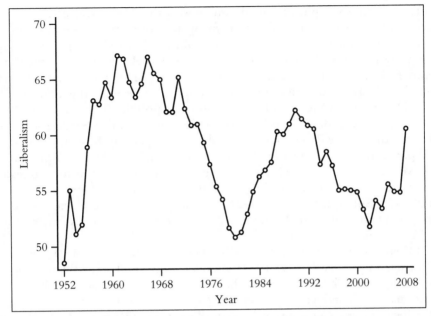

Figure 4.8 The public's policy "mood," 1952–2008. *Source:* James A. Stimson.

One can read the fluctuation in the national mood as the ebb and flow of the electorate's net demand for policy change. This demand is sensitive to changes in public policy. When Congress passes major liberal legislation in response to a liberal mood, as in the 1960s, the demand for liberalism is satisfied and the electorate's mood turns conservative. Similarly, when congressional action turns conservative in response to mood, as under Reagan's presidency in the 1980s, the demand for conservatism is satiated and national mood turns more liberal (Erikson, MacKuen, and Stimson 2002). The liberal surge of 2008 (necessary author change to adjust for recent events) can be accounted for as a reaction to the conservatism of the George W. Bush administration. Policy that pushes in one ideological direction induces the public to favor change in the opposite direction.

4-4 General Partisan Movement

From an electoral standpoint, one of the most important indicators is the distribution of party identification among the categories of Democrat, Republican, and Independent. The conventional view among political scientists regarding trends in party identification is that macrolevel partisanship is quite stable except for the rare shock of a "partisan realignment." Partisan realignments are precipitated by political parties making major changes in their policy orientations. As parties' policy images change in fundamental ways, the electorate responds with surprisingly large shifts in party identification.

The classic example of a realignment was the New Deal of the 1930s, when the electorate transformed from predominantly Republican to Democrat (Burnham 1970, 119–20; Sundquist 1973, 183–217). This change came in response to the Great Depression under a Republican president and Democratic president Franklin Roosevelt's response. Roosevelt was first elected in 1932, as the electorate demanded change with the onset of the Great Depression. Once in office, Roosevelt's policies, known as the New Deal, greatly expanded the role of the federal government to deal with the national emergency. People tended to align their partisanship anew based on their preferences for or against Roosevelt's economic liberalism. Although no polls were available until 1936, trends in election outcomes and voter registration clearly showed a major electoral shift in favor of the Democratic Party (Ladd 1970; Sundquist 1973, 183–217). To some extent, the electorate's division into Democrats and Republicans even today can be traced to the New Deal realignment.

If there had been polls in the 1920s, they would have shown a Republican dominance in partisanship. By 1937, when a national poll asked the party identification question for the first time, the Democrats predominated. In 99 percent of national polls conducted between 1937 and the present, Democrats outnumbered Republicans. On paper at least, the Democratic Party has had a decisive edge in identification.

In theory, the party system is stable for long periods punctuated only by realignment shocks such as the New Deal. Looking back on a half-century of political history, some scholars see signs of a more recent realignment (or something like it) in the 1960s, when issues like civil rights and social policy began to divide the parties nationally (Aldrich and Niemi 1995; Aldrich 2003). Others question the value of conceiving partisan history as equilibrium punctuated by sharp realignments (Mayhew 2002). In any case, it is now clear that the net direction of partisanship within the electorate is constantly moving over time.

As discussed in chapter 3, individual-level party identification is quite stable over time, as individuals rarely change their party preference. Still, when people do change partisanship (even if momentarily), they move in one-sided fashion in response to events. Figure 4.9 shows the annual reading of party identification in the Gallup Poll since 1945. Measured as the percentage of Democrats among combined Democrat and Republican identifiers, this macrolevel index has been dubbed "macropartisanship" (MacKuen, Erikson, and Stimson 1989). The graph shows palpable movement, with what usually is a Democratic edge that is sometimes quite narrow but at other times a hefty two to one advantage in the count of partisan identifiers. The partisan landscape changes via gradual evolution as well as realignment shock.

There were several changes in the nation's party identification over the last half of the twentieth century. The Democrats generally gained from World War II to a peak of support around 1964. Then the Republicans rebounded, only to show precipitous losses following the Watergate revelations of 1973 and 1974. The Democratic gain was followed by a strong Republican trend in the 1980s. Around the turn of the century, the electorate became almost evenly divided

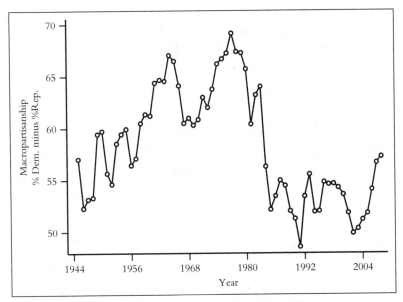

Figure 4.9   Macropartisanship, 1945–2009. Compiled from Gallup Polls.

between Democrats and Republicans. Then, toward the end of the George W. Bush administration, the Democrats more than recovered their losses.

Close investigation of partisan trends shows that macropartisanship tracks both presidential approval (or, more accurately, the causes of approval) and economic conditions (MacKuen, Erikson, and Stimson 1989; Erikson, MacKuen, and Stimson 1998, 2002; but see Green, Palmquist, and Schickler 1998, 2002 for another view). For instance, the combination of economic recovery and the positive appeal of President Reagan helped the Republicans gain in the 1980s. The George W. Bush presidency presents a mixed story. Following 9/11, the Republicans surged to a temporary lead, followed by substantial losses as Bush's popularity declined during his second term.

Interestingly, movement of party identification bears no resemblance to the movement of ideological mood or ideological identification previously discussed. The electorate's relative favor for Republicans or Democrats is totally unrelated to the electorate's swings between conservatism and liberalism. Although many people choose their partisanship based on ideology, the macrolevel movement of partisanship responds more to perceptions of party performance in office than to ideological preference.

One further trend of note in party identification is the growth in the proportion of the electorate who reject each major party, preferring to call themselves Independents. From World War II to about 1966, only between 22 and 25 percent of the public typically called themselves Independents. Then, as the nation faced the Vietnam War, youth unrest, and the peak of the civil rights revolution, a major rejection of the parties began. Since the late 1960s, about one-third of the electorate has called itself Independent. There is no general trend toward weakened partisanship, however. Recent decades have seen a resurgence in partisan strength, with a majority of those identifying with one of the major parties calling themselves a "strong" Democrat or "strong" Republican (Bartels 2000).

4-5   Presidential Approval

Without a doubt, the most closely watched political indicator in the United States is the president's approval rating. Unlike the other macrolevel attitudinal indicators we have discussed, presidential approval shows fluctuations so large as to attract attention from both politicians and the general public. The president's approval rating takes on importance because it is widely believed to measure the president's degree of political support at the moment. Congress may be more likely to enact the policy proposals of a president who shows popular support (Canes-Wrone and de Marchi 2002; Bond, Fleisher, and Wood 2003). Presidential approval also provides a guide to reelection prospects (Lewis-Beck and Rice 1982; Brody and Sigelman 1983; Erikson and Wlezien 2008).

While many polling organizations ask some variant of the presidential approval question, the standard measure is Gallup's question, asked regularly for over fifty years. When the Gallup Organization polls the American public, it regularly asks its respondents whether they "approve" of the president's performance, "disapprove" of the president's performance, or have no opinion. Attention generally focuses on the percentage (of all respondents) who approve of the president's current performance.

Gallup's sampling of presidential approval began with sporadic monitoring of Franklin Roosevelt in the late 1930s, when public opinion polling was in its infancy. However, regular readings of Roosevelt's approval rating were interrupted by World War II. Beginning with Harry Truman, presidents have been monitored in terms of public approval on virtually a continuous monthly basis. This database provides enough information that, in general terms at least, we now know which kinds of circumstances increase a president's popularity and which lead to its decline. In condensed form, Figure 4.10 depicts the history of presidential approval polling over a half-century, from Truman to Clinton. Figure 4.11 graphs the popularity, month to month, of the recent presidency of George W. Bush.[20]

All presidents enjoy some time above 50 percent approval, and most have unhappily spent some time below the 50 percent baseline. Presidents Truman, Nixon, Carter, and both Bushes all spent time near or below the 30 percent approval level. Three sources account for most variation in a president's approval rating: (1) the honeymoon effect, (2) the rally-round-the-flag effect, and (3) the economy.

The Honeymoon

Every president starts the term with a rather high level of political support, with approval ratings in the 70 percent range not unusual. Then, as the term unfolds, the approval rating undergoes a gradual but inevitable decline. It is not surprising to find that presidents start out with an aura of goodwill, with even supporters of

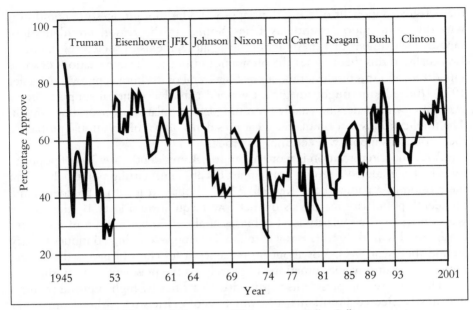

Figure 4.10   Presidential approval, Truman to Clinton. *Source*: Gallup Poll.

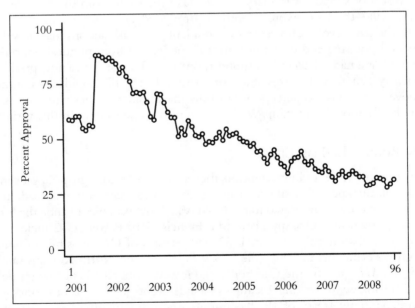

Figure 4.11   Presidential approval by month, George W. Bush. (Values for 9/01 and 3/03 include only polls post-9/11 and post-invasion, respectively.) *Source:* Gallup Poll.

the defeated opponent offering their approval. The more interesting question is why this honeymoon eventually fades. Some say the reason presidents lose support over time is that they cannot please all segments of society all the time. Eventually, so this theory goes, the president must upset the expectations of some supporters, and this disillusionment creates a spiral of declining approval (Mueller 1973). Indeed, one might imagine a general rule that political support decays over time, with leaders inevitably becoming less popular the longer they govern. The implication is that no matter what presidents do to solve national problems, their political support will continue to erode.

A second interpretation is more optimistic. A president's early loss of popularity is best considered a retreat from an artificially high starting point rather than the erosion of a natural base (Kernell 1978). About a year into a presidency, the president's popularity reaches its natural, lower equilibrium level. By the second year, a president's popularity level stabilizes at about 50 percent. From this point on, approval is as likely to rise as it is to fall. The approval rating continues to vary around the usual average of about 50 percent—a function of events that reflect sometimes positively and sometimes negatively on the president's stewardship.

The basic reason presidents begin with an artificially high approval rating is that newly elected presidents start out free of criticism—either from other politicians or from the media. This grace period arises in part because the president has just proved his popularity at the ballot box. It also arises because the new president is a blank slate; he has conducted few official acts to be second-guessed. Instead of criticizing a new president, politicians and the media respond with words of support. Ordinary citizens take their cue from these expressions of goodwill—they, too, express approval (Brody 1991).

As the term evolves, however, the president must take actions that are subject to second-guessing and criticism from the media and from political opponents. The result is a natural decline in support. But after the first year, a new president's popularity generally stabilizes at a more natural level. Still, popularity continues to move in response to perceptions of how the president copes with events and the task of national leadership. We examine next some sources in this variation.

Rally-Round-the-Flag Effect

From time to time, public attention focuses on some foreign policy event—perhaps an unexpected crisis or a major treaty or U.S. intervention abroad. In the past, most of these were related to the Cold War. Early examples include the Soviet shooting-down of a U.S. spy plane (the Francis Gary Powers U-2 incident) in 1960, the Cuban missile crisis in 1962, and seizures of U.S. ships by communist foreign governments in 1968 (the U.S.S. *Pueblo* by the North Koreans) and in 1975 (the *Mayaguez* by the Cambodians). However, not all salient foreign policy events are anxiety provoking. Examples include events such as major treaties (e.g., Nixon's Moscow Treaty of 1972), summits (starting with Eisenhower's Geneva summit conference with Soviet leaders in 1955), and peace efforts such as Johnson's bombing halt (1968) and Carter's Camp David accords (1978) establishing the foundation for peaceful relations between Israel and Egypt.

What these events have in common is a focus on foreign policy. Generally, major foreign policy events are followed by a short-term surge in support for the president—what is called the rally-round-the-flag effect. These are special moments when eyes turn to the president, and the media and national politicians are seen to unite behind the chief executive.

Going to war is a special case. In the short term, wars traditionally result in the showering of approval on the president. One example comes from the early days of polling. While Roosevelt's approval ratings in the late 1930s were no more than respectable (typically in the mid-50s), entry into World War II saw his numbers rise into the 70s. More recent wars show similar patterns. Truman gained 9 points following the start of the Korean War in 1950. Johnson gained 8 points following a major escalation of the Vietnam War in 1966. Lesser conflicts, such as Johnson's 1965 invasion of the Dominican Republic and Reagan's invasion of Grenada, were also followed by surges in presidential popularity. At one time, the record for the biggest gain from a war was the first President Bush's popularity surge to Gallup's record high of 87 percent in March 1991 following the brief first Gulf War against Iraq. The record was eclipsed by George W. Bush's even greater surge in popularity to 90 percent in some polls following 9/11.

But the political rewards from wars and invasions can be short lived (Mueller 1973, 1994; Berinsky 2009). Bush's popularity decline following the protraction of the Iraq War is fresh in memory. Vietnam provides the prime example. The Johnson administration miscalculated the American public's taste for a prolonged war in Vietnam. Johnson fell in a few short years from the 70s to the low 30s in approval. During the Korean conflict, Truman declined even further—into the 20s—as did Carter during the Iran hostage crisis. Both Truman and Johnson declined to seek reelection, and Carter was defeated in 1980. The first Bush's unique popularity after the first Gulf War shows what a short successful war can do to presidential popularity. But his approval decline in the war's aftermath (from 67 percent in August 1991 to 46 percent by January 1992) provides another lesson—that the political benefit from any presidential success may be short-lived.

The Economy

It is common knowledge that the president's approval rating rises and falls with the state of the economy. When unemployment or inflation rises, the president is blamed. When these indicators of economic gloom decline, the president is praised. Naturally, approval ratings reflect these tendencies. It is as if the electorate reads the state of the economy as a sign of the president's competence.

The exact mechanism by which the electorate converts economic perceptions into presidential approval has been the subject of considerable scholarly investigation. The simplest mechanism would be the straightforward response of personal pocketbook considerations—that when people face good economic times they support the president, and when they face hard times they do not. Consider, however, that most people, most of the time, know that they do not owe their current economic fortune to the president. If the economy is thriving, a person who just got fired or laid off is not likely to blame the president for his or her personal misfortune. Similarly, if the economy is clearly troubled, a person who earns a big raise and promotion is not likely to attribute this good fortune to the president.

But people *do* recognize the state of the general economy as having some relevance to their personal economic well-being. Consequently, citizens reward or punish the president not on the basis of their personal circumstances but rather their perceptions of the national economy. Such responses are called *sociotropic*, as people respond to how *society* is faring rather than how they personally are doing economically (Kinder and Kiewiet 1979). But the motive is still largely personal. People care about the national economy because they personally can be affected.

Evaluations of economic performance tend to be prospective rather than retrospective—that is, people update their evaluations based on prospects for the economy's future rather than evaluating its recent performance. We know this because, statistically, presidential approval tracks consumer expectations about the nation's economic future rather than consumer evaluations of current conditions (MacKuen, Erikson, and Stimson 1992; Erikson, MacKuen, and Stimson 2002). In sum, when people evaluate the president based on the economy, they do not wait until they feel the good or bad times directly in their pocketbook. Rather, they evaluate the president based on economic conditions generally, including the consensus of opinion regarding the economic future.

Presidential Approval and Presidential Success

Each president's record of approval follows its own arc, reflecting the public's often changing judgment of his performance. Approval is more volatile than other indicators of public opinion—one would not want to predict a president's approval numbers a year ahead from the president's numbers today. Approval is distinct for each president—one would not want to predict a new president's approval numbers based on those of his predecessor. And a president's approval numbers are not always a measure of his actual level of success, objectively measured.

A useful lesson is the approval record of President Harry Truman. Based on Gallup's numbers, Truman was one of the least popular presidents. But historians judge (and the public feels in retrospect) that Truman was among the most successful.

4-6 Conclusion: What Moves Public Opinion?

We have seen that public opinion has changed dramatically on many issues over the seventy years or so since the advent of reliable public opinion polling. Large shifts have sometimes occurred over short periods, or incremental moves have aggregated over the years to a fundamental reversal in American political sentiment.

Abrupt changes in public opinion normally can be traced to the public's reaction to current events. Explaining incremental change is more complex. Cohort replacement is certainly one factor. Almost 50 percent of the American electorate is replaced every twenty years (Abramson 1983, 54). When we see dramatic change in support for the ideals of the civil rights movement between 1960 and 1980, it is important to understand that only about half of those comprising the adult population in 1960 were still part of that population in 1980. The new 50 percent enter the electorate often socialized to a different set of political values. Thus, the change that appears in support for the ideas of the civil rights movement does not necessarily mean that people have changed their minds, although that may have happened as well.

Finally, the effects of modernization have certainly affected the political opinions of the American public. Included here are demographic trends such as rising levels of education, the decline of the rural population and growth of large cities, and the increasing penetration of the national mass media to all sectors of society. The advances of education, urbanization, and media penetration have undoubtedly played a role in the public's changing political attitudes and preferences.

Notes

1. Not everyone agrees that the "noise" in surveys is random. Althaus (2003) argues this noise is mostly not random, and often serves to the disadvantage of those in the lower economic strata as they are less likely to express opinions.
2. Responses to the services and spending question are based on a 7-point scale (see Appendix), where 1–3 are combined at one end, 4 is the midpoint, and 5–7 are combined at the other end.
3. On the 7-point scale, points 1, 2, and 3 are collapsed to indicate preference for a government health plan, and points 5, 6, and 7 are collapsed to indicate preference for a private plan.
4. In one poll, 93 percent with health insurance said they were very satisfied with the quality of their care. ABC News/USA Today/Kaiser Family Foundation Health Care Poll (September 7–12, 2006).
5. In 2009, 16 percent said "lower income people" paid too little in taxes. Only 5 percent of the same sample said "middle income" people paid too little, while 60 percent said "upper income people" paid too little.
6. Just 30 percent of blacks approved *Meredith v. Jefferson County Board of Education* (2007): Survey conducted for Newsweek by Princeton Research Associates, July 2–3, 2007. Dataset downloaded from IPOLL 5/11/2009 and analysis done by authors.
7. For more on trends in affirmative action attitudes, see Steeh and Krysan (1996), Sharp (1999), and Stoker (2001). Questions about affirmative action were rarely asked by pollsters in the 1960s and early 1970s, when affirmative action policies were pioneered.
8. According to this view, the racially prejudiced find a respectable outlet for expressing their views on symbolic issues such as the busing of school children for racial balance. It has been demonstrated, for example, that the most vocal opponents of busing are often nonparents with little direct stake in the matter (Sears, Hensler, and Speer 1979).
9. White racial attitudes are difficult to measure (Kuklinski, Cobb, and Gilens 1997) because racial appeals are often subtle. See Mendelberg (2001) regarding racial appeals to whites during election campaigns.

10. In 2003, 50 percent completely agreed that "It's best for the U.S. to be active globally." The percentage dropped to 42 percent in 2007, and then recovered to 51 percent in 2009. The largest gain between 2007 and 2009 (16 percent) came from Democrats (Pew).

11. Transatlantic Trend Survey, May 30–June 17, 2005; Pew April 23–May 6, 2007; May 27–June 10, 2009.

12. The question was first asked in 1993.

13. A 2000 ABC News /Washington Post Poll found 72 percent of respondents saying the death penalty issue was either "very" or "somewhat" important to them in deciding how to vote in the 2000 presidential election.

14. See Streb et al. (2008) for a significant qualification. They argue that the high level of support for a woman for president has a significant social desirability component, and present evidence to support their contention.

15. Respondents place themselves on a 7-point scale in answering this question, with 4 being neutral. Responses 1–3 were combined to indicate preference for an equal role of men and women in government and society. Respondents at 5–7 were combined to indicate a preference for women staying home. Category 4 (neutral) was deleted for this comparison.

16. Data from the Alan Guttmacher Institute at www.guttmacher.org, downloaded 05/28/2009.

17. Using the GSS data, Wilcox and Wade merged 2000–2006 data and divided the sample in four age groups. The 18–29-year-old group was the least pro-choice of these age groups, in contrast to previous GSS readings where the oldest age group was least pro-choice.

18. For a thorough discussion of trends in ideological identification and whether or not they can be explained, see Box-Steffensmeier, Knight, and Sigelman (1998).

19. For still another analysis of ideological trends using multiple survey items, see Smith 1990.

20. Figures 4.8 and 4.9 do not do justice to the many ups and downs of presidential approval. One excellent graphic presentation that overlays presidents' approval histories with the events of their administration can be found at the *Wall Street Journal's* Web site. See http://online.wsj.com/public/resources/documents/info-presapp0605-31.html

5 Political Socialization and Political Learning

JUST AS ONE LEARNS TO READ AND WRITE and identify fashionable clothing, one learns about politics. A considerable portion of this learning occurs before one is old enough to enter the voting booth. Adults, for example, tend to generalize from their idealization of childhood family authority structure to their preferred authority structure for the state (Barker and Tinnick 2006). A central premise in the study of childhood socialization to politics, called "the primacy principle," holds that what one learns as a preadult affects one's later political life. This assumption is crucial, for there is little reason for interest in the reaction of preadults to their political environment except insofar as it affects their adult attitudes and behaviors.

To *socialize* someone means "to make social, make fit for life in companionship with others" (*Random House Dictionary*). Thus, one perspective on political socialization focuses on the learning of attitudes, values, and acceptable forms of behavior necessary to fit into the established political and social order. It is the learning or failure to learn the lessons of being a good citizen, as defined by the politic status quo (Easton and Dennis 1969). Another perspective sees the field as more akin to generic political learning. The emphasis is on individual political change throughout the life cycle rather than on molding the person to fit the political community (Jennings 2004).

This chapter presents a journey through the political life cycle, starting with the formative years. We first trace the evolution of political learning from earliest childhood up to the approach of adult life, evaluating the agents of socialization along the way. We then analyze aspects of political socialization during adulthood.

5-1 The Preadult Years: Socialization to Citizenship

In every political system, children are indoctrinated from a young age to accept the ongoing political order. According to David Easton and Jack Dennis (1969, 5), pioneers in the study of political socialization, the persistence of the political system "may in part be dependent upon the success of a society in producing children most of whom acquire positive feelings about it. Childhood socialization involves encouraging the young to identify with the regime and inculcating a sense of loyalty and belonging to the political order." More than that, it also involves the transmission of the political culture from one generation to the next.

To analyze the development of preadult political orientations, we divide the early years into three periods: early childhood (ages three to nine), late childhood (ages ten to twelve), and adolescence (ages thirteen to eighteen). These are approximate categories, for just as children differ in their physical development, they differ in their political development. In conclusion, we discuss the consequences of socialization for citizenship.

Early Childhood

Much of what we know about early childhood socialization comes from studies conducted decades ago of children from preschool through the eighth grade. The dawning of political recognition begins before children commence their formal education. Perhaps the most important lesson children learn at this early stage is a sense of national identity. Preschoolers frequently confuse political authority with religious authority. In a study of kindergarten children in California, Moore, Lare, and Wagner (1985) report that when asked, "Who does the most to run the country?" 30 percent responded "God" or "Jesus." The most significant public figures for the young child are the president and the police officer. One school of thought contends that both officials play a major role in promoting the child's attachment to and identification with the political order. Schwartz (1975) found that 90 percent of her preschool sample were able to recognize the "man in the picture" as being "the policeman," and 75 percent were able to answer correctly when asked, "What does the policeman do?" The responses most frequently given concerned regulating traffic, helping lost children, and "catching bad people." The children, for the most part, saw the police officer as a benevolent authority figure symbolizing the State.

Public servants are not the only political symbols visible to preschool children. They also manifest a sense of political community. When presented with a picture showing nine different flags, the vast majority were able to identify the American flag. When asked, "Which flag is your favorite?" 60 percent chose the American flag and another 19 percent the Liberian flag, which closely resembles the American flag (Schwartz 1975, 242–43). Thus, preschool children both know and identify with the symbol of the American political community. We see the same pattern in other countries. In the Middle East, Arab and Jewish preschool children quickly develop a strong preference for the flag representing their own particular group. This early learning is thought to lay one of the foundations for national identity (Lawson 1975).

As the child begins early grade school, the content of the young person's political world begins to expand rapidly. However, the increase in content is almost entirely in terms of feelings and affect. Political understanding and critical thought have yet to emerge. The young child now becomes aware of the existence of the president. Government is personalized—that is, the child becomes aware of political authority by becoming aware of certain individuals—notably the president and the police officer. The child sees these figures as possessing great power and is aware that they stand above the family in the obedience hierarchy. Unlike adults, who tend to be cynical about politics, the young child sees the president and the police officer as trustworthy, helpful, and benevolent. Reasoning from the "primacy principle" and the "benevolent leader hypothesis," students of early childhood political socialization attached considerable importance to the idealization of authority by young children. According to the primacy principle, "what is learned early in life tends to be retained and to shape later attitudes and behavior" (Easton and Dennis 1969, 9). According to the benevolent leader hypothesis, the image of the president (the most visible symbol of political authority) that is formed in early childhood has a direct effect on the formation of attitudes and beliefs about other political figures and institutions. There is a hypothesized "spillover effect" from this early view of the president to later perceptions of other political authorities. Because the president is favorably viewed, they too tend to be viewed favorably. It is believed, therefore, significant that the child's introduction to politics is a positive one. Later in life, when the individual is able to make critical judgments about politics, this early idealization builds what David Easton (1965) refers to as "diffuse support"—a reservoir of goodwill toward the political system that is independent of any benefit the individual might receive. It helps legitimize the political order and, in times of political stress, the residue of this early idealization helps maintain a positive attitude toward government.

Late Childhood

Beginning about the age of ten or eleven, children start moving away from a personalized view of government to one based on a more sophisticated understanding. During this period the child learns the "civics book" norm of not always voting for the same political party but for the best person. In a national sample, 49 percent of fourth graders say a good citizen would join a political party and vote for its candidates instead of voting for the best person. But by the eighth grade, only 26 percent endorse this strategy (Hess and Torney 1967, 96). Views of what constitutes "good citizenship" also undergo change. Young children tend to see the good citizen as someone who is "helpful to others" and "always obeys the laws." But by late childhood, good citizenship is defined more in terms of adult conceptions: political interest, voting, and getting others to vote (Hess and Torney 1967, 37).

However, definitions of democracy in late childhood and even through adolescence seldom include the right to criticize government. Only 54 percent of the eighth graders in Hess and Torney's sample checked the option "you can say things against the government" as one possible definition of democracy. And 84 percent of eighth graders agreed that "the government usually knows what is best for the people." Such open acceptance of government and intolerance for dissent are generally regarded as unhealthy for democracy (see chapter 6).

Adolescence

The major spurt in a child's political learning usually comes during adolescence. An important aspect of this growth is the ability to comprehend the abstraction of community interest apart from self-interest. Ideals such as *community* and *society* are usually beyond the grasp of eleven-year-olds but not fifteen-year-olds (Adelson and O'Neil 1966). By midadolescence, the individual is in many ways politically beginning to resemble an adult. In a study of fifteen-year-old high school students, Conover and Searing (2000) found 61 percent said they think of themselves as citizens of the United States "all of the time." Only 3 percent said they never thought of themselves as U.S. citizens. When asked to define basic citizens rights, most students answered with a core set of rights, such as those of speech, religion, and privacy. By the ninth grade, children have some ability to think along a liberal–conservative continuum. Adult levels of political efficacy are also reached by the ninth grade (Merelman 1971; Hess and Torney 1967). One orientation that shows surprisingly little growth is support for democratic values (free speech, minority rights, rules of the game, etc.). Merelman (1971, 79) finds no increase in support for democratic values between the ninth and twelfth grades. This pattern has not improved in recent years. Conover and Searing (2000), for example, found levels of political tolerance among their sample of adolescents to be "disappointing low." As we note later, many blame the failure of this situation on the shortcomings of the public schools.

The Consequences of Preadult Socialization to Citizenship

The most dramatic findings in the literature on early socialization of citizenship are the extent to which young children (kindergarten through eighth grade) personalize government and the remarkable degree to which they idealize political authority. But do these findings really mean anything for adult behavior? The theory of diffuse support, born of childhood idealization, has a certain appeal but is difficult to verify empirically. First, the theory seems not to be general, as not all children idealize authority. African American (Greenberg 1970; Gimpel, Lay, and Schuknecht 2003), Mexican American (Garcia 1973), Native American (Fridkin, Kenney, and Crittenden 2006), and poor, isolated, rural white Appalachian children (Jaros, Hirsch, and Fleron 1968) are much more cynical about political authority than are middle-class white children. In fact, Jaros, Hirsch, and Fleron (1968) termed views of the president by Appalachian children as outright "malevolent."

When major political events arise, children can react as well as adults. One such event is the "Watergate" scandal of 1972–1974. Several studies investigated the impact of Watergate on preadults. They found that the dramatic negative shift in the portrayal of the president during Watergate had a deep impact on preadults, who underwent a "dramatic decline" in the positive image of the president (Arterton 1974; Dennis and Webster 1975; Hawkins, Pingree, and Roberts 1975; Rodgers and Lewis 1975). Christopher Arterton reports that based on a Boston-area sample, attitudes toward the president in fall 1973 "could only be described as wholly negative." The benevolent leader was transformed by Watergate into someone malevolent. In the early 1960s, anywhere from 50 to 66 percent (depending on grade) reported the president was their "favorite of all" or "of almost all." By 1973, the range was 5–23 percent, with the older children (fifth graders) being the least positive. Children in 1962 and 1973 were asked to "compare politicians" with "most people" in terms of power, selfishness, intelligence, honesty, and trustworthiness. The "spillover effect" of the president's image to other political authorities, which was positive in 1962, was negative in 1973. Particularly large differences between 1962 and 1973 exist on selfishness and trustworthiness. Fifty-four percent of the fifth graders in 1962 thought politicians were less selfish than other people; only 19 percent thought so in 1973.[1]

However, there is no evidence that this drastic swing in preadult views of the president due to Watergate had any effect in later life. For instance, ANES data shows that as adults those who would have been in grade school during Watergate have been no more or less trusting of government than other age cohorts. Similarly, the benevolent view of political authorities found among the children in the early socialization studies of the early 1960s must be reconciled with later radical protestors from the same age cohort. One possible explanation is that the samples chosen by the early researchers (eighth grade and younger) were not yet of impressionable age. We now know that political experiences have the most lasting long-term effect on people between the ages of seventeen and twenty-six ("the impressionable years thesis"). There is considerable support for this thesis, as we shall see shortly.

5-2 The Agents of Preadult Socialization

Having traced the development of political attitudes through the preadult years, we now attempt to sort out the agents most responsible for this development. The family seems to be the most influential source of preadult attitudes, but it certainly is not the only source. Schools make an effort to mold future citizens, and it seems probable that effort meets with at least some success. Other possible agents of early political socialization include childhood friends and the mass media. Finally, when important historical events occur, it seems likely that they leave an imprint on the young of impressionable age.

The Family

Political influence within the family is a function of numerous factors, but among the most important are communication and receptivity (Sears and Levy 2003). Parents score high on both these dimensions. First, children, particularly young children, spend a large amount of time with their parents. The opportunities for children to learn parental attitudes and for parents to exert influence on children is considerable. Second, in terms of receptivity, few bonds are as strong as the affective tie between parents and children. The stronger this tie and the more personal the relationship, the greater the parents' ability to exert influence.

A common assumption is that the political attitudes of family members are highly similar, with the presumed causal flow being from parents to children (rather than from sources outside the family that affect all family members alike).[2] Actually, the similarity depends on specific political issues and the time period during which parental socialization took place. The available data show there are differences between socialization in the 1960s and socialization in the 1990s (and presumably before and thereafter).

Much of what we know about the family and political socialization comes from the longitudinal parent–child socialization panel carried by the Survey Research Center at the University of Michigan. High school seniors and their parents were first interviewed in 1965. The students were then reinterviewed in 1973, 1982, and 1997. The parents were reinterviewed in 1973 and 1982. In 1997, children over the age of fifteen born to the original 1965 seniors were interviewed. Thus, we have an incredibly rich data set for understanding a wide range of social influences on political opinions, not just those of the family.

Shown in Table 5.1 is the relationship in 1965 between the attitudes of seniors and their parents on four policy issues (Jennings and Niemi 1968). Reading across the rows in the table, we can see that the students are much more likely to be pro-school integration and pro-school prayer when their parents favor these positions. For example, among the pro-integration parents, 83 percent have children who also favor school integration, but when parents oppose integration the percentage of children favoring integration drops to 45—a difference of 38 percent. What we are seeing is the effect of the 1960s political climate, where civil rights for African Americans were more attractive to the young than to their parents. We see something similar in the 1997 wave of the study. On issues like political tolerance, factors external to the family (notably the school climate) had more influence on the attitudes of the filial generation than did the parents (Jennings, Stoker and Bowers 2009).

Table 5.1 shows for 1965 that the relationship between parents and their children weakens considerably for the question of an elected Communist being allowed to hold office and virtually disappears on the question of allowing atheists to give speeches against churches. The best explanation is that these civil libertarian issues are of little importance to most families. In general, affect-laden issues with relatively long lives on the political agenda are most effectively transmitted from parents to children, regardless of the generation (Jennings, Stoker, and Bowers 2009). In 1997, for instance, a strong correlation was found again between parental and filial attitudes about whether prayers belong to schools. The strongest relationship between the 1997 parents and their children was on abortion, an issue not on the political agenda in 1965. In fact, in 1997 the correspondence between parents and children on abortion was stronger than for party identification (Jennings, Stoker and Bowers 2009).[3]

The most thoroughly documented successful transmission of an attitude from parent to child involves partisanship. One review notes that "party choices of parents and their offspring are correlated all over the world" (Ventura 2001). Again using the 1965 wave of the Michigan Socialization data, Table 5.2 documents the widespread agreement between parents and children on the question

TABLE 5.1 | Relationship Between High School Student and Parent Opinions on Four Policy Issues, 1965

Students	Federal Role in School Integration* (Parents)			Prayers in Public Schools* (Parents)			Elected Communists Can Hold Office (Parents)			Allow Speeches Against Churches (Parents)		
	Pro	*Depends*	*Con*	*Pro*	*Depends*	*Con*	*Pro*	*Depends*†	*Con*	*Pro*	*Depends*†	*Con*
Pro	83%	64%	45%	74%	62%	34%	45%	—	32%	88%	—	82%
Depends	7	17	14	3	8	7	1	—	0	0	—	0
Con	10	18	41	23	30	59	53	—	67	12	—	18
Total	100%	99%	100%	100%	100%	100%	99%		99%	100%		100%
	(961)	(202)	(453)	(1,253)	(68)	(238)	(1,337)		(1,337)	(1,376)		(523)
	$Tau_b = 0.34$			$Tau_b = 0.29$			$Tau_b = 0.08$			$Tau_b = 0.08$		

*Based on pairs in which both parents were "interested enough" to give a pro or con response.

†Ten or fewer cases.

Source: M. Kent Jennings and Richard G. Niemi, *The Political Character of Adolescence* (Princeton, NJ: Princeton University Press, 1974), p. 78. Reprinted by permission of Princeton University Press.

TABLE 5.2 | High School Student Party Identification by Parent Party Identification, 1965

Student	Parents			
	Democrat	Independent	Republican	Frequencies★
Democrat	66%	29%	13%	(43%)
Independent	27	55	36	(36%)
Republican	7	17	51	(21%)
Total	100%	100%	100%	
Frequencies★	(49%)	(24%)	(27%)	100%

★The frequency totals present the proportion of parents and students holding a particular party preference. For example, looking at the column frequencies we can see that 49 percent of the parents call themselves Democrats. Looking at the row frequencies, we can see that 43 percent of the students in the sample call themselves Democrats.

Source: M. Kent Jennings and Richard G. Niemi, *The Political Character of Adolescence* (Princeton, NJ: Princeton University Press, 1974), p. 41. Reprinted by permission of Princeton University Press.

of party preference. For instance, reading across the rows of the table, when we move from parents who are Democratic to those who are Independent to those who are Republican, the percentage of Democratic children drops dramatically and the percent who say they are Republicans increases. When parents agree between themselves on partisanship (74 percent do agree), 76 percent of the adolescents follow the preferences of their parents. This pattern was also reflected in the 1997 data. Interestingly, when parents disagree on partisanship (one is a Democrat, the other a Republican), the child is more likely to adopt the mother's partisanship than the father's. Also, with parental divergence on partisanship, the number of Independent children rises substantially, as one would expect given the cross-pressures (Jennings and Langton 1969). The success with which parents are able to transmit their partisanship to their children seems to have remained essentially static over the generations, despite vast changes in the family social structure. To generalize, the relationship between the partisanship of parents in 1997 (the 1965 high school seniors) and their own children is similar to that between parents and children in 1965 (Jennings and Stoker 2009). This generational continuity is important because it helps perpetuate existing party divisions across generations.

What is the mechanism by which parental transmission of political attitudes works? There are at least three possible explanations. One explanation is the simple matter of communication within the home. Children need to be aware of their parents' opinions. Second, the most politicized parents are likely to be most successful in socializing their children, since politics is important to those parents. Looking over the long haul (thirty-plus years), we expect those high school seniors who were most successfully socialized to their parents' political views will be those most likely to maintain those political attitudes over the life cycle. Third, transmission might not entirely be environmental. Genetics may play a role, as will be discussed shortly. The idea is not that there is a gene for partisanship or for particular political viewpoints. That is obviously not the case. Rather, the argument is that genetic transmission from parents to children includes genetic traits that predispose people toward particular views.

Communication. Party identification is passed from parent to child with much more success than other political orientations. One explanation grounded in social psychology is that most political questions are remote from the day-to-day concerns of the family. Few parents hold their political opinions strongly, and few children have an accurate perception of those opinions. In this regard, party identification is unique. It is one attitude that is normally of some consequence to parents and highly visible to children. At election time, young children often ask if "we" are Democrats or Republicans. In a study of high school seniors, Tedin (1974) found that while 72 percent were aware of parental party identification, no more than 36 percent were aware of parent attitudes on any one issue. But when issue attitudes were about as salient and well perceived as partisanship, parent–child correspondence approached that for partisanship. Anders Westholm (1999) finds a similar pattern in socialization study in Sweden. If children accurately perceive the political attitudes of their parents, socialization is quite successful. But misperception is frequent.

Politicization. We would expect the more politicized the parents, the more success they would have influencing their children. Thus, Andolina and her colleagues (2003) found that children from politicized families were more likely to vote and were more involved in a variety of political activities than were children from nonpoliticized families (see also McIntosh, Hart, and Youniss 2007). However, the politicization hypothesis is only partially borne out for political opinions (Beck and Jennings 1991; Jennings and Stoker 2009). Data from the Michigan panel show the most politicized families in 1965 successfully transmitted their partisanship, vote choice, and political trust, but for most other issues politicized parents were often less successful in transmitting political attitudes than nonpoliticized parents. The reason was the greater sensitivity to powerful environmental factors in the 1960s among politicized adolescents, such as the civil rights movement. On the other hand, in the less politically volatile 1990s, the 1997 parents were a good deal more successful in transmitting their issue preferences than were their own parents back in 1965. As before, partisanship and vote choice were successfully transmitted. However, in the case of issues, some of the correspondence between politicized parents and their children in 1997 is spectacularly higher than for nonpoliticized parents (Jennings and Stoker 2009). The reason is a lack of conflicting environmental counter influences in the 1990s that could push politically savvy adolescents away from the politics embraced by their parents.

By exploiting the Michigan panel's 1997 wave, it is possible to observe the successful parental socialization of 1965 high school students some thirty-two years later at the age of 50. For each issue, Jennings, Stoker and Bowers (2009) divided the 1965 high school seniors into two groups. One group agreed with their parents' position on the issue (giving identical responses to the question); the other did not. The authors then analyzed the extent to which these two groups (one "successfully" socialized and the other "unsuccessfully") retained in 1997 the political opinions they first inherited from their parents as found in the 1965 survey. In almost every instance, the continuity of political opinions was greater among those who acquired their parents' orientations back in 1965 than those who did not. For instance, 54 percent who adopted their parents' exact party identification in 1965 (as a Democrat, Republican, or Independent) retained that exact identification in 1997, compared to 33 percent among those who differed from their parents back in 1965. The inference is that early acquisition of parental political views has lifelong consequences.

The Peer Group

Like parents, the peer group enjoys considerable opportunity to influence attitudes and behavior. Strong affective ties are involved, and young people normally spend a substantial part of their time with friends. Parents and peers differ, however, at the point in the preadult's life when influence is greatest. Parents dominate the lives of their offspring until adolescence, at which point peers become increasingly important (Beck 1977). Despite the considerable attention paid to peer groups in the United States, there is relatively little research and (perhaps as a logical consequence) little agreement on the role of peers as an agent of political socialization. Some scholars argue that peer groups are the most important of all adolescent socialization agencies, while others assert that the influence of peers is largely redundant.[4] Peers are seen as simply reinforcing the lessons learned in the family and school. It is clear, however, that adolescent peers can be influential in areas involving the individual's status in the group. But these areas usually involve matters of taste in music, clothing, and hairstyles and "deviant" social practices rather than politics. For instance, numerous studies have demonstrated that peer influence (versus self-selection) is highly predictive of adolescent decisions to smoke—a practice discouraged by most parents (Kobus 2003; Hoffman et al. 2007).

In the Michigan Socialization Panel, a subset of the 1965 students were asked to indicate their best friend of the same sex, who was then included in the sample. As expected, for party identification the correlation between students and parents greatly exceeded that between students and peers. On the other hand, in the case of changing the voting age from twenty-one to eighteen (one had to be twenty-one to vote at the time of the survey), the student–peer correlation exceeded the student–parent correlation.[5] This is the pattern one would expect. Partisanship is learned during early childhood and is not a particularly youth-oriented issue. On the other hand, preadults were more likely to become aware of the eighteen-year-old vote issue during adolescence, and the issue is particularly relevant to high school seniors (Jennings and Niemi 1974). We would therefore expect more peer influence in the latter instance. In situations in which parents and peers disagree on partisanship, the student is more likely to follow the parent. But when parent and peer disagree on voting age, the student is more likely to follow his or her best friend (Sebert, Jennings, and Niemi 1974). Thus, peer versus parent influence seems to be issue-specific.

It is difficult to make any absolute assessment of peer influence, but it seems certain that even in adolescence, peers are not as important as parents. When politics are remote from one's day-to-day concerns, and when family social harmony as well as one's status in the peer group are only slightly affected by politics, parents probably have an advantage over peers in the socialization process. We have noted that one important precondition for influence is communication. Politics are more important to the thirty-five to fifty-year-old group (the common age of parents with adolescent children) than to those eighteen years old and under (Eskey 1995). If one assumes all other things are equal, adolescents are more likely to be aware of and receptive to parent attitudes simply because most contemporary political issues are more important to parents than to their peers (Tedin 1980). Moreover, there is strong evidence that adolescents have become less interested in politics over time; that is the finding from the "Monitoring the Future" surveys of high school seniors conducted yearly since 1975 by the University of Michigan[6] (see also Wattenberg 2008). Of course, when a matter is important to the esteem with which an adolescent is held by the peer group, parents usually cannot compete with peer influence. But for most American youth, everyday political issues are rarely of consequence for their standing in the peer group.

The Primary and Secondary School

Many political theorists, practical politicians, political reformers, and political revolutionaries believe or have believed that the school is an instrumental agent in the political training of the young. Examples abound. After the 1917 Russian revolution, children were removed from the family (presumably still attached to the old order and unsympathetic to Communist values) and required to spend long periods in school for political retraining. The Allied Powers followed a similar policy after the defeat of the Nazis in World War II. The schools were "de-Nazified," and German youths were instructed in the principles of democratic government as defined by the West. The same perspective on socialization is reflected in the fierce debate over a multicultural curriculum in American schools, or the teaching of "intelligent design" in the classroom along with the theory of evolution. The school is seen as an effective vehicle for instructing students in the values necessary for life in adult society.

Virtually all nations charge the public schools with the responsibility of teaching obedience to political authority. The practice is nearly universal, and from the standpoint of maintaining political stability and continuity, many believe it is a necessity. One need only observe the difficulties encountered by nations in which primary loyalties do not reside with the national government. For example, in some nations ethnic or tribal loyalty comes before national loyalty. The usual result is armed conflict. Political stability is highly dependent on the ability of the agents of socialization to produce in children feelings as to the rightness, the oughtness, the legitimacy of the political order. In all nations with an effective national government, this task is assigned to the schools. They are the one agent of political socialization over which the government has considerable control.

There can be little doubt, as we noted in the section on childhood political development, that preadults in the United States generally learn the lessons of patriotism and obedience. What is not clear is the relative role of the family and school in teaching these orientations. In an early landmark study of the public schools, Robert Hess and Judith Torney (1967, 126) declared that "compliance [with] roles and authority is the major focus of education in elementary schools." Most readers are undoubtedly aware of the patriotic rituals that characterize most classrooms—pictures of American heroes, the display of the American flag and proclaiming one's allegiance to it, singing patriotic songs, "young citizens leagues," and the emphasis on obedience to authority. Teaching methods change periodically in response to changes in thinking about what is and is not effective for student learning, but the goal of socializing the young to be loyal citizens is never divorced from changes in the curriculum (Ross 2004; Westheimer 2007). This goal, for example, is evident in *America 2000: An Educational Strategy*, a national civics curriculum for grades K–12 endorsed by both the first Bush and the Clinton administrations.[7] As Richard Merelman (1997, 56) observes, "the proposed national civics standards are mainly a symbolic ritual masked as educational policy for reinforcing cultural hegemony." In other words, the curriculum is focused on teaching a common American culture and values as opposed to teaching individual and group differences.

Students of political education agree that teaching loyalty and obedience is only one aspect of political education. There are other goals as well, such as teaching political knowledge, political participation skills, tolerance of competing political views, and acceptance and support for democratic values. An invigorated role for the schools in these areas would seem even more important in the twenty-first century than in the past, given the recent decline in adolescent interest and participation (Campbell 2005; Wattenberg 2008). One disappointment is that political education does not seem to generate much political enthusiasm or eagerness to participate in adult citizenship. For example, in a 2008 poll of high school seniors just 28 percent said they had "a lot" or a "great deal" of interest in current events.[8]

As political knowledge increases, people support democratic values and express faith in the political system (Dudley and Gitelson 2003; Galston 2004). Unfortunately, high school students' factual knowledge about politics is notoriously low. Niemi and Junn (1998) report that fewer than two-thirds of twelfth graders were aware that it is legal to participate in a boycott, organize a recall election, or impeach legislators. According to the National Assessment of Educational Progress, often called "the nation's report card," only 26 percent of high school seniors in 1999 had a "proficient" knowledge of how the government worked, and 35 percent failed the national civics test (Hedges 1999). Anderson and his colleagues (1990) report that only 61 percent of high school seniors recognized (in 1988) that having more than one political party was a fundamental difference between the United States and the Soviet Union; only 58 percent knew the United States has a two-party system, and just 50 percent knew the governor is a member of the executive branch.

Finally, surveys of high school youth suggest that support for democratic values is limited and fragile. A study of high school seniors back in the 1960s found 60 percent willing to allow the police and other groups to censor books and movies (Remmers and Franklin 1963, 62), and another in the 1970s found only 36 percent in favor of allowing a legally elected Communist to assume office (Jennings and Niemi 1974). Niemi and Junn's (1998) study from the 1990s finds that only 52 percent of high school seniors knew the right to religious freedom is part of the Bill of Rights, and only 47 percent knew there is a constitutional ban on double jeopardy. In a 2004 survey of high school students, 75 percent said flag burning was illegal, 50 percent said the government could censor the Internet, and more than a third said the First Amendment goes too far in guaranteeing individual rights.[9] With similar findings persisting over many decades, the inescapable conclusion is that adolescent youth typically are little interested in politics, possess little factual foundation, and are slow to learn democratic norms (Bennett 1997, 1998; Mann 1999).

The poor performance of adolescents on political quizzes and the desire of educational professionals to prepare adolescents for their adult role as citizens have engendered a lively debate over possible remedies. We need to start by asking to what extent traditional high school civics courses add an incremental improvement to commonly accepted standards for democratic citizenship. The thrust of early empirical research on this question indicated that the high school civics curriculum had little if any effect on political knowledge or political values (Langton and Jennings 1968; Jennings, Ehrman, and Niemi 1974; Anderson et al. 1990; Conover and Searing 2000). However, a more recent study of data from the National Assessment of Education Progress (NAEP) tells a more optimistic story. A detailed study of these data by Richard Niemi and Jane Junn (1998) turned up modest effects of the civics curriculum on trust in government—the more courses taken, the more trust in government—and stronger effects on political knowledge.[10] These effects hold up with multivariate controls for factors such as parents' education and plans for college. Moreover, Niemi and Junn find that if one looks at all factors relevant to civics instruction beyond simply hours in the classroom—the amount and recentness of coursework, variety of topics studied, and discussion of current events—the estimated effects increase.[11] Although the analysis of the NAEP data is mostly limited to gains in political knowledge, it serves to rehabilitate the curriculum as a contributor to political learning.[12]

It is not entirely clear how the curriculum in high school leads to higher levels of political knowledge or support for democratic values. There is, however, no doubt that those with a high school degree are more politically tolerant than those without. The 2008 GSS shows that while 57 percent of those with a grade school education support free speech for an atheist, 71 percent of those with a high school degree are supportive. Similarly, while 59 percent of those with a grade school education would allow a homosexual to teach in college, 75 percent of those with a high school degree would be willing. Numerous other examples can be offered. It may be that a high school education simply slots people into social, economic, and political positions in which they have a greater opportunity to learn democratic norms. Or it may be that the type of civics curriculum makes a significant difference. Studies contrasting an "open classroom" where high school students freely engage in discourse and debate on controversial real-world political problems, as opposed to the traditional "citizenship transmission" model, show that the former substantially elevates knowledge of democratic processes (based on response to a 49-item scale) and that students are more accepting of conflict as a normal part of the political process (Campbell 2008). Others show links between classroom discussion of civil liberties issues and the development of tolerant attitudes (Avery 2002). However, as explained by Ross (2004), critics of the open classroom model have effectively claimed that it is little more than a vehicle for political indoctrination, thus curtailing its appeal for many schools due to fear of public protests.

If the effect of formal civic education remains mixed, there is little doubt that participating in community activities in high school leads to higher rates of political activity in adult life. These activities, even when required by schools, are thought to foster a sense of civic identity that eventually results in elevated adult political participation. Metz and Youniss (2003) analyzed data from a school comparing the 1998–1999 graduating class, which had no community service requirement, to the 2001–2003 class, which had a forty-hour community service requirement. The students required to perform community service continued to do so at an even higher rate once the requirement was completed and expressed an intention to volunteer in the future at significantly higher levels than the 1998–1999 cohort of students who had no community service requirement. A panel study by McFarland and Thomas (2006) showed students who participated in high school activities such as student council, journalism clubs, music groups, and so on were significantly more likely to be politically involved as adults, even in the face of stringent statistical controls for background factors (see also Jennings 2002; Andolina et al. 2003; Torney-Purta and Amadeo 2003; Zukin et al. 2006).

However, overall rates of extracurricular activities among high school students dropped substantially between the mid-1960s and the late 1990s. High school students around the turn of the century simply do not participate in civic activities to the same extent as their parents did a generation earlier. For example, the Michigan Socialization Study shows that in 1965, 50 percent of high school seniors ran for an elected office in school while just 27 percent did so in 1997 (Jennings and Stoker 2004). The pattern for high school students is consistent with (and may be a precursor to the decline) an adult communal participation described by Robert Putnam in *Bowling Alone* (2000). More optimistically, these data suggest that a reversal in the decline in communal activity could start with an intervention at the high school level.

5-3   College: Higher Education and Its Impact

Although most students are legally adult when they enter college, the college experience is for many a transition period between life with the family and being on one's own. Today almost one of every two high school graduates goes to college. At the turn of the twentieth century, most young people did not even graduate from high school, let alone contemplate attaining a college degree.[13] Consequently, the proportion of the adult population with college experience has been rising steadily. For example, between 1950 and 1990, the proportion of adults with at least some college rose from 16 to 45 percent. In the short period between 1972 and 2008, the proportion of adults over twenty-five with college degrees rose from 13 to 30 percent (GSS). It is, however, important to understand that most of this recent increase is due to the departure of older, less-educated citizens rather than an increase in the number of citizens receiving college degrees. In fact, there is currently little growth in the educational attainment of the youngest age cohort. Thus, in future years we will likely see little gain in the overall percentage of the population that is college educated (Nie, Junn, and Stehlik-Barry 1998, 112–18).

The College Years

What are the political implications of the growth in the college-educated public? As a starting point, let us follow the evolution of the political attitudes of college freshmen, as monitored continually by the University of California at Los Angeles CIRP annual surveys and shown in Figure 5.1. Although the current crop of college students is more conservative in self-identification than students of the 1960s and 1970s, the popularity of the liberal label among college freshmen has been increasing in recent years. College freshmen are slightly

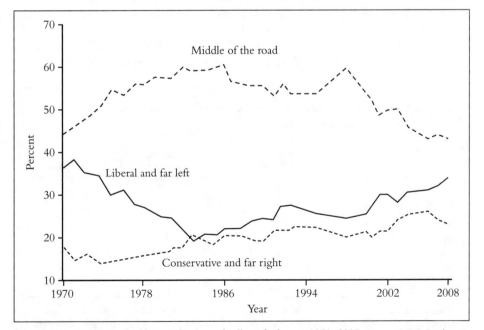

Figure 5.1 Ideological self-identification of college freshman, 1970–2008. *Source:* CIRP Freshman Study, Higher Education Research Institute, University of California, Los Angeles.

more conservative in the first decade of the twenty-first century than in 1970. Among freshmen in 1970, liberals outnumbered conservatives by about a 2 to 1 margin. By 1985, perhaps due to the Reagan Revolution, conservatives slightly outnumbered liberals. Since then, however, liberals have been gaining. In 2008 they outnumbered conservatives by 32 to 25 percent. This trend toward self-identified liberalism has been accompanied by an increasing liberalism on issues such as the death penalty, legalization of marijuana, and gay marriage. The 2008 UCLA study also showed students claiming no religious preference to be at an all-time high (21percent).

The move away from the political middle ground coincides with an increase in political interest among college freshmen. In 1966, 58 percent of freshmen said that "keeping up to date with political affairs" is very important; this number declined to 38 percent in 1979 and fell to an all-time low of 26 percent in 1998, increasing slightly to 31 percent in 2001, but then dramatically jumping to 51 percent in 2002—a likely consequence of the 9/11 terrorist attack—but falling back just modestly to 40 percent in 2008.

Acknowledging that students start their college experience somewhat more liberal than the adult population (see chapter 4), the next question is how the four years (or so) of the college experience shapes their attitudes. As we discuss at greater length in the following chapter, education is strongly correlated with political tolerance and support for democratic values. As the population has become better educated, its expression of support for these values has also increased. In addition, college generally has a liberalizing effect on noneconomic political opinions. Evidence in support of this view can be traced back to the 1920s. College seniors are consistently found to be less conservative than entering freshmen.[14]

Drawing on data from surveys from UCLA's CIRP, Table 5.3 nicely illustrates the likely liberalizing effect of the college experience with some recent

TABLE 5.3 | College Student Political Attitudes as Freshmen in 2004 and Seniors in 2008

	At College Entry (2004)	At End of College (2008)	Change
Liberal or Far Left	30	39	+9
Middle-of-the-Road	42	39	−3
Conservative or Far Right	29	23	−6
Legalize Marijuana	30	44	+14
Support Same Sex Marriage	57	69	+12
Abortion Should be Legal	49	61	+12
Abolish Death Penalty	40	46	+6

Source: Adapted from Amy Liu, Sylvia Ruiz, Linda DeAngelo, and John Pryor. 2009. "Findings from the 2008 Administration of the College Senior Survey (CSS): National Aggregates." Report from the Higher Education Research Institute, UCLA, Table 42.

data. The table compares attitudes of college freshmen in 2004 with the comparable attitudes of college seniors in 2008 when they would be graduating from college. In terms of ideological preference and on specific issues, this 2004 cohort of college freshmen (the class of 2008) becomes more liberal over time. The obvious inference is that something about the college experience caused attitude change. The interesting question is, what were the factors that may have been responsible?[15]

Three explanations are commonly advanced for these gains in liberalism: increased awareness, enlightenment, and indoctrination. None of these standing alone is entirely convincing. The awareness explanation is predicated on the fact that two of the stronger correlates of education are political knowledge and use of the media. Being informed about innovations and current events is directly related to education. As one scholar expressed it several decades ago, "thanks largely to wider personal contacts and greater exposure to the media of opinion, the better educated are the first to sense changes in the climate of opinion and quickly respond to new fashions in social thought" (Stembler 1961, 172). For example, in a study of support for the civil rights of women and blacks, one investigator found a large increase in support for women's rights occurring among the educated shortly after the media began devoting considerable attention to the issue. However, no parallel increase was found in support for black civil rights (which received no attention out of the ordinary), indicating that increased liberalism on women's issues was due to an awareness factor (Schreiber 1978). Early in the 1990s this same pattern appeared for "black" as opposed to "African-American" in terms of the preferred identifier for members of this racial group. Among blacks in the mass public, the college educated were the most likely to prefer "African-American."[16] The media (much influenced by the college educated) has also come to favor the newer label (Sigelman, Tuch, and Martin 2005). Because conservatism has an important status quo component and liberalism an important change component, a critic might argue that the awareness explanation is confusing becoming liberal with simply being trendy. The explanation is also time-bound. What is trendy at one point may be quite different at another.

A second argument asserts that education leads to "enlightenment," which in turn leads to liberalism. According to Lottes and Kuriloff (1994, 33) "during college, attitudes and values tend to become more open, humanitarian, altruistic, tolerant and liberal." However, as we demonstrate in chapter 7, education is not always a correlate of liberalism. On economic issues, the better educated tend to be more conservative. But as education increases, so does one's ability to think analytically and critically. The consequence is likely to be the rejection of stereotypes and prejudice, an increased tolerance of diverse lifestyles, and an increased liberalism across a variety of social issues.

A third explanation holds that the "liberal" college faculty indoctrinates students in the direction of their own political views. As Table 5.4 shows, college faculty members are more liberal than college seniors. But whether there is cause and effect is an open question. Woessner and Kelly-Woessner (2009) found that even in political science courses, students had at best only

TABLE 5.4	Political Orientations of College Faculty and College Seniors, 1984 and 1999		
Year	Liberal	Middle of the Road	Conservative	
Faculty				
1984	42%	27%	31%	100%
1999	45	37	18	100%
Students				
1984	35%	39%	26%	100%
1999	36	31	33	100%

Sources: For 1984 students and faculty, Ernest Boyer and Mary Jean Whitelaw, *The Condition of the Professoriate: Attitudes and Trends, 1989* (New York: Harper, 1989); for 1999 faculty, Denise E. Magner, "Faculty Attitudes and Characteristics: Results of a 1998–1999 Survey," *Chronicle of Higher Education* (Sept. 3, 1999), pp. A20–A21; the 1999 college seniors data are courtesy of Dr. Jerry Jacobs, Department of Sociology, University of Pennsylvania.

a hazy idea of the ideological orientation of their professors. Note also in Table 5.4 that while between 1984 and 1999, the percentage of conservative faculty dropped from 31 to 18 percent, conservative students over the same period increased from 26 to 33 percent. John Zipp and Rudy Fenwick (2006), analyzing the faculty data from 1989 through 1997, found centrists increasing at the expense of ideological extremes, with the social sciences faculty showing a modest drift in the conservative direction. It is also important to understand there is a significant ideological variation across academic disciplines. For the social sciences, the professoriate in 1997 were 67 percent liberal, 15 percent center, and 18 percent conservative. For the business schools, 32 percent were liberal, 20 percent were center, and 48 percent were conservative (Zipp and Fenwick 2006, 310). While the data for all faculty show liberals outnumber conservatives, the data show no ideological hegemony dominating the academy, and little evidence of faculty politically "indoctrinating" their students (Woessner and Kelly-Woessner 2009).

College Students Compared to Non-College Youth

Most observers would agree that college has an impact on student political views. Not only do college students become more liberal with increased years of college exposure (as noted above) but also there are substantial differences between young people in college and young people who do not attend college, as seen in Table 5.5 However, not all these differences can be attributed to the college experience. We know from panel studies (where respondents are reinterviewed over time) that many of the differences between those who go to college and those who do not already existed when the two groups were still in high school. In the Michigan Socialization Study, the 1965 high school seniors

Item	College	Noncollege
TABLE 5.5	**Youth Attending and Not Attending College**	
Registered to vote[*]	82%	69%
Liberal[†]	39	25
Disapprove Bush immigration Policy[*]	43	52
9/11 made me mistrust government[*]	35	29
Attended a political rally[*]	28	19
Getting involved in politics is honorable[*]	69	57
Approve abortion for any reason[†]	47	33
Allow antireligionist to teach in college[†]	80	68
Favor school prayer[†]	48	61
Women not suited for politics[†]	18	27

[*]2006 Biannual Youth Survey on Politics and Public Service, Institute for Politics, John F. Kennedy School of Government, Harvard University.

[†]1998–2008 pooled General Social Survey (18–23 year olds, whites only).

were reinterviewed eight years later, in 1973. With this panel design, we can compare those who went to college with those who did not, and compare the changes of the two groups between high school and their mid-twenties. The data show that college graduates were influenced both by their preadult socialization and their college experience. In some instances the opinion differences between college-bound high school seniors and those not bound for college were already apparent in high school. On questions of civic tolerance, the college-bound were already more liberal than their noncollege age cohorts. But by 1973 these differences had increased even further. Thus, there is both a self-selection factor at work as well as an impact of higher education. On the other hand, there was little difference in 1965 on questions of prayer in the public schools and support for racial integration. By 1973, however, there were substantial differences between those with a college degree and those who had not been to college, leading to an inference that college had caused opinion change in a liberal direction (Jennings and Niemi 1982, 257–60).

5-4 Personal Predispositions and Political Attitudes

So far, this chapter has discussed the various environmental factors from the formative years that shape political attitudes. But people are more than the sum of their environmental influences. They also contribute their personal dispositions to the mix. Ignoring politics for the moment, everybody knows that people vary considerably in terms of their unique personalities. These psychological differences are only partially traceable to socialization influences and may in large part be determined by one's genetic makeup. Research suggests that to some extent our political beliefs can be traced to our personalities and to the genes we were born with.

Personality and Political Attitudes

Social psychologists generally define "personality" as a set of mental traits or dispositions that govern cognitions and behavior. Importantly, personality tends to be quite permanent—generally stable throughout one's lifetime.

Today, most social psychologists see five major traits that define individual differences in personality—these are sometimes called the big five. They are as follows:

1. *Openness:* open to new experiences versus conforming and preferring routine
2. *Conscientious:* organized and disciplined versus careless and impulsive
3. *Extraversion:* sociable and affectionate versus somber and reserved
4. *Agreeableness:* trusting and helpful versus suspicious and uncooperative
5. *Neuroticism:* calm and secure versus anxious and self-pitying

These differences among individual personality types are easily recognizable. But what do they have to do with political opinions? For each trait we might hypothesize some pattern where people at the polar ends of the scale might differ politically. Numerous investigations have failed to find any connection to political attitudes for extroversion, agreeableness, or neuroticism. However, the first two traits listed above are convincingly related to political ideology and in a way we might expect: Liberals tend to be more open to new experiences while conservatives tend to be conforming. And to a lesser extent, conservatives tend to be conscientious and organized while liberals tend to be impulsive. This connection between personality and political ideology is known from numerous studies where subjects, typically college students, were given batteries of pencil-and-paper personality tests and their scores were compared with their self-declared ideological identification. Other studies have measured personality observationally. For instance, consistent with theory and common intuition, students who keep messy dorm rooms or workers who maintain messy offices tend to be liberals, while those who display their tidiness tend to be conservatives politically (see Carney, Jost, Gosling, and Potter 2009 for a review of recent evidence).

One of the most provocative studies involved an Internet survey of thousands of volunteers who took the "big five" personality inventory test as part of their interview. Respondents came from across the United States, including every state of the union. The researchers found that state-level personality helps to predict manifestations of liberalism–conservatism, such as the state's presidential voting (Rentfrow et al. 2009). The study showed that the divide between red states and blue states (in terms of recent presidential voting) is due in part to a geographical divide in terms of personality. Residents of red (Republican) states tend to be conforming and favoring order to their lives, while residents of blue (Democratic) states tend to be open to new ideas and impulsive. This result may be surprising because we might think that when comparing large groups like U.S. states, individual differences in personality would cancel out, particularly when considering the indirect impact on politics. But this is not the case. Just as some occupations may recruit people with conservative personality types (e.g., the military) and others may recruit people with liberal personality types (e.g., journalism), some states may recruit residents based on who might be attracted to the type of people who already live there. Or, it could be variation in state culture. Or, it could be genetic differences among the populations who comprise the various states. The possibilities are intriguing.

Genetic and Political Attitudes

At its most basic, children share the genetic makeup of their biological parents. The study of genetics has been prominent in the behavioral sciences, and for decades scholars having been trying to figure out how genetic and social influences contribute to a variety of personal characteristics such as simple happiness (Plomin 1997).

One way to answer questions about genetic versus social influence is through the study of identical (monozygotic or MZ) twins and fraternal (dizygotic or DZ) twins. MZ twins share identical genes, while DZ twins share 50 percent of their genes. DZ twins are no more genetically alike than any siblings. The hypothesis is that MZ twins should be more similar than DZ twins to the extent genetics determines behavior.

Several political scientists have recently advanced the notion that the parents not only influence political opinions through social interaction with their children, but add a genetic component as well. It is not that specific opinions are genetically based, but that genes determine deep-seated personality traits, which in turn influence political opinions. Genes may prime people to respond openly or cautiously to contemporary political issues. Thus, someone genetically programmed with an open disposition would be more likely to favor same-sex marriage than someone programmed with a cautious disposition.

The effect of genetic inheritance can be calculated by analyzing the difference in the rate that identical twins agree on political issues compared to the rate of fraternal twins. By comparing identical and nonidentical twins in terms of their political attitudes, researchers have found differences of the sort that on statistical grounds must be of genetic rather than environmental origin. Alford, Funk, and Hibbing (2005) suggest that as much as half of the variance in composite liberalism–conservatism (i.e., averaged over many issues) is the result of genetic transmission. Of course, this leaves about one half of the variance to be explained by environmental considerations.

One attitude that appears fairly resistant to genetic influence is party identification (Alford, Funk, and Hibbing 2005; Hatemi et al. 2009). Socialization exerts a particularly strong effect on the formation of partisanship and apparently overwhelms genetic factors. At the same time, genes may influence more than simply political opinions. The degree to which people participate in politics appears to be influenced by their genetic makeup. Fowler, Baker, and Dawes (2008) show this effect from their careful analysis of voting participation records of identical and nonidentical twins in Los Angeles. Pairs of identical twins were more alike in their frequency of voting than were pairs of nonidentical twins, and by an amount that suggested that genetic makeup was a contributing factor.

Still, not everyone is convinced (Beckwith and Morris 2008; Charney 2008). For the data to be compelling, one must accept the assumption of equal environments; that is, the assumption that MZ and DZ twins are treated alike. However, critics argue that because of their identical appearance, MZ twins are treated more alike by parents and others than are the more distinct DZ twins. It is also claimed that because they are identical, MZ twins bond more closely than do DZ twins. Both these environmental factors could account for the greater similarity we see in the political opinions and behavior of identical twins versus fraternal twins rather than genetics.

Discussion

Clearly, when it comes to politics, people are more than blank slates to be shaped by their environment. Even within the family, not all brothers and sisters are alike in politics just like they differ from each other in so many ways. Nor will any two adults in similar life environments (or even sharing a marriage) necessarily think alike politically. These differences are part of our unique political dispositions, which sometimes are traceable to our different personalities, which were largely in place by early childhood. They might also be traceable to factors in place at the time of their birth.

To speak of genetic variation accounting for political behavior does not of course mean that there are specific genes for specific political thoughts or acts. One plausible theory is that certain aspects of our genetic variation affect broad personality characteristics, which have ramifications for political orientations. Perhaps genes affect ideological dispositions by affecting how people rate on the personality traits of openness and conscientiousness, as we discussed earlier. Similarly, Alford, Funk, and Hibbing (2005) speculate about people's genetic makeup affecting their perspective on the world around them: "the very orientation of people to society, leadership, knowledge, group life, and the human condition" (Alford et al.2005, 16). In the case of genes affecting people's likelihood to vote, the connection could also be personality: a positive attitude toward society and/or a propensity to follow the lead of others (Fowler, Baker, and Dawes 2008).

5-5 Socialization During Adulthood

Preadult (and college-age) socialization is important because it influences the values and beliefs people hold at the outset of their adult political experience. But this takes the story only to the threshold of adulthood. What about subsequent socialization? Adult socialization is in part a story of stability. In the nonpolitical realm, increasing stability with age is the reason that commercial advertisers will pay higher rates for media programs that attract younger viewers. They believe ads can convert the product preferences of a younger audience but are less effective with an older audience. The political predispositions learned by one's mid-twenties persist to what might seem a surprising extent throughout adulthood. This fact only accentuates the importance of the early socialization experience. But early adulthood is also an important time of political awakening, as the political environment exerts a particularly strong pull during the first years of adult life. The implication is that generations (or birth cohorts) differ politically based on the collective experiences around the onset of their adulthood in what are called *generation effects*. Another aspect of adult socialization is that people *do* change politically as they grow older. When these changes are age-dependent, we call them *life-cycle effects*. An example is when people gradually get more politically conservative as they age (see Table 5.6). Finally, like children, mature adults change in response to commonly shared experiences, such as the turbulent 1960s, the end of the Cold War, and the tragedy of 9/11. These time-dependent changes are called *period effects*. By definition, period effects exert a common influence on people at all ages in the life cycle. They are responsible for the bulk of the short-term movement in opinion discussed in the previous chapter.

A life-cycle effect exists when people's political views are influenced by maturation. As a reference point, assume each new political generation enters political life with identical political attitudes. Then, any difference across generations would be due to aging. When we find, as we often do, that the young are more liberal than their elders, these age differences are explained by life-cycle effects. The implication is that the young, having few responsibilities, can afford to be idealistic. As they age, however, they take on the responsibility of raising a family, paying a mortgage, and holding down a full-time job. The effect is nicely

TABLE 5.6	Ideological Identification (% Conservative Minus % Liberal) by Birth Cohort, 1984, 1992, 2000, 2008			
Birth Year	**1984**	**1992**	**2000**	**2008**
1983–1990				2 (18–25)
1975–1982			–2 (18–25)	9
1967–1974		0 (18–25)	4	11
1959–1966	4 (18–25)	10	9	11
1951–1958	4	10	9	9
1943–1950	10	12	13	10
1935–1942	17	19	17	16
1927–1934	19	20	20	21
1919–1926	21	22	16	11 (82–89)
1911–1918	19	19	17 (82–89)	
1903–1910	29	25 (82–89)		
1895–1902	22 (82–89)			

Source: CBS News/*New York Times* Polls. Birth years are approximated from respondents' reported age.

captured in a comment about partisan politics by Winston Churchill: "Those at 18 who are not socialist have no heart; those at 40 who are still socialist have no head." In addition, it is often noted that learning continues throughout life, but reevaluation seems more frequent early in life than later (Sapiro 2004). Certain predispositions are reinforced over time, as people are more likely to expose themselves selectively to political stimuli with which they agree than to those with which they disagree. The life-cycle concept assumes a process that is similar for all age groups over time. It has been asserted, for example, that as people get older, political parties of the right become more attractive. This assertion (which we investigate below) posits an independent effect of aging on partisan predispositions.

A generational effect exists when a specific age cohort is uniquely socialized by a set of historical events. The logic of generational analysis dictates an interaction between age and experience. The usual assumption is that certain events in history make an indelible imprint on the young (defined approximately as the cohort of people age seventeen to twenty-six). It is argued that a generation's singular personality is shaped when its members leave the family and step out into the world on their own. Those who are younger remain shielded, to a certain extent, from the trauma of external events by the family. Those who are older are better equipped to resist its influence by their previous life experiences. For a distinct political generation to exist, something of historical consequence must have happened during their "impressionable years" (about the ages seventeen to twenty-six).[17] It is difficult to imagine anything occurring in the 1950s that would have distinctively stamped a generational cohort. On the other hand, one can easily conceive of the Vietnam War era (1965–1972) or the Great Depression of the 1930s as defining unique generations.

Period effects complicate matters further. Strong political shocks can affect young and old alike; for example, when the Cold War ended, all age groups relaxed their interest in further defense spending. When we observe all birth cohorts change in tandem as they grow older, we are tempted to see the changes as manifestations of life-cycle effects. But if the changes across all cohorts are time-bound, they can simply be "period effects" of shared experience rather than aging.[18]

The Life Cycle, Generations, and Party Identification

Much research on generational politics has focused on change in party identification. Generational effects are most important in the direction of party identification (Republican, Independent, or Democrat), but variation in the strength of partisanship (strong partisan, weak partisan, or Independent) responds most to movement through the life cycle.

Any survey will show that young adults have weaker partisan attachments than their elders due to life-cycle effects. For example, the 2008 ANES data shows 43 percent of those over age fifty-five claiming to be "strong" partisans, compared to only 22 percent under thirty. Similarly, only 27 percent of those over fifty-five are Independents, compared to 42 percent of those under thirty.

With figures such as these, one might forecast a general decline in partisanship as older cohorts with firm partisanship exit the electorate and are replaced by younger cohorts with weaker partisan attachments. But this does not happen—at least under equilibrium conditions—because each new generation acquires stronger partisan attachments as it ages. Under equilibrium conditions, the electorate's net partisan strength is stable, with each age cohort showing the same strength of partisanship as previous cohorts at the same point in the life cycle.

Maturation brings about a hardening of partisan commitment. Young adults start out disproportionately Independent in partisan choice, unsure of both parties. With age, they harden their choices. When they become senior citizens, the proportion calling themselves Independent is reduced by half. By the time it is necessary to enter a nursing home, most Americans have figured out whether they are Democrats or Republicans.[19]

Alternatively, the direction of partisanship is often imprinted on a political generation by historical events. We can see examples in Figure 5.2, which displays the relationship between age and the direction of party identification for an accumulation of Gallup Polls. The data are presented separately for 1990 and 1998. Comparing age groups at these points in history reveals clear generation effects.[20]

Let us look first at the data collected in 1990. We see that those citizens who were in their impressionable years during the 1930s depression (those between sixty-six and seventy-seven) were the most Democratic age cohort in the electorate. But note also the partisanship of those in their impressionable years during the boom times of the 1920s, when Republicans were ascendant. These citizens, in their eighties in 1990, were the most Republican age cohort. The difference in partisanship between those seventy-four to seventy-seven in 1990 and those eighty-two and over illustrates the profound effect of being socialized in the Roaring Twenties versus the Great Depression of the 1930s. The gap in partisan preference between these groups, who differ only modestly in chronological age, is quite startling, especially considering that the differentiation in the two groups' experiences had occurred decades earlier.[21]

At the other end of the age spectrum, the youngest cohorts in 1990 were more Republican than their elders (save those over eighty), having been socialized under the beleaguered President Carter and the optimistic years of the early Reagan administration. Moving forward to 1998, the youthful Republicans in 1990 were now between twenty-six and thirty-seven years old. They were still the most Republican cohort in the electorate as of 1998, but the fact that they experienced the good times of the 1990s while still in their impressionable years undercut their earlier, more Republican leanings. The most Republican cohort in 1990—those eighty-two years old and over and socialized under presidents Harding, Coolidge, and Hoover—had now exited the electorate. The New Deal generation is also now largely exiting the electorate, and the age differences within today's electorate on the direction of partisanship are leveling off.

The responses of new generations of young voters are particularly relevant to the understanding of partisan realignments. As discussed in earlier chapters, the United States has periodically undergone a partisan realignment. During

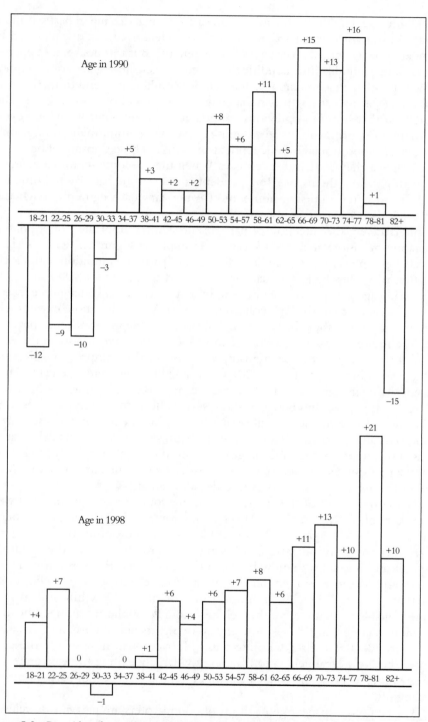

Figure 5.2 Party identification by age in 1990 and 1998 (percentage Democratic minus percentage Republican). *Source:* "America's Views and Mood 1998," *Public Perspective* (December/January 1999), p. 65.

realignments, the pace of partisan change quickens, with unusual numbers of voters changing their partisanship in response to new issues and events. The classic realignment occurred during the 1930s in response to the depression and New Deal, and it featured dramatic gains for the Democratic Party. Since the 1960s, pundits have occasionally forecast a massive new partisan realignment around the corner. If one arrives, what will it look like?

There is reason to believe that the vanguard of any new realignment will be young voters. Young voters lack strong partisan attachments, so they are particularly susceptible to political trends. For example, in 2008 with Bush's exit and Obama's election, the political winds favored the Democrats. Based on a merged set of Pew Research Center Polls from 2008 polls, totaling 17,543 respondents, the largest partisan difference by age group was for those between 18 and 29, where the Democrats had a 14 percentage point advantage over Republicans. But this is just one snapshot in time, due mostly to the Iraq War unpopularity of the Bush administration. The idea that young voters lead realignments is labeled the *mobilization theory* of realignment because it involves the mobilization of new voters. However, period effects also contribute to realignments, with both new voters and old voters showing equal rates of partisan conversion. If events are strong enough to cause a realignment, they may be strong enough to convert both old and young from one party to another. This view is known as the *conversion theory*.[22]

Will young voters lead the next realignment? Predictions based on the 1930s realignment are difficult because that realignment happened just as public opinion polling began. We saw, however, that the depression cohort, which began voting in the 1930s, even today leads other age groups in allegiance to the Democratic Party. But young voters in the 1930s were not numerous enough to account for a massive realignment by themselves. Examining early Gallup Polls and *Literary Digest* Polls (see chapter 2), Erikson and Tedin (1981) found evidence of considerable voter conversion during the realignment era. Realignments, it seems, are events of such force that even older generations of voters find the pressures difficult to resist.

Today it is recognized that partisan change occurs constantly, even without realignment-level shocks. The electorate's net party identification (or macropartisanship) constantly undergoes small changes, largely in response to whether the political and economic news favors the presidential party (Erikson, MacKuen, and Stimson 1998, 2002). In the short run, almost all the changes are due to period effects, as all age groups (generations) shift their partisanship more or less in tandem.[23]

Generations and Political Polarization

As discussed in previous chapters, there has been much commentary that like political elites the electorate too is becoming polarized. First, it is important to spell out what polarization does and does not mean. It *does not* mean that citizens are taking more ideologically extreme positions on political issues. What it *does mean* is that Americans holding liberal positions are increasingly identifying themselves with the Democrat Party, and those holding conservative positions are increasingly identifying themselves with the Republican Party. While no one disagrees this movement is taking place, there is lively disagreement about the magnitude of this sorting process (Abramowitz and Saunders 2008; Fiorina, Abrams, and Pope 2008).[24]

An analysis by Stoker and Jennings (2008) shows that the increased polarization of American electorate over time is driven by complex factors, but one of the keys is generational replacement. New entrants into the electorate evidence a greater level of polarization than those exiting the electorate. This pattern is consistent with the impressionable years thesis, where the recent increase in elite polarization affects the opinions of seventeen- to twenty-six-year-olds but does not much affect the older generations, whose opinions have now hardened. To the extent elite polarization continues, new generations will be socialized to a more polarized party system. As the electorate changes and the younger more polarized generations replace the older less polarized generations, party polarization of the electorate will increase until it reaches some new equilibrium point.

Generations, the Life Cycle, and Policy Issues

Understanding of generation and life-cycle effects is far less advanced when we turn from partisanship to policy issues. For one thing, policy issues are many, with a likelihood that each tells a different story. In chapter 4 we saw a variety of trends (often stationary) in opinion on many issues. The presumption is that these trends are mainly due to period effects, as all birth cohorts move in tandem to the ethos of the times. In rare cases there may be generational effects, as each new batch of adult citizens brings a new perspective to old problems like taxing and spending or the death penalty. We might expect to find life-cycle effects, with people starting out liberal but becoming more conservative as they age. But in some instances, such as the rise of white acceptance of racial integration in the 1960s and 1970s, change is so fast that the liberalism of the times must offset any conservative life-cycle effect, making specific birth cohorts become more liberal with age.

The supposedly liberalizing (or radicalizing) effect of the 1960s on the generation that came of age in that decade has been the focus of some study. Delli Carpini (1986) and Davis (2005) have made intensive studies of the 1960s generation and isolated a number of instances in which this generation differed from surrounding age cohorts. What we would expect among this generation, of course, is a leftist bent to their political ideology. For the most part, these authors found that the generation of the 1960s was more supportive than other cohorts of government involvement in the issues of race, civil liberties, economics, and social concerns. As the generation has aged, however, its distinctiveness has begun to erode. Society exerts a pull toward the political center as one moves through the life cycle (Delli Carpini 1986, 120–38).

If lasting effects of the 1960s generation are to be located, they would most likely be found among the subcohort of antiwar activists. An analysis was performed by Jennings (1987) using the Michigan socialization panel. From this group starting out as 1965 high school seniors, Jennings compared college graduates who protested the Vietnam War and the matching sample of college graduates who were not protesters. An advantage of the panel approach is that one can look back to high school and see if the differences are explained by self-selection. On many issues there were substantial generational effects. In 1965, while in high school, the (future) protesters were 8 percent less favorable to prayer in the public schools than the nonprotesters, but seventeen years later they were 30 percent less favorable than the nonprotesters. The protesters were 13 percent more supportive of a federal role in school integration in 1965, but 43 percent more supportive in 1982. On many other issue orientations, however, the once liberal protesters began to move in a conservative direction. While 83 percent of the protesters considered themselves liberals in 1973, only 63 percent did so in 1982. Declines of at least 20 percent also occurred on questions of government responsibility for providing jobs, legalization of marijuana, rights of accused, helping minorities, and equality for women. The protesters were still considerably more liberal than the nonprotesters in 1982, but they had lost at least some of their distinctiveness.

By 1982, the protesters' attitudes had been shaped by both generational and life-cycle effects. Their experience as antiwar protesters stamped them with an indelible liberal print, while life-cycle effects pushed them back in a conservative direction. Furthermore, their liberalism had been eroded by a period effect—exposure to the conservative ethos of the 1980s. In an interesting follow-up, Jennings (2002) showed that the offspring of the protestors were also a good deal more liberal than were the offspring of the nonprotestors. The experience as war protestors shaped not only the protestors' politics years later but also those of their children.

Thanks to extensive collection of data on the ideological preferences of Americans, ideological identification (as a liberal, moderate, or conservative) is the one issue-related variable for which we have strong evidence to document the nature of change and stability over time. Opposite the pattern for party identification, with its clear generational effects but no certain life-cycle effects, ideological identification shows clear life-cycle effects and no generational effects. As one might expect, each new generation starts out more liberal than average but then drifts toward the conservative with age. Moreover, each generation starts out with the same level of liberalism and drifts rightward at about the same rate. A regular pattern of newly entering liberals who then turn conservative works to keep the electorate's net division of ideological identification constant, at least under equilibrium conditions. We saw this in chapter 4, where unlike party identification, the division of ideological identification has been remarkably stable for over a quarter of a century.[25]

Table 5.6 illustrates the combination of birth cohorts and age cohorts for respondents in cumulated CBS/*New York Times* surveys for four years at eight-year intervals: 1984, 1992, 2000, and 2008. In each year, conservatism increases with age (read down the column). Showing life-cycle effects, each "generation" changes with the time. For instance, the youngest group (age twenty-five and under) in 1984 was only 4 percentage points more conservative than liberal in self-identification. Eight years later, when they became twenty-six to thirty-three, they were 10 percentage points more conservative than liberal. The cycle of entry by the new and exits among the old keeps the balance of liberals and conservatives more or less at a constant level. Interestingly, in recent years the oldsters who are the most conservative in ideological identification are also the most Democratic in terms of party identification. The generational effect of the depression apparently marked them for life.

One area we evidence both life-cycle effects and generational effects is political interest, which includes media use. Citizens become more interested in politics as they move through the life cycle. In 2004, 34 percent of those between eighteen and twenty-nine said they read a newspaper about the presidential campaign, rising to 39 percent for those between thirty and forty-four, 51 percent for those between forty-five and sixty-four, and 61 percent for those over sixty-five. While these data showing a strong life-cycle effect are not surprising, what is surprising is there also exists a strong generational effect. Those under thirty in the twenty-first century are much less likely to follow the political news than were those under thirty in the mid-1980s and earlier. In 1960, 84 percent of those under thirty said they followed the campaign in the newspaper; by 1980 it had dropped to 56 percent, and by 2004 it had fallen to 34 percent—clear evidence of a generational shift in traditional ways of following politics (Wattenberg 2008, 19). The evidence is still out as to whether the dot-com generation simply differs in the way it approaches politics from previous generations, but not, as some contend, in the quality of what constitutes "the good citizen" (Dalton 2008).

5-6 The Persistence of Political Orientations

At the outset of this chapter, we noted that a key assumption justifying the study of political socialization is that orientations formed early persist over time. There is a good deal of evidence that many important political predispositions do endure over a considerable span. There is also a good deal of evidence that people continue to learn and adjust their political perspective in response to their adult environment and the events in their lives. When we speak of long-term persistence, it is helpful to think of persistence as relative to one's peers rather than as an immunity from period effects—the impact of commonly shared events. Consider the mental experiment of imagining a group of young people at the onset of adulthood. Some are Democrats and some are Republicans, some are liberal and some are conservative, with further variation in other attitudes and opinions as well. The mental experiment is to ask whether or not the relative political positions of these young people stay the same throughout their lifetime. For instance, would the young liberals still be the most liberal and the young conservatives still be the most conservative during their old age? Obviously people can change, but the answer to this mental experiment is "yes." The young conservatives remain the most conservative among their peers in old age (likewise for liberals).

It is important to understand that when we speak of persistence, what mostly persist are core values and predispositions rather than specific opinions on issues of the day. Thus, overarching values such as partisanship, liberal–conservative orientation, and racial attitudes tend to persist, while trust in government or attitudes about defense spending tend to be more fleeting. Regarding persistence, two major points merit elaboration. First, political attitudes are malleable through the impressionable years. Second, after the impressionable years, political orientations harden considerably. Change still occurs, but stability markedly increases.

Once the impressionable years leading up to adulthood end, the stability of core political values increases greatly. There now exist three long-term panel surveys, all of which demonstrate this same point. The longest of these, and the most dramatic example of persistence, is the Bennington study originated by Theodore Newcomb. Young women (sixteen to twenty years old), mostly from conservative homes, matriculated at Bennington College, which at the time (in the 1930s) had an avowedly liberal faculty. Students were first interviewed between 1935 and 1938, then reinterviewed in 1960 and again in 1984. The data thus stretch over almost fifty years. Using a number of items to create a scale of liberal–conservative political orientations, Alwin, Cohen, and Newcomb (1991) found a high level of persistence over the fifty-year period. The authors concluded that 60 percent of the variance in the 1984 political predispositions could be predicted from the predispositions in the 1930s when the students were attending Bennington, whereas the remaining 40 percent reflected attitude change (Alwin, Cohen, and Newcomb 1991, 265). A second long-term panel survey (spanning thirty-seven years) is the Terman study of gifted children (Terman and Oden 1959). Respondents were interviewed four times, beginning in 1940 and ending in 1977 (when they were about thirty and sixty-seven years old). A reanalysis of these data by Sears and Funk (1999) showed that 65 percent held the same party preference and 54 percent held the same political ideology in 1977 that they had in 1940.[26] One conclusion is that socialization to core values for many people is largely complete by the late twenties.

Strong evidence for the persistence thesis comes from the Michigan socialization data. These data clearly support the impressionable years–later persistence hypothesis. Attitudes were subject to considerable change between eighteen and twenty-six years of age but became considerably more stable in the years following (Jennings and Stoker 1999). In Figure 5.3 we used the Michigan data for an even stronger test of persistence. We divided the 1965 high school seniors into Democrats and Republicans. We then looked at their reported vote choice for president between 1968 and 1996 based on their 1965 partisanship. The figure shows the 1965 Democrats consistently voted for Democratic presidential candidates and 1965 Republicans consistently voted for Republican presidential candidates over the following eight presidential elections for which we have data.[27] The foundation upon which the study of political socialization is based—what is learned young has a lifetime effect—is solidly supported by the evidence.

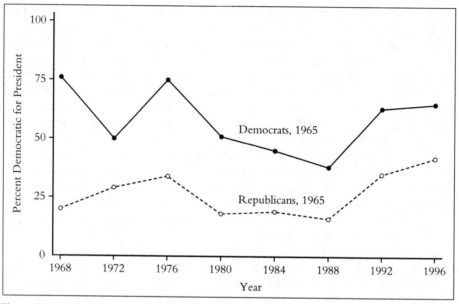

Figure 5.3   Vote for president as adults, by party identification as high school youth in 1965. *Source:* University of Michigan Political Socialization Study Data. Recalls of vote decisions are from 1973, 1982, and 1997 survey waves.

A Note on Marriage

Of course when people change their adult environment, change in political views sometimes follows. When one loses a job or gets a new one, or moves to a new community or joins a new circle of friends, their new political environment can change their political views. The biggest life change, however, may be marriage. It is not that we expect marriage to have a common effect on everyone. Rather, partners in marriage can shape each others' views about political issues.

Do couples become more alike over the course of a marriage? If so, who is influencing whom? Stoker and Jennings (2005) addressed these issues using the Michigan Socialization Study. Recall, the first interviews in this project began in 1965 when the respondents were high school seniors. These same respondents were then reinterviewed in 1973, 1982, and 1997. When they married, interviews were conducted with their marriage partners.

Even though few people use politics as the basis for selecting marriage partners, we would expect at the outset of marriage a positive relationship between the political opinions of husbands and wives, as people generally choose marriage partners from the same class, race, and religion. This is indeed what we see for the three data points. Over ten issues, there is a positive relationship between the political opinions of husbands and wives. In the case of party identification, in 1973 the correlation was .34, rising to .47 in 1982, and .54 in 1997. For the ten issues, the relationships tended to either grow stronger or remain the same over time. Of course, those who divorced before 1997 would not be in the 1997 sample, which may affect relationships. But on balance, the longer the marriage, the more alike the marital partners become in their political opinions.

In general, over time wives became more politically similar to husbands, rather than the reverse. Most of the movement occurred early in the marriage (1973–1982), with less movement occurring between 1982 and 1997. In the first period, there was significant movement for five issues, with wives becoming more like husbands in four cases, and husbands more like wives in one (the legalization of marijuana).[28] In the latter period (1982–1997) there is more evidence of mutual socialization, although husbands still had an edge.

Among the implications of these findings is that marriage serves to reduce the gender gap in partisanship, voting, and political opinions. A quite striking finding in this study is that among married couples in the 1997 data there was no gender gap, but among unmarried men and women in the sample there was a significant gender gap. For example, unmarried men were 41 percent more likely to vote Republican in the 1996 election than unmarried women, but there was no significant difference in vote choice among husbands and wives.

5-7 Conclusion

In this chapter we focused mainly on the preadult sources of political learning. Some political learning takes place in childhood, although the impressionable years (ages seventeen to twenty-six) seem to be the most important. While attitudes crystallize in later adulthood, political learning still takes place as individuals respond to their environment and life events. Even partisanship, the most stable of political predispositions, responds in adulthood to issues and political personalities (Markus 1979; Fiorina 1981; Erikson, MacKuen, and Stimson 2002). But generally speaking, political change in adulthood is incremental. It is the impressionable years that offer the greatest potential for a radical break from the past.

Notes

1. School children were also polled (by Gallup) during the heat of the Clinton impeachment controversy of 1998. As with Watergate, children (age 11–17) were critical of the president—more willing to impeach than were adult samples. Yet the same youth in the same poll were more trusting of government than adults (Owen and Dennis, 1999).
2. Evidence to support this belief came from a number of early studies (pre-1960) in which parents and children were not independently interviewed. Children (normally students) were interviewed and then asked to report the political attitudes of their parents. The parents themselves were not actually interviewed. We now know that this methodology grossly overestimates the amount of parent–child similarity on most political issues. In reporting parent attitudes, children tend to project their own attitudes onto parents, artificially inflating attitude correspondence.
3. In 1997 the correlation for party identification was .47; for abortion it was .70.
4. The former point is made by Harvey (1972, 601); the latter point is made by Silbiger (1977, 174).

5. For party identification, the student–parent correlation was .66; the student–peer correlation was .26. For the eighteen-year-old vote, the student–parent correlation was .08; the student–peer correlation was .29.

6. Data retrieved 9/7/2009 from www.monitoringthefuture.org

7. The U.S. Department of Education and the Pew Charitable Trusts awarded grants to the Center for Civics Education to develop a comprehensive, standardized curriculum for teaching civics in grades K–12. For a discussion of the proposal, see Mann (1996) and Dry (1996).

8. Monitoring the Future: A Continuing Study of American Youth; 2008 data downloaded from www.monitoringthefuture.org, 9/7/2009.

9. The survey was sponsored by the John S. and James L. Knight Foundation and conducted by the Survey Research Center at the University of Connecticut. www.knightfdn.org, downloaded 10/5/2005.

10. The principal difference is between little or no civics education to any degree (Niemi and Junn 1998, 72).

11. However, Greene (2000) in a reanalysis of these data finds much slimmer increases in knowledge as a consequence of taking civics courses, and an effect only for those students currently enrolled in a civics course.

12. In a seven-nation study (including the United States) of twelve- to eighteen-year-olds, Flanagan and his colleagues (1996) found democratic school climates had a weak but significant effect on the civic commitment of their respondents.

13. It is important to appreciate that the meaning of a college education in the twenty-first century is quite different from the 1930s or earlier. Prior to World War II, someone with a college education was a rarity. Now such education is an everyday part of the social landscape. Thus, the impact of a college degree today may be quite different than fifty years ago, particularly when it comes to slotting people in social and economic networks. For an extended discussion of this point, see Nie, Junn, and Stehlik-Barry (1998, ch. 6).

14. For a summary of the extensive literature on education and liberalism, see Feldman and Newcomb (1969). For a view challenging the notion that education leads to liberalism, see Jacob (1956). See also Nie, Junn, and Stehlik-Barry (1998).

15. Similarly, the 2006 nationwide *Youth Survey on Politics* shows that among college freshmen 51 percent called themselves "liberal" or "moderate leaning to liberal," rising to 69 percent among college seniors (Fall 2006 Biannual Youth Survey on Politics and Public Service, Institute for Politics, John F. Kennedy School of Government, Harvard University). See also, Sidanius et al. 2008.

16. In a reading of preferences for this term in March 1997, 30 percent of the racial group preferred "Black," 30 percent preferred "African-American," 8 percent preferred some other term, and 32 percent said either term was acceptable (Hart and Teeter for the *Wall Street Journal*). Currently, education does not predict a preference for these descriptors (Sigelman, Tuch, and Martin 2005).

17. There is no agreement about exactly what ages constitute the impressionable years, other than that they extend from adolescence through to early adulthood. However, the most frequently cited span is 17–26.

18. The alert reader of this section will learn, correctly, that the accounting of change in terms of generation, life-cycle, and period effects is fraught with more difficulties and ambiguities than one might think at first glance. When scholars study generation and life-cycle effects, they divide survey respondents by birth date or age. Dividing by birth date yields a set of birth cohorts, or people born during specific spans of years, like 1940–1944. Dividing by age yields "age cohorts," or people of specific age

segments, like people fifty-six to sixty years old. Suppose we check the survey responses of a birth cohort over time as it goes through the political life cycle. Any change that is observed could be a manifestation of either a life-cycle effect due to people changing as they grow older or a period effect due to people of all cohorts changing due to common experiences. Suppose we compare the survey responses of different age groups in a survey conducted at one specific period. Any observed variation by age could be a manifestation of life-cycle effects due to respondents at different stages of the cycle or to generation effects whereby respondents of different ages are affected by different experiences.

19. The socialization panel study provides a clue to why strength of partisanship increases throughout the life cycle. In the later life of the 1965 high school seniors, an increase in partisanship was found—but mainly among those who voted. Those who did not vote tended to remain Independents. Thus, one aspect of age that may lead to the acquisition of partisanship is simple learning based on experience (Jennings and Markus 1984).

20. The 1990 data are a compilation of Gallup Polls from 1989 to 1991 that contain 12,600 cases. The 1998 data are based on a single year. The exact number of cases was not reported in the original source.

21. A slightly different interpretation of differences between generations like the predepression and the postdepression generations is found in chapter 5 of Erikson, MacKuen, and Stimson (2002). Instead of dwelling on the unique events occurring as different generations came of age, they emphasize the extra experience of the older generation. For instance, the more experienced predepression generation differed from the postdepression generation mainly due to their added years of exposure to the "good" Republican years of the 1920s, before the depression. Both groups moved Democratic during the depression, but the older group's starting point was more Republican.

22. The best statement of the mobilization theory is found in Andersen (1979); an argument for the conversion hypothesis is found in Erikson and Tedin (1981); for a critique, see Campbell (1985); see Erikson and Tedin (1986) for a response. For a somewhat different approach to generations and changes in party identification, see Beck (1974).

23. Although not depicted in Figure 5.2, the 1960s generation (socialized between 1965 and 1973) also uniquely responded to the events of the time. If we look at a very special subcohort, those college graduates who protested the Vietnam War, and compare them to college graduates who did not protest, we find a strong, persistent generational impact. Jennings (1987) has made this analysis using a subset of the parent–child socialization panel. The panel contained 129 college graduates who had protested the war and a matching sample of college graduates (about twice as many) who had not been war protesters. These two groups differed little when they were in high school. Protesters-to-be were 39 percent Democratic; nonprotesters were 38 percent Democratic. By 1973, the two groups had shifted in opposite directions, with the protesters 48 percent Democratic and the nonprotesters 27 percent. By 1982, these percentages had changed little. The antiwar movement had clearly left its partisan mark on those who were actively involved.

24. Abramowtiz and Saunders (2008) show that between 1982 and 2004 the correlation between liberal–conservative ideological identification and party identification has more than doubled, but other measures show less support for party polarization thesis (Fiorina, Abrams, and Pope 2008).

25. The current steady state of ideological identification was preceded by a surge in conservative identification in the late 1960s and 1970s, contrary to the atmosphere of societal change at the time (see chapter 4). The possible role of different generations in this shift has not been systematically explored.

26. For party identification, 59 percent were perfectly stable over the four waves between 1940 and 1977, and another 6 percent moved around between waves but ended up in 1977 at the same place they started in 1940. For ideology, 42 percent were perfectly stable and 12 percent moved around but returned to their 1940 position by 1977.

27. It is important to distinguish between absolute and relative continuity. By *absolute continuity* we mean those who were strong liberals at Time 1 remain strong liberals at Time 2. By *relative continuity* we mean those who were most liberal at Time 1 are the most liberal at Time 2, but they may not have maintained their exact position on the scale. Correlation coefficients measure relative continuity, so what we are referring to in this section is the tendency, over time, for the most liberal respondents at Time 1 to be the most liberal at Time 2, not that they maintain the exact position on issues between time points. It would be unreasonable, for example, to think that in the Bennington study respondents would maintain the same issue position over a fifty-year period.

28. The four issues on which wives became more like husbands were race, gender equality, business versus labor, and school prayer. Husbands also had a slight advantage on party identification and vote choice.

6 Public Opinion and Democratic Stability

In a DEMOCRACY, public opinion is important because it can influence the decisions political leaders make. Certain aspects of public opinion take on special importance because they can influence the functioning of democratic government. In this chapter we analyze those attitudes and predispositions generally thought necessary to maintain a democracy and examine the degrees to which Americans appear to hold these attitudes.

Ideas about what is vital for the functioning of democratic government can be divided into four groups. First, there should be widespread tolerance of opposing points of view and support for the rules of democracy. An apt analogy here is the rules of the road for driving an automobile. If most people did not accept the rule that one must stop when the light is red, chaos would ensue. The rules of democracy involve guarantees that the civil liberties of all shall be protected—that majorities rule, but minorities have rights.

Second, democracy's stability may rest on a social consensus regarding values and goals. Disagreements must not be so fundamental that neither resolution nor compromise can be gained by institutionalized procedures. Too great a division may overtax even the best procedures for resolving conflict. Contemporary examples include the Hutu–Tutsi division in Rwanda, the Serb–Croat–Muslim division in Bosnia, and the division among the Shun, Kachin, and Karen peoples of Myanmar (formerly Burma), each of whom want an independent state. Strong cultural divisions are particularly vexing for the design of new democracies, as in Iraq, with its divisions between Shiites, Sunnis, and Kurds.

Third, it is important that people find reasons to trust their fellow citizens, trust government, and believe that democratic participation is meaningful. For people to accept government decisions, they must believe their political actions can be effective. They should feel that they can trust the government to respond to their interests. Should they be on the losing side in an electoral contest, they

161

should believe that while government officials will change, there will be no retribution against ordinary citizens. Widespread and intense distrust (political alienation) could threaten the stability of a democratic system.

Fourth, democracy is often thought to work best when people have certain kinds of what might be called *political personalities*. For instance, people should be open-minded rather than seek comfort for their problems by blaming others. They should accept the complexity of democratic decision making rather than seek solutions from a strong leader to override democratic discussion. When antidemocratic personalities are common, so the theory goes, minority rights become fragile and the stability of democracy is threatened.

6-1   Support for Democratic Values

One of the great threats to any political system, democracies included, is the desire on the part of those who hold political power to maintain it and to work their will free from constraints imposed by others. Ambition in political leaders is not, in and of itself, an undesirable trait. But history is strewn with examples of people in government warding off competition by the expeditious route of eliminating it. Consequently, democracies must anticipate that leaders may not suffer criticism gladly and may not want to share or give up political power if there is a way to avoid it. One solution to this problem, developed by the framers of the U.S. Constitution, was to build in a series of mechanisms designed to protect the rights of people outside government who aspire to political influence from those on the inside who hold political power. But constitutions can only go so far in making good on these protections. As Judge Learned Hand (1959, 144) once observed, "Liberty lies in the hearts and minds of men and women; when it dies there, no constitution, no laws, no court can save it." Some commitment to democratic values on the part of both political leaders and the public is essential.

In using the term *democratic values*, we are referring to procedural norms. These norms do not refer to the substance of legitimate political conflict, such as the desirable trade-off between inflation and unemployment or the merits of government paid health coverage versus private health insurance, but to the rules of the game in which that conflict takes place. One important set of procedural norms is found in the Bill of Rights. Here Americans are guaranteed the right to freedom of expression, freedom from unreasonable search and seizure, protection from self-incrimination, a speedy and public trial, free exercise of religion, and so on. Two related democratic values of great importance are majority rule and minority rights. At regular intervals, the population is mobilized into opposing camps. Each camp proclaims its own virtue and criticizes the opposition. An election is then held, and the winners take control of the government. The losers remain free to rouse popular hostility toward the new leaders in the hope of embarrassing them and ultimately replacing them in office. This procedure is normally the way decision makers are chosen in the United States. One therefore hopes to find an understanding among the electorate that these are the methods that should be employed to select public officials.

TABLE 6.1	Support for Democratic Values Stated in the Abstract		
Statement	**Democratic Response**	**Uncertain Response**	**Undemocratic Response**
People in the minority should be free to try to win majority support for their opinions.	89%	9%	2%
Public officials should be chosen by majority vote.	95	3	2
I believe in free speech for all, no matter what their views might be.	85	7	9
No matter what a person's political views are, he is entitled to the same legal protections as anyone else.	93	4	3
People should be allowed to express unpopular opinions★	95	0	5

★The Freedom Forum (June 12–July 5, 2002).

Source: John L. Sullivan, James Piereson, and George E. Marcus, *Political Tolerance and American Democracy* (Chicago: University of Chicago Press, 1982), p. 203.

As shown in Table 6.1, survey evidence does in fact demonstrate overwhelming support for democratic values when stated in the abstract. For instance, in 2002, 95 percent of the public agreed that "people should be allowed to express unpopular opinions." But note that these assertions are very general, with no reference to any specific person or group. These statements basically constitute an official American political ideology—the sort of lessons that are taught in a variety of both political and nonpolitical contexts by the family and the school and reinforced by the mass media.

However, when statements about the rules of the game have a double stimulus, with references both to democratic principles and to unpopular groups, support for these rules declines. Relevant evidence is presented in Table 6.2, in which the statements are two-pronged. Each refers to a democratic norm plus some specific group or activity. For example, in the statement "Members of the Ku Klux Klan should be banned from running for public office," individuals are asked to respond to both the norm of free elections and feelings about the Klan.

One interpretation of these data is that public support for procedural rights is less than ideal. In the cases of elections, 70 percent would ban a Klan member from running for public office (Gibson 1987). The pattern in Table 6.2 is clearly one of a lack of enthusiasm for the values of democracy when items refer to protests, demonstrations, or unpopular groups such as those "sympathetic to terrorists." Of course, we might avoid getting overly alarmed if we keep in mind that this evidence is not drawn from actual behavior and may simply represent ill-considered survey responses to hypothetical situations. However, when ordinary citizens are given the power to directly legislate using the ballot box, they often use that power to deprive

TABLE 6.2 | **Support for Democratic Values, by Specific Application**

	Democratic Response	Undecided	Undemocratic Response
[Should] people who want to overthrow the government by revolution [be] allowed to hold public meetings to express their views? (GSS 2006)	69%	1%	30%
[Should] books that contain dangerous ideas be banned from public libraries? (Pew 2009)	46	5	49
Freedom of speech should not extend to groups sympathetic to terrorists (Pew 2009)	45	6	49
The American press has too much freedom to what it wants (FAC 2005)	57	4	39
The police should be allowed to search house of people who might be sympathetic to terrorists without a court order (Pew 2009)	64	3	33
If a man is found innocent of a serious crime but new evidence is uncovered, do you think he should be tried for the same crime again? (CBS 1970)	38	4	58
If a person takes the Fifth Amendment and refuses to testify, the person is probably guilty of a crime (Fox News 2002)	36	14	50
If a person is suspected of a serious crime, do you think the police should be allowed to hold him in jail until they can get enough evidence to charge him? (CBS 2006)	48	4	48
The government should be allowed to access records to books people check out from the library (FAC 2005)	51	9	40
Newspapers which preach revolution should be banned from circulation (Harris 1973)	57	9	34
Judges should be able to censor the press in criminal cases so jurors are not biased (FF 1997)	21	14	65
Meetings to denounce the President should be banned (Harris 1973)	39	3	58
Government should be able to restrict media broadcasts that might be offensive to racial groups (FAC 2005)	48	N/A	52
[It is] a good idea for the government to keep a list of people who take part in demonstrations (Harris and Westin 1979)	25	26	50

Sources: John Sullivan, James Piereson, and George Marcus, *Political Tolerance and American Democracy* (Chicago: University of Chicago Press, 1982); General Social Survey (GSS), 1985; CBS: Robert Chandler, *Public Opinion* (New York: Bowker, 1972); Herbert McClosky, 1958; Herbert McClosky, "Consensus and Ideology in American Politics," *American Political Science Review* 58 (June 1964); CLS: Herbert McClosky and Alida Brill, *Dimensions of Political Tolerance* (New York: Russell Sage Foundation, 1983); Louis Harris and Alan F. Westin, *The Dimensions of Privacy* (Stevens Point, WI: Sentry Insurance, 1979); James L. Gibson, *Freedom and Tolerance in the United States* (NORC: unpublished codebook, 1987); *Washington Pos/CBS News 1970,2006*; Pew Research Center (PEW) 2009; The Freedom Forum, 1997; First Amendment Center (FAC), 2005; *Fox News* (2002).

unpopular minorities of their civil liberties and rights. Barbara Gamble (1997) looked at seventy-four ballot initiatives on public accommodations for minorities, school desegregation, gay rights, English language laws, and AIDS policies. She found that more than three-quarters of these elections resulted in the defeat of policies designed to protect minority rights.

A Growth in Democratic Tolerance?

There is a good deal of evidence that Americans are more tolerant of unpopular ideas today than in the past. Back in 1942, just 30 percent said that they believed "in free speech to the extent of allowing radicals to hold meetings and express their views in this community."[1] More recently, Table 6.3 shows the change in Americans' tolerance of selected unpopular groups from 1954 to 2008. One point attracts immediate attention: the appearance of a substantial increase in political tolerance over more than a half-century of polling. For example, note that tolerance for someone "speaking out against churches and religion" rose from 38 percent in 1954 to 76 percent in 2008. A simple conclusion is that the American public has become more tolerant of opposing points of view. A common explanation for this change is based on social learning theory. The assumption is that increases in exposure to social and cultural diversity lead to increases in support for democratic norms. Two changes of consequence for this explanation are rising levels of education and the move from rural to urban areas. The proportion of people who have been to college has more than doubled since the 1950s (ANES

TABLE 6.3	Public Tolerance for Advocates of Unpopular Ideas, 1954–2008								
	Person Should Be Allowed to Make a Speech			Person Should Be Allowed to Teach in College			Person's Book Should Remain in the Library		
	1954	1972	2008	1954	1972	2008	1954	1974	2008
An admitted communist	28%	52%	66%	6%	39%	61%	29%	53%	69%
Someone against churches and religion	38	65	76	12	40	63	37	60	73
Someone who favors government ownership of all railroads and large industries	65	77	★	38	56	★	60	67	★
Someone who believes that blacks are genetically inferior	★	61[†]	59	★	41	47	★	62	65

★Question not asked.

[†]General Social Survey, 1976.

Sources: 1954 data are from Samuel Stouffer, *Communism, Conformity, and Civil Liberties* (New York: Wiley, 1954); 1972 and 2006 data are from the General Social Survey.

1952–2008). Educated people are more likely to understand the importance of protecting democratic liberties, if only in their own self-interest. Also, social and cultural diversity, such as that found in the city, brings individuals into contact with people who are not like them. They learn that those who are different are not always dangerous (Williams, Nunn, and St. Peter 1976; Hillygus 2005).

A less obvious explanation for the rise in support for democratic values holds that there has been little real change between 1954 and 2008; rather, what we see is nothing more than an artifact of the question—that is, the groups used in 1954 to elicit tolerant or intolerant responses are not as threatening as they were in 1954. One undisputed conclusion from the research on democratic values is that perceived threat to the nation is the most powerful determinant of political intolerance. In 1954, the Cold War with the Soviet Union was hitting its stride. The climate of opinion in the United States was strongly influenced by the scare tactics of the ultra-right-wing junior senator from Wisconsin Joseph McCarthy. He claimed to have proof that communists had infiltrated the American government, and more than a few people believed him (Goldstein 1978). People were terminated from their jobs and blacklisted because they were presumed to harbor communist sympathies. At a minimum, low levels of support for democratic values among the public during the McCarthy era dissuaded many Americans from speaking out against these indefensible practices. The groups identified in the 1954 survey are those usually associated with the left—communists, atheists, and socialists. Tolerance may appear to have gone up simply because these groups no longer appear to pose the danger many once thought.[2]

In an ambitious project, Sullivan, Piereson, and Marcus (1982) devised a test to determine if the increased tolerance one sees in Table 6.3 is real or simply an illusion. They suspected that support for the civil liberties of a specific group was largely driven by emotion rather than considered judgment. If someone liked atheists, that person would have no problem allowing them the right of free speech. It takes no tolerance to put up with someone with whom one agrees or someone who is promoting a political agenda with which one concurs. On the other hand, the same person might heartily dislike members of the Ku Klux Klan and be quite willing to deny them free expression. The acid test for tolerance, according to Sullivan and his colleagues, is putting up with those whose ideas one finds repugnant. In other words, they suspected that support for procedural rights depended on whose ox was being gored.

Sullivan, Piereson, and Marcus (1982, 60–63) devised a "content-controlled" question in which respondents were given a list of groups and asked which one they liked least (with an option to supply a group not on the list). Respondents were then queried as to whether they would "put up with" (i.e., be tolerant of) the procedural rights of) their least liked group.

As Table 6.4 demonstrates, tolerance using a least liked approach does not seem to have improved much since 1954.[3] For example, only 18 percent would allow a member of their least liked group to teach in the public schools. These levels of tolerance are not much different from the 1950s. If true, this finding has disturbing implications. It calls into question the inherent willingness of Americans to embrace one of the pillars of democratic thought: tolerance.

TABLE 6.4	Levels of Tolerance Using Content-Controlled Items (1987)	
		Percentage Tolerant of Least Liked Group
Members of the [least liked group] should be allowed to teach in public schools.		19
The [least liked group] should not be outlawed.		31
Members of the [least liked group] should be allowed to make a speech in this city.		50
The [least liked group] should not have their phones tapped by our government.		63
The [least liked group] should be allowed to hold public rallies in our city.		32

Source: James Gibson, *Freedom and Tolerance in the United States* (National Opinion Research Center: unpublished codebook, 1987).

It also seems to offer little hope for improvement. The early studies showed a strong relationship between education and support for democratic values. One might suppose as aggregate levels of education increased, so would political tolerance. However, the revisionist thesis holds this is not the case, as Americans are no more tolerant now than they were during the McCarthy era of the 1950s. Thus, improvements in the general level of education, according to this viewpoint, are not the answer to what is seen as a dangerously low level of support for democratic values.

Not surprisingly, this line of research has been subject to substantial criticism. Among the most telling critiques is a claim that the questions used are inherently incapable of determining the true level of support for democratic values. The questions are flawed because by their very nature they have double stimuli—support for a general principle and reactions to an unpopular group or political act. Further, these stimuli are not balanced. A strong stimulus (one's single most disliked group) is contrasted to a much weaker stimulus (abstract democratic values).

In the typical survey setting, in which respondents must give answers in a few seconds, it is not unexpected that the strong stimulus frequently overwhelms the weak one (or first comes to mind). Most people know whom they do and do not like, and whom they do not like they often find threatening. Coming to grips with an abstract principle is more difficult (Brady and Sniderman 1985; Zaller and Feldman 1992). Thus, initially, the strong stimulus dominates. But importantly, several studies show that people can often be talked out of—or talked into—antidemocratic positions (Chong 1993; Cobb and Kuklinski 1997). Gibson (1996) demonstrates that of Americans who initially gave an intolerant response, 38 percent changed their minds when given subsequent counterarguments for the tolerant alternative. But counterarguments were even more effective among those initially giving a tolerant response. Sixty-three percent changed their minds and gave the intolerant response. Davis and Silver (2004) show a similar pattern in their study of the trade-off between civil liberties and national security following 9/11. It was easier to get people to abandon pro–civil liberties attitudes than to abandon pro-security attitudes. It seems quite clear that people have great difficulty reconciling their desire to support the principles of democratic procedure with their fears and apprehensions about unconventional groups and national security.

Still, the data shown in Table 6.3 show the importance of the target group when assessing change in tolerance over time. Note the difference in change in the tolerance for "an admitted communist" and for "someone who believes blacks are genetically inferior." Between 1972 and 2008, the public moved from 52 percent saying an admitted communist should be allowed to speak to 66 percent. But for the race and genetics question, the change was slightly in the other direction moving from 61 percent down to 59 percent saying a person holding racist views should be allowed to speak.

Mondak and Sanders (2003) offer yet another wrinkle on the target group problem. The General Social Survey (GSS) contains a total of fifteen questions that address intolerance across a variety of target groups. Mondak and Sanders argue that an intolerant response for any one of these groups on any one legal activity (or any one of the fifteen questions) is an indicator of intolerance. In other words, instead of tolerance being measured by a continuous scale ranging from 0 to 15, any score greater than zero indicates intolerance. People are tolerant only to the extent that they are willing to grant full legal democratic activity to all groups without exception. So tolerance is conceptualized as a dichotomy—one either is or is not tolerant. This is a demanding standard, and using it the proportion scoring as tolerant in the GSS was only 15 percent in 1997, 20 percent in 1987, and 21 percent in 1997.

The 1987 GSS also included the Sullivan, Piereson, and Marcus (1982) "least liked" measures of tolerance. It turns out that a very large percentage of those giving tolerant answers to all 15 of the conventional GSS items gave at least one intolerant answer to the "least liked" measure. Thus, if we require tolerant responses to each of the conventional GSS measures *plus* the least liked measure, less than 5 percent of Americans (in 1987) would be classed as tolerant (Gibson 2005). This number is so low that it would seem to undermine the utility to the concept of "political tolerance." Even after 50 years of research on political tolerance, there is still no widely accepted way to measure it.

Democratic Values and 9/11

It is real and not hypothetical circumstances that provide the acid test for citizen commitment to democratic values. In everyday life, concerns over civil liberties are usually remote. In that regard, the 9/11 terrorist attack on the World Trade Center in New York and the Pentagon near Washington, D.C., provides a unique circumstance to test the willingness of citizens to trade off liberties protected by the Bill of Rights for more domestic security. In the wake of 9/11, the government proposed and enacted a number of measures to increase national security, but at a cost in terms of personal liberty. The public debate has turned on the need to protect civil liberties as the government seeks greater powers to defeat a mostly foreign enemy, but one that also poses risks to domestic security.

To properly test for the effect of 9/11, we must examine data both before and after the terrorist attack. As shown in Figure 6.1, starting with the Oklahoma City bombing in 1995, the public has been repeatedly asked, "In order to curb terrorism in this country, do you think it will be necessary for the average person to give up some civil liberties, or not?" Immediately following the Oklahoma City bombing, 49 percent thought it would be necessary to give up some civil liberties. As time passed, the percentage taking this position declined. However, shortly after 9/11, 63 percent thought it would be necessary to give up some personal liberties to fight terror, but again these percentages declined over time. As of July 2005, 40 percent believed we may have to give up some civil liberties to fight terrorism, which was just a single percentage point lower than just after the bombing of the Murrah Federal Building in Oklahoma City on April 19, 1995. However, by 2009 just 27 percent thought we might have to give up some civil liberties to fight terrorism, the lowest percentage point in the time series. Perhaps worries over terrorism were supplanted by worries over the economy, or by lack of any terrorist event on U.S. soil since 9/11.

The data in Figure 6.1 underscore the persistent finding in the literature on democratic values that the perception of threat against society or cherished beliefs is the single most important factor that drives people to cede fundamental liberties to government (Marcus and MacKuen 2001; Huddy et al. 2005). Unfortunately, the chain of causal inference stops here, as there is almost no

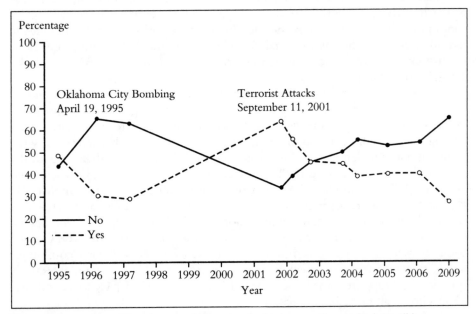

Figure 6.1   *Question:* "In order to curb terrorism in this country, do you think it will be necessary for the average person to give up some civil liberties, or not?" *Sources:* Surveys by *Los Angeles Times, Newsweek,* Pew Center.

reliable research on why some people see foes to their nation's way of life so much more threatening than do others.

For their study of post-9/11 attitudes toward civil liberties, Davis and Silver (2004; see also Davis 2007) constructed a nine-item scale that addressed the trade-off between civil liberties and personal security. In addition to the items shown in Figure 6.1 they asked, for example, if high school teachers should "have the right to criticize America's policies toward terrorism" or should high school teachers "defend America's policies in order to promote loyalty to our country." Sixty percent of a national sample said teachers should promote loyalty. On the other hand, 77 percent opposed the government being able to search a suspected terrorist's property without a warrant. Davis and Silver conclude that on the whole Americans are not unreasonable on these matters. Among the best predictors of a willingness to yield liberal liberties to the government was the perception of threat and trust in government. The more people feared the possibility of another terrorist attack in the next three months and the more they trusted government, the more likely they were willing to cede fundamental liberties to the government in order to fight terror.

The Theory of Democratic Elitism

If the public is as equivocal about or nonsupportive of democratic values as many believe, how does democracy in the United States survive? American colleges and universities contain substantial numbers of atheists (Gibson and Bingham 1985, 15). In 2006, 37 percent of the public would not allow atheists to teach in these institutions (GSS). Why has there been no mass movement to root out the nonbelievers? Beyond the obvious observation that what people say has no one-to-one link with actual behavior, one influential accounting for this circumstance is "the theory of democratic elitism" (Stouffer 1955; McClosky 1964; Rose 1964).

The starting point for the theory of democratic elitism is the observation that support for democratic values is not evenly spread throughout the population. Perhaps not surprisingly, surveys show the least commitment to democratic values among the least educated and the politically inactive. Conversely, surveys show the most support for democratic values among the highly educated and politically alert, and especially among public officials. For example, Nunn, Crockett, and Williams (1978) demonstrated that 83 percent of a community leader sample could be classified as "more tolerant" compared to only 56 percent of a comparable mass sample. Even today, the mass public is not as verbally supportive of democratic values as political elites in the late 1970s or even the mid-1950s. The 2008 General Social Survey shows 66 percent of the public favors free speech for a communist and 65 percent favors free speech for a militarist. Comparable figures for elites show greater verbal support going back as far as 1954 (Stouffer 1955; McClosky and Brill 1983; Gibson and Bingham 1985).

Perhaps the most important predictor of support for democratic values is education. Several investigators have presented data showing people who are better educated tend to be more supportive of democratic procedures than those with less education (Stouffer 1955; Nunn, Crockett, and Williams 1978; Nie, Junn, and Stehlik-Barry 1998). The 2008 General Social Survey shows that 48 percent of those with a grade-school education would allow a homosexual to teach at a college or university, while 93 percent of those with a college degree would do so. Most now believe that the causal link between education and support for democratic values runs through verbal cognitive proficiency— the ability to gather, analyze, and comprehend information and discover where one's self-interest truly lies (Nie, Junn, and Stehlik-Barry 1998; Hillygus 2005).

In addition, some go even further and argue that within categories of education, political elites are more tolerant than the public. One author inferred from the Stouffer data (part of which is presented in Table 6.3) that the "differences between leaders and the community at large does not seem due simply to education, since 79 percent of the college-educated leaders are among the more tolerant as compared to 66 percent for the general college-educated population" (Kornhauser 1970, 67). According to the theory of democratic elitism, political leaders are more tolerant than their education alone would predict because of their exposure to the democratic values that permeate the American elite political culture (McCloskey 1964; McClosky and Brill 1983). The system works, therefore, because those who are least attached to democratic values are unlikely to be active or influential in politics. On the other hand, those most committed to democratic tolerance are the ones who have the most influence on actual political outcomes because of their high interest and high levels of political participation. Proponents of democratic elitism can point to countries like Argentina, where government had historically been unstable, and find confirmation of their theory in the fact that educated political activists in that nation are very low in their support for democratic values (Dahl 1971, 139; Stevens, Bishin, and Barr 2006). That American political elites score high on these values is then interpreted as an explanation for democratic stability in the United States.

In the words of one of the pioneer scholars on the subject, "Democratic viability is . . . saved by the fact that those who are the most confused about democratic ideas are also most likely to be politically apathetic" (McCloskey 1964, 365). The implication would seem to be a cautionary note that too much democracy is a bad thing if, once actively engaged, the masses can pose a substantial threat to democratic values. Democracy works best, it would seem, when people are content to passively vote for competing sets of elites who control the political parties but to otherwise leave political decisions to elected leaders.

Considerable criticism has been directed at this theory. Any explanation of democratic stability that portrays political activists and officeholders as saviors and common people as potential saboteurs of democratic government will be found immediately suspect by many. Reanalysis of the Stouffer data by Robert Jackman (1972), for example, casts considerable doubt on the claim that political influentials are more supportive of democratic values than are others who share their education, gender, region of origin, and other distinguishing characteristics. The Sullivan, Piereson, and Marcus (1982) least-liked-group analysis found that the differences in tolerance between political activists and nonactivists were spurious, caused by other factors related to both support for democratic values and tolerance. Sniderman et al. (1989) found that conservative elites were particularly less tolerant than the conservative mass public, and much less tolerant than the liberal mass public. In their study of post-9/11 attitudes, Davis and Silver (2004) found that even liberals, who in normal times are the strongest defenders of civil liberties, are, under perception of threat, willing to make civil liberties concessions.

Elite support for democratic values is most crucial when these values face an actual threat. One can point to examples in U.S. history when most elites—regardless of their political persuasions—failed to come to the rescue when democratic values were actually under siege. One instance was the lack of elite opposition to the internment of Japanese Americans during World War II. Another was the failure of elites to respond critically to violations of traditional norms of free speech and due process during the persecution of alleged communists in the McCarthy era of the early 1950s.

In the case of the McCarthy era, James Gibson (1988) has correlated the tolerance scores of the mass and elite samples from the 1954 Stouffer survey, aggregated by state, with an index measuring repressive legislation passed by the states during that period. He found no evidence of demands for the repression of American communists emanating from the mass public. But he did find evidence of a link between intolerant state elites and repressive state legislation, with the role of the public perhaps being best described as acquiescence.

We should not make too much of the educated elite's greater support for civil liberties when confronted with attitudinal surveys on the matter. The better educated may simply learn what are socially desirable and "appropriate" answers to questions about tolerance (Jackman 1978, Weissberg 1998). Doubts about the tolerance-inducing effect of education can be drawn from the often-noted pressure for "political correctness" within certain provinces of society. In the 2008 GSS, a surprisingly high 26 percent of college-educated whites would not allow someone who believed blacks are genetically inferior to give a speech in their community. Using this same item, Chong (2006) breaks the GSS data into pre– and post–political correctness eras (which he pegs as before and after 1986) and examines the willingness of eighteen- to twenty-three-year-old college students to allow someone who believes blacks are genetically inferior to speak freely. Among the college students, there is a 6 percent *decrease* in tolerance post-1986, compared to an overall gain of 3 percent for the sample as a whole. Chong argues that the change in political culture condemning "hate speech" that peaked in colleges in the mid-1980s had the effect of lowering tolerance for free expression, particularly among self-identified liberal students. In some instances, the norms transmitted in the education process can provide the intellectual rationale for rejecting the right to express controversial ideas.

In a similar vein, when it comes to endorsing the ideals of the civil rights movement, well-educated whites are considerably more supportive of these ideals than those with less education. However, in demanding applied situations (such as government action to benefit racial minorities), the well educated are no more likely to be supportive than are the less educated. (For details, see chapter 7.) Jackman and Mulha (1984) stress that education does not so much increase tolerance as it increases awareness of the socially acceptable and the ability of those in the privileged class to develop sophisticated rationales for their privileged position. Of course, not everyone agrees with this interpretation.

Pluralistic Intolerance

In another approach to reconciling an intolerant public with continuing democratic government, Sullivan, Piereson, and Marcus (1982) offer a theory of "pluralistic intolerance." While the public may be quite intolerant, their data show no consensus as to what group should be suppressed. There was a great deal of diversity among the groups Americans like least. In the Sullivan, Piereson, and Marcus (1982) survey, the least liked group was American communists at 29 percent, followed by the Ku Klux Klan at 24 percent. Because there is no agreement on what groups to suppress, elites receive mixed signals and consequently have the freedom to act on the basis of their own (presumably democratic) preferences. In other words, with no intolerant consensus, there is no demand for political repression of any particular group.[4]

The most recent survey in 2005 (Gibson 2008) shows the most disliked group is the Klan at 44 percent, followed by radical Muslims at 13 percent, Nazis at 12 percent, and atheists at 6 percent. On a list of the three most disliked, only the Klan and Nazis garnered mention by a majority of Americans. But one in five (21 percent) listed atheists as one of their three most disliked groups (more than for communists). Is this most current distribution "pluralistic"? Since no group gathers a "least liked" 50 percent majority, a defensible answer is "yes," particularly since in the twenty-first century the Klan and Nazis are fringe groups with virtually no political impact and just a smattering of followers. Their current status as the most disliked in 2005 seems a relic of the past and leads one to question whether their selection as "least liked" simply indicates ritualistic responses to now toothless bogymen.

The theory of pluralistic intolerance implies that when one vulnerable group is very unpopular among the general public, political repression will occur. In the 1950s, intolerance was focused on communists and people of the political left. Repression of those persons has been amply documented (Goldstein 1978). Following the decline and fall of McCarthyism in the mid-1950s, intolerance became unfocused and repression was much less evident. The post-9/11 atmosphere presents concern about a new focus on public intolerance of Muslims and people of Arab extraction. The 2005 survey shows that 13 percent of Americans mentioned radical Muslims as their most disliked group, and 37 percent mentioned them as one of their three most disliked groups (Gibson 2008).

But is public hysteria over outgroups the major factor when repression occurs? The direction of causation here is very much open to question. It is possible that both the policy of repressing the left during the McCarthy era and mass public opinion opposing communists and the like were determined by political elites.[5] In fact, a common interpretation of mass–elite linkage is that independent of any effect of opinion on policy, elite opinion and behavior shape mass opinion (e.g., Zaller 1992; Jacobs and Shapiro 2000; Page 2002). The danger in focused intolerance at the mass level may be that demagogic elites can find a receptive audience to fuel an antidemocratic political movement.

Intolerant Beliefs and Intolerant Behavior

How much significance should we allot to responses to survey questions about tolerance and civil liberties? Intolerant beliefs may be of consequence only if they lead to intolerant behavior, and there is little evidence of any meaningful link. It is important to realize that behavior has multiple causes, of which attitudes are only one (Deutscher 1973). For example, a person would probably look for group support before attempting to prevent an atheist from speaking or before removing books by a communist from the public library. The opinions measured in studies of political tolerance are so uniquely distant from intolerant behavior as to render them little more than hypothetical (Weissberg 1998). For instance, do the expressed fears of some citizens in an opinion survey about libraries stocking their shelves with inflammatory books by Marxists really capture an enduring predisposition for antidemocratic behavior? Translating antidemocratic beliefs into behavior is likely to be a much less frequent occurrence than translating a preference for a political candidate into the behavior of casting a vote for that candidate.

6-2   Political Consensus

Clearly, a democracy is more stable if citizens agree, or are in consensus, on basic values and goals. Some conflict over issues is inevitable in a democracy because public policies generally cannot benefit or penalize all persons or groups equally. Intense or severe political conflict, however, is undesirable because it may threaten the stability of democracy. Robert Dahl defines *intensity of conflict* as a function of the extent to which each side sees the other as an enemy to be destroyed by whatever means necessary (Dahl 1971, 335). As issues become more intensely debated, the language of conflict becomes harsher; opponents are accused of acting out of less than honorable motives, and tactics that were once regarded as illegitimate are given serious consideration. The Hutu–Tutsi split in Rwanda and Muslim–Christian split in Lebanon are classic examples of political divisions that make democratic government and the protection of civil liberties extremely difficult.

The United States has clearly experienced political conflict in its history. Now, in the twenty-first century, some even see the growing polarization of public opinion leading to a "culture war" over basic values. But unlike many other countries, there has not been significant controversy over a number of fundamental issues. Evidence from several surveys indicates the following: (1) The broad elements of the constitutional order are widely endorsed; 90 percent agree that America is unique because it is founded on the ideals of freedom, equality, and opportunity[6];

(2) there is a consensus that defects should be remedied by legal processes of change; (3) most people are satisfied with the economic order, with 94 percent agreeing that we "must be ready to make sacrifices if necessary . . . to preserve the free enterprise system"; few want to nationalize large corporations; big business is widely accepted; labor unions are less popular, but few want to see them eliminated; (4) Americans believe that opportunities exist for personal achievement—the doors of success are open for those willing to work; and (5) most people are content with their lot.[7] When asked, 80 percent say they feel extremely good or very good when they see the American flag fly (ANES 2004); 86 percent say they own an American flag; 87 percent say they are "patriotic,"[8] and 89 percent profess extreme or very strong love for their country (ANES 2004). Seventy-nine percent are "very proud" to be American (GSS 2004), and 89 percent say they would rather be a citizen of the United States than of any other country (GSS 2004).

Traditional sources of cleavage that have posed problems in other countries have, for the most part, been moderate in the United States. Among the most important of these are class, regionalism, and religion. Particularly important is the fact that political attitudes are only weakly related to these divisions (see chapter 7). Regional differences (at least currently) also tend not to be intense. The American public is mobile. The Bureau of the Census reports that in a typical year, 20 percent of the population moves, with about one-third moving a considerable distance. Even the South, on the question of race, is beginning to lose some of its uniqueness. Religious antagonisms, too, do not lead to severe issue conflicts. One reason is that religious preference is only slightly related to social class. One's religion does not determine one's opportunities or economic well-being. The low salience of these conflicts is evidenced in the data that, in 2007, 92 percent of opinion-holders said they would vote for a Jew for president, 94 percent said they would vote for a black (and of course Barack Obama was elected president in 2008), 95 percent said they would vote for a Catholic, 87 percent would vote for a Hispanic, 86 percent would vote for a woman, and 82 percent would vote for a Mormon (Gallup 2007).[9] Despite these observations, there have been important divisions within American society.

Race and Ethnicity

Racial divisions have existed since the beginning of the republic. The historic struggles to end slavery, racial segregation, and racial discrimination are well known. Today, there still exists a wide gap between the opinions of white Americans and African Americans on a substantial range of issues. These differences are most pronounced on questions of what constitutes fair treatment for blacks (again, see chapter 7), but exist in other domains as well. The possibility for conflict between the races is intensified by the fact that socioeconomic differences reinforce issue disagreements. Compared to whites, blacks are disproportionately working class and unemployed.

While blacks clearly have specific policy grievances and tend to view partisan politics from a different perspective than whites, they do not reject the central tenets underlying the American political system. In 1981, 76 percent of a national sample of black respondents thought the United States had a special role to play in the world; 86 percent said the United States was the best place in the world to live (Gallup 1986); in 1988 (ANES) only 3 percent of blacks said they were "not proud" to be an American; in 2004 (NES), 83 percent of blacks professed an "extremely strong" or "very strong" love for the country; and in 2009, 88 percent of blacks agreed "I am very patriotic" (Pew).

Today, the fastest growing minority group is Hispanic Americans, who are already overtaking African Americans as the largest minority group in the United States. Like previous waves of immigrants when they came to the United States, newcomers from Mexico and elsewhere in Latin America have been seen as threats by many Americans fearful of change. One prominent social scientist, the late Samuel Huntington (2004), has even expressed concern that Hispanic Americans differ from previous immigrant groups by resisting assimilation into the mainstream American culture. However, studies of Hispanic Americans (themselves a culturally diverse group of different national origins and races) suggest such fears to be unfounded. For instance, when asked questions about pride in the United States and American citizenship, Hispanic Americans answer affirmatively at rates similar to non-Hispanic whites and African Americans (de la Garza, Falcon, and Garcia 1996).

But should we even be singling out minorities as if to ask whether they pass the test of democratic citizenship or American patriotism? If a danger to democracy exists, it may come not from minorities rejecting mainstream American values or resisting assimilation, but rather from some members of the dominant white majority who resist their aspirations. At the fringe are white "super patriots" who though low in number have shown a willingness to engage in unlawful acts including violence. They may offer the greatest threat of civil disorder today.

6-3   Political Support: Trust and Efficacy

A common assumption is that political systems work better when citizens both trust their fellow citizens and trust their government. Social trust (trusting fellow citizens) is a key component of *social capital*, often cited as the lubricant that makes democracy work. *Political trust* (trusting government) is the affective component of support. Those high in political trust are satisfied with the procedures and products of government. The opposite of trust is *political cynicism*, or the evaluation that the political system is not producing policies according to expectations. *Efficacy* is the cognitive or belief component of support; it is the extent to which a person believes his or her political activities will influence government.

Political Trust

The performance of government drives political trust. No government, of course, ever has the complete trust of all its citizens. However, many argue that it is important for democratic government to maintain some minimal (usually unspecified) level of trust among its citizens. One argument is pitched at the normative level. If the distinctive character of democracy is the substitution of voluntary consent for coercion, it is no small moral shortcoming when citizens withdraw trust out of a conviction that the government is not acting in their best interests (Nye 1997). Others make claims of a more practical bent. Levels of trust are thought to affect the leadership strategies available to political decision makers. Leaders must be able to make decisions and commit resources without first consulting those persons who will be affected by the decisions and called upon to supply the resource materials. As William Gamson (1968, 45–46) wrote, when trust is high, "the authorities are able to make new commitments on the basis of it and, if successful, increase support even more. When it is low or declining, authorities may find it difficult to meet existing commitments and govern effectively." Thus, when trust was high in 1964, the government could draw on its credit rating with the electorate and send troops to fight an overseas police action in Vietnam with little public debate. That sort of freedom was considerably constrained after 1972.

Levels of trust are particularly important in the economic area, where the government needs maneuvering room to pursue long-term policy goals. For example, if inflation becomes entrenched, the government must sometimes call upon citizens to endure the pain of recession for the promise of stable prices at a point in the indeterminate future. Citizens must have faith in the fairness and competence of government and not demand a premature accounting based on a short-term appraisal of cost and benefits (Weatherford 1987; Hetherington and Rudolph 2008.) More concretely, low trust among citizens can undermine the willingness of bright people to go into government and the willingness to voluntarily comply with the law (Nye 1997). It has also been shown that political trust influences support for redistributive policies—that is, a willingness to make financial sacrifices to help minorities and the poor or provide foreign aid. According to Hetherington (2005), when trust is high, Americans are more willing to approve the spending of dollars necessary for these programs. The effect of trust on willingness to spend on redistribution may be particularly important for conservatives, who see redistribution of tax money as a sacrifice rather than a benefit. When trust in government is high, conservatives are more willing to support government spending programs; when trust is low, they are likely to oppose them (Rudolph and Evans 2005; Hetherington and Rudolph 2008).

If political trust drops sufficiently low, the result can be social disruption. Disruption may serve as an impetus to needed reform, or it may threaten the stability of an existing regime. At the very least, a portion of state resources must be diverted to cope with the disturbances. Lack of trust is particularly dangerous when the system is not performing in an adequate fashion—as, for example, in an economic depression. During the worldwide depression of the 1930s, many democratic governments ceased to be effective. Those with a reservoir of trust among their citizens were able to withstand the strain, while those not so advantaged (such as Austria, Germany, and Spain) succumbed to severe antidemocratic movements. To those who remember that era and its consequences, concern about trust is more than an academic exercise. See the pathbreaking work of Lipset (1960) and Almond and Verba (1963).

The level of political trust serves as a barometer indicating how well government is performing. It is, therefore, no surprise that scholars have paid considerable attention to the fluctuations in trust over time.[10] Figure 6.2 presents the trend in political trust between 1958 and 2008 taken from the American National Election Studies. The data from 1958 to 1966 reflect the tranquility of the Eisenhower years, the Camelot years of Kennedy, and the landslide election of Lyndon Johnson. After 1966 trust began to decrease at a steady pace until 1980. Common explanations include the government's handling of the civil rights movement, the Vietnam War, Watergate, the pardon of Richard Nixon, and the economic and foreign policy problems associated with the Carter administration. The decrease in trust during this period came about equally from the dissatisfied left and the dissatisfied right. For example, cynics on the left tended to think the government had moved too slowly on civil rights; cynics on the right tended to think it had moved too rapidly (Miller 1983).

The most severe decline in trust came between 1972 and 1974. The most plausible explanation is Watergate. Daily accusations of break-ins, slush funds, wiretapping, extortion, cover-ups, and the like are not designed to encourage enthusiasm for government. But even after President Nixon left office, there was no immediate decline in cynicism. In fact, trust did not rebound until Ronald Reagan took office and proclaimed it was "morning in America." The Reagan administration's attack on big government and an improving economy helped boost the level of trust. By 1984, trust had rebounded considerably, although it

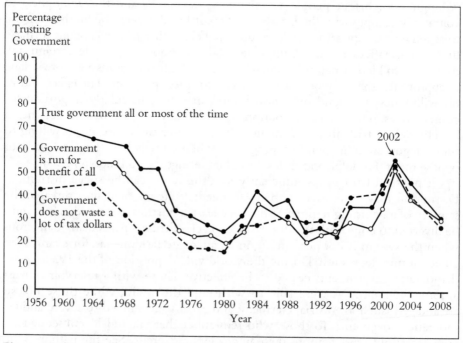

Figure 6.2 Trends in public trust by item. *Source:* National Election Studies (1958–2008).

was nowhere close to the levels of the late 1950s and early 1960s. Following this uptick, trust again declined, mostly in response to the Iran-Contra scandal and the breaking of the "read my lips—no new taxes" pledge by the first President Bush. With a thriving economy, and despite the Monicagate scandal, trust grew again with an upward movement in political trust that began about the time of Clinton's second term.

With the events of 9/11, trust in government skyrocketed. In January 2001, a CBS/*New York Times* poll showed a mere 31 percent of Americans claiming to trust the government in Washington to do what is right "most of the time" or "just about always." Two weeks after 9/11, an ABC News/*Washington Post* poll showed 64 percent trusted government "most of the time" or "just about always." A CBS/*New York Times* poll in early October 2001 found 55 percent trusted government. The *New York Times* proclaimed "Suddenly Americans Trust Uncle Sam" (Langer 2002). One had to go back to the presidency of Lyndon Johnson in 1966 to see trust at this elevated level. However, the surge in trust was not to last. CBS/*New York Times* Polls showed trust in government at 46 percent in January 2002, falling to 36 percent in July 2003—about where it stood before 9/11. By September 2005, trust in government "all" or "most of the time" had fallen to just 29 percent, holding at 31 percent in late 2008 (ANES).

Reconsidering Political Trust. The rapid surge and decline in trust following 9/11 forced students of public opinion to reconsider the theoretical underpinnings of political trust. The long decline in trust starting in 1966 already had been subject to a good deal of speculation. Inglehart (1997a) saw the decline simply as part of an overall decline in confidence in all major institutions due to a rise in postmaterialist values, which encourage the denigration of authority. And, in fact, data from other advanced industrial countries show the same general pattern of declining trust that we see for the United States (Dalton 2004). Confidence in American business over the three decades prior to 2000 had dropped from 55 to 21 percent, in universities from 61 to 30 percent, and in medicine from 73 to 29 percent.[11] Government is simply part of this overall pattern.

A recent perspective contends that changes in political trust are a function of what problem the public sees as most important at the time. Like the "rally around the flag" spike in presidential approval during an international crisis, political trust increases when the public is primed to focus on international events, such as 9/11, as opposed to domestic matters (Bishop 2004; Hetherington and Rudolph 2008). Hetherington and Rudolph claim priming provides one explanation for the high level of political trust in the 1950s, as the public was primed to view the Soviet threat as a major problem facing America. Paradoxically, when the Soviet empire collapsed in 1989, trust in government actually declined.

Political trust is linked to the economy, with declines in trust often accompanying economic downturns. Unlike an international crisis, when the government receives positive press coverage (witness the early months of the Iraq War), economic problems lead to negative press coverage of government. A decline in trust usually follows (Citrin and Green 1986; Hetherington 1998; Hetherington and Rudolph 2008).

Today's low level of trust of course does not approach the depths that lead to rejection of the political order. Nevertheless, there may still be worrisome consequences. Orren (1997) argues that people turn to quick, simpleminded fixes—for example, direct legislation, third parties, and term limits—for perceived problems when trust is low. In two-party presidential elections, the distrustful are more likely to vote for the challenger than the incumbent. In three-party contests, the distrustful are more inclined to vote for third-party candidates than the Republican or the Democrat. In voting for president, those low in trust opt for candidates promising the most far-reaching change (Hetherington 1999). A similar pattern appears on the issue of term limits for elected officials. The strongest predictor of those voting for term limits in state referenda is low political trust (Karp 1995). Scholz and Lubell (1998) show trust in government significantly influences compliance with tax laws. Those scoring low on trust in government tended to underreport their taxable income.

None of the possible consequences listed earlier, however, threatens democratic stability. How low, then, must political trust fall before it makes a difference? One obvious observation is that in the mid-1970s, when trust was at its nadir, the process of government did not operate with any appreciable difference from the 1950s. The weapons of war were still being built, pensions were paid, and the garbage was collected. The survival of democracy and the functioning of government were not threatened. Further, one could argue that if there had *not* been a plunge in trust in the wake of Watergate, it would have been the more disturbing outcome. Leaders (e.g., Nixon) whose actions threaten the democratic fabric presumably deserve the distrust of "small d" democrats.

Finally, we note that in monitoring the level of public trust, the location of trust within groups is important. In the United States, support is highest among the white, non-Southern, non-Jewish, middle-aged upper middle class. In other words, trust is concentrated in people who are most rewarded by the existing system. Extending broad trust beyond this group may be a key to democratic stability. We should also be mindful that one's trust in government at the moment is partially a function of whether one's preferred political party is in power. Everything else being equal, partisans are most likely to trust their government when their own party controls Congress and the presidency (Keele 2005).

Political Efficacy

The concept of *political efficacy* was originally developed in the early 1950s to explain variations in voting turnout. The four questions used to measure it have been repeated frequently and over a longer period than almost any other survey indicator. Efficacy can be best described as a belief that one can influence the political process. It is a feeling that an active citizen can play a part in bringing about social and political change and that one's input counts (Campbell, Gurin, and Miller 1954, 187). Since it was first developed, the concept has been generalized to account for a wide variety of political activities. Given its long use and history, the original four-item efficacy scale has been the subject of an extensive methodological review. Some of the original items proved to be poor indicators of the concept, but in recent years considerable effort has gone into the development of more reliable items (Niemi, Craig, and Mattei 1991; Morrell 2003).

Data from two large-scale studies of political participation show a strong relationship between political efficacy and many types of political activity (Verba and Nie 1972; Verba, Schlozman, and Brady 1995). Beyond its relationship to voting, these studies generally show that the higher the sense of political efficacy, the greater the likelihood that one will participate in political activities of a relatively demanding sort. Conversely, a low sense of efficacy is one of the factors normally associated with political apathy (Verba and Nie 1972; Lewis-Beck et al. 2008). Some current research is directed toward how to increase young people's sense of political efficacy through the school curriculum and extra-curricular activities (Pinkleton, Austin, and Fortman 1998; Bowler and Donovan 2002; Kahne and Westheimer 2006). However, the best predictor of efficacy remains the one identified back in the 1950s—years of formal education (Campbell, Gurin, and Miller 1954).

It should come as no surprise that political efficacy and trust are related—that those who feel they can influence government also tend to trust it. According to the 2008 ANES, only about 10 percent of the American public scored in the top 25 percent in efficacy but also in the bottom 25 percent in political trust.[12] Thus, there seems to be a nontrivial segment of the population that could be mobilized for active opposition to the status quo given the appropriate circumstances. It might be noted, for example, that the low-trust/high-efficacy group voted at almost twice the rate for third-party candidate Ross Perot in 1992 than did the rest of the population.

Considerable research has been conducted on the behavior patterns of those low on trust but high on efficacy. Shingles (1981), in a reanalysis of the Verba-Nie participation data, finds that the combination of low trust and high efficacy overcomes the disadvantages of low income and low education in motivating political participation. This combination was a particularly important antecedent of political activity among African Americans. Jennings and Andersen (1996) find the same pattern in support for the confrontational tactics used by the AIDS Coalition to Unleash Power (ACT-UP), which demanded that the Food and Drug Administration (FDA) release experimental AIDS drugs.[13] Finally, in a variety of research settings, Edward Muller (Muller and Jukam 1983; Muller and Opp 1986; Muller and Seligson 1987) and his colleagues have demonstrated that nontraditional political activity is most likely to occur among people who are distrustful of and alienated from government and who also believe that their actions (sometimes violent) will get them what they want.[14] One might speculate that many "tea party" activists consist of those high in efficacy but low in political trust.

Social Trust

Social trust can be differentiated from political trust. Social trust is generalized trust in others. It is trust in other people, people you have never met. It is often measured with the question, "Do you believe that most people can be trusted or that you can't be too careful in dealing with people?" Social trust has little in common with political trust, as the two have different origins (Uslaner 2002; Delhey and Newton 2003; Mishler and Rose 2005). Looking across a variety of nations, the level of social trust is strongly related to the existence of democratic institutions. The higher the level of interpersonal trust among citizens, the more likely a nation will have democratic institutions and the more likely a nation is able to maintain long-term democratic stability (Inglehart 1997a; Newton 2007). Among the reasons for this are that democratic institutions depend on a trust among citizens that those voted into power will not use extralegal methods to stay there or use the power of state to suppress political opposition. People who trust others tend to be tolerant, participate in politics, contribute to charity, serve on juries, have high levels of confidence in political institutions such as Congress and the Supreme Court, and generally display the hallmarks of civic virtue (Putnam 2000). According to some, generalized trust is the oil that lubricates democracy (Warren 1999; Uslaner 2002; Zmerli and Newton 2008).

Like political trust, social trust has been declining. In 1960, 57 percent of the public said they trusted most people (Almond and Verba 1963). By 1978, social trust had dropped to 40 percent and by 1994 to 33 percent, a range where it has more or less stayed (GSS 1972–2008). Almost all of this decline can be attributed to generational replacement (Putnam 2000, 140; Jennings and Stoker 2004). Trusting seniors are being replaced in the electorate by less trusting new entrants. With the events of 9/11 came an increase in social trust, but it did not skyrocket like political trust. In November 2001, 42 percent said they trusted most people (Pew), but by February 2002 social trust had dropped to 34 percent, and stood at 32 percent in 2008 (GSS). Still, compared to other nations, Americans tend generally to trust others. Only the Scandinavian countries routinely exceed the United States when it comes to generalized social trust.

Social trust also matters because it can influence public opinion. Brewer and colleagues (2004) show that social trust influences the level of trust in the benign intentions of most foreign countries, which in turn promotes an internationalist perspective in foreign affairs. More famously, social trust matters because it is an essential component of social capital. Many students of democracy believe that the development and maintenance of a civic culture is greatly aided by high levels of social capital.[15] Robert Putnam (1995a, 182) writes that "democratic government is strengthened, not weakened, when it faces a vigorous civil society." Social capital involves membership in voluntary associations and networks that create a sense of political efficacy. It allows people to work together effectively to influence government, which in turn mitigates the intensity of conflict that can threaten democratic government (Verba, Schlozman, and Brady 1995; Fukuyama 1995). Associational life in civil society, in the words of Verba and his colleagues, "operates as the school of democracy" (Brady, Verba, and Schlozman 1995, 285).

Levels of social capital have attracted much attention in recent years because of the provocative claim by Putnam (1995a, 1995b, 2000) that civic engagement in the United States has undergone a serious decline (see also Lance Bennett 1998). As evidence, Putnam notes that membership in voluntary associations ranging from the Red Cross to bowling leagues has declined appreciably over the last three decades. The primary culprit, according to Putman, is the widespread appeal of television beginning in the mid-1950s.[16] The more one watches television, the less time one has for life in voluntary associations. In addition, data show that the more one watches television, the lower one's level of interpersonal trust. Television emphasizes violence, crime, and duplicitous personal relationships. According to the "mean world" thesis of George Gerbner (1998), heavy television users confuse its content with the real world. They see the world as unrealistically mean and dangerous, which has a negative effect on social trust. Not everyone, however, is convinced by the decline-in-social-capital thesis. Some have challenged the evidence of a decline (Pettinico 1996; Ladd 1998; Shapiro 2002); others doubt its connection to democratic stability (Jackman and Miller 1996; Tarrow 1996).

6-4 Personality and Democratic Citizenship

In chapter 5, we discussed certain personality traits that can affect political opinions—such as why some people are liberals and others are conservatives. In this chapter we discuss those personality traits that are sometimes posited as making one more or less conducive to democratic citizenship. Could it be that certain personality types are attracted to authoritarian leadership, whereas other personality types make healthy democratic citizens?

The Authoritarian Personality

Influenced by events in Germany during Hitler's rule, a group of scholars from the University of California at Berkeley began a systematic investigation into the personality structure of individuals particularly susceptible to anti-Semitic and fascist political appeals. Was there something about the personality of some individuals that led them to actively support or passively sympathize with a program of genocide against Jews, homosexuals, and gypsies, and the replacement of democratic government by dictatorship (as happened in Germany between 1932 and 1945)? The study (Adorno et al. 1950) has had a profound influence on all branches of the social sciences.

The thesis of the book is straightforward. Prejudice, suspicion, distrust, and hostility are manifestations of attempts to resolve deep-seated psychological conflicts. At the heart of these conflicts is a highly ambivalent orientation toward authority. To compensate for feelings of personal weakness, authoritarians present a tough façade. They are critical of those they see as beneath them, particularly those who are different, such as members of minority groups or those living "deviant" lifestyles such as gays and lesbians. Authoritarians are submissive to those above them in the social order and condescending toward those below. As depicted in German folklore, they are like a person on a bicycle—above they bow, below they kick. While such persons are outwardly deferential, they in fact harbor considerable hostility toward authority. This hostility, however, is mostly unconscious, and authoritarians are only intermittently aware of the hate side of this love–hate amalgam. Rather, negative feelings are repressed by primitive ego defensive mechanisms. Authoritarians are extremely servile toward authority, driving from consciousness the malice they feel toward those above them. Other characteristics of authoritarian syndrome include (1) conventionalism—a rigid adherence to conventional middle-class values; (2) anti-intraception—opposition to the tender-hearted, subjective, and imaginative; (3) superstition—a belief in mystical determinants influencing one's fate; and (4) ethnocentrism—a strong attachment to one's own group and hostility to outgroups (Kirscht and Dillehay 1967, 5–6).

Authoritarianism is thought to originate primarily with childhood family relationships.[17] Peterson, Smirles, and Wentworth (1997), for example, demonstrate the strong tendency for authoritarian parents to have authoritarian children.[18] Persons displaying the authoritarian syndrome often describe parental affection as being given only as a reward for good behavior. Their parents employed rigid, punishment-oriented disciplinary practices, as opposed to discipline based on love withdrawal. Family roles were clearly defined in terms of dominance and submission (Milburn, Conrad, and Carberry 1995). The implications of *The Authoritarian Personality* for public opinion and democratic stability became obvious to students of politics soon after its publication. One of the first tasks investigators set for themselves was to determine the political correlates of authoritarianism (Are authoritarians prejudiced toward minorities? Do they hold antidemocratic political beliefs? and so on.) This undertaking was greatly aided by the fact that *The Authoritarian Personality*, unlike other such studies, provided a ready-made paper-and-pencil test to measure the extent to which the syndrome exists. This instrument, the *California F-scale* (the *F* is for fascism), early after its publication, became virtually synonymous with authoritarianism. Typical agree/disagree items from the original F-scale include the following (Adorno et al. 1950, 167):

- What young people need most of all is strict discipline by their parents.
- Most people who don't get ahead just don't have enough willpower.
- Sex criminals deserve more than prison; they should be whipped in public or worse.

Investigators soon discovered severe methodological problems with the F-scale. Among the most difficult to resolve was response set. All twenty items in the original F-scale were worded in a positive direction (to agree was authoritarian). As we indicated earlier, people with low education tend to be yea-sayers, making it difficult to separate the effects of education from the effects of personality when all questions in a scale suffer from response set. One solution is to reverse some of the items so that disagreeing with the question is the authoritarian response. While this strategy has merit, it is less than a completely satisfactory solution. Also, one essential requirement of a personality measure is that it not be contaminated by political content. It is now generally agreed that the F-scale is biased in the direction of right-wing authoritarianism. For example, one agree/disagree item from the F-scale states: "Homosexuals are hardly better than criminals and ought to be severely punished." Such a question may tap both personality traits and right-wing political outlooks. Consequently, the F-scale might not be sensitive to authoritarians of the left (such as American communists), and is likely overly sensitive to authoritarians on the right (such as neo-Nazis or skinheads).

Because of these problems, the original F-scale is no longer used. However, there have been three important attempts to measure authoritarianism in a more scientific fashion. The first, by Milton Rokeach (1960), was the development of a new measure—the *dogmatism scale*—which Rokeach claimed could tap authoritarianism of both the left and the right. Currently, the dogmatism scale is one of the most frequently used measures of authoritarian tendencies (although it suffers from response set, because to be "dogmatic" is to agree with scale items). It also is better able to predict extreme conservative opinion than extreme liberal opinion. Typical dogmatism agree–disagree items state, "there are two types of people in the world—those who are for the truth and those against it," or that "most of ideas that get printed today are not worth the paper they are written on."

The second solution was simply to recognize the ideological problem and reformulate the concept. Bob Altemeyer (1981, 1988, 1997) developed a highly reliable scale of thirty-four items free from response set which he labels "Right Wing Authoritarianism" (RWA). He argues that authoritarianism naturally leads to right-wing political views. Unfortunately, since much of what is to be explained by authoritarianism contains conservative political content, this approach runs the risk of being tautological. He reorganizes the concept into three domains: submission to established authorities, aggression toward outgroups, and adherence to tradi-tional social conventions. Typical agree–disagree items from Altemeyer's RWA scale are "Once our government leaders and authorities condemn the dangerous elements in our society, it will be the duty of every patriotic citizen to help stomp out the rot that is poisoning our country from within" and "It is best to treat dissenters with leniency and open mind, since new ideas are the lifeblood of progressive change." Altemeyer found no evidence of authoritarianism on the political left, even among those holding extreme opinions. Authoritarianism, in his studies, was limited to those on the political right (1988, 329).

Karen Stenner (2005) offers a third solution. She uses a scale consisting only of items that ask respondents about the qualities they think are most important for childrearing. For instance, do people believe it is more important for a child to be obedient or self-reliant; considerate or well-behaved? Stenner argues that attitudes about childrearing are independent of political content and are a valid measure of authoritarian tendencies; that is, tendencies to desire society to be structured in a way to maximize sameness and minimize diversity among people, beliefs, and behavior.[19] Her scale proves to be a robust predictor of racial intolerance, political intolerance, and moral intolerance. In addition, she finds over time that authoritarianism is becoming a more, not less, powerful predictor of these forms of intolerance (Stenner 2005, 190).

Regardless of approach, one consistent finding for authoritarianism is its clear association with social conformity (Altemeyer 1997; Feldman 2003; Stenner 2005). For instance, in a typical study a persuasive message was presented (from a variety of sources) to a number of different groups. Those scoring high on the F-scale were particularly likely to change their attitude when the message was delivered by a high-status source (Harvey and Beverly 1961, 125–30). Interestingly, authoritarians generally claim to hold their political opinions strongly, even though they tend not to be particularly informed politically (Peterson, Duncan, and Pang 2002; Lavine, Lodge, and Freitas 2005).

Researchers studying democratic values have found authoritarianism—measured in a variety of fashions—to consistently be related to political intolerance. Sullivan, Piereson, and Marcus (1982) found "large and significant" differences (in the predicted direction) between those scoring high and those scoring low on the dogmatism (D) scale with regard to the toleration of respondents' least liked group, as did McClosky and Brill (1983, 342) using the traditional F-scale. Gibson and Tedin (1988) report similar findings in a study of tolerance for gay rights. They found that dogmatism contributed to an intolerance for gays by reducing support for norms of democracy (see also Mirels and Dean 2006). Feldman and Stenner (1997; Stenner 2005) find authoritarianism contributes to intolerance by increasing the perceived threat of disliked groups. Lavine, Lodge, and Freitas (2005) find a difference between authoritarians and others in how they solve problems under threat. Where nonauthoritarians tend to be open to new information to solve the problem, authoritarians are more likely to seek new information to reinforce their existing opinions.

Even with extensive statistical controls, those scoring high on authoritarianism are more likely to trade civil liberties for national security than are those scoring low (Davis 2007). Huddy and Khatib (2007) report a strong relationship between authoritarianism and "uncritical patriotism." Huddy et al. (2005) found authoritarians more likely to endorse government surveillance, extended security checks, and visa restrictions on Arab Americans than did nonauthoritarians. Kam and Kinder (2007) show that authoritarians are more likely to favor increased spending on homeland security, border control, support the war in Iraq, and approve of President George W. Bush's response to 9/11. Stevens, Bishin, and Barr (2006) find authoritarianism related to greater confidence in order-maintaining institutions.

Decades of research have also found a substantial linkage between authoritarianism and racism. The correlation between these constructs is one of the most enduring in the social science literature. John Ray (1988, 673), one of the most trenchant critics of the authoritarianism concept, concedes that "despite all the other failures of their theory, Adorno et al. would appear to have succeeded in at last one of their basic aims—to find something that would predict who is a racist and who is not." Meloen, van der Linden, and De Witte (1996) have demonstrated strong relationships between authoritarianism and voting for political parties with a racist agenda. Sniderman and Piazza (1993) have shown that authoritarian values among whites lead to the negative stereotyping of both Jews and African Americans. These groups are so different from each other in terms of educational accomplishment, material success, intact families, and other characteristics that factual considerations can hardly explain why the same people who hold negative stereotypes about Jews also hold them about blacks. Rather, the explanation is authoritarian values. It is not the actual characteristics of blacks, any more than it is the actual characteristics of Jews, that evoke prejudice and dislike. Rather, it is the ethnocentric dimension of the authoritarian personality—the generalized hostility to outgroups—that is part of the syndrome.

One particularly interesting study on authoritarianism involved the classic experiment developed by Stanley Milgram (1969) to measure obedience to authority. In this experiment, a naive subject ("the teacher") is required by the study director ("the authority figure") to administer an electrical shock each time "the learner" fails to perform a rote memorization task satisfactorily. The teacher is not aware that the learner is in league with the person running the experiment and is in fact receiving no shock at all. However, each time the learner fails the task, the authority figure (the experimenter) orders the teacher to shock the learner at an ever higher level of voltage. As the shocks presumably become stronger, the learner cries out in pain. The object is to see how long the teacher will obey the authority figure and continue to administer the shocks. One disturbing feature of this study is that many subjects continue to administer the shocks until the learner is in an apparent state of unconsciousness. Alan Elms (1972) administered the "teachers" the F-scale before conducting the Milgram experiment. He found that those who scored high on authoritarianism were most eager (as predicted) to obey the authority figure and continue the experiment to completion. It is important to appreciate that Milgram's studies go beyond a simple pencil-and-paper approach and are a measure of how people really act in a highly realistic setting. Milgram's work was in fact so realistic that it could not be conducted today due to human subjects considerations.

After years of criticism and recent neglect, the study of authoritarianism is experiencing something of a revival. While many of the hypotheses advanced more than fifty years ago in *The Authoritarian Personality* were more provocative than rigorously tested, some of these ideas have withstood the test of time and continue to be core concepts for research on public opinion. One argument, pursued by Hetherington and Weiler (2009), is that the growing polarization of American politics has its roots in ever increasing conflicting worldviews about core values, traced to the degree to which one favors an authoritarian order versus one that is open and permissive.

Is There a Democratic Personality?

Considerably less attention has been paid to the possibility that certain personality traits might promote support for democratic principles. Much of what has been written is either speculative or consists of inferences based on intensive interviews with small samples. Authors like Lasswell (1951), Lane (1962), Inkeles (1961), and Sniderman (1975) write about the democratic character as being warm, outgoing, high in self-esteem and ego strength, flexible, and tolerant of ambiguity. One characteristic of this literature is a rather cavalier tendency to portray the democratic personality as the "healthy" personality and the nondemocratic personality as having psychological maladjustments.

It is misleading to talk about a democratic personality as if it were a distinct psychological type. But there may be certain personality traits that elicit support for democratic values as these values interact with particular environmental situations. The emphasis on environment is important because personality traits that encourage support for democratic principles (the accepted norm) among citizens of the United States probably encouraged support of totalitarian communism (the accepted norm) among citizens of the former Soviet Union. In other words, some personality types work well within the given rules of the political game—whatever those rules might be. It is not surprising, therefore, that many politicians who were successful when communism was the accepted norm in the Soviet Union are also successful under the norms of democracy in Russia and the independent states. For example, Russian prime minister Vladimir Putin is a former colonel in the Soviet KGB (the intelligence agency).

6-5   Conclusion

There seem to be two fundamental prerequisites for the existence and maintenance of democratic rights and freedoms. One is economic and the other is psychological. In the former, considerable research indicates that some minimal level of economic affluence and development is necessary before a democracy can operate successfully. If people must worry about feeding themselves and their children, concern about democratic government will be a low priority for most (Inglehart 1990; Huntington 1991). Beyond simple sustenance, the most relevant factor associated with democratic development is communication networks. Without sufficiently developed channels of communication, interests cannot be articulated and aggregated, and conflicting groups cannot exchange information on goals and desires (Lipset 1959). But once a minimal level of economic development has occurred in tandem with associated communication networks, psychological and cultural factors become important (Inglehart 1997b).

This chapter has analyzed a number of political attitudes commonly thought to affect the stability of democracy. All may be of consequence, but none alone, or even in combination, provides a total explanation for the continued protection of democratic values in the United States. America has perhaps been most fortunate in that it has experienced few intense group or issue cleavages dividing the population. As long as a modest consensus exists and most of the population has a minimal degree of economic security, the system seems able to tolerate a wide variety of personality types, a relatively low level of trust in government, and considerable lack of enthusiasm (although perhaps not outright hostility) for procedural democratic norms.

Notes

1. Data are from the U.S. Office of Public Opinion Research and were downloaded from iPOLL. Thirty percent responded "yes," 63 percent said "no," and 6 percent had no opinion.
2. One bit of evidence for this thesis is the rather substantial increase in support for the civil rights of communists that occurred between 1988 and 1993, the period

surrounding the fall of the communist Soviet Union. According to th[e]
1988, 60 percent would allow an admitted communist to speak; in 199[ ]
71 percent would. In 1988, 59 percent would allow an admitted comm[ ]
book to remain in the library; by 1993, 70 percent would. Increases in tolerance
for other groups addressed in this battery of questions (e.g., atheists, militarists, and
so on) were not nearly as large, so the explanation must be that with the fall of the
Soviet Union, communists do not seem so dangerous.

3. Sullivan, Piereson, and Marcus (1982, 67) concede that tolerance may have
   increased somewhat between 1954 and 1978, but not as much as the items in
   Table 6.3 would lead one to believe.
4. A point first noted by Herson and Hofstetter (1975).
5. For additional critiques of the theory of pluralistic intolerance, see Gibson (1986)
   and Sniderman et al. (1989).
6. Greenberg, Quinlan, Rosner Research (August 2007; from IPOLL).
7. Surveys reported in Dahl (1982), Ladd (1989), and McLean (1999), Freedom
   Forum (August 16–26, 2007; from IPOLL).
8. Greenberg, Quinlan, Rosner Research (August 2007; from IPOLL).
9. However, just 51 percent of opinion–holders said they would vote for a Muslim.
   Princeton Research Associates for *Newsweek*, July 11–12, 2007 (from IPOLL).
10. The literature on trust is voluminous. Among the better, more recent studies are
    Craig (1993); Nye, Zelikow, and King (1997); and Hetherington (2005).
11. Based on Harris Polls, cited in Nye (1997, 283).
12. The 2008 ANES efficacy scale is based on three agree/disagree items: "Sometimes
    politics and government seem so complicated that a person like me can't really
    understand what's going on"; "People like me have no say in what government
    does"; and "I don't think public officials care much what people like me think."
    For each, to disagree is to give the efficacious response. The trust scale is based on
    the items in Figure 6.2.
13. The tactics used by ACT-UP members included stopping trading on the floor of
    the New York Stock Exchange, disrupting political speeches, locking themselves
    inside the offices of major pharmaceutical companies, and conducting "die-ins" on
    streets with heavy traffic (Jennings and Andersen 1996, 313).
14. The best statement of this perspective can be found in Finkel, Muller, and Opp (1989).
15. Although there is conflicting evidence, it appears that high levels of trust lead to
    greater community involvement, not the reverse (Brehm and Rahn 1997; Uslaner
    2002; Jennings and Stoker 2004).
16. In 1950, only 10 percent of all households had television. By 1960, 90 percent of
    all households had television. Americans typically watch three to four hours of
    television a day. The more television they watch, the less active they are in
    voluntary associations (Putnam 1995a).
17. For an argument that the authoritarian syndrome originates in Darwinian
    evolution, see Somit and Peterson (1997).
18. Peterson, Smirles, and Wentworth (1997) report a significant path coefficient
    ($r = 0.47$) between authoritarianism in parents and authoritarianism in children.
    Altemeyer (1997) finds a similar relationship ($r = 0.40$).
19. The 2004 and 2008 ANES contains a four-item battery of attitudes about child-
    rearing designed to measure authoritarianism.

7 Group Differences in Political Opinions

PEOPLE OFTEN THINK OF THEMSELVES as belonging to a specific group. This group identification may influence political opinions, as people see certain policies as being beneficial to the group with which they identify. Thus, we are not surprised if blacks are more favorable to affirmative action than whites, or people with high incomes more opposed to social welfare programs than those living near the poverty line. However, not all group differences are the result of calculated self-interest. Many political opinions are based on sociotropic considerations—that is, on the well-being of the nation as a whole rather than on that of the individual or the group (Kinder and Kiewiet 1981). Life experiences can also shape political outlooks. For instance, individuals with a college education differ sharply from those without on a variety of cultural or social issues, such as abortion. Growing up as a white person in the South once virtually ensured an allegiance to the Democratic Party, although obviously no longer.

In this chapter, we explore the validity of generalizations made about group differences in public opinion. In earlier chapters, we observed that Americans are becoming more polarized—with ideology increasingly driving party attachments and vote choice. Here we examine the degree to which group differences contribute to this polarization. For example, do we see increasing political divisions between the rich and the poor? Is the nation becoming more divided by geography, as if a political gulf exists between Democratic "blue" states and Republican "red" states? Do differences in education, age, and religion divide people more than before, especially on cultural issues? On some group dimensions, are Americans becoming more alike rather than different? Long-standing racial and ethnic divisions may now be less distinct than in the past.

7-1 Socioeconomic Class and Political Opinions

Because a great many issues in political life concern the distribution of benefits within society, the rich and the poor often seem to have quite different economic interests. The haves and the have-nots are expected to disagree, for example, on questions involving taxation and government services. In most European democracies, the major political battle lines are drawn between working-class parties and parties of the middle class. As indicated by the fact that the United States has never had an appreciable socialist movement, America has escaped the more extreme forms of class polarization and conflict. There are, nevertheless, class differences on many political issues.

How do we measure economic or social class? One approach, called *subjective social class*, is simply to ask people into which social class they fall—the lower class, working class, middle class, or upper class. When asked, almost everyone is willing to place himself in one of these classes. In the 2008 GSS, 7 percent identified themselves with the lower class, 46 percent with the working class, 43 percent with the middle class, and 4 percent with the upper class. This division has remained virtually unchanged since the GSS first asked the question in 1972.

An alternative to the subjective approach is to use the objective indicators of occupation, income, and education. Each indicator has its problems. The connections among the three are often far from perfect. Many blue-collar workers have greater incomes than white-collar workers. Also, education is an imperfect predictor of income because many college graduates often have lower incomes than skilled manual workers. We could focus on income, but the same dollar amounts buy distinctly different lifestyles in various parts of the country. A $40,000 annual income in rural Montana might allow a pleasant middle-class lifestyle, while a family would have to struggle to live on that amount in New York City. Subjective class identifications are actually quite predictable from education, income, and occupation (Jackman and Jackman 1983).

Class Differences on Economic Issues

Income is more concentrated at the upper levels of society in the United States than it is in any other Western democracy save Russia and Mexico (Rector and Hederman 2004). In 2006, the richest 1 percent of all Americans had more money than the bottom 50 percent, and the share of the richest 1 percent is now at its highest level since 1928 (Saez 2008). Rather than decreasing, the level of income concentration in recent years has been increasing, fueled significantly by wealth generated through the technology revolution. In 1991, conservative analyst Kevin Phillips (1991, 10) wrote that "no parallel upsurge of riches has been seen since the nineteenth century, the era of the Vanderbilts, Morans, and Rockefellers." With the advent of the dot-com boom and the tax cuts of the second President Bush, which greatly advantaged the wealthy, that upsurge is even more pronounced in the twenty-first century (Phillips 2002, 157–61; Bartels 2008). In 1977, the richest one-fifth of the population took home 44.2 percent of all income; in 2006 they took home 49.7. In 1977, the richest 1 percent received 7.3 percent of all income; in 2006 they received 22.0 percent (Johnstone 2003; Saez 2008). The public is not blind to this accelerated inequality. An increasing number of Americans see society as divided into the haves and have-nots. In 1988, just 26 percent said the nation was split along class lines, compared to 39 percent in 2005.[1] The 2008 ANES reports that 70 percent of the public believe that the national income gap between the rich and poor is "much greater" than it was twenty years ago. Yet by European standards, political cleavages along class lines in the United States are rather muted. Perhaps one reason is a belief among Americans that the opportunity to succeed financially is readily available to those with the energy and ability. For example, one poll found only 12 percent saying there is little or no chance of becoming rich in the United States if one is willing to work hard. When a British sample was asked a similar question, 63 percent said they did not think they had a chance to become rich if they really wanted to.[2]

Table 7.1 shows the relationship between subjective social class and beliefs regarding whether the government should spend more money on programs such as health care, education, retirement benefits, aid to cities, and science and technology. For most of these programs, the working class is the group most likely to favor increased government spending. The greatest opinion difference among the classes is on Social Security benefits, aid to poor people, child care, and AIDS research. Obviously, the working class has real concerns about the well-being of their children when they are away from home, for their own financial security after retirement, and the AIDS epidemic. On the other hand, there is no meaningful difference in opinion on spending for roads and bridges, which benefits all classes. The opinions on these spending increases seem predictable from one's station in life. Social Security and unemployment are of much more concern to

TABLE 7.1	Subjective Social Class and Opinions about Spending on Selected Government Programs		
Percentage Wanting to Spend More On	**Working Class**	**Middle Class**	**Upper Middle/ Upper Class**
AIDS research*	60%	51%	38%
Education[†]	71	71	61
Aid to poor people[††]	54	49	37
Space program[†]	11	14	22
Social security[†]	69	54	39
Child care[§]	60	49	45
Health care[†]	80	74	63
Helping large cities[†]	47	51	38
Road and bridges[†]	44	46	48
Science and technology[†]	35	46	49
Foreign aid[†]	13	11	13

*ANES, 2000

[†]GSS, 2008

[††]GSS, 2006

[§]ANES, 2008

the working class than the more affluent classes. On the other hand, the most affluent class is a potential beneficiary of increasing spending on science and technology, and its members tend to support such spending increases. There is virtually no constituency for an increase in spending on foreign aid.

For the 2008 ANES, Figure 7.1 shows how family income, an objective indicator of social class, is related to opinion on the issues of increasing domestic spending and services and support for a government-guaranteed job and good standard of living. (Nonwhites are excluded here in order to show the effect of income independent of race.) We would expect for reasons of simple economic self-interest that people in the lower-income categories would support public policies designed to promote employment and fund social programs, with a commensurate lack of support among the more financially secure. As one goes from poor to affluent, one does in fact see a decline in the percentage of people holding liberal positions on these economic issues. Despite the repeated findings that rich and poor divide on redistributive issues like taxing and spending, it may seem puzzling that this class division is not stronger than shown in surveys. The angles of the lines in Figure 7.1 are remarkably shallow once we pass the $30–40,000 income level. Clearly, more than direct self-interest is at work. Many wealthy individuals support government programs, paid for by their tax dollars, for which the direct benefits go to those less fortunate, while many of the less fortunate oppose programs for which they pay little tax but receive benefits.

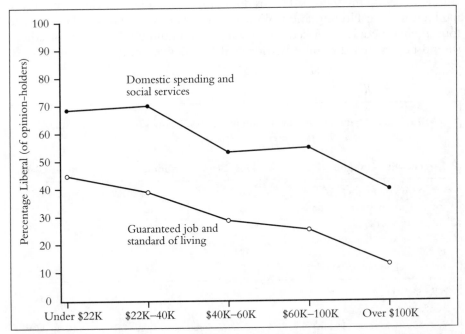

Figure 7.1   Social welfare opinions by family income (whites only). *Source:* American National Election Studies, 2008.

One instance of this puzzle was the general public acceptance of President George W. Bush's tax cuts, which predominantly benefited the wealthy. According to polls, a plurality accepted Bush's tax cuts, including even repeal of the estate tax, which benefits only the wealthiest 2 percent. Why did ordinary people not object? One reason is that those of modest income often do not understand the complexities of the tax code. Also taxes are unpopular. Since the 1970s, more than 70 percent have said the government wastes "a lot" of tax money (ANES). It is of no small psychological importance that while the Bush tax cuts put the most dollars in the pockets of the wealthy, everyone got a tax cut. It was apparently of little consequence that the primary beneficiaries were the rich. The results raise intriguing questions. Would more voters oppose tax cuts for the rich if they were better informed? Or, as some say, is it simply that citizens favor benefits for the rich because they hope to join them someday? Americans are economic optimists. One poll showed that 76 percent believe that one can start out poor, work hard, and become rich (Page and Jacobs 2009, 51).

Class Differences on Noneconomic Domestic Issues

On noneconomic issues, liberalism tends to increase rather than decrease as one goes up the status ladder. Typical are the relationships between social class and opinions on the death penalty, abortion, gay marriage, and legal immigration shown in Table 7.2. While the differences are not large, they are consistent. Reading the table across the columns, we see that support for gay marriage rises as one moves up the status ladder, as does support for abortion rights, and favoring increased legal immigration. Similar relations between status and opinion are found when people are asked about whether communists, socialists, or atheists should be granted the full range of civil liberties. Among whites, high-status

---

TABLE 7.2 | **Opinions on Noneconomic Domestic Issues by Subjective Social Class (Whites Only)**

Percent with Opinion	Working Class	Middle Class	Upper Class
Oppose death penalty★	20%	27%	28%
Favor abortion for any reason†	18	38	49
Allow gay marriage★	53	54	60
Allow books by homosexuals in library†	37	77	82
Increase legal immigration★	08	15	19

★ANES, 2008

†GSS, 2008

Note: Opinion-holders include only those with a clear pro or con opinion. Those with a middle response, e.g., "4s" on ANES seven-point scales, are excluded.

respondents express less racial prejudice than do low-status respondents (Kinder and Sanders 1996; Sniderman and Carmines 1997; Gomez and Wilson 2006).

Those with higher incomes tend to be conservative on economic issues, but on issues outside the economic realm status differences are complicated by the role of education. We saw in chapters 5 and 6 that educational achievement promotes political tolerance and political liberalism. This liberalizing effect of education is, however, almost entirely limited to noneconomic issues. If we separate the effects of income and education on political attitudes, we find different patterns for economic and noneconomic issues. On noneconomic issues, high education but not high income is associated with liberalism. On economic issues, high income is negatively related to liberalism, but education is not.

Table 7.3 shows relevant examples. This table indicates that within low and high income categories, liberal opinions on the noneconomic issue of gay marriage increases with educational attainment. Note, for instance, the increase in support for gay marriage in the high income group when we compare those with a high school education to those with some college to those with a college education. We see 47 percent of those with high income and a high school degree favor gay marriage compared to 58 percent with high income and a college degree.

The reverse pattern is apparent on the economic issue of domestic spending. As family income goes up, individuals become more conservative on domestic

TABLE 7.3	Joint Effect of Income and Education on Selected issues, Whites Only		
		Education	
	High School Only	**Some College**	**College Graduate**
For gay marriage			
Income Low	45%	60%	64%
Medium	41	63	61
High	47	49	58
For more domestic spending			
Income Low	75	67	62
Medium	56	48	55
High	60	39	48
For more government aid to blacks			
Income Low	22	29	33
Medium	13	11	20
High	1	19	19

Source: American National Election Studies, 2008 election data. Numbers represent the percent of opinion-holders. Percentages are based on opinion-holders (pro or con) only. For the full texts of the opinion questions, see the Appendix.

spending within categories of education. Thus, 64 percent of college graduates with low incomes want increased spending, compared to only 58 percent of college graduates with high incomes.

The third issue—aid to blacks—taps both the economic dimension of financial aid and the noneconomic dimensions of attitudes toward minorities. On this issue we can see the joint effect of higher education (which affects the noneconomic part of the issue) and the conservative effect of income (which affects the economic part of the issue). Thus, we see that among those with low income, college graduates are the most favorable to aid for blacks. But among college graduates, those with the highest incomes are the least favorable.

Class Differences on Foreign Policy

The major class difference on foreign policy attitudes is that people in the lower educational strata more readily take the isolationist position than the more internationally minded, better educated strata. These sorts of class differences can be traced to the 1930s and 1940s, when isolationism had great appeal to the working class, while the middle and upper classes favored an active role for the United States in world affairs (Mueller 1977). In 1948, for example, 92 percent of the college educated favored an active role for the United States compared to only 59 percent with less than a high school education (Page and Shapiro 1992). As shown by the more contemporary data in Table 7.4, the better educated continue to favor an active role for the United States in world affairs, want a more powerful United Nations, are more willing to normalize relations with Cuba, believe that

TABLE 7.4	Education and Internationalism		
Percent with Opinion	**Less Than High School**	**High School Graduate**	**College Graduate**
U.S. should take an active role in world affairs (2006)★★	49%	57%	76%
United Nations has too little power (2004)★★	15	25	36
U.S. should reestablish relations with Cuba (2008)†	40	53	73
Communism worst kind of government (1993)★★	63	49	36
Diplomacy better than use of threats in foreign relations (2004)††	39	53	62

★Princeton Survey Research Associates
†Gallup
★★General Social Survey
††ANES

diplomacy is a better approach to international problems than military threats, and did not (back in 1993) view communism as harshly as those with less education.

We might expect that high-status people would be more willing to support military action abroad, as it is in some ways a logical extension of internationalism, just as isolationism implies keeping the troops at home. The accumulation of survey evidence presented in Table 7.5 shows a modest tendency on the part of those with higher levels of education to support American military adventures. In the case of Vietnam, support for the war in 1968 among the college educated may seem surprising because the most visible war opponents were found on college campuses. Only if we refine the educational index to isolate the small segment of people with graduate degrees or four-year degrees from the most prestigious universities was there disproportionate anti-Vietnam War sentiment at the top of the educational ladder (Rosenberg et al. 1970, 54–65). Regarding the Gulf War of 1991, the education differences are considerable when respondents were asked if they agree that "all things considered, the [1991 Persian] Gulf War was worth the cost." We also see those with higher education are more likely to approve the handling of the current conflict in Iraq. Twenty-six percent of college graduates in 2008 approved the handling of the war compared to 17 percent of those without a high school degree (ANES). The same pattern held for the war in Afghanistan.

Class Differences in Voting and Party Preference

Ever since the 1930s, socioeconomic class has been the principal factor dividing people into Republicans and Democrats. We can see this division persisting into the twenty-first century, using data from the 2008 American National

TABLE 7.5	Education and Opinion on U.S. Involvement in Foreign Countries		
Issue	**Less Than High School**	**High School Graduate**	**College Graduate**
U.S. should expand the Vietnam War (1968)*	24%	21%	25%
U.S. should be more involved in Central America (1986)*	19	21	25
The Persian Gulf War was worth it (1992)*	48	56	61
U.S. should commit peacekeeping troops to Kosovo (1999)[†]	44	49	63
Approve government handing of Iraq War (2008)*	17	24	28
Approve government handling of Afghanistan War (2008)*	16	23	26

*American National Election Studies
[†]Gallup

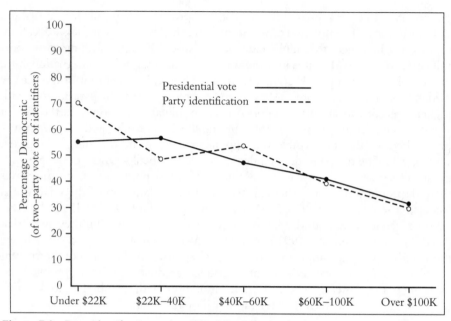

Figure 7.2 Party identification and presidential vote by family income, 2008 (whites only). *Source:* American National Election Studies, 2008 election data.

Election Study. Figure 7.2 divides white respondents into five income groups from low to high, arranged as quintiles, with each group representing roughly one-fifth of whites in the sample. As one would expect, the figure shows that as one moves up the income ladder, the frequency of Democratic Party identification and frequency of Democratic presidential voting both decrease. Among the poorest fifth, 70 percent of the white partisans call themselves Democrats, while 55 percent of voters chose Obama. Among the richest fifth of white voters, Republicans outnumber Democrats 70 to 30 percent in party identification, while McCain outpolled Obama 68 to 32.

As measured by family income, class differences in politics have clearly grown. Figure 7.3 shows the trend, with a comparison of the voting behavior of the top and bottom thirds of family income (for whites only) from 1952 through 2008. As a general trend, clearly the rich and poor have grown farther apart politically.[3] Even as cultural issues have become more salient to voters, the partisan polarization of the rich and poor has increased (see also Stonecash 2000; Abramowitz and Saunders 2008; Bartels 2008).

The growth in class voting may appear counterintuitive. It is sometimes presumed that the increased salience of cultural issues trumps economic issues to push working class voters into the arms of the Republican Party. But this is not generally the case. It is true that the Democrats are challenged to win working-class votes if the working class is (awkwardly) defined as those without a college education. Education cuts differently than income. At one time, Republicans drew their strongest support from the best educated, just as they do now from the most affluent. But this trend has eroded so that in some surveys the

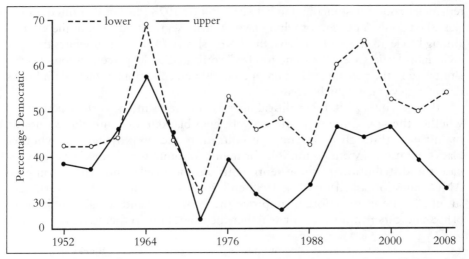

Figure 7.3 Major party Democratic presidential vote (whites only) by top third and bottom third of family income, 1952–2008. *Source:* National Election Studies data.

most educated—particularly professionals with advanced university degrees—are the most Democratic. (Educated business leaders continue to lean Republican.) While the increased importance of cultural issues is largely responsible for the attraction of educated citizens to the Democrats, the poor as a group are decidedly more Democratic than the rich.[4]

7-2 Race and Political Opinions

The most profound political division between groups in the United States is between blacks and whites. While progress has surely been made, there is a wide gulf between blacks and whites on most political issues, particularly on those involving discrimination and its remedies. Of course, African Americans are not the only racial or ethnic minority in America. The proportion of Latinos (Hispanics) and Asians is growing at a rapid rate, and the former now outnumber blacks as the largest minority group in the United States. However, neither group has the distinctive political opinions that characterize the black population.[5]

Blacks, Whites, and Political Opinions

Until the late 1970s, the central division of opinion in the United States concerning the role of African Americans was the very issue of a racially integrated society. In a 1964 ANES, respondents were asked if they favored "strict segregation" of the races, "desegregation," or "something in between." Not surprisingly, 73 percent of blacks favored desegregation, while only 6 percent favored segregation, with 21 percent favoring something in between. Among whites, about equal numbers chose strict segregation (25 percent) as desegregation (27 percent), with the remainder choosing something in between. But by 1978 (the last year this question was asked), only 5 percent of whites favored strict segregation—about the same as among blacks (6 percent). In 1964, the ANES shows 74 percent of whites thought civil rights leaders were "pushing too fast" compared to 11 percent among blacks. But by 1980 the percentage had dropped to 40 percent among whites, with blacks remaining essentially unchanged.

By the late 1970s, the political agenda on race shifted to the question of whether the government should actively help blacks move into the economic mainstream through preferences in education and employment or whether blacks themselves were responsible for their economic well-being. We can compare the distribution of these sentiments among blacks and whites using an ANES question asked in 1974, 1988 and 2008 as to whether the government should "make every effort to improve the economic and social condition of blacks and other minorities" or whether they should help themselves.

	Whites			**Blacks**		
	1974	**1988**	**2008**	**1974**	**1988**	**2008**
Government should help blacks	25%	25%	15%	63%	58%	52%
Unsure	26	54	23	25	21	21
Blacks should help themselves	50	51	63	12	21	27
	101%	100%	100%	100%	100%	100%

These are substantial differences between blacks and whites. At the same time, both racial groups have become less supportive of government intervention. Either there has been a declining belief in the ability of government to solve racial problems or an increasing belief that such assistance is not as necessary as was once the case.

In recent years, much of the debate over racial policies has shifted to the arena of affirmative action. Given the dual emphasis in the American political tradition on equality and individualism, many well-intentioned citizens appear caught in a dilemma. First, there is a recognition that blacks historically have not had the same opportunities as whites, but there is also a belief that educational opportunities and jobs should be filled on merit, without reference to race, sex, or religion.

As one would expect, blacks are more supportive of affirmative action than whites. In 2008, the GSS asked if due to past discrimination blacks should be given preferences in hiring and promotion, or whether such preference is wrong because it discriminates against whites. The data show:

	Whites	**Blacks**
Favor preferences for blacks in hiring and promotion	11%	44%
Undecided	4	5
Oppose preferences for blacks in hiring and promotion	85	51
	100%	100%

As seen here, programs that imply preferences or quotas for minorities are highly unpopular with whites, while dividing blacks.[6] A majority of blacks, in fact, oppose affirmative action in this instance. As noted in chapter 4, questions on affirmative action are sensitive to question-wording effects, as many of the terms employed, such as *quotas* and *racial preferences*, are politically charged. We can see this from the divisions in responses to a very similar question to the one above (this one from the NBC News/*Wall Street Journal* poll, 2003), where the affirmative action alternative rejects "rigid quotas."

	Whites	Blacks
Affirmative action programs needed "as long as there are no rigid quotas"	43%	79%
Not sure	6	12
Affirmative action programs "should be ended because they unfairly discriminate against whites"	49	14
	100%	100%

In this instance, whites are divided while blacks are one-sidedly favorable.[7] These opinion gaps are rooted in differences between blacks and whites concerning perceptions of the continued existence of racial discrimination. However, these differences, while not trivial, are declining. An ABC poll in 1996 showed 70 percent of blacks called racism "a big problem," compared to 44 percent in 2009. Among whites, the figures were 52 percent in 1996, declining to 22 percent in 2009.[8]

But still there are vast differences in the extent to which blacks and whites see discrimination in their own communities. Among whites, in 2009, 83 percent believed blacks receive equal treatment in employment, compared to just 38 percent of blacks. Eighty-one percent of whites see equal opportunity in housing compared to 47 percent of blacks. Whites are less optimistic about blacks receiving equal treatment from the police (60 percent), but only 22 percent of blacks believe the police afford them equal treatment. On a more upbeat note, 56 percent of blacks believe they have achieved racial equality or will do so soon; just 18 percent said it will never occur (*ABC News*, 2009).

Even on issues that are tangential to civil rights, blacks are more likely than whites to take the liberal position. Some examples are shown in Table 7.6. As we would expect, there are substantial black–white differences on economic issues such as the pace of domestic spending and whether or not the government should guarantee everyone a good standard of living. For whites, social class is a consistent correlate of opinion on these social welfare issues. However, for blacks there is no relationship. Upper-income blacks are about as supportive as lower-income blacks. The mostly likely explanation is the "linked fate" hypothesis (Dawson 1994). Most blacks believe their own economic well-being is linked to the overall progress of blacks as a group—a position most strongly held by upper-income blacks (Tate 1993). In 2008, 66 percent of blacks said their personal life is affected by what happens to blacks as a group (ANES). Upper-income blacks are more likely to

TABLE 7.6 | Race and Opinion on Selected Non–Civil Rights Issues

Percent with Opinion of Opinion-Holders	Whites	Blacks	Difference
Government should provide more services and increase spending (2008)★	44%	67%	23%
Favor government health insurance plan (2008)★	44	75	31
Should be more restrictions on handguns (2004)[†]	68	87	19
Oppose death penalty for those convicted of murder (2008)[†]	27	54	27
Disapprove of handling of war in Iraq (2008)★	58	83	25
Government collects too much information about people like me (2003)[‡]	54	74	20

Note: Opinion-holders include only those with a clear pro- or con-opinion. Those with a middle response, e.g., "4s" on ANES seven-point scales are excluded.

★American National Election Studies

[†]GSS

[‡]*Washington Post* poll

identify with their race than with their social class. Upper-class whites, on the other hand, are more likely to identify with their social class. Blacks are also much less supportive of the death penalty than are whites, perhaps because those on death row are disproportionately black. Note, however, that the death penalty is still supported by close to a majority of black citizens. Blacks are also less supportive of American military action abroad. For example, we see a sizable difference in support for American involvement in the two Iraq wars. Blacks were much less supportive of the Vietnam War than were whites and have been less enthusiastic about other American military adventures, whether in Nicaragua, Grenada, and Panama in the 1980s or in Bosnia and Kosovo in the 1990s. These racial differences may stem from the Vietnam War, where a disproportionate number of African Americans bore the brunt of the fighting. In conflicts since then, the Pentagon has been careful to ensure that blacks and other minorities are not overrepresented (given their numbers in the armed services) among those assigned to combat zones.

Further survey evidence points toward an easing of strains in racial relations. Between 1981 and 1997, there was a 14 percentage point increase in the number of blacks who said they had a "close personal friend" who was white and a 17 percentage point increase among whites saying they had a "close personal friend" who was black.[9] American neighborhoods have become more racially integrated. Between 1980 and 2006, the GSS shows a 22 percentage point increase among white respondents saying they have black neighbors.

Racial Groups and the Vote

In terms of the vote and party identification, there are major differences between blacks and whites. According to the 2008 NEP exit poll, 95 percent of African Americans, but only 43 percent of whites cast their vote for Barack

Obama. Latinos and Asian-Americans voted predominantly Democratic, although not nearly to the same extent as blacks. The 2008 vote choice for the four major ethnic groups in the United States is as follows:

2008 Vote	Asian Americans	Blacks	Latinos	Whites
Obama	62%	95%	67%	43%
McCain	35	04	31	55
Percent of electorate	(02%)	(13%)	(09%)	(74%)

Minorities not only voted more Democratic than usual in 2008 but they also turned out at a greater rate than usual in the polls. In fact, according to the U.S. Census, eligible African Americans for the first time turned out to vote at the same rate as eligible whites. It can be argued that if blacks had voted at the same frequency in 2008 as in 2004, and had they voted Democratic at the slightly lower 2004 rate, Obama would have lost the presidential election to McCain (Ansolabehere, Persily, and Stewart 2010).

The voting differences we see among the races are also found in terms of the underlying attitude of party identification. Following are the racial divisions in party identification from pooled Pew surveys (N = 31,201) over the 2008 presidential campaign: [10]

Party Identification	Asians	Blacks	Latinos	Whites
Democrat	38%	77%	45%	31%
Independent	42	20	35	35
Republican	20	4	21	34
	100%	100%	100%	100%

Whites as a group are slightly more likely to identify with the Republican Party than with the Democrats. In contrast, within each of the three minority groups, the Democrats hold solid pluralities in terms of party allegiance.

Over time, American blacks have undergone a long-term reversal in their party allegiance. Between the Civil War and Franklin Roosevelt's presidency, most blacks who could vote opted for the Republican Party because it was the party of Lincoln. From the 1930s to the present, however, most blacks have supported the Democratic Party. Initially, this shift was a response to economic issues rather than any consequential attempt on the part of the Democratic Party to remove racial barriers or explicitly appeal to blacks. Only in recent decades could the Democratic Party be identified as the party with clearly greater sympathy for the civil rights cause. As a result of the Democrats' increasing image as the more pro–civil rights party, Democratic voting among blacks at the presidential level has changed from a tendency to near unanimity. The solidifying event was the 1964 election, in which President Lyndon Johnson took a strong stand in favor of the Civil Rights

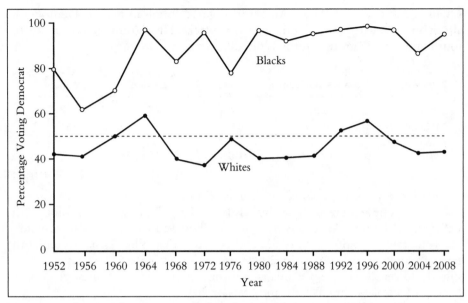

Figure 7.4 Race and the two-party presidential vote, 1952–2004. *Sources:* Gallup Poll, 1952–1976; National Election Studies, 1980–1992; Voter News Service, 1996–2000; NEP, 2004–2008.

Act and Republican challenger Barry Goldwater opposed and voted against it in Congress (as an infringement on states' rights). The change over time is shown in Figure 7.4. Clearly the black vote is a pivotal factor for the Democratic Party in presidential elections. In only one such election since World War II (1964) has the Democratic candidate received a majority of the total white vote.

7-3 Age and Political Opinions

When we examine the breakdowns by age on the scores of political issues found in polls, we find instances of three possible patterns. On the majority of issues there are no meaningful age-group differences; on a sizable minority of issues, those older are more conservative than those younger; only on a small number of issues are the young more conservative than their elders. As discussed in chapter 5, there are two major reasons why older cohorts might differ from younger ones. First, there may be life-cycle effects in which the process of maturation results in changes throughout adulthood. People growing more conservative with age is the typical example. Second, there may be generational effects, with each group of young voters differing from those in the past. While increasing conservatism with age creates an age gap in opinions, so could generational differences of the type where each cohort of new citizens is more liberal than those that came before.[11]

The Politics of Age

This section focuses mainly on issues where young and older citizens have unique political perspectives on some issues, perhaps because of competing self-interest. For instance, advocates for children often blame inadequate funding for programs benefiting youngsters on the political power of older Americans, whom they accuse of greedily siphoning off more than their fair share of government dollars, or voting against school bond referendums to keep their property taxes low (Tedin, Matland, and Weiher 2001).

Recently, many have voiced concern that the Social Security and Medicare benefits enjoyed by older Americans will bankrupt the system before those currently paying the bill are eligible to receive benefits. Social Security reform seems—for the moment at least—to be stalled. On the other hand, in 2003 Congress passed and the president signed into law a new Medicare drug benefits program. On January 1, 2006, those over sixty-five became eligible for government-subsidized prescription drug benefits. The program is estimated to cost $1.2 trillion over the next decade (Connolly and Allen 2005). Issues such as these have raised the specter of intergenerational political conflict.

We see meaningful differences between the age groups on many economic issues. Younger adults are more likely to feel the government should provide a variety of increased services to its citizens, and are generally more likely to endorse new economic trends. For instance, those between eighteen and twenty-five are significantly more acceptant than their elders of outsourcing jobs to foreign countries rather than keeping them for American workers, and believe that the growing number of immigrants "strengthens American society" (Pew 2006).[12] Reflecting its self-interest, the younger cohort is considerably more liberal on the issue of increased spending for student loans. On the issue of government health insurance, the generational differences are complicated. Senior citizens endorse government health care, but express concern about reform when it appears that extending benefits to others besides seniors might threaten the quality of care under Medicare (Blendon and Benson 2009).

When we turn to cultural issues, we find younger cohorts consistently more liberal than older ones. The young are more receptive to new ideas since they are, for the most part, not committed to old ones. This point can be illustrated using the 39 percentage point gap between those under thirty and those over fifty-five on the issue of gay marriage in Table 7.7 (ANES 2008). For those over fifty-five, it was inconceivable during most of their lives that this item would even be on the political agenda. Alternatively, those over thirty have heard dialog on the issue much of their lives.

On the issue of racial discrimination in housing, a once robust generation gap has now largely disappeared. The reasons are instructive. For the 2008 GSS, there is just an 12 point gap between those under twenty-five and those over fifty-five who say they would allow homeowners to discriminate based on race when selling their property. This age gap was much greater in the past, for instance, 25 percentage points in 1996 and 32 points in 1988 (GSS). The age gap shrunk because those who grew up when it was commonplace to believe people could discriminate based on

TABLE 7.7 | **Age and Opinion on Selected Issues**

	Percentage Support Among Opinion-Holders		
	Under 30	55 and Over	Difference
Economic Issues			
Favor more government services if it means more spending★	44%	33%	11%
Favor government health versus private medical insurance (2008)★	55	42	13
Favor allowing Social Security funds invested in stock market (2008)★	61	32	29
Increase spending on student loans (1996)★	70	42	28
Social Issues			
Home owners can't discriminate by race when selling a house (2008)★	78	66	12
Oppose death penalty for murder (2008)★	37	27	10
Allow same-sex marriage (2008)★	60	22	38
Allow abortion for any reason (2008)★	48	30	18
Foreign Policy/Military Issues			
U.S. should decrease military spending (2008)★	72	69	03
Iraq War not worth fighting (2008)?‡	74	65	09
Civic Orientations			
Extremely/very interested in national campaign (2008)★	30	41	−11
Read news about 2008 campaign (2008)★	46	76	−30
View Internet information about presidential campaign (2008)★	55	23	32
Try to influence the vote of others (2008)★	42	48	06
Liberal/Conservative Ideological Identification (2008)§			
Liberal	46	32	14
Moderate	38	37	01
Conservative	33	46	−13

★National Election Studies.

†General Social Survey.

‡ABC News

§Pew combined surveys ($n = 31,201$)

race are from an older generation that is rapidly departing the electorate and being replaced by a younger generation who reject discrimination.

On foreign affairs, it is often thought that the young are more wary of foreign intervention than their elders. However, the truth of that claim often depends on circumstances. In past conflicts, including World War II, Korea, and even Vietnam, the younger cohort has in fact been more supportive of U.S. involvement than those over fifty-five were (see Wittkopf 1990). Currently, however, the younger generation is slightly more dovish on defense issues and military intervention.

Importantly, younger Americans in general are less interested and involved in politics than older generations (Bennett 1996; Wattenberg 2008). These differences are reflected in Table 7.7. For instance, in 2008 those over fifty-five were 11 percentage points more interested in the national campaign than those under thirty. Strikingly, they were 30 percentage points more likely to read about the campaign in the newspaper. On the other hand, following politics on the Internet was far more frequent among the young.

The lack of political involvement among the young is clearest when it comes to voting participation. According to the Current Population Survey conducted by the U.S. Census, in the midterm election of 2006 only 22 percent of eligible voters under twenty-five cast a ballot compared to 62 percent of those sixty-five and above. This is part of the political life cycle. Young people are preoccupied with other things besides politics—school, social life, learning to make a living, and so on—and often lack attachments to their local community. As they mature, they pay more attention to the world of politics, an interest that often does not reach its peak until well into old age. Especially in low-turnout elections, seniors greatly outweigh young people at the polls.

Of course an event such as Obama's campaign can temporarily arouse young people toward greater activity. According to the Bureau of the Census, the only group to show a significant increase in turnout between 2004 and 2008 were those between eighteen and twenty-four, who voted at a 49 percent rate, upto 2 percentage points from 2004. Seniors sixty-five and older, by contrast, voted at a 70 percent rate.[13] In casting their votes, the young surged toward Obama to a degree not found among their elders. Exit polls show that in 2008 those under thirty gave 67 percent of their vote to Obama compared to 51 percent by the rest of the electorate. Similarly, in terms of party identification, youth in 2008 were almost twice as likely to call themselves Democratic than Republican, whereas as recently as 1992 the allegiance of young voters (under thirty) was virtually evenly divided between the two parties (Keeter, Horowitz, and Tyson 2008). Whether the recent cohort of young voters will continue to vote more Democratic as they age remains to be seen.

7-4 Religion and Political Opinions

Compared with other nations, Americans are religious (Norris and Inglehart 2004). In 2005, respondents in the World Values Survey were asked if they were or were not a religious person.[14] As we can see from the following table, the

United States stands out in the high proportion of its citizens who find religion important in their lives.

	Am a Religious Person	Am Not Religious	Other/Don't Know★
United States	72%	24%	04%
Canada	66	27	07
Australia	52	38	10
Britain	49	41	10
Spain	46	47	07
France	47	36	17
Germany	43	38	19
Sweden	33	49	17
Japan	24	62	14
China	22	60	18

★ *Volunteered.*

Most Americans belong to churches, although that was not always the case. At the time of the American Revolution, only 17 percent were church members. By the end of the Civil War the number had doubled to 35 percent, then increased to 53 percent by 1916, to 63 percent in the 1990s (Finke and Stark 1994), dropping slightly to 62 percent in 2008 (Gallup).[15]

Protestants, Catholics, Jews, and "Nones"

Table 7.8 presents a basic inventory of religious preferences in the United States, drawn from the authoritative 2004 National Survey of Religion and Politics, with a large sample of 4,000 respondents.[16] The table shows 53 percent of American adults are Protestant, 22 percent are Catholic, 2 percent are Jewish, 6 percent are "other," and 17 percent profess no religious preference ("Nones").[17] Some major religious streams are further broken into subgroups. Protestants are divided into evangelical and mainline denominations, with evangelicals being the largest of the various religious subgroups. Churches considered to be evangelical are theologically conservative, stress being "born again," and believe in the inerrancy of the Bible, although this characterization is somewhat of an oversimplification. Predominantly, black and Hispanic denominations are considered separately. Catholics are divided into Anglo (White non-Hispanic) and Hispanic. The table treats Jews as a single group, as well as the "nones."

Table 7.8 shows evangelical Protestant denominations are the most Republican, the most conservative, and the most pro-life on abortion. At the other end, atheists/agnostics are generally the most liberal (although black Protestants are the most Democratic). "Nones" in general tend to be liberal. To be unchurched is to be outside the American cultural mainstream, and such marginality tends to result in a liberal political outlook. Mainline Protestants tend to be Republican and conservative, but less pro-life on abortion than the

TABLE 7.8	Religious Denomination and Political Opinions, 2004 (%)					
	Party Identification		Political Ideology		Abortion	Size of Group
	Republican	Democrat	Conservative	Liberal	"Pro-Life"	
All Respondents	38%	42%	40%	28%	48%	100%
Protestant	48	39	47	22	56	(53)
Evangelical	58	26	58	16	70	25
Mainline	44	40	41	30	35	16
Black	11	71	31	26	54	9
Hispanic	38	44	35	25	63	3
Catholic	36	47	39	31	50	(22)
Anglo	41	44	40	29	48	18
Hispanic	15	62	35	36	56	5
Jewish	22	68	22	57	16	2
Other	27	38	28	32	46	5
None	26	43	25	39	27	17

Source: Adapted from Corwin Smidt, Lyman Kellsteadt, and James Guth "The Role of Religion in American Politics." In Corwin Smidt (ed), *Oxford Handbook of Religion and American Politics* (Oxford: Oxford Press, 2009).

sample as a whole. Despite the doctrinal position of the Catholic Church on abortion, Anglo Catholics are no more pro-life than the sample as a whole. Hispanic Catholics tend to be Democratic and liberal, but are decided pro-life on the abortion issue. Only evangelicals exceed them. Thus, it is possible that both major parties can appeal to the growing Hispanic population—the Democrats on economic issues and the Republicans on cultural issues. Jews are notably Democratic, liberal, and pro-choice.

Historically, religious cleavages between Protestants, Catholics, and Jews were at their pinnacle in 1960, when Democrats broke with tradition and nominated a Catholic, John F. Kennedy, for president. Presented below is the presidential vote by religion (among northern whites) in 1960 (ANES).[18]

Northern Whites	Protestant	Catholic	Jewish
Voting Democratic (Kennedy)	28%	83%	83%
Voting Republican (Nixon)	72	17	17
	100%	100%	100%

Almost three-fourths of the Protestant vote among Northern whites was for Nixon, while over 80 percent of the Catholic and Jewish vote went for Kennedy. In more typical elections, without a Catholic candidate, the same ordering exists, but the differences are smaller. The table below shows the presidential vote divisions among (Northern white) Protestants, Catholics, Jews, and Nones in the 2008 ANES. Among Northern whites, Protestants tilted slightly to McCain while Catholics tilted slightly to Obama. Jews and those with no religious preference were the most strongly for Obama. The religious breakdown of the vote in 2008 was decisively milder than in 1960, almost a half century earlier, when Kennedy's religion was such a matter of contention.

Northern Whites	Protestant	Catholic	Jewish	Nones
Voting Democratic (Obama)	47%	53%	79%	67%
Voting Republican (McCain)	53	47	21	33
	100%	100%	100%	100%

The temporal stability of partisan differences between Protestants, Catholics, and Jews is shown in Figure 7.5. For Northern whites, the figure displays the party identification (as percent Democrat of partisan identifiers) for the three religious groups between 1956 and 2008. The relative ordering of the three religious groups has been stable over the half century of polling: Jews most Democratic, followed by Catholics and then Protestants. Historically, Catholics have been more Democratic than Protestants, although this gap has noticeably narrowed in recent years.

One explanation for this once persistent Democratic voting among Catholics is that in the past American Catholics were less affluent than their Protestant neighbors—a condition that would naturally cause them to gravitate to the Democratic Party for economic reasons. But there is more than economics at work, because during the 1940s, surveys showed that even affluent Catholics

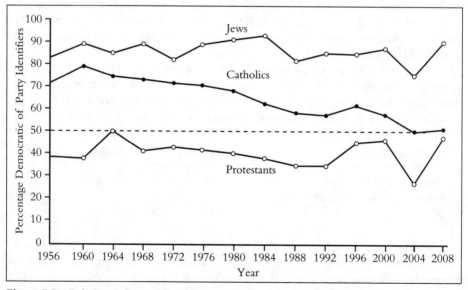

Figure 7.5 Religion and party identification (Northern whites only), 1956–2008. *Source:* American National Election Studies, 2008 election data.

tended to be Democratic, much as affluent blacks are today (Berelson, Lazarsfeld, and McPhee 1954, 64–66). Besides, the Protestant–Catholic gap in income closed decades ago. The Democrats had traditionally wooed immigrant voters, most of whom were Catholic. The payoff of this policy for the Democratic Party has been the continued allegiance of many members of Catholic ethnic groups—the Irish, Italians, Polish, East Europeans, Filipinos, and Mexicans—who continue to identify and vote more consistently Democratic than Protestants, despite having incomes that place them solidly in the middle class. Perhaps the best explanation for the Democratic allegiance of Catholics is simply the socialization of partisanship from one generation to the next. Even though the social and economic reasons for remaining Democratic no longer exist, there is a family tradition of Democratic partisanship among Catholics that keeps them from turning Republican in spite of the erosion of the once firm Catholic allegiance to the Democratic Party.

Evangelicals, Mainline Protestants, Catholics, and Seculars

Of course to talk about religion and politics today, more is involved than the historical division between Protestants and Catholics. As discussed earlier, an important division today is between evangelical and mainline Protestants. Another is between those who regularly attend religious services and those who do not. This suggests the four-way classification (Catholic churchgoers, evangelical churchgoers, mainline Protestant churchgoers, and "seculars" who do not go to church) shown in Table 7.9.

In Table 7.9, the four groups are compared in terms of their partisanship and opinion in the 2008 American National Election Study. We distinguish evangelical Protestants from mainline Protestants by the shorthand of whether they claim to be "born again."[19] Seculars include those who either claim no religion or if they do, say they "never" attend services, as one would not expect religion to have much sway over people who ignore their professed religion.[20] To facilitate the estimation of religion's effects on political views, the table compares white respondents only. Basically, the table reveals seculars to be (relatively) on the left, evangelical churchgoers on the right, with Catholic and mainline Protestant churchgoers in the middle.

First, we look once again at partisan differences by religion. Among white voters, the one group that strongly supported McCain and opposed Obama was evangelicals. One might have expected religion would play a lesser role in 2008 than in 2004, when support from evangelicals helped to reelect George W. Bush. Bush's appeal to the religious right and the cultural issues so strongly highlighted in the 2004 campaign gave way to economic issues in 2008. In 2008, McCain was not a favorite of conservative Christians. Yet he received almost the same share of the evangelical vote as Bush had four years earlier. Among white voters, the one group where McCain lost ground was among mainline Protestants. Otherwise, from the standpoint of the religious vote, the 2008 election looked very much like 2004—albeit with a different political party claiming victory (Smidt, Kellstedt, and Guth 2009).

TABLE 7.9	Religious Divisions and Political Views Among Whites, 2008			
Percent of Opinion-Holders	**Secular [Not a Church Goer](40%)**	**Catholic Church Goer (14%)**	**Mainline Protestant Church Goer (15%)**	**Evangelical Protestant Church Goer (29%)**
More domestic spending	62	58	56	45
Less defense spending	43	33	47	25
For national health insurance	62	55	57	39
Government should help blacks	21	27	22	12
For guaranteed job, standard of living	34	35	24	23
Permit all or most abortions	67	51	68	38
Allow gay marriage	6951	5536	6844	2115
For more gun control	45	50	47	32
Against death penalty	25	39	13	23
For Iraq troop withdrawal timetable	61	54	55	42
Democrat (of party identifiers)	57	52	47	31
Liberal (of ideological identifiers)	54	30	38	17
Vote for Obama, 2008	57	50	52	23

Note: Opinion-holders include only those with a clear pro or con opinion. Those with a middle response, e.g., "4s" on ANES seven-point scales, are excluded. Seculars include those with no religion, and those who claim a religious denomination but "never" attend services. Evangelical church attenders claim membership in a Protestant church and to be "born again." Mainline church attenders are all other members of Protestant faiths. Religiously observant members of the Jewish faith and non-Judeo-Christian faiths are omitted from the analysis.

Source: 2008 National Election Study.

The one set of political issues that divide religious groups more than any other is, of course, the cultural issues. Historically, people of strong religious faith tend to hold to traditional moral values, while seculars hold more modernistic values. Thus, the seculars are the most liberal on cultural issues, such as abortion and gay rights, and evangelicals stand out uniquely for their conservatism. This is not only true for abortion, as we saw in Table 7.8, but also for allowing gay marriage (as shown in Table 7.9).

Further differences by religious orientation can be found on domestic spending and foreign policy issues. Wilson (2009) analyzes the three survey questions on government spending programs used consistently in the ANES time series (services/spending, job guarantee, and health care). Over the years, the most consistently economically conservative have been evangelical Protestants. Table 7.9 shows this once again to be true in 2008. The most likely explanation is distrust of government, commitment to the Protestant notion of personal self-reliance, reinforced by messages from the Pulpit (Wald, Owen, and Hill 1989; Jelen 1992; Djupe and Gilbert 2002). Closely following evangelicals are mainline Protestants, who are only slightly less conservative. Catholics have a history of liberalism on economic issues.

Unlike the claims made in some studies (Holsti 2004; Kohut and Stokes 2006) other research shows links between religion and opinions about foreign policy. In particular, evangelicals stand out as distinct from other religious groups—they tend to distrust the UN, favor increases in defense funding, support Israel and oppose a Palestinian state, and favor combating terrorism through military action (Page 2006).[21] Some current research focuses on the link between religion and support for U.S. engagement in preemptive military action such as in Iraq. The data from a variety of sources point to evangelicals as key supporters for this doctrine (Barker, Hurwitz, and Nelson 2008; Guth 2009). Table 7.9 shows the distinctive foreign policy militancy of evangelicals on the issues of defense spending and Iraq withdrawal.

The political differences we see between evangelicals and others—and to a lesser extent between the religious and the secular—are relatively new to American politics. Fifty years ago, evangelical churches rarely got involved in politics and one's religiosity had little bearing on one's political views. But back then there were few cultural issues on the political agenda to spur some religious people to defend traditional values and others, usually less religious, to push for change. To some extent, religion has contributed to today's polarization, as politics can sometimes seem like ideological combat between strident conservative and liberal political foes. At the same time, we should be cautious about stereotyping people politically from their religious beliefs. A significant minority of seculars are conservative just as a significant minority of evangelicals are on the liberal side of the political spectrum.

7-5   Geography and Political Opinions

People commonly think of American public opinion as differing along regional lines. The South stands out in particular for its political conservatism, particularly on civil rights and cultural issues. Outlandish fads (political and otherwise) are thought to start in the West, most notably in California. The East is often characterized as being liberal (every New England congressional district elected a Democrat in 2008). There have been other regional stereotypes that once may have been valid but seem less so today. The South, for example, was once the most international-minded region in foreign policy, largely because of the cotton growers' interest in free trade with other nations. The Midwest at one time had the reputation, seemingly deserved on the basis of poll results, for being the most isolationist (least internationalist) region of the country (Hero 1973).[22] The long-term trend shows little loss of regional distinctiveness in party preference.

Several factors, however, serve to undermine the impact of region. Americans are mobile (20 percent move each year) and dilute the native citizenry. Only 40 percent of adults say they currently live in the same locale as they did when they were sixteen years old (GSS 2008). The near-universal penetration of the national media would seem to have a homogenizing effect on regionalism. But we should not overstate the case. On many issues, meaningful regional differences persist, especially between the South and the remainder of the country.

In the twenty-first century, the media introduced a new set of geographic terms to the political lexicon. It became common to identify states as "red" (Republican) or "blue" (Democrat) based on their presidential voting. Fiorina Abrams, and Pope (2006) analyzed differences in public opinion between blue and red states using the 2000 and 2004 ANES. They found surprisingly small opinion differences, and no evidence of a "culture war."

Using data from the 2008 ANES, we compare residents of "red" states which went Republican in the 2000–2004–2008 elections with those of "blue," states which went Democrat in those elections. For comparison, we use the summary 21-point ten-issue scale of liberalism–conservatism introduced in chapter 3. With a possible range of +10 to −10, the red states lean slightly to the right (mean = 1.3) and the blue states to the left (mean = −1.0). Out of ten issue questions, the average citizen in a Republican state will give the conservative response to about 5.5 questions compared to 4.5 for the average citizen in a Democratic state. While this is a real difference, it is hard to make argument for severe issue polarization based on how states cast their Electoral College vote (for a somewhat different take on polarization, see Abramowitz 2010).

It is only recently that commentators have been talking about red and blue states. The most common way to divide the country has been by region (Northeast, Midwest, South, and West) and by urban/rural. Taking region first, analysis of public opinion data from the millennium forward shows that on virtually all cultural issues—such as school prayer, gay rights, allowing communists to speak in one's community, abortion, and gun control—the South is markedly conservative. The South is also markedly conservative on foreign policy issues. Its residents want to spend more on defense and are more likely to endorse the use of military force to settle international conflicts. These distinctive opinions represent the cultural conservatism of the South.

Just as on some issues the South is uniquely conservative, the Northeast is uniquely liberal. We illustrate with some examples from a 2009 Pew poll. For example, 67 percent in the Northeast favor legal abortions in all or most cases, compared to 49 percent in the South, and 59 percent in the West.[23] Similar patterns can be found for civil liberties, prayer in the schools, and gun control. For instance, 60 percent of people in the Northeast favor allowing gay marriage versus just 30 percent in the South. The other two regions fall in between. Fifty-eight percent in the South believe books with dangerous ideas should be banned, compared to 41 percent for the rest of the country. Those in the South are also most likely to favor protecting gun ownership over gun control (52 percent) versus just 35 percent in the Northeast. Again, the Midwest and the West fall in the middle. The South also stands out as having citizens most likely to believe that the best way to insure peace is through military strength (64 percent). For the rest of the country, it is 52 percent. In the South, 58 percent say torture is often justified against suspected terrorists, compared to 43 percent in the West, with the other two regions falling in between. On immigration, the West is unique in that 78 percent favor providing illegal immigrants with a route to citizens, while a lesser 62 percent of the South and Midwest favor this position. One area where there is almost no difference among regions is attitudes toward business. In terms of ideological self-identification, 46 percent in the South call themselves conservative, compared to 40 percent in the Midwest, 37 percent in the Northeast, and 34 percent in the West.

But are regional differences in fact related to a regional culture, or are they simply compositional effects? For instance, the South's cultural conservatism is at least partially due to its adherence to evangelical Christianity. While composition does account for much of the observed regional differences, there is certainly some truth to this view; individual state culture does make some contribution to one's partisanship and political ideology (Erikson, Wright, and McIver 1994). For example, even with demographic factors held constant, residents of, say, Minnesota are more liberal than, say, Oklahoma. There is something about state culture that affects partisanship and ideology beyond the fact that residents may differ in their religion, income, education, or race.

Other than state residence and regional groupings, the most common geographical division is between cities, suburbs, small towns, and rural areas. It is generally thought that urban areas are sources of liberal and nonconventional political attitudes, with rural and small-town America being the bastions of conservatism. This is the pattern we see in the 2008 Pew merged data set, where (for whites only) among rural respondents, 38 percent identify as conservatives, compared to 23 percent classified as living in urban places. Earlier analyses by Yang and Alba (1992), using GSS data and focusing on nonconventional opinions, show that residents of urban areas are much more liberal on these domains than are those living in small towns and rural areas. A study by Wilson (1985) shows urban residence has a positive association with political tolerance.

At least part of this variation is due to composition effects. City residents show up as more liberal in surveys because they have a large proportion of people with liberal group characteristics, such as blacks, gays, Jews, and secular nonchurchgoers. Small towns and rural areas are conservative because they are disproportionately evangelical and, outside the South, contain few blacks. But not all these urban/rural differences disappear when controls for composition effects are introduced. In fact, most remain statistically significant, although reduced in magnitude. Fischer (1975, 428) advances an "urban subculture" theory, which holds that urban residents are more nonconventional in their political opinions because urban life provides a *critical mass*, meaning "the congregation of numbers of persons sufficient to maintain viable unconventional subcultures." In other words, there is something about urban life—perhaps social diversity or the existence of support groups—independent of the social background of the residents that attracts liberals to move there and influences residents to become more liberal or nonconventional than those living in small towns and rural areas.

The Changing American South

The once distinctive South (the old Confederacy) is gradually losing its unique political character. The reasons are complex but certainly involve the economic boom that began after World War II, migration (many blacks left the region in search of jobs, while many Northern whites moved into the region for the same reason), plus rapid industrialization of the region with attendant liberalizing consequences.

The South's original distinctiveness spans many elements of opinion and political behavior. We have discussed the South's conservatism on cultural issues. The uniqueness of the South was associated even more with a conservative stance on racial questions and overwhelming support for the Democratic Party. In recent years, surveys show only small differences between white Southerners and the rest of the nation on race. In terms of partisanship, white southerners have shifted from being predominantly Democratic (but conservative) to overwhelmingly Republican.

Over the past half century, the white South has adapted to the end of racial segregation. Table 7.10 shows the dramatic decline in the difference between Southern and non-Southern whites in response to the question of whether or not one favors the principle of black and white children attending the same school. In 1956, the differences between the South and the rest of the nation were substantial. By 1985 (the last year the question was asked), there was almost no difference of consequence between the whites in the South and whites in the rest of the nation on whether black and white children should attend the same schools.[24] For the 1994 ANES question on whether "the federal government should see to it" that blacks and whites attend the same schools, there was no difference between whites in the South and the rest of the nation (38 percent in both regions favored government action).

Not all are convinced by the New South argument. Measuring racial hostility is difficult, given the social norms that surround the race issue. The most racially

TABLE 7.10	School Integration Opinion Among Whites by Region and Education, 1956 and 1985	
	Favor Blacks and Whites Attending the Same School	
Non-South	**1956**	**1985**
Less than high school	58%	86%
High school	67	98
Some college or more	79	99
South		
Less than high school	8	67
High school	20	93
Some college or more	30	98

Sources: 1956 data adapted from Howard Schuman, Charlotte Steeh, and Lawrence Bobo, *Racial Attitudes in America* (Cambridge, MA: Harvard University Press, 1985), p. 78; the 1985 data are from the General Social Survey.

prejudiced may in fact be the most likely to hide their true feelings. Using a method to disguise racially sensitive questions, Kuklinski, Cobb, and Gilens (1997) report considerably more racial resentment among white Southerners than among whites outside the South.[25] For example, 42 percent of white Southerners expressed anger at the thought of a black family moving in next door, compared to 10 percent of non-Southern whites (Kuklinski, Cobb, and Gilens 1997, 329–30). Their conclusion is that many white Southerners are giving insincere answers when asked directly about racial issues.

The initial attachment of the South to the Democratic Party goes back, of course, to the Civil War, but it was reinforced by economics. The South was long the poorest region of the country—a plus for the Democratic Party, given its image of providing jobs and benefits to the average person. Until the Voting Rights Act of 1965, blacks were effectively disenfranchised in much of the South, meaning that the Democratic Party of the South was largely a white party. Strategically, the white South had gained by staying with the Democrats because its prominent position stymied the party's Northern liberal wing to act on blacks' pressing demands for civil rights legislation. Then, the parties began to diverge on civil rights at about the moment that blacks began voting in heavier numbers. The next forty years or so saw a rapid decline in the white South's allegiance to the Democratic Party. Today, whites are more Republican in the South than in any other region, and the South has become the most dependably Republican region in terms of voting, first only for president but now more generally for other offices as well.

Figure 7.6 documents Republican gains in the white South in terms of party identification. In 1952, Democrats outnumbered Republicans by an 8–1 ratio in the white South. As can be seen in Figure 7.6, the major Republican gain followed the presidential candidacy of Republican Barry

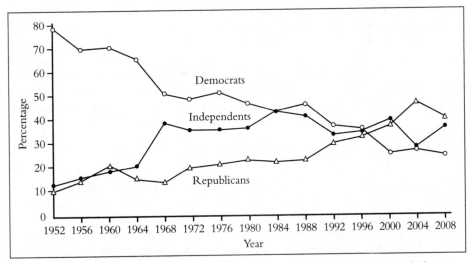

Figure 7.6 Party identification among white Southerners, 1952–2008. *Source:* National Election Studies.

Goldwater in 1964. Goldwater voted against the 1964 Civil Rights Act on the grounds that it violated states' rights. Since then, the decline has been gradual but steady. By 2008, 40 percent of Southern whites were calling themselves Republicans and just 24 percent were calling themselves Democrats.

The survey evidence regarding the white South's growing Republicanism reveals the importance of long-standing party attachments. Older Southern whites who grew up during the Democratic era have been more resistant to Republicanism than young Southerners, who flock to the Republican Party unburdened by the habits of lifelong Democratic identification (Wattenberg 1998; Erikson, MacKuen, and Stimson 2002; Green, Palmquist, and Schickler 1998). We can see this pattern even today in the following table, based on pooling multiple Pew surveys from 2008. Among whites outside the South, it is older partisans who are the most likely to call themselves Republicans, as expected. Among white Southerners, however, age makes little difference, with one exception: It is the very oldest partisans, now eighty-five years of age or older, who are the most resistant to the Republican label. The gradual exit of this older generation of Southern whites has contributed to the growing Republicanism in the South.[26]

| | Percent Republican Identifiers | | | | |
2008	18–24	25–44	45–64	65–85	85–
Southern Whites	63	63	63	59	51
Non-Southern Whites	45	49	45	48	52

It is not just that young white Southerners have become more Republican; they are now considerably more Republican than their white counterparts in the North. It is paradoxical that younger Southerners show the most movement to the Republican Party even though polls have shown them to be more liberal on racial and cultural issues than their elders. The nature of this attraction has been debated by scholars. Some emphasize a latent racism among Southern whites as the cause (Carmines and Stimson 1989; Valentino and Sears 2004). Others insist that the source is the white South's cultural conservatism on social issues and foreign policy (Abramowitz 1994). The matter remains unresolved.

7-6   Gender and Political Opinions

Over the years, survey researchers began to see growing differences between the opinions of men and women. This difference has entered common parlance as the "gender gap." Among the consistently documented differences are party identification, voting, opinions on force, violence and war, compassion issues, political efficacy, participation beyond voting, and political knowledge (Schlesinger and Heldman 2001; Kanthak and Norrander 2004; Mondak and Anderson 2004). However, observed gender differences are only the beginning of the story. Of much consequence is the explanation. Among the frequently cited are differences in socialization, gender roles, biology, occupations (Norris 2006), and even genetics (Hatemi, Medland, and Eaves 2009).

The Gender Gap in Voting and Partisanship

In the early days of survey research, it was thought that there were few differences between men and women in partisanship, voting, and political opinions. Although women participated less than men, they were thought to be indistinguishable from them on questions of party and voting, with perhaps a few minor differences on issue positions. In fact, according to ANES data, between 1952 and 1964 women voted more Republican than men, with the largest gap being 6 percent in 1956. Had the 1960 election been decided by women only, Richard Nixon would have defeated John F. Kennedy—despite the lore about Kennedy's boyish good looks being an asset among female voters.

In 1968, women began voting more Democratic than men, but it was not until the 1980 election that considerable media attention was devoted to the gap between male and female voting for president. In 1980, the gap between male and female vote choice was 8 percent. The gender gap weakened somewhat between 1984 and 1994, but emerged again strongly in 1996, when women voted 13 percent more Democratic than did men—currently the largest gap (in terms of presidential voting) for which we have data. In 2008, women voted 7 percent more Democratic than men (NEP Exit Poll).[27]

The pattern we see for voting also appears for party identification. Since 1988 women have been about 10 percentage points more Democratic than men (ANES). This Democratic tendency in identification is particularly noticeable among unmarried and well-educated women, but disappears when comparisons are made between male and female married respondents. For instance, the 1997 wave of the Michigan socialization panel shows that for the 1996 presidential election unmarried men were 41 percent points more likely to vote Republican than unmarried women, but there was no difference between husbands and wives (Stoker and Jennings 2005).[28]

The conventional wisdom about the gender gap is that over the years women became more Democratic as greater numbers entered college and the workforce, and became more attuned to their own political agenda. However, the notion that the gender gap was created by women becoming more Democratic in their partisan preference and vote choice is wrong. The data show just the opposite. The voting behavior and partisan behavior of women has remained within a narrow band since 1980. Meanwhile, men moved decidedly in the Republican direction. It is this decisive movement among men that accounts for most of the gender gap in partisanship and vote choice (Kaufmann and Petrocik 1999; Kaufman 2006).

Still the gender gap expands and shrinks. We might initially conclude that this shifting around has to do with the candidates and issues in particular elections. Mostly, that is not the case. Rather, the gender gap is a dynamic process that exists independently of elections. Box-Steffensmeier, De Boef, and Lin (2004) use CBS Polls aggregated quarterly between 1977 and 2004 to study the gender gap in partisanship between elections. Poor economic conditions hurt women more than men. In periods of high unemployment, women are more likely to gravitate to the Democratic Party than are men—increasing the gender gap. But that is only part of the story. The gender gap also increases with the rise in the percentage of adults who claim to be conservative and with the percentage of the unmarried women in the electorate. However, the state of the economy is the most important determinant of the partisan gender gap. As economic conditions improve, the gender gap in partisanship shrinks.

The Gender Gap in Political Knowledge

One of the largest and most analyzed gender gaps occurs between men and women on political knowledge (Verba, Burns, and Schlozman 1997; Delli Carpini and Keeter 2000; Kenski and Jamieson 2000). Media polls frequently report large knowledge gaps between men and women. For instance, in 2007 Pew queried the political knowledge of the public using a 23-item test. Forty-five percent of men scored in the "high" knowledge category compared to 25 percent of women.[29] Holding key background factors constant (such as education, age, and race) has only a modest effect in reducing these differences.

However, men and women respond differently to multiple-choice questions, creating the illusion of a larger gender gap than really exists. Given a multiple-choice knowledge test, men are more likely than women to guess at the correct answer than say "don't know" (Rapoport 1982, 1985). Perhaps this gap is a residual of childhood socialization where boys are taught to be aggressive and girls to be more nurturing. Obviously, if men are guessing more than women, some of the guesses are going to be right, while "don't know" answers can never be right. The consequence is that men score higher on measures of political knowledge. Mondak and Anderson (2004) estimate that this different propensity to guess accounts for as much as half the gender gap in political knowledge. Still, even with background controls and corrections for guessing, there exists a nontrivial political knowledge gap between men and women that has yet to be fully explained.

The Gender Gap in Issue Opinions

Women and men often differ in their opinion on issues. Table 7.11 presents gender differences in selected issue domains. Since the 1930s, surveys have shown that women are less prone to endorse violence and aggression in any form, be it at the personal level, regarding capital punishment, or in foreign affairs regarding matters such as war (Berinsky 2009). The table shows the same 18 percentage point gender gap in 2004 regarding the war in Iraq as it does for 2009 regarding the war in Afghanistan. These gender differences have also appeared in other conflicts. Women were 12 percent more likely than men to say it was wrong for the United States to get involved in the 2001 Gulf War (ANES 1992). There was a similar gender difference in support of the Korean

TABLE 7.11 | Gender and Political Opinions

Opinion	Percent Among Opinion-Holders		
	Men	Women	Difference
Force, Violence, and Aggression			
Government should decrease defense spending (2008)★	31%	49%	+18
Want stricter gun control laws (2008)★	36	57	+21
Oppose death penalty over life in prison for capital murder (2009)[†]	38	54	+16
Iraq War not worth fighting (2004)[‡]	38	46	+18
Oppose Afghanistan War (2009)[†]	40	58	+18
Compassion			
Spend budget surplus on social programs, not tax cut (1999)★	49	64	+15
Government should provide health insurance (2008)★	46	54	+8
Government should provide more spending and services (2008)[†]	44	53	+87
Increase spending on the poor (2008)[‡]	65	75	+10
Civil Liberties/Civil Rights			
Legalize same-sex marriage (20092008)★	36	42	+6
Favor legalization of marijuana (2008)[‡]	42	35	−7
Allow communists to speak (2008)[‡]	72	64	−8
Reduce crime by solving social problems (1996)[†]	27	33	+6
Favor government aid to blacks (2008)★	20	22	+2
Favor affirmative action for minorities (2008)[‡,★]	17	18	+1
Gender-Related Issues			
Abortion should be available for any reason (2008)[‡]	42	40	−2
Deny women seeking equality demand special favors (2004)[†]	28	26	−2
Men and women equally suited for politics (2008)[★, §]	63	67	+4
Draft men only into the military (1998)★	56	51	−5
Increase spending for child care (2008)[‡]	50	59	+9

Note: Opinion-holders include only those with a clear pro or con opinion. Those with a middle response, e.g., "4s" on ANES seven-point scales, are excluded. But note exception on the women's role question.

★American National Election Studies.

[†]CNN/ORC

[‡]General Social Survey.

§

War and the Vietnam War, with women typically being 8–10 percent less enthusiastic than men. This gender difference on foreign affairs has important electoral consequences. When elections tend to turn on questions of human rights and issues of war and peace, the gender gap in voting increases, with women moving to favor Democratic candidates.

These differences on violence and aggression are probably due to the interplay of socialization and biology. There is a large body of research showing that men have a greater predisposition than women do to use force (Schlesinger and Heldman 2001). The socialization of young boys frequently emphasizes aggression (witness playground games), while such aggression is discouraged in young girls. Another possible explanation is that women are more risk averse than men (Tedin and Yap 1993). For example, 31 percent of men but only 5 percent of women favor building more nuclear power plants (ANES Pilot 1991).

Women are generally more supportive of a compassionate approach to political issues than are men, but the differences are not as large as the gap for the use of force and violence. Still, there are meaningful gender differences on spending for social programs, health insurance, and assisting the poor, as seen in Table 7.11. When large differences appear, they are usually on issues that address specific hazards rather than more general society-wide problems. For example, in addition to differences in support for building nuclear power plants, substantial gaps have been documented in support for the 55-mile-per-hour speed limit, for state laws requiring seatbelts, and for stiff jail terms for drunk drivers.

On civil liberties issues, men and women usually do not differ. One exception is that women have historically been more supportive of gay rights than men, although the 2008 ANES shows a modest 6 percentage point difference on same-sex marriage and a 10 percentage point difference on favoring laws to protect homosexuals from job discrimination. Note the 9 percent difference favoring men on willingness to allow a communist to "speak in your neighborhood." These differences are not limited to the United States but show up in Western Europe and the former Soviet Union as well (Norris 1988; Tedin and Yap 1993; Tedin 1994a). Controls for background factors reduce, but do not eliminate, these differences. In the case of civil rights, even though women sometimes benefit from affirmative action programs, they generally differ little from men in their opinions. There is only a 2 percent difference on aid to blacks and a 1 percent difference on affirmative action for minorities.

Perhaps surprisingly, on most gender-related issues the gender gap is small to nonexistent. Women are more in favor of increased spending for child care, but on most other gender issues there are either quite modest gender differences or, occasionally, differences that seem to run counter to self-interest. In twenty-one successive readings of the General Social Survey, men have been at least as supportive of abortion "for any reason" as have women. In some early GSS surveys, men were as much as 10 percentage points more supportive, although the gender gap on abortion has essentially disappeared in recent years (as shown in Table 7.11).

One reason for this pattern is that on many issues that directly concern women there is a greater gap among women themselves than between women and men. Take, for instance, the label *feminist*. In 2008, 36 percent of women answered "yes" to the question "Do you consider yourself a feminist?" (Gallup).[30] Women accepting this label tend not to be "average." Rather, they are highly educated and affluent. Their voting patterns are also atypical. In 2004, nonfeminist women gave 83 percent of their vote to George W. Bush, while feminist women gave him only 27 percent (ANES 2004).[31]

We see clearly the class division among women by looking at the 2008 ANES question that asks if "women should have an equal role with men in running business, industry, and government," or whether "women's place is in the home." Women disagree among themselves on the answer to this question more than they disagree with men. The line of stratification divides working women and homemakers and divides on level of education. Sixty-seven percent of working women chose the most equalitarian category (option 1 on a seven-point scale), compared to only 44 percent of the homemakers. Among working women with a college degree, 71 percent chose the most egalitarian option. Only 36 percent of homemakers with no more than a high school education chose this option. Although support for women in the workforce continues to increase as full-time working women have become commonplace, there are nevertheless lifestyle distinctions about what makes one an important and worthwhile person that split the political opinions of women.

7-7 Conclusion

Group characteristics can clearly make a difference in how people see the political world. Belonging to a group is part of one's self-identification. Many groups have a vested political interest. Being prosperous and economically secure encourages one to believe that through one's own effort success can be achieved, and government should be limited in its ability to spend tax money to aid those who have not been successful in life's competition. Being poor encourages the opposite perspective. Race, religion, gender, region, and age also intrude on one's life in a fashion not entirely neutral, consequently coloring the way one sees the desirable organization and ends of the polity.

Over time, certain group distinctions may increase or decrease in importance. Some see cultural differences in terms of religion leading to further political polarization. Group distinctions that may increase in political relevance are those between the young and the old, the Sun Belt and the Frost Belt, and the technologically skilled and unskilled. These potential cleavages may at some point replace traditional sources of voting alignments, such as partisanship or class. If that happens, the benefits that government bestows on its citizens, as well as the obligations it demands, may also change.

Notes

1. The Pew Research Center, poll conducted between March 17 and March 27. In 2004, the NES asked if there had been a change in the income gap between the rich and the poor in the last twenty years. Seventy-nine percent said the gap had grown larger, and 58 percent said it had grown "much larger."
2. "Public Opinion and Demographic Report," *Public Perspective* 4 (May/June 1993): 85.
3. The increased partisan divide based on income is also found when party identification is substituted for the vote. Even occupational class has held its own as a predictor of the vote when multivariate controls are imposed (Manza and Brooks 1999).
4. It can also be observed that the richest states tend to vote more Democratic than the poor states. While the reasons for this are complex, it is also true that within each state, the rich vote more Republican than the poor. The poorer the state, the more the rich vote Republican (Gelman et al. 2008).
5. On contemporary public opinion among Latinos, including variations by nation of origin, see Uhlaner and Garcia (2002), Barreto et al. (2002), and de la Garza and Jang (2008).
6. There is greater racial division on questions involving racial preferences in education than on jobs, with blacks more one-sidedly favorable to affirmative action in the realm of education opportunities. More blacks, as well as more whites, are likely to endorse programs that create equality of opportunity rather than equality of outcomes.
7. Sigelman and Welch (1991) analyzed answers to a large number of affirmative action questions and found that depending on question wording, as many as 96 percent of blacks and 76 percent of whites were favorable, or as few as 23 percent of blacks and 9 percent of whites were favorable. They also found that those affirmative action programs that get the most support from blacks also get the most support from whites.
8. ABC News/Washington Post Poll, conducted January 13–19, 2009. Downloaded from ABC polling Web site.
9. Data from polls taken by the *Washington Post* reported in *The Public Perspective* (Oct./Nov. 1997): 17.
10. Analysis by authors.
11. Generational differences can be a function of compositional effects, as when more recent political generations hold opinions different from their elders because of their greater levels of education.
12. Among those between eighteen and twenty-five, 41 percent say outsourcing jobs helps American workers, compared to just 8 percent of those over forty; 45 percent of those between eighteen and twenty-four say the growing number of immigrants helps American workers versus 21 percent of those over forty (Pew Research Center, "How Young People View Their Lives, Futures and Politics" (Released January 9, 2007).
13. The ratio of the senior voting rate to the youth voting rate, which approaches 3 to 1 in midterm years, drops to about 3 to 2 in presidential elections.
14. Data available at www.worldvaluessurvey.org.
15. The Gallup questions is, "Do you happen to be a member of a church or synagogue?"
16. For a detailed description of the survey, see Green (2007).
17. These percentages have changed little since the 2004 survey.

18. We use northern whites only so as not to confuse the effect of denominational preference with race and region. The South is largely Protestant and conservative; blacks are largely Protestant and liberal.

19. In Table 7.8, recall, the division between mainline versus evangelical Protestants was based on the denomination. Smidt, et al. (2010) offers a thoughtful discussion of alternative ways of measuring the politically relevant divisions within American Protestanism.

20. Due to their small sample size, religiously observant members of the Jewish faith and non-Judeo-Christian faiths are omitted from the analysis of Table 7.9.

21. Page (2006) argues these links are indirect, a function of partisanship and political ideology.

22. To take an example of one-time regional differences in foreign policy isolationism, Southerners, when asked in 1945 whether the United States and Russia "should make a permanent military alliance," responded favorably by a ratio greater than 2 to 1. At the other extreme, a slight majority of Midwesterners opposed such an alliance (Cantril 1951, 961). By the late 1950s, such disparities had largely disappeared (Key 1961a, 134).

23. Pews Values Survey conducted April 14–20, 2009. Data set downloaded 11/6/2009, data analysis by authors.

24. As almost everyone now endorses the principle of white and black students attending the same school, the question has not been asked by the GSS since 1985.

25. Kuklinski and colleagues randomly gave one-half of the sample a list of three nonracial items and asked how many of the items make them angry—importantly, not *which one*, just *how many*. The other half of the sample got the same three items plus an additional item addressing race, such as "a black family moving in next door." Again, the respondents were asked how many make them angry. Only the additional item for half of the sample getting four options addresses race. Thus, respondents saying two of four items anger them assume the interviewer cannot know which two—which indeed he or she cannot. However, statistical methods can be used to determine the level of anger about "a black family moving in next door" among Southerners and non-Southerners as a group.

26. Even as the oldest generation of white southerners resisted the Republican label, they still voted Republican for president at a rate similar to their younger counterparts.

27. In 2000 the gender gap was 10 percent and 2004 it was 5 percent (VNS and NEP Exit Polls).

28. This trend was already evident in the 1980s. See Weisberg (1987) for a statistical demonstration.

29. Pew Research Center, "Public Knowledge of Current Affairs Little Changed by News and Information Revolutions" (Released April 15, 2007).

30. Based on a survey by Yankelovich Partners (May 18, 1998) for *Time* and the Cable News Network.

31. Women were defined as "feminists" or "nonfeminists" using the 100 NES point feeling thermometer. Those one-third of women rating feminists highest on the feeling thermometer were classified as "feminists"; those one-third rating them lowest were classed as "nonfeminists." The 2008 ANES did not ask the feminist question, but a Gallup preelection survey (September 5–9, 2008) showed 70 percent of women calling themselves feminist favored Obama, compared to 28 percent of women who said they were not feminists.

8 The News Media and Political Opinions

OUR POLITICAL BELIEFS ARE SHAPED by the political information we receive, and most of this information is transmitted through the mass media. In totalitarian political systems, the regime attempts to shape this information by controlling outlets for the news. In democracies, the mass media is relatively free of government control. Indeed, it is difficult to imagine free democratic elections without a free flow of competing information in the mass media.

However, the proper flow of political information requires more than the government simply allowing an unfettered mass media to print or broadcast free from political interference. Today, most of what we read, see, or hear in the mass media comes from newspapers, magazines, television, radio, and Internet outlets that are owned by large private conglomerates, such as General Electric, Disney, and News Corp. Within these institutions, individuals with complex motives and incentives decide what to print, broadcast, or post. These motives and incentives range from a commitment to report the news thoroughly and objectively, to packaging the news for profit like any other commercial product, to using corporate power over the media to preserve the economic and political status quo.

Defined most broadly, the content of the mass media extends beyond matters of politics to include all aspects of information and entertainment. Although it can be tempting to read political implications in the entertainment portions of media content, that is not our concern here. Our focus is on political news and commentary in newspapers and on the radio, television, and the Internet. In this chapter, we discuss the nature of the news media, its possible biases, and the effect of the media on public opinion.

8-1 The Evolution of the American Media

The evolution of the media can be divided into five eras (West 2001).[1] The first is the Era of the Partisan Press (1787–1832). During this period, the press was simply an arm of the political parties, with parties or factions reaching out to their supporters via newspapers. At one time, the newspaper of the Federalists, the party of Alexander Hamilton, was the *Gazette of the United States*. For the Democratic-Republicans, the party of Thomas Jefferson, it was the *National Intelligencer*. It was the parties that arranged financial support and appointed the editors. The job of each newspaper was to promote the party's issue positions and criticize opponents. The *Gazette*, for example, ran numerous stories about sexual misconduct between Thomas Jefferson and his slave Sally Hemmings. Due to limited population literacy and high subscription costs, these were not mass circulation newspapers. Rather, they were directed at the elite of each party, providing some news and instructing the faithful about the issue positions the party championed. It was fully understood that objectivity was not a goal in reporting the news.

The Era of the Commercial Media began in 1833 with the advent of the penny press. Newspapers now sold for a penny (vs. 6 cents in the earlier era), which—along with rising literacy—allowed for mass circulation. With the invention of the telegraph, newspapers in 1848 organized the Associated Press, which gathered information from around the world. Political news could be delivered to newspaper editorial desks from all parts of the country hours or even minutes after it happened.

The penny press also entertained its readers with human interest stories and sensational reports of crimes and disasters. Importantly, the press now made a profit—often a substantial profit. This financial success allowed the press to free itself from control by the political parties and gave rise to powerful independent editors who could package news stories as they saw fit. However, this packaging was often strongly partisan and sensationalistic, a practice referred to as *yellow journalism*. Among the most flamboyant practitioners of yellow journalism was William Randolph Hearst. He used his newspapers to promote his politics. By claiming that the explosion which sunk the U.S. battleship *Maine* in Havana harbor was the work of Spanish agents, he provoked a public outcry for a war between the United States and Spain.[2] The practice of yellow journalism tended to undermine the credibility of the press. The media would have to transform itself yet another time before gaining the confidence and respect of the public (Bettig and Hall 2003).

The new century (1900) saw the dawning of the Era of the Objective Media. Previously, reporters were not professionals; they had no specialized training or professional values that guided their work. Recognizing a need, newspaper magnate Joseph Pulitzer provided funding to establish a school for journalism at Columbia University. Other schools soon followed. Journalists were trained to be *objective*, defined by the American Society of Newspaper Editors as "free of opinion or bias of any kind." Commensurate with their new status, reporters now had bylines—that is, the reporter's name appeared along with the story. This innovation allowed the public to hold reporters accountable for what they wrote.

The coverage of the Vietnam War and Watergate represented the high point for the objective press. The glaring light of publicity was brought to bear on matters of the highest importance by investigative journalists. Woodward and Bernstein became household names for investigations that ultimately brought down the Nixon White House. Walter Cronkite, anchor of the CBS evening news, was once cited as the most trusted man in America. Public confidence in the media was at an all-time high. There was talk of the media establishment as a coequal "fourth branch of government" (Cook 2007).

The fourth era of interpretive journalism began about 1980 and soon cascaded into a fifth, which can be labeled the era of fragmented media. The era of interpretive media ushered in a rejection of the ideal of objective journalism for a more interpretive style. This trend accelerated with the new availability of cable/satellite TV and the Internet, which fragmented the market for news considerably. With the two trends of interpretative journalism and fragmentation, media sources have become increasingly diverse and often partisan, allowing people to seek out media outlets fitting their political perspective. A feedback process commenced, leading the current state of affairs where one can easily find media outlets that cater to any partisan political taste.

Interpretive Journalism

The trend toward interpretative journalism reflects a general skepticism about the possibility of holding to a standard of strict objectivity that arose in intellectual circles in the 1980s. Facts do not speak for themselves; rather, they need to be understood in context. This development coincided with the career aspirations of journalists, who want to add their independent and unique contribution to the political debate—their "journalistic voice." They do not simply want to report the news; they want to analyze it. Reporters became less inclined to behave as lapdogs for politicians, as some have characterized their role during the Era of the Objective Press (Sabato 1993).

This shift to interpretive journalism is not simply a changing taste on the part of working reporters; it reflects a change in how editors and executive producers see the market for news. In the realm of politics, news consumers demand more than hearing and reading what the politicians have to say (Iyengar, Norpoth, and Hahn 2004). Journalists today do not see their job as helping politicians get their story out directly to the public. Rather, journalists see themselves as standing between politicians and the public. Politicians do not talk to citizens; politicians talk to journalists. It is the journalists who talk to the public. They see their job as analyzing and interpreting for the public the often ambiguous or misleading messages being delivered by political leaders. Thomas Patterson (1996) argues that this interpretative style empowers journalists by giving them significant control over the news message. It places the journalist at the center of the news story.

There are substantial empirical data to document this change. For example, journalists increasingly speak for candidates rather than candidates speaking for themselves. The average length of the candidate sound bite (candidates speaking for themselves) on the network news has decreased dramatically. In 1968 these sound bites averaged 43.1 seconds. By 2000 and again in 2004 they averaged only 7.8 seconds. In fact, 2000 Democratic presidential candidate Al Gore got more speaking time during his one appearance on David Letterman's TV show than he did on the news broadcasts of all three major networks combined during the month of October.[3] On the other hand, speaking time allotted to journalists has increased commensurately (Owen 2002). A similar pattern can be found in the print media. For the *New York Times* in the 1960s, the vast majority of the news stories (91 percent) were descriptive. In the 1990s, the vast majority (84 percent) were interpretative (Patterson 1994, 82; see also Gilens, Vavreck, and Cohen 2007). Rather than direct communication from politicians, much of what the public hears today is the analysis of journalists.

The Fragmentation of the Media

Thanks to deregulation and technological innovation the actual number of media outlets has skyrocketed over what was available just a few years ago. Cable and satellite TV gave rise to channels like MSNBC, CNN, and the Fox News Network, which cover the political news twenty-four hours a day, seven days a week. The Internet revolution, beginning in 1991, offers unlimited access to political information any time of day. Anyone can set up their own political blog, and some have become quite popular and even profitable. Depending on one's preferences, there is news with a liberal slant and news with a conservative slant.

Figure 8.1 shows the dramatic decline in two sources of political news— daily newspapers and the networks' evening news shows on broadcast television.

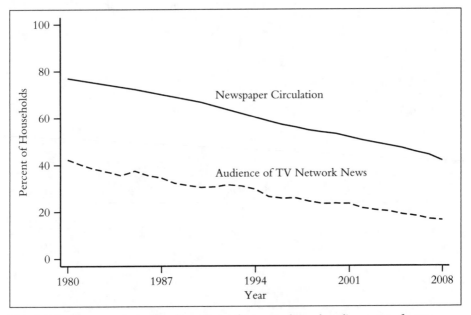

Figure 8.1   Downward trends in the audience for two traditional media sources of news. *Source:* Data compiled from Tables 4.1 and 4.2 in Harold W. Stanley and Richard G. Niemi, *Vital Statistics on American Politics 2007–2008* (Washington: CQ Press, 2008), augmented by data from *Editor and Publisher* and Pew Web sites.

Measured on a per household basis, newspaper circulation and the audience for the traditional network evening news shows have both declined by about half since 1980. The bulk of the defectors have moved to the newer media sources, such as cable television and the Internet. Table 8.1 offers further details of the change in audience, based on Pew surveys.[4]

Of course, some of these trends started before our first data point in 1993. The percentage of households subscribing to a daily newspaper peaked in 1950. The percentage getting news from the network television peaked in 1970 (West 2001, 131). Meanwhile, the first cable news channel came online in 1980. Talk radio was not a major factor for political discourse until 1988, when it was reinvented by Rush Limbaugh. And no one got their news from the Internet prior to the mid-1990s.

While the trend toward newer media outlets is clear, it is important to note that most people still get their news from traditional sources. Perhaps surprisingly, as shown in Table 8.1, local TV news remains the primary source of information for most people. It is also important to understand that television

TABLE 8.1	Audience for Traditional Media and New Media			
	Traditional Media			
	1993–1994	**1998**	**2004**	**2008**
Local TV news	77%	64%	59%	52%
Nightly network news	60	38	34	29
Newspapers	58	48	42	34
Radio news	47	41	40	35
Print news magazine	16	15	13	12
Network TV magazines	52	23	22	18
Network morning shows	—	—	22	22
Sunday morning talk shows	—	—	12	13
	New Media			
	1993–1994	**1998**	**2004**	**2008**
CNN	35%	23%	22%	24%
Fox News Channel	—	17	25	23
MSNBC	—	8	11	15
Talk radio	16	13	17	17
National Public Radio	9	15	16	10
Online news	6	18	25	27

Sources: Pew Research Center, "Public's News Habits Little Changed by September 11" (June 9, 2002); "News Audiences Increasingly Politicized" (June 8, 2004); "Key News Audiences Now Blend Online and Traditional Sources" (August 17, 2008).

as a news source is not in decline; it has simply fragmented. There is now a wider menu from which to choose.

The fragmentation of news media outlets has had several important effects on how people get the news. One consequence of the greater competition among news outlets may be the quality of news reporting and the amount of information about current events that people receive. With twenty-four–hour news channels and Internet news sources, interested news consumers can catch up with current events at a speed previously unimaginable. Yet, despite the new diversity of choices and contrary to American culture's celebration of the virtues of competition, some observers conclude that the fragmented media has actually lowered the quality of the news. John Zaller (2004b) presents evidence that in-depth coverage of issues decreases as competition increases. He concludes that journalists produce better-quality news when insulated from market pressures.

The diversity of choices has had further consequences. Today's consumer of television news can choose from a menu of cable all-news outlets—Fox on the right, CNN more mainstream, and MSNBC with mainly liberal commentary. For more information, opinion, and analysis, the avid news consumer can turn to the incredible diversity of the Internet, where each network and major newspaper has its Web page, or to sites for political opinions and analysis of all ideological stripes. In a fragmented media market, people have the ability to ideologically customize their sources of political information. Thus, studies by the Pew Research Center show that the audience for Fox News are predominantly Republican, while the audience for CNN and especially MSNBC lean equally Democratic.[5]

The ability of people to ideologically customize their sources of political information contributes to the increasing ideological polarization of the electorate discussed previously. Before cable television and then the Internet, everybody who watched the news on television observed a common content from the assertively nonpartisan network news programs. Now when people can rely solely on news sources that fit their ideological niche, they become less open to alternative view-points. As a result, initial opinions intensify and are reinforced, possibly contributing to rancor in public discourse that had previously been absent (Mutz 2007).

Paradoxically, the expansion of the media menu may contribute to a decline in political information—at least in some segments of society. At one time the evening news had a monopoly on television viewing. There was no competition for the nightly news, so a person either watched nothing or watched the news. In the current media environment, the news has to compete with entertainment for its audience. The result is that those most interested in politics with access to cable/satellite TV and the Internet have many choices, resulting in high levels of political information. Those with access to cable/satellite TV and the Internet with little or no interest in the news can avoid it entirely and turn to strictly entertainment channels.

The result is an increased division of information levels between the politically interested and knowledgeable on the one hand and the disinterested and voluntarily ignorant on the other. Prior (2007) demonstrates that for those without cable or Internet access, interest in politics has little relationship to political knowledge. But among those with access to the Internet, cable/satellite

TV, or (especially) both, interest leads to increased knowledge and disinterest leads to increased ignorance. The least informed of Prior's subjects were those with potential access to many sources of information but who were uninterested in politics. With Internet and cable/satellite, this group was able to tune out politics in favor of other pursuits.[6]

A related consequence of the fragmented media is a decline in the power of the president and other leaders to hold the people's attention (Baum and Kernell 1999; Cohen 2008). Cable/satellite TV had ended the "golden age" of presidential influence via television. The multiplicity of media options has significantly diminished the president's ability to reach a large national audience. Previously, when presidents chose to address the nation, they had a monopoly on prime-time television. Viewers could either watch the address or seek entertainment other than television. In 1969, a routine press conference of President Richard Nixon drew 59 percent of the potential national TV audience. In 1995, a major prime-time news conference by President Clinton attracted only 6.5 percent of households with television. While access to cable news may allow greater attention to the details of contemporary politics, television viewers are freed from reliance on the broadcast networks. Analyzing the 1996 presidential debates, Baum and Kernell found when controlling for key background variables, those without cable television—a captive audience—were 7 percent more likely to have watched the first debate and 9 percent more likely to have watched the second debate than those with cable television.[7] This fragmentation is not lost on network executives, who appreciate that the cost of carrying a prime-time presidential address is the loss of audience share to cable competitors. "Going public" is an important leadership tool for the modern presidency (Tedin, Rottinghaus, and Rodgers 2010). The current focus on audience share and profits may mean the president has lost an asset that will be difficult to replace (Baum and Kernell 1999).

It is widely believed that the rise of the Internet has one important victim—the American newspaper. Just in 2008 alone, newspaper circulation dropped 5 percent, despite the exciting presidential race. Ad revenue dropped an alarming 15 percent (Pew 2009). Newspapers have adapted by developing their own Web sites and as a result, paradoxically, some are now actually reaching more readers than ever before. But by generally offering free access on the Web, newspapers online must make money by advertising on their Web sites, which to date has yielded disappointing revenue. As a result, news content suffers, reporters are laid off, and a downward spiral persists. News media decision makers are vexed by this set of circumstances. For now, readers on the Internet enjoy wide access to newspaper content. But over time the content of what they read will suffer in quality unless newspapers can find an alternative revenue model.

8-2   Bias and Negativity in the News

Although the news media prides itself on the fairness of its news coverage, critics from both the left and the right complain that the news media is biased and lacks objectivity. Could it be the case that the media *are* seriously biased, or are ideological critics too quick to blame the messenger when they dislike the message? *Objectivity* has proven notoriously difficult to define. Like beauty, it is very much in the eye of the beholder. Objectivity is so elusive that it was dropped from the code of ethics by the Society of Professional Journalists. It was replaced in the ethics code by "truth, accuracy and comprehensiveness" (Bennett 2003, 192). One reason is that objectivity can imply passing along messages from government officials without subjecting them to critical scrutiny—a practice some would say on its face is nonobjective, given the ability of those in government to dominate the news. But to what extent does the media cover the news with truth, accuracy, and comprehensiveness? Given the complexity of the question, it is not surprising there is no agreed-upon answer.

Critics on the political left charge that as business operations are dependent on business advertising for their profits, the media tilt their coverage to the right. Critics on the political right see a liberal bias to the media, with liberal journalists slanting the news to the left. Both liberals and conservatives have nonprofit organizations with Web sites devoted exclusively to exposing press bias. Accuracy in the media (http://www.aim.org) and newsbusters.org (http://newsbusters.org) are two Web sites devoted to exposing liberal bias in the news. On the other side of the spectrum, fairness and accuracy in reporting (http://www.fair.org) and media matters (http://mediamatters.org) are designed to ferret out bias in the conservative direction. Neither side lacks compelling examples. On the other hand, the academic literature has concluded—at a minimum—there is no systematic and pervasive ideological bias in the media (Patterson 1994; Groeling and Kernell 1998; Farnsworth and Lichter 2007).

Criticism of the mainstream media is occasionally subtle and can extend beyond blanket charges of bias based on ideology. Some say because the mainstream media try to appeal to the broadest possible audience, they constrict the flow of ideas in the safe middle range (Bennett 1980, 304–44). Some see the media as too uncritical of government officials out of a need to protect their access to news sources (Hertsgaard 1988; Press and Verburn 1988). But others see the reverse, with journalists giving a particularly hard time to incumbent officeholders (Patterson 1994). As we will discuss, one of the more serious charges against the media is that to maintain the interests of its audience, news outlets promote an overly cynical outlook as they focus excessively on negative news.

In this section we discuss two sorts of claims about the content of the media. First, is the news biased in a liberal or conservative direction? Second, as some charge, are the news media unduly negative in their reporting?

Liberal Journalists

Is there a liberal bias to the news media? One foundation for the claim that the news is biased in a liberal direction comes from the fact, confirmed by many studies, that journalists themselves tend to be much more liberal and Democratic than the American public as a whole. Further, the most liberal and most Democratic journalists tend to work for the prestige news sources, such as the *New York Times* or network news (Weaver and Wilhoit 1996). Shown in

TABLE 8.2	Views of General Public and Journalists on Selected Issues		
		Public	**Journalists**
Consider Self	Left (liberal)	18%	47%
	Right (conservative)	34	22
Consider Self	Democrat	34	44
	Republican	33	16
Sympathize with	Business	33	27
	Labor	32	31
Government should reduce income inequality	Favor	55	50
	Oppose	23	39
Increase defense budget	Favor	38	15
	Oppose	51	80
Allow women to have abortions	Favor	49	82
	Oppose	44	14
Prayer in public schools	Favor	74	25
	Oppose	19	67
Death penalty for murder	Favor	75	47
	Oppose	17	47

Sources: David H. Weaver and G. Cleveland Wilhoit, *The American Journalist in the 1990s* (Mahwah, NJ: Erlbaum, 1996), pp. 15–18; William Schneider and I. A. Lewis, "Views on the News," *Public Opinion* 8 (August–September 1985), p. 7.

Table 8.2 are data contrasting the opinions of journalists and everyday citizens from a 1985 *Times-Mirror* survey and a 1992 survey sponsored by the Freedom Forum (see also Dautrich and Deneen 1996). Although the findings may seem dated, there is no reason to believe that the distinctions shown between journalists and the public have narrowed. A 2004 Pew survey of the press found liberals outnumbering conservatives among journalists by a margin of 33 to 7 percent (with the remainder mainly self-described "moderates") (Pew 2004b).

Journalists are particularly more liberal than the public on cultural issues like abortion and the death penalty, as can be seen in Table 8.2. However, journalists may be more conservative than the public when it comes to economic issues. At a time when only 23 percent of the public opposed government action to reduce income inequality, 39 percent of the journalists were opposed (Schneider and Lewis 1985). The national press corps in Washington is relatively highly paid, and these data may reflect their class interest.

It is interesting to speculate why journalists lean to the left politically. Although some conservatives might argue differently, there is no evidence that news organizations reward reporters and other workers based on their political ideology. The reason news employees show a liberal political tendency is not that conservative aspirants are cast aside for their political views. To some extent, the liberalism of journalists, especially outside the economic sphere, simply reflects the values of young urban college-educated professionals—the class from which journalists are drawn. Another factor may be that journalism attracts people with liberal personality traits, much the same way that a military career attracts conservative personalities.

Conservative Ownership

If some claim that the media are biased to the left because of the political views of news media employees, what about the opposite charge that there exists a conservative bias to the news media? The foundation for the claim of conservative bias starts with media ownership. The major networks are owned or controlled by giant multinational corporations—whose managers and major stockholders are not noted for their liberal sentiments. And while the *New York Times* and the *Washington Post* remain independent, most other newspapers are part of media conglomerates most interested in the financial bottom line. Gilens and Hertzman (2000) found significant differences in how newspapers covered congressional debate on the 1996 Telecommunications Act, designed to ease restrictions on corporate ownership of multiple media outlets. The newspapers owned by those who would benefit from the passage of legislation downplayed monopoly issues. The authors concluded that financial self-interest not only affected the editorial page but leaked into the straight news reporting as well. Because of newspaper owners' special interest in the fate of monopoly ownership, Gilens' and Hetzman's finding of biased news coverage may be more the exception than the rule. A study by Gentzkow and Shapiro (2010) of the general ideological slant of newspapers finds news coverage to be generally unrelated to newspapers ownership. Corporations that own multiple newspapers in different markets leave little imprint on the content. Rather, to the extent they slant their news left or right, it is toward the direction as reader opinion.

If there is a conservative tendency to the American news media, the most obvious manifestation is on the newspaper editorial pages. Unlike most television and radio stations, newspapers regularly take positions on issues. And while television and radio stations do not formally endorse candidates during election season (due to FCC rules about equal time), newspapers routinely endorse political candidates on their editorial pages. Going back at least to the 1930s, newspapers have endorsed far more Republican than Democratic candidates. This historic tendency makes it all the more remarkable that in recent presidential races most newspapers endorsed the Democratic candidates, first Kerry against Bush in 2004 and then by an even larger margin for Obama over McCain in 2008.

Two factors readily account for newspaper publishers' tradition of Republicanism and conservatism. First, newspaper publishers are businesspeople. Their conservative Republicanism is a natural extension of the prevailing orthodoxy of the business community. Second, a newspaper's advertisers also represent the conservative business community. Although major advertisers only rarely threaten to withdraw their ads from newspapers because of their political stands, newspaper publishers know they must depend on advertising for the major share of their revenue.

Biased News?

The liberalism of journalists does not necessarily mean that their ideological preferences filter into news stories, nor does the conservatism of their bosses (and newspaper editorial pages) necessarily spill over into the reporting of the news. It is plausible that both the liberalism of journalists and the conservatism of their bosses influence the presentation of the news, with each offsetting the other. Objective measurement of possible bias is difficult, complicated by loud voices on the left and right claiming to quantify the existence of bias by the other side.

The public discussion of bias tends to bog down in narrow debates between competing protagonists, with each side presenting its own mostly anecdotal evidence. For instance, the conservative former CBS newsman Bernard Goldberg (*Bias in the News* 2001) claims to have identified one way in which TV newscasts promote liberalism as the mainstream. He charges that network newscasts repeatedly label conservative political figures as "conservatives" while leaving their liberal counterparts unidentified ideologically. Goldberg claims the networks see liberal positions as the norm and identify those taking positions on the right as "conservative" to alert viewers they are out of the mainstream. Liberal media critic Eric Alterman (*What Liberal Media?* 2003) dissents, saying Goldberg presents only anecdotal evidence to support his contention. Alterman cites counterevidence where the networks label conservatives and liberals even-handedly. Even if it were true that network newscasts disproportionately pin ideological labels on conservative politicians more than liberal politicians, this would fall far short of proof that the network newscasts, or the media at large, routinely distort the news to favor the liberal point of view. On the other hand, critics say this tendency is simply one sign of a much larger problem.

Does the political ideology of reporters affect the way they cover the news? There is no conclusive answer to this question, but in their study of the Washington-based media, Dautrich and Deneen (1996) asked journalists for a self-assessment of whether their opinions ever affected their reporting. Seventy-eight percent said it did so at least "occasionally" and virtually no reporter said "never." Still, most reporters hold professional values that mandate a conscious effort to keep personal politics out of their reporting. In one experimental study, a sample of reporters was asked to describe how they would cover a variety of hypothetical stories. Political ideology had only a minor (but statistically significant) effect (Patterson and Donsbach 1996). In addition, while stories are written by reporters, editors responsible to CEOs and owners decide what gets published or aired. These gatekeepers, who themselves are decidedly less liberal than their reporters, are unlikely to be promoting a liberal agenda.

Academic studies of presidential campaign network news coverage show that the networks attempt to achieve balance. Network news shows devote roughly equal time to both major party candidates, and network journalists insist that their news judgment is unaffected by personal political preferences. But are they evenhanded in the tone of their stories about presidential candidates? Over the six most recent presidential campaigns, the "nonpartisan" Center for Media and Public Affairs has attempted to measure network bias in presidential campaigns. Its researchers have content-analyzed all campaign stories that appeared on network news shows from Labor Day through Election Day (Farnsworth and Lichter 2007; Media Monitor 2009). Their accounts are based on judgments of the tone (positive or negative) of each (non–horse-race) statement by a nonpartisan source presented on the network news. As shown in Table 8.3, Farnsworth and Lichter judge the tone of most campaign coverage to be more negative than positive. In terms of balance (more positive toward one candidate or the other), they find variation from campaign to campaign. Averaged over the last six presidential elections, they found about two-thirds of the stories to be negative about the Republican candidate. According to their report, the general tone of stories about the Democrat candidate varied by year, in some years almost as negative as stories about the Republican. Their trend line is clearly that Democrats get more favorable treatment, with Barack Obama in 2008 receiving the most favorable treatment of any candidate in their analysis. As Center for Media and Public Affairs (CMPA) authors see it, on balance, and especially in 2008, the network news tilts—intentionally or not—in favor of Democratic presidential candidates.

The CMPA findings are, however, subject to multiple interpretations and caveats. Like all other claims to measure media bias, their analysis ultimately rests on coding schemes and subjective interpretations of whether statements about candidates are mainly positive or mainly negative. Critics point out, fairly or unfairly, that the seemingly neutral CMPA has received funding from conservative foundations.[8] Other scattered accounts that purport to measure objectivity and bias in television news claim greater partisan balance (and less negativity) than Farnsworth and Lichter and their CMPA associates record.[9] Readers should employ a certain "buyer beware" approach to studies claiming to have uncovered ideological bias in the media.

In evaluating claims of bias or favoritism in the news, we must consider that an observable tilt in the tone to favor one candidate over the other could represent the actual reality of the news rather than a distortion. "Good" news for one candidate and "bad" news for the other can easily represent the reality of campaign events. For instance, by the CMPA methodology, candidates who do well in debates (e.g., Bush in 2000 and Kerry in 2004) get scored with

TABLE 8.3	General Election News: Tone of Coverage, 1988–2008					
	Percent Negative					
	1988	**1992**	**1996**	**2000**	**2004**	**2008**
Democratic nominee	62%	48%	50%	60%	41%	32%
Republican nominee	59	71	67	63	63	67

Sources: Adapted from Farnsworth and Lichter, 2007; Media Monitor, 2009.

more favorable media treatment (Farnsworth and Lichter 2007). Presumably, no one would argue the press should shy away from positive coverage about a candidate who seems to capture public enthusiasm or manufacture good news about a candidate who falters.

In another investigation of bias, Groseclose and Milyo (2005) examined the "think tank" and advocacy groups cited as sources over a ten-year period by the print and broadcast media. They scored the left–right ideology of policy think tanks and advocacy groups based on the ideology of Congress members who cited these sources in the *Congressional Record*. Then they counted the frequency with which the various media cited these sources in their news coverage. The bottom line is that media outlets more often cited liberal sources than conservative sources. Policy advocacy groups favored by conservatives in Congress are relatively ignored as sources by the media. The authors conclude that the news media interpret the news with a liberal slant.

Not surprisingly, this study has been criticized for its own possible ideological bias. What the study does show is a fact with multiple interpretations. One rival interpretation is that instead of indicating bias, Groseclose and Milyo's results arise because congressional conservatives cite conservative sources with inferior intellectual credentials. If so, the media are not likely to use them as sources.

In a more recent paper, Gentzkow and Shapiro (2010) scored phrases used by members of Congress by the ideological leanings of those who used them. Based on these same phrases, they then scored several newspapers by the "slant" of their news coverage based on the extent the same political phrases were found in the news pages. While their research shows that newspapers slant their coverage in accord with readership ideological taste, they find little evidence of a general pattern of bias to either the left or the right.

The search for an overall bias in the media may be a fruitless quest. For example, all studies show that Fox News Hour is to the right of the broadcast networks' evening news shows. The argument is over the location of a possible neutral point. And we should pause before using the preferences of the average Congress member as the standard. The goal of a free press ought not be the successful mirroring of government preferences.

Whatever the final verdict on bias in news reporting, there exists no even balance when we turn from the reporting of the news to opinion, or commentary. Any liberal favoritism in news reporting is offset by the conservative tilt of media commentary. Particularly in the era of fragmented media, conservative voices have come to significantly outnumber liberal voices. To the conservative dominance of newspaper editorial pages, which has long been in place, one must add talk radio and cable news punditry. Talk radio, in particular, is dominated by conservatives. On national radio, there are no liberal equivalents to Rush Limbaugh, Laura Ingraham, and Michael Savage. The tilt is not as pronounced on cable news channels. But Fox News's stable of conservative commentators—Bill O'Reilly and farther on the right, Shawn Hannity, and Glenn Beck—consistently draw larger audiences than MSNBC's Keith Olberman, Rachel Madow, and others on the left.

The Public's View of Media Bias

Among the general public, many believe that the media are not entirely objective in covering the news. When people were asked about "bias in the media" in a 2009 Gallup Poll, 45 percent said the "news media" were "too liberal," while only 15 percent said it was "too conservative" (35 percent said it was "about right"). However, when asked about "bias in election coverage," the public sees the media as more evenhanded. In a Pew Research Center poll in September 2008, 36 percent of the public said the media were biased in favor of Barack Obama, 14 percent said the media were biased in favor of John McCain, and 40 percent said "no bias." When people are asked if press criticism does more good than harm, surveys from the Reagan to Obama administrations show opinion depends on which party is in power. Those who share the partisanship of the incumbent president are always the least likely to applaud media criticism, although typically majorities within both parties say it does more good than bad (Pew 2009b).

Some degree of skepticism about the media is probably healthy. Still, if taken too far it can undercut the ability of the press to credibly inform the public in a fashion necessary for citizens to hold elected officials accountable. Despite the numbers, there is reason to doubt that the situation is as gloomy as it might appear. There is a tendency for partisans to see any unfriendly criticism as media bias and, as we saw earlier, criticism is the norm in today's news. Provocatively, Dalton, Beck, and Huckfeldt (1998) demonstrated there is virtually no connection between the liberal–conservative tilt taken by newspapers and reader perceptions of that tilt. Dalton and his colleagues used content analysis and a representative sample of newspapers in forty counties to measure the actual ideological slant of the news and a survey to measure the perception of that slant by newspaper readers. They found no meaningful correspondence. What they did find was that in the 1992 presidential race, strong Republicans saw their paper as slanted toward Clinton and strong Democrats saw their paper as slanted toward Bush.

The results reported by Dalton and his associates (1998) are consistent with a good deal of experimental research on the hostile media phenomenon, which holds that people are predisposed to see bias when the press covers topics important to them. In one study, two groups on opposite sides of the Middle East issue (either pro-Arab or pro-Israeli) were given a news story about conflict in the area and asked to evaluate it. Both sides tended to see the story as biased against their position. However, the two sides read exactly the same account (Vallone, Ross, and Lepper 1985).

As we detail in the following section, it is apparent why some people at both ends of the political spectrum might see the news as biased. Much of the content of the media is negative in tone. As citizens look at media content through the colored glasses of partisanship, it is easy to conclude that one's own political values are not getting a fair shake.

Negativity in the News

While there remains disagreement about ideological bias in the news, a much stronger case can be made that in recent years the tone of the media has turned profoundly negative, and not just in campaign coverage by network news. According to Thomas Patterson, the real bias in the media is an "ingrained cynicism" (Patterson 1996). In an analysis of stories in *Time* and *Newsweek* about presidential campaign coverage, Patterson (1994) found the negative content of this coverage increased dramatically beginning in 1980. In 1960, only 25 percent of the stories were negative, but by 1976, 40 percent were negative. Over half were negative in 1980, and in 1992, 60 percent of the stories were negative. According to Groeling and Kernell (1998), in 1991 when the popularity of George H. W. Bush reached 90 percent in some polls, barely half his media coverage was positive.

Why has the press become more negative toward politicians over recent decades? One explanation holds that relations between politicians and the press have become increasingly adversarial. In recent years, politicians have aggressively tried to control the flow of the news, which detracts from the ability of journalists to do their job. A mutual dislike has arisen resulting in the negative coverage of political personalities (Zaller 2004b). A second explanation is economic. The conviction in financial quarters that the news must be entertaining to be profitable has led to a focus on sensational stories, scandal (real or imagined), and "gotcha" news coverage of those in public life (Sabato, Stencel, and Lichter 2000; Farnsworth and Lichter 2007).[10] Whatever the reason, the media are a good deal more aggressive in exposing potentially embarrassing actions by public officials than they were in past.

While there is agreement that cynicism in the news has increased substantially when compared to the past, there is disagreement about how this trend affects public opinion. Some make the controversial claim that the decline in political trust and/or the continuing low levels of political trust can largely be blamed on the negative media (Patterson 1994, 22; but for a different view, see O'Keefe 1980). Experimental studies show that people exposed to negative stories about government are more likely to be distrusting than an equivalent control group (Cappella and Jamieson 1997), as are people exposed to the "incivility" currently so common on cable television's political talk shows (Mutz and Reeves 2005; Mutz 2007). Basing their findings on survey evidence, others claim that the more one is exposed to the political news, the greater the mistrust of government (Hetherington 2001). Another claim is that the approval rate of Congress suffers due to relentless negative portrayals of the institution in the media (Mann and Ornstein 1994, 4). About nine out of ten media evaluations of Congress are negative. Hibbing and Theiss-Morse (1998) found that the greater the exposure to the media, the more likely people had a negative emotional reaction to Congress.

Has increased negativity in the media caused a decline in political trust? Not all are convinced. While the decline in political trust coincides with the rise in media negativity, cause and effect have yet to be clearly demonstrated. And, before getting unduly concerned about alleged harm from a negative press, we should stop to consider the opposite problem. Would the public be better served by a docile press that goes out of its way to report only happy news about politicians and their antics? Some media critics complain precisely about such an imbalance, objecting that the press is overly timid and overly reluctant to challenge the political leaders to whom they owe their access (Cook 1998; Fritz,

Keefer, and Nyhan 2004).The media's acquiescence with the Bush administration in spring 2003 on the rationale for the Iraq War is a case in point.

8-3 Models of Media Effects

In the 1938 radio broadcast "War of the Worlds," Orson Welles described an invasion of New Jersey by Martians from outer space. Although the story was fiction, many believed it to be true, causing something of a panic in the New Jersey area. For many scholars, this was an example of the powerful sway the media can have over citizens.The use of media propaganda by Benito Mussolini in Italy and Adolf Hitler in Germany to gain and hold political power was seen as another example of pervasive media effects. This model of media influence has been dubbed the *hypodermic effect*, as it is similar to getting a drug injection. The effect is immediate and powerful. However, with the advent of scientific public opinion surveys, scholarly consensus shifted in the opposite direction. Early studies found media influences in political campaigns to be trivial, giving rise to a new perspective, called the *minimal effects model*. In recent years, the minimal effects model has also fallen into disfavor. Current media scholars favor a more nuanced approach that emphasizes the search for subtle but meaningful consequences of media exposure, including some that are easy to overlook.

The Minimal Effects Model

The first attempts to examine empirically the political influence of the mass media were the early studies of voting behavior: panel studies of voters in Erie County, Ohio, in 1940 and voters in Elmira, New York, in 1948 (Lazarsfeld, Berelson, and Gaudet 1948; Berelson, Lazarsfeld, and McPhee 1954).These early studies presented a viewpoint regarding the influence of the media that has since become known as the minimal effects model of media influence. Perhaps because the researchers for these projects moved into voting research from market research, they expected to find campaign messages in the mass media (at that time, essentially newspapers and radio) to be quite influential on individual voters.They envisioned voters waffling in their choice of candidates somewhat in the way a consumer might change his or her choice of toothpaste from purchase to purchase, depending on the effectiveness of the latest advertising.

These early researchers on presidential choice, however, made three discoveries that seemed to dismiss the mass media's influence. First, they discovered the anchor of partisanship. A substantial number of citizens interviewed as early as May of election year had already decided how they were going to vote in November. This suggests that most voters had a "product loyalty" to one or the other of the two major political parties. Second, the researchers discovered perceptual screening. Voters paid particular attention to the messages from the candidate they preferred, which served to maintain their "product loyalty." They avoided exposure to campaign messages for the opposition, even misperceiving these messages when exposure was unavoidable.Third, the researchers discovered the importance of personal conversations. When someone was about to change his or her viewpoint due to a persuasive message in the media, that person would often return to the original opinion after talking to others who shared that original opinion.

For these reasons, the messages on the mass media are less influential than they might appear. Because people's political views are anchored by their past beliefs, perceptual screening, and interpersonal communications, it is not likely that any particular revelation in the evening news will create massive changes in people's political likes and dislikes. Two interesting examples are the responses to President Reagan's Iran-Contra scandal in 1986 and 1987 and the scandal involving President Clinton and Monica Lewinsky in 1998 and 1999.

In late 1986, the American public was first shocked to learn that President Reagan was selling arms to Iran and then shocked again to learn that one purpose was to illegally fund the Contras in Nicaragua. The national media gave this scandal the coverage and the treatment usually reserved for a constitutional crisis of the order of Watergate. In one month, popular approval of Reagan's performance dropped about 20 percentage points, which (until 9/11) perhaps defines the outer limit of how quickly public opinion can respond in the short run. Twenty percentage points is the greatest one-month drop in presidential approval ever recorded. Yet, if one sets a high threshold regarding what constitutes a "major" opinion change, an upper limit of 20 percentage points may seem like not much at all. At least two-thirds of those who approved of Reagan before the scandal continued to do so despite the Iran-Contra revelations.

The 1998 Lewinsky scandal surpassed the Iran-Contra scandal in shock value. Within days of the first revelations, pundits were discussing whether the president would be or should be impeached. The news being reported appeared disastrous for the president at a time when Clinton was basking in the glow of a record level of popularity for a president so late in his presidency. Given the new revelations involving sex, lies, and audiotape, most political experts were sure that Clinton's standing with the public would plunge like a rock. Instead, it rose. In fact, over the first week of the scandal, Clinton's approval rating rose 10 points, close to a record for short-term presidential gain. What occurred was a seeming disconnection between the negative media stories and the public's evaluation of the president—a development that remains far from fully understood (Zaller 1998; Fischle 2000; Just and Crigler 2000; Owen 2000; Cohen 2008). What is clear from this episode is that public opinion does not automatically flow in the direction of the news. People judged the facts of the Lewinsky case in a way that allowed them to support the president in spite of negative revelations and speculation in the media.

Contemporary Perspectives on Media Effects

The Iran-Contra and Lewinsky examples illustrate the obvious limits of the media's power. Consistent with the minimal effects interpretation of media influence, shifts in public evaluations are limited even in response to one-sided news stories, and sometimes not even in the expected direction. However, many mass media researchers reject the minimalist interpretation. They concede the media has limited ability to change vote preferences in partisan elections or change opinions deeply rooted in partisanship or group identification. Instead, they search for more modest influences on political beliefs that perhaps can be detected only by experimental designs, imposing complex statistical controls on the data, or by isolating influences that exist only under restricted circumstances (e.g., see Bartels 1993; Finkel 1993).

It is well understood that media effects are circumscribed because message awareness and message acceptance push in opposite directions. Consider that the possibility of opinion change in response to a new political message depends on both the likelihood of becoming aware of the message and the likelihood of accepting it once becoming aware. For many people, when the likelihood of accepting a message from the media is high, the likelihood of hearing it is low—and vice versa. Individuals most susceptible to media effects are those with moderate levels of political sophistication—sufficiently interested to be aware of media content but lacking the sophistication to completely resist media messages (Converse 1962; Zaller 1997).

Finally, there is a recognition that the net influence of the mass media so often seems to be slight because it represents a balance among conflicting points of view (Zaller 1992, 1996). If the media messages were truly one sided, like the flow of propaganda in a nondemocratic regime, their cumulative impact might well be substantial. Even in a democratic society, there is often a consensus at the elite level that results in a one-sided media message. Examples include the president's honeymoon period and rally effects following crises, both discussed in chapter 4. In these instances, presidents receive exceptional popularity levels because media voices are uniformly supportive (Brody 1991).

Contemporary thinking about media effects focuses on three processes by which the media are believed to influence public opinion: (1) agenda setting, where the media influences the issues citizens think are most important; (2) priming, which influences how citizens use these issues to evaluate political figures; and (3) framing, which can influence opinion by the way issues are presented to the public.

Agenda Setting

The potential influence of the mass media on political thinking is not limited to influence on policy preferences. As Bernard Cohen famously remarked, the media "may not be successful much of time in telling people what to think, but it stunningly successful in telling [people] what to think about" (Cohen 1963).

Ever since a pioneering study by McCombs and Shaw (1972) of the 1968 presidential election, it has been known that people talk about the same issues that are being discussed in the media at the time. Is this media manipulation, or are the media and the citizens simply reacting to the same salient events when they occur?

Ideally, the best way to ascertain a causal inference whereby the mass media influences the agenda is to experimentally manipulate what people read or watch. This approach was used by Iyengar and his associates (Iyengar, Peters, and Kinder 1982; Iyengar and Kinder 1987) in a study of the network news. Ordinary citizens were divided into four groups, and for six consecutive days they watched the nightly news. Unknown to the subjects, each group saw a different version. For one group, a news story about defense preparedness was edited into each news program. For a second, a news story about pollution was inserted. The third group saw an economic inflation story, and a fourth group saw an unedited version of the news. Thus, each group got a weeklong dose of messages concerning one particular problem.

The most interesting result was the set of responses to the "most important problem" question before and after the experiment. Those given pollution stories and those given defense stories registered significant increases in concern about pollution and defense, respectively. The inflation group did not change much, apparently because they already expressed a strong concern about inflation in their questionnaires prior to the experiment and could hardly increase the level of their response. Further analysis suggested that the subjects in each group began to evaluate President Carter according to how they saw Carter's handling of their manipulated topic. Iyengar and his colleagues showed not only that the content of the media can influence the agenda but also that the choice of issues for the agenda can influence people's evaluation of the president.

An important issue is how individual political sophistication relates to agenda setting. Iyengar, Peters, and Kinder (1982) report that their least sophisticated respondents were the most responsive to experimental manipulation of the agenda. This finding seems reasonable, as less sophisticated people lack the stored information that helps discount messages in the media at odds with their current opinions. However, the subjects were shown news programs under artificial experimental conditions. Would they have been as attentive and persuaded in a natural setting? MacKuen (1984) finds the least sophisticated respondents to be the most immune to changes in the media's agenda. As we noted earlier, at least a moderate level of political sophistication seems necessary for the media to lead. To be persuaded by the media requires some minimal attention to the media. In a natural setting, that attention apparently does not exist among the least sophisticated.

It is now understood that when an issue becomes the subject of media attention, the net public opinion change will be slight as long as both sides of the issue are presented (although people on each side may become more polarized). When the media present only one side of an issue, public opinion responds to the dominant message (Zaller 1992; Baumgartner and Jones 1993; Jacobs and Shapiro 2000; Sniderman and Theriault 2004; Gershkoff and Kushner 2005). The door is thus open for possible media manipulation. However, objective circumstances mostly drive the media agenda. For example, the media covers inflation when inflation is high and therefore newsworthy (Behr and Iyengar 1985).

Priming

The concept of "priming" political attitudes was introduced by Iyengar and Kinder (1987). By setting the agenda, the media not only increase the perceived importance of an issue but they can also "prime" the public by directing it to consider certain aspects of the question and not others when they make their political evaluations. For example, when the 1991 Gulf War was in the daily headlines, the popularity of the first President Bush soared to record heights.

The public was being primed by the media to evaluate Bush based on how he was handling the war. However, by November 1991 the attention of the media shifted to the economy. By placing the economy at the top of the public agenda, the media was priming the public to evaluate Bush not on his past successes in the Persian Gulf but on an allegedly stalling economy (Krosnick and Brannon 1993; Hetherington 1996). When the media shifted its focus from the war to the economy, the president's approval rating rapidly declined (Zaller 1994).

There are two ways priming might work. First, it can increase the accessibility of information in short-term memory. When the media focus attention on combating terrorism, "considerations" about the war on terrorism rise to "the top of the head." Second, when the media focus attention on an issue they make it clear, either explicitly or implicitly, that reporters and editors feel this issue is important. It is not unexpected that many people come to share this media perspective—at least if they place some minimal level of trust in the media. Once a person comes to believe an issue is important, it is only natural to place significant weight on that issue when evaluating the president (Miller and Krosnick 2000).

Framing Issues

A media frame provides meaning to unfolding events. It is the central or organizing theme or story line in a news report. A frame highlights what is important about an issue, such as its causes, morality, the people involved, and proposed solutions (Cappella and Jamieson 1997; Price, Nir, and Cappella 2005; Chong and Druckman 2007). While agenda setting and priming concern the importance the media place on an issue, framing concerns the way media present issue content to the public. A frame determines what is in the picture and what is left out. According to the framing hypothesis, the slant or angle journalists take on newsworthy issues that can affect opinions about these issues. We are all familiar with the way news stories can be framed. News about poverty programs can stress a "helping hand" or a "government handout." Combatants in foreign conflicts can be "freedom fighters" or "terrorists." Antiabortion protestors can be portrayed as idealists committed to the sanctity of life or as religious zealots intent on enforcing their views on everyone else.

A recent example of a powerful and successful frame concerns the war in Iraq. When the United States went to war on March 19, 2003, it was supported by more than 70 percent of the population—despite opinion polls showing Americans expected a long, costly war with significant adverse economic consequences that in the short term would likely increase rather than reduce terrorism. The best explanation for the high level of support is that the Bush administration was able to frame the Iraq invasion as an extension of the war on terrorism. This view went unchallenged by Democrats and quickly became the dominant media frame, which had a major influence on political attitudes regarding the war (Gershkoff and Kushner 2005). Once critics began to challenge the evidence for weapons of mass destruction, the old frame was quickly undermined, as was the approval of the president.

Mediating Media Influence

We should be careful not to overstate the influence of the mass media on political beliefs. We saw in chapter 3 a distinction between the long-term stability of peoples' political dispositions and the volatility of their responses to survey questions, as the nature of the stimuli affects the short-term response. This note of caution applies here. For instance, experimental studies that involve manipulation of media presentations rarely report effects to be long lasting (e.g., Mutz and Reeves 2005). Arguably, evidence of framing and priming is little more than a demonstration that one can influence what bubbles to "the top of the head" (Zaller 1992) without generating a long-term impact. And we should always keep in mind that the relationship between the journalistic source and the recipient does not go unfiltered. People immunize themselves from media influence not only by their personal belief systems but also by talking to others (Druckman and Nelsen 2003; Druckman 2004).

Moreover, we must recognize that the source of agenda setting, priming, and framing is not some mass media monolith. News stories are prepared by journalists who themselves are influenced by the competing voices clamoring for their attention—such as competing politicians and interest groups trying to get their story out to the public. Finally, it must be recognized that if the mainstream media ever could keep the gates closed regarding what people think or think about, that is no longer possible in the age of the Internet. Political stories often appear first on political blogs. When they draw interest, they force the mainstream media to give them attention.

8-4   Media Content and Political Opinions

While the minimal effects model holds that the media do little more than reinforce preexisting opinions, recent research has demonstrated meaningful media effects on political opinions among those who regularly follow politics on television and talk radio and in the newspapers. In this section we discuss the findings of some of these studies.

Television Network News

In an ambitious study, Page and Shapiro (1992) estimated the influence of television news reports on the content of public opinion. They collected eighty instances from the late 1960s into the early 1980s where the same survey question about an important question of public policy was administered to national samples over a period of years. They then determined whether television news content between the two surveys could account for the observed change in public opinion. This exercise involved extensive monitoring and coding for more than a decade's worth of network news programs.

On the average, opinion did not change much in the short run of even a few years. But when change occurred, the direction tended to be consistent with the preponderant direction of the messages on network news. The authors examined the impact of many sources of information on network news (e.g., presidents, the opposition party, and interest groups). The source that best predicted opinion change was television commentary—from anchorpersons, reporters in the field, and special commentators. According to the estimates, each viewpoint presented in a commentary could bring about as much as 4 percentage points of opinion change. But Page and Shapiro are cautious when interpreting why television commentary predicts opinion change. They do not claim that individual newscasters are themselves the major source of opinion change. Rather, their message frequently overlaps or reinforces the dominant elite message that filters to the public via the media. Or news commentators and others with whom they agree may be perceived as simply reflecting an agreed-upon consensus that may strongly influence the formation of citizen opinions (Page and Shapiro 1992).

In other words, when the messages on television news are predominantly one sided and advocate a particular change of policy, it is a good bet that public opinion will change at least modestly in the same direction. But instead of television messages *causing* the opinion change, another possibility could be that both television messages and public opinion are both *responding* independently (but in a common direction) to the same events. In this way, public opinion and elite opinion (via the media) could be moving in tandem but with neither causing the other.

The Fox News Effect

Now, of course, less of our news viewing is from network news and more is from the cable news outlets. With its conservative slant, Fox News has grown to be the most heavily watched cable news channel. Because of Fox News' success at attracting viewers, it would seem obvious that its entry into the news field has had a significant impact on public opinion.

One ambitious and careful study has attempted to measure just that. The Fox News Channel did not exist until October 1996, when it began its twenty-four–hour news service in a few scattered cable markets. By 2000, it had become available to about 20 percent of the U.S. public. The pattern of its spread was idiosyncratic. DellaVigna and Kaplan (2008) examined the voting trends between the presidential elections of 1996 and 2000 in the towns where Fox News became available by 2000 with the trends in comparable towns where cable viewers were not yet able to receive Fox News. To get the best estimates, they compared towns with the Fox News Channel with towns in the same county where it was not yet available and utilized further statistical controls.

What they found was a small but quite statistically significant effect of about one-half of a percentage point on the vote. Republican George W. Bush received about half a percent more of the vote where Fox News was available on cable television. Half a point may not seem like much, although like any factor it could have been decisive in the close 2000 election. But to see why this impact is impressive, consider the size of the pool of potential converts available for Fox to push toward Bush. Where Fox became available, only some potential viewers subscribed to cable and of these, not all found their way to the upstart

Fox News Channel. Of these, roughly half were going to vote for Bush anyway. Thus, one half of one percent of all voters being swayed represent a much more sizeable chunk of would-be Gore voters who had cable and followed the campaign on Fox News.

In its early days, new viewers to Fox News might have been more influenced by its conservative tilt because they were not yet aware of its conservative reputation. Today, television viewers are generally aware of Fox News's conservative slant and this awareness can inoculate them from the full impact of its content. Undoubtedly, Fox News continues to influence its most faithful conservative viewers by reinforcing their already conservative beliefs. Others who are aware of Fox News's reputation but are not particularly predisposed toward its conservatism may use this knowledge to discount its conservatism when they do watch it or to ignore it by switching to rival news channels. Further studies of the impact of the diverse choices people have of cable news channels would be welcome.

Talk Radio

In recent times, nowhere has the merger of the news and entertainment been more successful than talk radio. Thirty-six percent of Americans say they listen to talk radio at least occasionally (Barker 2002, 19). Its champions claim talk radio serves to empower everyday people. However, as Davis and Owen (1999) forcefully note, talk radio is first and foremost about making money. The content of talk radio is simply a by-product of what sells best to the public. Currently, conservatives dominate the talk radio format. However, if some other format drew a larger audience, many conservative talk shows would quickly disappear.

The audience for talk radio tends to be older white males—particularly in the case of conservative talk radio. For the medium's best-known personality, Rush Limbaugh, 67 percent of listeners are male, 45 percent are over fifty years old, and 95 percent are white. Those who listen to talk radio tend to be more conservative than nonlisteners, but not by a large margin. Davis and Owen (1999, 168–70) found that 57 percent of listeners call themselves conservative, compared to about 40 percent of their public sample. Listeners were also more Republican (Davis and Owen 1999, 168–70). The fact that talk show hosts are generally a good deal more conservative than their audiences leads some analysts to conclude that entertainment is as big a drawing card as is political content (Lee and Cappella 2001).

A plausible interpretation is that the audience for talk radio leans to the right mainly because conservatives self-select to listen. Talk show hosts are essentially preaching to the choir. Mostly, that is the correct conclusion. However, several studies have shown that for issues frequently discussed on talk radio, hosts can have an independent influence on political opinions. In the mid-1990s, Rush Limbaugh spent considerable time bashing Ross Perot and Bill Clinton. David Barker (2002) found that with other factors held constant, regular listeners to Limbaugh were more negative in their evaluations of Perot and Clinton than were nonlisteners. On the other hand, listeners and nonlisteners did not differ on issues rarely covered by Limbaugh, such as the death penalty or school prayer. In the 2000 Republican primary, Limbaugh came out early in favor of George W. Bush over his principal primary opponent, Senator John McCain of Arizona (who Limbaugh said was not a "real" Republican). Using a design where respondents could be tracked over time, Barker (2002) found the more one listened to Limbaugh, the more likely was a change toward a favorable opinion of Bush and an unfavorable opinion of McCain. Because the sample was entirely composed of Republicans and tracked change over time, one can reasonably rule out the alternative explanation of self-selection.

Newspapers

In principle, political reporting in newspapers is not supposed to reflect an ideological position. Professional ethics dictate that journalists not let their own political feelings color their reporting. However, for the editorial pages, that is neither the expectation nor the case. Here, columnists such as conservative George Will and liberal Paul Krugman analyze political events through an ideological prism. In addition, the owners and managers of newspapers often endorse candidates for public office—a rare practice for the owners of television and radio stations. Because they use the public airwaves, radio and television stations would have to provide equal time for other candidates to respond.

As in the case of television and talk radio, there is evidence that the editorial content of newspapers can affect the political opinions of its readers. One reason is that editorial opinion can leak from the editorial page to straight news coverage. For example, in an analysis of media coverage of seventy-nine senate races between 1988 and 1992, Kahn and Kenney (2002) found that when a newspaper endorsed an incumbent senator on its editorial pages, the tone of its campaign coverage of that senator was significantly more positive than when it made no endorsement. Thus, to the extent there is spillover from the editorial pages to the straight news, the potential is greater for newspapers to influence political opinions (but see Dalton, Beck, and Huckfeldt 1998 for a somewhat different take).

Newspapers generally endorse Republicans for president, which makes it difficult to match voters who read Republican newspapers with those who read Democratic newspapers. But one exception to the Republican endorsement habits of American newspapers provided a unique opportunity to study endorsement effects. In the 1964 presidential election, more newspapers endorsed President Lyndon Johnson (42 percent) than his Republican opponent, Barry Goldwater (35 percent). With this relatively even division, Erikson (1976c) was able to compare the vote in communities where the local newspaper(s) endorsed the Democrat with the vote in communities where the local newspaper(s) endorsed the Republican. Statistical controls were imposed for the community's previous vote, the particular state, and the size of the city. Even with these controls, the 1960–1964 vote shift was about 5 percentage points more in the Democratic direction where the endorsements were Democratic than where they were Republican.

Various researchers (Entman 1989; Kahn and Kenney 2002; Druckman and Parkin 2005) have examined public opinion surveys to search for possible evidence that the newspapers people read influence their opinions or vote. With statistical controls for the influence of other variables, these analyses reveal evidence of newspaper influence. Interpretation should be cautious, however, because even the most careful statistical analysis might not be able to control fully for selective exposure—the tendency to select reading material based on ideological affinity. Also, newspapers tend to offer the slant their readers want to read (Gentzkow and Shapiro 2010).

Gerber, Kaplan, and Bergen (2009) avoided the selective-exposure problem by conducting a field experiment. Prior to the 2005 Virginia governor's election, they randomly assigned treatments of newspaper subscriptions to either the liberal *Washington Post* or the conservative *Washington Times*. Control subjects got neither. Surprisingly, they found that newspaper reading from either paper led to a boost in support for the Democratic candidate compared to the control group. They probably obtained this result because the flow of the news during this period (post-Katrina) was generally favorable to Democrats and critical of the Bush administration. Apparently, even conservative newspapers were not immune—another indicator of minimal media effects.

The Internet

With the Internet era still in its adolescence, much is yet to be learned about its impact on political attitudes. It should first be stated that politics is only one aspect of Internet content. For instance, tracking data show that pornographic Web sites gather three times the traffic of news sites and a full 100 times the traffic of strictly political sites (Hindman 2009). Still, as we shall see, the Internet obviously is a major source of political news for many people.

Internet political content—news sources and blogs—can be found on both the political left and the right. But as if to counterbalance talk radio as the comfort zone of the political right, the Internet provides a haven for the political left. Left-wing blogs for instance have more traffic than those on the right, and liberals read far more about politics on the Internet than do conservatives (Hindman 2009). Just as with talk radio, the ideological tilt can be partially explained by demographics—heavy Internet users are younger, more educated, and more Democrat than the average Internet user or nonuser (Smith 2009).

As discussed earlier, the Internet creates the opportunity for people to focus only on sources of information that are ideologically congenial with their current political beliefs. The net effect is a growth in polarization. Indeed, research shows that most people who read political blogs read mainly those that fit their ideological taste. The division between blog readers on the left and on the right is greater than between the viewers of "mainstream" television news (tilting left) and Fox News on the right. Further, one can argue that the two groups of blog readers are more polarized ideologically than even Democrats and Republicans in Congress (Lawrence, Sides, and Farrell 2009).

8-5 Media Change and the Quality of Electoral Decision Making

In political campaigns, the public must rely on the news media for information. Over the past half century there have been important changes in where prospective voters have sought their campaign news and also in the content of the media's campaign coverage. In this section we examine this change and its possible consequences.

News Consumption During Presidential Campaigns

Earlier in this chapter, we documented the general changes in news media consumption. Here we expand this discussion to focus on attention to the media during presidential campaigns, going back as far as 1952. Starting in 1952, the American National Election Studies asked voters if they followed the campaign in four media: newspapers, television, radio, and magazines. The responses to these questions from 1952 through 2008 are recorded in Figure 8.2. It shows the by now familiar decline in dependence on newspapers and the growth of television. For 2008, the ANES survey also asked about following the campaign on the Internet and almost half of the respondents said they did.

Next, we take a closer look at media consumption during the 2008 campaign using ANES data. Table 8.4 shows the reported frequencies of exposure to campaign news from the three main sources—television, newspapers, and the Internet. As usual, watching television dominates newspapers as the

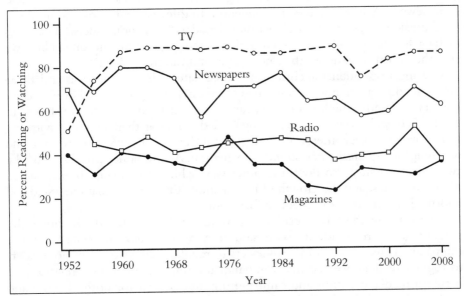

Figure 8.2 Sources of presidential campaign news. *Source:* ANES election studies. Percent yes to questions "Did you read about [watch] [heard about] the campaign in [on] . . . " Some questions were not asked for some years.

TABLE 8.4 | Media Usage in 2008 Presidential Campaign

	Attention to National Politics		
How many [items]?	Television	Newspapers	The Internet
None, just one or two	29%	47%	70%
Several	28	25	17
A good many	32	17	13

Note: Respondents were asked how often they "watched" [TV], "read" [newspapers], or "read, watched, or listened" [Internet] stories about the campaign.

Source: National Election Studies, 2008 election data.

reported source of campaign news. By 2008, the Internet had become a rival to newspapers as a frequent news source. Most tellingly, whereas about one-fifth claimed to ignore the campaign on television, about half said they paid no attention to it on the newspapers. And while more than half ignored the Internet as a source of campaign news, about one-fifth followed the campaign closely on the Internet.

Do people who follow the campaign closely on television tend to be the same people who follow the campaign closely in print, whether in print via newspapers or online via the Internet? We divided 2008 ANES respondents into three categories of television news watching: "Regular viewers," "occasional viewers," and "nonviewers." We also divided respondents into three categories of reading about the campaign: "regular readers," "occasional readers," and "nonreaders." The notes to Table 8.5 describe the details. Note that in scoring respondents on reading, we pool the information about their newspaper and Internet habits.[11]

Rating respondents according to three categories on viewing and three categories on reading gives a combined set of categories with a total of nine cells. Frequencies with which people appear in each of the nine cells are shown in Table 8.5. Regular viewing and reading tended to go together. So did nonviewing and nonreading. Our interest is in sorting out the separate effects of reading and watching on political interest and information. At the same time, we must be aware that causality also flows the other way; while monitoring the media can stimulate interest and the growth of information, it is also true that interested and informed citizens seek out media information.

We can see the basic results in part (a) of Table 8.6, which shows the percentage of respondents who said they were "very interested" in the campaign. As we move from nonviewers to regular viewers or from nonreaders to regular readers, we see that campaign interest increases. This relationship between media attention and campaign interest is clear for both viewing and reading. For each level of television news viewing, readers are more interested than nonreaders. For each level of reading, television news viewers are more interested than nonviewers. All this fits with common sense. Interest in the

TABLE 8.5 | **Patterns of Attention to Newspaper and Television News, 2008**

Newspaper and Internet Reading	Television News Viewing			
	Regular viewer	Occasional viewer	Non-viewer	All cases
Regular reader	16*	10	3	29
Occasional reader	7	14	6	27
Nonreader	9	14	21	43
All cases	32	37	31	100

Note: Regular readers are those who read "a good many" stories either on the Web or in newspapers. Nonreaders read no more than "just a bit" on either the Web or newspapers. Occasional readers are in-between. Regular viewers watch "a good many" stories about the campaign on TV. Nonreaders read none or "just a bit." Occasional viewers are in-between.

*Cell entries are percentages of total sample.

Source: American National Election Studies, 2008 election data.

TABLE 8.6 | **Responsiveness in the 2008 Presidential Campaign, by Media Attention**

(a) Percentage "Very Interested" in the Election

Newspaper and Internet Reading	Television News Viewing		
	Regular viewer	Occasional viewer	Non-viewer
Regular reader	51	36	50
Occasional reader	44	25	17
Nonreader	34	30	22

(b) Percentage with High Information About Candidate Positions*

Newspaper and Internet Reading	Television News Viewing		
	Regular viewer	Occasional viewer	Non-viewer
Regular reader	56	45	51
Occasional reader	40	38	34
Nonreader	28	24	9

*Categories same as for Table 8.5.

Source: National Election Studies, 2008 election data.

campaign should make one want to follow the campaign more closely both in print and on television, and following the campaign either in print or on television makes one more interested.

In part (b) of Table 8.6, note what happens when we substitute percentages with "high" information about candidate policy positions for campaign interest. We define high scorers as those who correctly rated McCain to the right of Obama on all four issues examined. News reading is sharply related to information level, especially among people who are not regular consumers of national news reports on television. The degree to which one follows the campaign on television, however, is not strongly related to information level (except among nonreaders). We do not find a pattern where at each level of newspaper/Internet reading, television watching is related to being informed. For instance, regular readers who watch no television news are among the most informed.[12]

How should this pattern be interpreted? Obviously one contributing factor may be that people learn more about political campaigns by reading newspapers or reading online than they do from watching stories about the campaign on television. Equally obvious, this pattern must partially be a matter of self-selection. People who choose the written word over television are more cognitively skilled and therefore more informed to begin with.

The Content of Television Campaign News

We might ask whether the increased reliance on television rather than newspapers for campaign news has made the electorate any less capable. People say the news they see on television is more credible than the news they read in the papers (and presumably now on the Web) (Roper 1997). But from which medium do people actually learn most?

It is commonly believed that people learn more about politics by reading newspapers than by watching television (e.g., Drew and Weaver 2006; Druckman 2005). The reasons are several. First, newspapers can carry far more in-depth information than brief newscasts can. Second, it is possible to browse the newspaper (and now the Internet) for detailed information in a way that is not possible or practical with television. Third, as the proportion of the voters who watch network news has declined by about half, people get their news from even less informative sources such as local news programs or entertainment shows. Fourth, as discussed further below, television has focused increasingly on covering campaigns as horse races, at the expense of presenting the candidate's actual campaign activities and policy proposals. Are voters worse off as a result?

Some say that the media tend to frame the campaign not as a clash of ideas but as a strategic game. Issues are seldom covered, and even less often covered in any depth. Rather, the news media are fixated on the game of politics—the "horse race." A consistent finding for elections in the past thirty years is that the primary focus of the network news is on who is leading, who is gaining, and who is losing electoral support, with stories often supported by polling data. Since television news pays little attention to issues, it is not surprising that viewers gain little substantive knowledge. As Larry Bartels (1988, 32) notes,

"In covering a presidential campaign, the media tell us more about who is winning and losing than they do about who is fit to be president."[13]

Horse-race journalism has not always characterized the media campaign coverage. Until the 1970s, reports on candidate issue positions more than held their own with reports of campaign conduct (Iyengar, Norpoth, and Hahn 2004). The most frequently identified reason for this change is the need the media have for novelty, currency, appealing pictures, and human interest stories—all of which feed into the corporate requirement to maximize profits. The proliferation of public opinion polls has accentuated this tendency. As we noted in chapter 2, two-thirds of all campaign stories include information from polls.[14] The evidence is mixed on whether the public really prefers horse-race journalism or wants the media to focus more on issue substance. On the one hand, Farnsworth and Lichter (2007) cite a number of polls and other evidence supporting the claim that people really want more substance. On the other hand, Iyengar, Norpoth, and Hahn (2004) find that when given an unambiguous choice in a real-world setting, more people prefer strategic information than issue information.

Evaluation

With the historical increase in television as the source for campaign news and the decline in the quality of campaign coverage, one might despair about the quality of the information voters have at hand when they vote for political candidates. We have seen that readers tend to be more informed than watchers, although the direction of causality is ambiguous. But even careful statistical analysis suggests that reading helps voters make more informed decisions than does watching TV. For instance, a careful analysis by Druckman (2005) of a Minnesota contest for the U.S. Senate found that the more newspaper content people read (controlling for other relevant variables), the more they learned about the candidates' positions. Television had no similar impact.

So in a given election, more information might be gained from reading than watching. But does this mean that the growing reliance on television has meant a decline in the information voters possess, or a reliance on superficial aspects of the campaign as opposed to the supposedly more noble policy positions of the candidates? Gilens, Vavreck, and Cohen (2007) analyze ANES electoral data from 1952 through 2000, looking for the effects of media reliance on the concerns of voters. While they found that the quality of news coverage (both television and newspapers) declined over the half-century, they also found that this made little difference in terms of whether the public framed of campaigns in terms of issues or in terms of personalities and other presumably less relevant criteria.

8-6 Political Advertising

Much of what people learn about political campaigns is incidental—from political advertisements that interrupt entertainment and news shows alike on television (and radio). The typical complaint about political ads is that they are overly negative. But, as we will see, some say that the ads actually are educational—and might even tell the voters more about political candidates than the voters can learn from television news.

Negativity in Political Ads

Negative ads are not new but seem to have increased significantly since 1980. By one account, only about 10 percent of paid ads were negative in 1960, while in 2000, 68 percent were negative and in 2008 about 60 percent were negative (West 2009, 67). Still, coding an ad as "negative" is very subjective, and percentages vary considerably from one study to another (Lau et al. 1999). In particular, there is often a fine line between "contrast ads" where candidates are compared and "negative ads" in which opponents are personally attacked.

The study of negative advertising was pioneered by Ansolabehere and Iyengar (Ansolabehere et al. 1994; Ansolabehere and Iyengar 1995, 111). They came to very harsh conclusions about the effect of negative ads on the public, asserting that negative ads lead to political cynicism and lower efficacy because "people infer from negative advertisements that the entire process, not the just the targeted candidate, is deeply flawed." According to their data, negative ads account for a 5 percent decrease in voter turnout.

The original work on negative ads has spawned a cottage industry of elaborations and refutations (prominent examples are Finkel and Geer 1998; Freedman and Goldstein 1999; Kahn and Kenney 1999; Sigelman and Kugler 2003; Lau and Pomper 2004; Geer 2005; Mutz and Reeves 2005; Krasno and Green 2008). Some studies make the counterclaim that negative ads actually increase turnout by signaling to voters that election is about something important. Other replications have failed to detect decreases in efficacy, political trust, and turnout due to negative ads (Finkel and Geer 1998; Freedman and Goldstein 1999). Sigelman and Kugler (2003) found almost no overlap between the way academics code negative ads and the extent to which citizens actually perceive advertising as negative in real-world electoral contests. Lau and his associates (1999) conducted a "meta-analysis" of 55 studies on the effect of negative political advertising.[15] When integrating the results of these 55 studies, they found no support for any of the effects attributed to negative ads—including increasing likes or dislikes of the competing candidates. A 2007 follow-up confirms these findings (Lau, Sigelman, and Royner 2007). People mostly do not like political ads, but whether they are negative, positive, or contrast ads makes little difference for most everyday citizens.

Ads and Political Information

Surprising as it may seem at first glance, citizens learn more about substantive policy issues from the content of paid candidate campaign ads than they do from television news coverage. The superior issue content of political ads was first claimed by Thomas Patterson and Robert McClure in a study of the 1972 presidential campaign and was reconfirmed in studies of the 1992 and 2000 elections (Brians and Wattenberg 1996; Freedman, Franz, and Goldstein 2004). Patterson and

McClure (1976) found that people who claimed to regularly watch the network news increased their knowledge of candidate issue positions by 28 percent on average between September and November 1972. But people who claimed to not watch network news at all gained about as much, 25 percent, indicating the network news had almost no effect. On the other hand, those who (by self-report) watched "many" political ads gained 36 percent in awareness of candidate issue positions, compared to 25 percent among those who watched only "a few" ads.

While cynics often charge that political advertising is without substance and designed simply to fool the voters, research indicates that ads provide considerable information about candidate policy positions. Based on a study of the almost one million television ads run in the 2000 election, Freedman, Franz, and Goldstein (2004) make an even bolder claim for the pedagogical merits of campaign commercials, calling them the "multi-vitamins" of American politics. They note that 95 percent of all presidential ads and 90 percent of all general election ads contained issue content. Campaign advertising, they claim, "is rich is informational content." Comparing those most exposed to these ads with those least exposed, they found exposure significantly increased political information, political interest, and voter turnout. And importantly, exposure had its greatest effect among those least politically engaged.

Gilens, Vavreck, and Cohen's (2007) analysis of ANES electoral data from 1952 through 2000 finds surprising evidence for the positive impact of ads. The more political ads were shown on television, the more the public focused on policy issues. The more advertisements accented policy differences between the candidates, the more voters evaluated candidates based on their policy positions.

Battleground versus Nonbattleground states Because of the Electoral College's winner-take-all feature at the state level, presidential candidates concentrate their ads in "battleground" states where the vote is expected to be closest, and largely ignore the other "blackout" states. One half of the nation is exposed to an unrelenting barrage of ads, while the other half receives virtually none. Researchers are beginning to explore what difference this makes for the quality of electoral decisions.

Gimpel et al. (2007) find that battleground state residents, because they are exposed to more ads, become more interested and engaged in the campaign, especially low income voters. Panagopoulos (2009) finds that over the campaign, candidate preferences are more volatile in battleground states, where they are exposed to most of the information. In effect, by their exposure to the campaign, battleground state residents sometimes shift their aggregate preferences, while blackout state residents rarely do so. And Gilens, Vavreck, and Cohen (2007) find that voters focus on issues more in battleground states than in blackout states.

Do the ads in battleground states also affect votes for president? This is hard to estimate, because candidates tend to place ads in media markets where they think they can harvest the most votes. Huber and Arseneaux (2007) got around this problem with the aid of a natural experiment—the spread of ads to unintended targets—residents of blackout states who reside in media markets centered in battleground states. (An example would be Kentuckians receiving Ohio television from the Cincinnati market in battleground Ohio.) They do find an effect on vote choices in 2000. The more ads there were for Bush relative to Gore, the better Bush did among accidentally exposed nonbattleground state voters.

8-7 Conclusion

Like citizens and politicians, the media has a crucial role to play in the American democracy. Self-government depends on the free exchange of ideas among reasonably well-informed men and women. How the media provides the necessary information for this exchange of ideas in the years to come will have important consequences for democratic accountability in the United States.

Developments in the past twenty years lend cause for both optimism and pessimism. The advent of multiple sources of political information can certainly be cause for optimism. Detailed information and in-depth analysis about political matters are there to be had for anyone who wants them. However, politics is a low priority for most Americans. They mostly look for shortcuts, and it is only rational for citizens to seek the minimal amount of information necessary to hold decision makers accountable. Unfortunately, the information that is easily found is often not very useful. The focus on candidate strategy and the horse race has almost no lasting educational value, and it provides virtually no useful policy insights upon which citizens might draw. And one cannot help but feel that the rampant negativity that characterizes the political news can have only a corrosive effect on the relations between citizens and government, although cause and effect have yet to be convincingly demonstrated.

With rapid advances in technology and some human ingenuity, it may yet be possible to make the political news appealing and profitable while at the same time genuinely informative. However, even under the best of circumstances, one should not overestimate the influence of the media for either good or bad. While the minimal effects model, taken to its extreme, is certainly not correct, the realistic alternative could perhaps be labeled something like *minimal effects plus a little bit more.*

Notes

1. We adopt West's (2001) timeline with some modifications.
2. There is still debate over what actually sunk the *Maine*. The most plausible explanation is that the ship hit a mine, causing its munitions to explode. Others believe the cause was internal; perhaps its munitions were ignited by a spark from its boilers.
3. Center for Media and Public Affairs, "Press Release," Oct. 30, 2000.
4. As the size of the audience for network news declines, the remaining audience grows older. Between 1991 and 2003, the median age of television viewers rose from fifty-five to sixty. Nielsen Media Research as reported in the *New York Times,* Feb. 9, 2004, C6.
5. In a survey conducted at the height of the campaign in October 2008, Pew (2008) found that those who claimed to get most of their campaign news from Fox News were three times more likely to call themselves Republicans than Democrats.

Democrats outnumbered Republicans by an even higher ratio among those who claimed to get most of their campaign news from CNN or from MSNBC. These partisan tilts were considerably higher than those in earlier Pew surveys.

6. In the new fragmented media, one strategy candidates increasingly use to reach those with low political interest is appearing on entertainment talks shows like *Oprah Winfrey*, the *Tonight Show* with Conan O'Brien, the *Late Night With David Letterman*, or even Jon Stewart's fake news, *The Daily Show*. One bonus for these appearances is that the tone of the coverage they receive is overwhelmingly positive.

7. While households not wired for cable comprise a captive audience for television networks, the amount of news presented by broadcast networks has declined appreciably. Much political news of the type once reported by broadcast networks (e.g., coverage of party conventions) is now relegated to cable news networks.

8. Reported by the Web site Media Transparency, 2004, "Recipient Grants: Center for Media and Public Affairs," http://www.mediatransparency.org/recipientgrants. php? 573, accessed Jan. 2, 2006.

9. See (for 1996), for instance, Domke, Shah, and Wackmanl. (1998); the reports from the Project for Excellence in Journalism at www.journalism.org (for 2000 and 2004); and (for 2004) the study by Media Tenor as reported in Stanley and Niemi (2006, 184–185). Farnsworth and Lichter only code the tone of news stories as positive or negative, while Media Tenor reports them as positive, negative, or could assign "no clear rating." Scoring the matter similar to Media Tenor, PEJ finds a mostly positive tone to network news coverage. With the results largely driven by debate coverage, PEJ studies find media treatment favoring Bush in 2000 but Kerry in 2004. PEJ evaluations are not directly comparable to the others, however, because they include both print broadcast media and incorporate statements about campaign tactics and the horse race.

10. Still another contributing factor to the news media's increased negativity is that they take the lead from the increased negativity of candidate advertising. As candidates increasingly run negative campaigns attacking their opponents, these attacks become part of the news story and hence reported by the media.

11. We take some license by referring to Internet users as "readers." A small portion of the time people spend on the Internet regarding political campaigns involves watching videos.

12. While watching and reading about the campaign are correlated (Table 8.5), the two components of reading about the campaign—following the campaign in newspapers and on the Internet—are virtually unrelated. One cannot predict the degree to which a person followed the 2008 campaign in the newspapers from the degree the person followed it on the Internet. The two sources of news may be interchangeable. Of regular readers, those who get most of the news from the Internet are the most knowledgeable.

13. The Center for the Study of Media and Public Affairs has monitored the content of the major networks' news coverage since 1988. With 2004 being a slight exception, it has found more coverage of the horse race than of policy content.

14. One downside of the media's reliance on polls is inaccurate reporting, as reporters often misinterpret poll results. Stephanie Larson (2001) gives a number of examples of how reporters come to wrong conclusions based on polling data.

15. A "meta-analysis" is a study of the findings of all work in a specific area. The results of each study are quantified and entered into a database. Standard statistical tests are used to determine if the studies taken as a whole support a particular conclusion.

9 Elections as Instruments of Popular Control

IN A DEMOCRACY, THE PUBLIC supposedly controls the behavior of its public officials by exercising its influence at the ballot box in a rational fashion—in accordance with what we call the *rational-activist model*. Ideally, each voter selects the candidate who best represents his or her views on matters of public policy. At least in a two-candidate election, the collective choice is then the candidate who is closer to most voters on the issues. The policy result is the closest correspondence possible, given the choice of candidates, between the collective preferences of the electorate and government policy.

But representation of the public interest via democratic elections is not as simple in practice as it is in theory. It is possible, for instance, to hold elections in which none of the candidates on the ballot offer policy choices that voters find attractive. Even when the candidates present a relevant menu of policy choices, the electorate may—through some combination of misguidance, ignorance, and indifference—vote "irrationally" by voting into office a candidate who does not represent their interests. Also, if officeholders perceive that the electorate is not watching, or that it does not care, they may feel free to make policy decisions without consideration of public opinion.

Looking at the matter positively rather than negatively, we can state the conditions that *do* allow elections to be an effective instrument for inducing policy decisions that are responsive to public opinion. First, the candidates should offer a meaningful choice of policy options that appeal to voters, and once elected, the winner should try to carry out campaign pledges. Second, the voters should be informed about the issues that separate the candidates and vote for the candidate who best represents their own views. Clearly, the fulfillment of each of these conditions depends on the other. For example, political leaders pay the greatest attention to public opinion when they believe the public is alert enough to throw them out of office if they do not. Similarly, voters have the greatest opportunity to vote intelligently on the basis of policy issues when the politicians act on the assumption that the public is going to do so.

In this chapter, we examine the behavior of the electorate when it carries out its assigned responsibility. In chapter 10, we examine the responsiveness of political elites to public opinion.

9-1 Political Campaigns and the Voter

During every political campaign, voters are bombarded with news and propaganda about the candidates who seek their favor. Judging by the attention politicians give to the voters at election time, one might conclude that the voter reacts to campaign stimuli in the same fluid manner as a consumer reacting to advertising stimuli in the mass media. Just as the person about to purchase a product, such as a detergent, might vacillate in his or her choice of brands until the moment of purchase, so might the voter waver between the candidates until entry into the voting booth forces a final decision. But as we saw in chapter 8, this image of the voting process underestimates the voter's ability to resist political messages.

As discussed in chapter 3, most American voters have a more or less permanent attachment to either the Republican or the Democratic Party. It is through this filter of party identification that most voters view the partisan aspects of the political world. The anchor of party identification prevents voters from changing the party they vote for from one election to the next and from wavering in their choice of candidates during a campaign.

From one election to the next, only a small minority of those who vote both times switch sides. Converse (1962) reports 20 percent changed the party of their presidential vote from 1956 to 1960 among the ANES's 1956–1960 panelists. In the ANES's 1992–1996 panel, the percent switching sides deflates to 11 percent if third-party votes for Perot are excluded. And in the ANES 2000–2004 panel, of those who voted in both presidential elections, only 10 percent switched their presidential vote from Republican to Democratic or vice versa. Over the past half century, voters have become more polarized in their vote choice.

On a day-to-day or week-to-week basis over a campaign, vote choices are even more stable. The greatest change is observed following major campaign events such as party conventions or candidate debates. Hillygus and Jackman's (2003) panel study of Internet respondents in the 2000 campaign finds only about 10 percent of prospective voters with a candidate choice prior to the two conventions or prior to the first debate changing their mind after the event. The vast majority of changers simply became undecided rather than switch to the other major candidate. Over the course of a fall campaign, few change from one major party's candidate to the other.

The ANES presidential polls interview their respondents both before and after the election. About one-fourth of the initial interviews take place from 45 to 60 days before the election—at the early stage of the fall campaign. Over a half century of polling, over 3,000 from this set of respondents offered a preelection preference for a major party candidate, and then reported voting for a major party candidate when reinterviewed after the election. These respondents offer a window regarding the degree of switching over in the final two months of the campaign. Only 7 percent switched their vote preference between the preelection interview and the Election Day. In the intense Obama–McCain campaign of 2008, the switching rate was merely 6 percent. Of the 2008 campaign's 532 ANES respondents who (a) were interviewed 45–60 days in advance, (b) offered an initial preference, and then (c) voted for a major party candidate, 5 percent were McCain voters switching to Obama and only 1 percent were switchers from Obama to McCain.[1]

Below the presidential level, the percentage of voters who stick with their party's choice is even higher. For lower offices, the amount of information that reaches voters is often too slight to give them any reason to go against their party. Only in nonpartisan elections and primary contests (where party identification cannot be a criterion of choice) do voters vacillate in an erratic manner. In fact, vote preferences in primary contests are so fluid that pollsters have great difficulty predicting outcomes, even when they monitor opinion as late as a day or two before the election.

Of course, if party identification were the sole determinant of how people vote, election results would simply reflect the balance of Democratic and Republican identifiers. And since the ratio of Democratic to Republican identifiers changes only modestly in the short run, election results would be almost identical from one election to the next. In fact, election results often depart considerably from the voter division that would occur with a strict party-line vote.

When an election is decided on a party-line basis, the result is called the *normal vote*. At one time, the normal vote was considered a constant of politics. The calculation was that assuming a 50–50 split by Independents and a balanced, minimal defection rate by partisans (about 10 percent on each side), the nation-level normal vote would be a narrow Democratic win by about 54 percent Democratic to 46 percent Republican (Converse 1966; see also Petrocik 1989). This calculation reflects the Democratic edge in party identification that more than counterbalances the higher turnout rate among Republicans than Democrats.

Figure 9.1 presents a sixty-two–year approximation of the normal vote, between 1946 and 2008, derived from the national division of party identification.[2] Note the disappearance of the Democrats' once-dominant edge over the Republicans. Nationally, the normal vote is approximated by the national vote in congressional elections. As Figure 9.1 shows, the national House vote between 1948 and 1992 never varied from between 50 and 59 percent Democratic, averaging at the expected 54 percent Democratic. The Democrats' prior large advantage in party identification thus explains why the Democrats controlled the House of Representatives (and usually the Senate) for forty years, running from 1954 to 1994. In 1994 the Republicans suddenly gained control of the House after their forty-year drought. This could not have happened without a change in the normal vote brought about by Republican gains in party identification.

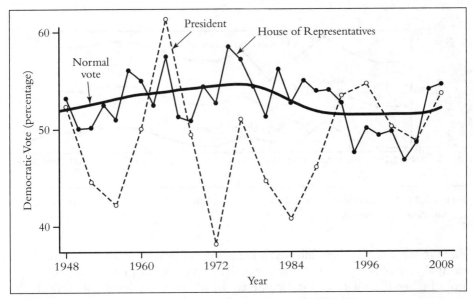

Figure 9.1   The national two-party vote (percent Democratic), 1948–2008.

The difference between the actual vote and the normal vote represents the *short-term partisan forces* of the election. When it comes to voting for Congress, national issues are of only modest importance. National-level short-term forces are modest for congressional elections, so party control of Congress is largely determined by the normal vote. But for the presidency, short-term forces can be of major importance. As Figure 9.1 shows, the national vote for president often departs significantly from the normal vote. In fact, during the post–World War II era, the presidency has been won more often by the Republicans than by the Democrats.

Deviations of election results from the normal vote do not signify that the usual role of party identification in shaping election results has broken down. Instead, one finds that the party favored by short-term forces is the beneficiary of most of the short-term party defections, and it also wins the majority of the Independent vote. Figure 9.2 shows this pattern over the sixteen presidential elections from 1948 through 2008.

When short-term forces favor the Republicans, Democrats defect beyond their usual rate; Republicans are even more loyal to their party than usual, and Independents vote overwhelmingly Republican. With pro-Democratic short-term forces, the pattern is the reverse—with unusually frequent Republican defections and a Democratic trend among Independents.

Short-Term Forces Below the Presidential Level

For state and local elections, the normal vote reflects the partisan balance of the particular state or local constituency rather than the nation as a whole. Due to the kinds of people who reside in the area, the local normal vote is often one

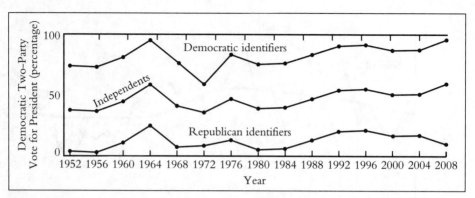

Figure 9.2   Party identification and the vote for president, 1952–2008. *Source:* American National Election Studies election data.

sided in favor of the Republicans or Democrats. Election results reflect the local normal vote plus any short-term forces that carry over from national politics (or from higher-level state or local contests). In addition, the local vote reflects the short-term forces generated by the local candidates and their campaign. One way of thinking about local short-term forces is as the personal vote generated by the candidates themselves (Cain, Ferejohn, and Fiorina 1987).

Although candidates for local office run less visible races than presidential candidates, their own campaigns help determine their electoral fate. The importance of local campaigns is indicated by the fact that as many as half the voters in a national election report that they split their ticket rather than vote for one party's candidate for all offices (Burden and Kimball 2002). Because of this ticket splitting, the same constituency often votes the Democratic candidate into one office and the Republican candidate into another.

As for president, election outcomes below the presidential level depend in large part on the short-term forces of the specific campaign. By one estimate, short-term forces for the statewide offices of governor and U.S. senator are about as large as for president (Erikson, Wright, and McIver 1994, ch. 9). The implication is that statewide (and perhaps local) outcomes readily depart by 10 or 15 percentage points from the state (or local) normal vote. Even where one party dominates, the disadvantaged party often can win when it fields the stronger candidate.

Who Are the Floating Voters?

Election outcomes are the result of both the normal vote and short-term partisan forces of the campaign. Voters whose choice is determined by the campaign rather than a long-term partisan commitment are called *floating voters*. An important question remains: How informed are the floating voters? If the floating voters were more politically informed than the average, we would think that election trends are essentially the response of the most politically alert segment of the public. But if the reverse is true—that floaters are more politically *ignorant* than the average—then we might be pushed toward the more dismal conclusion that election trends are largely the result of campaign propaganda of the sort that appeals to the voters least capable of making an informed evaluation.

Thanks to a classic article by Converse (1962) and a more recent elaboration by Zaller (1992, 2004a; see also Alvarez 1997), we have a good but complicated theory regarding floating voters. Consider a candidate's decision to pitch the campaign at inattentive and unsophisticated voters or at attentive and sophisticated voters. On one hand, the more attentive voters are easier to reach with new campaign messages. On the other hand, these attentive voters are more hardened in their views. Their accumulated storage of political information helps bolster their initial views against intruding information. For example, a Republican who is highly informed about politics is better equipped to discount Democratic propaganda than one who is more politically ignorant. Less attentive voters are more easily swayed, but only if new information reaches them.

Given these complications, the information level of floating voters depends considerably on the intensity of the campaign and the flow of information. When the information flow is low, the least attentive voters are so uninformed that they lack any basis for switching between candidates. They vote according to their initial partisan predisposition, if they vote at all. Attentive voters, meanwhile, although more resistant to influence from campaign propaganda, sometimes change their candidate choice when new information reaches them. However, when the information flow is high, even the least attentive voters receive some information. Because these least attentive voters are the most influenced by new information they receive, they contribute disproportionately to electoral volatility.

The battle for the presidency attracts great interest and large voter turnout, with almost all voters receiving some campaign exposure. For example, in ANES surveys during presidential campaigns, voters are almost universally aware of the names of the presidential candidates. The universal intake of new information during a presidential campaign loosens a great number of voters from their partisan moorings—particularly among the least attentive voters. The tiny fraction of presidential voters who manage completely to avoid the campaign maintain stable candidate preferences throughout. But setting these few cases aside, partisan defections and preelection wavering in candidate choice are most frequent among voters with the least exposure to presidential campaign information.

Table 9.1 illustrates the relationship between our information scale, introduced in chapter 3 and defined in the Appendix, and partisan defection in the 2008 presidential election. Defectors are partisans who vote against their party. First, let us consider the Democratic identifiers in 2008. Although the vast majority voted for Obama, the few defectors were drawn mainly from "low" information voters; "high information" Democrats were the most steadfast for Obama. Among Republicans, similarly, the few defectors were mainly among the less informed voters. (Overall, Republicans defected at a slightly lower rate than did Democrats in 2008; McCain's loss is due to there being fewer Republican identifiers than Democrats.)

Table 9.1 also shows the voting behavior of self-proclaimed Independents in the 2008 presidential election. In 2008, most Independent voters cast their

TABLE 9.1 | Vote for President, 2008, by Information Level and Party Identification*

	Information		
	Low	Medium	High
Democratic identifiers			
Obama	86%	91%	96%
McCain	14	9	4
	100%	100%	100%
Independent identifiers			
Obama	60%	62%	49%
McCain	40	38	51
	100%	100%	100%
Republican identifiers			
Obama	9%	8%	6%
McCain	91	92	94
	100%	100%	100%

*Information scale based on correctness of relative placement of candidates on issues. For details, see the Appendix.

Source: American National Election Studies, 2008 election data.

ballots for Obama, although those with the most information were an exception. Generally, Independents flock disproportionately to the winner, especially the *least* informed Independents. In 1996, for instance, Clinton did well among all Independents, particularly the least informed. In 1988, the last time a Republican won a decisive presidential victory, the first President Bush did well among the Independents, especially the least informed.

Knowledgeable voters tend to sort as Democratic and Republican partisans based on their beliefs and stick to them. Less informed voters enter the campaign as relatively blank slates, available to persuasion by the short-term forces of the campaign. We see this when we follow the vote over the presidential elections from 1984 to 2004 separately for high-information voters and low-information voters. Among the ANES's "highly informed" presidential voters (by criteria similar to those used here for the 2008 election), the 1984–2004 trend in the two-party vote was slight:

	1984	1988	1992	1996	2000	2004	2008
% Dem. among high-information voters	46%	48%	56%	48%	48%	48%	47%

But among ANES's low-information voters, we see considerable volatility:

	1984	1988	1992	1996	2000	2004	2008
% Dem. among low-information voters	44%	48%	61%	77%	63%	50%	60%

As Converse argues, it sometimes seems that "not only is the electorate as a whole quite uninformed, but it is the least informed members within the electorate who seem to hold the critical 'balance of power' in the sense that alternatives in the governing party depend disproportionately on shifts in their sentiment" (Converse 1962, 578).[3]

We might even be tempted to conclude that the most effective presidential campaign would be one aimed directly at the voter who is normally inattentive and uninformed about politics. But recall that the inattentive voter is a less accessible target of campaign messages. Note, too, the tendency of the least informed to dilute their influence by not voting. Based on self-reports, the 2008 vote turnout within the least and most informed categories was as follows:

	Low Information	High Information
Voted	60%	88%
Did not vote	40	12
	100%	100%

The electoral contribution of the least informed citizens is diluted by their low motivation to vote.

9-2 Policy Issues and Voters

Despite our current knowledge about voting behavior, scholars do not fully agree on the precise role of policy issues in elections. From what we know about the capabilities of average American voters, we are not surprised that many scholars are skeptical of the capacity of candidates' policy proposals and ideological leanings to affect many voter decisions. Among the most pessimistic are the authors of *The American Voter*, undoubtedly the single most influential book on voting behavior. They found the electorate almost wholly without detailed information on the issues of the day, unable to judge the rationality of government policies, and unable to appraise the appropriateness of the means necessary to arrive at desirable ends (Campbell et al. 1960, 543).

The American Voter, however, was based on the two Eisenhower elections from the quiescent 1950s. Several studies of more recent elections—with titles such as *The Changing American Voter* (Nie, Verba, and Petrocik 1976), *The New American Voter* (Miller and Shanks 1996), and *The American Voter Revisited* (Lewis-Beck et al. 2008)—offer a rather different interpretation of the capabilities of the American voter. Beginning with the Johnson–Goldwater election of 1964, political issues and ideologies have become increasingly important as determinants of the vote in the United States. The reason for this growth of issue voting is that parties and candidates have become more polarized on liberal versus conservative lines (Abramowitz 2010). But just how important issues have become remains controversial.

For voters to be influenced by policy issues when they cast their ballots, two conditions must be met. First, the voters must be aware of the differences between the policy views of the candidates. Second, the voters must be motivated to vote on the basis of the issues that divide the candidates. Evidence of issue voting is strongest when the divergence between the candidate stances is strong and the issue is of considerable importance to the electorate.

Here, we examine the evidence of policy voting in presidential elections. Most of the data analysis that follows is from the ANES survey of the 2008 presidential election. As measured via survey analysis, the degree of issue voting in 2008 was typical of recent presidential elections.

Voter Perceptions of Candidate Differences, 2008

A necessary condition for voting on the basis of candidates' policy positions is that the voters perceive actual policy differences between the candidates. Following their usual procedure, in 2008 the ANES researchers asked respondents for their perceptions of the presidential candidates' positions on a series of seven-point scales representing several issues. Table 9.2 arranges these data to show how voters rated the Democratic victor Barack Obama relative to his opponent, John McCain, on five issues.

Individuals could rate Obama to the left of McCain (correct), rate McCain to the left of Obama (incorrect), or place the two candidates in a tie (presumably incorrect). In addition, on each issue scale some voters (generally around 10 percent) gave incomplete ratings, claiming not to know the position of one or both of the major candidates. We also scored responses as incomplete in all instances where the respondent had no opinion on the issue.

Table 9.2 shows voter perceptions of the candidates' relative positions on issues where Obama and McCain clearly differed. On all these issues, a majority of voters ordered the candidates correctly. Obama was seen as to McCain's left by anywhere between 56 and 62 percent of the respondents; meanwhile, between 8 and 10 percent mistakenly placed McCain to the left of Obama.

The first four respondent ratings of candidate ideology shown in Table 9.2 provided the basis for classification on our information index. Among voters in

---

TABLE 9.2 | **Voter Perceptions of Issue Differences Between Presidential Candidates, 2008**

	Obama left of McCain	McCain left of Obama	Same or incomplete ratings
Liberal/conservative ideology	58%	9%	33%
Domestic spending	56	10	33
Defense spending	62	8	30
Abortion	58	9	33
Medical Care	59	10	31

Source: American National Election Studies, 2008 election data. Each percentage is based on voters only. Relative positions are determined by voters' responses on a seven-point scale, except for the abortion issue, where the question presents a four-point scale. For full question wording, see the Appendix.

the 2008 election, a respectable 36 percent were "high-information" scorers, meaning they saw Obama to McCain's left on all four items. "Low-information" scorers constituted 23 percent of the voting total, as they correctly identify the relative placement of the candidates on no more than one of the four issues. The remaining 41 percent were in between. Thus, roughly speaking, one-third of the voting electorate is clearly tuned in to the candidates' ideological differences, about one quarter are not, with the remainder somewhere in between. As usual, our picture of the electorate is mixed.

Policy Issues, Ideology, and Votes, 2008

In order to vote on the basis of policy issues, it is not enough for voters to become aware of the candidates' policy differences. In addition, they must find these choices sufficiently important to influence their vote choices. With policy voting, we would observe people voting for the candidate closest to their own views. This would usually mean liberals voting Democratic and conservatives voting Republican.

Table 9.3 presents simple evidence of policy voting in the 2008 presidential election. This table shows that over a variety of issues, voters who prefer the liberal position gave the most support to Obama, while voters preferring the conservative position gave the most support to McCain. Of these ten issues, what divided the electorate most in terms of influencing their vote choice (with vote gaps in the 50 percent range) were withdrawal of forces from Iraq, domestic spending, and aid to blacks. Not far behind were health care, defense spending, and gay marriage. Trailing in importance were the so-called "cultural" issues of abortion, capital punishment, and gun control.

It is typical that voters vary most on the basis of economic issues and less on the basis of cultural issues. Iraq also interjected itself as an issue in the 2008 presidential race. The strong influence of foreign policy on the campaign was unusual, in that in normal times voters supposedly do not put foreign policy as their top priority. But a war and nation-building in the Middle East during the midst of a war on terror are not normal times.

It is worth noting also the polarization on gay marriage, which of course is a prime cultural issue. Gay rights have not been a strong source of division. And neither Obama nor McCain endorsed gay marriage during the campaign. Even so, it emerged as an issue to divide people's votes.[4]

Because so many issues seem to matter, we should be able to improve our vote predictions by taking into account voter positions on many issues simultaneously rather than one issue at a time. Table 9.4 shows the relationship between general liberal–conservative ideology and the 2008 vote in two different ways. First, the table shows the vote as a function of ideological self-identification, where ideological identification is measured using the full seven-point scale from "extremely liberal" to "extremely conservative." Ideological identification predicts fairly well, particularly for voters on the liberal side of the spectrum. Of the 24 percent who placed themselves at one of the three positions on the liberal side of the spectrum, 90 percent voted for Obama over McCain. Of the 35 percent on the conservative side, 71 percent chose McCain over Obama. Thus, for most

TABLE 9.3 | 2008 Presidential Vote by Policy Opinions

Policy	Obama (%)	McCain (%)	(%)	Difference
Impose Iraq Withdrawal Deadline				
Favor	76	24	= 100%	+50
Oppose	26	74	= 100%	
Defense Spending				
Less	77	23	= 100%	+39
More	38	62	= 100%	
Aid to Blacks				
Favor	88	12	= 100%	+54
Oppose	34	66	= 100%	
Domestic Spending				
More	71	29	= 100%	+51
Less	20	80	= 100%	
National Health Care				
Favor	73	24	= 100%	+47
Oppose	26	74	= 100%	
Guaranteed Job, Standard of Living				
Favor	81	19	= 100%	+45
Oppose	36	64	= 100%	
Death Penalty				
Oppose	73	27	= 100%	+27
Favor	46	54	= 100%	
More Gun Control				
Favor	69	31	= 100%	+26
Oppose	43	57	= 100%	
Abortion				
Permit	64	36	= 100%	+26
Restrict	38	62	= 100%	
Legalize Gay Marriage				
Favor	79	21	= 100%	+42
Oppose	41	59	= 100%	

Source: American National Election Studies, 2008 election data. Votes for minor-party candidates are ignored.

voters with an ideological leaning, the vote choice was in line with their ideological preference. But not all voters identify with one of the ideological sides. Of the 41 percent of voters either moderate or without an ideological preference, more than two-thirds chose Obama over McCain.

The second part of Table 9.4 shows the vote as a function of the ten-item composite liberal–conservative index introduced in chapter 3. Here the degree of

TABLE 9.4 | **Presidential Vote by Two Summary Measures of Liberalism–Conservatism, 2008**

Self-Identification on Ideological Scale

| | Extremely Liberal | | | | | Extremely Conservative | | |
	1	2	3	4	5	6	7	None
Obama (%)	99	95	81	62	31	11	10	71
McCain (%)	1	6	19	38	69	89	90	29
(Percentage of voters)	(4)	(11)	(9)	(21)	(12)	(20)	(3)	(20)

Ten-Item Composite Issue Index★

| | Most Liberal | | | | | | Most Conservative |
	−10 to −8	−7 to −5	−4 to −2	−1 to +1	+2 to +4	+5 to +7	+8 to +10
Obama%)	100	93	78	62	39	14	0
McCain(%)	0	7	22	38	61	86	100
(Percentage of voters)	(6)	(10)	(17)	(22)	(20)	(15)	(10)

★For construction of the ten-item composite issue index, see the Appendix.

Source: American National Election Studies, 2008 election data.

prediction is, if anything, even better. The ten-item scale has a twenty-one–point range from +10 (perfect liberal) to −10 (perfect conservative). Among the 16 percent on the far left, from −5 to −10, 96 percent voted for Obama over McCain. Similarly, among the 25 percent who are on the far right, from +5 to +10, 91 percent chose McCain.

From this demonstration, voters with consistently liberal or conservative views are highly predictable in their vote choice. But most voters are not at either ideological extreme. Nearly one-fourth (22 percent) are near the exact center—in the −1 to +1 range on the ten-point scale—and must be described as decidedly moderate or centrist. Many others appear only vaguely liberal or conservative, and their votes do not always follow from their ideological direction.[5]

In part, the predictability of votes from ideology as shown in Table 9.4 is due to voters simply responding to their partisan background. Liberals tend to identify with the Democratic Party and conservatives with the Republicans (chapter 3). Thus, just by voting their party identification, voters tend to support the candidates closest to their views. Issue voting is further enhanced by party defections and Independents. Table 9.5 illustrates this tendency by showing the relationships between ideology and the vote within the three categories of party identification. Conservative Democrats and liberal Republicans, while rare, are the partisan groups most prone to defect in their presidential voting. Meanwhile, Independents

TABLE 9.5 | **2008 Presidential Vote by Ideology, with Party Identification Controlled**

	Democrats			Independents			Republicans		
	Ideological Self-Identification								
	Lib.	**Mod.**	**Con.**	**Lib.**	**Mod.**	**Con.**	**Lib.**	**Mod.**	**Con.**
Obama (%)	94	87	81	91	61	20	34	14	4
McCain (%)	6	13	19	9	39	80	68	86	96
(Percentage of voters)	(19)	(10)	(6)	(8)	(14)	(11)	(1)	(5)	(26)
	Democrats			Independents			Republicans		
	Ten-Item Issue Index★								
	Lib.	**Center**	**Con.**	**Lib.**	**Center**	**Con.**	**Lib.**	**Center**	**Con.**
Obama (%)	96	85	74	75	64	24	41	21	2
McCain (%)	4	17	26	25	36	76	59	79	98
(Percentage of voters)	(16)	(9)	(2)	(15)	(17)	(7)	(4)	(11)	(20)

★Ideology scale collapsed so −10 to −3 = liberal; −2 to +2 = center; +3 to +10 = conservative.
Source: American National Election Studies, 2008 election data.

present the clearest example of issue voting. Neutral in terms of partisanship, they generally vote Democratic if liberal and Republican if conservative.

Information and Ideological Voting

As one would expect, ideological voting is most prevalent among voters who are highly informed about candidate positions. In surveys, the observed relationship between ideology and vote choice becomes most pronounced when we select the most informed voters (Knight 1985; Jacoby 1991). Figure 9.3 illustrates how issue voting rises with information.

The figure divides 2008 respondents into those low, medium, and high on our scale of information about candidate differences on issues. For each group, Figure 9.3 shows the relationship between the ten-item index of respondent liberalism–conservatism and the vote. Graphed percentages represent the Obama proportion of the two-party vote.

The graph shows that the sharpness of the tendency for liberals to vote Democratic and conservatives to vote Republican varies with the voters' level of information. Among the "high-information" voters, there were few exceptions to the rule that liberals voted Democratic and conservatives Republican. In fact, even a slight ideological tilt (in the 22–24 or 12–14 range) was sufficient to push most informed voters to vote consistent with their ideological tendency. Among "medium-information" voters, ideological voting is also present, although in a more muted form. Among "low-information" voters, we see the mildest tendency toward ideological voting.

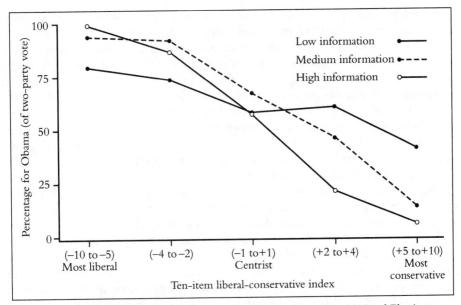

Figure 9.3 Issue voting by level of information, 2008. *Source:* American National Election Studies election data.

We learn from this exercise that when voters are informed about the ideological differences among candidates, ideology is a strong influence on vote choice. The degree to which voters choose candidates based on ideology depends in large part on the degree of ideological division between the candidates and the degree to which these differences are publicized. When Democratic and Republican candidates are ideologically similar, ideological differences between Democratic and Republican voters are negligible except for those that derive from voting on the basis of party identification. Studies of different elections (e.g., Nie, Verba, and Petrocik 1976) show that the stronger the candidates' ideological differences, the more ideological voting follows.

Issue Voting and Candidate Advantage

So far we have seen evidence of ideological and issue voting whereby the most liberal voters based on a survey item or set of items vote Democratic while the most conservative vote Republican. We might also wonder, which issues help or hurt the various candidates? On a given issue in 2008, who did the voters see as closer to them: Obama or McCain? To set up the test, we analyze responses to the 2008 ANES items regarding ideological leanings plus four issues where the candidates took divergent stands and on which the voters were asked to place the candidates on the same scale as the voters. On most issues, these scales were the ANES seven-point scales where voters were asked to rate themselves and the candidates from 1 (liberal) to 7 (conservative). We identified respondents who were closer to Obama or McCain based on these scales. Many respondents of course placed themselves equidistant between the candidates or assigned identical scale scores to the two candidates and thus could not be counted as closer to one candidate over the other on the particular issue. Others were excluded due to missing data on one or more of the three necessary scale scores needed for a comparison. Importantly, even if a voter's ratings indicated a greater proximity to one candidate over the other, we excluded the relative rating if the voter mistakenly scored McCain to the left of Obama on the issue. The argument behind this exclusion is that voters who assign the "wrong" relative positions to the candidates are mainly "guessing" (and guessing wrong) and would not likely have been influenced by the issue in the election.

Table 9.6 shows the results. For each item, the table presents the proportion of voters closer to each candidate by the criteria outlined plus each group's vote choice. On the five issues, 86 to 92 percent of the voters saw themselves as closer to one candidate than the other. McCain held a slight edge on ideological identification. (More voters saw themselves as closer to McCain's conservatism than to Obama's liberalism.) More also saw themselves closer to McCain on government spending. However, on defense spending, medical care, and especially abortion, most preferred Obama's more liberal position to McCain's. Typically, there was about a 70-percentage point differential in the vote choices of those who saw themselves closer to Obama versus those seeing themselves closer to McCain on an issue.

Overall, a perusal of Table 9.6 would suggest a very close contest in terms of which candidate was, on balance, closer to the voters. McCain wins on ideology

TABLE 9.6	Presidential Vote Choice and Relative Closeness of Voters to Candidates, 2008			
	Percent Closer to		**Vote of Those Closer to**	
	Obama	McCain	Obama	McCain
Liberal–conservative ideological identification	40	52	89% Obama 11% McCain	12% Obama 88% McCain
Domestic spending	43	49	95% Obama 5% McCain	20% Obama 80% McCain
Defense spending	46	40	83% Obama 17% McCain	12% Obama 88% McCain
Government versus private health care	49	41	83% Obama 17% McCain	15% Obama 85% McCain
Abortion rights	61	32	75% Obama 25% McCain	15% Obama 85% McCain

Respondents scored in terms of closeness only if they perceived McCain to the right of Obama on the issue.

Source: American National Election Studies, 2008 election data.

plus spending, while Obama wins on the remaining three issues. Consider voters' net balance on the five items shown in Table 9.6. Summing across issues, we find that 38 percent of all voters in the 2008 ANES sample saw themselves as closer to Obama and 89 percent of these cast their ballots for Obama. On the other side of the ledger, 37 percent saw themselves closer to McCain and 88 percent of this group voted for McCain. Meanwhile, a pivotal 25 percent were in the middle when summing across issues, and they supported Obama by a decisive 68 to 32 ratio. In terms of wooing voters on issues, the contest between Obama and McCain was very close. Obama may owe his victory to other factors, such as general likeability. We should be somewhat cautious, however, in assigning one candidate with the advantage in terms of issue proximity. Note how relative closeness depends on the item under discussion. For instance, on domestic policy, McCain wins on the general question of spending and taxation while Obama wins on the specific issue of medical care. How we do the scoring depends on survey researchers' decisions regarding which issues are sampled.[6]

Easy Versus Hard Issues

For voters, questions of public policy are hard issues in the sense that they require a certain amount of attention and sophistication. Many voters lack the political resources necessary to monitor and evaluate the candidates' policy proposals. Recall from chapter 3 that no more than a quarter of the electorate (sometimes less) can be classified as sophisticated ideologues who evaluate parties and candidates in left–right policy terms. But even if unsophisticated voters do not make judgments about the desirability of specific policies, they can evaluate candidates in terms of relatively easy issues. One example of an easy issue evaluation is whether a candidate appears to favor or represent the interests of certain groups more than others. This, recall from chapter 3, is a group benefit response to voting. Another easy kind of issue evaluation is to decide whether conditions seem good or bad under the incumbent or incumbent party. This, recall from chapter 3, is nature-of-the-times voting. Neither group benefit nor nature-of-the-times voting requires direct knowledge of either specific policies or what the candidates claim they would do if elected. But each allows the voter to cast a seemingly informed vote with a minimum of information costs.

Group-Based Voting Voters can orient themselves to parties and candidates on the basis of which groups they are for or against. In this way, voters must recognize which groups they like and dislike and learn the party with which each of these groups is aligned. No investment in determining candidate positions or the relative benefits from these is required. Group-based voting is voting on the basis of "ideology-by-proxy" (Campbell et al. 1960, 219–20). For example, a relatively prosperous citizen can learn to vote Republican simply by adopting the belief that Republicans favor the rich. In this way, our prosperous citizen votes the same as if he or she were able to develop a conservative ideology to rationalize economic self-interest.

Nature-of-the-Times Voting Still another voter shortcut is nature-of-the-times voting—evaluating whether times are good or bad (or will improve or worsen) and rewarding or punishing the incumbent party accordingly. Especially when little other information is available, the recent performance of the incumbent (or incumbent party) may be the best forecast of future prospects under a continuation of the existing regime. Nature-of-the-times voters may not have specific policies in mind, but they can throw the rascals out if the obvious signs indicate that it is time, in Angus Campbell's words, to let "a new bunch of fellows run things for a while" (1964, 755).[7]

The ANES regularly asks its respondents to evaluate the recent economy, asking whether over the previous year the nation's economy "has gotten better, stayed the same, or gotten worse." Responses to this question are usually consistent with vote choice. Typical was the pattern in 2004:

Vote	Economy has gotten better	Economy has stayed about the same	Economy has gotten worse
Kerry	12%	41%	78%
Bush	88	59	22
	100%	100%	100%
Percentage of voters	(26)	(31)	(43)

A full 88 percent of those saying the economy had grown voted to reelect Bush, while a slightly lesser 78 percent of the larger group who insisted the economy was moving backward voted for Kerry. With statistics like these, the economy clearly seems to matter on Election Day. Still, these numbers undoubtedly exaggerate the actual influence of economic perception on vote choice. One reason for the consistency between economic perception and vote choice in surveys is that respondents often respond to economic questions with rationalizations of their vote choice. For instance, a respondent who has signaled enthusiasm for the president may feel a need to praise the president's economy out of a need to appear consistent.[8]

So how did economic perceptions relate to vote choice in 2008, when the campaign was waged in the midst of an economic collapse? A full 91 percent of voters in the preelection ANES survey said the economy had "gotten worse," with only 2 percent insisting it was improving. The relationship between reported economic perceptions and the vote was as follows:

Vote	Economy has gotten better	Economy has stayed about the same	Economy has gotten worse
Obama	31%	43%	56%
McCain	69	57	44
	100%	100%	100%
Percentage of voters	(2)	(7)	(91)

In all likelihood, the few respondents who did not say the economy was in decline were mainly inattentive to the economy while basing their vote decision on other factors. Even most McCain voters had to admit that the economy was in trouble.

Candidate Evaluations

Still another important set of voter motivations has nothing to do with issues. We refer to voters' evaluations of the personal characteristics and leadership abilities of the candidates. Simply put, voters tend to support candidates whom they like and trust. Whether a voter likes a candidate may transcend policy differences or even overcome a strong party identification.

To examine candidate evaluations in the 2008 presidential contest, we turn to the open-ended evaluations of candidates. ANES respondents were asked what they liked and what they disliked anything about each presidential candidate. We score relative liking for Obama versus McCain by subtracting McCain likes and Obama dislikes from Obama likes and McCain likes. Thus, we end up with voters who appear to like Obama better, others who are neutral (offsetting likes and dislikes) and voters who appear to like McCain better.[9] Net candidate evaluations predicted 2008 votes as follows:

Vote	Like Obama better	Neutral	Like McCain better
Obama	96%	60%	6%
McCain	4	40	94
	100%	100%	100%
Percentage of voters	(42)	(24)	(34)

In terms of general appeal, voters were more attracted to Obama than to McCain and most voters with a preference in terms of candidate appeal vote for the candidate they liked best. Thus, the advantage in terms of attractiveness went to Obama.

Prediction and Causation

Policy issues, ideological identifications, group attitudes, retrospective evaluations, candidate evaluations, and party identifications all seem to predict the vote. The more variables we take into account, the better the prediction. To see that most votes can be predicted, let us simultaneously predict year 2008 presidential votes from the three best predictors: (1) party identification, (2) the ten-issue ideological scale, and (3) net candidate evaluations. We simply score each predictor as pro-Democratic, neutral, or pro-Republican, and sum them to make a scale from -3 (liberal Democrats who like Obama better) to +3 (conservative Republicans who like McCain better). The results are shown in Table 9.7.

Table 9.7 scores 9 percent at zero with balanced positions on the three predictors; these seemingly neutral voters gave a slight margin to Obama over McCain, 58 to 42 percent, evidently due to other factors such as concern over the economy. For the remaining 89 percent with a partisan tilt to their relevant attitudes, the vast majority—93 percent—voted in accord with the direction of their partisan attitudes. At the extreme, 40 percent of the voters found all three relevant attitudes in partisan agreement; they were either liberal Democrats who liked Obama better or the slightly larger group of conservative Republicans

TABLE 9.7 | **Predicting 2008 Presidential Votes from the Summary of Partisan Attitudes**

	Pro-Obama		Neutral			Pro-McCain	
	−3	−2	−1	0	+1	+2	+3
Obama (%)	99	95	87	57	27	6	2
McCain (%)	1	5	13	43	73	94	98
	100	100	100	100	100	100	100
(Percentage of voters)	(17)	(15)	(12)	(9)	(10)	(14)	(23)

Note: Index scores represent sum of partisan directions (+ = Republican, − = Democratic) on party identification, ten-item ideological scale, and net candidate evaluations. −3 voters are liberal Democrats who like Obama better. +3 voters are conservative Republicans who like McCain better.

Source: American National Election Studies, 2008 election data.

who liked McCain better. Of the 17 percent with clear pro–Obama attitudes, 99 percent voted for Obama. Of the 23 percent with clear pro-McCain attitudes, 98 percent chose McCain. The lesson to be learned is that when voters possess consistent reasons to vote one way or another, their votes are usually consistent with those reasons.[10]

We must be cautious, however, in attributing causal connections. Voters have a need to maintain cognitive consistency between their partisan attitudes and their vote. Of course, the obvious way to achieve this consistency is to vote according to one's partisan attitude. The problem is that when people decide whom to vote for, they may also rearrange their political attitudes to fit their vote decision. Once citizens decide to vote Democratic, for example, they tend to develop new attitudes even more favorable to the Democratic point of view. Thus, when a 2008 Obama supporter asserted the economy was in bad shape, that Obama would make a great leader, or that Obama was right on the issues, we might suspect that some of these attitudes are generated to support the vote choice rather than the reverse. Of special concern is the voters' need to maintain cognitive consistency between their issue stances, their perceptions of the candidates' issue stances, and their choice of candidate.

Consider the voter whose views are initially out of alignment—for example, the voter might have liberal views combined with an initial attraction to the more conservative Republican candidate. How this voter would resolve this dilemma depends on which of the three elements—perceptions of the candidates, policy views, and candidate preference—is the weakest link. If the voter feels strongly about his or her policy views and is certain the favored candidate opposes them, the voter could resolve the dilemma by reversing the candidate choice. This would be an example of policy voting. If the candidate's stands are only vaguely known, the easiest way out might be to shift one's estimate of the candidate stances. This process, known as *projection*, is a frequent way out of the dilemma. Voters who see conservative candidates as liberals or vice versa are often projecting their favored views onto their favored candidates (or projecting views they dislike onto candidates they dislike).[11]

A third possible resolution would be for the voter to change a relatively weak policy stance to make it consistent with the position of the favored candidate. Because of such *rationalization*, it becomes impossible to disentangle fully the causal process that produces a correlation between voters' policy views and their candidate choice. Consider, for example, the many voters in 2008 observed to be both liberals and Obama supporters. Presumably liberals supported Obama because they were attracted to his liberalism. But in theory, part of the explanation could be that liking Obama—for whatever reason—made his supporters think better of his policy positions.

Does rationalization seriously contaminate survey analyses of the vote? In an analysis of panel data from various electoral contexts, Lenz (2009) finds several instances of voter rationalization. One clear instance involved the issue of social security in the close 2000 presidential campaign. George W. Bush campaigned hard in favor of allowing social security recipients to invest their funds in the stock market; his opponent Al Gore emphasized the dangers of this approach, offering the metaphor of insuring the funds in a "lockbox." This distinction became clearer over the campaign, especially when the two candidates emphasized their positions in their first debate.

Over the 2000 campaign, voters increasingly became aware of the candidates' divide on the social security issue and their vote choices became increasingly consistent with their personal preferences on social security (Johnston et al. 2004). This of course is consistent with the notion that upon learning the candidates' positions, voters shift their candidate choice based on this new information. But no such shift occurred. Instead, Lenz found that voters shifted their positions on social security to become consistent with their candidate choice; Bush supporters increasingly saw the investment plan as a good idea while Gore voters saw it as increasingly risky. This was a classic example of voter rationalization, revising their views on issues to make them consistent with their candidate choice.

Every report of a relationship between voter attitudes and voter decisions should be read cautiously with an eye to the possibility that the seeming evidence of policy voting may be contaminated by widespread voter projection or rationalization. Still, we should consider the context. The social security example involved complex considerations—a "hard" issue—upon which most voters lacked expertise. Thus, voters rarely switched their candidate choice based on a candidate's social security spiel. The result would be different if the voter learning involved candidate positions on an "easy" issue like race or whether government should spend more to help poor and middle-class voters. Besides, we should remember that voters tend to stand firm in their candidate choice during a campaign. Thus, we should not expect that new information about candidate issue positions would change many minds. Partisanship in particular keeps voter choice grounded in their policy preferences. As a standing decision, liberals generally vote Democratic because their ideology leads them to the Democratic Party and conservatives generally vote Republican because their ideology leads them to the Republican Party.[12]

9-3   Explaining Election Outcomes

Explaining election outcomes requires a different level of analysis than explaining voter decisions. At the microlevel, analysts try to account for why people vote the way they do. At the macrolevel, analysts try to account for short-term forces and electoral trends—for example, why Obama defeated McCain in 2008, whereas Bush had won in 2004. In this section, we explore the sources of electoral change. We identify four sets of influences for our discussion: the electorate's partisanship, the economy and other aspects of government management, the relative attractiveness of the candidates, and the ideological (issue) proximity of the candidates to the voters.

Partisanship

As we discussed in chapter 4, the partisanship of the national electorate (often called "macropartisanship") changes over time, but usually in small increments. For most of the post–World War II period, the Democrats had a numerical edge over the Republicans in macropartisanship. This Democratic advantage declined in fits and starts beginning in the early 1980s and by the early part of the twenty-first century became virtually nonexistent, leaving the two parties in a state of virtual parity in terms of their allegiance by the general public. Starting about 2006, the trend switched again, with a new tilt toward the Democrats following the unpopularity of George W. Bush during the later years of his presidency. Future trends, of course, are unpredictable.

We have seen in this chapter that party identification matters mightily in the accounting of individual votes: Everything else being equal, Democrats usually vote Democratic and Republicans vote Republican. Therefore, the recent Democratic gains in party identification can only be seen as good news for the Democrats. The Democratic Party has an easier time in terms of winning national elections than it did in the recent past when the parties were at near parity in national allegiance.

We see the importance of macropartisanship when we turn to elections for the House of Representatives. For nineteen straight elections spanning forty years—from the 1954 to the 1994 elections—the Democrats won the most votes and controlled the most seats. During this period, the Democrats were the dominant party as the nation's "normal vote" favored the Democrats. With minimal short-term forces interfering with the national vote for Congress, a Democratic House (and almost always a Democratic Senate) was guaranteed. Following the forty-year Democratic reign, the Republicans enjoyed twelve years of firm but narrow control of the House (and, usually, the Senate), helped greatly by the more even division of the electorate's party preferences. The year 2006 ushered the Democrats back into control of Congress.

As discussed in section 9-1, for one party to hold the edge in terms of the normal vote is not necessarily a guarantee of electoral success. In elections for governor, for example, both the Democrats and Republicans are competitive in most states even when one party holds the edge in terms of party identification. At the national level, the Democratic edge in partisanship and the normal vote has not prevented the Republicans from winning their share of presidential elections. The lesson is that the dominated party can overcome its electoral handicap by choosing candidates and programs that appeal to the electorate.

Retrospective Performance Evaluation: The Economy and Wars

Recall that voters are often motivated by their reaction to the nature of the times—their personal evaluation of government performance and their attribution to the presidential party. The electorate's net evaluation of the nature of the times is partially captured by its evaluation of the president. Especially when the incumbent president runs for reelection, a useful electoral predictor is simply the incumbent president's popularity as Election Day approaches. An axiom of politics is that when presidents seek reelection, an approval rating above 50 percent (Eisenhower, Johnson, Nixon, Reagan, and Clinton) is followed by victory, while an approval rating below 50 percent (Ford, Carter, and the first Bush) augurs defeat. George W. Bush's approval rating was only about 50 percent throughout the 2004 campaign, and he won reelection only by a narrow margin.

As we saw in chapter 4, foreign policy helps drive presidential approval. Presidents gain popularity when they are seen as coping with foreign policy crises. George W. Bush's boost in the aftermath of 9/11 is the most visible example. However, prolonged wars (e.g., Vietnam and Iraq), prolonged crises (e.g., the Iran hostage crisis), and foreign policy folly (Iran-Contra) certainly do not help. It is a reasonable proposition that George W. Bush would have won a larger victory in 2004 if the fighting in Iraq had been contained or if the war had not been fought at all.

The perceived management of the economy is a particularly important aspect of presidential popularity. Beyond its effect on presidential popularity, the degree of economic prosperity is a key determinant of presidential election results. Prosperity on Election Day benefits the incumbent presidential party regardless of whether the president seeks reelection.

The effects of the economy on presidential elections can be observed directly. For thirteen post–World War II elections, Figure 9.4 graphs the vote (for the incumbent party) as a function of per capita income growth in the election year. Clearly, the more the election year growth in per capita income, the stronger the national vote for the president's party. It might even seem that all a president must do for his party to win the next election is to time the upward swings of the economic cycle to coincide with election years in the political cycle. Perhaps fortunately, it is not always that simple. Some presidents (e.g., Carter and the first Bush) have found themselves presiding over election-year economic recessions instead of prosperity. And the incumbent party does not win with great regularity anyway. Of the sixteen presidential elections from 1948 through 2008, the incumbent party won eight and lost eight.

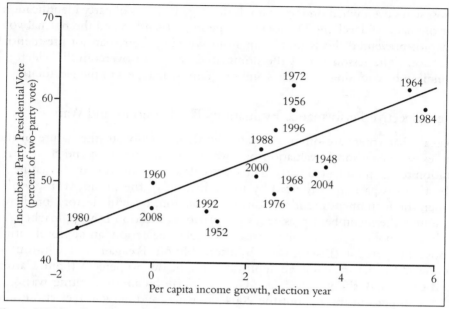

Figure 9.4   Presidential vote by income growth, 1948–2008.

Candidate Evaluations

One important source of changing short-term electoral forces is the changing cast of candidates. For election to any level of office, the personal attractiveness of the major-party candidates can be a decisive factor. At the presidential level, the electorate's attraction to the Republican and the Democratic candidates can vary dramatically from one election to the next. One set of estimates that are comparable over the years is generated from ANES respondents' candidate evaluations of the likes and dislikes expressed about candidates' personalities and leadership abilities. Analysts add the respondent's number of personal likes for a candidate and subtract the dislikes. The difference serves as a measure of the net candidate attractiveness to the respondent. Using multivariate statistical techniques, analysts have shown that these evaluations of candidate personalities and capabilities constitute a major determinant of electoral change (Stokes 1966; Kagay and Caldeira 1980; Erikson 2002).

Figure 9.5 presents a simplified version of these data. It shows the percentage who "like" each major presidential candidate better plus those whose net likes and dislikes are neutral, from 1952 to 2004. (Comparable data are not yet available for 2008.) By this measure, Republicans typically run the most attractive candidates, which helps to offset the one-time Democratic edge in party identification. The most popular presidential candidate as recorded by the ANES' likes-and-dislikes measure was Dwight ("Ike") Eisenhower, elected twice in the 1950s as the Republican standard-bearer. Eisenhower was a popular World War II general who engaged the voters with his warm smile. Early voting studies such

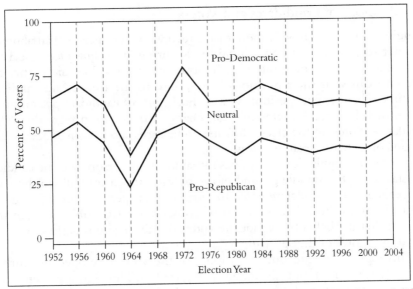

Figure 9.5   Net evaluations of presidential candidates (1952–2004) from ANES likes and dislikes of candidate leadership and personality. *Source:* American National Election Studies data.

as *The American Voter* (Campbell et al. 1960) emphasized Eisenhower's personal popularity to account for his easy victories following five straight Democratic presidential wins and the consistent persistence of a Democratic dominance in terms of party identification. The lesson was party identification matters, but personality counts too.

Most presidential candidates are favorably viewed by voters, but not to the extent that the 1950s voters "liked Ike." Two candidates who were viewed particularly negatively were Barry Goldwater (Republican in 1964) and George McGovern (Democrat in 1972). According to the estimates, each cost their party about 4 percentage points just in terms of likeability and leadership. Each lost in a major landslide.

Are elections greatly determined simply by which candidate the people seem to like as personalities and leaders? It is not easy to disentangle the electorate's collective reactions to the candidates' personal attributes from the candidates' ideological reputations. We saw that two of the candidates with the least personal appeal were Goldwater (Republican, 1964) and McGovern (Democrat, 1972). Were these candidates seen as unattractive because they lacked personal charm and leadership? Or were voters responding to cues from their political environment, as these two candidates were persistently vilified as ideological extremists during their runs for the presidency? Similarly, was Eisenhower's popularity due in part to the fact that his ideological imagery was that of a moderate? Was Reagan popular because of or despite his conservatism? It is to the candidates' ideological closeness to the voters that we turn to next.

Issue Positions of Candidates and Voters

Changing candidates provide more than a revolving set of personal attributes for the voter to judge. Each new candidate also brings a unique ideological tone and a new set of policy positions. Moreover, candidates (like the parties they represent) can shift their positions in response to the times. And candidates sometimes change their position as well. Each shift of candidate positioning or shift in the electorate's preference can change the equation regarding which candidate is closest to the electorate's net preferences and in turn affect the election outcome. Let us examine how.

Part of the popular lore of politics is that in a two-person race, the candidate who stakes out the middle ground of the political spectrum will win by virtue of appealing to the moderate voter. In terms of their personal views, candidates tend to be more liberal (Democrat) or conservative (Republican) than their electorate. Yet the belief that moderate voters decide elections pushes candidates toward the center of the spectrum.

This logic is spelled out in a model of the vote developed by Anthony Downs (1958, ch. 8) and illustrated in Figure 9.6. This figure presents voter positions as a bell-shaped distribution on the liberal–conservative spectrum. The Downs model assumes policy voters who prefer the candidate closest to their views on this spectrum. If both candidates are stationed near the center, as in Figure 9.6(a), neither will have the policy edge. But if one candidate veers toward one of the ideological extremes—as does the conservative in Figure 9.6(b)—then policy voters in the middle will support the opponent, giving that more moderate candidate the victory.

The Downs model predicts that Democratic candidates get more votes when they take moderate rather than liberal positions and that Republican candidates get more votes when they take moderate rather than conservative positions. These hypotheses have received considerable support in research on congressional (U.S. House and Senate) elections (Erikson 1971; Johannes and McAdams 1981; Wright and Berkman 1986; Erikson and Wright 2001; Canes-Wrone, Brady, and Cogan 2002; Erikson and Wright 2009).

Legislators create their own record of roll-call votes, which can be arrayed on a scale from extreme liberal to extreme conservative. Both Democrats and Republicans usually get ideological satisfaction from voting with their party's ideological extreme, but they gain electoral benefit from moderation. By one estimate, Congress members in the middle of the ideological spectrum generate almost 10 percentage points more of the vote than they would at their party's ideological extreme (Erikson and Wright 2009).[13]

Table 9.8 offers a simple illustration. Nationally in 2008, the major-party vote divisions for the House of Representatives and the presidency were very similar. The Democrats won 54.6 percent of the House vote and Obama won 53.7 percent of the presidential vote. We can compare extremist and moderate Congress members of each party to see how they fared in the 2008 election compared to their presidential ticket; that is, by how much did their personal vote margins exceed or fall below that of their party's presidential ticket in their district. For a Republican, the question is how much did the representative lead

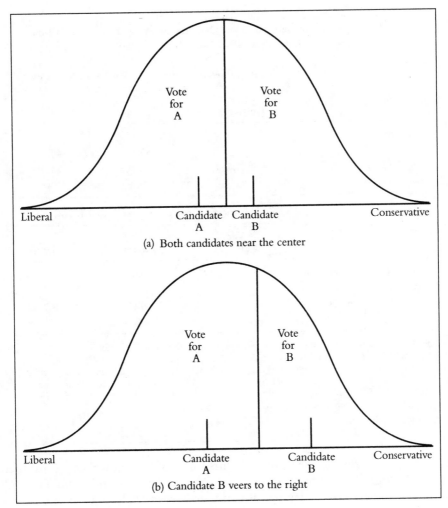

Figure 9.6   Candidate ideology and voter responses (hypothetical).

(or lag) McCain. For a Democrat, the question is how much was the representative's lead (or lag) over Obama.

Table 9.8 shows the data where for each party incumbent representatives are grouped according to the ideological tendency of their roll-call votes. The range for Republicans is from very conservative to moderate; for Democrats it is from very liberal to moderate. For each party, we see that the extremist members (very conservative or very liberal) enjoy slimmer leads over their more moderate counterparts. In 2008, the difference between having an extreme roll-call position and being moderate was about 10 points for Republicans and about 6 points for Democrats in terms of their lead over the party ticket.

Of special interest are the representatives whose roll-call voting record is against partisan type—somewhat liberal Republicans and somewhat conservative Democrats. On average, these incumbents represented districts that voted for the

TABLE 9.8 | Vote for House Incumbent Candidates (as Lead over Presidential Ticket) by Incumbent Roll-Call Ideology, 2008

	Republican Incumbents' Roll-Call Ideology		
	Very Conservative	Conservative	Moderate
Mean % for Rep. Incumbent	61.9	61.1	58.6
Mean% for McCain in district	58.5	55.4	45.4
Mean % Lead over McCain	**3.4%**	**5.7%**	**13.2%**
(*N* in parentheses)	(63)	(80)	(10)

	Democrat Incumbents' Roll-Call Ideology		
	Very Liberal	Liberal	Moderate*
Mean % for Dem. Incumbent	77.8	70.6	63.1
Mean % for Obama in district	75.0	64.6	53.4
Mean % Lead over Obama	**3.8%**	**6.0%**	**9.7%**
(*N* in parentheses)	(41)	(88)	(52)

Note: Ideology is measured as the weighted mean of the first and second dimension DW-NOMINATE scores, where the second dimension is weighted 0.35 times the first. This index measures the relative liberalism and conservatism of members of the House of Representatives and is based on their roll-call votes in 2007 and 2008. See Poole and Rosenthal (2007) for a discussion of DW-NOMINATE methodology. The cutpoints separating the ideological groups are -0.45,-0.15, 0.15, and 0.45. High numerical scores signify conservatism.

*includes eight conservatives.

opposition party for president. Typically, members of Congress vote against their party's ideological tilt only when electoral survival depends on it. And Table 9.8 shows that their atypical ideological behavior may indeed be necessary, as they gain far more votes (over their presidential ticketmate) than if they had voted typically for their party. For Republican moderates, we even see that although they tended to represent districts that went for Obama over McCain, they personally did almost as well as very conservative Republicans, who tended to represent safe Republican districts that went overwhelmingly for McCain.[14]

If congressional contests can be decided by candidate ideology, the same must certainly be true for presidential elections. We have already seen that citizens' votes are determined by their personal positions on the left–right scale. Presidential election outcomes are partially determined by both the voters' and the candidates' ideological positions—which candidates (and which parties) best reflect the preferences of the voting electorate.

To shed some light, we can examine ANES survey data. Since 1972, respondents have been asked not only to place themselves on the seven-point version of the ideological scale but also to locate the two major presidential candidates. Figure 9.7 traces the historical record, comparing the mean positions

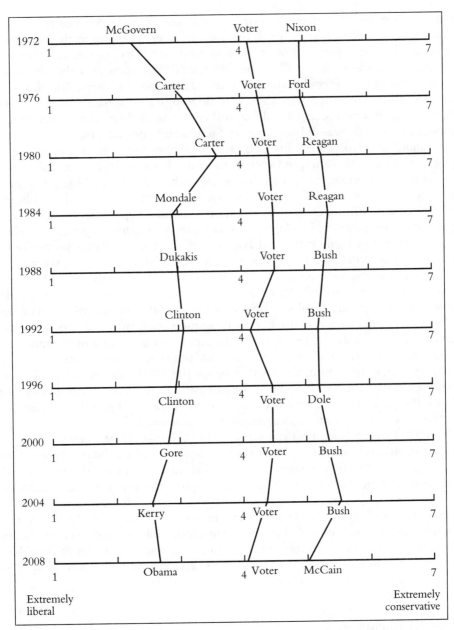

Figure 9.7   Mean ratings by voters of their own positions and candidates' positions on seven-point liberal–conservative scales, 1972–2008. *Source:* American National Election Studies data.

over time of the electorate and also the candidates as they are perceived by the ANES voters.

Of the nine elections shown in Figure 9.7, the 1972 contest stands out as one clear case where most voters were closer ideologically to one candidate than the other. In 1972, Richard Nixon was decisively reelected over the Democratic nominee, George McGovern, who most voters saw as too liberal. Figure 9.7 also shows that in elections since 1972, the average voter was close to the midpoint between the mean perceptions of the two candidates' positions. A close scan of the figure also shows that in all but one contest (1980), voters were slightly closer ideologically to the Republican than to the Democratic candidate. But this may be deceptive. Voters comfortable with ideological language tend to vote Republican and on average are about as Republican as their relative ideological proximity from the candidates suggests. Some voters do not rate themselves or the candidates ideologically in ANES surveys. Those voters tend toward liberal positions on specific issues, and vote Democratic. If we look at voter evaluations of candidate positions on specific issues rather than general ideology, they give the edge to the Democrats on some issues (e.g., abortion) and to the Republicans on others (e.g., affirmative action). Based on mean ideological identifications and perceptions of candidate ideologies in ANES surveys, Figure 9.7 presents a rather static portrayal of Democratic and Republican candidates' relative proximity to the voters over time. Greater volatility can be obtained by measuring voter preferences and actual party positions over specific issues. *The Macro Polity* (Erikson, MacKuen, and Stimson 2002) measures the rival candidates' proximity to the voters in terms of the ideological distance between the liberalism–conservatism of the party platforms and the liberalism–conservatism of the electorate measured by Stimson's mood. Perhaps out of necessity to overcome their numerical handicap, it was the Republicans who took positions closer to the voters for most of the elections from the 1950s through the 1980s. Starting with Clinton, however, the Democrats have been the more moderate party. According to *The Macro Polity*, ideological proximity is a powerful predictor of presidential election outcomes once the electorate's partisanship is controlled.[15]

In the final analysis, what can we say about the role of issues and ideology in deciding election outcomes? Most political analysts and candidates believe that ideological issues divide Americans and that voters evaluate the ideological positions of candidates when they go to the polls. Because issues and ideology matter, ideological mood swings by the public and the ideological responses of candidates and party leaders contribute to the relative fortunes of the Democratic and Republican Parties in American politics. Moreover, the belief that issues and ideology matter drives politicians to respond to changes in public preferences when they become visible. We examine how politicians respond to public opinion in the next chapter.

9-4 Conclusion

When the rational-activist model is fulfilled, elections are decided by voters choosing candidates on the basis of their policy views. By this standard, the record of recent presidential elections is mixed. Tracing back to the 1964 presidential election, Democratic and Republican presidential candidates have polarized on liberal versus conservative grounds sufficiently to give the voters a clear ideological choice. At the microlevel, many individual voters are motivated by the ideological menu when they cast their ballots. But they are also motivated by nonpolicy considerations. At the macrolevel, the electorate's collective reactions to candidate positions help shape their electoral verdict, but in conjunction with other considerations.

Apart from policy issues and ideology are additional determinants of the vote. As we have seen, people sometimes vote for or against the incumbent party on the basis of its past performance. One would find difficulty condemning this behavior as irrational. In addition, two important predictors of individuals' votes are their party identification and their evaluation of the personal characteristics of the candidates. To the extent that people vote on the basis of a party identification that is grounded in policy or ideological considerations (as when a staunch conservative is committed to the Republican Party) and to the extent that the candidates are ideologically typical of their party (see chapter 10), party voting can be viewed as rational.

But what about voting on the basis of the candidates' personal characteristics? One of the best predictors of a person's vote is simply whether the voter likes the personal qualities of the Democratic candidate more than that of the Republican. We may be tempted to view voting on such a nonissue (or even apolitical) basis to be voting on the basis of irrelevant considerations. But this view may be mistaken. Writing almost a quarter century ago, Morris Fiorina puts the question well:

> Various authors have suggested that voting on the basis of candidate qualities is irrational, or at least of lower order of rationality than voting on the issues. . . . Such suggestions apparently stem from the erroneous belief that attitudes toward the candidates reflect no more than Ike's smile, Nixon's beard, or Kennedy's accent. Actually, the bulk of the citizenry's impressions of the candidates focuses on qualities which are of legitimate relevance to the latter's capacity to govern: experience, leadership ability, and so on. . . . Why should a candidate's intelligence, administrative ability, etc., be any less a legitimate issue than where he stands on Medicare or aid to Israel? (1977, 618)

That voters choose the candidate they find to have the greatest character, competence, or trustworthiness is quite reasonable, even if their candidate is not the one that is closest to the voters on policy issues. Unfortunately, however, voters do not always have the necessary information to make good judgments about a candidate's character until after they are elected president.

The collective decisions voters make at election time contain elements of both stability and change. That most voting decisions are based on long-standing partisan loyalty adds an element of stability. Electoral shifts are normally only temporary because voters shifting toward the advantaged party or candidate do not change their identification in the process. Consequently, they may surge in the opposition partisan direction in a subsequent election, or even do so when voting in another contest held on the same date. Yet, it is also true that partisan loyalties continually evolve, in part due to the entry of new voters and the departure of old and in part due to partisan conversions (see chapters 4 and 5). In extreme, the change is sufficiently major to be labeled an electoral realignment.

The most recent such realignment period, centered in the 1930s, produced a change from a considerable Republican advantage in national voting loyalties to a long-term Democratic edge in party identification that has persisted until recently. If another realignment is on the near horizon, it could restore the Republican Party to the predominant position it once held before the New Deal era of the 1930s. Or, it could restore the Democratic dominance of the latter twentieth century. Also possible is a major change in the focus of the issues that separate the two parties but without any net change in the distribution of party loyalties. If any of these possibilities comes to pass, the public will have arranged its partisan loyalties as a long-term electoral response to the decisive issues of the day.

Notes

1. As for all data presentations from the 2008 ANES survey, the reported findings are based on the properly weighted sample.
2. In Figure 9.1, the normal vote is constructed as the prediction of the House vote by regressing the vote on macrolevel party identification in quarter three of the election year and then smoothing the trendline via the LOWESS procedure.
3. The reader might be curious regarding information level and the rate of switching sides during the campaign. As discussed earlier, only 6 percent of ANES respondents switched their presidential choice over the final sixty days of the campaign. The switching rate was only 1 percent among those high in political knowledge, but 11 percent among those in the lowest knowledge category. Clearly, late changes were mainly among the least informed.
4. The relative importance of the issues as shown in Table 9.3 is maintained if one predicts the vote from positions on the ten issues in a multivariate probit analysis. The two shifts are plunges in relative importance of health care and (less so) gay marriage. The probit equation estimates the impact of each variable, while holding the others statistically constant.
5. For more on ideology and the vote, see Knight (1985), Tedin (1987), and Miller and Shanks (1996).
6. The 2008 ANES ascertained perceptions of candidate positions on additional issues, which we ignore here on the grounds that arguably Obama and McCain did not hold distinctly different positions on them, particularly in the way the questions were framed. These four issues are a guaranteed job/standard of living and aid to blacks (on which the public saw itself more in line with McCain) and the environment-jobs trade-off and women's role (on which the public saw itself more in line with Obama.)
7. Zaller (2004a) shows evidence that the least informed voters tend to be the ones who react to the economy.
8. On voters' motivations for reacting to the economy, there is a long and extensive literature. See Kiewiet (1983), Fiorina (1981), Lewis-Beck and Stegmeier 2000, Duch and Stevenson 2008, Bartels 2008, and Erikson 2009 for various points of view.
9. In past editions where we analyzed earlier elections, we were able to separate responses to the ANES likes and dislikes questions into those that refer to a candidate's personal characteristics—from leadership and experience (e.g., "Bush is a proven leader") to personal characteristics (e.g., "Kerry cares"; "Kerry can't be trusted"). At the time of this writing, these details were not yet coded and available

from the ANES data. Thus, we caution that our categorization of candidate likes and dislikes in 2008 includes the full range of reasons, including matters of partisan attraction and policy. Also, at this writing we have only the information regarding whether the respondent offers a like or dislike for a particular candidate but not the exact number. Our like–dislike index simply sums the existence rather than the count of likes for Obama plus dislikes of McCain minus dislikes of Obama minus likes of McCain. Some studies have measured candidate evaluations from "thermometer" ratings of the candidates. Such ratings measure more than candidate likeability and perceived leadership ability and usually predict the vote so well that they may be considered surrogates for the vote decision. The result is the relatively empty prediction that people vote for the candidates they like best.

10. It has long been recognized that it is easy to predict voting decisions from known attitudes; for instance, see Campbell, Gurin, and Miller (1954) and Kelley (1983). The best statistical procedure for predicting vote decisions from multiple attitudes is via a probit equation. Some readers may be interested in the probit equation predicting the vote from our three attitudinal predictors. We estimated the probit equation predicting 2008 presidential votes (Obama versus McCain) from the seven-point party identification scale, the twenty-one-point left–right scale, and the five-point candidate effect scale. Using the McKelvay–Zavoina procedure for estimating a pseudo-R squared, the three variables together account for 81 percent of the variance in the latent dimension that accounts for vote decisions.

11. Projection, for example, can account for many of the instances of misperception shown in Table 9.2. For discussions on projection, see Conover and Feldman (1989) and Lodge, McGraw, and Stroh (1989).

12. Our discussion of voters and campaigns only scratches the surface in terms of the available literature. In addition to the literature cited elsewhere in this chapter, see Campbell 2008, Lau and Redlawsk 2006, and Hillygus and Shields 2008.

13. See note 11 for more on the estimate of House members' vote gain from moderating. The estimate of a ten-point differential is higher than sometimes found in the literature. For instance, Gelman (2008) sees the maximum gain in the single digits.

14. The findings of Table 9.8 are supported by a conventional regression analysis predicting the House vote from the district presidential vote and the member's ideology. Separate analyses area run for Democratic and Republican House candidates. Ideology is measured by the weighted average of the member's DW-Nominate score on dimensions 1 and 2, where scores on the second dimension are weighted 0.35 times as much as scores on the first dimension. (Although analysts often ignore the second dimension, it arguably has as much impact on voter decision making as do first-dimension scores.) The coefficient for (conservative) ideology predicting the district vote is 5.2 for Democratic incumbents and 12.5 for Republican incumbents (statistically significant at .08 and .001, respectively). Ideology scores have a range of 0.94 points for Democrats and 0.83 for Republicans.

15. In Erikson, MacKuen, and Stimson (2002), the median voter's position and candidate-party positions are measured on different scales—Stimson's mood and platform ratings by McDonald, Budge, and Hofferbert (1999). The problem of comparing apples and oranges is solved by treating both variables separately in a regression analysis predicting the vote. The more liberal the mood and more conservative the two party platforms, the stronger is the Democratic vote.

10 The Public and Its Elected Leaders

As SHOWN IN THE PREVIOUS CHAPTER, voters often use elections as a policy expression, as prescribed by the rational-activist model. Voters tend to reelect officeholders who show evidence of policy competence (e.g., presidents who produce economic prosperity or foreign policy success). Moreover, voters generally support candidates who are close to them in terms of their policy positions. By sorting candidates for office into winners and losers, voters do their part to achieve agreement between public preferences and public policy.

The degree of policy representation depends on the behavior not only of voters but also of politicians. The rational-activist model is one of five models of linkage between public opinion and policy that were introduced in chapter 1. In this chapter, we consider the four additional models by which public opinion translates into policy: the sharing model, the political parties model, the delegate model, and the interest groups model. To understand these models, our focus is on politicians and their relationship with the public.

By the sharing model, representation is achieved because politicians are drawn from the same culture as their constituents. By the parties model, Republican and Democratic politicians diverge ideologically to provide the convenient cue of party affiliation, allowing voters to vote rationally using their habit of party identification. By the delegate model, politicians are sufficiently fearful of public opinion that they follow public opinion in their policies in advance of the next election. By the interest groups model, politicians respond to public opinion when they respond to articulated interest group opinion.

10-1 Opinion Sharing Between Policymakers and the Public

In this section, we consider political leaders as a class. We ask how different they are from the general public. If leaders (elected officials) and followers (the general public) are essentially alike in their interests and preferences, it matters less whether leaders' decisions follow from their own preferences or from trying to satisfy public opinion. In the extreme, public opinion and leader opinion could be the same thing.

The simplest form of linkage between public opinion and the policy decisions of political leaders is the simple sharing of common opinions by followers and leaders. Consider, for example, the result if we elected members of the House of Representatives by lottery. Just as a randomly selected sample of survey respondents is representative of the general population within a certain margin of error, so would an assembly of 435 randomly selected people acting as a House of Representatives be representative of the population. If such an assembly could act without being distracted by the demands of powerful interest groups or the actual rules of Congress that impede change, then—for better or worse—its decisions would reflect public opinion. In actuality, the Congress (and other legislatures) is less representative than a random sample, if for no other reason than that members are supposedly chosen for their superior capabilities rather than their typicality.

How then do members of Congress and other political leaders differ from the general population? To answer this question, we must find the traits that motivate some people but not others to pursue a political career and the traits that favor success in achieving this goal. When people who are active in politics—whether as a local party official or an elected legislator—are interviewed, they often report that a spur to their political career was a politically active family. The consensus, based on several early studies, is that about 40 percent of the people who are presently politically active grew up in politically active homes. Thus, assuming only 10 percent of the public (at the most) are active in politics themselves, almost half of our political leaders come from the 10 percent of the nation's families that are most politically active (Prewitt 1970). Current evidence suggests that the influence of political upbringing on office seeking persists. In their recent study of the causes of political ambition, Fox and Lawless (2005) find growing up in a politically active family to be a major cause of interest in a career in politics.

Intense political interest alone cannot push a person into a political leadership role. It helps to be recruited by others. To contest an election seriously, the would-be political leader must attract the base of support necessary to win. In some cases, the political leader is a self-starter who, because of his or her political interest and ambition, announces candidacy and is then able to accumulate support. In other cases, the future leader is selected by the local business or party elite for the task of getting elected.[1]

Because the wealthiest and best educated people are most likely to be politically interested and articulate and have the visibility to be tapped for a leadership role, we are not surprised that these are the people who become some of our political leaders. Put simply, there is an upper-status bias to the political leadership opportunity structure. For example, as Table 10.1 shows, the occupations of the members of Congress are predominantly professional or managerial. In a society where only 18 percent of the workforce is engaged in such occupations, lawyers and businesspeople are particularly overrepresented in Congress. Lawyers and businesspeople are somewhat overrepresented in state legislatures as well.

TABLE 10.1	Occupations of Members of Congress Compared with the Public (2008) (in Percentages)		
Occupation	U.S. Senate	U.S. House	U.S. Labor Force
Farmer	6	5	1
Manager (business)	27	38	11
Teacher	14	20	6
Lawyer	59	37	1
Journalist	8	2	★
All others	—	—	84

★Less than 0.5 percent. Senate and House percentages include multiple listings.
Sources: Stanley and Niem, 2009. Table 5.4., Bureau of Labor Statistics.

Additionally, greater percentages of legislators are white, male, Protestant, and middle-aged than in the general adult population.[2]

In part, the overrepresentation of the affluent and educated in the councils of government stems from the middle-class leadership structure of the two major political parties. Even the Democratic Party—supposedly the more representative of the working class—draws its leaders from the middle class. By contrast, in many other democracies, the presence of a Socialist or Labor Party draws working-class people into greater political activity. Although Socialist and Labor parties do not draw their leaders exclusively from the working class they represent, they do at least open the door for the political recruitment of blue-collar workers, a door that is rather closed in this country.

The disproportionate concentration of political leadership skills in the hands of the better educated and prosperous may make the class bias all but inevitable. For example, delegates to Democratic National Conventions are better educated and more affluent than the general population, even though representative on the basis of race, sex, and age. Even movements of economic protest draw their leaders from the most affluent strata within the protest group. For example, Lipset (1950, 166) discovered that within agricultural protest movements: "the battle for higher prices and a better economic return for their labor has been conducted by the farmers who need it least."

The status bias to the leadership structure does not necessarily mean that the views of political leaders typify their class instead of that of the general public. For example, Democratic Convention delegates do not express the prevailing views of the economically comfortable. Still, a general consideration is that whatever their individual ideology, the generally affluent leaders might resist wealth-redistribution legislation that would work against their self-interest. For example, a study of the attitudes of national convention delegates (in 1956) found that one of the few issues on which delegates of both parties were clearly more conservative than the public was their resistance to making the rich pay a greater share of taxes (McClosky, Hoffman, and O'Hara 1960).

Of course, one could argue that virtually all political viewpoints found in the general population are also shared by some of the prosperous and better educated—and these might be our leaders. Those who run for office do not always represent the political views of their economic group. Thus, one can hope there is sufficient diversity of viewpoint among the candidates for office from which the people make their selections at the polls. And if not, there is still the possibility that electoral pressure can divert the behavior of political leaders from unrepresentative personal preferences.

We can try a direct approach to the question of whether political leaders and the general public share opinions by comparing the political attitudes of the two groups. In chapter 6, we already discussed one difference between public and leadership attitudes—leaders' greater support for civil liberties. For routine policy issues, however, only a few sets of data exist from which to assess the correspondence between the policy views of the public and its elected leaders.

One opportunity to assess the correspondence between public and leader opinion derives from CBS/*New York Times* polls that compare public and congressional responses to current political issues: in 1970 (by CBS) and in 1978 and 1982 (by CBS/*New York Times*). Examples for 1978 are shown in Table 10.2. For both the 1970 and 1982 surveys, the distributions of responses by the public sample and by U.S. House members generally differ by only a few percentage points.[3] Small differences between the views of the public and their elected officials were also found by Herrera, Herrera, and Smith (1992) in their later public versus Congress comparison and by Uslaner and Weber (1983) in their study of state legislators.

That the public and its elected leaders have similar opinions on a variety of issues may seem a surprise, given the differences of the two groups in income, education, and other background characteristics. The biases of leadership selection could have us expect that elected officials would share the opinions of the affluent and most educated rather than the opinions of the public as a whole. Instead, the

---

TABLE 10.2 | **Comparison of Public and Congressional Opinion on Selected Policy Issues, 1978 (in Percentages)**

	Public	U.S. House Members
Defense: In favor of decreasing money for national defense	23	26
SALT: In favor of SALT II	67	74
Health Insurance: In favor of "National Health Insurance fully paid by government"	47	45
Tax cut: Opposed to a "large federal income tax cut"	53	51
Abortion: In favor of "government paying for abortions for the poor"	41	35

Source: Kathleen A. Frankovic and Laurily K. Epstein, "Congress and Its Constituency: The New Machine Politics," paper delivered at American Political Science Association Meeting, Washington DC, September 1979.

apparent absence of bias in leadership opinions suggests that electoral politics works to weed out political candidates whose views are incongruent with public opinion.

10-2 Political Parties and Representation

So far we have compared politicians generally with the voting public. Averaged out, politicians might approximate a mirror image of the electorate. But this similarity can be misleading in that U.S. politicians come in two dominant and distinct flavors—as Democrats and as Republicans. In this section we look at this partisan distinction with an eye to determining the choice it affords voters.

According to the political parties model, party labels clarify the political choices available to the voters, allowing them to cast informed ballots with minimal search for information about candidates. Based on the history of their parties' behavior, Democratic politicians earn reputation as liberals and Republican politicians earn reputation as conservatives. These stereotypes then provide useful cues regarding what Democrats and Republicans will do once in office. This simplifies the task of the policy-oriented voter. Instead of monitoring each candidate's campaign statements and hoping they reflect what he or she would do if elected, the voter need only learn the differences between the parties and use party labels as a cue to rational voting.[4]

As we have seen (chapter 3), ideological considerations compete with other factors (such as family history) as motivations for party choice. Increasingly, citizens are polarizing ideologically, with liberals as Democrats and conservatives as Republicans. This trend is present when comparing aggregated constituencies as well as individual citizens, with a growing tendency for local electorates to use ideology as their basis of partisan sorting. Figure 10.1 shows this ideological sorting among states electorates as measured in the 2004 state exit polls. With exceptions, the most liberal states in terms of ideological identification also tended to be the most Democratic in terms of party identification.[5]

Just as individuals tend to vote according to their party identification, geographic constituencies tend to vote according to their net party identification. We can see this at the state level, as state electorates are strongly influenced by their partisan tendencies when they select their U.S. senators. Table 10.3 shows that predominantly Republican states (in identification) elect mainly Republicans to the Senate while predominantly Democratic states elect mainly Democrats.[6] Whether voters can achieve ideological representation by using party labels depends on the existence of actual differences between the programs of the two parties. Next we examine the extent to which Republican and Democratic leaders actually differ in their policy presences, in the programs they offer to the voters, and in their behavior in office.

Ideology and Party Leaders

In chapter 3, we saw that ideology is a modest source of partisan division between ordinary Republican and Democratic Party identifiers. Especially among those

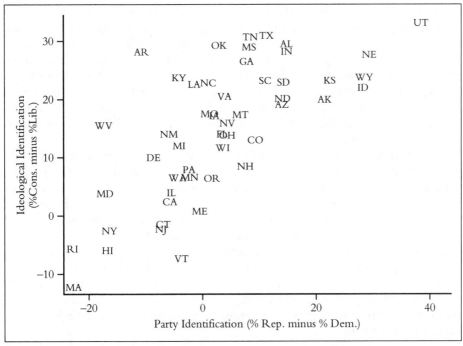

Figure 10.1 Partisanship and ideology of state electorates, 2004. *Source:* NEP Exit Polls.

TABLE 10.3 | **Partisanship of Senate Delegations by Partisanship of State Electorates**

Partisanship of State Senate Delegation, Post-2004 Election	Partisanship of State Electorate		
	Republican States (0–47% Dem., Macropartisanship)	Competitive States (47–53% Dem., Macropartisanship)	Democratic States (57–100% Dem., Macropartisanship)
Both Republicans	13	8	0
Split	5	6	2
Both Democrats	1	2	12

Note: Numbers in cells represent the number of states. Macropartisanship is the percentage of Democrats and Republicans in the state's 2004 NEP Exit Poll.

highly aware of party differences on issues, ordinary voters sort themselves ideologically, with liberals identifying as Democrats and conservatives as Republicans. Among political activists and politicians, ideology is an even stronger motivation force. When a strong ideology motivation spurs an individual to political activism, the individual usually develops an affinity for the ideologically appropriate party.

For instance, in studies of delegates to the national conventions going back to 1956, each party's delegates are more ideologically extreme than the party rank and file. Republican delegates are to the right of Republicans in the electorate and Democratic delegates are to the left of Democrats in the electorate (McClosky, Hoffman, and O'Hara 1960; Miller and Jennings 1987). In terms of ideological identification, Democratic delegates tend to be liberal or moderate, but rarely conservative; Republican delegates tend to be conservative or moderate, but rarely liberal. Table 10.4 displays these patterns for delegates over six sets of national conventions.

Political parties obtain their political energy from their activists. But while the classic role of party leader is to balance the ideological preferences of the activists with the pragmatism necessary for winning elections, party activists may be more concerned with ideological correctness than with electoral victory. Increasingly, with the decline of traditional party organizations and the growing openness of party conventions brought by reforms of party rules beginning in the early 1970s, ideologues have increasingly dominated party leadership positions. There is an irony here. As the leadership structures of the political parties have become more internally democratic, the potential for greater policy choice between the parties is created. This increases the conflict between the parties' policies and the preferences of their less active rank-and-file supporters.

Public Opinion Relative to the Public's Perceptions of the Parties

Here we examine party differences through the eyes of ordinary citizens as they perceive their personal positions in relation to the parties. As discussed in chapter 3, about one-third of the respondents in the 2008 ANES survey were scored as in the "high information" category, due to their recognizing Obama to the left of McCain on all five of the selected issues. For this group, who hold a recognition of the candidates' and parties' positions on the liberal–conservative continuum, we can place their personal issue positions relative to the two candidates.

TABLE 10.4	Ideological Identification of National Convention Delegates, 1984–2004										
	1984		**1988**		**1992**		**1996**		**2000**		**2004**
Ideology	**Dem.**	**Rep.**	**Dem.**	**Rep.**	**Dem.**	**Rep.**	**Dem.**	**Rep.**	**Dem.**	**Rep.**	**Dem.**	**Rep.**
Liberal (%)	48	1	43	0	47	1	43	0	36	1	41	1
Moderate (%)	42	35	43	35	44	32	48	27	56	34	52	33
Conservative (%)	4	60	5	58	5	63	5	70	5	63	3	63

Source: Harold W. Stanley and Richard G. Niemi, *Vital Statistics of American Politics, 2005–2006* (Washington, DC: Congressional Quarterly Press, 2006), p. 75.

We examine averages over five issues—liberalism–conservatism, domestic spending, defense spending, health care, and abortion rights. On each issue, 2008 ANES respondents were asked their own position, Obama's position, and McCain's position. Selecting only respondents who saw Obama to McCain's left on all five issues, we ask whether the respondent saw his or her position as, on average, to the left of both parties, to the right of both parties, or in between. (Those who, according to our measure, perceive their average position as perfectly represented by one party—e.g., seeing McCain as just right but Obama as too liberal—are scored with those between the parties.)

Table 10.5 displays the relevant data. Overall, slightly more than half of those who correctly order the major presidential candidates ideologically see themselves as between the Democrat on their left and the Republican on their right. The remainder are about evenly split between conservatives who see themselves even to the right of the Republican and liberals who see themselves even to the left of the Democrat.[7]

Table 10.5 also shows perceptions of candidate positions broken down by party identification. The most interesting groups are the "strong Republicans" and "strong Democrats." Forty percent of the strong Republicans were sufficiently conservative as to see themselves to the right of both Obama and McCain. Similarly, 30 percent of the strong Democrats (and even 40 percent of weak Democrats) saw themselves to the left of both candidates. The two parties need to satisfy these polarized partisans, but they also need to woo the portion of the electorate—mainly weak partisans and Independents—in the middle of the ideological spectrum.

Each party's strong identifiers are typical of the party's primary electorate. Activists tend to dominate low-turnout party primaries, with an important

TABLE 10.5	Public Perceptions of Their Policy Positions Relative to the Two Major Party Candidates, 2008					
Respondent's Perceived Position	Strong Dem.	Weak Dem.	Ind.	Weak Rep.	Strong Rep.	All Cases
Respondent left of Obama	30%	40%	17%	4%	0%	15%
Respondent in between the two candidates*	70	60	68	69	54	65
Respondent right of McCain	0	02	14	31	46	20
	100%	100%	100%	100%	100%	100%

*Includes respondents who see themselves in the same location as one of the candidates (11 percent).

Source: National Election Studies, 2008 election data. Based on respondent (voters only) perceptions of self and candidate positions on ideology, domestic spending, defense spending, and health care. Includes only voters who saw Obama (the Democrat) to the left of McCain (the Republican) on all four issues.

segment urging the party in a more extreme ideological direction. But to the extent the primary electorate chooses extreme candidates over moderates, the party risks alienating voters in the center. Each party's more moderate candidates may have the greatest chance to become general election winners, but they face the problem first in securing the nomination from a hostile primary electorate.[8]

And what of that majority of the relevant electorate who appear ideologically located between the two parties? These centrist voters seemingly face a distasteful choice of giving power either to a party that is too conservative or a party that is too liberal. However, these voters also have the opportunity to split their ticket, voting for a balance of Democrats and Republicans. The desire of moderates for an ideological balance of party power may help explain the frequent pattern of divided party control. Arguably, moderate voters should prefer the ideological balance of one party controlling the presidency and the other controlling Congress to unified control by either party (Fiorina 1992; Alesina and Rosenthal 1995).

The Relevance of Party Platforms

At national conventions every fourth year, each party devotes considerable time to spelling out the details of its platform in order to detail the party's official position on the issues of the day. Party platforms are often dismissed as mere ritualistic documentation because they are rarely read, quickly forgotten, and not officially binding on a party's candidates. Nevertheless, as research by Gerald Pomper with Susan Lederer (1980, chs. 7 and 8) shows, careful reading of party platforms provides clues to what the parties would do if they came to power.

Pomper examined the content of the Democratic and Republican platforms from 1944 to 1976. He found about half the platform statements to be relatively meaningless rhetoric ("The American Free Enterprise System is one of the greatest achievements of humankind") or statements about the issues that are too vague or broad to be meaningful ("The Anti-Trust Laws must be vigorously enforced"). About another quarter of the platform statements qualify as policy approval ("In the Nuclear Test Ban Treaty, we have written our commitment to limitations on the arms race"). Finally, about one-quarter are detailed policy statements like "The Security of the American Trade Unions must be strengthened by repealing 14B of the Taft-Hartley Act." Although people rarely read party platforms directly, platform statements reach voters indirectly "through interest groups, mass media, candidates' speeches, and incomplete popular perceptions" (Pomper with Lederer 1980, 152).

Of particular relevance is whether parties keep their policy promises once in office. Pomper finds that about two-thirds of the winning presidential party's pledges become at least partially fulfilled during the next four years. Somewhat over half the pledges of the nonpresidential party do as well. When both parties offer the same pledge in their platforms, the pledge is fulfilled in some fashion about 80 percent of the time. Pomper concludes, "We should take platforms seriously, because politicians take them seriously" (1980, 176). An analysis of more recent platform data through 2004 by Lee Payne (2008) finds that both major parties continue to act consistently with platform promises the vast majority of the time.

A statistical analysis by Ian Budge and Richard Hofferbert (1990) also showed the impact of party platforms. They were able to connect changing federal expenditure patterns to changing priorities in party platforms, particularly the platform of the presidential party (see also McDonald, Budge, and Hofferbert 1999). And the ideological messages in platforms reflect the party positions revealed to voters. The more moderate a party's platform (as opposed to representing the party's ideological extreme), the stronger is the party's showing in presidential elections (Erikson, MacKuen, and Stimson 2002).

Party Voting in Legislatures

Ideally, from the standpoint of the political parties model, the electorally dominant party not only would articulate a program that achieves voter approval but would also be in a position to enact that program once in power. The dominant congressional party, for example, would be able to enact its preferred legislation, particularly if the president is of the same party and gives encouragement.

As is well known, events do not always work out this way in the American political system. About as often as not, the presidency and Congress are controlled by different parties, leading to the potential for gridlock or stalemate. Even when the president's party is in the congressional majority, the president still has difficulty pushing his proposals through Congress. For instance, President Clinton was unable to pass his health care legislation in 1993 and 1994, even though the Democrats held a healthy majority in both House and Senate.

This discussion may seem to suggest that party labels are not relevant in Congress. However, that is far from the truth. In fact, party affiliation is the single best predictor of roll-call voting in Congress. By almost all accounts, the degree of party polarization in Congress is increasing rather than decreasing (McCarty, Poole, and Rosenthal 2006).

Figures 10.2 and 10.3 show visually the differences between the two parties' roll-call voting in Congress. Figure 10.2, for the House of Representatives in the 110th Congress (2007–2008), presents individual members' voting records along two dimensions known as DW-Nominate scores (Poole and Rosenthal 2007).[9]

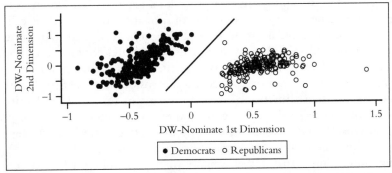

Figure 10.2 House of Representatives members scored on two dimensions of liberalism–conservatism, 2007–2008. *Source:* http://voteview.com.

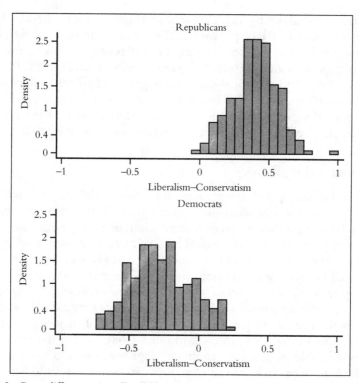

Figure 10.3   Party differences in roll-call liberalism–conservatism, U.S. House of Representatives and Senate, 2007–2008. Roll-call ideology is measured as the weighted average of dimension 1 and dimension 2 of DW-Nominate scores, where dimension 2 is weighted 0.35 that of dimension 1. *Source:* http://voteview.com.

The dominant first dimension is liberal–conservative ideology. It shows clear party differences where all Democrats (shown on the left side of the graph) are more liberal than all Republicans (on the right side). In other words, this dimension represents traditional left–right issues that divide the parties, such as the role of the federal government. It may exaggerate somewhat the parties' ideological differences because it captures in part procedural issues within Congress (such as voting on amendments) as well as matters of substance to voters. Roll-call voting on the second dimension is unrelated to party but still taps aspects of liberalism–conservatism. This second dimension captures congressional voting on certain issues involving civil liberties or reform, such as campaign finance reform. Fewer roll-call votes are cast on the second dimension than the first dimension.[10]

Because the first dimension is so dominant in terms of explaining how members vote on roll calls, the second dimension is often ignored in political science analysis. But because variation along the second dimension does appear to matter to voters (and to the representation process), we consider it here. A useful working assumption is that voters weigh Congress members' behavior along the second dimension about 0.35 times as much as they do their behavior on the first dimension. Thus, in the analysis below (and of voters' congressional voting in chapter 9), we compress congressional voting records to one dimension, but as a blend of one part dimension 1 and 0.35 parts dimension 2. We call it, simply, liberalism–conservatism. (In Figure 10.2, this composite score is the degree to which the voting record is distant, perpendicularly, to the diagonal line.)

Using our measure of congressional liberalism–conservatism, Figure 10.3 displays the distributions of Democrats and Republicans in both the House and Senate for the 2007–2008 110th Congress. Note that even when we allow the second DW-Nominate dimension to influence the ideology scores, there is little overlap between Democrats and Republicans. Almost all Democrats are to the left of almost all Republicans. Know the Congress member's party affiliation, and you have a near flawless idea of his or her ideological tendencies.

State legislatures show considerable variation in their degree of party polarization (Aldrich and Coleman Battista 2002). At one extreme, Nebraska elects its legislators on a nonpartisan basis, with the result being a noticeable lack of ideological structure to roll-call votes (Wright and Schaffner 2002). At the other extreme, some state legislative parties behave as disciplined units, resulting in parties even more polarized than the U.S. Congress.

In Congress, the source of growing party polarization is the subject of considerable debate among political scientists. Some say the visible increase in party differences reflects an increase in party discipline, as party leaders pressure members to support their position (Cox and McCubbins 1993, 2004; Aldrich and Rohde 2001; Aldrich, Berger, and Rohde 2002). Others say rather than the product of coercion, the polarization simply reflects the growing differences of opinion between Democratic and Republican activists (Krehbiel 1993, 1999, 2000). Resolving this debate empirically has been particularly challenging (Sinclair 1997; Krehbiel 2000; Snyder and Groseclose 2000; McCarty, Poole, and Rosenthal 2001; Roberts and Smith 2003). In any event, it is clear that the polarization of congressional parties provides voters with an ideological choice.

Party Labels as a Basis for Policy Choice

Although elected leaders from the Democratic and Republican parties differ ideologically, one might think this results simply because Democrats and Republicans represent distinct geographic constituencies rather than ideological competition within constituencies. What is required by the parties model is that prospective voters are provided a choice within specific constituencies. In this section, we examine the ideological choice provided by the Republican and Democratic parties at the constituency level. Our focus is on candidates in individual contests for the U.S. House of Representatives.

In U.S. House races, the electorate's choice is not between the typical congressional Democrat and the typical congressional Republican because (as we will demonstrate) congressional candidates often adjust their issue stances according to the prevailing constituency views. A liberal district is generally given a choice between a relatively liberal Democrat and a relatively liberal Republican. Similarly, a conservative district is given a choice between Democrat and Republican candidates who are both relatively conservative for their party. We are interested in the extent to which candidates at the district level diverge and give the constituency voters a meaningful choice.

It is no understatement to say that almost always, when a constituency's congressional candidates differ on important issues, the Democrat is more liberal than the Republican. For instance, a study of congressional candidates in 2002 found the Republican to the right of the Democratic candidate in all 168 districts sampled (Erikson and Wright 2005), with no exceptions (see also Ansolabehere, Snyder, and Stewart 2001). The expectation is that similar patterns would be found in most U.S. Senate elections (and for state legislature and most local offices).

A congressional voter has an easy decision rule for casting a partisan ballot: To help elect the most conservative candidate, vote Republican; to help elect the most liberal candidate, vote Democratic. When the public desires a more conservative or liberal Congress, it can simply elect more Republicans or Democrats accordingly. On the one hand, changes in the party composition of Congress are often attributed to such factors as economic conditions, presidential coattails, and Watergates—not to changes in policy preferences by the public. On the other hand, one can marshal statistical evidence that the over-time variation in the numbers of Republicans and Democrats in Congress is partially due to ideological shifts by the public (Erikson, MacKuen, and Stimson 2002). The mechanism of choice is available for the public to create a policy shift in Congress—and in state legislatures and other political arenas as well.

The Importance of Party Competition

The importance of parties is evident under circumstances when parties cease to play a major role—when elections are held on a truly nonpartisan basis, as in many American cities and sometimes for state offices. Reformers once saw nonpartisan elections as ideal because they weaken the role of corrupt political parties. But it is now generally believed that nonpartisan elections make it more difficult for voters to get their preferred policies enacted and to hold leaders accountable for their actions (Cassel 1986).[11]

When both major parties compete effectively for the electorate's favor, we would expect close elections. Sometimes, however, party competition breaks down and one party enjoys a monopoly. This has not happened at the national level since the Era of Good Feelings—which was around 1820. Often at the state and local levels, however, one party becomes so dominant that it wins almost every election.

In theory, the effect of strong party competition should be to enhance representation. With election outcomes uncertain, each party has an added incentive to woo the marginal voter who otherwise would be ignored. The opposite result occurs under one-party dominance. The dominant party does not need to make policy appeals to a public whose loyalty (or apathy) they have already won.

V. O. Key (1949) argued that the lack of party competition in the American South allowed the once dominant Democratic Party to ignore public opinion, with the result that the haves enacted public policy at the expense of the have-nots. There is, largely as a result of Key's position, a conviction among political scientists that parties become more responsive to public opinion when there exist two strong parties competing for votes. Until recently, the states had been moving more toward two-party systems, both in the South and nationwide. When the parties are evenly matched in the contests for control of governorships and state legislatures, this can only be a positive step in terms of the political parties model, yielding increased influence in the political process by everyday citizens.

Does Party Control Matter?

Readily following from our discussion, which party controls the levers of power can have important policy consequences. We have already seen that elected politicians do often turn party platform pledges into law. We can also see different policies under different types of party control. Liberal innovations in domestic policy, for example, are most frequent when Democrats control Congress and, especially, when the Democrats hold the White House (Kiewiet and McCubbins 1985; Browning 1986; Erikson, MacKuen, and Stimson 2002). Statistically speaking, unemployment (a major concern of the less affluent) is more likely to decline under Democratic presidents. And inflation (a major concern of the more affluent) is more likely to decline under Republican presidents (Hibbs 1987, ch. 7; Alesina and Rosenthal 1995). There is also statistical evidence that the income gap between the rich and the poor goes up under Republican presidents and down under Democratic presidents (Hibbs and Dennis 1988; Bartels 2008).

Of course there are important limits to the policy consequences of party control. The U.S. system of separation of powers and checks and balances slows the connection between policy proposals and policy enactment. For citizens with a radical perspective, the choices between the policies of the Democrats and Republicans can be viewed as merely slight variations on the status quo. If one's taste runs toward policies like government ownership of industry, legalization of drugs, or abandonment of the public school system, one will not be represented by either major party.

Actually, many see the major problem with today's parties as not the lack of choice but rather that they are too ideologically polarized. Faced with a choice between liberal Democrats and conservative Republicans, the moderate voter in the middle can achieve ideological satisfaction only by massive ticket-splitting. In theory, either party could gain votes by moving toward the center. But they do not do so, possibly because of the ideological extremism of primary voters or the parties' ideological reputations are so hardened that party leaders believe that voters will not respond to centrist gestures. Still, individual politicians sometimes move from the dominant ideological position of their party, moderating their policy positions in order to stay elected rather than pleasing their parties' ideological constituents. We turn to this aspect of democratic representation next.

10-3 Leadership Responsiveness to Public Opinion

When in office, politicians face the choice of pursuing their personal policy agenda or following the dictates of the voters who elect them. In this section we ask whether politicians, even as partisan ideologues, respond to public opinion in a way that overrides their own policy taste. When they do respond to public opinion rather than personal taste, they play the role of the people's delegate or agent. This is the delegate model at work. By this model, politicians anticipate the next election, responding to public opinion in advance of the potential fury of the voters.

Officeholders are driven by two often conflicting motivations: to win elections and to make good policy (as they see it). How strongly they respond to public opinion depends both on the relative strengths of these two motivations and on how strongly they believe their reelection goals are affected by their behavior. For instance, suppose, counterfactually, that voters are incapable of responding to the policy choices candidates present. If voters ignore what politicians do, even electorally sensitive politicians are free to ignore the nominal policy preferences of the public when they make policy. On the other hand, suppose, again counterfactually, that voters are hypersensitive to candidate policy choices, always electing the candidate closest to their views. If voters care only about policy choices, even policy-centered politicians are compelled to follow the public's wishes because that is the only way to win elections.

In truth, citizen attention is highly variable—on average somewhere between no attention and full attention. Thus, the responses of politicians—with their mixed goals of election and policy—are also in between. They try to follow public opinion but are also guided by their personal policy preferences.

For the delegate model to work, the representative must have an incentive to choose the public's preference over his or her own. While this incentive may be the representative's belief that following public opinion is ordinarily the right thing to do, more likely it is the representative's fear that electoral defeat would be the consequence of ignoring public opinion. For reelection to properly motivate, the elected official must believe the public is watching. The official must also want to be reelected. Finally, for the model to work well, the representative must know what public opinion is, a task made easier by modern public opinion polling.

Political Ambition

The belief that their reelection chances hinge on how well they represent constituency opinion will not influence officeholders much unless they care about being reelected. When officeholders retire rather than seek reelection, the fear is that they shirk their responsibility to represent constituency opinion (Rothenberg and Sanders 2000). As Joseph Schlesinger (1966, 2) described the positive functions of political ambition, "no more irresponsible government is imaginable than one of high-minded men unconcerned for their political futures."

Politicians at the top of the political ladder usually try to continue in office as long as possible. For example, presidents normally want to stay in office for their constitutional allotment of two full terms. Even Truman and Johnson, who both opted for retirement in the spring of their reelection years, did so only after the results of the first presidential primaries indicated that even renomination by their party would have been a hurdle.

Most governors (about 75 percent) also seek reelection when not constitutionally prohibited by term limits. Ambition also runs high for Congress members.

When up for reelection, about 80 percent of senators and 90 percent of House members try for another term (see Davidson and Oleszck 2002 for historical details). Even when Congress members retire, they rarely leave political life; most House members who decline to run again for their congressional seat do so to seek another political office or to serve as highly paid lobbyists in Washington.

Preoccupation with reelection is a persistent theme in studies of congressional behavior. Douglas Arnold (1990) claims that staying elected is the dominant congressional motivation. Kingdon (1973) shows that representatives aim to please constituency interests even on routine legislation, while Fenno (1978) finds that representatives spend much of their time in their districts explaining their roll-call votes to constituents. Mayhew (1974) argues that the structural organization of the House of Representatives is best understood as a collective response to the members' need to stay elected, while Adler (2002) shows how the reelection concern has thwarted reform of the House committee system. Of course the desire to stay elected is not the sole congressional motivation. Parker (1992) reminds us that representatives focus on generating safe reelection prospects to free themselves in order to pursue their policy agendas.

Promoters of term limits for officeholders argue that the continuous preoccupation with staying elected detracts from the policymaking function. One concern is that elected officials may overrespond to the less enlightened aspects of public opinion. As V.O. Key (1961a, 490) observed, "Public men often act as if they thought the deciding margin in elections was cast by fools; moreover, by fools informed enough and alert enough to bring retribution to those who dare not demonstrate themselves equally foolish."

Interestingly, the inclination to hold onto office for several terms is a relatively recent phenomenon. In the nineteenth century, House and Senate members quite frequently returned to private life after a term or two (Price 1971). This is the pattern in many state legislatures even today, particularly in states offering low legislative pay (Squire 1988, 1992). With variation from state to state, perhaps one-fifth of state legislators retire before each election (Jewell and Breaux 1988; Montcrief 1999). Many retirements actually are to pursue alternative electoral opportunities.

Having strong policy goals does not free representatives from electoral concerns. Surely, many politicians are strongly motivated to advance their conception of the public interest. But this pursuit of accomplishments only feeds their ambition for further public service, which requires reelection. This reasoning suggests the hypothesis that the political leaders with the strongest policy motivations tend to feel the most electoral pressure to satisfy public opinion—at least on matters that concern them least.

Following Public Opinion

The legislator's role is as an agent, serving the interests of the constituency. The classic question is whether the legislator should serve these interests as the legislator thinks best or should the legislator heed public opinion and follow the wishes of the constituency (the "delegate" model). Ascertaining politicians' concern about public opinion is difficult. As V.O. Key lamented in 1961, "We have practically no systematic information about what goes on in the minds of public men as they ruminate about the weight to be given to public opinion in governmental decision" (Key 1961a, 490). If we take seriously the reported attitudes of politicians and the public when they are surveyed, it would seem that neither puts much credence in the delegate model. When asked, politicians are more likely to claim they act in their constituents' best interests as they see them rather than by slavishly following constituency preferences (Friesema and Hedlund 1981). Similarly, citizens are more likely to claim they prefer their politicians to be of independent mind rather than asking them (the voters) what to do (Hedlund 1975).

Citizens and politicians alike claim to reject the notion that elected officials should follow the wishes of their constituents even if those wishes are contrary to their own. To be sure, many legislators would find it too humiliating to admit to being merely the voice of others. Indeed, most of us applaud the courage of the statesmanlike legislator who votes with his independent judgment rather than pander to the views of his constituency—particularly when we agree with that judgment.

Examining what elected representatives do rather than what they say produces strong circumstantial evidence that politicians follow district preferences (are delegates), at least in terms of broad ideological outline. Numerous studies have examined the statistical relationship between constituency opinion on one hand and legislative behavior on the other. For instance, Snyder (1996) was able to compare the votes cast in the California state legislature with constituency choices on several referenda issues. He found a strong statistical connection between constituency preferences and legislative behavior. For U.S. House districts, we have no direct measure of constituency opinion, although the constituency's vote for president is a serviceable indicator of district ideological preferences. For members of each party, district presidential voting correlates strongly with the ideological tendencies of the member's roll-call behavior; the more Democratic the district, the more liberal the member (Erikson and Wright 2001). Figure 10.4 shows this pattern for roll-call voting in the 110th Congress (2007–2008). Each party's most ideologically extreme members represent districts that voted one-sidedly for their party's candidate for president. Safe districts allow ideological voting, while competitive (moderate) districts require moderation of issue positions for electoral survival.

In the U.S. Senate, we can measure constituency preferences directly from the liberal–conservative preferences in statewide surveys. State-level liberalism–conservatism in surveys is strongly related to roll-call liberalism by the states' senators (Wright and Berkman 1986; Erikson 1990; Wood and Anderson 1998), even after controlling for the senator's party. Figure 10.5 summarizes this pattern for 2007–2008. For both Democrats and Republicans, the more liberal the state's opinion as measured by the 2000 exit polls, the more liberal is the senator's roll-call liberalism as measured by our DW-Nominate–based index of legislative liberalism. Thus, despite the general tendency for senators to be ideologically polarized by party, they moderate their views when faced with an ideologically adverse constituency.[12]

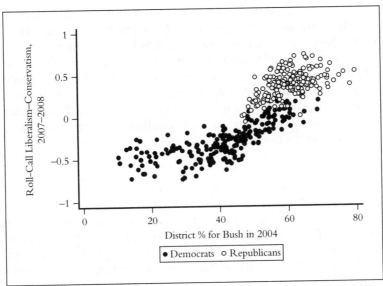

Figure 10.4   House of Representatives roll-call liberalism, 2007–2008, by district 2004 presidential vote, by party of representative. Roll-call ideology is measured as the weighted average of dimension 1 and dimension 2 of DW–Nominate scores, where dimension 2 is weighted 0.35 that of dimension 1. *Source:* http://voteview.com.

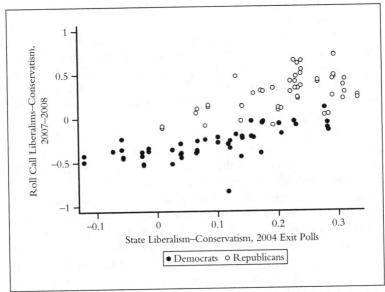

Figure 10.5   Senate roll-call liberalism, 2007–2008, by state opinion (2004 NEP Exit Polls), by party of senator. State opinion = percent conservative minus percent liberal in ideological identification in state exit polls. Roll-call ideology is measured as the weighted average of dimension 1 and dimension 2 of DW–Nominate scores, where dimension 2 is weighted 0.35 that of dimension 1. *Source:* http://voteview.com.

We can also find evidence of responsiveness to public opinion when comparing the paths of public opinion and congressional legislation over time (Erikson, MacKuen, and Stimson 2002). Controlling for the presidential party and party composition of Congress, Congress enacts more liberal legislation when public opinion (lagged) is in a liberal mood. Similarly, policy conservatism follows from public conservatism. Thus, the electorate's ideological mood not only helps determine election outcomes (e.g., electing Republicans when conservative); in anticipation of electoral sanctions, Congress also takes public opinion into account when it legislates.

Electoral Timing

The alert reader will notice the circumstantial nature of much of our evidence of responsiveness to constituencies. While politicians' positions correlate with constituency preferences (while holding party affiliation constant), there are other possible sources besides legislator attentiveness (the delegate model). The source could be simply the sharing of interests by constituents and representatives (the sharing model). The reason why each party's most conservative politicians represent conservative districts, for instance, could be that they are drawn from their constituencies and share their values rather than (or in addition to) a response to constituency concerns.

Not to be forgotten as a source of the correlation between constituency opinion and the representative's behavior is the rational-activist model, discussed in chapter 9. The delegate model—whereby representatives respond to constituency preferences—works best when voters are paying attention and ready to reward or punish their representatives at the polls. By voting into office the candidate closest to its collective views, an attentive constituency becomes the source of consistency between its opinions and the policy preferences of its representative. For instance, one reason there are few liberal Congress members from conservative constituencies is that the conservative constituencies usually reject liberal candidacies at the ballot box.

For the delegate model we would like a stronger test of responsiveness to constituency concerns. One test might be to see whether responsiveness increases with the approach of the next election. Another is whether or not politicians adapt ideologically when their constituency boundaries change. Here we examine evidence from state legislators and the U.S. Congress.

In a study of California legislators, Kuklinski (1978) assessed representation by means of the correlation between constituency liberalism (as expressed in frequent referendum results) and the legislator's roll-call liberalism. He found that California assembly members in the lower house—who face reelection every two years—show a consistent pattern of responsiveness throughout the years examined. For California state senators, however, who face reelection only every four years, the pattern is more cyclical; more responsive in the two years before election than in the two years after election. These examples suggest that representatives do respond to perceived electoral threats by seeking to better reflect their constituents' views as election time approaches.

The six-year senatorial term makes the U.S. Senate a particularly useful laboratory for watching elected leaders respond to public opinion. We might presume that senators act more constrained by opinion in their state late in their six-year term, as reelection time approaches, than early in the six-year cycle just after being elected. Democratic senators, whose personal beliefs are generally more liberal than those of their statewide constituencies, would act less liberal as their term progresses but then return to more liberal positions once reelected. Republican senators, whose personal beliefs generally are more conservative than those of their statewide constituencies, would act less conservative as their term progresses but then return to more conservative positions once reelected. In a study of Senate roll-call voting, Martin Thomas (1985) reports exactly these patterns. Both Democratic senators and Republican senators moderate their roll-call record as reelection time approaches. This is true, however, only for senators who seek reelection. Interestingly, Thomas shows that senators who do not run again moderate their views through the fifth year and then return to their original positions in the sixth year when the retirement decision has been made.[13]

With their two-year term, U.S. House members must continually try to stay elected. Although we cannot watch their behavior change with the election cycle, an opportunity is sometimes present to watch them change when their constituency changes. U.S. House constituencies change every ten years following the U.S. Census, as district lines must be redrawn to reflect population changes. Amihai Glazer and Marc Robbins (1985) have statistically demonstrated that U.S. House members respond to these district changes in their roll-call voting. They measure changes in constituency opinion by comparing the past presidential voting of the new and the old district. By this measure, when the House member gets a more liberal district, the member usually becomes more liberal; when the member gets a more conservative district, the member usually becomes more conservative (see also Stratmann 2000).

Legislators are not the only politicians who respond to the electoral cycle. Brandice Canes-Wrone (2006) offers a "conditional pandering theory" to explain the behavior of U.S. presidents as a function of the election cycle. For presidents in their first term, the closer to the election, the more their stands are consistent with ("pander to") public opinion. The tighter the reelection battle seems to be according to advance indicators, the greater the pandering late in the election cycle. If they succeed to a second term and thus become ineligible for reelection, the election cycle no longer governs a president's behavior (Canes-Wrone, Herron, and Shotts 2001; Canes-Wrone and Shotts 2004; Canes-Wrone 2006).

This latter observation reminds us that electoral timing works two ways. Politicians can move in the direction of their constituents when Election Day approaches. But if they plan to retire or become ineligible for reelection, they can move in the other direction—away from their constituency toward their party's extreme. Snyder and Ting (2003) have conducted the most rigorous investigation of this phenomenon, technically known as "last period shirking." They find that when Republican House members retire they shift to the right, whereas when Democrats retire they shift left. In each case this is what we expect from ideologically motivated politicians once liberated from constituency pressure.

Political Leaders as Educators

When we observe policy agreement between constituencies and their elected officials, it is natural to assume that the causal mechanism is public opinion influencing the officials' position. Consider again the dilemma of public officials torn between their personal beliefs about good public policy and the contrary sentiment of public opinion. Their options are not limited to following public opinion or ignoring it altogether. A tempting alternative is to try to educate public opinion about their point of view. When this strategy works, the opinion–policy connection is instigated by the politicians rather than the public they represent. Just as public opinion can influence politicians, so too can politicians influence public opinion.

Politicians who can influence voters toward their point of view enjoy a win-win situation. They win on policy and electorally. Lawrence Jacobs and Robert Shapiro (2000) document this educating behavior among the contestants in the battle over national health care in the early Clinton administration. Rather than pandering to public opinion, both supporters and opponents of national health care drew their positions based on principle and then tried to influence the public. (The opponents won the battle.) More generally, when we observe Democrats and Republicans challenging each other with ideological rhetoric, they are not pandering to the median voter's point of view; they are trying to shift the median position in their direction. That politicians engage in this behavior in no way detracts from the importance of public opinion in the electoral process. They try to influence public opinion precisely because public opinion decides their electoral fates.

10-4 Do Elected Officials Need to Follow Public Opinion?

We have seen that politicians apparently try to consider public opinion when making decisions—partly from fear of electoral retribution if they do not. Actually, one might suspect public officials do not need to weigh public opinion heavily in order to be reelected. Incumbent officeholders do not lose reelection bids at a rate that stimulates electoral anxiety. Furthermore, most people do not monitor their leaders' policy with sufficient attention to produce massive voter reactions. Could it be that elected officials have more freedom from public opinion than they realize?

Incumbency

Judging from their reelection rates, it may seem that elected politicians have little reason to fear the wrath of the voters. In the 1990s, 94 percent of U.S. House incumbents who sought reelection were returned to office. For U.S. senators, the reelection rate was only slightly lower (Davidson and Oleszck 2002). State legislators are also secure, with reelection rates above 90 percent—but with important variations among states (Jewell and Breaux 1988).

There are five clear reasons incumbents almost always win reelection. First, many elections are partisan contests, decided along partisan lines. Consequently, elections tend to favor the locally dominant party. Where one party dominates the other, even an officeholder with a low personal standing can win repeated victories. District lines for legislative elections are typically carved in a way that creates one-party districts that are safe for incumbents. Statewide elections are far more competitive than district-level elections, which accounts for the greater electoral vulnerability of U.S. senators and state governors.

Second, incumbents generally win because the status of incumbency gives them an advantage over their opponents. In U.S. House elections, incumbents gain 5 percent or more of the vote between their first victory and their first reelection attempt (Alford and Brady 1993). State legislators enjoy a similar incumbency advantage (Barry, Berkman, and Schneiderman 2000). The process that accounts for this incumbency advantage is not fully understood, but it seems House members and state legislators are able to exploit their office in terms of constituency service and easy publicity. Interestingly, the more visible U.S. senators and state governors do not seem to gain much of an advantage from incumbency status.

Third, incumbents generally win due to electoral selection. Candidates with strong personal appeal tend to win elections. Winners in one election tend to be strong candidates in future elections. So when winners seek reelection as incumbents, they generally do well due to their personal appeal. In other words, winning creates incumbency status in addition to the other way around.[14]

Fourth, incumbents gain votes by scaring off strong challenges. Potentially strong candidates tend not to run in elections they are likely to lose. Thus, potentially strong challengers avoid challenging strong incumbents, preferring to wait until the incumbent retires. In addition, the weaker candidates who do run against strong incumbents have few resources at their disposal, as potential supporters prefer not to concentrate their time and money on contests with little hope of success (Jacobson and Kernell 1983; Cox and Katz 1996).

A final reason why incumbents rarely lose is that anticipation of defeat makes incumbents more likely to retire. Candidates are most likely to retire when their reelection prospects are at a low ebb, due for instance to scandal or the prospect of a strong challenger (Fukumoto 2009). Representatives are most prone to retire when their party's national election prospects are at a low ebb (Wolak 2007). The retirement of vulnerable incumbents in advance of potential voter wrath helps lower the observed rate of incumbent defeat. Far more incumbents would lose if they were forced to seek reelection rather than take their graceful exit by quitting.

The electoral success of incumbents may signal both something wrong and something right about the status of representation. When elected officials are repeatedly returned to office because people vote for the dominant party or because people vote for the security of the familiar incumbent, they can act unbound by constituency opinion. Under these circumstances, representation suffers. But there is also a positive side. Part of the reason for incumbent success is that candidates who do things to please voters are allowed to stay in office.

Incumbents who represent their constituencies on policy issues are allowed to stay in office the longest.[15]

The Public's Attention to Policy Positions

To what extent do citizens react to the content of their leaders' policy decisions and policy proposals for the future? In the previous chapter we saw evidence of policy voting, particularly at the presidential level. But especially in subpresidential contests, the public's information is usually too low to allow the expectation of much policy voting. The best data in this regard concern people's awareness of the U.S. House of Representatives and their particular representative. Let us consider how visible House members' actions are to their constituents.

First, the local news media rarely gives much coverage to the roll-call stands of members of Congress or to the substantive issues of congressional campaigns. Consequently, even if more people had the urge to follow the congressional politics of their district, they would have great difficulty in doing so (Hutchings 2003).

Less than half the public can recall the name of their congressional representative. Similarly, at election time only about half claim to have read or heard anything about their representative in Washington or the opposing candidate. When interviewers probe to find out what respondents have read or heard about the incumbent congressional candidate, the answer is typically a vague reference such as "he (or she) is a good person," or "he (or she) knows the problems." In the National Election Studies, only about 15 percent express reactions to their U.S. House member in terms of positions taken on specific legislation (Jacobson 1987).

On even hotly debated congressional issues, few people know where their Congress member stands. Consider the following examples. After Congress's passage of the 1991 resolution authorizing the first President Bush to conduct the first Gulf War, ANES respondents were asked how their individual House member had voted on this contentious issue. Fifty-six percent correctly identified their member's position, while 30 percent got it wrong (Alvarez and Gronke 1996; Lapinski 2001).[16] In one of the biggest congressional votes of Clinton's presidency, Congress narrowly assented to Clinton's tax-raising, budget-balancing Budget Resolution of 1993. Following the vote, ANES respondents were asked about their House member's vote. Sixty-three percent reported their member's vote correctly on this highly partisan issue, while 21 percent got it wrong (Lapinski 2001). More recently, respondents in a 2005 poll were asked their representative's positions on a proposed constitutional amendment banning gay marriage and a bill banning partial birth abortions. The percent correct and incorrect were thirty-eight and twenty, respectively, on gay marriage and forty-eight and fifteen, respectively, on partial birth abortions. Assuming as many were guessing the correct answer as gave the wrong answer, still less than half knew their Congress member's positions on these important votes (Ansolabehere and Jones 2006).

Looking at these survey findings, one might well wonder whether the representatives need to pay attention to the views of their constituency when they weigh the alternatives of each legislative decision. As Warren Miller and Donald Stokes (1963, 54) observed in a pioneering study, "Congressmen feel that their individual legislative actions may have considerable impact on the electorate, yet some simple facts about the representative's salience to his constituents imply that this could hardly be true."

Indeed, we may have a major political linkage between mass opinion and leader response that is generally overlooked—although the public is not watching, leaders sometimes do what they think the public wants because they mistakenly believe the public is paying attention! If this is true, then leaders' responsiveness to public opinion would quickly evaporate once somebody points out to them that surveys show the public to be rather indifferent to what they do. On the other hand, maybe the politicians do not exaggerate the importance of their record to their electoral fate as much as the polls seem to suggest. Let us explore the reasons officeholders must tread carefully when they consider violating public opinion.

First, the high reelection rate of incumbent officeholders does not actually provide much security because the officeholder may want to win not only the next election but also several thereafter. Consider the case of U.S. House members, who have a success rate of over 90 percent per reelection attempt. Most survive their next election, but in the long run about one-third eventually leave office via an electoral defeat (Erikson 1976a). Such odds on long-term electoral survival can give House members reason to pay special attention to constituency desires.

Second, the easiest way for citizens to become aware of their elected leader's record is for it to be exploited by an opponent as a stand against public opinion. Therefore, although name recognition generally wins votes, lack of public knowledge of a political leader's policy stands may sometimes actually be a sign of successful representation. Put another way, if members of Congress became more casual in their consideration of constituency views—for example, if representatives of liberal districts started acting like conservatives and vice versa—the polls might show much more evidence of constituency awareness, and on Election Day, more incumbents would be defeated. David Mayhew explains it this way:

> When we say "Congressman Smith is unbeatable," we do not mean there is nothing he could do that would lose him his seat. Rather we mean, "Congressman Smith is unbeatable as long as he continues to do the things he is doing." If he stopped answering his mail, or stopped visiting his district, or began voting randomly on roll calls, or shifted his vote record eighty points on the ADA scale, he would bring on primary or November election troubles in a hurry. (1974, 37)

Third, one should note that there does exist a sprinkling of informed voters who shift their political weight according to the policy views of the candidates. Even if these alert voters compose a tiny fraction of the total, their opinion leadership allows them to influence election outcomes to an extent beyond what their number would indicate. As information about the representative diffuses downward from relatively informed opinion leaders to the mass public, many voters may "get simple positive or negative cues about the Congressman which were provoked by his legislative actions but no longer have a recognizable policy content," as Miller and Stokes (1963, 55) suggest. By responding to such cues, a significant number of voters may act as if they are relatively informed about their representative's record. As a result, the collective electoral decisions in congressional contests may be more responsive to roll-call records than our knowledge about individual votes would indicate.

In the previous chapter, we saw the result of this process is visible in election returns. Members of Congress lose votes when they take ideologically extreme public positions. Normally such vote loss due to policy stands is not sufficient for defeat, as the representative is often protected by a modest incumbency advantage and a one-party district. But the few who do lose can often blame their own policy stands for their misfortune.

10-5   Interest Groups and Democratic Representation

Public opinion is generally treated as a passive input for the consideration of elected officials, with politicians absorbing the costs of interpreting public preferences from polls and other indicators. But public opinion can take on an active voice when people try to gain attention by such actions as protesting, ranting on the Internet, and lobbying officials. Often people coordinate their activity so it becomes group activity. Then, politicians pay extra attention due to the power of numbers. At its best, this is the interest groups model at work.

Like the political parties model, the interest groups model allows for an intermediate agent (in this case, organized groups) between individuals and their government leaders. Group members need not engage in extensive activity themselves but can instead rely on their group's leaders and lobbyists to represent their interest. Members may be called on, however, to contribute to the group's strength by giving money, writing letters to officials, participating in demonstrations, or voting for the group's endorsed candidates. Elected leaders, according to the model, satisfy public opinion when they respond to (and anticipate) group pressures. To the extent the interest groups model is working, the influence of different interest groups reflects their membership and the intensity with which their views are held. When conflicting demands of different interest groups collide, the policy result is a compromise, with each side getting its way in proportion to the strength of its membership support.

Interest Groups Opinion as Public Opinion

By organizing as political interest groups, people take the initiative to get the attention of politicians. An argument can be made that organized interest groups facilitate the representation of public opinion. Policymakers want to be informed about public opinion so they can act without electoral surprises. Thus, they listen to spokespersons for the various groups with interests in the matter at hand (Herbst 1993). Without organized groups to facilitate their understanding of the varying interests of the public, politicians would be operating from ignorance. In the ideal case, the aggregation of group opinion represents public opinion.

Politically active interest groups include business groups (e.g., the National Association of Wholesale Distributors), labor unions (e.g., the United Auto Workers), professional groups (e.g., the American Nurses Association), issue advocates (e.g., the National Rifle Association and the Sierra Club), identity groups (e.g., National Organization of Women and Mexican American Political Association), and ideological groups (e.g., Americans for Democratic Action and the American Conservative Union). This diversity masks the challenge that the various groups holding a political interest do not face equal costs of organizing or enjoy equal persuasive powers when they do. In fact, the startup costs for group action are considerable, so the advantage goes to the groups organized in advance (Olson 1968). Wealthy and educated people gain an advantage in influence via the group process, with studies repeatedly finding citizens at the high end of the socioeconomic ladder belonging to more political groups than those at the low end (e.g., Verba and Nie 1972). The wealthy and educated gain a further advantage because officeholders tend to empathize more with higher status citizens. For instance, elected officials are more likely to attend to the concerns of business leaders than to those of advocates for the homeless.

Implicit in any discussion of interest group success is the group's power to dispense or withhold rewards to elected officials. The most obvious source of reward or punishment is the group's vote on Election Day. Yet it is not always clear that group leaders speak for their members' interests or whether their endorsements of candidates can influence voters (Lupia and McCubbins 1998).

Groups may lobby most effectively on issues outside the public spotlight. Generally, a group is successful if its goal would greatly benefit the group and cost little to others. Examples of such benefits include tax breaks, agricultural subsidies, oil import quotas, veterans' benefits, and land tariffs on commodities. Unfortunately, from the standpoint of the interest groups model, the beneficiaries of such policies are special interests that cannot claim to represent public opinion. Narrow but specialized interests have an advantage not only because they have a unity of purpose but also because the public is often not aware of their activities. Meanwhile, groups that depend on a large mass membership for support are often handicapped when their members become satisfied by public relations gestures and symbolic rewards (Edelman 1965).

Money, PACs, and the Electoral Process

Interest groups have additional political resources besides the power of the vote. For instance, they are often able to offer the government their technical expertise. Most important of all, interest groups dispense cash to finance politicians' campaigns. While most campaign contributions originate with individual citizens directly rather than groups, organized groups' Political Action Committees (PACs) play a special role in campaign financing by drawing money from their membership base, bundling it, and dispersing it to political candidates.

The role of PACs in campaign finance is widely regarded as giving too much power to well-financed groups at the expense of ordinary citizens. More is involved than simply the effect of money on election outcomes. The argument goes as follows. Contributors give to campaigns not as philanthropic generosity to the deserving class of righteous politicians but as policy investments. Otherwise, why would groups contribute so much to unopposed candidates or concentrate their contributions on electorally safe members of congressional committees that must vote on legislation relevant to the group? Although contributions are often given in gratitude for legislative support of the group's positions in the past rather than for explicit future favors, legislators can enhance their expectation of future group support if they support the group position in advance. Once they receive a PAC's support, individual legislators become even more receptive to the group's position. A legislator who votes against a PAC's interest can find its future contributions withdrawn or even given to an electoral opponent. Even when a PAC mistakenly backs the losing horse in an election, the PAC often recovers influence by funding the winner. In fact, PACs often spread their investment by contributing to both candidates in an election.

With reelection rates of over 90 percent, and with evidence showing that the money they spend in a campaign is rarely crucial to their reelection, we might ask why members of Congress could not boldly act independently of PAC influence. One argument is that politicians do not like to take electoral chances they can avoid. Certainly many politicians take PAC money without being influenced by it, and many others avoid all PAC money on principle. But there can be little doubt that PAC money buys access if not actual influence. Elected officials generally pay extra attention to the views of those who give them money.

Does PAC activity distort the political process in favor of groups with advantages in resources? Political scientists tend to be somewhat cautious in their conclusion because testing for statistical evidence of PAC influence is not easy. Scholars who have reviewed the evidence do see a tentative statistical pattern whereby Congress members give more weight to contributor opinion than their overall voting record, constituency preferences, and party affiliation would suggest.[17] However, one could argue that is exactly the pattern one would find if contributors gave to like-minded candidates, expecting nothing in return.

Although it stands to reason that people who give money to campaigns expect something in return (Snyder 1992), the statistical evidence suggests elected officials rarely take abrupt U-turns in policy in response to bursts of campaign cash (Wawro 2001). While corrupt deals undoubtedly occur behind closed doors, the evidence is elusive regarding the influence of political money on the ideological direction of national policy making (Ansolabehere, de Figueirido, and Snyder 2003).

Many informed observers doubt that significant reform of campaign financing would greatly diminish the overall role of interest groups in the policy process because organized groups would still possess the advantages of information, expertise, and direct monitoring of government officials—which the general public does not possess. The hoped-for change would be that a group's bankroll would play a smaller role in determining its degree of influence. When elected leaders respond to potential votes rather than potential cash, the different organized groups compete on a more level-playing field.

Interest Groups: An Assessment

Because the positions voiced by influential organized groups do not necessarily correspond to even the most strongly held views within the general public, the actual group process seldom follows the prescription of the interest groups model. If group activity were the sole input into governmental decision, the result would be a distortion of public opinion. The problem is that the group process results in some opinions carrying more weight than others.

Although some people obtain more representation from group activity than others, this does not mean that interest groups' freedom to operate in the political arena works against the public interest. A fact of political life is that some people—particularly the wealthy, educated, articulate, and already politically powerful—are in the best position to advance their political preferences. This fact is only made clearer when we examine the role of interest groups in politics.

One could conduct a mental experiment of imagining a political world where all interest group access to government officials is somehow eliminated. While the "special interest" would lose access, so would the spokespersons for the general public. Rather than wishing for the wholesale reduction in interest group influence, perhaps we should concentrate on ways to make the process of interest group access more equitable.

10-6 Conclusion

This chapter has explored sources beyond the direct mechanism of elections for additional linkages between public opinion and public policy. Four models were explored. The sharing model generates representation because politicians are drawn from the same community as their voters. The parties model generates representation because parties provide voters with an easy cue to cast rational ballots. The delegate model generates representation because elected leaders anticipate the need to please future voters. Finally, although it can lead to distortion, the interest groups model generates representation because the politicians' response to group interest can indirectly reflect the opinions of the general public.

A public that is not well informed gets its policy views represented by government, perhaps to a degree greater than it seems to deserve. In the next and final chapter, we assess the net influence of public opinion on policy in the United States, and we discuss possible ways to make the public's influence stronger.

Notes

1. In an early study of nonpartisan city councils, Kenneth Prewitt (1970) found many "lateral entrants" who were encouraged by friends and associates to run for office. In an early study of the partisan Connecticut legislature, James Barber (1965) identified many "reluctants"—serving not because of their raw ambition or political interest but because of the insistence of others.
2. In 2008, women comprised only 16 percent of both the House and the Senate. Nine percent of House members were African American and 5 percent were

Hispanic. The Senate contained one (1 percent) African American and three (3 percent) Hispanics. Only 5 percent of the House members were under forty years of age. No senator was under forty (Stanley and Niemi 2010, Table 5.2). Women and minorities are less likely than white males to consider political careers in the first place, even when they have the occupational stature that normally leads to political success. See Fox and Lawless, (2004, 2005).

3. Comparing opinions of the mass public with those of the elites is difficult because the results of the comparison can depend on the issues that are chosen. In 1982, the CBS/*New York Times* survey included questions about school prayer and a constitutional amendment to balance the budget. Elites appear more liberal on these issues because they are more aware of the complexities than the mass public, who treat questions about prayers and balanced budgets as referenda on God and the virtue of thrift, respectively. On the practical issues of what Congress should spend its money on, the 1982 mass and congressional samples were remarkably similar.

4. Ansolabehere and Jones (2006) find strong survey evidence that voters often use their Congress member's party affiliation as a cue regarding their votes on important bills.

5. As recently as 1988 there had been virtually no statistical relationship between state-level ideology and state-level partisanship (Erikson 2001). Much—but not all—of the change in the states has been due to conservative Southern states converting to the Republican party.

6. Table 10.3 uses the Republican year of 2004 as a base. In 2004, Republicans had the edge in most states and they held a modest majority in the Senate. Just as the Democrats gained Senate seats in 2006 and 2008, achieving a majority, they also enjoyed a corresponding gain in party identification.

7. For previous editions, we estimated voter positions relative to their perceptions of the parties, unlike the comparisons to candidates in 2008, shown here. (The 2008 ANES includes no questions about party positions, only candidate positions.) While in 2004 three-quarters saw themselves between the two parties ideologically, the comparable number from the 2000 ANES data was two-thirds. This mild shift is a sign that either voters are moderating toward the center or that the parties are (in the voters' view) moving farther apart. We suspect the latter.

8. Although the image of primary elections as driven by the preferences of ideologues of the left (for Democrats) and right (Republicans) is a common one, support from survey analysis is elusive; see Norrander (1989).

9. DW-Nominate scores can be obtained from the Web site http://voteview.com.

10. Figure 10.2 shows one outlier at the far right on dimension 1. This is Congressman Ron Paul, who contested the Republican presidential nomination in 2008 offering a libertarian appeal.

11. If nonpartisan officials are generally less responsive to public opinion, an exception to this conventional wisdom can be found in the judicial branch. Caldarone, Canes-Wrone, and Clark (2009) show that elected state supreme courts are most responsive to state opinion on abortion rights when they are elected on a nonpartisan basis. The argument is that nonpartisan judicial candidates must pander to public opinion, whereas partisan candidates are protected from scrutiny by the reputations of their party labels.

12. For the House of Representatives, the correlations between the presidential vote and our roll-call liberalism measure are .84 (all cases), .76 (Democrats), and .56 (Republicans). For senators, the correlations between roll-call liberalism and our measure of state opinion are .74 (all cases), .70 (Democrats), and

.56 (Republicans). Overall, our composite index incorporating dimension 2 as well as dimension 1 of the DW–Nominate scores correlates more strongly with measures of constituency opinion than scores on either dimension treated separately.

13. It is not only legislators who modify their behavior in election years to respond to an anticipated public opinion. Huber and Gordon (2004) find that elected judges (in Pennsylvania) rule more punitively in criminal cases during years when they are up for reelection.

14. The original use of the term "electoral selection" as a source of incumbent electoral strength was probably in Erikson and Wright, (1997). Zaller (1998) presents the analogy from boxing. Champion boxers generally defeat their challengers. It would be foolish to attribute their success to their incumbency advantage. Rather, their ability to repeat as champion is due to their skill in the ring.

15. For further discussion, see Erikson and Wright (2001).

16. Voter knowledge of positions on the first Gulf War was equally slim regarding senators and representatives (Alvarez and Gronke 1996).

17. Consider two classic discussions of money and politics. Jacobson (1989, 141) concludes: "Still, at least some [Congress] members, on some issues (those drawing little public or district attention) seem to vote in a way that reflects prior PAC contributions independent of ideology, partisanship, or local interests." Sorauf (1988, 312) states it this way: "The results have been disappointingly mixed and ambiguous. Some studies find modest relationships and an independent effect of contributions but others do not—an outcome probably the result of the different methodologies and the different groups and votes in the various projects."

11 Public Opinion and the Performance of Democracy

ACCORDING TO DEMOCRATIC THEORY, the health of a democracy depends on the existence of a politically informed and active citizenry. By carefully monitoring government affairs, citizens can develop informed opinions about policies that represent their interests. By working for and voting for candidates who represent their views, and by making their views known to elected leaders, citizens can collectively translate their policy preferences into government action. The resulting set of policies that governments enact represents a reasonable compromise between competing claims of equally powerful and informed citizens. This description is the democratic ideal. In this concluding chapter we assess the degree to which American democracy approaches the ideal and speculate about possible ways to achieve improvement.

11-1 Assessing the Impact of Public Opinion on Policy

We have discussed five models that have the potential to provide public policy consistent with what the public prefers. By voting for leaders who share their views, the public can fulfill the basic needs of the rational–activist model. If reliable voting cues are furnished by political parties, policy-oriented voters can fulfill the political parties model by choosing the party platform most compatible with their views. Aside from voting, people can influence policymakers by bringing the preferences of the group to which they belong to bear on officials, thus fulfilling the interest groups model. In addition, linkage between opinions and policy can be furnished by two models that do not demand public coercion of leaders. If policymakers try to follow public opinion and perceive that opinion accurately, the role-playing model is fulfilled. Finally, because leaders and followers share many political beliefs, the sharing model provides political linkage.

By itself, each of these sources of political linkage may provide only a small increase in the degree to which officials are responsive to the public. Their total effect may in fact be slight, as to show that public opinion can influence policy is not a demonstration that public opinion is followed all or even most of the time. Perhaps the evidence we need is some sort of counting of the frequency with which government policies are in accord with public opinion. A truly definitive study following this design would require information at the national, state, and local levels across a broad range of policies as to whether the process of political linkage results in public policy consistent with public opinion. We would want to be able to say which of the linkage models proves most viable, and on what issues. We would want to assess the consequences of linkage failure for the public's opinions about its government, for its participation in political affairs, and, ultimately, for political stability. Unfortunately, such a study does not exist.

Because presently available evidence of the frequency of political linkage is limited, conclusions based on it must be tentative—perhaps limited to the specific issues studied, the level of government considered, and the period involved. Moreover, congruence of majority opinion and government policy may not always be the best indicator of political linkage, as government decisions can be responses to the intense opinions of a minority rather than the preferences of the majority. Also, as we have seen, majority opinion on an issue fluctuates with the exact wording of a survey question. Keeping these cautions in mind, let us see what the evidence shows about the congruence of public opinion and government policy.

Evidence at the National Level

If acts of Congress were determined by the demands of public opinion, then Congress would act whenever public opinion built to majority support or higher behind a proposed program. Because polls do not regularly monitor opinions on specific proposals before Congress, we seldom know how much the public supports a policy before its enactment. However, polls can offer clues to how well Congress serves the broad policy guidelines preferred by the public.

Government policy on health care has been a major national issue for over half a century. The central event in the history of government health care was the passage of Medicare in 1965, extending government-subsidized health care to senior citizens. Medicare is a good issue for examining the connection—or its lack—between opinion and policy. As early as 1935, a presidential commission proposed a plan for national health insurance that would have provided universal coverage. In 1945, President Truman endorsed such a plan. Twenty years later, Congress created Medicare, a comprehensive health insurance plan, but only for the elderly. Why was there such a delay? One reason is that although most people favored government assistance, they were not insistent. For example, consider the results of an ANES poll in 1956 (when the health care issue was dormant) that asked people whether the government should "help people get doctors and health care at low cost" and also asked for an appraisal of government performance to date (too much, less than it should, about right, or "haven't heard yet what government is doing"). Although opinion was more than 2 to 1 in favor of government participation, only 30 percent said government was doing less than it should. The crystallized opposition—taking the position of both opposing government participation as well as saying the government either was doing about right or was going too far—made up only 15 percent of the sample (recomputed from Key 1961b, 269). Most people apparently did not have a coherent opinion one way or the other. Even when Medicare became a central issue in the 1960s, few were attentive. In a 1962 quiz of the public, only 57 percent of the respondents said they had heard of Medicare (then only a proposal) and had any understanding of it. In fact, only 7 percent knew the basic facts—that it would be financed by Social Security and limited to people receiving old-age insurance (Nadel 1972, 540). Only after Medicare became law in 1965 did most people become aware of its general provisions.

Perhaps if people had been politically mobilized by their views on medical care, Medicare or a program even more extensive would have been enacted much sooner. As things stood, the powerful American Medical Association was able to forestall satisfaction of a feeble-voiced public. In fact, neither Medicare nor its predecessors emerged from the House Ways and Means Committee in more than very diluted form until the 1964 Democratic landslide tipped the committee's balance in favor of such legislation (Marmor 1970; Jacobs 1993).

While the importance of public opinion in the enactment of Medicare remains ambiguous, we need to analyze more than a single issue. To develop a strong statistical argument that policy corresponds (or seems to follow) public opinion, we must find a consistent pattern of congruence over many issues. One form of congruence would be a pattern of policy changes usually following the direction of majority opinion. Even stronger evidence would be both opinion and policy changing in the same direction such that opinion change predicted a corresponding policy change.

Alan Monroe (1979, 1998) has examined opinion–policy congruence over the period from 1960 to 1974 and again from 1980 to 1993. For a variety of poll questions, Monroe ascertained whether or not the public preferred a specific change in national policy. For each issue, he then determined whether the public's preferred policy change eventually took place. His findings for the earlier period are shown in Table 11.1. On the seventy-four issues for which the public favored the status quo, the desired outcome of no change occurred 76 percent of the time. On the forty-eight issues on which the public preferred change, the desired outcome of designated change occurred 59 percent of the time. Evidently, the public is less likely to get its way when it prefers change than when it prefers the status quo. Of course, that the American political system tends to be status quo oriented has often been observed—that is, an intense minority (e.g., opponents of gun control) can often block change. But in either case, the public's preference becomes policy more often than not. Over all cases—preferences for change and preferences for the status quo—Monroe finds policy corresponding to public opinion almost two-thirds of the time. For the later period (1980–1993), the rate of policy correspondence was somewhat lower for reasons that are not clear.

In a related study, Page and Shapiro (1983) examine over 300 instances of opinion change recorded by polls between 1935 and 1979. They find a healthy

TABLE 11.1	Congruence of Policy Preference Among the Mass Public and Policy Outcomes at the National Level

	Preference	
Outcome	Status Quo	Change
Status quo	76%	41%
Change	24	59
	100%	100%
	(n = 74)	(n = 148)

Source: Alan D. Monroe, "Consistency Between Public Preferences and National Policy Decisions," *American Politics Quarterly* 7 (Jan. 1979), p. 9. Copyright © 1979 by Sage Publications. Reprinted by permission of Sage Publications, Inc.

correspondence between the direction of the change in public preferences and the direction of change in public policy. In the 231 instances where opinion and policy both changed, they changed in the same direction 66 percent of the time. Page and Shapiro do not entirely rule out the possibility of some spurious relationship: Political elites could educate the public on the policies they prefer and then convince the public of their merit. Support for the inference that opinion causes policy is strengthened, however, by the fact that observed policy changes almost always followed the change in opinion rather than the other way around.

The relationship between national opinion and national legislation seems to have weakened in the past decade or two. Monroe's 1998 report shows a linkage that is weaker than in his earlier 1978 study. Jacobs and Shapiro (2000) concur that the relationship between opinion and policy on specific issues has become frayed. A case in point is the relationship between opinion and policy on raising the minimum wage. (Because the minimum wage is not indexed, congressional action is required to keep up with inflation.) Polls consistently show decisive majorities favoring further increases, and until the 1990s, Congress would respond willingly. Then, eleven years, from 1996 to 2007, went by without a minimum wage increase even though Gallup Polls in 2001 and 2005 showed more than 80 percent of the public favoring an increase. When the minimum wage was finally increased in 2007 (from $5.15 to $7.15 an hour), it had been at its lowest in terms of real dollars since the early 1950s.

One important nuance about the opinion–policy relationship is that the public is most likely to get its way when the matter is highly salient. With passage of the 2010 Health Care Bill one arguable exception, Congress rarely passes major legislation without a plurality of support from the public.[1] One cannot say the same about legislation that is obscure. Burstein (2006) shows that on issues that are rather invisible to the public, the nominal views of the public as expressed in polls have little bearing on policy.

Recently, scholars have been exploring long-term relationships between opinion and national policy in search of statistical evidence of opinion influencing policy. Several positive results have been reported. The clearest evidence is for defense spending, with changes in defense spending seemingly following from shifts in public perceptions of need (Bartels 1991; Hartley and Russett 1992; Wlezien 1995b). Spending levels for domestic purposes also appear responsive to public preferences (Wlezien 1995a). Statistical evidence even suggests that Supreme Court decisions respond to shifts in public opinion (Mishler and Sheehan 1993; Flemming and Wood 1997).

Time-series evidence of an opinion–policy linkage at the national level can also be presented in terms of the electorate's ideological mood on the one hand and a composite of national policies on the other. As our measure of public opinion, we use Stimson's "mood" indicator of public liberalism. Recall (chapter 4) that mood represents a composite of trends over several survey questions regarding national policy. As a measure of national policy, we count the number of major liberal laws minus the number of major conservative laws for each Congress, 1953 to 2006.[2] Figure 11.1 overlays public opinion (mood) and policy (laws) over the last half of the twentieth century, revealing a connection between public opinion and policy. When public opinion turns more liberal or conservative, the index of national policy appears to follow: the more liberal the national mood, the more major laws in the liberal direction. And (although not directly evident from Figure 11.1) the passage of liberal laws lessens the demand for liberal legislation as measured by mood, while conservative legislative records raise it (Erikson, MacKuen, and Stimson 2002).

In Figure 11.1, one clear break in this pattern appears at the end of the time series. The G.W. Bush administration's conservative policies pushed mood in the liberal direction, generating a bigger gap than usual between mood and laws in the early twenty-first century. This pent-up liberal demand set the stage for the

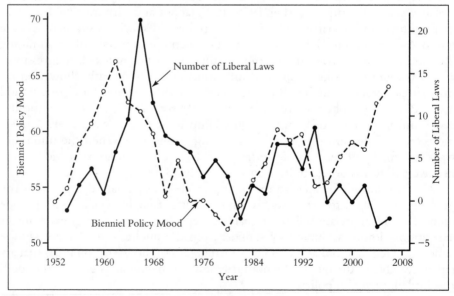

Figure 11.1   Public opinion (mood) and policy liberalism (laws) over time. *Source:* Updated from Erikson, MacKuen, and Stimson (2002, Figure 9.1).

election of President Obama in 2008 and the Democrats poised to pass a liberal agenda.[3] A first success was the health care reform act of 2010. The thermostatic response would of course be a conservative reaction and the eventual return to power by the Republicans.

Evidence at the State Level

At the state level, the opinion–policy linkage can be analyzed by seeing whether the policy preferences of state electorates are related to the actual policies in the states. One such approach is to compare the general policy preferences of the state (e.g., the population's relative liberalism–conservatism) to the general ideological tone of state policy. Another approach is to estimate the general liberal–conservatism of a state's population and compare that to the state's liberal–conservative policy outputs. For a broad analysis of state policy, Erikson, Wright, and McIver (1994) pooled several CBS/*News York Times* surveys from the 1976–1988 period. Pooling of several surveys provided over 100,000 national respondents and large samples within states. Their measure of state opinion is based on the ideological self-identification (liberal, moderate, or conservative) of the state samples. Their measure of state policy is a composite of eight policies with a liberal versus conservative content. They find a large correlation (0.81) between the opinion measure and the policy measure.

This relationship is shown in Figure 11.2, where the ideological tendency of state public opinion and the ideological tendency of state policy are seen to almost always go together. The most liberal states enact the most liberal policies, and the most conservative states enact the most conservative policies. Although we cannot be certain about the causal direction, these data strongly suggest that public opinion matters when states make important policy decisions.

Other studies have examined the relationship between state opinion on specific topics and state policymaking on that topic. Recent years have seen research on the opinion–policy connection in the states on specific policies—notably abortion rights (Wetstein 1995; Norrander and Wilcox 1999), capital punishment (Mooney and Lee 2000; Norrander 2000), environmental policy (Johnson, Brace, and Arceneaux 2005), and gay rights (Haider-Markel and Kaufman 2006; Lax and Philips 2009). These studies find modest to strong relationships between state opinion on the specific topic and relevant state policy.[4] And at a lower-level government, Berkman and Plutzer (2006) find evidence that local preferences on school spending influence school boards' spending policy.

An Opinion–Policy Connection

Although the evidence is certainly incomplete, the few relevant studies that test for an opinion–policy linkage suggest that public opinion is far from inconsequential. At the national level we find that opinion and national policy are in agreement more often than not. At the state level we find that state opinion can be a good predictor of state policy. These findings should not be surprising because, as we have seen, several linkages work to translate even feebly voiced public opinion into

Figure 11.2   State policy liberalism and public opinion. *Source:* Robert S. Erikson, Gerald C. Wright, and John P. McIver, *Statehouse Democracy* (New York: Cambridge University Press, 1994).

policy. This information, however, should not be cause for complacency about the current state of American democracy. Other forces besides public opinion shape government decisions—and we must keep in mind that collective public opinion at best moves incrementally and is often simply uniformed.[5]

We should of course be wary of assigning the United States an inflated grade for its current level of responsiveness to public opinion. It is sometimes suggested that observed correlations between public opinion and policy are not what they seem. In some instances when the electorate's preferences are statistically related to policy outcomes, it is conceivable that the true causal connection is reversed—that is, that politicians are educating the public rather than the public influencing the politicians (Page 2002; Hurley and Hill 2003). Certainly the political and economic leadership—the elite—play a role in shaping public opinion. To contend that public opinion influences policy does not require that the driving force of politics must be some sort of populist will of the masses that arises independent of elite influence. When public opinion changes course, it usually follows the lead of elite discourse. A case in point is public attitudes toward homosexuality and gay rights. Over recent decades, public opinion became increasingly acceptant and legislation proliferated to advance the rights of homosexuals. There is no doubt that it took a shift in elite opinion to drive the public's growing tolerance toward homosexuality (Zaller 1992). But there can also be no doubt that public opinion sets the limits on how far policy will go in terms of advancing the agenda of the gay rights movement.

Do all Opinions Count Equally?

Although legislators' policy positions are highly predictable from constituency opinion (chapter 10) and that policy direction is often predictable from public opinion (here in chapter 11), we must ask whether this is evidence that elected politicians respond to public opinion generally, or just to a selected few. In other words, all opinions may not count equally. As we saw in chapter 3, the opinions of the informed are often different from those of the less informed. These informed opinions are likely to have disproportionate influence, which of course means that many are underrepresented (Althaus 2003). Those with "no opinion" in surveys may be the most powerless of all (Berinsky 2004). As we saw in chapter 9, it is the most informed about and interested in politics who vote and cast votes based on issues. As we saw in chapter 10, politicians listen to these voices to stay elected. According to one recent study, despite strong statistical evidence that the opinions of a state's voters influence its senators' roll-call behavior, senators appear to ignore the views of their states' nonvoters (Griffin and Newman 2005).

The considerable attention has been focused on the gap between the political influence of the rich and the poor. In addition to the advantage that the affluent have over the poor in terms of political information, they also have greater access to elected leaders. Politicians listen to those who finance their campaigns, and of course campaign contributors are wealthier than others. And politicians listen most attentively to people like themselves, which usually means the affluent.

Based on a detailed analysis of state public opinion and Senate roll-call voting, Bartels (2008) has compared the responsiveness of senators to their constituents at different income levels. He finds that senators respond more to the views of the rich than to those of the poor. In an ambitious study, Gilens (2005, 2010) compares the preferences found in almost two thousand opinion polls with subsequent policy outcomes—except that he performs this exercise separately for respondents at different income levels. He finds that the richer are more likely to receive their desired policy changes. Similarly, at the state level, Rigby and Wright (2010) find that policy responds more to the views of the affluent than those less well off. And on foreign policy, a domain where the influence of public opinion has been understudied, Jacobs and Page (2005) find that the influential voices are those of business leaders and other elites—and not public opinion at all.

Other statistical analyses find less evidence of unequal representation across income groups (Ura and Ellis 2008; Bhatti and Erikson 2010; Enns and Wlezien 2010; Stimson 2010). One challenge is that opinions of the rich and the poor are often similar and move in tandem, making their effects hard to disentangle. The truth might be that by attending to the rich, the politicians do not depart much from the wishes of the poor. If so, the puzzle shifts. The usual assumption is that the poor would demand more liberal policies, particularly those that involve some redistribution of resources. But, as we saw in chapter 7, the income divide in terms of policy preferences is weaker than one might think. From the perspective of the political left, the first question is why don't the poor understand their own political interests? Second, what can be done to awaken them sufficiently that the politicians heed their views?.

11-2 Interpreting the Public's Role in Democracy

As we have seen throughout this book, the public generally does not live up to its prescribed activist role. Moreover, while public opinion can often influence government policy, in reality it is not the sole determinant of policy outcomes. Why not? Public control of government decisions depends on both the extent to which people actually participate in politics and the equality of people's resources for effective participation. The first point is obvious: It seems logical that the more people participate in politics, the more they can influence government decisions. But some people can participate more effectively than others because they command a greater share of the necessary resources, such as money, information, articulateness, and access to decision makers. How inequitable one views the distribution of these political resources can determine one's view of how democratic the political system actually is. Some observers see effective political power concentrated in the hands of an elite that controls policy outcomes for its own interests. Others more optimistically see the inequality in the distribution of power limited basically to the different political skills that individuals have and their interest in using them.[6] Because this debate over the equality of the distribution of political power is not easily decided by scientific inquiry, we do not enter it directly here. But, taking into account that the tools of effective political participation are not equally distributed, how can we assess the less than active political role of the public? We discuss four plausible conclusions.

Public Apathy as Mass Political Incompetence

Perhaps the easiest view of the public's limited role in government affairs is that people are simply incapable of doing better. The frequency with which people fail to hold political opinions, the rarity of the liberal or conservative ideologue, and the difficulty in locating rational policy-oriented voters may all indicate that people generally lack the skills necessary to make sophisticated judgments about their political leaders and policies. Worse yet, the political views that people do hold may be intolerant, naive, or simply wrong. Viewed from this perspective, an increase in public participation would only make the situation worse because "bad" public opinion would drive "good" policymakers toward undesirable acts.

If the mass public is viewed as being inherently incapable of playing a useful role, then the remedy of trying to uplift public opinion becomes ineffective. Instead, one might have to rely on the proper training or careful recruitment of political leaders as a means of producing desired outcomes. If such desired outcomes include the preservation of the substance of democracy, then one must prescribe both a limited public role and the instillation of a heavy dose of democratic values among political elites. Thomas Dye and Harmon Ziegler (2009), who arrive at this position, call it the "irony of democracy."

Public Apathy as Rational Disengagement

Possibly the reason most people do not allow politics to intrude far into their lives is that to do so would be irrational. From a strict cost-benefit standpoint, one should not follow public affairs closely because the investment would get one nowhere. One person's vote is useless because it is fantasy to assume that a single vote can decide an election's outcome except in the most extraordinary circumstances. Even when an individual's economic interest is directly at stake in the political arena (which may be rare), organizing like-minded people for collective political pressure is irrational because the costs of organization outweigh the possible benefits one could expect (Olson 1968). The cynic might also suggest that increased public knowledge of governmental affairs would produce only greater political withdrawal, as people who learn about their leaders' corruption and unresponsiveness would feel even more helpless at the prospect of changing things.

If this logic is correct, then people who participate in politics are usually motivated by something other than tangible personal gains. Perhaps they "irrationally" participate in order to gratify a felt obligation or civic duty. If the major determinant of an individual's sense of obligation to participate is preadult political socialization, then a reformer might hope to increase public participation by improving the training of the next generation of citizens. Alternatively, one might hope to eliminate rational withdrawal from politics by somehow increasing the rewards of political participation.

Public Apathy as Elite Manipulation

One can also interpret the public's low participation in politics as the result of manipulation by leaders and their allies (Domhoff 2002; Page 2002). When one observes political docility on the part of people who seemingly should have strong reasons for political protest, one can easily draw the conclusion that the individuals are being misled by elite propaganda. By this view, people are quiet and content because a ruling elite distracts them with bread and circuses.

One need not believe in a complex conspiracy in order to view political quiescence as the result of elite manipulation. Because most political events are remote from people's everyday lives, people willingly view these events through the interpretation of their leaders. Also, because people want to believe their political system is benign rather than corrupt or evil, they readily find reassurance from optimistic interpretations of the existing order and resist the voices that tell them otherwise (Edelman 1965).

If one sees people as unwilling to accept the "truth" because they do not want to disturb their cherished beliefs, the obvious remedy would appear to be heavy doses of correct information. But how to make this remedy effective remains unclear.

Public Apathy as Public Contentment

Rather than viewing public apathy as a sign that the classical democratic model does not hold, one can interpret apathy as an indicator of public contentment. If people do not concern themselves with political matters, then they must not have any additional demands to make on their government. Conversely, when many people do participate in politics, it is a distressing signal either that government has ignored public needs or that conflicts between societal groups are no longer being successfully resolved by political leaders.

Actually, the view that public apathy means public satisfaction rests on the assumption that the public is rather politically sophisticated. It assumes that people are capable of articulating grievances, that they feel their expression of grievance would be effective, and that they are not easily led to ignore their interests. Only if these assumptions are made can one conclude that the lack of political participation indicates that people's needs are met by the proper working of a democratic system.

Evaluation

Although they contradict one another, each of these four possible explanations of the public's lack of political participation contains a grain of truth. For example, the public may not be capable of participation in all government decisions, particularly when the decision depends on proper evaluation of advanced technical knowledge. Equally obvious is that people can take only limited time from their personal affairs to participate in politics. Moreover, people may decide not to participate because they feel (perhaps mistakenly) they can trust their political leaders. Finally, people may retire from the political arena because they indeed have no grievances.

Simply holding them up to the light of scientific evidence cannot determine which of the explanations of low participation in politics is most valid, as individual observers will view the evidence through the filter of their own preconceptions and values. How observers view such matters as human nature, people's basic interest, and the benevolence of government can shape how strongly they conclude that political inactivity signifies incapability, rational withdrawal, manipulation, or contentment. Similarly, the extent to which observers see their own opinion in harmony with majority opinion might influence their views of whether public control of government should increase or decrease.

11-3 The Expansion of Political Participation

Whether or not increased public political participation is desirable also depends on the type of political participation. Few would applaud increased mass participation that results in civil war or mass mobilization in support of an antidemocratic movement. But few would fear an increase in informed, democratic participation—particularly if we ignore possible disagreement over what *informed democratic participation* means. When there is little mass participation, the burden of responsibility falls on the political elites—both to ensure the continuation of the democratic rules and also to make policy decisions that are fair and equitable. But if one agrees that the purpose of democracy is to ensure political leaders are held accountable to the people, one can hardly applaud when people do not actively seek to protect their own interests. Are there ways to increase the number of active participants while at the same time ensuring this participation is rational and democratic?

Seemingly, part of the answer involves some way of creating a more politically informed public. The public can hardly be blamed for its political ignorance when it is given little information with which to make political judgments. One can readily endorse more thorough political reporting by news media and other efforts to induce a more informed public. Hopes should not be set too high, however, because information campaigns do not always reach the people most in need of them. Also, we must recognize the possible side effects produced by increased public knowledge, such as greater public cynicism or an intensification of conflicts among politically aroused mass groups.

However difficult the task of boosting information might be, we can readily imagine that a more informed public would be better able to serve its function in the American democracy. Furthermore, we can speculate about how different the opinions of a truly informed public would be from the actual public we know. Increasingly, political scientists are taking this matter seriously, asking in what ways an informed public would act differently and how a more informed public might be achieved (Delli Carpini and Keeter 1996; Bartels 1996, 2008; Fishkin 1997, 1999; Lupia and McCubbins 1998; Althaus 1998, 2003; Gastil 2000; Gilens 2001; Luskin 2003).

Answering these questions is difficult. A particular challenge is that the public may not want to be thrust into the policymaking spotlight. Citizens see their job as keeping a watch over the rascal politicians at the helm rather than taking the helm themselves (Hibbing and Theiss-Morse 2002).

Apart from inducing the development of a more informed public, a related and equally daunting task is to induce more people to participate in politics. The most obvious way of doing so would be to legislate changes that lower the costs and burdens of participation. For instance, motor-voter legislation and other reforms reduce or eliminate the initial barriers to voter registration. If we register the unregistered, maybe they will vote and maybe they will become informed and cast informed votes. We await the evidence. In recent years, the voting rate (among eligible voters) threatened to fall to record lows, a disturbing phenomenon at a time when most of the entry costs for voter participation have been removed. Increasing numbers of Americans are *choosing* to be nonparticipants. Political scientists have failed to understand this trend and its underlying causes.

Perhaps the existing methods for translating public opinion into government policy are inaccurate relics of a technically primitive time when ballot casting, face-to-face communication, and geographic representation were the only feasible conduits for public expression. New methods might be tried to encourage greater citizen participation, giving people greater opportunity to participate directly in local decisions, including perhaps more participatory democracy in nongovernmental groups such as the workplace, school, and religious organizations. Also, people could play a more direct role by deciding policy questions in referenda instead of letting their elected leaders decide them. Finally, it is now technologically feasible to allow people to vote in referenda via the Internet from the comfort of their home.

There is no question that greater citizen participation is a desired democratic value. But it is debatable whether additional opportunities to participate would lead to wiser government decisions than elected leaders currently make. While proposals for expanding participation deserve serious consideration, their practicability and desirability remain uncertain.

Notes

1. For instance, most if not all of the legislation defined as "major" by Mayhew (1991) either was supported by poll majorities or went unpolled. In retrospect, it is sometimes said that the landmark Voting Rights Act of 1965, which helped to ensure the exercise of voting rights by African Americans and other minorities, was an instance of Congress passing major legislation even though it was unpopular in its day. This is incorrect. The VRA received majority support in polls at the time of passage. Similarly, passage of its companion civil rights bill, the Public Accommodation Act of 1964, was eased by the fact that it received majority support in the polls. In chapter 4, we considered the case of the Bush tax cuts, a major legislation that received majority support in most polls, but arguably by the manipulation of question wording. Although strictly speaking not in the category of "legislation," the one clear instance of Congress acting against public opinion is the impeachment of President Clinton by the House of Representatives in 1998. The Republicans suffered electorally in the short term.

2. Important laws are determined using the format of Mayhew (1991).

3. Earlier, less visible gaps between mood and policymaking occurred in the early 1960s, when a liberal mood led to the Kennedy–Johnson administrations and eventually the great society, and then in the late 1970s, when the conservative tone of mood led to the conservatism of the Reagan presidencies.

4. To estimate state opinion requires drawing large samples from within states. To do so, studies that estimate state opinion typically pool multiple surveys and collect state-level subsamples. Back in the 1930s, the Gallup Poll collected much larger state-level samples than national polls do today. This allowed the testing of the relationship between state opinion and policy on selected issues—capital punishment, women on juries, and the failed child labor amendment to the Constitution. On each of these three issues, opinion on the issue was strongly related to state policy. Opinion from the 1930s on capital punishment was also related to state capital punishment policy in the 1970s (Erikson 1976b).

5. As an example of opinion based on misinformation, consider opinion on crime. Public perceptions of the severity of the crime problem do not track well with the objective crime rate (Sharp 1999).

6. The debate is framed by two classic studies, now decades old: Mills (1956), claiming rule by a "power elite," and Dahl (1961), arguing for the presence of pluralism.

Appendix   The American National Election Study and the General Social Survey Questions

TWO MAJOR NATIONAL SURVEYS, DESIGNED SPECIFICALLY for academic analysis, are conducted on a regular basis. These are the American National Election Study (ANES), done by the Center for Political Studies at the University of Michigan (conducted in even-number years), and the General Social Survey (GSS), done by the National Opinion Research Center at the University of Chicago (usually conducted yearly). For academic purposes, these surveys are usually more valuable than surveys done by commercial polling organizations. One reason is that the interviews are done in person rather than over the phone. Another is that the questionnaires are quite lengthy, usually including hundreds of items administered over a period of more than one hour. Also, many items are repeated over time, allowing for the analysis of changes.

In recent years, surveys conducted by the Pew Research Center have also proved valuable for academic analysis. Pew will usually do several surveys a year focused on a specific topic that has sufficient questions for academic analysis. Also, commercial surveys such as Gallup or ABC News have increased in value as they now have repeated many questions over a sufficient period of time to allow for inferences about opinion change. However, the ANES and GSS remain our principal sources of data.

Throughout this book, responses to opinion questions asked by various survey organizations are examined. As their content usually appears in abbreviated form, the complete wordings for the most frequently used questions in the book are presented below. Where appropriate, responses are labeled as [L] for liberal and [C] for conservative, according to how these terms are applied to the response alternative within the text.

A-1   Questions from the American National Election Studies

1. Party Identification

Two questions are used to measure party identification. First, respondents are asked:

> Generally speaking, do you usually think of yourself as a Republican, a Democrat, an Independent, or what?

This basic question provides the division between the three kinds of partisans. For the second question, partisans are probed regarding the strength of their partisanship, and Independents are probed to see whether they lean toward one of the major parties.

Republicans and Democrats are asked:

> Would you call yourself a strong Republican [Democrat] or not so strong Republican [Democrat]?

Independents are asked:

> Do you think of yourself as closer to the Republican Party or to the Democratic Party?

Independents who choose a party are called *Independent Leaners*. Many Independents respond that they lean toward neither party. They are often called *Pure Independents*.

The net result is a seven-point scale of partisanship.

1. Strong Democrat
2. Not so strong (or "weak") Democrat
3. Independent, leaning Democrat
4. Pure Independent
5. Independent, leaning Republican
6. Not so strong (or "weak") Republican
7. Strong Republican

Unless otherwise noted, we use the simpler three-way division: Democrats (1 and 2), Independents (3, 4, and 5), and Republicans (6 and 7).

2. Liberal/Conservative Ideology

People are asked to choose an ideological position on a seven-point scale. Respondents are first asked:

> We hear a lot of talk these days about liberals and conservatives. Here is a seven-point scale on which the political views that most people might hold are arranged from extremely liberal to extremely conservative.

Then they are asked:

> Where would you place yourself on this scale, or haven't you thought much about it?

1. Extremely liberal
2. Liberal
3. Slightly liberal
4. Moderate, middle-of-the-road
5. Slightly conservative
6. Conservative
7. Extremely conservative
8. Don't know
9. Haven't thought much about it

Where we show the basic division between self-identified liberals and conservatives, we combine responses 1, 2, and 3 as *liberal* and 5, 6, and 7 as *conservative*.

In recent years, the ANES has used the following variation of the seven-point scale for most of its issue questions. Respondents are first presented with two extreme positions on the issue. Then they are asked to place themselves with regard to the issue on a scale ranging from 1 to 7. Shown the scale, respondents are asked: "Where would you place yourself on this scale, or haven't you thought much about it?" The scale position 1 generally represents the extreme liberal viewpoint and scale position 7 generally represents the extreme conservative viewpoint. For convenience, we often compress the scale, combining the responses 1, 2, and 3 as *liberal* responses and 5, 6, and 7 as *conservative* responses, with neutral "4" respondents and those who admit they "haven't thought much about it" combined as "nonopinion holders."

Following are the five seven-point issue scales used in our ten-item index of respondent liberalism–conservatism.

3. Government Services/Spending Scale

Some people think the government should provide fewer services, even in areas such as health and education, in order to reduce spending. . . . Other people feel it is important for the government to provide many more services even if it means an increase in spending. . . . Where would you place yourself on this scale? . . .

[C] Government should provide many fewer services, reduce spending a lot.
[L] Government should provide many more services, increase government spending a lot.

(On this one item, ANES scores 1 to 7 as conservative to liberal. We reverse the polarity so that 1 represents the liberal and 7 the conservative end of the scale, consistent with the other items.)

4. Government Job and Standard of Living Scale

Some people feel the government in Washington should see to it that every person has a job and a good standard of living. Others think the government should just let each person get ahead on his own. . . . Where would you place yourself on this scale? . . .

[L] Government see to a job and a good standard of living
[C] Government let each person get ahead on own

5. National Health Insurance

There is much concern about the rapid rise in medical and hospital costs. Some people feel there should be a government insurance plan that would cover all medical and hospital expenses for everyone. . . . Others feel that all medical expenses should be paid by individuals and through private insurance plans like Blue Cross or other company plans. . . . Where would you place yourself on this scale? . . .

[L] Government insurance plan
[C] Private insurance plan

6. Aid to Blacks Scale

Some people feel that the government in Washington should make every effort to improve the social and economic positions of blacks. . . . Others feel that the government should not make any special effort to help blacks because they should help themselves. Where would you place yourself on this scale? . . .

[L] Government should help blacks
[C] Blacks should help themselves

7. Defense Spending Scale

Some people believe that we should spend much less for defense. . . . Others feel that spending should be greatly increased. . . . Where would you place yourself on this scale? . . .

[L] Greatly decrease defense spending
[C] Greatly increase defense spending

Items 3–7 are used as a part of our ten-item composite index of liberal–conservative policy positions from the 2008 ANES Survey. For this composite scale, each component item is added as a -1 (liberal), $+1$ (conservative), or 0 (other or in between). The remaining five issues for the composite scale are the following five items from the 2008 ANES Survey.

8. Timetable for Withdrawal from Iraq

Do you favor, oppose, or neither favor nor oppose setting a deadline for withdrawing all U.S. troops from Iraq?

[L] Favor
[C] Oppose

9. Gun Control

Do you think the federal government should make it more difficult for people to buy a gun than it is now, make it easier for people to buy a gun, or keep these rules about the same as they are now?

[L] More difficult
[C] Make it easier or keep same

10. Death Penalty

Do you favor or oppose the death penalty for persons convicted of murder?

[L] Favor
[C] Oppose

11. Gay Marriage

Should same-sex couples be allowed to marry, or do you think they should not be allowed to marry?

[L] Favor
[C] Oppose

12. Abortion

There has been some discussion about abortion during recent years. Which of these opinions on this page best agree with your view?

1. By law, abortion should never be permitted.
2. The law should permit abortion only in case of rape, incest, or when the woman's life is in danger.
3. The law should permit abortion for reasons other than rape, incest, or danger to the woman's life, but only after the need for abortion has been clearly established.
4. By law, a woman should always be able to obtain an abortion as a matter of personal choice.

For purposes of ideological classification, responses 1 and 2 are coded as conservative, and responses 3 and 4 are coded as liberal.

Some of the items for the ten-item liberal–conservative scale were administered to only half of the 2008 sample. Thus, the ten-item liberal–conservative scale and the political information scale (derived from the ten items as described below) can be applied to only half of the 2008 ANES sample.

13. Political Information Scale

For some items, the ANES asked respondents to locate the positions of the major presidential candidates on the same scale. We used the candidate placements for items 2, 3, 5, and 7 to form the political information scale used in chapters 3, 8, 9, and 10. To construct this scale, every correct answer (McCain to the right of Obama) was scored as 1. All others were scored as zero. These scores were summed to create a composite knowledge score ranging from 0 to 4 (all correct).

A-2   Questions from the General Social Survey

14. Abortion

Please tell me whether or not you think it should be possible for a pregnant woman to obtain a legal abortion.

a. If there is a strong chance of a serious defect in the baby?
b. If she is married and does not want any more children?
c. If the woman's own health is seriously endangered by the pregnancy?
d. If the family has very low income and cannot afford any more children?
e. If she became pregnant as a result of a rape?
f. If she is not married and does not want to marry the man?
g. If the woman wants it for any reason?

15. Political Tolerance

The GSS asks tolerance questions with a variety of groups as the target. The general form of the question, using atheists as the target group, is

There are always some people whose ideas are considered bad or dangerous by other people. For instance, somebody who is against all churches and religion. . . .

a. If such a person wanted to make a speech in your (city/town/community) against churches and religion, should he be allowed to speak or not?
b. Should such a person be allowed to teach in a college or university, or not?
c. If some people in your community suggested that a book he wrote against churches and religion should be taken out of your public library, would you favor removing this book, or not?

References

Abramowitz, Alan I. 1994. "Issue Evolution Reconsidered: Racial Attitudes and Partisanship in the U.S. Electorate." *American Journal of Political Science* 38 (Feb.): 1–25.

———. 2010. *The Disappearing Center: Engaged Citizens, Polarization and American Democracy* (McGraw-Hill).

Abramowitz, Alan, and Kyl L. Saunders. 1998. "Ideological Realignment in the U.S. Electorate." *Journal of Politics* 60: 634–652.

———. 2008. "Is Polarization a Myth." *Journal of Politics* 70 (Apr.): 542–555.

Abramson, Paul R. 1983. *Political Attitudes in America*. San Francisco: Freeman.

Achen, Christopher H. 1975. "Mass Political Attitudes and the Survey Response." *American Political Science Review* 69 (Dec.): 1218–1231.

Adelson, Joseph, and Robert P. O'Neil. 1966. "Growth of Political Ideas in Adolescence: The Sense of Community." *Journal of Personality and Social Psychology* 4 (July): 295–306.

Adler, Scott E. 2002. *Why Congressional Reforms Fail: Reelection and the House Committee System*. Chicago: University of Chicago Press.

Adorno, Theodore W., et al. 1950. *The Authoritarian Personality*. New York: Harper.

Aldrich, John H. 2003. "Electoral Democracy During Politics as Usual—and Unusual." In *Electoral Democracy*, eds. George Rabinowitz and Michael B. MacKuen. Ann Arbor: University of Michigan Press.

Aldrich, John, Mark M. Berger, and David W. Rohde. 2002. "The Historic Variability in Conditional Party Government, 1877–1994." In *Party, Process, and Political Change in Congress*, eds. David W. Brady and Matthew D. McCubbins. Stanford, CA: Stanford University Press.

Aldrich, John, and James S. Coleman Battista. 2002. "Conditional Party Government in the States." *American Journal of Political Science* 46: 164–172.

Aldrich, John, and Richard Niemi. 1995. "The Sixth American Party System: Electoral Change, 1952–1992." In *Broken Contract?* ed. Stephen Craig. Boulder, CO: Westview Press.

Aldrich, John, and David W. Rohde. 2001. "The Logic of Conditional Party Government: Revisiting the Electoral Connection." In *Congress Reconsidered*, 7th ed., eds. Lawrence C. Dodd and Bruce I. Oppenheimer. Washington, DC: Congressional Quarterly Press.

Alesina, Alberto, and Edward L. Glaeser. 2004. *Fighting Poverty in the U.S. and Europe*. Oxford: Oxford University Press.

Alesina, Alberto, and Howard Rosenthal. 1995. *Partisan Politics, Divided Government, and the Economy.* New York: Cambridge University Press.

Alford, John R., and David W. Brady. 1993. "Personal and Partisan Advantage in U.S. Congressional Elections." In *Congress Reconsidered,* 5th ed., eds. Lawrence C. Dodd and Bruce I. Oppenheimer. Washington, DC: Congressional Quarterly Press.

Alford, John R., Carolyn L. Funk, and John R. Hibbing. 2005. "Are Political Orientations Genetically Transmitted?" *American Political Science Review* 99 (May): 153–169.

Almond, Gabriel A. 1950. *The American People and Foreign Policy.* New York: Harcourt.

Almond, Gabriel A., and Sidney Verba. 1963. *The Civic Culture.* Boston, MA: Little, Brown.

Altemeyer, Bob. 1981. *Right Wing Authoritarianism.* Winnipeg, MB: University of Winnipeg Press.

———. 1988. *Enemies of Freedom: Understanding Right Wing Authoritarianism.* San Francisco: Jossey-Bass.

———. 1997. *The Authoritarian Spector.* Cambridge, MA: Harvard University Press.

Alterman, Eric. 2003. *What Liberal Media?* New York: Basic Books.

Althaus, Scott L. 1998. "Information Effects in Collective Preferences." *American Political Science Review* 92 (Sept.): 545–558.

———. 2003. *Collective Preferences in Democratic Politics.* Cambridge, UK: Cambridge University Press.

Althaus, Scott L., and Devon M. Largio. 2004. "When Osama Became Saddam: Origins and Consequences of Change in America's Public Enemy #1." *PS: Political Science and Politics* 37 (Oct.): 795–799.

Alvarez, R. Michael. 1997. *Information and Elections.* Ann Arbor: University of Michigan Press.

Alvarez, R. Michael, and John Brehm. 2002. *Hard Choices, Easy Answers: Values, Information, and American Public Opinion.* Princeton, NJ: Princeton University Press.

Alvarez, Michael, and Paul Gronke. 1996. "Constituents and Legislators: Learning About the Persian Gulf Resolution." *Legislative Studies Quarterly* 21: 105–127.

Alwin, Duane F., Ronald L. Cohen, and Theodore M. Newcomb. 1991. *Political Attitudes over the Life Span.* Madison, WI: University of Wisconsin Press.

Anderson, David D. 1981. *William Jennings Bryan.* Boston, MA: Twayne.

Anderson, Lee, et al. 1990. *The Civics Report Card.* Princeton, NJ: National Assessment of Educational Progress, Educational Testing Service.

Andolina, Molly W., Krista Jenkings, Cliff Zukin, and Scott Keeter. 2003. "Habits from Home, Lessons from School: Influences on Youth Civic Engagement." *PS: Political Science and Politics* 36 (Apr.): 275–280.

Ansolabehere, Stephen, John de Figueirido, and James Snyder. 2003. "Why Is There So Little Money in U.S. Politics?" *Journal of Economic Perspectives* 17 (Winter): 105–130.

Ansolabehere, Stephen, and Shanto Iyengar. 1995. *Going Negative.* New York: Free Press.

Ansolabehere, Stephen D., Shanto Iyengar, Adam Simon, and Nicholas Valentino. 1994. "Does Attack Advertising Demobilize the Electorate?" *American Political Science Review* 88 (Sept.): 829–838.

Ansolabehere, Stephen, James Snyder, and Charles Stewart. 2001. "Candidate Positioning in House Elections." *American Journal of Political Science* 45 (Jan.): 136–159.

Ansolabehere, Stephen, and Phil Jones. 2006. "Constituents, Policy Preferences and Approval of Their Members of Congress." Cooperative Congressional Election Study Working Paper 6–01, downloaded from: web.mit.edu.poliasci/port1/cces/material/ansolabehere_jones.pdf

Ansolabehere, Stephen, Nathaniel Persily, and Charles Stewart III. 2010. "Race, Region and Voce Choice in the 2008 Election: Implications for the Future of the Voting Rights Act." *Harvard Law Review* (forthcoming).

Ansolabehere, Stephen, James Rodden, and James M. Synder, Jr. 2008. "The Strength of Issues: Using Multiple Measures to Gauge Preference Stability, Ideological Constraint, and Issue Voting." *American Political Science Review* 102 (May): 215–232.

Arnold, Douglas. 1990. *The Logic of Congressional Action.* New Haven, CT: Yale University Press.

Arterton, F. Christopher. 1974. "The Impact of Watergate on Children's Attitudes Toward Authority." *Political Science Quarterly* 89 (June): 269–288.

Avery, P. G. 2002. "Political Tolerance, Democracy, and Adolescents." In *Education for Democracy: Contexts, Curricula, Assessments,* ed. Parker, Walter. C. Greenwich, CT: Information Age Publishing, 113–130.

Baker, C. Edwin. 2006. *Media Concentration and Democracy.* Cambridge, UK: Cambridge University Press.

Barabas, Jason. 2004. "How Deliberation Affects Policy Opinions." *American Political Science Review* 98 (Nov.): 687–701.

Barber, James D. 1965. *The Lawmakers.* New Haven, CT: Yale University Press.

Barker, David C. 2002. *Rushed to Judgment: Talk Radio, Persuasion, and American Political Behavior.* New York: Columbia University Press.

Barker, David C., and James D. Tinnick. 2006. "Competing Visions of Parental Roles and Ideological Constraint." *American Political Science Review* 100 (May): 249–265.

Barker, David C., Jon Hurwitz, and Traci L. Nelson. 2008. "Of Crusades and Culture Wars: 'Messianic' Militarism and Political Conflict in the United States." *Journal of Politics* 70 (Apr.): 307–323.

Barry, William D., Michael B. Berkman, and Stuart Schneiderman. 2000. "Legislative Professionalism and Incumbent Reelection: The Development of Institutional Boundaries." *American Political Science Review* 94: 859–874.

Bartels, Larry. 1988. *Presidential Primaries and the Dynamics of Public Choice.* Princeton, NJ: Princeton University Press.

———. 1991. "Constituency Opinion and Congressional Policy Making: The Reagan Buildup." *American Political Science Review* 85 (June): 457–474.

———. 1993. "Messages Received: The Political Impact of Media Exposure." *American Political Science Review* 87 (Mar.): 267–286.

———. 1996. "Uninformed Voters: Information Effects in Presidential Elections." *American Journal of Political Science* 40: 194–230.

———. 2000. "Partisanship and Voting Behavior, 1952–1996." *American Journal of Political Science* 44: 35–51.

———. "Democracy with Attitudes." 2003. In *Electoral Democracy*, eds. Michael B. MacKuen and George Rabinowitz, pp. 48–82. Ann Arbor: University of Michigan Press.

———. 2005. "Homer Gets a Tax Cut: Inequality and Public Policy in the American Mind." *Perspectives on Politics* 3 (Mar.): 15–31.

———. 2008. *Unequal Democracy.* Princeton, NJ: Princeton University Press.

Baum, Matthew A., and Samuel Kernell. 1999. "Has Cable Ended the Golden Age of Presidential Television?" *American Political Science Review* 93 (Mar.): 99–114.

Baumgartner, Frank R., and Bryan D. Jones. 1993. *Agendas and Instability in American Politics.* Chicago: University of Chicago Press.

Baumgartner R. Frank, Suzanna L. De Boef, and Amber E. Boydstun. 2008. *The Decline of the Death Penalty and the Discovery of Innocence.* Cambridge, UK: Cambridge University Press.

Bawn, Kathleen. 1999. "Constructing 'US': Ideology, Coalition Politics, and False Consciousness." *American Journal of Political Science* 43: 303–334.

Beck, Paul Allen. 1977. "The Role of Agents in Political Socialization." In *Handbook of Political Socialization,* ed. Stanley A. Renshon. New York: Free Press.

Beck, Paul Allen, and M. Kent Jennings. 1991. "Family Traditions, Political Periods, and the Development of Partisan Orientations." *Journal of Politics* 53 (Aug.): 742–763.

Beckwith, Jon, and Corey A. Morris. 2008. "Development of Partisan Orientations." *Journal of Politics* 53 (Aug.): 742–763.

———. 2008 "Twin Studies of Political Behavior: Untenable Assumptions." *Perspectives on Politics* 6 (Dec.): 785–791.

Behr, Roy, and Shanto Iyengar. 1985. "Television News, Real-World Cues, and Changes in the Public Agenda." *Public Opinion Quarterly* 49 (Spring): 38–57.

Bennett, Stephen. 1997. "Why Young Americans Hate Politics, and What We Should Do About It." *Politics and Political Science* 30 (Mar.): 47–52.

———. 1998. "Young Americans' Indifference to Media Coverage of Public Affairs." *Political Science and Politics* 31 (Sept.): 535–541.

Bennett, W. Lance. 1980. *Public Opinion in American Politics.* New York: Harcourt.

———. "The Uncivic Culture: Communication, Identity, and the Rise of Lifestyle Politics." *Political Science and Politics* 31 (Dec.): 741–762.

———. 2003. *News: The Politics of Illusion.* New York: Longman.

Berelson, Bernard, Paul Lazarsfeld, and William McPhee. 1954. *Voting.* Chicago: University of Chicago Press.

Berinsky, Adam J. 2004. *Silent Voices: Public Opinion and Political Participation in America.* Princeton, NJ: Princeton University Press.

———. 2009. *In Time of War.* Chicago: University of Chicago Press.

Berinsky, Adam, and Tali Mendelberg. 2005. "The Indirect Effects of Discredited Stereotypes in Judgments of Jewish Leaders." *American Journal of Political Science* 49 (Oct.): 845–864.

Berkman, Michael B., and Eric Plutzer. 2006. *Ten Thousand Democracies.* Washington, DC: Georgtown University Press.

Bettig, Ronald V., and Jeanne Lynn Hall. 2003. *Big Media, Big Money.* New York: Rowan-Littlefield.

Bhatti, Yosef, and Robert S. Erikson. 2010. "How Poorly Are the Poor Represented in the U.S. Senate." In *Who Gets Represente*, eds. Peter Enns and Christopher Wlezien. New York: Russell Sage.

Bishop, George. 2002. "Illusion of Change." *Public Perspective* (May/June): 38–43.

———. 2004. *The Illusion of Public Opinion.* New York: Rowman and Littlefield.

Bishop, George F., et al. 1980. "Pseudo-Opinions on Public Affairs." *Public Opinion Quarterly* 44 (Summer): 198–209.

Blendon, Robert J., and John M. Benson. 2009. "Understanding How Americans View Health Care Reform." *The New England Journal of Medicine* 361 (Aug.): E13.

Bloch-Elkon, Yaeli, and Robert Y. Shapiro. 2005. "Deep Suspicion: Iraq, Misperception, and Partisanship." Public Opinion Pros (June): www.PublicOpinionPros.com. Accessed Jan. 16, 2006.

Blumberg, Stephen, Julian V. Luke, Geustur Davidson, Michael Davern, Tyz-Chyi Yu, and Karen Soderberg. 2009. "Wireless Substitution: State-Level Estimates from the National Health Interview Survey, January–December 2007." *National Health Statistics Reports* 14 (Mar.): 1–16.

Blumberg, Stephen, and Julian V. Luke. 2009. "Wireless Substitution: Early Release of Estimates from the National Health Interview Survey, July–December 2008." Centers for Disease Control and Prevention (May 5).

Blumer, Herbert. 1948. "Public Opinion and Public Opinion Polling." *American Sociological Review* 13 (Oct.): 542–554.

Bond, Jon R., Richard Fleisher, and B. Dan Wood. 2003. "The Marginal and Time-Varying Effect of Public Approval on Presidential Success in Congress." *Journal of Politics* 65: 92–110.

Bowler, Shaun, and Todd Donovan. 2002. "Democracy, Institutions, and Attitudes about Citizen Influence over Government." *British Journal of Political Science* 32 (July): 371–390.

Box-Steffensmeier, Janet., Suzanna De Boef, and Tse-min Lin. 2004. "The Dynamics of the Partisan Gender Gap." *American Political Science Review* 98 (Aug.): 515–528.

Box-Steffensmeier, Janet, Kathleen Knight, and Lee Sigelman. 1998. "The Interplay of Macroideology and Macropartisanship: A Times Series Analysis." *Journal of Politics* 60: 131–149.

Brady, Henry E., and Paul M. Sniderman. 1985. "Attitude Attribution: A Group Basis for Political Reasoning." *American Political Science Review* 79 (Dec.): 1061–1078.

Brady, Henry E., Sidney Verba, and Kay Lehman Schlozman. 1995. "Beyond SES: A Resource Model of Political Participation." *American Political Science Review* 89 (Mar.): 271–292.

Brehm, John. 1993. *The Phantom Respondents.* Ann Arbor: University of Michigan Press.

Brewer, Paul R., Kimberly Gross, Sean Aday, and Lars Willnat. 2004. "International Trust and Public Opinion About World Affairs." *American Journal of Political Science* 48 (Feb.): 93–112.

Brewer, Paul R., and Clyde Wilcox. 2005. "Trends: Same-Sex Marriage and Civil Unions." *Public Opinion Quarterly* 69 (Winter): 599–616.

Brians, Craig L., and Martin P. Wattenberg. 1996. "Campaign Issue Knowledge: Comparing Reception from TV Commercials, TV Shows, and Newspapers. *American Journal of Political Science* 40 (Feb.): 172–193.

Brody, Richard A. 1991. *Assessing the President.* Stanford, CA: Stanford University Press.

Brody, Richard A., and Lee Sigelman. 1983. "Presidential Popularity and Presidential Elections: An Update and Extension." *Public Opinion Quarterly* 47 (Fall): 325–328.

Browning, Robert X. 1986. *Politics and Social Welfare Policy in the United States.* Knoxville, TN: University of Tennessee Press.

Bryce, James. 1900. *The American Commonwealth.* New York: Macmillan.

Budge, Ian, and Richard I. Hofferbert. 1990. "Mandates and Policy Outputs: U.S. Party Platforms and Federal Expenditures, 1950–1985." *American Political Science Review* 84 (Mar.): 248–261.

Burden, Barry C., and David C. Kimball. 2002. *Why Americans Split Their Tickets: Campaigns, Competition, and Divided Government.* Ann Arbor: University of Michigan Press.

Burnham, Walter Dean. 1970. *Critical Elections and the Mainsprings of American Politics.* New York: Norton.

Burstein, Paul. 2006. "Why Estimates of the Impact of Public Opinion on Public Policy Are Too High: Empirical and Theoretical Implications." *Social Forces* 84: 2273–2289.

Cain, Bruce, John Ferejohn, and Morris Fiorina. 1987. *The Personal Vote.* Cambridge, MA: Harvard University Press.

Caldarone, Richard P., Brandice-Canes-Wrone, and Tom S. Clark. 2009. "Partisan Labels and Democratic Accountability: An Analysis of State Supreme Court Abortion Decisions." *Journal of Politics* 71 (May): 560–573.

Campbell, Andrea. 2010. *How Americans Think About Taxes: Public Opinion and the American Fiscal State.* Princeton, NJ: Princeton University Press.

Campbell, Angus. 1964. "Issues and Voters: Past and Present." *Journal of Politics* 26 (Nov.): 745–757.

Campbell, Angus, Philip E. Converse, Warren E. Miller, and Donald E. Stokes. 1960. *The American Voter.* New York: Wiley.

Campbell, Angus, Gerald Gurin, and Warren E. Miller. 1954. *The Voter Decides.* Evanston, IL: Row.

Campbell, David E. 2005. "Voices in the Classroom: How an Open Classroom Environment Facilitates Adolescents' Civic Development." Circle Working Paper 28. Downloaded from www.civicyouth.com, November 4, 2005.

Campbell, David E. 2008. "Voice in the Classroom: How an Open Classroom Climate Fosters Political Engagement among Adolescents." *Political Behavior* 30: 437–454.

Campbell, James E. 1985. "Sources of the New Deal Realignment: The Contribution of Conversion and Mobilization to Partisan Change." *Western Political Quarterly* 38 (June): 357–376.

Campbell, James B. 2008. *The American Campaign,* 2nd ed. College Station, TX: Texas A&M University Press.

Canes-Wrone, Brandice. 2006. *Who Leads Whom? Presidents, Policy, and the Public.* Chicago: University of Chicago Press.

Canes-Wrone, Brandice, David W. Brady, and John F. Cogan. 2002. "Out of Step, Out of Office: Electoral Accountability and House Members' Voting." *American Political Science Review* 96: 127–140.

Canes-Wrone, Brandice, and Scott de Marchi. 2002. "Presidential Approval and Legislative Success." *Journal of Politics* 64: 491–509.

Canes-Wrone, Brandice, Michael C. Herron, and Kenneth W. Shotts. 2001. "Leadership and Pandering: A Theory of Executive Policymaking." *American Journal of Political Science* 43: 532–550.

Canes-Wrone, Brandice, and Kenneth W. Shotts. 2004. "The Conditional Nature of Presidential Responsiveness of Public Opinion." *American Journal of Political Science* 48 (Oct.): 690–706.

Cantril, Albert H. 1991. *The Opinion Connection.* Washington, DC: Brookings.

Cantril, Albert H., and Susan Davis Cantril. 1999. *Reading Mixed Signals: Ambivalence in American Public Opinion About Government.* Baltimore, MD: Johns Hopkins University Press.

Cantril, Hadley. 1951. *Public Opinion 1935–1946.* Princeton, NJ: Princeton University Press.

Cappella, Joseph, and Kathleen Jamieson. 1997. *Spiral of Cynicism: The Press and the Public Good.* New York: Oxford University Press.

Carmines, Edward G., and James A. Stimson. 1980. "The Two Faces of Issue Voting." *American Political Science Review* 74 (Jan.): 78–91.

————. 1989. *Issue Evolution: Race and the Transformation of American Politics.* Princeton, NJ: Princeton University Press.

Carney, Dana, John T. Jost, Samuel D. Gosling, and Jeff Potter. 2009. "The Secret Lives of Liberals and Conservatives: Personality Profiles, Interaction Styles, and the Things They Leave Behind." *Political Psychology* 29 (6): 807–840.

Carsey, Thomas M., and Geoffrey C. Layman. 2006. "Changing Sides or Changing Minds? Party Identification and Policy Preferences in the American Electorate." *American Journal of Political Science* 50 (Apr.): 464–477.

Cassel, Carol A. 1986. "The Non-Partisan Ballot in the United States." In *Electoral Laws and Their Consequences*, eds. Bernard Grofman and Rend Lipjart. New York: Agathon.

Chadwick, Andrew. 2005. *Internet Politics: States, Citizens, and New Communication Techniques.* Oxford: Oxford University Press.

Charney, Evan. 2008. "Genes and Ideologies." *Perspectives on Politics* 6 (June): 299–319.

Childs, Harwood. 1965. *Public Opinion: Nature, Formation and Role.* Princeton, NJ: Van Nostrand.

Chong, Dennis. 1993. "How People Think, Reason, and Feel About Civil Liberties." *American Journal of Political Science* 37 (Aug.): 867–899.

Chong, Dennis. 2006. "Free Speech and Mulitculturalism In and Out of the Academy." *Political Psychology* 27 (Jan.): 29–54.

Chong, Dennis, and James N. Druckman. 2007. "Framing Theory." *Annual Review of Political Science* 10: 103–126.

Citrin, Jack, and Donald Philip Green. 1986. "Presidential Leadership and the Resurgence of Trust in Government." *British Journal of Political Science* 16 (Dec.): 973–988.

Cobb, Michael D., and James H. Kuklinski. 1997. "Changing Minds: Political Arguments and Political Persuasion." *American Journal of Political Science* 41 (Jan.): 88–121.

Cohen, Bernard. 1963. *The Press and Foreign Policy.* Princeton, NJ: Princeton University Press.

Cohen, Jeffrey E. 2008. *The Presidency in the Era of 24 Hour News.* Princeton, NJ: Princeton University Press.

Connolly, Ceci, and Mike Allen. 2005. "Medicare Drug Benefit May Cost $1.2 Trillion." *Washington Post.* Feb. 9, A1.

Conover, Pamela J., and Stanley Feldman. 1989. "Candidate Perceptions in an Ambiguous World: Campaigns, Cues, and Inference Processes." *American Journal of Political Science* 33 (Nov.): 912–941.

Conover, Pamela J., and Donald D. Searing. 2000. "A Political Socialization Perspective." In *Rediscovering the Democratic Purposes of Education*, eds. Lorraine M. McDonnell, P. Michael Timpane and Roger Benjamin. Lawrence, Kansas: University of Kansas Press.

Converse, Jean. 1987. *Survey Research in the United States: Roots and Emergence 1890–1960.* Berkeley, CA: University of California Press.

Converse, Philip E. 1962. "Information Flow and the Stability of Partisan Attitudes." *Public Opinion Quarterly* 26 (Winter): 578–599.

————. 1964. "The Nature of Belief Systems in Mass Publics." In *Ideology and Discontent*, ed. David Apter. New York: Free Press.

————. 1966. "The Concept of the Normal Vote." In *Elections and the Political Order*, eds. Angus Campbell et al. New York: Wiley.

————. 1987. "Changing Conceptions of Public Opinion in the Political Process. *Public Opinion Quarterly* 51 (Spring): 12–24.

————. 1990. "Popular Representation and the Distribution of Information." In *Information and Democratic Processes*, eds. John Ferejohn and James Kuklinksi. Urbana, IL: University of Illinois Press.

Converse, Philip E., Aage R. Clausen, and Warren E. Miller. 1965. "Electoral Myth and Reality: The 1964 Election." *American Political Science Review* 59 (June): 332–335.

Converse, Philip E., and Gregory B. Markus. 1979. "Plus Ça Change: The New CPS Election Study Panel." *American Political Science Review* 73 (Mar.): 32–49.

Cook, Timothy E. 1998. *Governing with the News: The News Media as a Political Institution*. Chicago: University of Chicago Press.

————. 2007. *Governing with the News: The News Media as a Political Institution*, 2nd ed. Chicago: University of Chicago Press.

Cox, Gary, and Jonathan N. Katz. 1996. "Why Did the Incumbency Advantage in the U.S. House Grow?" *American Journal of Political Science* 40: 478–497.

Cox, Gary W., and Matthew D. McCubbins. 1993. *Legislative Leviathan: Party Government in the House*. Berkeley, CA: University of California Press.

————. 2004. *Setting the Agenda*. Cambridge, UK: Cambridge University Press.

Craig, Stephen G. 1993. *The Malevolent Leaders*. Boulder, CO: Westview.

Craig, Stephen C., James G. Kane, and Michael D. Martinez. 2002. "Sometimes You Feel Like a Nut, Sometimes You Don't: Citizens' Ambivalence About Abortion." *Political Psychology* 23: 285–300.

Crespi, Irving. 1988. *Pre-Election Polling: Sources of Accuracy and Error*. New York: Russell Sage.

Curtin, Richard, Stanley Presser, and Eleanor Singer. 2005. "Changes in Telephone Survey Nonresponse over the Past Quarter Century." *Public Opinion Quarterly* 69 (Spring): 87–98.

Dahl, Robert A. 1961. *Who Governs?* New Haven, CT: Yale University Press.

————. 1971. *Polyarchy*. New Haven, CT: Yale University Press.

————. 1982. *Democracy in the United States*. Chicago, IL: Rand.

————. 1989. *Democracy and Its Critics*. New Haven, CT: Yale University Press.

Dalton, Russell J. 2004. *Democratic Challengers, Democratic Choices: The Erosion of Political Support in Advanced Industrial Democracies*. Oxford: Oxford University Press.

————. 2008. *The Good Citizen*. Washington, DC: CQ Press.

Dalton, Russell J., Paul A. Beck, and Robert Huckfeldt. 1998. "Partisan Cues and the Media: Information Flows in the 1992 Presidential Election." *American Political Science Review* 92 (Mar.): 111–126.

Dautrich, Kenneth, and Jennifer Necci Deneen. 1996. "Media Bias: What Journalists and the Public Say About It." *Public Perspective* 7: 7–19.

Davidson, Roger H., and Walter J. Oleszck. 2002. *Congress and Its Members*, 8th ed. Washington, DC: Congressional Quarterly Press.

Davis, Darren. 2007. *Negative Liberty: Public Opinion and the Terrorist Attacks on America*. New York: Russell Sage Foundation.

Davis, Darren, and Brian Silver. 2004. "Civil Liberties Versus Security: Public Opinion in the Context of the Terrorist Attacks on America." *American Journal of Political Science* 48: 47–61.

Davis, Richard, and Diana Owen. 1999. *New Media and American Politics*. New York: Oxford University Press.

Davis, James A. 2005. "Did Growing Up in the 1960s Leave a Permanent Mark on Attitudes and Values? Evidence from the General Social Survey." *Public Opinion Quarterly* 68: (Summer): 161–183.

Dawson, Michael C. 1994. *Behind the Mule: Race and Class in African-American Politics*. Princeton, NJ: Princeton University Press.

Delhey Jan, and Kenneth Newton. 2003. "Who Trusts: The Origins of Social Trust in Seven Societies." *European Sociological Review* 21 (Dec.): 311–327.

DellaVigna, Stefano, and Ethan Kaplan. 2008. "The Fox News Effect: Media Bias and Voting." *Quarterly Journal of Economics* 122 (Aug.): 1187–1234.

Delli Carpini, Michael X. 1986. *Stability and Change in American Politics: The Coming of Age of the Generation of the 1960s.* New York: New York University Press.

Delli Carpini, Michael X., Fay Lomax Cook, and Lawrence R. Jacobs. 2004. "Public Deliberations, Discursive Participation, and Citizen Engagement: A Review of the Empirical Literature." *Annual Review of Political Science* 7: 315–344.

Delli Carpini, Michael X., and Scott Keeter. 1996. *What Americans Know About Politics and Why It Matters.* New Haven, CT: Yale University Press.

———. 2000. "Gender and Political Knowledge." In *Gender and American Politics: Women, Men and the Political Process*, eds. Sue tolleson Rinhart and Jyl J. Jopsephson. Armonk, NY: M.E Sharpe.

Dennis, Jack, and Carol Webster. 1975. "Children's Images of the President and Government in 1962 and 1974." *American Politics Quarterly* (Oct.): 211–238.

Deutscher, Irwin. 1973. *What We Say/What We Do.* Glenview, IL: Scott.

Dillman, Don A. 2008. *Mail and Internet Surveys: The Tailored Design Method.* 2nd ed. New York: John Wiley.

Domhoff, G. William. 2002. "The Power Elite, Public Policy and Public Opinion." In *Navigating Public Opinion*, eds. Jeff Manza, Fay Loxmax Cook, and Benjamin I. Page. Oxford: Oxford University Press.

Domke, David, David P. Fan, Michael Fibison, Dhavan V. Shah, Steven S. Smith, and Mark D. Watts. 1997. "Mass News Media, Candidates and Issues, and Public Opinion in the 1996 Presidential Campaign." *Journalism and Mass Communications Quarterly* 74: 718–737.

Domke, David, Dhavan V. Shah, and Daniel Wackman. 1998. " 'Moral Referendums': Values, News Media, and the Process of Candidate Choice." *Political Communication* 15: 301–321.

Downs, Anthony. 1958. *An Economic Theory of Democracy.* New York: Harper.

Drew, Dan, and David H. Weaver. 2004. "Voter Learning in the 2004 Presidential Election: Did the Media Matter?" *Journalism and Mass Communication Quarterly* 83 (1): 25–42.

Drezner, Daniel. 2008. "The Realist Tradition in American Public Opinion." *Perspectives on Politics* 6: 51–70.

Druckman, James N. 2004. "Political Preference Formation: Competition, Deliberation, and the (Ir)relevance of Framing Effects." *American Political Science Review* 98 (Nov.): 671–686.

Druckman, James N. 2005. "Media Matter: How Newspapers and Television News Cover Campaigns and Influence Voters." *Political Communication* 22: 463–481.

Druckman, James N., and Kjersten R. Nelsen. 2003. "Framing and Deliberation: How Citizens' Conversations Limit Elite Influence." *American Journal of Political Science* 47 (Oct.): 729–745.

Druckman, James N., and Michael Parkin. 2005. "The Impact of Media Bias: How Editorial Slant Affects Voters" *Journal of Politics* 67: 1030–1049.

Dry, Murray. 1996. "Review of National Standards for Civics and Government." *Political Science and Politics* 29 (Mar.): 49–52.

Djupe, Paul A., and Christopher P. Gilbert. 2002. "The Political Voice of the Clergy." *Journal of Politics.* 64 (May): 596–609.

Duch, Raymond M., and Randolph T. Stevenson. 2008. *The Economic Vote.* Cambridge, UK: Cambridge University Press.

Dudley, Robert L., and Alan R. Gitelson. 2003. "Civic Education, Civic Engagement, and Youth Civic Development." *Political Science and Politics* 36 (Apr.): 263–267.

Dye, Thomas R., and Harmon Ziegler. 2009. *The Irony of Democracy*, 14th ed. Belmont, CA: Wadsworth.

Easton, David. 1965. *A Systems Analysis of Political Life.* New York: Wiley.

Easton, David, and Jack Dennis. 1969. *Children and the Political System*. New York: McGraw.

Edelman, Murray. 1965. *The Symbolic Uses of Politics*. Urbana, IL: University of Illinois Press.

Edwards, George C. 2003. *On Deaf Ears: The Limits of the Bully Pulpit*. New Haven, CT: Yale University Press.

Elms, Alan. 1972. *Social Psychology and Social Relevance*. Boston, MA: Little, Brown.

Engelberg, Stephan. 1993. "A New Breed of Hired Hands Cultivates Grass-Roots Anger." *New York Times*, Mar. 27, sec. A1, 11.

Entman, Robert M. 1989. "How the Media Affect What People Think: An Information Processing Approach." *Journal of Politics* 51 (May): 347–370.

Erikson, Robert S. 1971. "The Electoral Impact of Congressional Roll Call Voting." *American Political Science Review* 65 (Dec.): 1018–1032.

———. 1976a. "Is There Such a Thing as a Safe Seat?" *Polity* 8 (Summer): 613–632.

———. 1976b. "The Relationship Between Public Opinion and State Policy: A New Look at Some Forgotten Data." *American Journal of Political Science* 20 (Feb.): 25–36.

———. 1976c. "The Influence of Newspaper Endorsements in Presidential Elections: The Case of 1964." *American Journal of Political Science* 20 (May): 207–234.

———. 1979. "The SRC Panel Data and Mass Attitudes." *British Journal of Political Science* 9 (Jan.): 89–114.

———. 1990. "Roll Calls, Reputations, and Representation in the U.S. Senate." *Legislative Studies Quarterly* 15: 623–642.

———. 1993. "Counting Likely Voters in Gallup's Tracking Poll." *Public Perspective* 4 (Mar./Apr.): 22–23.

———. 2001. "The 2000 Election in Historical Perspective." *Political Science Quarterly* 116 (Spring): 29–52.

———. 2002. "National Election Studies and Macro Analysis." *Electoral Studies* 21: 269–281.

———. 2008. "The American Voter and the Economy, 2008." *PS: Political Science* 41 (July): 467–471.

———. 2009. "The American Voter and the Economy." *PS: Political Science & Politics* 42, 3 (July): 467–471.

Erikson, Robert S., Michael B. MacKuen, and James A. Stimson. 2002. *The Macro Polity*. New York: Cambridge University Press.

Erikson, Robert S., Costas Panagopoulos, and Christopher Wlezien. 2004. "Likely (and Unlikely) Voters and the Assessment of Campaign Dynamics." *Public Opinion Quarterly* 68 (Winter): 588–601.

Erikson, Robert S., and Kent L. Tedin. 1981. "The 1928–1936 Partisan Realignment: The Case for the Conversion Hypothesis." *American Political Science Review* 75 (Dec.): 951–962.

———. 1986. "Voter Conversion and the New Deal Realignment." *Western Political Quarterly* 39: 729–732.

Erikson, Robert S., and Christopher Wlezien. 1999. "Presidential Polls as a Time Series: The Case of 1996." *Public Opinion Quarterly* 63 (Summer): 163–178.

Erikson, Robert S., Michael B. MacKuen, and James A. Stimson. 1998. "What Moves Macropartisanship? A Reply to Green, Palmquist, and Schickler." *American Political Science Review* 92: (December): 901–912.

———. 2008. "Leading Economic Indicators, the Polls and the President Vote." *PS: Political Science and Politics* 39 (October): 703–709.

———. 1997. "Voters, Candidates, and Issues in Congressional Elections." In *Congress Reconsidered*, 6th. ed., eds. Lawrence C. Dodd and Bruce I. Oppenheimer. Washington, DC: Congressional Quarterly Press.

Erikson, Robert S., and Gerald C. Wright. 2001. "Representation of Constituency Ideology in Congress." In *Continuity and Change in Congressional Elections*, eds. David Brady and John Cogan (Ch. 8). Stanford, CA: Stanford University Press.

————. 2005. "Voters, Candidates, and Issues in Congressional Elections." In *Congress Reconsidered*, 8th ed., eds. Lawrence C. Dodd and Bruce I. Oppenheimer. Washington, DC: Congressional Quarterly Press.

————. 2009. "Voters, Candidates, and Issues in Congressional Elections." In *Congress Reconsidered*, 9th ed., eds. Lawrence C. Dodd and Bruce I. Oppenheimer. Washington, DC: Congressional Quarterly Press.

Erikson, Robert S., Gerald C. Wright, and John P. McIver. 1994. *Statehouse Democracy: Public Opinion and Policy in the American States*. New York: Cambridge University Press.

Erskine, Hazel. 1962a. "The Polls: Race Relations." *Public Opinion Quarterly* 26 (Winter): 137–148.

————. 1962b. "The Polls: Attitudes." *Public Opinion Quarterly* 26 (Winter): 293.

————. 1975. "The Polls: Health Insurance." *Public Opinion Quarterly* 39 (Spring): 128–143.

Eskey, Kenneth. 1995. "American Youth Not Very Interested in Politics." *Houston Chronicle*, Jan. 9, 5A.

Farnsworth, Stephen J., and S. Robert Lichter. 2007. *The Nightly News Nightmare,* 2nd ed. New York: Rowman-Littlefield.

Farrand, Max. 1961. *The Records of the Federal Convention of 1787*, vol. 1. New Haven, CT: Yale University Press.

Fearon, James. 1999. "Electoral Accountability and the Control of Politicians: Selecting Good Types Versus Sanctioning Poor Performance." In *Democracy, Accountability, and Representation*, eds. Adam Przeworski, Susan C. Stokes and Bernard Manin. Cambridge, UK: Cambridge University Press.

Feaver, Peter D., and Christopher Gelpi. 2004. *Choosing Your Battles*. Princeton, NJ: Princeton University Press.

Federico, Christopher M. 2006. "Race, Education, and Individualism Revisited." *Journal of Politics* 68 (Aug.): 600–610.

Feldman, Kenneth, and Theodore M. Newcomb. 1969. *The Impact of College on Students*, vol. 2. San Francisco: Jossey-Bass.

Feldman, Stanley. 1988. "Structure and Consistency in Public Opinion: The Role of Core Beliefs and Values." *American Journal of Political Science* 32 (June): 416–440.

————. 1989. "Reliability and Stability of Policy Positions: Evidence from a Five-Wave Panel." *Political Analysis* 1: 25–60.

————. 2003. "Enforcing Social Conformity: A Theory of Authoritarianism." *Political Psychology* 24: 41–74.

Feldman, Stanley, and Leonie Huddy. 2005. "Racial Resentment and White Opposition to Race-Conscious Programs: Principles of Prejudice?" *American Journal of Political Science* 49 (Jan.): 168–183.

Feldman, Stanley, and Karen Stenner. 1997. "Perceived Threat and Authoritarianism." *Political Psychology* 18: 741–769.

Feldman, Stanley, and John Zaller. 1992. "The Political Culture of Ambivalence: Ideological Response to the Welfare State." *American Journal of Political Science* 36 (Feb.): 268–291.

Fenno, Richard F., Jr. 1978. *Home Style: House Members in Their Districts*. Boston, MA: Little, Brown.

Ferejohn, John. 1999. "Accountability and Authority: Toward a Theory of Political Accountability. In *Democracy, Accountability, and Representation*, eds. Adam Przeworski, Susan C. Stokes, and Bernard Manin. Cambridge, UK: Cambridge University Press.

Ferree, G. Donald. 1993. "Counting Likely Voters: A Reply to Erikson." *Public Perspective* 4 (Mar./Apr.): 22–23.

de Figueiredo, Rui J. P., and Zachary Elkins. 2003. "Are Patroits Bigots? An Inquiry into the Vices of In-Group Pride." *American Journal of Political Science* 47 (Jan.): 171–188.

Finke, Roger, and Rodney Stark. 1994. *The Churching of America, 1776–1990*. New Brunswick, NJ: Rutgers University Press.

Finkel, Steven E. 1993. "Reexamining the Minimal Effects Model of Recent Presidential Campaigns," *Journal of Politics* 55 (Feb.): 1–21.

Finkel, Steven E., and John G. Geer. 1998. "A Spot Check: Casting Doubt on the Demobilization Effect of Attack Advertising." *American Journal of Political Science* 42 (Aug.): 573–595.

Finkel, Steven E., Edward N. Muller, and Karl-Dieter Opp. 1989. "Personal Influence, Collective Rationality, and Mass Political Action." *American Political Science Review* 83 (Sept.): 885–903.

Fiorina, Morris P. 1977. "An Outline for a Model of Party Choice." *American Journal of Political Science* 21 (Aug.): 601–625.

———. 1981. *Retrospective Voting in American National Elections.* New Haven, CT: Yale University Press.

———. 1992. *Divided Government.* New York: Macmillan.

Fiorina, Morris P., Samuel Abrams, and Jeremy Pope. 2003. "The 2000 US Presidential Election: Can Retrospective Voting Be Saved?" *British Journal of Political Science* 33 (Apr.): 163–187.

Fiorina, Morris P., with Samuel J. Abrams and Jeremy C. Pope. 2006. *Culture War: The Myth of a Polarized America,* 2nd ed. New York: Longman.

Fiorina, Morris P., with Samuel J. Abrams and Jeremy C. Pope. 2008. "Polarization in the American Public: Misconceptions and Misreadings." *Journal of Politics* 70 (Apr.): 556–560.

Fiorina, Morris, and Paul Peterson, Betram Johnson and William G. Meyer. 2009. *The New American Democracy.* New York: Longman.

Fischer, Claude S. 1975. "Toward a Subcultural Theory of Urbanism." *Social Forces* 53 (Mar.): 420–432.

Fischle, Mark. 2000. "Mass Response to the Lewinsky Scandal: Motivated Reasoning or Bayesian Updating?" *Political Psychology* 21: 135–159.

Fishkin, James S. 1997. *The Voice of the People: Public Opinion and Democracy.* New Haven, CT: Yale University Press.

———. 1999. "Toward a Deliberative Democracy: Experimenting with an Ideal." In *Citizen Competence and Democratic Institutions*, eds. S. Elkin and K.E. Soltan. State College: Pennsylvania State Press: 279–290.

Flanagan, Timothy J., and Dennis R. Longmire. 1996. *Americans View Crime and Justice: A National Public Opinion Survey.* Thousand Oaks, CA: Sage.

Flemming, Roy B., and B. Dan Wood. 1997. "The Public and the Supreme Court: Individual Justice Responsiveness to American Policy Moods." *American Journal of Political Science* 41: 468–498.

Fowler, James H., Laura A. Baker, and Christopher T. Dawes. 2008. "Genetic Variation in Political Participation." *American Political Science Review* 102 (May): 231–248.

Fox, Richard L., and Jennifer L. Lawless. 2004. "Entering the Arena? Gender and the Decision to Run for Office." *American Journal of Political Science* 48: 264–280.

———. 2005. "To Run or Not to Run for Office: Explaining Nascent Political Ambition." *American Journal of Political Science* 49: 642–659.

Franklin, Charles H., and John E. Jackson. 1983. "The Dynamics of Party Identification." *American Political Science Review* 77 (Dec.): 957–973.

Frankel, Martin R., and Lester R. Frankel. 1987. "Fifty Years of Survey Sampling in the United States." *Public Opinion Quarterly* 51 (Winter): S127–S138.

———. 1997. "Public Opinion and Polling." In *The Politics of News, The News of Politics*, eds. Doris Graber, Denis McQuail, and Pippa Norris. Washington, DC: CQ Press.

———. 2003. "News Organizations' Responses to the Mistakes of Election 2000: Why They Continue to Project Elections." *Public Opinion Quarterly* 67 (Spring): 19–31.

Free, Lloyd A., and Hadley Cantril. 1967. *The Political Beliefs of Americans.* New York: Simon and Schuster.

Freedman, Paul, Michael Franz, and Kenneth Goldstein. 2004. "Campaign Advertising and Political Citizenship." *American Journal of Political Science* 48 (Oct.): 723–741.

Freedman, Paul, and Kenneth Goldstein. 1999. "Measuring Media Exposure and the Effects of Negative Campaign Ads." *American Journal of Political Science* 43 (Nov.): 1189–1208.

Fried, Amy. 2006. "The Forgotten Lindsay Rogers and the Development of American Political Science." *American Political Science Review* 100 (Nov.): 555–562.

Friesema, H. Paul, and Ronald D. Hedlund. 1981. "The Reality of Representational Roles." In *Public Opinion and Public Policy*, ed. Norman R. Luttbeg. Itasca, IL: Peacock.

Fridkin, Kim L., Patrick J. Kenney, and Jack Crittenden. 2006. "On the Margins of Democratic Life: The Impact of Race and Ethnicty on the Political Engagement of Young People." *American Politics Quarterly* 34: 605–262.

Fritz, Ben, Brian Keefer, and Brendan Nyhan. 2004. *All the President's Spin*. New York: Touchstone.

Fritz, Sara, and Dwight Morris. 1992. *Handbook of Campaign Spending*. Washington, DC: Congressional Quarterly Press.

Fukumoto, Kentaro. 2009. "Systematically Dependent Competing Risks and Strategic Retirement." *American Journal of Political Science* 53 (Aug.): 740–754.

Fukuyama, Francis. 1995. *Trust: Social Virtues and the Creation of Propriety*. New York: Free Press.

Gallup, George, and Saul Rae. 1940. *The Pulse of Democracy*. New York: Simon.

Gallup Organization. 2003. "Poll Analysis: Public Remains Skeptical of News Media." May 30, 2.

Galston, William A. 2004. "Civic Education and Political Participation." *PS: Political Science and Politics* 32 (Apr.): 263–266.

Gamble, Barbara. 1997. "Putting Civil Rights to a Popular Vote." *American Journal of Political Science* 32 (Jan.): 245–269.

Gamson, William. 1968. *Power and Discontent*. Homewood, IL: Dorsey.

Garcia, F. Chris. 1973. *Political Socialization of Chicano Children*. New York: Praeger.

Gartner, Scott S., and Gary M. Segura. 1998. "War Casualties and Public Opinion." *Journal of Conflict Resolution* 42 (June): 278–300.

de la Garza, Rodolfo O., Angelo Falcon, and F. Chris Garcia. 1996. "Will the Real Americans Please Stand Up: Anglo and Mexican-American Support of Core American Political Values." *American Journal of Political Science* 40 (2): 335–351.

de la Garza, Rodolfo O., and Seung-Jin Jang. 2008. "Latino Public Opinion." In *Oxford Handbook of American Public Opinion and Media*, eds. Robert S. Shapiro and Larry Jacobs (forthcoming).

Gastil, John. 2000. *By Popular Demand: Revitalizing Representative Democracy Through Deliberative Elections*. Berkeley, CA: University of California Press.

Geer, John G. 1996. *From Tea Leaves to Opinion Polls*. New York: Columbia University Press.

———. 2005. *Attacking Democracy: A Defense of Negativity in Presidential Campaigns*. Chicago: University of Chicago Press.

Gelman, Andrew, David Park, Boris Shor, Joseph Bafumi, and Geronimo Cortina. 2008. *Red State, Blue State, Rich State, Poor State: Why Americans Vote the Way They Do*. Princeton, NJ: Princeton University Press.

Gelpi, Christopheri, Peter D. Feaver, and Jason Reifler. 2005–2006. "Casualty Sensitivity and the War in Iraq." *International Security* 30: 7–46.

Gerber, Alan S., Dean Karlan, and Daniel Bergan. 2009. "Does the Media Matter? A Field Experiment Measuring the Effect of Newspapers on Voting Behavior and Political Opinions." *American Economic Journal: Applied Economics* 1 (2): 35–52.

Gerbner, George. 1998. "Who Is Shooting Whom? The Content and Analysis of Media Violence." In *Bang Bang, Shoot Shoot! Essays in Guns and Popular Culture*, eds. Murray Pomerance and John Sakeris. Needham Heights, MA: Simon and Schuster.

Gershkoff, Amy, and Shana Kushner. 2005. "Shaping Public Opinion: The 9/11-Iraq Connection in the Bush Administration's Rhetoric." *Perspectives on Politics* 3 (Sept.): 525–538.

Gentzkow, Mathew, and Jesse M. Shapiro. 2010. "What Drives Media Slant? Evidence from U.S. Daily Newspapers." *Econometrica* 78 (forthcoming).

Gibson, James L. 1986. "Pluralistic Intolerance in America." *American Politics Quarterly* 14 (Oct.): 267–293.

———. 1987. "Freedom and Tolerance in the United States." NORC (unpublished codebook).

———. 1988. "Political Intolerance and Political Repression During the McCarthy Red Scare." *American Political Science Review* 82 (June): 512–529.

———. 1996. "The Paradoxes of Political Tolerance in the Process of Democratization." *Politikon: South African Journal of Political Science* 23: 2–21.

———. 2005. "On the Nature of Tolerance: Dichotomous or Continuous?" *Political Behavior* 27 (Dec.): 313–323.

———. 2008. "Intolerance and Political Repression in the United States: A Half Century After McCarthyism." *American Journal of Political Science* 52 (Jan.): 96–108.

Gibson, James L., and Richard D. Bingham. 1985. *Civil Liberties and the Nazis: The Skokie Free-Speech Controversy.* New York: Praeger.

Gibson, James L., and Kent L. Tedin. 1988. "The Etiology of Intolerance for Homosexual Politics." *Social Science Quarterly* 69 (Sept.): 587–604.

Gibson, James L., and Gregory A. Caldeira. 2009. "Knowing the Supreme Court? A Reconsideration of Public Ignorance about the High Court." *Journal of Politics* 71 (Apr.): 429–441.

Gilens, Martin. 1999. *Why Americans Hate Welfare: Race, Media, and the Politics of Welfare Policy.* Chicago: University of Chicago Press.

———. 2001. "Political Ignorance and Collective Policy Preferences." *American Political Science Review* 95: 379–398.

———. 2005. "Inequality and Democratic Responsiveness." *Public Opinion Quarterly* 69: 778–796.

———. 2009. "Preference Gaps and Inequality in Representation." *PS: Political Science and Politics* 42 (Apr.): 335–342.

———. 2010. "Income Inequality in Democratic Responsiveness." In *Who Gets Represented*, eds. Peter Enns and Christopher Wlezien. New York: Russell Sage.

Gilens, Martin, and Craig Hertzman. 2000. "Corporate Ownership of News Bias: Newspaper Coverage of the 1996 Telecommunications Act." *Journal of Politics* 62 (Aug.): 369–389.

Gilens, Martin, Lynn Vavreck, and Martin Cohen. 2007. "The Mass Media and the Public Assessment of Presidential Candidates." *Journal of Politics* 69 (Nov.): 1160–1175.

Gilljam, Mikael, and Donald Granberg. 1993. "Should We Take Don't Know for an Answer?" *Public Opinion Quarterly* 57 (Fall): 348–357.

Gimpel, James G., J. Celeste Lay, and Jason E. Schuknecht. 2003. *Cultivating Democracy.* Washington, DC: Brookings Institution Press.

Gimpel, James G., Karen M. Kaufman, and Shanna Pearson Merkowitz. 2007. "Battleground States versus Blackout States: The Behavioral Implication of Modern Presidential Campaigns." *Journal of Politics* 64 (Aug.): 786–797.

Ginsberg, Benjamin. 1982. *The Consequences of Consent: Elections, Citizen Control and Popular Acquiescence.* Reading, MA: Addison-Wesley.

———. 1986. *The Captive Public.* New York: Basic.

Glazer, Amihai, and Marc Robbins. 1985. "Congressional Responsiveness to Constituency Change." *American Journal of Political Science* 29 (May): 259–273.

Goldberg, Barnard. 2001. *Bias in the News.* Washington, DC: Regnery.

Goldstein, Robert. 1978. *Political Repression in Modern America: From 1870 to the Present.* Cambridge, MA: Schenkman.

Gomez, Brad T., and J. Mathew Wilson. 2006. "Rethinking Symbolic Racism: Evidence of Attribution Bias." *Journal of Politics* 68 (Aug.): 611–625.

Goren, Paul. 2004. "Political Sophistication and Policy Reasoning: A Reconsideration." *American Journal of Political Science* 48 (July): 462–478.

———. 2005. "Party Identification and Core Political Values." *American Journal of Political Science* 49 (Oct.): 881–896.

Green, Donald, Bradley Palmquist, and Eric Schickler. 1998. "Macropartisanship: A Replication and Critique." *American Political Science Review* 92: 883–899.

———. 2002. *Partisan Hearts and Minds: Political Parties and the Social Identities of the Voters.* New Haven, CT: Yale University Press.

Green, John C. 2007. *The Faith Factor: How Religion Influences American Elections.* Westport, CT: Praeger.

Greenberg, Edward. 1970. "Black Children and the Political System." *Public Opinion Quarterly* 34: 335–348.

Greene, Jay P. 2000. "Review of Civic Education: What Makes Students Learn." *Social Science Quarterly* 81: 696–697.

Griffin, John D., and Brian Newman. 2005. "Are Voters Better Represented?" *Journal of Politics* 67: 1206–1227.

Groeling, Timothy, and Samuel Kernell. 1998. "Is Network News Coverage of the President Biased?" *Journal of Politics* 60: 1063–1087.

Groseclose, Timothy, and Jeffrey Milyo. 2005. "A Measure of Media Bias." *Quarterly Journal of Economics* 120 (4): 1191–1237.

Groves, Robert, and Mick Couper. 1998. *Nonresponse in Household Surveys.* New York: John Wiley and Sons.

Groves, Robert. 2006. "Nonresponse Rates and Nonresponse Bias in Household Surveys." *Public Opinion Quarterly* 70 (Winter): 646–675.

Guth, Mathew. 2009. "Religion and American Public Opinion: Foreign Policy Issues." In *The Oxford Handbook of Religion and American Politics,* eds. Corwin E. Smidt, Lyman A. Kellstedt, and James L. Guth. Oxford: Oxford University Press.

Hacker, Jacob S., and Paul Pierson. 2005. "Abandoning the Middle: The Bush Tax Cuts and the Limits of Democratic Control." *Perspectives on Politics* 3 (Mar.): 33–53.

Haider-Markel, Donald P., and Mark R. Joslyn. 2008. "Beliefs about the Origins of Homosexuality and Support for Gay Rights: An Empirical Test of Attribution Theory." *Public Opinion Quarterly* 72 (Summer): 291–310.

Haider-Markel, Donald P., and Matthew S. Kaufman. 2006. "Public Opinion and Culture Wars. Is There a Connection Between Opinion and State Policy on Gay and Lesbian Issues?" In *Public Opinion in State Politics,* ed. Jeffrey E. Cohen. Stanford, CA: Stanford University Press.

Hand, Learned. 1959. *The Spirit of Liberty: Papers and Addresses.* New York: Knopf.

Hansen, John Mark. 1998. "Individuals, Institutions, and Public Preferences over Public Finance." *American Political Science Review* 92 (Sept.): 513–531.

Harris-Kojetin, Brian, and Clyde Tucker. 1999. "Exploring the Relation of Economic and Political Conditions with Refusal Rates to a Government Survey." *Journal of Official Statistics* 15 (June): 167–184.

Hartley, Thomas, and Bruce Russett. 1992. "Public Opinion and the Common Defense: Who Governs Military Spending in the United States?" *American Political Science Review* 86 (Dec.): 905–915.

Harvey, G. Ted. 1972. "Computer Simulation of Peer Group Influence on Adolescent Political Behavior." *American Journal of Political Science* 16 (Nov.): 588–621.

Harvey, O. J., and G. Beverly. 1961. "Some Personality Correlates of Concept Change Through Role Playing." *Journal of Abnormal and Social Psychology* 27 (Mar.): 125–130.

Hatemi, Peter K., John Hibbing, John Alford, Nicholas Martin, and Lindon Eaves. 2009. "Is There a Party in Your Genes?" *Political Research Quarterly* 62: 584–600.

Hatemi, Peter K., Sarah E. Medland, and Lindon J. Eaves. 2009. "Genetic Sources for the Gender Gap." *Journal of Politics* 71: 262–276.

Hawkins, Robert P., Suzanne Pingree, and Donald Roberts. 1975. "Watergate and Political Socialization." *American Politics Quarterly* 4 (Oct.): 406–436.

Hedges, Chris. 1999. "35% of High School Seniors Fail National Civics Test." *New York Times,* Nov. 12, 1999, sec. 1, p. 17.

Hedlund, Ronald D. 1975. "Perceptions of Decisional Referents in Legislative Decision-Making." *American Journal of Political Science* 19 (Aug.): 527–542.

Herbst, Susan. 1993. *Numbered Voices: How Public Opinion Has Shaped American Politics*. Chicago: University of Chicago Press.

Herson, Lawrence J. R., and C. Richard Hofstetter. 1975. "Tolerance, Consensus, and Democratic Creed." *Journal of Politics* 37 (Dec.): 1007–1032.

Hero, Alfred O. 1973. *American Religious Groups View Foreign Policy: Trends in Rank and File Opinion, 1937–1969*. Durham, NC: Duke University Press.

Herrera, Cheryl Lyn, Richard Herrera, and Eric R. A. N. Smith. 1992. "Public Opinion and Congressional Representation." *Public Opinion Quarterly* 56 (Summer): 185–205.

Herrera, Richard. 1992. "The Understanding of Ideological Labels by Political Elites: A Research Note." *Western Political Quarterly* 45 (Dec.): 1021–1035.

Hertsgaard, Mark. 1988. *On Bended Knee: The Press and the Reagan Presidency*. New York: Farrar.

Hess, Robert D., and Judith V. Torney. 1967. *The Development of Political Attitudes in Children*. Chicago, IL: Aldine.

Hetherington, Marc J. 1996. "The Media's Role in Forming Voters' National Economic Evaluations in 1992." *American Journal of Political Science* 40 (May): 372–395.

———. 1998. "The Political Relevance of Political Trust." *American Political Science Review* 91 (Dec.): 791–808.

———. 1999. "The Effect of Political Trust on the Presidential Vote, 1968–1996." *American Political Science Review* 93 (June): 311–326.

———. 2001. "Declining Trust and Shrinking Policy Agenda: Why Media Scholars Should Care." In *Communication in U.S. Elections: New Agendas*, eds. Roderick P. Hart and Daron R. Shaw. Lanham, MD: Rowman-Littlefield.

———. 2005. *Why Trust Matters: Declining Political Trust and the Demise of American Liberalism*. Princeton, NJ: Princeton University Press.

Hetherington, Marc J., and Thomas J. Rudolph. 2008. "Priming, Performance, and the Dynamics of Political Trust." *Journal of Politics* 70 (Apr.): 498–512.

Hetherington, Marc J., and Jonathan D. Weiler. 2009. *Authoritarianism and Polarization in American Politics*. Cambridge, UK: Cambridge University Press.

Hibbing, John, and Elizabeth Theiss-Morse. 1998. "The Media's Role in Public Negativity Toward Congress: Distinguishing Emotional Reactions and Cognitive Evaluations." *American Journal of Political Science* 42 (May): 475–498.

———. 2002. *Stealth Democracy: Americans' Beliefs About How Government Should Work*. Cambridge, UK: Cambridge University Press.

Hibbs, Douglas A., Jr. 1987. *The American Political Economy: Macroeconomics and Electoral Politics in the United States*. Cambridge, MA: Harvard University Press.

Hibbs, Douglas A., Jr., and Christopher Dennis. 1988. "Income Distribution in the United States." *American Political Science Review* 82 (June): 467–490.

Hilderbrand, Robert. 1981. *Power and the People: Executive Management of Public Opinion in Foreign Affairs*. Chapel Hill, NC: University of North Carolina Press.

Hillygus, D. Sunshine. 2005. "The Missing Link: Exploring the Relationship between Higher Education and Political Engagement." *Political Behavior* 27: 25–45.

Hillygus, D. Sunshine, and Simon Jackman. 2003. "Voter Decision Making in Election 2000: Campaign Effects, Partisan Activation, and the Clinton Legacy." *American Journal of Political Science* 47: 583–596.

Hillygus, Sunshine, and Todd G. Shields. 2008. *The Persuadable Voter*. Princeton, NJ: Princeton University Press.

Hindman, Mathew. 2009. *The Myth of Digital Democracy*. Princeton, NJ: Princeton University Press.

Hoffman, Beth R., Peter R. Mone, Chich-Ping Chou, and Thomas W. Valente. 2007. "Perceived Peer Influence and Peer Selection on Adolescent Smoking." *Addictive Behaviors* 32: 1546–1554.

Holbrook, Allyson L., Jon A. Krosnick, and Alison Pfent. 2008. "The Causes and Consequences of Response Rates in Surveys by the News Media and Government Contractor Research Firms." In *Advances in Telephone Survey Methods,* eds. James Lepkowski, Clyde Tucker, Michael Brick, Edith Leeuw, Lilli Japec, Paul Lavrakas, and Rioberta Snagster. New York: Wiley Interscience.

Holsti, Ole. 2004. *Public Opinion and American Foreign Policy.* Ann Arbor: University of Michigan Press.

Hopkins, Daniel J. 2009. "No More Wilder Effect, Never a Whitman Effect: When and Why Polls Mislead about Black and Female Candidates." *Journal of Politics* 71 (July): 769–781.

Huber, Gregory A., and Sanford C. Gordon. 2004. "Accountability and Coersion: Is Justice Blind When It Runs for Office?" *American Journal of Political Science* 48 (Apr.): 247–263.

Huber, Gregory A., and Kevin Arceneaux. 2007. "Identifying the Persuasive Effects of Political Advertising." *American Journal of Political Science* 51: 957–977.

Huber, Gregory A., and John S. Lapinski. 2006. "The 'Race Card' Revisited: Assessing Racial Priming in Policy Contents." *American Journal of Political Science* 48 (May): 375–401.

———. 2008. "Testing the Implicit-Explicit Model of Racialized Political Communication." *Perspectives on Politics* 6 (Mar.): 125–134.

Huddy, Leonie, Stanley Feldman, Charles Taber, and Gallya Lavhav. 2005. "Threat, Anxiety, and Support of Antiterrorism Policies." *American Journal of Political Science* 49 (July): 593–608.

Huddy, Leonie, and Nadia Khatib. 2007. "American Patriotism, National Identity and Political Involvement." *American Journal of Political Science* 51 (Jan.): 63–77.

Hugick, Larry, and Guy Molyneux. 1993. "The Performance of the Gallup Tracking Poll: The Myth and the Reality." *Public Perspective* 4 (Jan./Feb.): 12–14.

Huntington, Samuel P. 1991. *The Third Wave: Democratization in the Late Twentieth Century.* Norman: University of Oklahoma Press.

———. 2004. *Who Are We?* New York: Simon and Schuster.

Hurley, Patricia A., and Kim Quaile Hill. 2003. "Beyond the Diamond-Input Model: A Theory of Representational Linkages." *Journal of Politics* 65 (2): 304–326.

Hurwitz, Jon, and Mark Peffley. 1987. "How Are Foreign Policy Attitudes Structured? A Hierarchical Model." *American Political Science Review* 81 (Dec.): 1099–1120.

———. 2005. "Playing the Race Card in the Post-Willie Horton Era." *Public Opinion Quarterly* 69 (Spring): 99–112.

Hutchings, Vincent L. 2003. *Public Opinion and Democratic Accountability.* Princeton, NJ: Princeton University Press.

Hutchings, Vincent L., and Ashley E. Jardina. 2009. "Experiments on Racial Priming in Political Campaigns." *Annual Review of Political Science* 12: 397–402.

Inglehart, Ronald. 1990. *Culture Shift.* Princeton, NJ: Princeton University Press.

———. 1997a. "Postmaterialist Values and the Erosion of Institutional Authority." In *Why People Don't Trust Government,* eds. Joseph S. Nye, Philip D. Zelikow, and David C. King. Cambridge, MA: Harvard University Press.

———. 1997b. *Modernization and Postmodernization.* Princeton, NJ: Princeton University Press.

Inkeles, Alex. 1961. "National Character and the Modern Political System." In *Psychological Anthropology: Approaches to Culture and Personality,* ed. Francis L. K. Hsu. Homewood, IL: Dorsey.

Iyengar, Shanto, and Donald R. Kinder. 1987. *News that Matters.* Chicago: University of Chicago Press.

Iyengar, Shanto, Helmut Norpoth, and Kyu S. Hahn. 2004. "Consumer Demand for Election News: The Horserace Sells." *Journal of Politics* 66 (Feb.): 157–175.

Iyengar, Shanto, Mark D. Peters, and Donald R. Kinder. 1982. "Experimental Demonstrations of 'Not-So-Minimal' Consequences of Television News Programs." *American Political Science Review* 76 (Dec.): 848–858.

Jackman, Mary. 1978. "General and Applied Tolerance: Does Education Increase Commitment to Racial Integration?" *American Journal of Political Science* 22 (May): 302–324.

Jackman, Mary R., and Robert W. Jackman. 1983. *Class Awareness in the United States.* Berkeley, CA: University of California Press.

Jackman, Mary, and Michael J. Mulha. 1984. "Education and Intergroup Attitudes: Moral Enlightenment, Superficial Democratic Commitment or Ideological Refinement." *American Sociological Review* 49 (Aug.): 751–769.

Jackman, Robert W. 1972. "Political Elites, Mass Publics, and Support for Democratic Principles." *Journal of Politics* 54 (Aug.): 753–773.

Jackman, Robert W., and Robert A. Miller. 1996. "A Renaissance of Political Culture?" *American Journal of Political Science* 40 (May): 632–659.

Jackman, Simon, and Paul Sniderman. 2006. "The Limits of Deliberative Discussion: A Model of Everyday Political Arguments." *The Journal of Politics* 68: 272–283.

Jacob, Philip E. 1956. *Changing Values in College.* New Haven, CT: Hazen Foundation.

Jacobs, Lawrence R. 1993. *The Health of Nations: Public Opinions in the Making of American and British Health Policy.* Ithaca, NY: Cornell University Press.

Jacobs, Lawrence R., and Benjamin I. Page. 2005. "Who Influences U.S. Foreign Policy?" *American Political Science Review* 99: 107–123.

Jacobs, Lawrence R., and Robert Y. Shapiro. 2000. *Politicians Don't Pander: Political Manipulation and the Loss of Democratic Responsiveness.* Chicago: University of Chicago Press.

Jacobson, Gary C. 1987. *The Politics of Congressional Elections,* 2nd ed. Boston, MA: Little, Brown.

———. 1989. "Parties and PACs in Congressional Elections." In *Congress Reconsidered,* 4th ed., eds. Lawrence C. Dodd and Bruce I. Oppenheimer. Washington, DC: Congressional Quarterly Press.

Jacobson, Gary C., and Samuel Kernell. 1983. *Strategy and Choice in Congressional Elections,* 2nd ed. New Haven, CT: Yale University Press.

Jacoby, William G. 1988. "The Impact of Party Identification on Issue Attitudes." *American Journal of Political Science* 32 (Aug.): 643–661.

———. 1991. "Ideological Identifications and Issue Attitudes." *American Journal of Political Science* 35 (Feb.): 178–205.

Jaros, Dean, Herbert Hirsch, and Frederick Fleron. 1968. "The Malevolent Leader: Political Socialization in an American Sub-Culture." *American Political Science Review* 62 (June): 564–575.

Jelen, Ted. G. 1992. "Political Christianity: A Contextual Analysis." *American Journal of Political Science* 36 (Aug.): 662–692.

Jennings, M. Kent. 1987. "Residuals of a Movement: The Aging of the American Protest Generation." *American Political Science Review* 81 (June): 365–381.

———. 1992. "Ideological Thinking among Mass Publics and Political Elites." *Public Opinion Quarterly* 56 (Winter): 419–441.

———. 2002. "Generational Units and the Student Protest Movement in the United States: An Intra- and Intergenerational Analysis." *Political Psychology* 23 (June): 303–325.

———. 2004. "Political Socialization." In *The Oxford Handbook of Political Behavior,* eds. Russell Dalton and Hans-Dieter Klingman. Oxford: Oxford University Press.

Jennings, M. Kent, and Ellen Ann Andersen. 1996. "Support for Confrontational Tactics among AIDS Activists: A Study of Intra–Movement Divisions." *American Journal of Political Science* 40 (May): 311–334.

Jennings, M. Kent, Lee H. Ehrman, and Richard G. Niemi. 1974. "Social Studies Teachers and Their Students." In *The Political Character of Adolescence,* eds. M. Kent Jennings and Richard G. Niemi. Princeton, NJ: Princeton University Press.

Jennings, M. Kent, and Gregory B. Markus. 1984. "Partisan Orientations over the Long Haul: Results from the Three-Wave Political Socialization Panel Study." *American Political Science Review* 78 (Dec.): 1000–1018.

Jennings, M. Kent, and Kenneth P. Langton. 1969. "Mothers Versus Fathers: The Formation of Political Orientations among Young Americans." *Journal of Politics 31* (Nov.): 724–741.

Jennings, M. Kent, and Richard G. Niemi. 1968. "The Transmission of Political Values from Parent to Child." *American Political Science Review* 62 (Mar.): 1579–1592.

———. 1974. *The Political Character of Adolescence*. Princeton, NJ: Princeton University Press.

———. 1982. *Generations and Politics*. Princeton, NJ: Princeton University Press.

Jennings, M. Kent, and Laura Stoker. 1999. "The Persistence of the Past: The Class of 1965 Turns Fifty." Paper presented at the Midwest Political Science Convention, April 1999. Chicago.

Jennings, M. Kent, and Laura Stoker. 2004. "Social Trust and Civic Engagement Across Time and Generations." *Acta Politica* 39 (July): 342–379.

Jennings, M. Kent, Laura Stoker, and Jake Bowers. 2009. "Politics Across Generations: Family Transmission Reexamined." *Journal of Politics* 71 (July): 782–799.

Jensen, Richard. 1968. "American Election Analysis: A Case of History and Methodological Innovation and Diffusion." In *Politics and Social Science*, ed. Seymour Martin Lipset. New York: Oxford University Press.

Jerit, Jennifer, and Jason Barabas. 2006. "Bankrupt Rhetoric: How Misleading Information Affects Knowledge about Social Security." *Public Opinion Quarterly* 70 (Fall): 278–303.

Jewell, Malcolm E., and David Breaux. 1988. "The Effect of Incumbency on State Legislative Elections." *Legislative Studies Quarterly* 13 (Nov.): 495–514.

Johannes, John R., and John P. McAdams. 1981. "The Congressional Incumbency Effect: Is It Casework, Policy Compatibility, or Something Else? An Examination of the 1978 Election." *American Journal of Political Science* 25 (Aug.): 512–552.

Johnson, Martin, Paul Brace, and Kevin Arceneaux. 2005. "Public Opinion and Dynamic Representation in the States: The Case of Environmental Attitudes." *Social Science Quarterly* 86 (Mar.): 87–108.

Johnston, Richard, Michael G. Hagan, and Kathleen Hall Jamieson. 2004. The 2000 Presidential Election and the Foundation of Party Politics. Cambridge, UK: Cambridge University Press.

Johnstone, David Cay. 2003. "At the Very Top, A Surge in Income in '03." *New York Times*. Oct. 5, D1.

Joslyn, Mark R. 2003. "The Determinants and Consequences of Recall Error About Gulf War Preferences." *American Journal of Political Science* 47: 127–139.

Just, Marion, and Ann Crigler. 2000. "Leadership Image-Building: After Clinton and Watergate." *Political Psychology* 21: 179–188.

Kagay, Michael R., and Gregory A. Caldiera. 1980. "A 'Reformed' Electorate? Well, at Least a Changed Electorate, 1952–1976," In *Paths to Political Reform*, ed. William Crotty. D. C. Heath.

Kahn, Kim Fridkin, and Patrick J. Kenney. 1999. "Do Negative Campaigns Mobilize or Suppress Turnout? Clarifying the Relationship Between Negativity and Participation." *American Political Science Review* 93: 877–889.

———. 2002. "The Slant of the News: How Editorial Endorsements Influence Campaign Coverage and Citizens' Views of Candidates." *American Political Science Review* 96 (June): 381–394.

Kahne, Joseph, and Joel Westheimer. 2006. "The Limits of Political Efficacy: Educating Citizens for Democratic Society." *PS: Political Science and Politics* 39 (Apr.): 289–298.

Kam, Cindy D., and Donald R. Kinder. 2007. "Terrorism and Ethnocentrism: Foundations of American Support for the War on Terror." *Journal of Politics* 69 (May): 320–338.

Kanthak, Kristin, and Barbara Norrander. 2004. "The Enduring Gender Gap." In *Models of Voting in Presidential Elections*, eds. Herbert F. Weisberg and Clyde Wilcox. Stanford, CA: Stanford University Press.

Karp, Jeffrey A. 1995. "Support for Legislative Term Limits." *Public Opinion Quarterly* 59 (Fall): 373–391.

Kaufmann, Karen M., and John R. Petrocik. 1999. "The Changing Politics of Men: Understanding the Source of the Gender Gap." *American Journal of Political Science* 43 (July): 864–887.

Kaufman, Karen M. 2006. "The Gender Gap." *PS: Political Science and Politics* 39: 447–453.

Keele, Luke. 2005. "The Authorities Really Do Matter: Party Control and Trust in Government." *Journal of Politics* 87 (Aug.): 872–886.

Keeter, Scott, Carolyn Miller, Andrew Kohut, Robert M. Groves, and Stanley Presser. 2000. "Consequences of Reducing Nonresponse in a National Telephone Survey." *Public Opinion Quarterly* 64: 125–148.

Keeter, Scott. 2006. "The Impact of Cell Phone Noncoverage Biases on Polling in the 2004 Presidential Election." *Public Opinion Quarterly* 70 (Spring): 88–98.

Keeter, Scott, Juliana Maenasce Horowitz, and Alec Tyson. 2008. "Gen Dems: The Party's Advantage Among Young Voters Widens." Pew Research Center (Apr.). http://pewresearch.org/pubs/813/gen-dems

Kelley, Stanley J., Jr. 1983. *Interpreting Elections*. Princeton, NJ: Princeton University Press.

Kelly, Nathan J. 2009. *The Politics of Income Inequality in the United States*. New York: Cambridge University Press.

Kenski, Kate, and Kathleen Hall Jamieson. 2000. The Gender Gap in Political Knowledge: Are Women Less Knowledgeable Than Men About Politics? In *Everything You Think You Know About Politics And Why You are Wrong*, ed. Kathleen Hall Jamieson. New York: Basic Books.

Kerlinger, Fred N. 1984. *Liberalism and Conservatism*. Hillsdale, NJ: Erlbaum.

Kernell, Samuel. 1978. "Explaining Presidential Popularity." *American Political Science Review* 72 (June): 506–523.

———. 1993. *Going Public: New Strategies for Presidential Leadership*. Washington, DC: Congressional Quarterly Press.

Key, V. O., Jr. 1949. *Southern Politics in State and Nation*. New York: Knopf.

Key, V.O., Jr. 1961a. "Public Opinion and the Decay of Democracy." *Virginia Quarterly Review* 37 (Autumn): 481–491.

———. 1961b. *Public Opinion and American Democracy*. New York: Knopf.

Kiewiet, D. Roderick. 1983. *Macroeconomics and Micropolitics*. Chicago: University of Chicago Press.

Kiewiet, D. Roderick, and Matthew D. McCubbins. 1985. "Congressional Appropriations and the Electoral Connection." *Journal of Politics* 47 (Spring): 59–82.

Kinder, Donald R., and D. Roderick Kiewiet. 1979. "Economic Grievances and Political Behavior: The Role of Personal Discontents and Collective Judgments in Congressional Voting." *American Journal of Political Science* 23 (Aug.): 495–527.

———. 1981. "Sociotropic Politics." *British Journal of Political Science* 11 (Apr.): 129–161.

Kinder, Donald R., and Lynn M. Sanders. 1996. *Divided by Color*. Chicago: University of Chicago Press.

Kinder, Donald R., and Nicholas Winter. 2001. "Exploring the Racial Divide: Blacks, Whites and Opinions on National Policy." *American Journal of Political Science* 45: 439–452.

Kingdon, John W. 1973. *Congressmen's Voting Decisions*. New York: Harper.

Kirscht, John P., and Ronald C. Dillehay. 1967. *Dimensions of Authoritarianism: A Review of Research and Theory*. Lexington: University of Kentucky Press.

Knight, Kathleen. 1985. "Ideology in the 1980 Election: Political Sophistication Matters." *Journal of Politics* 47 (Aug.): 828–853.

Kobus, Kim. 2003. "Peers and Adolescent Smoking." *Addiction* 98 (Suppl. 1): 37–55.

Kohut, Andrew, and Bruce Stokes. 2006. *American Against the World. How We Are Different and Why We Are Disliked*. New York: New York Times Books.

Koch, Jeffery W. 1998. "Political Rhetoric and Political Persuasion." *Public Opinion Quarterly* 62 (Summer): 209–229.

Kornhauser, William. 1970. *The Politics of Mass Society*. Chicago, IL: Markham.

Krehbiel, Keith. 1993. "Where's the Party?" *British Journal of Political Science* 23: 235–266.

———. 1999. "The Party Effect from A to Z and Beyond." *Journal of Politics* 61: 832–841.

———. 2000. "Party Discipline and the Measures of Partisanship." *American Journal of Political Science* 44: 212–227.

Krasno, Jonathan S., and Donald P. Green. 2008. "Do Television Presidential Ads Increase Voter Turnout: Evidence from a Natural Experiment." *Journal of Politics* 70 (Jan.): 245–261.

Krosnick, Jon A., and Laura Brannon. 1993. "The Impact of the Gulf War on the Ingredients of Presidential Evaluations: Multidimensional Effects of Political Involvement." *American Political Science Review* 87 (Dec.): 963–975.

Krosnick, Jon A., and Matthew K. Kerent. 1993. "Comparisons of Party Identification and Policy Preferences: The Impact of Survey Question Format." *American Journal of Political Science* 37 (Aug.): 941–964.

Kuklinski, James H. 1978. "Representatives and Elections: A Policy Analysis." *American Political Science Review* 72 (Mar.) 165–177.

Kuklinski, James H., Michael D. Cobb, and Martin Gilens. 1997. "Racial Attitudes in the New South." *Journal of Politics* 59 (May): 323–349.

Kuklinski, James H., Paul J. Quirk, Jennifer Jerit, and Robert Rich. 2001. "The Political Environment of Citizen Competence." *American Journal of Political Science* 41 (Oct.): 410–429.

Kull, Steven, Clay Ramsey, and Evin Lewis. 2003–2004. "Misperception, the Media, and the Iraq War." *Political Science Quarterly* 118: 369–398.

Ladd, Everett Carl. 1970. *American Political Parties: Social Change and Political Response*. New York: Norton.

———. 1989. *The American Polity*. New York: Norton.

———. 1998. *America's Social Capital: Change and Renewal in Civil Life*. New York: Free Press.

Lane, Robert. 1962. *Political Ideology*. New York: Free Press.

Langer, Gary. 2002. "Trust in Government." *Public Perspective* (July/Aug.): 7–10.

Langton, Kenneth P., and M. Kent Jennings. 1968. "Political Socialization and the High School Civics Curriculum in the United States." *American Political Science Review* 62 (Sept.): 852–877.

Lapinski, Daniel. 2001. "The Effect of Messages Communicated by Members of Congress: The Impact of Publicizing Their Votes." *Legislative Studies Quarterly* 26: 81–100.

Larson, Stephanie G. 2001. "Poll Coverage of the 2000 Presidential Campaign on the Network News." Paper delivered at the annual meeting of the American Political Science Association, Sept., San Francisco.

Lasswell, Harold D. 1951. "Democratic Character." In *The Political Writings of Harold D. Lasswell*. Glencoe, IL: Free Press.

Lau, Richard R., and Gerald M. Pomper. 2004. *Negative Campaigning: An Analysis of U.S. Senate Elections*. New York: Rowland and Littlefield.

Lau, Richard, and David P. Redlawsk. 2006. *How Voters Decide: Information Processing During Election Campaigns*. New York: Cambridge University Press.

Lau, Richard R. Lee Sigelman, and Iry Brown Royner. 2007. "The Effects of Negative Political Campaigns: A Meta-Analytic Reassessment." *Journal of Politics* 69 (Nov.): 1176–1209.

Lau, Richard R., Lee Sigelman, Caroline Heldman, and Paul Babbit. 1999. "The Effects of Negative Political Advertisements: A Meta-Analytic Assessment." *American Political Science Review* 93 (Dec.): 851–876.

Lavine, Howard, Milton Lodge, and Kate Freitas. 2005. "Threat, Authoritarianism, and Selective Exposure to Information." *Political Psychology* 26: 219–244.

Lawson, Edwin D. 1975. "Flag Preference as an Indicator of Patriotism in Israeli Children." *Journal of Cross-Cultural Psychology* 6: 490–499.

Lawrence, Eric., John Sides, and Henry Farrell. 2009. "Self-Segregation or Deliberation: Blog Readership and Polarization in American Politics." *Perspectives on Politics* (Forthcoming).

Lax, Jeffrey, and Justin Philips. 2009. "Gay Rights in the States: Public Opinion and Policy Responsiveness." *American Political Science Review* (Forthcoming).

Lazarsfeld, Paul, Bernard Berelson, and Hazel Gaudet. 1948. *The People's Choice*. New York: Columbia University Press.

Lee, Gahgheong, and Joseph N. Cappella. 2001. "The Effects of Political Talk Radio on Political Attitude Formation: Exposure Versus Knowledge." *Political Communication* 18: 369–394.

Lenz, Gabriel. 2009. "Learning and Opinion Change, Not Priming: Reconsidering the Evidence for the Priming Hypothesis." *American Journal of Political Science* 53 (Oct.): 812–837.

Lepkowski, James M, and Clyde Tucker, J. Michael Brick, and Eeith D. De Leeuw. 2008. *Advances in Telephone Survey Methodology.* New York: Wiley Interscience.

Lewis-Beck, Michael S., William S. Jacoby, Helmut Norpoth, and Herbert F. Weisberg. 2008. *The American Voter Revisited.* Ann Arbor, MI: University of Michigan Press.

Lewis-Beck, Michael, and Tom Rice. 1982. "Presidential Popularity and the Presidential Vote." *Public Opinion Quarterly* 47 (Winter): 534–537.

Lewis-Beck, Michael S., and Mary Stegmeier. 2000. "Economic Determinants of Electoral Outcomes." *Annual Review of Political Science* 3: 183–219.

Light, Paul C., and Celinda Lake. 1985. "The Election: Candidates, Strategies, and Decision." In *The Elections of 1984*, ed. Michael Nelson. Washington, DC: Congressional Quarterly.

Lindeman, Michael. 2002. "Opinion Quality and Policy Preferences in Deliberative Research" In *Research in Micropolitics: Decision-Making, Deliberation and Participation.* Greenwich, CT: JAI Press.

Lippmann, Walter. 1922. *Public Opinion.* New York: Harcourt.

———. 1925. *The Phantom Public.* New York: Harcourt.

Lipset, Seymour Martin. 1950. *Agrarian Socialism.* Berkeley, CA: University of California Press.

———. 1959. "Some Social Requisites of Modern Democracy: Economic Development and Political Legitimacy." *American Political Science Review* 53 (Mar.): 69–105.

———. 1960. *Political Man.* Garden City, NY: Doubleday.

Lodge, Milton, Kathleen McGraw, and Patrick Stroh. 1989. "An Impression-Driven Model of Candidate Evaluation." *American Political Science Review* 83 (June): 399–419.

Lodge, Milton, Marco R. Steenbergen, and Shawn Brau. 1995. "The Responsive Voter: Candidate Information and the Dynamics of Candidate Evaluation." *American Political Science Review* 89 (June): 309–331.

Lodge, Milton, and Patrick Stroh. 1993. "Inside the Mental Voting Booth: An Impression-Driven Process." In *Explorations in Political Psychology*, eds. Shanto Iyengar and William J. McGuire. Durham, NC: Duke University Press.

Lottes, Ilsa L., and Peter J. Kuriloff. 1994. "The Impact of College Experience on Political and Social Attitudes." *Sex Roles* 31: 31–54.

Luker, Kristin. 1984. *Abortion and the Politics of Motherhood.* Berkeley, CA: University of California Press.

Lupia, Arthur, and Mathew D. McCubbins. 1998. *The Democratic Dilemma: Can Citizens Learn What They Need to Know?* New York: Cambridge University Press.

Lupia, Arthur, Adam Seth Levine, Jesse O. Manning, and Giesela Sin. 2007. "Were Bush Tax Cut Supporters 'Simply Ignorant?' A Second Look at Conservatives and Liberals in 'Homer Gets a Tax Cut'." *Perspectives on Politics* 4 (Dec.): 773–784.

Luskin, Robert C. 1987. "Measuring Political Sophistication." *American Journal of Political Science* 31 (Nov.): 856–899.

———. 2003. "The Heavenly Public: What Would a Fully Informed Citizenry Be Like?" In *Electoral Democracy*, eds. George Rabinowitz and Michael B. MacKuen. Ann Arbor: University of Michigan Press.

Luskin, Robert, James Fishkin, and Roger Jowell. 2002. "Considered Opinions: Deliberative Polling in Britain." *British Journal of Political Science* 32: 455–487.

Luttbeg, Norman R. 1968. "Political Linkage in a Large Society." In *Public Opinion and Public Policy*, ed. Norman Luttbeg. Homewood, IL: Dorsey.

MacDougall, Curtis D. 1966. *Understanding Public Opinion.* Boston, MA: Little, Brown.

————. 1984. "Exposure to Information, Belief Integration, and Individual Responsiveness to Agenda Change." *American Political Science Review* 78 (June): 372–391.

MacKuen, Michael B., Robert S. Erikson, and James A. Stimson. 1989. "Macropartisanship." *American Political Science Review* 83 (Dec.): 1125–1142.

————. 1992. "Peasants or Bankers? The American Electorate and the U.S. Economy." *American Political Science Review* 86 (Sept.): 597–611.

Magner, Denise. 1999. "Faculty Attitudes and Characteristics: Results of a 1998–1999 Survey." *Chronicle of Higher Education* (Sept. 3): A20–A21.

Meloen, J. D., G. van der Linden, and H. de Witte. 1996. "A Test of the Approaches of Adorno et al., Ledere, and Altemeyer of Authoritarianism in Belgian Flanders: A Research Note." *Political Psychology* 17: 643–656.

Manin, Bernard, Adam Przeworski, and Susan C. Stokes. 1999. "Elections and Representation." In *Democracy, Accountability, and Representation*, eds. Adam Przeworski, Susan C. Stokes, and Bernard Manin. Cambridge, UK: Cambridge University Press.

Mann, Sheilah. 1996. "Symposium: Political Scientists Examine Civic Standards." *Political Science and Politics* 29 (Mar.): 47–48.

————. 1999. "What the Survey of American College Freshman Tells Us About Their Interest in Politics and Political Science." *Political Science and Politics* 32 (June): 263–268.

Mann, Thomas E., and Norman J. Ornstein, eds. 1994. *Congress, the Press, and the Public.* Washington, DC: Brookings.

Manza, Jeff, and Clem Brooks. 1999. *Social Cleavages and Political Change: Voter Alignments and U.S. Party Coalitions.* New York: Oxford University Press.

Mansbridge, Jane. 2003. "Rethinking Representation." *American Political Science Review* 97: 515–528.

Marcus, George E., W. Russell Neuman, and Michael B. MacKuen. 2000. *Affective Intelligence and Political Judgment.* Chicago: University of Chicago Press.

Marcus, George E., and Michael B. MacKuen. 2001. "Emotions and Politics: The Dynamic Functions of Emotionality." In *Citizen and Politics: Perspectives from Political Psychology*, ed. James Kuklinski. Cambridge, UK: Cambridge University Press.

Markus, Gregory B. 1979. "The Political Environment and the Dynamics of Public Attitudes." *American Journal of Political Science* 23 (May): 338–359.

Markus, Gregory B., and Philip E. Converse. 1979. "A Dynamic Simultaneous Equation Model of Public Choice." *American Political Science Review* 73 (Dec.): 1055–1070.

Marmor, Theodore R. 1970. *The Politics of Medicare.* Chicago, IL: Aldine.

Mayhew, David R. 1974. *Congress: The Electoral Connection.* New Haven, CT: Yale University Press.

————. 1991. *Divided We Govern: Party Control, Lawmaking, and Investigations, 1946–1990.* New Haven, CT: Yale University Press.

————. 2002. *Electoral Realignments: A Critique of the American Genre.* New Haven, CT: Yale University Press.

McCarty, Nolan, Keith T. Poole, and Howard Rosenthal. 2001. "The Hunt for Party Discipline in Congress." *American Political Science Review* 95: 673–688.

————. 2006. *Polarized America: The Dance of Ideology and Unequal Riches.* Cambridge: MIT Press.

McCloskey, Herbert. 1964. "Consensus and Ideology in American Politics." *American Political Science Review* 58 (June).

McClosky, Herbert, and Alida Brill. 1983. *Dimensions of Political Tolerance.* New York: Russell Sage.

McClosky, Herbert, Paul J. Hoffman, and Rosemary O'Hara. 1960. "Issue Conflict and Consensus Among Party Leaders and Followers." *American Political Science Review* 59 (June): 406–427.

McCombs, Maxwell E., and Donald L. Shaw. 1972. "The Agenda-Setting Function of the Mass Media." *Public Opinion Quarterly* 35 (Summer): 176–187.

McDermott, Monika L., and Kathleen A. Frankovic. 2003. "Horserace Polling and the Survey Method: An Analysis of the 2000 Campaign." *Public Opinion Quarterly* 67 (June): 244–264.

McDonald, Michael D., Ian Budge, and Richard I. Hofferbert. 1999. "Party Mandate Theory and Time Series Analysis: A Theoretical and Methodological Response." *Electoral Studies* 18: 587–596.

McFarland, Daniel A., and Reuben J. Thomas. 2006. "Bowling Young: How Youth Voluntary Associations Influence Adult Political Participation." *American Sociological Review* 71 (June): 401–425.

McIntosh, Hugh, Daniel Hart, and James Youniss. 2007. "The Influence of Family Political Discussion on Youth Civil Development: Which Parent Qualities Matter." *PS: Political Science and Politics* 40 (July): 495–499.

Media Monitor. 2009. "Election Watch: Campaign 2008 Final: How TV News Covered the General Election Campaign." Vol. 23 (Winter).

Meloen, Jos D., Gert Van der Linden, and Hans De Witte. 1996. "A Test of the Approaches of Adorno et al., Lederer, and Altemeyer of Authoritarianism in Belgian Flanders: A Research Note." *Political Psychology* 17: 643–656.

Mendelberg, Tali. 2001. *The Race Card: Campaign Strategy, Implicit Messages, and the Norm of Equality.* Princeton, NJ: Princeton University Press.

———. 2002. "The Deliberative Citizen: Theory and Evidence." In *Research in Micropolitics: Decision-Making, Deliberation and Participation.* Greenwich, CT: JAI Press.

———. 2008. "Racial Priming Revived." *Perspectives on Politics* 6 (Mar.): 109–123.

Merelman, Richard. 1971. *Political Socialization and Educational Climates.* New York: Holt.

———. 1997. "Symbols and Substance in National Civics Standards." *Political Science and Politics* 29 (Mar.): 53–56.

Metz, Edward, and James Youniss. 2003. "A Demonstration that School-Based Required Service Does Not Deter—but Heightens—Volunteerism." *PS: Political Science and Politics* 36 (Apr.): 281–286.

Milburn, Michael A., S. D. Conrad, and S. Carberry. 1995. "Childhood Punishment, Denial, and Political Attitudes." *Political Psychology* 16: 447–478.

Milgram, Stanley. 1969. *Obedience to Authority.* New York: Harper.

Miller, Arthur H. 1983. "Is Confidence Rebounding?" *Public Opinion* (June/July): 16–21.

Miller, Joanne M., and Jon A. Krosnick. 2000. "News Media Impact on the Ingredients of Presidential Evaluations: Politically Knowledgeable Citizens Are Guided by a Trusted Source." *American Journal of Political Science* 44 (Apr.): 301–315.

Miller, Warren E., and M. Kent Jennings. 1987. *Parties in Transition: A Longitudinal Study of Party Elites and Party Supporters.* New York: Russell Sage.

Miller, Warren E., and J. Merrill Shanks. 1996. *The New American Voter.* Cambridge, MA: Harvard University Press.

Miller, Warren E., and Donald W. Stokes. 1963. "Constituency Influence in Congress." *American Political Science Review* 57 (Mar.): 45–56.

Mills, C. Wright. 1956. *The Power Elite.* New York: Oxford University Press.

Mirels, Herbert L., and Janet B. Dean. 2006. "Right-Wing Authoritarianism, Attitude Salience, and Beliefs about Matters of Fact." *Political Psychology* 27 (Dec.): 839–866.

Mishler, William, and Reginald S. Sheehan. 1993. "The Supreme Court as a Countermajoritarian Institution? The Impact of Public Opinion on Supreme Court Decisions." *American Political Science Review* 87 (Mar.): 87–101.

Moncrief, Gary. 1999. "Recruitment and Retention in U.S. Legislatures." *Legislative Studies Quarterly* 24: 173–208.

Mondak, Jeffery J., and Mitchell S. Sanders. 2003. "Tolerance and Intolerance, 1976–1998." *American Journal of Political Science* 47 (July): 492–502.

Mondak, Jeffery J., and Mary Anderson. 2004. "The Knowledge Gap: A Reexamination of Gender-Based Differences in Political Knowledge." *Journal of Politics* 77 (Aug.): 492–512.

Monroe, Alan D. 1979. "Consistency Between Public Preferences and National Policy Decisions." *American Politics Quarterly* 7 (Jan.): 3–21.

———. 1998. "Public Opinion and Public Policy: 1980–93." *Public Opinion Quarterly* 62: 6–28.

Montaigne, Michel de. 1967. *The Complete Works of Montaigne.* Stanford, CA: Stanford University Press.

Mooney, Christopher Z., and Mei-Hsien Lee. 2000. "The Influence of Values on Consensus and Contentious Morality Policy: U.S. Death Penalty Reform, 1956–1982." *The Journal of Politics* 62: 223–239.

Moore, David W. 1992. *The SuperPollsters.* New York: Four Walls, Eight Windows.

Moore, David W. 2008. *The Opinion Makers.* Boston, MA: Beacon Press.

Moore, Stanley W., James Lare, and Kenneth A. Wagner. 1985. *The Child's Political World.* New York: Praeger.

Morrell, Michael. 2003. "Survey and Experimental Evidence for a Reliable and Valid Measure of Internal Political Efficacy." *Public Opinion Quarterly* 67 (Winter): 589–602.

Mueller, John E. 1973. *War, Presidents, and Public Opinion.* New York: Wiley.

———. 1977. "Changes in American Attitudes Toward International Involvement." In *The Limits of Military Intervention*, ed. Ellen Stern. Beverly Hills, CA: Sage.

———. 1994. *Policy, Opinion, and the Gulf War.* Chicago: University of Chicago Press.

———. 1996. "Fifteen Propositions About American Foreign Policy and Public Opinion in An Era Free of Compelling Threats." Paper presented at he National Convention for the International Studies Association, April 16–20. San Diego, CA.

———. 2005. "The Iraq Syndrome." *Foreign Affairs.* 84: 44–54.

Muller, Edward N., and Thomas O. Jukam. 1983. "Discontent and Aggressive Political Participation." *British Journal of Political Science* 13 (Apr.): 159–179.

Muller, Edward N., and Karl-Dieter Opp. 1986. "Rational Choice and Rebellious Collective Action." *American Political Science Review* 80 (June): 471–488.

Muller, Edward N., and Mitchell A. Seligson. 1987. "Inequality and Insurgency." *American Political Science Review* 81 (June): 425–452.

Murphy, Mike, and Mark Mellman. 2007. "The Heisenberg Primaries—Candidates and Media Beware: You can't Measure what Hasn't Happened." *Los Angeles Times* (July 5).

Mutz, Diana. 2007. "Effects of 'in-your-face' Television Discourse on Perceptions of Legitimate Opposition." *American Political Science Review* 101 (Dec.): 621–636.

Mutz, Diana C., and Byron Reeves. 2005. "The New Videomalaise: Effects of Televised Incivility on Political Trust." *American Political Science Review* 99 (Feb.): 1–16.

Newton, Kenneth. 2007. "Social and Political Trust." In *The Oxford Handbook of Political Behavior*, eds. Russell Dalton and Hans-Dieter Klingemann. Oxford: Oxford University Press.

Neyman, Jerzy. 1934. "On the Two Different Aspects of the Representational Method: The Method of Stratified Sampling and the Method of Purposive Selection." *Journal of the Royal Statistical Society* 558: 217–234.

Nie, Norman, and Kristi Anderson. 1974. "Mass Belief Systems Revisited: Political Change and Attitude Structure." *Journal of Politics* 36 (Aug.): 540–591.

Nie, Norman H., Jane Junn, and Kenneth Stehlik-Barry. 1998. *Education and Democratic Citizenship in America.* Chicago: University of Chicago Press.

Nie, Norman H., Sidney Verba, and John R. Petrocik. 1976. *The Changing American Voter.* Cambridge, MA: Harvard University Press.

Niemi, Richard G., Stephen C. Craig, and Franco Mattei. 1991. "Measuring Internal Political Efficacy in the 1988 National Election Study." *American Political Science Review* 85 (Dec.): 1407–1413.

Niemi, Richard G., and Jane Junn. 1998. *Civic Education: What Makes Students Learn.* New Haven, CT: Yale University Press.

Niemi, Richard G., John Mueller, and Tom W. Smith. 1989. *Trends in Public Opinion.* New York: Greenwood.

Norrander, Barbara. 1989. "Ideological Representatives of Presidential Primary Voters." *American Journal of Political Science* 33 (Aug.): 570–587.

———. 2000. "The Multi-Layerd Impact of Public Opinion on Capital Punishment implementation in the American States." *Political Research Quarterly* 53: 771–794.

Norrander, Barbara, and Clyde Wilcox. 1999. "Public Opinion and Policymaking in the States: The Case of Post-Roe Abortion Policy." *Policy Studies Journal* 27 (Dec.): 707–722.

Norris, Pippa. 1988. "The Gender Gap: A Cross–National Trend?" In *The Politics of the Gender Gap*, ed. Carol M. Mueller. Beverly Hills, CA: Sage.

———. 2006. "The Feminist Challenges to the Study of Political Engagement." In *The Oxford Handbook of Political Behavior*, eds. Russell Dalton and Hans-Dieter Klingemann. Oxford England: Oxford University Press.

Norris, Pippa, and Ronald Inglehart. 2004. *Sacred and Secular: Religion and Politics Worldwide.* Cambridge, UK: Cambridge University Press.

Nunn, Clyde Z., Harry J. Crockett, Jr., and J. Allen Williams, Jr. 1978. *Tolerance for Nonconformity.* San Francisco: Jossey-Bass.

Nye, Joseph S. 1997. "The Decline of Confidence in Government." In *Why People Don't Trust Government*, eds. Joseph S. Nye, Philip D. Zelikow, and David C. King. Cambridge, MA: Harvard University Press.

Nye, Joseph S., Philip D. Zelikow, and David King. 1997. *Why People Don't Trust Government.* Cambridge, MA: Harvard University Press.

O'Keefe, Garrett J. 1980. "Political Malaise and Reliance on Media." *Journalism Quarterly* 57: 122–128.

Olson, Mancur, Jr. 1968. *The Logic of Collective Action.* New York: Schocken.

Orren, Gary. 1997. "Fall from Grace: The Public's Loss of Faith in Government." In *Why People Don't Trust Government*, eds. Joseph S. Nye, Philip D. Zelikow, and David C. King. Cambridge, MA: Harvard University Press.

Owen, Diana. 2000. "Popular Politics and the Clinton/Lewinsky Affair: The Implications of Leadership." *Political Psychology* 21: 161–177.

———. 2002. "Media Mayhem: Performance of the Press in Election 2000." In *Overtime*, ed. Larry Sabato. New York: Longman.

Owen, Diana, and Jack Dennis. 1999. "Kids and the Presidency: Assessing Clinton's Legacy." *Public Perspective* 10 (Apr./May): 41–44.

Panagopoulos, Costas. 2009. "Campaign Dynamics in Battleground and nonBattleground States: *Public Opinion Quarterly* 73: (Spring): 119–129.

Page, Benjamin. 1996. *Who Deliberates.* Chicago: University of Chicago Press.

———. 2002. "The Semi-Sovereign Public." In *Navigating Public Opinion*, eds. Jeff Manza, Fay Loxmax Cook, and Benjamin I. Page. Oxford: Oxford University Press.

———2006. *The Foreign Policy Disconnect.* Chicago: University of Chicago Press.

Page, Benjamin, and Lawrence Jacobs 2009. *Class War.* Chicago: University of Chicago Press.

Page, Benjamin I., and Robert Y. Shapiro. 1983. "Effects of Public Opinion on Public Policy." *American Political Science Review* 77 (Mar.): 175–190.

———. 1989. "Foreign Policy and the Rational Public." *Journal of Conflict Resolution* 32 (June): 211–247.

———. 1992. *The Rational Public.* Chicago: University of Chicago Press.

Palmer, Paul A. 1936. "The Concept of Public Opinion in Political Theory." In *Essays in History and Political Thought*, ed. Carl F. Wittke. London: Oxford University Press.

Parker, Glen R. 1992. *Institutional Change, Discretion, and the Making of the Modern Congress.* Ann Arbor: University of Michigan Press.

Patterson, Thomas E. 1989. "The Press and Its Missed Assignment." In *The Election of 1988*, ed. Michael Nelson. Washington, DC: Congressional Quarterly Press.

———. 1994. *Out of Order.* New York: Vintage.

————. 1996. "Bad News, Period." *Political Science and Politics* 29 (Mar.): 17–20.

————. 2002. *The Vanishing Voter*. New York: Alfred A. Knopf.

————. 2005. "Of Polls, Mountains: U.S. Journalists and Their Use of Election Surveys." *Public Opinion Quarterly* 69 (Special Issue): 716–724.

Patterson, Thomas E., and Wolfgang Donsbach. 1996. "News Decisions: Journalists as Partisan Actors." *Political Communication* 13: 453–468.

Patterson, Thomas E., and Robert D. McClure. 1976. *The Unseeing Eye*. New York: Putnam.

Payne, Lee. W. 2008. *Responsive and Responsible Parties: Public Opinion, Polarization, and Platform Promise Keeping*. (Ph.D. dissertation, Department of Political Science, University of Houston).

Peterson, B. E., L. E. Duncan, and J. Pang. 2002. "Authoritarianism and Political Impoverishment: Deficits in Knowledge and Civic Disinterest." *Political Psychology* 23: 97–112.

Peterson, B. E., K. A. Smirles, and P. A. Wentworth. 1997. "Generativity and Authoritarianism: Implications for Personality, Political Involvement, and Parenting." *Journal of Personality and Social Psychology* 72: 1202–1216.

Pettinico, George. 1996. "Civic Participation Alive and Well in Today's Environmental Movement." *Public Perspective* 31 (June/July): 27–30.

Petrocik, John R. 1989. "An Expected Party Vote: New Data for an Old Concept." *American Journal of Political Science* 33 (Feb.): 44–66.

Pew Research Center for the People and the Press. 2004a. "Survey Experiment Shows Polls Face Growing Resistance, but Still Representative" April 20. http://people-press.org/report/211/.

————. 2004b. "Bottom-Line Pressures Now Hurting Coverage, Say Journalists" May 23. http://people-press.org/report/214/.

————. 2007. "Political Knowledge and Current Affairs Little Changed by News and Information Revolution." Apr. 15. http://people-press.org/report/319.

————. 2008. "Internet Major Source of Campaign News" Oct. 31. http://pewresearch.org/pubs/1017/.

————. 2009a. "The State of the Mass Media, 2009" Mar. 16. http://pewresearch.org/pubs/1151/.

————. 2009b. "Public Praises Science; Scientists Fault Public, Media" July 9. http://people-press.org/report/528/.

————. 2009c. "Press Accuracy Rating Hits Two Decade Low: Public Evaluations of the News Media: 1985–2009." Sept. 13. http://pewresearch.org/pubs/1341/.

Phillips, Kevin. 1991. *The Politics of Rich and Poor*. New York: Harper.

————. 2002. *Wealth and Democracy*. New York: Broadway Books.

Pinkleton, Bruce E., Erica Weintraub Austin, and Kristine K. J. Fortman. 1998. "Relationships between Media Use and Political Disaffection to Political Efficacy and Voting Behavior." *Journal of Broadcasting and Electronic Media* 42: 34–49.

Plomin, Robert. 1997. *Behavioral Genetics*. New York: W. H. Freeman.

Plutzer, Eric, and Michael Berkman. 2008. "Trends: Evolution, Creationism, and the Teaching of Human Origins in Schools." *Public Opinion Quarterly* 72 (Fall): 540–553.

Pomper, Gerald M., with Susan S. Lederman. 1980. *Elections in America: Control and Influence in Democratic Politics*, 2nd ed. New York: Longman.

Poole, Keith T., and Howard Rosenthal. 2007. *Congress: A Political-Economic History of Roll Call Voting*. Oxford: Oxford University Press.

Popkin, Samuel L. 1991. *The Reasoning Voter*. Chicago: University of Chicago Press.

Press, Charles, and Kenneth Verburn. 1988. *American Politicians and Journalists*. Boston, MA: Scott.

Prewitt, Kenneth. 1970. *The Recruitment of Political Leaders: A Study of Citizen Politicians*. New York: Bobbs-Merrill.

Price, H. Douglas. 1971. "The Congressional Career—Then and Now." In *Congressional Behavior*, ed. Nelson W. Polsby. New York: Random.

Price, Vincent. 1992. *Public Opinion*. Newbury Park, CA: Sage.

Price, Vincent, Lilach Nir, and Joseph N. Cappella. 2005. "Framing Public Discussion of Gay Civil Unions." *Public Opinion Quarterly* 69 (Summer): 179–212.

Prior, Markus. 2002. "Political Knowledge After September 11." *PS: Political Science and Politics* 35 (Sept.): 523–529.

———. 2007. *Post-Broadcast Democracy.* New York: Cambridge University Press.

———. 2009. "Improving Media Effects Research Through Better Measurement of News Exposure." *Journal of Politics* 71 (July): 893–909.

Prior, Markus, and Arthur Lupia. 2008. "Money, Time, and Political Knowledge: Distinguishing Quick recall and Political Learning Skills." *American Journal of Political Science* 52 (Jan.):169–183.

Putnam, Robert. 1995a. "Bowling Alone: America's Declining Social Capital." *Journal of Democracy* 6: 65–78.

———. 1995b. "Tuning In, Tuning Out: The Strange Disappearance of Social Capital in America." *Political Science and Politics* 28: 664–683.

———. 2000. *Bowling Alone: The Collapse and Revival of American Community.* New York: Simon and Schuster.

Putz, David. 2002. "Partisan Conversion in the 1990s: Ideological Realigment Meets Measurement Theory." *Journal of Politics* 64: 199–209.

Rapoport, Ronald B. 1982. "Sex Differences in Political Expression: A Generational Explanation." *Public Opinion Quarterly* 46 (Spring): 86–96.

———. 1985. "Like Mother, Like Daughter: Intergenerational Transmission of DK Response Rates." *Public Opinion Quarterly* 49 (Summer): 198–208.

Ray, John J. 1988. "Why The F Scale Predicts Racism: A Critical Review." *Political Psychology* 9: 671–679. Rector, Robert, and Rea Hederman. 2004. "Two Americas: One Rich, One Poor?" The Heritage Foundation. www.heritage.org, downloaded Nov. 29, 2005.

Remmers, H. H., and Richard D. Franklin. 1963. "Sweet Land of Liberty." In *Anti-Democratic Attitudes in American Schools*, ed. H. H. Remmers. Evanston, IL: Northwestern University Press.

Rentfrow, Peter, John T. Just, Samuel D. Gosling, and Jeffrey Potter. 2009. "Statewide Differences in Personality Predict Voting Patterns in 1996–2004 US Presidential Elections." In *Social and Psychological Bases of Ideology and System Justification,* eds. John T. Jost, Aaron C. Kay, and Hulda Thorisdottir. Oxford: Oxford University Press, pp. 324–347.

Rigby, Elizabeth, and Gerald C. Wright. 2010. "Whose Statehouse Democracy? How State Policy Choices Align with the Preferences of Poor, Middle-income and Wealthy Segments of the Electorate." In *Who Gets Represented*, eds. Peter Enns and Christopher Wlezien. New York: Russell Sage.

Roberts, Jason M., and Steven S. Smith. 2003. "Procedural Contexts, Party Strategy, and Conditional Party Voting in the U.S. House of Representatives, 1971–2000." *American Journal of Political Science* 47: 305–317.

Robinson, Claude. 1932. *Straw Votes: A Study of Political Predicting.* New York: Columbia University Press.

Rodgers, Harrell R., and Edward B. Lewis. 1975. "Student Attitudes Toward Mr. Nixon." *American Politics Quarterly* 4 (Oct.): 432–436.

Rogers, Lindsay, 1949. *The Pollsters: Public Opinion, Politics, and Democratic Leadership.* New York: Alfred A. Knopf.

Rohde, Paul W., and Koleman S. Strumpf. 2004. "Historic Presidential Betting Markets." *Journal of Economic Perspectives* 18: 127–142.

Rokeach, Milton. 1960. *The Open and Closed Mind.* New York: Basic.

Rosenberg, Milton J., Philip E. Converse and Howard Schuman. 1970. *Vietnam and the Silent Majority.* New York: Harper.

Rose, A. M. 1964. "Alienation and Participation." *American Sociological Review* 27 (Dec.): 151–173.

Ross, E. Wayne. 2004. "Negotiating the Politics of Citizenship Education." *PS: Political Science and Politics* 32 (Apr.): 249–251.

Rothenberg, Lawrence C., and Mitchell S. Sanders. 2000. "Severing the Electoral Connection: Shirking in the Contemporary Congress." *American Journal of Political Science* 44: 316–326.

Rotunda, Ronald D. 1986. *The Politics of Language: Liberalism as Word and Symbol.* Iowa City: University of Iowa Press.

Rudolph, Thomas J., and Jillian Evans. 2005. "Political Trust, Ideology, and Public Support for Government Spending." *American Journal of Political Science* 49 (July): 660–671.

Russett, Bruce, and Thomas W. Graham. 1989. "Public Opinion and National Security Policy: Relationships and Impacts." In *Handbook of War Studies*, ed. Manus J. Midlarsky. Boston, MA: Unwin Hyman.

Ruttenberg, Jim. 2005. "Pollsters Faulted for Failure to Predict Edward's Surge and for Subsequent News Coverage." *New York Times*, Feb. 19, A19.

Sabato, Larry J., Mark Stencel, and S. Robert Lichter. 2000. *Peep Show: Media and Politics in an Age of Scandal.* Lanham, MD: Rowman-Littlefield.

Saez, Emmanuel. 2008. "Striking it Richer: The Evolution of Top Incomes in the United States." *Pathways Magazine* (Winter): 6–7.

Sabato, Larry. 1993. *Feeding Frenzy: How Attack Journalism Has Transformed American Politics*, 2nd ed. New York: Free Press.

Sapiro, Virginia. 2004. "Not Your Parents' Political Socialization." *Annual Review of Political Science* 7 (May): 1–23.

Schlesinger, Mark, and Caroline Heldman. 2001. "Gender Gap or Gender Gaps? New Perspectives on Support for Government Action and Policy." *Journal of Politics* 63 (Feb.): 59–92.

Schlesinger, Joseph. 1966. *Ambition and Politics.* Chicago, IL: Rand.

Schreiber, E. M. 1978. "Education and Change in American Opinions on a Woman for President." *Public Opinion Quarterly* 42 (Summer): 171–182.

Scholz, John T., and Mark Lubell. 1998. "Trust and Taxpaying: Testing the Heuristic Approach to Collective Action." *American Journal of Political Science* 42 (Apr.): 398–417.

Schuman, Howard, and Stanley Presser. 1996. *Questions and Answers in Attitude Surveys.* Thousand Oaks, CA: Sage.

Schuman, Howard, Charlotte Steeh, Lawrence Bobo, and Maria Krysan. 1997. *Racial Attitudes in America.* Cambridge, MA: Harvard University Press.

Schwartz, Sandra K. 1975. "Preschoolers and Politics." In *New Directions in Political Socialization*, eds. David C. Schwartz and Sandra K. Schwartz. New York: Free Press.

Sears, David O., and Carolyn L. Funk. 1990. "Self-Interest in Americans' Political Opinions." In *Beyond Self-Interest*, ed. Jane J. Mansbridge. Chicago: University of Chicago Press.

———. 1999. "Evidence of the Long-Term Persistence of Adults' Political Predispositions." *Journal of Politics* 61 (Feb.): 1–28.

Sears, David O., and Donald R. Kinder. 1971. "Racial Tensions and Voting in Los Angeles." In *Los Angeles: Viability and Prospects for Metropolitan Leadership*, eds. W. Z. Hirsch. New York: Praeger.

Sears, David O., and Richard R. Lau. 1983. "Inducing Apparently Self-Interested Political Preferences." *American Journal of Political Science* 27 (May): 223–252.

Sears, David O., and Sheri Levy. 2003. "Childhood and Adult Political Development." In *Oxford Handbook of Political Psychology*, eds. David O. Sears, Leonie Huddy, and Robert Jervis. New York: Oxford University Press.

Sears, David O., Colette Van Laar, Mary Carrillo, and Rick Kosterman. 1997. "Is It Really Racism?" *Public Opinion Quarterly* 61 (Spring): 16–53.

Sebert, Suzanne K., M. Kent Jennings, and Richard G. Niemi. 1974. "The Political Texture of Peer Groups." In *The Political Character of Adolescence*, ed. M. Kent Jennings and Richard G. Niemi. Princeton, NJ: Princeton University Press.

Shapiro, Michael J. 2002. "Post-Liberal Civil Society and the Worlds of Neo Tocquevillean Social Theory." In *Social Capital: Critical Perspectives on Community and 'Bowling Alone,* eds. Scottt L. McLean, David A Schultz, and Manfred B. Steger. New York: New York University Press.

Sharp, Elaine B. 1999. *The Sometimes Connection: Public Opinion and Social Policy.* Albany: State University of New York Press.

Sheehan, Colleen A. 2004. "Madison v. Hamilton: The Battle over Republicanism and the Role of Public Opinion." *American Political Science Review* 98 (Aug.): 405–424.

Sidanius, Jim., Shana Levin, Colette Van Laar, and David O. Sears. 2008. *The Diversity Challenge: Social Identity and Intergroup Relations on a College Campus.* New York: Russell Sage Foundation.

Sigelman, Lee. 1981. "Question-Order Effects on Presidential Popularity." *Public Opinion Quarterly* 45 (Summer): 199–207.

Sigelman, Lee, and Mark Kugler. 2003. "Why is Research on the Effects of Negative Campaigning So Inconclusive? Understanding Citizens' Perceptions of Negativity" *Journal of Politics* 65 (Feb.):142–160.

Sigelman, Lee, Steven A. Tuch, and Jack K. Martin. 2005. "What's in a Name? Preference for 'Black' versus 'African-American' among Americans of African Descent." *Public Opinion Quarterly* 69 (Fall): 429–438.

Sigelman, Lee, and Susan Welch. 1991. *Black Americans' View of Racial Inequality: The Dream Deferred.* Cambridge, UK: Cambridge University Press.

Silbiger, Sara S. 1977. "Peers and Political Socialization." *Youth and Society* 5 (Mar.): 169–178.

Sinclair, Barbara. 1997. *Unorthodox Lawmaking: New Legislative Processes in the U.S. Congress.* Washington, DC: Congressional Quarterly Press.

Smidt, Corwin E, Lyman A. Kellstedt, and James L. Guth. 2009. "The role of Religion in American Politics: Explanatory Theories an Associated Analytical and Measurement Issues." In *The Oxford Handbook of Religion and American Politics,* eds. Corwin E. Smidt, Lyman A. Kellstedt, and James L. Guth. Oxford: Oxford University Press.

Smidt, Corwiln E., Kevin R. den Dulk, Bryan T. Froehle, James M. Penning, Stephen V. Monsma, and Douglas L. Koopman. 2010. *The Disappearing God Gap: Religion in the 2008 Presidential Election.* New York: Oxford University Press.

Smith, Aaron. 2009. "The Internet's Role in Campaign 2008." Pew Internet and American Life Project. Jan. 11. http://www.pewinternet.org/Reports/2009/6—The-Internets-Role-in-Campaign-2008.aspx

Smith, Eric R. A. N., and Peverill Squire. 1990. "The Effects of Prestige Names in Question Wording." *Public Opinion Quarterly* 54 (Spring): 97–116.

Smith, M. B., J. S. Bruner, and R. W. White. 1956. *Opinions and Personality.* New York: Wiley.

Smith, Tom W. 1984. "Nonattitudes: A Review and Evaluation." In *Surveying Subjective Phenomena,* vol. 2, eds. Charles F. Turner and Elizabeth Martin. New York: Russell Sage.

———. 1990. "The First Straw? A Study of the Origins of Election Polls." *Public Opinion Quarterly* 54 (Spring): 21–36.

Smith, Tom W., and Paul Sheatsley. 1984. "American Attitudes toward Race Relations." *Public Opinion Quarterly* (Oct./Nov.): 14–15.

Sniderman, Paul M. 1975. *Personality and Democratic Politics.* Berkeley: University of California Press.

Sniderman, Paul M., Philip E. Tetlock, James N. Glaser, Donald Philip Green, and Michael Hout. 1989. "Principled Tolerance and the American Mass Public." *British Journal of Political Science* 19 (Feb.): 25–45.

Sniderman, Paul M., and Thomas Piazza. 1993. *The Scar of Race.* Cambridge, MA: Harvard University Press.

Paul M. Sniderman, Gretchen C. Crosby, and William G. Howell, 2000. "The Politics of Race," In *Racialized Politics: The Debate About Racism in America,* eds. David O. Sears, Jim Sidanius, and Lawrence Bobo. Chicago: University of Chicago Press, 236–279.

Sniderman, Paul M., and Edward G. Carmines. 1997. *Reaching Beyond Race*. Cambridge, MA: Harvard University Press.

Sniderman, Paul M., and S. M. Theriault. 2004. "The Structure of Political Argument and the Logic of Issue Framing." In *Studies in Public Opinion*, eds. W.E. Saris and P.M. Sniderman. Princeton: Princeton University Press, 133–165.

Snyder, James M., Jr. 1992. "Long-Term Investments in Politicians, or Give Early, Give Often." *Journal of Law and Economics* 35 (Apr.): 15–44.

———. 1996. "Constituency Preferences: California Ballot Propositions, 1974–1990." *Legislative Studies Quarterly* 21: 463–488.

Snyder, James M., Jr., and Tim Groseclose. 2000. "Estimating Party Influence in Congressional Roll Call Voting." *American Journal of Political Science* 44: 193–211.

Snyder, James M., Jr., and Michael Ting. 2003. "Roll Calls, Party Labels, and Elections." *Political Analysis* 11: 419–444.

Somit, Albert, and S. A. Peterson. 1997. *Darwinism, Dominance, and Democracy: The Biological Bases of Authoritarianism*. Westport, CT: Praeger.

Sorauf, Frank J. 1988. *Money in American Elections*. Boston, MA: Scott.

Soss, Joe, Laura Langbein, and Alan R. Metelko. 2003. "Why Do Americans Support the Death Penalty." *Journal of Politics* 65 (May): 397–421.

Spitz, Elaine. 1984. *Majority Rule*. Chatham, NJ: Chatham House.

Squire, Peverill. 1988. "Why the 1937 *Literary Digest* Poll Failed." *Public Opinion Quarterly* 52 (Spring): 123–133.

———. 1992. "Changing State Legislative Careers." In *Changing Patterns in State Legislative Careers*, eds. Gary F. Moncrief and Joel A. Thompson. Ann Arbor: University of Michigan Press.

Steeh, Charlotte, and Maria Krysan. 1996. "Trends: Affirmative Action and the Public, 1970–995." *Public Opinion Quarterly* 60 (Spring): 128–158.

Stanley, Harold, and Richard Niemi. 2006. *Vital Statistics on American Politics 2005–2006*. Washington, DC: Congressional Quarterly Press.

———. 2008. *Vital Statistics on American Politics 2007–2008*. Washington, DC: Congressional Quarterly Press.

———. 2010. *Vital Statistics on American Politics 2009–2010*. Washington, DC: Congressional Quarterly Press.

Stein, Robert M., and Greg Vonnahme. 2008. "Engaging the Unengaged Voter: Vote Centers and Voter Turnout." *Journal of Politics* 70 (Apr.):487–497.

Stembler, Charles H. 1961. *Education and Attitude Change: The Effect of Schooling on Prejudice Against Minority Groups*. New York: Institute of Human Relations.

Stenner, Karen. 2005. *The Authoritarian Dynamic*. New York: Cambridge University Press.

Stevens, Daniel, Benjamin G. Bishin, and Robert R. Barr. 2006. "Authoritarian Attitudes, Democracy, and Policy Preferences among Latin American Elites." *American Journal of Political Science* 50 (July): 606–620.

Stimson, James A. 1975. "Belief Systems: Constraint, Complexity, and the 1972 Election." *American Journal of Political Science* 19 (Aug.): 393–417.

———. 1999. *Public Opinion in America: Moods, Cycles, and Swings*, 2nd ed. Boulder, CO: Westview.

———. 2004. *Tides of Consent*. New York: Cambridge.

Stoker, Laura. 2001. "Citizen Value Judgments." In *Citizens and Politics*, ed. James H. Kuklinksi. New York: Cambridge University Press.

Stoker, Laura, and M. Kent Jennings. 2005. "Political Similarity and Influence Between Husbands and Wives." In *The Social Logic of Politics*, ed. Alan S. Zuckerman. Philadelphia: Temple University Press.

Stoker, Laura, and M. Kent Jennings. 2008. "Of Time and Partisan Polarization." *American Journal of Political Science* 52 (July): 619–635.

Stokes, Donald E. 1966. "Some Dynamic Elements of Contests for the Presidency." *American Political Science Review* 60 (Mar.): 19–28.

Stonecash, Jeffrey M. 2000. *Class and Party in American Politics*. Boulder, CO: Westview.

Stouffer, Samuel A. 1949. *The American Soldier*. Princeton, NJ: Princeton University Press.

——. 1955. *Communism, Conformity, and Civil Liberties*. New York: Doubleday.

Stratmann, Thomas. 2000. "Congressional Voting over Congressional Careers: Shifting Careers and Changing Constraints." *American Political Science Review* 94: 665–676.

Streb, Mathew J., Barbara Burrell, Brain Frederick, and Michael A. Genovese. 2008. "Social Desirability Effects and Support for a Female American President." *Public Opinion Quarterly* 72 (Spring): 76–89.

Sturgis, Patrick, Caroline Roberts, and Nick Allum. 2005. "A Different Take on the Deliberative Poll: Information, Deliberation, and Attitude Constraint." *Public Opinion Quarterly* 69 (Spring): 30–65.

Sullivan, John L., James E. Piereson, and George E. Marcus. 1982. *Political Tolerance and American Democracy*. Chicago: University of Chicago Press.

Sundquist, James L. 1973. *Dynamics of the Party System*. Washington, DC: Brookings.

Surowiecki, James. 2004. *The Wisdom of Crowds*. New York. Doubleday

Tarman, Christopher, and David O. Sears. 2005. "The Conceptualization and Measurement of Symbolic Racism." *Journal of Politics* 67 (Aug.): 731–761.

Tarrow, Sidney. 1996. "Making Social Science Work Across Space and Time: A Critical Reflection on Robert Putnam's Making Democracy Work." *American Political Science Review* 90 (June): 389–397.

Tate, Katherine. 1993. *From Protest to Politics: The New Black Voters in American Elections*. New York: Russell Sage.

Tedin, Kent L. 1974. "The Influence of Parents on the Political Attitudes of Adolescents." *American Political Science Review* 68 (Dec.): 1579–1592.

——. 1980. "Measuring Parent and Peer Influence on Adolescent Political Attitudes." *American Journal of Political Science* 24 (Feb.): 136–154.

——. 1987. "Political Ideology and the Vote." In *Research in Micro-Politics*, vol. 2, ed. Samuel Long. Greenwich, CT: JAI.

——. 1994a. "Mass Support for Competitive Elections in the Soviet Union." *Comparative Politics* 27 (Apr.): 241–271.

——. 1994b. "Self Interest, Symbolic Values, and the Financial Equalization of the Public Schools." *Journal of Politics* 56 (Aug.): 628–649.

Tedin, Kent L., Richard E. Matland, and Gregory R. Weiher. 2001. "The Politics of Age and Race: Support and Opposition to a School Bond Referendum." *Journal of Politics* 63 (Feb.): 270–294.

Tedin, Kent L., and Richard W. Murray. 1979. "Public Awareness of Congressional Representatives: Recall Versus Recognition." *American Politics Quarterly* 7: 509–517.

Tedin, Kent L., and Gregory R. Weiher. 2004. "Racial/Ethnic Diversity and Academic Quality as Components of School Choice." *Journal of Politics* 66 (Nov.): 1109–1133.

Tedin, Kent L., and Oi-Kuan Fiona Yap. 1993. "The Gender Factor in Soviet Mass Politics: Survey Evidence from Greater Moscow." *Political Research Quarterly* 46 (Mar.): 179–211.

Tedin, Kent L., Brandon Rottinghaus and Harrell Rodgers. 2010. "When the President Goes Public: The Consequences of Communication Mode for Opinion Change Across Issue Types and Groups." *Political Research Quarterly* (forthcoming).

Terman, Lewis M., and Melinda H. Oden. 1959. *Genetic Studies of Genius V: The Gifted Group at Midlife*. Stanford, CA: Stanford University Press.

Thomas, Martin. 1985. "Electoral Proximity and Senatorial Roll Call Voting." *American Journal of Political Science* 29 (Feb.): 96–111.

Tocqueville, Alexis de. 1966. *Democracy in America*, eds. J. P. Mayer and Max Lerner. New York: Harper.

Torney-Purta, Judith, and Jo-Ann Amadeo. 2003. "A Cross-National Analysis of Political and Civic Involvement Among Adolescents." *Political Science and Politics* 36 (Apr.): 269–274.

Traugott, Michael W. 2005. "The Accuracy of the National Pre-Election Polls in the 2004 Presidential Election." *Public Opinion Quarterly* 69 (Special Issue): 642–654.

Traugott, Michael, Benjamin Highton, and Henry Brady. 2005. "A Review of Recent Controversies Concerning the 2004 Presidential Election Exit Polls." Available from http://elections.ssrc.org, downloaded June 15, 2005.

Traugott, Michael W., and Mee-Eeun Kang. 2000. "Push Polls as Negative Persuasive Strategies." In *Election Polls, the News Media, and Democracy*, eds. Paul J. Lavrakas and Michael W. Traugott. Chatham, NJ: Chatham House.

Traugott, Michael W, and Paul L. Lavrakas. 2008. *The Voter's Guide to Election Polls* 4th ed. Lanham, MD: Rowan and Littlefield.

Uhlaner, Carole Jean, and F. Chris Garcia. 2002. "Latino Public Opinion." In *Understanding Public Opinion*, 2nd ed., eds. Barbara Norrander and Clyde Wilcox. Washington, DC: Congressional Quarterly Press.

Ura, Joseph Daniel, and Christoper R. Ellis. 2008. "Income, Preferences and the Dynamics of Policy Responsiveness." *PS: Political Science and Politics* 41 (Oct.): 785–794.

Uslaner, Eric M. 2002. *The Moral Foundations of Trust*. New York: Cambridge University Press.

Uslaner, Eric M., and Ronald E. Weber. 1983. "Policy Congruence and American State Elites: Descriptive Representation Versus Electoral Accountability." *Journal of Politics* 45 (Feb.): 183–196.

Valentino, Nicholas A., and David O. Sears. 2004. "Old Times There Are Not Forgotten: Race and Partisan Realignment in the Contemporary South." *American Journal of Political Science* 49 (July): 672–688.

Vallone, Robert, Less Ross, and Mark Lepper. 1985. "The Hostile Media Phenomenon: Bias Perception and Perceptions of Media Bias in Coverage of the Beirut Massacre." *Journal of Personality and Social Psychology* 49 (Sept.): 577–588.

Vavreck, Lynn. 2009. *The Message matters: An Economic Theory of Campaigns*. Princeton: Princeton University Press.

Ventura, Raphael. 2001. "Family Socialization in Multiparty Systems." *Comparative Political Studies* 34: 666–691.

Verba, Sidney. 1996. "The Citizen as Respondent: Sample Surveys and American Democracy." *American Political Science Review* 90 (1): 1–7.

Verba, Sidney, and Norman H. Nie. 1972. *Participation in America*. New York: Harper.

Verba, Sidney, Kay Lehman Schlozman, and Henry E. Brady. 1995. *Voice and Equality: Civic Voluntarism in American Democracy*. Cambridge, MA: Harvard University Press.

Verba, Sidney, Nancy Burns, and Key Lehman Schlozman. 1997. "Knowing and Caring About Politics: Gender and Citizen Engagement." *Journal of Politics* 59 (Nov.): 981–998.

Visser, Penny, Allyson Hobrook and Jon A. Krosnick. 2008. "Knowledge and Attitudes." In *The Sage Handbook of Public Opinion Research*, eds. Wolfgang Donsbach and Michael Traugott. Thousand Oaks, CA: Sage.

Wald, Kenneth D., Dennis E. Owen, and Samuel S. Hill. 1989. "Churches as Political Communities." *American Political Science Review* 82 (June): 532–548.

Wallis, Allen, and Harry Roberts. 1956. *Statistics*. Glencoe, IL: Free Press.

Warren, Kenneth F. 2001. *In Defense of Polling*. Boulder, CO: Westview.

Warren, Mark. 1999. "Democratic Theory and Trust." In *Democracy and Trust*, ed. Mark Warren. London: Cambridge University Press.

Wattenberg, Martin P. 1998. *The Decline of American Political Parties*. Cambridge, MA: Harvard University Press.

————. 2008. *Is Voting for Young People.* New York: Longman.

Wawro, Gregory. 2001. "A Panel Probit Analysis of Campaign Contributions and Roll Call Votes." *American Journal of Political Science* 45: 563–579.

Weaver, David H., and Dan Drew. 1993. "Voter Learning in the 1990 Off-Year Election: Did the Media Matter?" *Journalism Quarterly* 70: 356–368.

Weaver, David H., and G. Cleveland Wilhoit. 1996. *The American Journalist in the 1990s.* Mahwah, NJ: Erlbaum.

Weisberg, Herbert. 1987. "The Demographics of New Voting Gap: Marital Differences in American Voting." *Public Opinion Quarterly* 51 (Fall): 335–343.

Weissberg, Robert. 1998. *Political Tolerance: Balancing Community and Diversity.* Thousand Oaks, CA: Sage.

West, Darrell M. 2001. *The Rise and Fall of the Media Establishment.* Bedford, MA: St. Martins Press.

————. 2009. *Air Wars: Television Advertising in Election Campaigns, 1952–2008,* 5th ed. Washington, DC: Congressional Quarterly Press.

Westheimer, Joel. 2007. *Pledging Allegiance: The Politics of Patriotism in America's Schools.* New York: Teachers College Press.

Westholm, Anders. 1999. "The Perceptual Pathway: Tracing the Mechanisms of Political Value Transfer Across Generations." *Political Psychology* 20: 525–552.

Wetstein, Matthew E. 1993. "A LISREL Model of Public Opinion on Abortion." In *Understanding the New Politics of Abortion,* ed. Malcolm Goggin. Newbury Park, CA: Sage.

Williams, J. Allen, Jr., Clyde Z. Nunn, and Louis St. Peter. 1976. "Origins of Tolerance: Findings from a Replication of Stouffer's Communism, Conformity, and Civil Liberties." *Social Forces* 44 (Dec.): 394–408.

Wilcox, Clyde, and Patrick Carr. 2010. "The Puzzling Case of the Abortion Attitudes of the Millennial Generation." In *Understanding Public Opinion,* eds. Barbara Norrander and Clyde Wilcox. Washington, DC: CQ Press.

Wilson, Thomas C. 1985. "Urbanism and Tolerance: A Test of Some Hypotheses Drawn from Wirth and Stouffer." *American Sociological Review* 50: 117–123.

Wilson, J. Mathew. 2009. "Religion and American Public Opinion: Economic Issues." In *The Oxford Handbook of Religion and American Politics,* eds. Corwin E. Smidt, Lyman A. Kellstedt and James L. Guth. Oxford: Oxford University Press.

Wittkopf, Eugene R. 1990. *Faces of Internationalism: American Public Opinion and Foreign Policy.* Durham, NC: Duke University Press.

Wlezien, Christopher. 1995a. "Dynamic Representation: The Case of US Spending on Defense." *British Journal of Political Science* 26: 81–103.

————. 1995b. "The Public as Thermostat: The Dynamics of Public Preferences for Spending." *American Journal of Political Science* 39: 981–1000.

Wlezien, Christopher, and Robert S. Erikson. 2000. "Temporal Horizons and Presidential Election Forecasts." In *Before the Vote: Forecasting American National Elections,* eds. James E. Campbell and James C. Garand. Thousand Oaks, CA: Sage.

————. 2002. "The Time Line of Presidential Campaigns." *Journal of Politics* 64: 969–993.

Wolak, Jennifer. 2007. "Strategic Retirements: The Influence of Public Preferences on Voluntary Departures from Congress." *Legislative Studies Quarterly* 32 (May): 285–308.

Wood, B. Dan, and Angela Hinton Anderson. 1998. "The Dynamics of Senatorial Representation, 1952–1991." *Journal of Politics* 60: 705–736.

Woessner, Mathew and April Kelly-Woessner. 2009. "I Think My Professor is a Democrat: Considering whether Students Recognize and React to Faculty Politics." *PS: Political Science and Politics* 42: 342–352.

Wright, Gerald C., Jr., and Michael Berkman. 1986. "Candidates and Policies in United States Senate Elections." *American Political Science Review* 80 (June): 567–588.

Wright, Gerald C., and Brian F. Schaffner. 2002. "The Influence of Party: Evidence from the State Legislatures." *American Political Science Review* 96: 367–380.

Wyer, Robert S., Jr., and Victor C. Ottati. 1993. "Political Information Processing." In *Explorations in Political Psychology*, eds. Shanto Iyengar and William J. McGuire. Durham, NC: Duke University Press.

Yang, Soon Joon, and Richard D. Alba. 1992. "Urbanism and Nontraditional Opinion: A Test of Fischer's Subcultural Theory." *Social Science Quarterly* 73 (Sept.): 596–609.

Zaller, John. 1992. *The Nature and Origins of Mass Opinion*. Cambridge, UK: Cambridge University Press.

———. 1994. "Elite Leadership of Mass Opinion: New Evidence from the Gulf War." In *Taken by Storm: The Media, Public Opinion, and U.S. Foreign Policy in the Gulf War*, eds. W. Lance Bennett and David L. Paletz. Chicago: University of Chicago Press.

———. 1996. "The Myth of Massive Media Impact Revived: New Support for a Discredited Idea." In *Political Persuasion and Attitude Change*, ed. Diane C. Mutz, Paul M. Sniderman, and Richard A. Brody. Ann Arbor: University of Michigan Press.

———. 1997. "A Model of Communication Effects at the Outbreak of the Gulf War." In *Do the Media Govern? Politicians, Voters, and Reporters in America*, eds. Shanto Iyengar and Richard Reeves. Thousand Oaks, CA: Sage.

———. 1998. "Monica Lewinsky's Contribution to Political Science." *Political Science and Politics* 31: 182–189.

———. 1998. "Politicians as Prize Fighters: Electoral Selection and Electoral Advantage." In *Politicians and Party Politics,* ed. John Geer. Baltimore, MD: Johns-Hopkins Press.

———. 2004a. "Floating Voters in U.S. Presidential Elections, 1948–2000." In *Studies in Public Opinion*, eds. Willem E. Saris and Paul M. Sniderman. Princeton, NJ: Princeton University Press.

———. 2004b. *A Theory of Media Politics*. (UCLA: unpublished manuscript).

Zaller, John, and Stanley Feldman. 1992. "A Simple Theory of the Survey Response: Answering Questions and Revealing Preferences." *American Journal of Political Science* 36: 579–616.

Zipp, John F., and Rudy Fenwick. 2006. "Is the Academy a Liberal Hegemony? The Political Orientations and Educational Values of Professors." *Public Opinion Quarterly* 70: 304–326.

Zmerli, Sonja, and Kenneth Newton. 2008. "Social Trust and Attitudes Toward Democracy." Public Opinion Quarterly 72 (Winter): 706–724.

Zukin, Cliff, Scott Keeter, Molly Andolina, Krista Jenkings, and Michael X. Delli Carpini. 2006. *A New Engagement*. Oxford: Oxford University Press.

Index